THE BIRDWATC.
and DIA

Designed and published by
Hilary Cromack

Edited by
David Cromack

BUCKINGHAM PRESS

in association with

SWAROVSKI
OPTIK

Published in 2002 by:
Buckingham Press
55 Thorpe Park Road, Peterborough
Cambridgeshire PE3 6LJ
United Kingdom

01733 561739
e-mail: buck.press@btinternet.com

© Buckingham Press 2002

ISBN 0 9533840 55
ISSN 0144-364 X

Cover: Slavonian Grebes, an acrylic by Chris Rose.
Chris has illustrated *Grebes of the World*, a large-format book published by
Bruce Coleman (end of 2002). More of his work can be seen on his
web-site; which includes originals, limited edition prints, illustrations and
works in progress.
Address: Maple Cottage, Holydean, Bowden, Melrose, Scotland, TD6 9HT;
(Tel/Fax)01835 822547. e-mail: chrisroseswla@onetel.net.uk

Printed and bound in Great Britain by:
Biddles Ltd Book Manufacturers, Guildford, Surrey.

CONTENTS

CONTENTS

CONTENTS

Key contributors in this Edition

GORDON HAMLETT, a freelance writer, is a regular contributor to *Bird Watching* magazine, both as a reviewer of books and computer software and also as sub-editor of the UK Bird Sightings section. Gordon is not only an active committeeman of both the Greater Peterborough Ornithological Group and Peterborough Bird Club, but an incorrigible Net surfer. Who better to evaluate club sites from around Britain?

CHRIS MEAD, since retiring as head of the British Trust for Ornithology's ringing section, has devoted much time to researching garden birds, and continues to spearhead the Trust's dealings with the media. A prolific writer, Chris was greatly praised for his latest book, *The State of the Nation's Birds*, which charted the decline in many familiar species. In this edition of *The Yearbook*, Chris reviews the most interesting ornithological discoveries of the past 12 months.

CHRIS ROSE, an award-winning artist whose work appears in many leading ornithological publications, exhibits at: The Wildlife Art Gallery, Suffolk; Nigel Stacy-Marks Gallery, Perth; Society of Wildlife Artists, Mall Galleries, London; On the WildSide, Malvern.

PREFACE

WELCOME to the 23rd edition of *The Birdwatcher's Yearbook & Diary* – I hope you will find it as useful and stimulating as all its predecessors. When Dr John Pemberton realised how difficult it was to track down the various individuals and organisations within the ornithological world, he deployed all his dogged librarian skills to fashion the original edition in 1981.

John's rigorous attention to detail ensured that the *Yearbook* became a trusted resource for trade and ornithological professionals and amateur birdwatchers and we trust we have maintained the high standards he set for himself.

Last year's introduction of colour to the Reserves section and other design changes were well received. Published reviews were universally positive, while sales couldn't have been better (less than 20 copies of the 2002 edition remain unsold) and we are delighted to report that Swarovski has agreed to sponsor *The Yearbook* for a further three years, at least.

In addition to updating core information, we want to add useful new categories. Last year we introduced listings for bird artists, photographers and lecturers, plus a diverse selection of businesses catering for the needs of birdwatchers and this continues in 2003. Many of you have told us how valuable it is to be able to find so much useful information in one place: you will help us maintain this feature into the future if you remember to mention the *Yearbook* whenever you speak to listed contacts. Thank you.

For 2003's edition we have compiled a listing of English-language bird magazines from around the world. This is by no means all-inclusive and we welcome feedback from readers about other useful titles that might be added in future years.

Regular readers will quickly realise that the 'tried and trusted' selection of bird reserves featured in *The Yearbook* has been considerably refreshed this year. We have introduced a considerable number of new sites to broaden your birding horizons and get a better geographical spread. Again, we welcome reader input about other places that should be considered for future editions so that we can have a rolling programme of new introductions.

The inclusion of new sites has meant that some old favourites have been shortened in this edition. Generally speaking, we selected reserves where the information provided in 2002 has not altered, but recognising that many bird group leaders like to double check their facts before a visit we have included phone numbers for all the ammended sites.

On the eve of going to press, the British Ornithologists' Union announced that it was altering the taxonomic order of species in the British List. As such changes tend to be controversial, we have retained the old order for this issue and welcome reader comment about adopting the changes for the 2004 edition.

The increasing use of the Internet meant that Gordon Hamlett's selection of 150 top birding web-sites was well received last year. This time around our intrepid net surfer has produced a county-by-county assessment of bird group sites. If you want to plan a birding trip to an unfamiliar part of the country, clicking onto a local club site may be a great way to get information about birding locations. Gordon's guide will help you identify the most helpful web-sites.

Once again, we have asked Chris Mead to summarise some of the most interesting pieces of ornithological research published since our last edition, and some of these are adorned by the artwork of Steve Cale, a Norfolk-based artist who has taken the plunge and given up the 'day job' to concentrate on painting and drawing for a living. Our partnership with *British Birds* continues this year with short-listed entries from the BB Bird Illustrator of the Year competition being shown throughout this edition.

The cover painting of Slavonian Grebes on a Scottish loch shows the sublime skills of artist Chris Rose to perfection and we feel confident it will bring an enormous amount of pleasure to our readers and make the 2003 edition a collector's item. It certainly exerted a magic spell on my wife and I when we removed the original painting from its packaging – so much so we bought it to hang on our wall.

Compiling the *Yearbook* is an immense undertaking each year, with thousands of facts having to be assembled and checked. The task would be immensely harder without the enthusiastic support of so many people but the contributions made by Derek Toomer (BTO), Chris and Gordon Hamlett and Cherry Hadley deserve special mention. We are exceedingly grateful to all our contributors and supporters.

Hilary A Cromack
Publisher

David Cromack
Editor

A message from our sponsor

IT HAS BEEN pleasing to know that the partnership formed between Buckingham Press and Swarovski UK that enabled the 2002 Edition of *The Birdwatcher's Yearbook and Diary* to undergo a major transformation in presentation values was rewarded with sell-out success.

You will see that important new features such as the web-site guides have been continued into the 2003 *Yearbook*. Both companies are committed to making constant improvements to our products and if you have any ideas you'd like to see incorporated into future Editions, do not hesitate to contact publisher Hilary Cromack.

To help bring such a useful book to the attention of ever greater numbers of British birdwatchers, Swarovski will use the 2003 Edition in a major nationwide promotional campaign at all of our approved dealers. We look forward to a long and fruitful association with *The Yearbook* and its growing audience of readers.

John Brinkley, Sales and Marketing Director of Swarovski Optik

CONTINUING ARTISTIC PARTNERSHIP

Yearbook continues to work with *British Birds*

GRACING this edition of *The Yearbook* is a selection of black and white drawings entered for the 2002 *British Birds* Illustrator of the Year contest. The quality of the competition is so high that none of these works won prizes, but we are delighted to ensure they are seen by a wider public.

The competition to find the Bird Illustrator of the Year has been run by *British Birds* since 1979, and the list of past winners contains a large proportion of Britain's top bird artists. Amateur and professional artists alike can enter, and must submit four line-drawings (of precise, specified dimensions) to be eligible for the main award. The subjects should be birds recorded in the Western Palearctic.

Two additional awards and one further category are included in the competition. The Richard Richardson Award, for the best work submitted by an artist under 22 years of age, was established in 1979, in honour of Richard Richardson, the renowned Norfolk ornithologist and artist, while the PJC Award, for a single work of merit, was established in 1987 by David Cook, in memory of his wife Pauline. Finally, entrants may also submit a colour painting, suitable for use on the cover of *British Birds*. Sponsorship of the event by Christopher Helm (an imprint of A & C Black Publishers Ltd) ensures that winners of the various categories are suitably rewarded for their efforts.

All the winning entries are displayed at the Society of Wildlife Artists annual exhibition, and at the British Birdwatching Fair, where a presentation ceremony for the winners take place.

For further details of the award, contact Roger Riddington, *British Birds*, Chapel Cottage, Dunrossness, Shetland ZE2 9JH. e-mail: editor@britishbirds.co.uk

Norman McCanch submitted this study of a Shore Lark

FEATURES

Despite the rigours of a maritime existence, Manx Shearwaters are setting longevity records (see page 10).

SCIENTIFIC DISCOVERIES IN 2002

(A REVIEW OF THE YEAR'S LITERATURE)

Renowned ornithologist Chris Mead provides a resume of some results from the scientific literature relevant to Britain's birds and their conservation, published during the last year. Most come from surveys run by the British Trust for Ornithology or research undertaken by its staff or the staff of the RSPB. All illustrations by Steve Cale.

Age shall not wither them

MOST wild birds live short lives but two amazing British longevity records for wild living birds have been reported in 2002.

On April 3, ringers on Bardsey, the Welsh island off the tip of the Lleyn peninsula trapped a Manx Shearwater *P. puffinus* that was first ringed as an adult on May 22, 1957 – an elapsed time of 16,387 days or almost 45 years.

This bird's first ring was aluminium and was replaced on July 8, 1961, with a modern hard version, and again on April 16, 1977. These birds are very hard on their rings and the older ones need to be renewed regularly.

The other ancient bird was a female Fulmar *Fulmarus glacialis* that was first marked at its nest on Eynhallow (Orkney) in 1951. She was also colour-ringed to allow her to be monitored easily from year to year. She produced 21 chicks up to her last breeding in 1996 (when she still managed to fledge a chick) but recent updating of the Eynhallow database shows that she has not been recorded since. This makes her, again, 45 years old and, since females generally do not breed until they are more than five years old, she will have been more than 50 years old! The previous record-holder (1996) was almost 41 years old.

Both these species are petrels – large tube-nosed seabirds weighing a bit over 500 grams. They have only one attempt at breeding each year and always lay a single egg. Most of them do not breed until they are at least five years old, so the adults must reach a really ripe old age or the species would be in great trouble.

One hundred years ago there were only a few hundred pairs of Fulmars in Britain, apart from a large colony (20,000-plus) on St. Kilda but there are now well in excess of 500,000 breeding pairs round the coasts of Britain and Ireland and more than 60,000 on

St. Kilda. This is a direct result of their ability to exploit by-catch from trawlers. Fulmars move around the Arctic oceans and the North Atlantic, while Manx Shearwaters go much further and winter off Brazil, Argentina and Uruguay – there is even a ringed bird record from Australia!

Based on its direct migration flights, the Bardsey shearwater must have travelled in excess of 500,000 miles (800,000 kms) – the equivalent of the moon and back! If you allow for the daily feeding flights, the distance the old bird has covered during its life probably is in excess of five *million* miles.

These old birds are, of course, known as individuals since they are ringed and recaptured by ringers. There will be more and more records of older and older birds as studies continue. Calculations indicate it is possible that half a dozen or so Fulmars on St Kilda that were hatched before 1900 may still be alive!

The British seabirds were not quite the oldest wild birds. After they had been reported, Chan Robbins from America reported that he had retrapped a Laysan Albatross *Diomedia immutabilis,* originally ringed on Midway Island some 47 years earlier. The oldest record is Grandma, the Royal Albatross *D. epomorpha* from New Zealand that was last seen at the age of 51.5 years and was certainly 60 years old then.

Double-use nestboxes prove a big success

AN IMPROBABLE house-sharing scheme in South-western Britain between a migrant bird species and a cuddly rodent is paying dividends for both.

Following the discovery of a pair of Pied Flycatchers *Ficedula hypoleuca* nesting in a local village, BTO member Gordon Vaughan decided to erect nestboxes to encourage them to breed in the Okehampton area. This was 30 years ago, when there were as few as 20 pairs in the entire county.

His first pair nested in 1974 and since then he has had more than 1,000 nests with 5,000 fledged young! What really surprised him was the fact that a couple of dormice *Muscardinus arvellanarius*, which were not known in the area at all, started using the boxes in 1978.

Pied Flycatchers now have tenants in some Devon nestboxes.

They were not entirely welcome, since they have been known to predate Pied Flycatchers and are dominant over the bird in case of disputes. This is not simply a question of size since the

11

dormice are only a little heavier than the bird. It is more to do with teeth as they can do much more damage than the soft bill of the bird.

Gordon's loyalty was torn between the undoubtedly rare and unexpected mammal and the locally rare bird, so he decided to continue to study both, but now has to put up with losses of something like 10% of the Pied Flycatchers' breeding attempts each year.

Mice occupied eight boxes in 1984 and 27 in 1985 with five litters of young. Breeding, which happens after the birds vacate the boxes in June, rather startled him, as they are not normally expected to use bird boxes to raise their young. The drought of 1995 meant that 56 boxes had dormice (13 litters were reared) and 1999 had 28 litters from 69 boxes occupied.

Gordon removes the old bird nests as soon as the chicks have fledged – they do not return once they have made their first flight – and now has 84 instances of birds breeding successfully followed by dormice. These concerned 38 Blue Tits *Parus caeruleus*, 27 Pied Flycatchers *Ficedula hypoleuca*, 16 Great Tits *Parus major* and three Nuthatches *Sitta europea*.

Apart from the rather small number of predated bird nests, this is a doubly successful story. Gordon's nest boxes now have one of the biggest colonies of Pied Flycatchers in the South West, and the biggest dormouse city of the region too!

Times are hard for nesting Lapwings

HUNDREDS of records of Lapwing *V vanellus* nests have been analysed to find out what is driving the continuing decline of this species (49% between 1987 and 1998 according to two British Trust for Ornithology surveys).

Overall, there seems to be an increase in failures in recent years and four causes:
• nest abandonment
• unfavourable weather
• nest destruction (usually by agricultural machinery)
• predation
have been plotted by decade.

The weather was judged not to have been very significant, but may have been worse in the 1980s and 1990s. Nests lost to destruction have halved between the 1960s and 1990s, possibly because spring sowing of crops is rarer now, so the birds were not even trying to nest in actively cultivated fields.

The 1990s were worst for predation, possibly because the birds were forced to use less suitable habitats that made nests easier for predators to find. In upland areas nest losses are about three times that in the early 1960s.

Nest losses on arable land, particularly, but also on pasture, declined to about 1980 and then increased again. On the other hand, marginal areas had increasing nest losses until the early 1980s and now they are doing better. The increased losses on pasture and upland areas might be associated with the higher stocking rates of sheep. This might have a knock-on effect as the reported results for nests only refer to the period while the birds are on eggs. When chicks are running around heavily grazed pasture, they might lack cover and become more at risk from predators such as crows and foxes.

• If you would like to join in The Nest Records Scheme – you only need to record half a dozen nests a year – contact Andy Simpkin at BTO (andy.simpkin@bto.org or 01842 750050).

Spotted Crakes heard, not seen

ONE of Britain's most secretive birds, the Spotted Crake *P. porzana* seems to be booming. During an organised search in 1999 it was reported in more places than for many decades. Though usually almost impossible to see, they have a characteristic call, a strange repeated whipcrack-like song, and this is easy to hear at night.

The increase in Spotted Crake numbers has been hidden - because they are such expert skulkers.

They use wet, tangled vegetation and, during 1999, 18 out of 19 most likely sites were checked and 85% of about 100 less likely places were also visited. No fewer than 73 singing birds were found in May and June – much higher than previously recorded in recent times. There were also a further seven singing birds recorded outside the two months of the survey and youngsters were found at another three sites.

Report author Gillian Gilbert concluded in *Bird Study* that Spotted Crakes should now be considered as established and much more than a sporadic breeding visitor to Britain. We need better monitoring to understand its population trends.

The species may have been very much more widespread and numerous 150 or 200 years ago when there was more wetland in Britain's undrained countryside. However, in recent years, there have been few records (only 14 in 1997 and a peak of 31 in 1993) and there were regular records only in two regions (Eastern England and the Highlands).

The birds migrate south to winter in Africa and return to Britain in April. The survey's insights into the bird's habitat preferences will provide a starting point for further studies and help reserve managers, who might wish to make suitable areas for the birds. Initial results seem to show that low-level grazing of wet sites may produce the right conditions.

Gillian Gilbert has also been working for the RSPB on Bitterns *Botaurus stellata* and has been recording their calls. The booms are characteristic for each individual bird and they can be identified from year to year. Though to human ears one Spotted Crake call sounds very much the same as any other, slowing down recordings, may lead to individual identification for them as well.

Hurricane blow for Hawfinches?

MYSTERY surrounds the continued widespread decline of Britain's biggest finch – the Hawfinch *C. coccothraustes*. Thought by some ornithologists not to have colonised Britain until some 200 years ago, the species now breeds sparsely over most of England and parts of Wales and southern Scotland. The major concentrations are in Kent, Sussex and Hampshire, along the Chilterns, in the Forest of Dean, the Lake District and a few places elsewhere.

Hawfinch - what lies behind its recent decline?

STEVE CALE. 02.

SCIENTIFIC DISCOVERIES IN 2002

A new survey indicates that the population increased from the mid-1970s for ten years, remained at a high level for a few years and then declined steeply over the last ten years. The birds like to be in areas near oaks and hornbeams, trees that were badly affected by the hurricanes in the late 1980s, but most experts think there are other, unknown, causes for the decline.

Gloucestershire and Lincolnshire are bucking the trend with more records in recent years. On the other hand, other major areas – Buckinghamshire, Cumbria, Essex, Norfolk, Northumberland, Oxford, Somerset and the West Midlands – report sightings down by at least 50%.

These large pinkish birds with massive bills and broad shoulders feed by cracking the toughest of nuts and readily eat the kernels from cherry stones – pressures of 150 pounds per square inch are required to get into these, so the birds are seriously dangerous in the hand. They can take chunks out of you like an apple corer!

Ringing records show that most don't move far from where they are ringed but migrants to and from Germany and from Norway have been found in Britain – two of them in the Shetland Islands where they do not breed.

The report, published in *British Birds* (95: 166-173) by Rowena Langston, Richard Gregory and Roy Adams, used some 830 published records for 1998 for a species that was thought to have between 3,000 and 6,500 breeding pairs in the United Kingdom as recently as 1990!

Predator pressure on Shetland Kittiwakes

KITTIWAKES are in serious decline on the Shetlands and a recently-published study shows that predation by an even rarer bird species may be part of the problem.

Twenty years of annual counts show a 70% decline in the main Shetland Kittiwake colonies. On Fair Isle, a few miles south of the main islands, decreases started later (about 1990) but the numbers are now down to 8,204 breeding pairs from 19,340 in 1988. This is now almost exactly a third of the Shetland breeding population – Fair Isle had about a quarter of Shetland's Kittiwakes in 1981.

Report author Martin Heubeck, who spends much of summer in a small inflatable carefully counting Kittiwake nests in colonies that cannot be observed from land, reports many of the traditional sites are now totally deserted.

Two reasons are postulated for the losses. The birds feed on sand-eels but the fish's behaviour has changed and they often now seem to be hidden in the sand when the birds need them. This has affected other species as well and the lack of seabirds flying around with sand-eels in their beaks has stopped the aggressive Great Skuas *Catharacta skua* from stealing food. Some have changed to direct predation on the seabirds – and particularly the Kittiwakes.

Many of the remaining Kittiwake colonies and particularly those doing relatively well, are in more sheltered areas where the Great Skuas find it more difficult to get access.

The Shetlands contain about 10% of Britain's breeding population of Kittiwakes and rather more than 1% of the North Atlantic population. Great Skuas are rare in most areas but Shetland has more than 40% of the world population, so they are of great conservation interest even though they are very destructive of the Kittiwakes! More details are given in *British Birds*, by Martin Heubeck (95: 118-122**).**

Capercaillie extinction looms again

THE BIGGEST and most spectacular of Britain's game birds, Capercaillie *Tetrao urogallus*, is on the brink of extinction for a second time. A repeat winter survey in its only British breeding area in the Highlands of Scotland was conducted in 1998/99 using exactly the same transects as in 1992-1994 and 51% of the population had been lost! This represents a 13% annual decline and the females are going down at a faster rate than the males.

The published report is in *Bird Study*, the journal of the British Trust for Ornithology. Earlier research, surveying in the summer, indicated that the national population fell by 16% per year from 1992 to 1997. The most recent results are not quite so bad but such declines are not sustainable for long.

The causes of the decline probably include the loss of the bird's habitat. The study shows that they do best in areas of Scots pine and blaeberry and cannot survive in very small patches. Breeding success may be limited by bad weather, while predation by crows and foxes and collisions with deer fences also play a part.

Capercaillie became extinct in the 1770s but was reintroduced from Sweden in 1837. The sought-after gamebird rapidly increased, reaching a maximum in the early part of the last century.

Hills no longer alive with Ring Ouzels

WIDESPREAD fears that Ring Ouzel *Turdus torquata* was in serious trouble in Britain have been confirmed. Research in 1999 to provide a population estimate for this scarce bird, to act as the basis for regular surveys, documents a bad decline and contraction of range.

A total of 284 plots were surveyed in the regions where the birds were found during the two Breeding Bird Atlas surveys and the new total population was estimated at between just more than 6,000 and a maximum of 7,549. This is at the lower end of the estimate made for 1988-1991 (of 5,500 to 11,000 pairs) and gives considerable cause for concern.

Why is it harder to see Ring Ouzels these days?

The biggest population is in Scotland (minimum 4,341 and maximum of 5,503), followed by Northern England (just over 1,500), Wales (between 300 and 400) and very few in the Southwest (seven to 16). None at all were found in Northern Ireland.

Further research is being undertaken to try to find out what has caused the decline. Suggestions include the increased rate of stocking of animals in the uplands, afforestation destroying habitat, or soil acidification affecting food supplies. Climate change may be pushing them north and Ring Ouzels may now face increased predation as gamekeepers become both rarer and more ethical. Yet other causes could be disturbance by the increasing numbers of walkers, competition with Blackbird *Turdus merula* and Mistle Thrush *Turdus viscivorus* and, quite possibly, changes to the ecology of the winter quarters.

Siren calls may be a Swift solution

COLD, wet weather this summer has put extra pressure on Britain's adult Swifts *A. apus* as they have had a hard time finding food. Their misery has been compounded by the loss of many traditional breeding sites, almost invariably in roof spaces, by people who have their rooves repaired.

The birds are long-lived and come back, year after year, to the same site. Modern building regulations are often interpreted to exclude nesting Swifts and as many as 80% of Swifts have been lost in one area of Northamptonshire due to demolition and re-roofing over a period of 15 years.

I am a member of a group of ornithologists called *Concern for Swifts,* formed a few years ago to promote the bird's interests and we are very worried that the numbers breeding are declining each year. Leaflets advising home-owners how to keep their Swifts in old buildings and also showing a very neat way of allowing them to nest in the louvres of the local church's bell tower – a truly traditional sort of site – are available from Chris Mead, The Nunnery, Hilborough, Thetford, Norfolk IP26 5BW. Please include an SAE. Another leaflet shows how to allow Swifts access to nest in new buildings.

SCIENTIFIC DISCOVERIES IN 2002

A special CD, especially for Swifts, is also available to attract them to new nesting sites or special nest boxes. To humans it is very boring, consisting of one track lasting more than 70 minutes of the screaming and squealing calls of Swifts actually recorded on their nests.

These are the calls of birds to their mates and also males advertising that they have a nice nest site available. The screaming parties of flying birds, such a feature of July evenings, are mainly young birds that have not bred yet and are the birds that need to be attracted to new breeding sites, which they can use in subsequent years.

As my roof design is not suitable for Swifts, I erected nest boxes and was sad not to have any real interest in them for several years. This all changed when I played the CD by the nest boxes last July. They are only about 150 yards from the nearest nesting birds and I was very impressed by the interest shown in the boxes – much more than any previous year. This year they are going into the nest box!

A new CD can encourage Swifts to use nest boxes.

One aim of the campaign is to alert local councils to the plight of their Swifts. Some are already helping by making sure that Swift-friendly repairs are made to their housing stock – for example in Norwich City. The best that could happen is that the birds get a specific mention in the local planning guidance documents.

BRITISH WEB-SITES AND MAILING LISTS

Gordon Hamlett trawls the internet to find the web-sites that will be of greatest help to acive birdwatchers in Britain. He also draws your attention to leading mailing lists – the modern-day parish pumps, where information and opinion can be exchanged.

THE WEB-SITES SECTION this year looks at bird clubs in the UK and other local birding resources. As a lot of bird organisations – especially local RSPB groups – cater solely for their members, I have tended to avoid bringing these to your attention. Instead, I have looked at various sites that have something to offer someone visiting the area for the first time, maybe for a day out or holiday, or perhaps someone who has just moved into the area.

In particular, I've been looking for suggestions for local sites to go birding and news of recent sightings (not necessarily just rare birds). As the web-site acts as a huge advertisement for a club, it's also possible to get a feel for how friendly and welcoming the group is. It soon became clear that this varies enormously across the country.

Many hours were devoted to checking websites for all counties. My published assessments are based on what I found on the latest possible date and I apologise if clubs have affected major improvements between then and now. I hope my comments are viewed as constructive criticism, as I am a real enthusiast for the service they provide. If you feel I have missed any valuable sites, please let me know for inclusion in next year's guide.

One strange thing that emerged was the patchy nature of web presence across the UK. Some counties, like Kent, have a large number of local sites, but for others, I really struggled to find anything at all.

This is also true for the mailing lists (see page 20). Some counties have very active discussion groups. With others, you can go for months without anyone posting a single message. Are you listening Norfolk?

Mailing lists

The idea of mailing lists is simple. Once you have signed up for a list and been accepted (this usually involves nothing more than sending an e-mail to the addresses listed in this article and then a confirmatory one later on), every time you send an e-mail to the group, it is automatically forwarded to every other member of that group.

Obviously, many groups use this as a method of passing round the latest sightings, but you can also use them discuss tricky identification problems, publicise your next meeting or whatever. All that most groups ask is that you keep your messages relevant to that particular group. In other words, don't post something about Cornish birds on the Lincolnshire group.

When we started the Peterborough Bird Club, and in particular, the Peterbirder mailing list, the first thing we noticed was that the number of bird records submitted went up astronomically. It is so easy to send off an e-mail just after you have visited a site rather than wait until the end of the year and then forget to send in anything at all.

Birders interested in a particular species can seek information from fellow subscribers. For instance, when word of mouth suggested that Bullfinch sightings were down we werw able to appeal to club members for all sightings to be submitted.

For that reason alone, I would encourage all clubs to accept casual records submitted in this way. While insisting that regular contributors download the correct form for submitting records, occasional visitors to your area will be unlikely to bother to go to that extra degree of trouble.

Of course, this may mean extra work for the recorder, but it will encourage a better coverage of each area. I know of one recorder who ignored a full description of what would have been a county first, simply because it wasn't written on the correct form! And did the person involved resubmit the record. Of course I didn't.

NB: A number of web-site addresses in the following directory are too long to fit on one line. We have divided the address where necessary, but when entering it on your search-engine remember there is no space between the last word of line one and the first word of line two.

ENGLAND

AVON

http://www.avonwildlifetrust.org.uk/
This is a really well-designed web-site. As well as information on 37 reserves run by the Trust, there are all sorts of news stories and events detailed, which were bang up to date.

BERKSHIRE

http://www.roc.care4free.net/
Any site featuring a collection of photos by Gordon Langsbury is on to a winner. The Reading Ornithological Society is a good example of what a local club can do. Their newsletter is online as well as their current programme. It would be nice to have details of local birding sites and sightings though.

http://www.berksbirds.co.uk/
There is a database of recent sightings and a huge gazetteer of local sites with links to maps so you can find your way around. Unfortunately, this is just a list of grid references – there is nothing to suggest some good places for the casual visitor to try.

Mailing lists
To join, send a blank e-mail to:
berksbirdnews-subscribe@yahoogroups.com
BERKSBIRDS-subscribe@yahoogroups.com

BEDFORDSHIRE

http://www.btinternet.com/~picus/ bedsbirdclub/
Everything you wanted to know about birding in the county, including where-to-watch guides and electronic versions of the club's newsletter. You can also submit your sightings online.

http://fly.to/blows.downs
A detailed description of this local migration hotspot, even going so far as to suggest exactly where various migrants are likely to be found. Site navigation is slightly clumsy – you have to return to the home page every time you want to move on.

Mailing lists
To join, send a blank e-mail to:
bedsbirds-subscribe@yahoogroups.com

BUCKINGHAMSHIRE

http://www.hawfinches.freeserve.co.uk/
Apart from some garish colour schemes and unnecessary flashing bits, the Buckinghamshire Bird Club's web page has a lot of useful information including site guides and county lists. What is useful is a section telling people what not to publish on the mailing list. Beginners and visitors often get this wrong and let slip sensitive information.
Mailing lists
To join, send a blank e-mail to:
BBirds-subscribe@yahoogroups.com

CAMBRIDGESHIRE

http://www.cambridgebirdclub.org.uk/
The Cambridge Bird Club's site is fairly basic in terms of information provided, though there is a large section on gulls and gull watching in the county. Another section details the current records for bird races and garden lists.

http://www.peterboroughbirdclub.org.uk/
Peterborough Bird Club's recording area covers parts of Lincs and Northants as well as Cambs. There is an excellent section on local sites as well as reports of recent club outings and bird races, together with a complete area checklist. The club is happy to accept sightings via an ordinary e-mail – no spreadsheets or whatever required.

http://www.paxton-pits.org.uk/
Boasting more visitors per annum than Minsmere, the locals are justifiably proud of their nature reserve, which is fully detailed here. One useful section tells the prospective visitor what wildlife to expect in the month ahead. You will also find information on local archaeology and geology as well as bird life.

BRITISH WEB-SITES AND MAILING LISTS

Mailing lists
To join, send a blank e-mail to:
cambirds-subscribe@yahoogroups.com
peterbirder-subscribe@egroups.com

CHESHIRE

http://www.10x50.com/index.htm
The Knutsford Ornithological Society site has lots
of interesting stuff including historical archives.
There is a lot on recent field trips but little or
nothing on recent sightings or places to go apart
from Tatton Park. I couldn't find anything advising
me how to join the group.

http://www.hems.u-net.com/opener.html
The Mid-Cheshire Ornithological Society runs its
own reserve at Hatton's Hey and there is plenty of
information about the place, plus the usual
forthcoming programme notes and brief reports
from previous field trips.

http://www.deeestuary.freeserve.co.uk/
Most birders visiting Cheshire or North Wales are
likely to head to the Dee Estuary and they are very
well served by this site with tide tables, maps of
the best places to go, recent sightings, bird
counts, monthly newsletters etc. An excellent
amateur site.

CLEVELAND

http://www.teesmouthbc.freeserve.co.uk
It is obvious from this site that the Teesmouth Bird
Club and its members are very active. Records are
archived on a monthly basis and there is a
gazetteer of sites. There is a mailing list but it is
restricted, by and large, to club members only.

**http://
www.barlowsathome.freeserve.co.uk/
birdwatching.html**
These home pages have a few suggestions for
local birdwatching sites. There are accompanying
maps for South Gare and North Tees Marshes but
not for the moorland or miscellaneous habits
pages.

Mailing lists
To join, send a blank e-mail to:
**NorthEastBirding-subscribe@
yahoogroups.co.uk**

CORNWALL

http://sennen-cove.com/birds.htm
Anyone visiting the western end of Cornwall should
look here for the latest weather and rarity news
and photographs – for insects and cetaceans as
well as birds. There is a comprehensive selection
of local sites and seawatching guide.

**http://www.surfbirds.com/
kernowbirds.html**
Considering what a major county Cornwall is for
birds, it is very poorly served on the Net. This site
has details of quite a few sites to visit but the rarity
news was eight months old when I last checked it.

Mailing lists
To join, send a blank e-mail to:
**CornishWildlife-subscribe@
yahoogroups.com**
Kernowbirds-subscribe@yahoogroups.com
thelizard-naturally-subscribe@egroups.ca

CUMBRIA

**http://www.lakesfd.co.uk/
osprey%20home.htm**
Cumbria is justifiably proud of its breeding
Ospreys, the first English pair in recent times not
involving re-introduced birds. This site has
everything you want to know – images, diaries,
biology and a web-cam of the nest, with pictures
updated every 30 minutes.

**http://
www.cumbriabirdclub.freeserve.co.uk**
This is a fairly modest site from the Cumbria Bird
Club. Recent sightings are archived, though they
were two months out of date when I checked. Six
local sites are detailed and some of their
newsletter items are available online.

Mailing lists
To join, send a blank e-mail to:
**BirdingCumbria-subscribe@
yahoogroups.com**

DERBYSHIRE

http://www.derbyshireos.org.uk
The Derbyshire OS has opted to have an online
message board rather than a separate mailing list.
Apart from this, there are recent sightings (bang
up to date), a guide to eight top sites in the county
and various articles of local interest.

http://www.carsingtonbirdclub.co.uk
A nice local web-site, highlight of which is an annotated map, not just showing the area, but also detailing what species can be expected at different seasons. There are recent sightings and details of recent club activities. The whole thing suggests a very friendly club.

http://www.ogstonbirdclub.co.uk/
Ogston Bird Club has no less than 20 main sections ranging from a virtual trip around the area to items for sale. The recent sightings page is the most comprehensive I have come across anywhere, listing every species recorded, every day. Again, there is an online message board. Does the lack of a county-wide mailing list mean that the different groups don't like sharing information?

DEVON

http://www.devonwildlifetrust.org/
The local Wildlife Trust pages list 14 reserves but there is very little information given as to what wildlife to look out for. It is just the same on the Dartmoor pages; no entry for wildlife at all. For a top bird county, it is a shame there is so little on offer for locals and visitors alike.

DORSET

http://www.portlandbirdobs.btinternet.co.uk/
Just what you want from an observatory site. The Portland Observatory has all the latest news – both bird and other wildlife and is updated daily. There are plenty of other sections giving information, latest weather, monthly summaries and advice on visiting the area. The database is fully searchable too.

http://www.naturalist.co.uk/nothe/
These pages show just what can be achieved with one man's devotion to his local patch – the Nothe in Weymouth. Records for some 180 species go back more than 20 years, all broken down and summarised. There is a regularly updated diary as well as plenty of other details about the area.

http://www.chog.org.uk
The Christchurch Harbour Ornithological Group web-site – which covers the area round Stanpit Marsh and Hengistbury Head – has details of some of the local hotspots, recent sightings and a systematic list. Your own sightings can be sent by e-mail.

DURHAM

http://www.durham-rspb.org.uk/
The local RSPB group's site has plenty of information for anyone wishing to join – indoor and outdoor meetings, trip reports etc but there is nothing to interest the casual birding visitor to Durham.

http://www.wwt.org.uk/visit/washington/
Part of the larger Wildfowl and Wetlands Trust site, this was something of a disappointment with nothing at all listed under 'Bird Sightings' and 'What's New' and even the admission prices left off the section on 'Admission Prices'.

Mailing lists
To join, send a blank e-mail to:
NorthEastBirding-subscribe@yahoogroups.co.uk

ESSEX

http://www.essexbirdwatchsoc.co.uk/
The Essex Birdwatching Society's site is in desperate need of an update – latest news was four months old and all the programme details well out of date. There was little in the way of additional information to interest the casual browser. A turquoise and pink colour scheme does not aid readability.

http://www.southendrspb.co.uk/
Southend-on-Sea has always had one of the most dynamic RSPB groups and this is carried forward into their web-site. As well as a huge site guide, you can also get information to find key species. There are polls and a discussion forum as well as all the latest news, though this is dominated by general observations rather than rarities.

http://www.geocities.com/RainForest/Wetlands/6757/index.html
Here's another local patch site, this time East Tilbury. The design is classically simple and uncluttered, complete with a checklist of birds seen, guided walks and recent sightings. Makes you want to go there.

GLOUCESTERSHIRE

http://beehive.thisisgloucestershire.co.uk/default.asp?WCI=SiteHome&ID=1285
The contents page of the Cheltenham Bird Club is

a bit of a hotchpotch with new pages seemingly added to the end of the list with no thoughts of structure. It features plenty of foreign trip reports but apart from forthcoming activities and some recent sightings, not very much about birding locally.

http://www.birder.pwp.blueyonder.co.uk/
Web pages of the Gloster Birder. Here you will find some recent sightings, various lists and trip reports and even a page of local dialect names. There are a few major sites mentioned but unfortunately, no map or directions included. This site bubbles with enthusiasm.

GREATER LONDON

http://web-site.lineone.net/~andrewself/Londonsbirding.htm
London's Birding aims to offer a one-stop site for all your birding needs in the capital. There is a full diary of forthcoming events, recent sightings, site guide (though these are external links rather than self written and so variable in quality) and 'for sale' section. There are plenty of links to other London birding sites.

http://www.janja.dircon.co.uk/rspb/index.html
The pages of the Central London RSPB group contain details of 27 sites within relatively easy access of the city centre. In addition, there are details of the club's indoor and outdoor programmes and an archived copy of the last newsletter. Not surprisingly, most of the links are RSPB oriented.

http://www.brentres.com/
Brent Reservoir (aka Welsh Harp) has turned up an impressive 245 species over the years. As well as bird reports, there are lists, for mammals, butterflies, flora etc. There is a discussion forum to report any sightings and details of a full programme of walks.

Mailing lists
To join, send a blank e-mail to:
LondonOrnithology-subscribe@yahoogroups.com

GREATER MANCHESTER

http://www.gmbirds.freeserve.co.uk/
No fancy frills whatsoever, but a good spot to get to grips with birding in Greater Manchester. There is a comprehensive site guide and plenty of contacts for other groups, few of whom have actually made it onto the Net though. The previous month's sightings are summarised.

http://www.mike.hill.care4free.net/
Though titled 'Birding in Wigan', there is a fair bit of information (and links) to the Leigh Ornithological Society. The site guide could do with a few more details on what birds are actually to be seen at each location and the odd map wouldn't go amiss. Needs a bit of updating.

HAMPSHIRE

http://www.hants.gov.uk/hos/
There is plenty to keep you occupied on the pages of the Hampshire Ornithological Society, even if site navigation is a bit clumsy. Plenty of local sites are detailed though you still feel that coverage is somewhat patchy. There is an excellent series of events with guided walks seemingly every week.

http://www.hants.gov.uk/countryside/titchfield/
A huge site devoted to Titchfield Haven NNR. All wildlife, not just birds, is covered in a comprehensive sightings section run about two weeks in arrears. Other information includes everything from disabled access to volunteering your services.

http://members.lycos.co.uk/trevorc28/
An unusual presentation of data in the Hampshire Calendar of Birds. This is a collection of interesting facts and figures, cross referred to different days and months. The county list and record counts are also included. Just the sort of quirky site I like.

Mailing lists
To join, send a blank e-mail to:
hoslist-subscribe@yahoogroups.com

HEREFORDSHIRE

http://www.herefordshirebirding.net/
The Herefordshire Ornithological Society has the most surreal web-site I looked at. When I clicked on the page for club contacts, it started playing Debussy while a link to a bookshop on that page invited me to browse for erotica! Apart from that, the usual bird club fare is present and seems strangely normal.

BRITISH WEB-SITES AND MAILING LISTS

HERTFORDSHIRE

http://www.hertsbirdclub.org.uk/
The Herts Bird Club has a very well presented site with up-to-date sightings and an easy method for submitting sightings online. The only thing missing is any form of bird site information, so it's of minimal use to the non-local birder.

http://www.tringreservoirs.btinternet.co.uk/
Tring Reservoirs is one of the best known reserves in the county and this site, run by the Friends of Tring Reservoirs does it full justice with recent sightings, calendar of likely species, detailed maps and details of current management plans and other wildlife. The use of the club's logo as a watermark on most pages decreases readability considerably.

http://www.leevalleypark.org.uk/
There's an awful lot of information here about all sorts of outdoor activities in the Lee (Lea) Valley Park, not just birdwatching and not just about the famous site for wintering Bitterns either. A link **(http://www.acmiddleton.pwp. blueyonder.co.uk/localbirds.htm)** takes to you a page devoted to recent sightings.

ISLE OF WIGHT

http://dbhale.members.beeb.net/
This personal site dealing with birding on the Isle of Wight has sections devoted to latest sightings, an excellent and comprehensive where-to-watch guide for the visiting birder and dozens of photographs of local birds. Monthly lists of species seen are included, plus details of the Isle of Wight Ornithological Group.

KENT

http://www.kentos.org.uk/
The many, many pages here give full value for the Kent Ornithological Society. This is a massive resource as befits one of our major birding areas and should be your number one stop if you live in, or are visiting the county. The only minor gripe was that it hadn't been updated for over a week when I last looked. There are links to many other Kent birding resources.
At the time of writing, one of Kent's premier spots – RSPB Cliffe Pools and the rest of the North Kent Marshes – is under severe threat of being turned

into an overspill airport for London. An excellent section of this site is devoted to the latest news and messages of support for the campaign to say 'No'.

Mailing lists
To join, send a blank e-mail to:
kosnet-subscribe@yahoogroups.com

LANCASHIRE

http://libweb.lancs.ac.uk/ldbws.htm
All the information you want about the Lancaster & District Birdwatching Society is here, though navigation is somewhat tricky. These are the home pages for the club, but articles from the club's newsletter appear on a different web-site and recent sightings on a third. Best item is a massive systematic list detailing all recent records.

http://www.eastlancashirebirding.nstemp.net/index.htm
East Lancashire is a well-kept secret, appreciated by locals but not known by visiting birders. This site is a fairly standard format – sightings, site guide etc. It would be useful to have details of the local meetings, while much bigger print on the home page for selecting the different sections wouldn't go amiss either.

http://www.lancashire.police.uk/wildlife.html
This is one of the few police forces I've come across so far that has part of its web-site devoted to wildlife crime. There is some good basic information, though it would be useful to increase the section on Frequently Asked Questions, which currently stands at just one! Possible topics might be 'What to do if you find a dead bird' or 'Who can shoot what, when?'

LEICESTERSHIRE (AND RUTLAND)

http://www.lros.org.uk
The Leicestershire and Rutland Ornithological Society's web pages are a perfect example for other clubs to follow: enjoyable to read with everything you need in an easy-to-find format. It's enthusiastic too, something not always obvious in other clubs. The one major niggle is the antiquated system of insisting that all records be sent in on the prescribed slips – guaranteed to discourage casual sightings being submitted.

BRITISH WEB-SITES AND MAILING LISTS

http://www.eyebrook.org.uk/
There is plenty of information here about one of the county's premier sites with a comprehensive systematic list and detailed ringing records. It would benefit from someone checking the poor spelling and grammar, which spoils an otherwise fine local site.

http://www.rutlandwater.u-net.com/rw/ RW.home.htm
The Rutland Water pages include excellent sections on their Tree Sparrow and Osprey projects as well as all the other pages you might expect. Site navigation is not all it might be, as you have to return to the home page every time you want to choose another section.

LINCOLNSHIRE

http://www.lincsbirdclub.co.uk
There's plenty of information and articles on the Lincolnshire Bird Club site but not all of it is up to date. For example, the 'Recent sightings' were several months old, though there are plenty of recent rarity photos. The site guide needs expanding and there is nowhere to submit records online. Unusual sections include a 'Kids puzzle page' and computer wallpaper to download.

http://www.cix.co.uk/~lincstrust/reserves/ gib/gib.html
While the Gibraltar Point web-site has a fair bit of information about the place it all seems so sterile and hardly makes you want to visit. The only bird information is a small section on 13 wintering species and a page on the Shore Lark ringing project. Even a complete species list or month-by-month guide to what birds to look for would help.

Mailing lists
To join, send a blank e-mail to:
Lincsbirdnews-subscribe@yahoogroups.com

NORFOLK

http://www.accessbs.com/narvos/
Norfolk is another major birding county with absolutely atrocious coverage on the net. Nar Valley Ornithological Society's site is one of the best and that is, at best, limited in its scope. There are a few recent sightings, while the site guide gives grid references only, rather than maps or directions. There is a good local weather page and a quiz.

http://www.birdguides.com/birdnews/ county.asp?a=25
The Birdguides web page has a major section on Norfolk with details of 37 major birdwatching sites and many more minor sites. In addition, there is a list of recent sightings, rarity photos and an excellent summary of the previous month's birds. Contacts and a book list complete this excellent resource. Now if outsiders can produce something like this, why can't the locals?

http://freespace.virgin.net/ralph.bateman/ index.html
The pages of the West Norfolk RSPB Member's Group have details of the club's current indoor and outdoor programmes but nothing else to interest a casual visitor.

Mailing lists
To join, send a blank e-mail to:
**Norfolkbirdnews-subscribe@yahoogroups.com
norfolkbirds-subscribe@yahoogroups.com**

NORTHAMPTONSHIRE

http://www.treen.freeserve.co.uk/
Apart from a few recent sightings and summaries of birds seen over the last couple of months, most of the information about the Northants Bird Club is devoted to the club itself. There is no county list nor site guide to interest the general browser.

http:// www.northamptonshirewildlife.co.uk/
This excellent site covers all the county's wildlife. Of most interest to birds though, is not the link to the 'birds' section, which is pretty limited, but rather to the complete text of *The Birds of Northamptonshire* .
(**http:// www.northamptonshirewildlife.co.uk/ npton/NPTONIND.HTM**) which is a complete systematic list, showing all records up to the end of 1997 with a few further updates included. There are illustrations and sound recordings to enhance your reading.

NORTHUMBERLAND

http://www.ntbc.org.uk/
The pages of the Northumberland and Tyneside Bird Club don't claim to be anything other than a vehicle for club activities with details of trips and meetings etc. There are extracts from previous

club bulletins and a nice touch is that prospective members can send off for a free sample copy of the bulletin.

http://www.northumberland.gov.uk/vg/birds.html
The Visitor Guide for Northumberland County Council might not be the first place you think of looking for bird information, so congratulations to them for realising that birders are tourists too. There are three sections – coastal, upland and lowland birds with suggestions and links for places to go and birds to see.

Mailing lists
To join, send a blank e-mail to:
NorthEastBirding-subscribe@yahoogroups.co.uk

NOTTINGHAMSHIRE

http://www.nottm.birds.care4free.net/home.htm
There are plenty of where-to-watch sites listed on the pages of the Nottinghamshire Birdwatchers as well as a brief list of recent sightings with previous month's records being archived. You can submit sightings from here though it is user-unfriendly. The rest of the pages are devoted to club activities.

http://www.notts-rspb.org.uk/
The Nottingham RSPB site is one of the more dynamic Local Members' Group offerings, even if the map on the front page does resemble a swastika. What is offered is extremely well presented though the site guide needs expanding. You feel as if you would be made really welcome if you joined.

http://www.colwick2000.freeserve.co.uk/
The Colwick Park web pages have everything you want about your local park with one major exception. Different pages tell you what butterflies and dragonflies are on the wing and what birds have been seen recently. There are some excellent tales from the warden and all sorts of events. So what's missing? Something telling me how to get there! Preferably, a location map with another more detailed map showing all the different parts of the park will soon be added.

Mailing lists
To join, send a blank e-mail to:
Nottsbirdsnews-subscribe@yahoogroups.com

OXFORDSHIRE

http://www.oos.org.uk/
A quick look at the pages of the Oxford Ornithological Society leaves you with a real feeling that this club brooks no nonsense.The site guide is excellent with some first class maps. Sightings are only discussed via the mailing list. You can submit your own sightings but only in the most exacting format imagineable. Would I send mine in like this? No.

http://homepage.ntlworld.com/thomas.stevenson/benson.htm
This is another of those quirky little sites that shows just what can be achieved. The Birds of Benson Parish is just that, details of sightings collated from one tiny part of the county. There are systematic lists and graphs and line drawings, showing just what happens to populations of the commoner birds throughout the year – species that are often ignored by larger organisations. I bet that you will learn something if you take a look.

Mailing lists
To join, send a blank e-mail to:
Oxonbirds-subscribe@yahoogroups.com

ISLES OF SCILLY

http://www.scillybirding.co.uk/
As you might expect, there is a lot of stuff and photos of various rarities. Pelagic voyages feature strongly too, but there is no site guide and the recent sightings section seems a bit thin. One interesting feature is a list of species requiring a full description. Would you think of filling out a rarity form for a Coal Tit?

SHROPSHIRE

http://www.shropshirewildlifetrust.org.uk/
This is another county with little representation on the web. The best offerings are the pages of the local Wildlife Trust, which has a good section on 37 different reserves to visit.

SOMERSET

http://www.somornithosoc.freeserve.co.uk/
Though still under construction, the pages of the Somerset Ornithological Society show some

promise. Not only is there a site guide for the county, but plans to cover the four surrounding counties are being advertised. Recent sightings can only be accessed by a slightly quirky message board system. In the fullness of time, it might be better to extract all the information and put it on one page.

http://www.somerset.gov.uk/levels/
This site – which starts off as a simple clickable map – has many pages showing just why different parts of the Somerset Levels are of national or international importance. It feels like a typical government site, full of really useful information but as dull as it is possible to make.

http://www.mitchley18.freeserve.co.uk/
Another one-man site, this time from someone who spends most of his time birding in Somerset. Most likely to be useful if you are planning a visit to Weston-super-Mare where there are a number of local patch sites detailed. Also many photos and a few foreign trip reports.

STAFFORDSHIRE
(see also West Midlands)

http://www.wildlifetrust.org.uk/staffs/
There doesn't seem to be too much on the net about birding in Staffordshire. The local Wildlife Trust site mentions a few reserves but only gives very limited information about some of them and nothing more than a map reference. The local North West Group **(http://www.staffswildlifetrust-nwgroup.co.uk/)** seems slightly more dynamic.

http://www.keele.ac.uk/university/nathist/
Keele University may not be the most obvious place to go birding but these pages have annotated lists and maps for birds (110 species) as well as a variety of other wildlife.

SUFFOLK

http://home.clara.net/ammodytes/
Don't be put off by the jokey 'Lounge Lizards' title. The Lowestoft Birding Club has some excellent material with comprehensive sightings and site guide, plus a whole range of articles and foreign trip reports.

http://www.wildlifetrust.org.uk/suffolk/
Compared to the pages of the Staffs WT (above),

the nature reserves section of the Suffolk WT's pages are a total joy. You read the reserve descriptions and you want to visit. There are clear colourful maps, to help you find even the smallest meadow. Many counties would do well to copy.

SURREY

http://www.sbclub.ukonline.co.uk/
Nothing too ambitious from the Surrey Bird Club. There are details of recent sightings and news stories, recent trip reports plus details of forthcoming trips and not a lot else.

http://www.sdbws.ndo.co.uk/
The Surbiton and District Birdwatching Society is very much a local club though they undertake plenty of survey work. Recent records are listed a month in arrears and there are various trip reports. Again, there is no site guide to encourage the casual visitor.

http://myweb.tiscali.co.uk/johnnyallan/index.html
Everything you need to know about Surrey listers and Beddington Sewage Farm in particular can be found at this personal site. The lack of margins and continual use of capitals do not make the pages easy to read.

Mailing lists
To join, send a blank e-mail to:
SurreyBirders-subscribe@yahoogroups.com

SUSSEX

http://www.susos.org.uk/
An excellent resource for anyone interested in Sussex birding – this should definitely be your first port of call. The only weakness is that though there is a gazetteer of some 2,800 sites, complete with links to maps, there is nothing as yet telling you the best places to visit.

http://home.clara.net/yates/lnr.html
Rye Harbour has always been one of my favourite reserves and this site does it full justice with all sorts of information on the 3,257 different species of bird, insect, flower etc. so far recorded. There are details on guided walks, recent sightings and a month-by-month calendar of what to look out for. First class.

BRITISH WEB-SITES AND MAILING LISTS

Mailing lists
To join, send a blank e-mail to:
**Rye_Bay_Wildlife-subscribe@
yahoogroups.com**

WARWICKSHIRE
(see also West Midlands)

http://www.warwickshirebirding.co.uk/
The main Warwickshire pages could do with a little upgrading; too many of the links were broken when I tried them. The sightings section was up to date but the sites section doesn't make you want to visit at all.

http://www.draycotebirding.co.uk/
The Draycote Reservoir pages were also something of a mixed bag. When I tried the link to the latest sightings it didn't work. Though there is a heavily annotated map, there is nothing to explain what all the markings mean. Elsewhere I read that access details had been changed, so I fear a major overhaul is needed. One daft thing is that when you click on a link, it changes colour to one that can no longer be easily read (orange on green).

Mailing lists
To join, send a blank e-mail to:
warwickbirds-subscribe@yahoogroups.com

WEST MIDLANDS

http://www.westmidlandbirdclub.com/
The West Midlands Bird Club serves Staffordshire, Warwickshire and Worcestershire as well as the Metropolitan County of the West Midlands. The site is a model of clarity and very easy on the eye. There is a large where-to-watch section though this is of variable quality as it is simply links to other sites rather than being self-penned. There are no recent sightings and rather than a mailing list, the club still uses a telephone hotline service. How quaint.

http://www.thomas1976.freeserve.co.uk/
This is a mini where-to-watch guide for the area and covers the counties mentioned above. Highlights are included for each season. Brief directions are included though you can click on a link to get a map of the appropriate area.

WILTSHIRE

http://www.wiltshire-web.co.uk/wildlife/
The Wiltshire Wildlife Trust has a good section on the 40 or so reserves it manages, though the slant is to general wildlife watching rather than just birds. Excellent maps.

WORCESTERSHIRE
(see also West Midlands)

http://www.worcswildlifetrust.co.uk/
The pages of the Worcestershire Wildlife Trust have a good selection of reserves but only written directions are included – there's not a map in sight.

YORKSHIRE

http://www.bradfordbirders.co.uk/
There is a lot of information about birding in the Bradford area here, as well as many articles from previous newsletters. The only problem is, they're all in downloadable form rather than present as web pages so you will need to have Adobe's Acrobat installed to read them. The recent sightings page is straightforward.

http://www.tka.co.uk/yoc/
The pages of the York Ornithological Club look very slick but I found the content to be disappointing. The recent sightings section was three months out of date and the where-to-watch section was little more than a series of links to other sites – of varying quality. I know that clubs are trying to raise as much money as possible but pop-up adverts are a huge turn-off and likely to turn potential browsers away.

**http://www.spurnpoint.com/
Spurn_bird_observatory.htm**
Plenty of archived sightings and an interesting article on the history of Spurn Observatory. The birding details are disappointing though, with a useless map and no tips on where to look for the best bird species.

http://www.filey2000.co.uk/birding.html
Though it is mainly concerned with the reserve at Filey Dams, this site also includes recent sightings from Filey Brigg as well (though there is more information about the Brigg at **http://
www.fbog.fsnet.co.uk/**). Joy of joys, you can easily submit your own sightings online.

http://www.sbsg.org/
There is a somewhat antiseptic feel to the Sheffield Bird Study Group's site – plenty of information but not a scrap of emotion. You would never guess that birding is something to be enjoyed. Recent sightings can be sorted by date or site but there are no specific site details telling you how to get to sites other than a grid reference.

Mailing lists
To join, send a blank e-mail to:
airebirding-subscribe@yahoogroups.com
YorkshireBirds-subscribe@yahoogroups.com

SCOTLAND

ABERDEENSHIRE

http://www.abdn.ac.uk/~src074/main.htm
Aberdeen University has a very active bird club and been on the web for many years now. There is lots of stuff here but updating is at the vagaries of term-time and it is noticeable that there have been no newsletters this year.

http://www.wildlifeweb.co.uk/
This is one of the longest running web-sites around, now in its 12th year. There is a recent sightings section – both for birds and other wildlife – and a where-to-watch-guide, aiming to cover the whole of Scotland though it is a bit patchy in places.

Mailing lists
To join, send a blank e-mail to:
ABZ-Rare-Birds-subscribe@yahoogroups.com

ANGUS AND DUNDEE

http://angusbirding.homestead.com/
A few recent sightings for birds and other wildlife are listed. The where-to-watch guide takes the form of listing some key species and suggesting places where they might be found.

http://www.montrosebasin.org.uk/
A few pages detailing the wildlife of Montrose Basin reserve. Needs updating and a map of where to find it would be appreciated.

ARGYLL AND BUTE

http://www.mullbirds.com/
A lovely little site describing the bird life on Mull. Recent sightings are included and there are plenty of suggestions for places to go, including the best places on the island to encounter the likes of White-tailed Eagle and Corncrake.

http://www.islaywildlife.freeserve.co.uk/inhtindex.htm
The Islay Natural History Trust has an excellent section on the best places to go birding on the island. There is also a major section on geology, assorted checklists, and details of recent sightings.

AYRSHIRE

http://www.ckrw3.fsnet.co.uk/index.htm
The Ayrshire branch of the Scottish Ornithologists Club has a huge web-site complete with archived newsletters, plenty of local sites, news, photos, checklist and extracts from the annual report. It all comes across as a very friendly club.

Mailing lists
To join, send a blank e-mail to:
ayrshirebirding-subscribe@yahoogroups.com

DUMFRIES AND GALLOWAY

Mailing lists
To join, send a blank e-mail to:
DumfriesandGallowayBirding-subscribe@yahoogroups.com

BRITISH WEB-SITES AND MAILING LISTS

FIFE

The only information I found on birding in Fife was on the pages of the Scottish Ornithologists' Club (**http://www.the-soc.fsnet.co.uk/**). If you go to the 'where to birdwatch' section, there are a couple of site guides there.

HIGHLAND

http://www.kincraig.com/rspb.htm
The local Kincraig pages have a detailed section on RSPB Insh Marshes.

http://www.wildcaithness.org/
These pages cover all sorts of wildlife watching in Caithness, from seabirds to whales.

Mailing lists
To join, send a blank e-mail to:
Highland_and_Moray_Birds-subscribe@ yahoogroups.com

LOTHIAN

http://www.andrewsi.freeserve.co.uk/ lothian-sites.htm
This impressive where-to-watch guide for the Lothian region covers some 37 main areas.

http://www.geocities.com/lothianbirding/ LSOC/Index_pagex.html
The Lothian branch of the SOC has a site that is still under development so there is no site guide or bird finding guide at the moment. There are a few recent sightings as well as the usual details of club meetings.

http://www.lothrare.org/rarebirds1.1.htm
This site is setting out to detail the occurrence of every single rare bird recorded in the area. It is a massive resource, but curiously has been put on just one absolutely huge page

Mailing lists
To join, send a blank e-mail to:
lothianbirdnews-subscribe@ yahoogroups.com

ORKNEY

http://www.nrbo.f2s.com/
The North Ronaldsay Bird Observatory site has a good range of information though perhaps not as much as might have been hoped for. For example, there are no ringing records or archived details of past migrations. The latest sightings page was four months out of date.

http://w8.demon.co.uk/www.charles-tait.com/guide/birdwatching.html
Extracts from the Orkney Guide Book offers a reasonable selection of birdwatching sites, though no location maps are given.

SHETLAND

http://www.wildlife.shetland.co.uk/
At first sight, the Shetland Wildlife web-site looks really impressive; it's only when you start to use it that a few quirks become apparent. There is a section on reserves but no detail at all for several on the map. Navigation is a bit hit or miss and of the many thousands of web-sites I've looked at, this is the only one with the menu on the right of the screen. Having said that, there is still a lot of useful information here on all sorts of wildlife.

http://www.fairislebirdobs.co.uk/
Given that Fair Isle is home to our most famous observatory, this site was something of a disappointment, being little more than a glorified advert for the place. There is no ringing data available, island bird list or anything other than the most basic guide to what birds turn up when – you have to go through previous reports and work it out for yourself.

STRATHCLYDE

http://www.baronshaugh.co.uk/
Plenty of information about Baron's Haugh RSPB reserve is complemented with recent sightings. These are all linked to the map of the reserve so that you know what has been seen and where.

http://kilbrydebirds.net/
This is a small club based in East Kilbride. There are only about 20 members at the moment but they are desperate for more. A friendly welcome is guaranteed.

WESTERN ISLES

http://www.wildlifehebrides.com/
A well presented site that should be your first port of call if you are interested in any sort of wildlife on the Western Isles.

WALES

CLWYD

http://www.deeestuary.freeserve.co.uk/
Last year's award-winning web-site needs no further recommendation. Even though it only covers part of the coast, it was the only birding reference to Clwyd I could find. Fortunately, it's a first class site with maps, sightings, tide tables and newsletters etc.

DYFED

http://hometown.aol.com/skokholm/holm.htm
There's practically no design and the site hasn't been updated for five years but I thought that this was a great site! The authors were obviously in love with the island and that love comes cascading through. Guaranteed to make you want to visit Skokholm.

http://stdavids.co.uk/nonprofit/ramsey/index.htm
Another island – this time Ramsey. Again, a simple site and not updated for over a year but there are details of how to get there, a calendar of what you might see in the different seasons and a list of birds, both breeding and regular migrants.

GLAMORGAN

http://homepage.ntlworld.com/johndw/gbc.html
A fine, very friendly site for the Glamorgan Bird Club. As well as the usual features, there are plenty of write-ups from previous club trips that make you wish you had been there. The where-to-watch section could do with a few more entries.

GWENT

http://www.gwentbirds.org.uk/
Obviously designed by the person doing the Glamorgan site, the pages of the Gwent Ornithological Society have the same look and feel to them though there are certain differences. There is no site guide as such but the entire latest newsletter is available, either to read online or download to print off and read later.

http://www.wildlifetrust.org.uk/gwent/
The local Wildlife Trust's site has a basic guide to their nature reserves but no maps.

GWYNEDD

http://mysite.freeserve.com/cambrianos
The Cambrian Ornithological Society offers both a site guide and bird finding section. Though you are encouraged to submit your records, there is no facility to do so online. Colour scheme is garish.

http://www.bbfo.org.uk/index.html
The pages of Bardsey Bird Observatory are somewhat disappointing. Apart from the fact that they haven't been updated for a year, the content is rather lacking too. I'd advise the members take a look at the Portland Bird Observatory site to see how it should be done.

POWYS

http://www.rspb.vyrnwy.org/english.htm
Though the maps are fairly disappointing, there is still some useful information here about RSPB Lake Vyrnwy, including video clips of a dozen or so key species. There is a section on recent news but this was a couple of months old when I looked.

http://www.gigrin.co.uk/index.html
Gigrin Farm is the best known of the various Red Kite feeding stations. The web-site positively bubbles with enthusiasm. There are pages about the kites themselves, loads of pictures and stories and information about other wildlife in the area. The only change I would make would be to make the map and directions a lot easier to find.

ENGLISH-LANGUAGE BIRD MAGAZINES

RECOGNISING that birdwatchers in Great Britain increasingly want information about birds and birding opportunities overseas, we have compiled this Directory of English language magazines (a mix of commercial and society-based titles) that we know of personally. We welcome further reader recommendations for future Editions of *The Yearbook*.

GREAT BRITAIN

Birding World

 A subscription-only title produced by the Bird Information Service team that runs the national Birdline telephone news service. The magazine caters for serious birders with a keen interest in UK rarities and overseas travel. Each monthly issue details the most significant bird sightings in Britain and the remainder of the Western Palearctic. Other regulars include first-person accounts of the finding of rare birds in the UK and accounts of overseas birding trips.
Editor: Steve Gantlett
Contact details: Birding World, Sea Lawn, Coast Road, Cley-next-the-Sea, Holt, Norfolk NR25 7RZ. Tel: 01263 740 913.
E-mail: Steve@birdingworld.co.uk
Web-site: www.birdingworld.co.uk

Birds

The quarterly members-only magazine issued by the Royal Society for the Protection of Birds is a full-colour super-A4 magazine that promotes the organisation's work in conservation and education. In addition to an extensive general news section, the magazine carries features on RSPB reserves, international initiatives with partner organisations, tips on developing birdwatching skills, members' letters and book reviews. *Birds* is available on tape for visually-impaired members.
Editor: Rob Hume
Contact details: Birds magazine, The Lodge, Sandy, Bedfordshire SG19 2DL. Tel: 01767 680 551. Web-site: www.rspb.org.uk

Birdwatch

A monthly full-colour A4 magazine available on subscription and from main newsagents in Britain. Contains a range of features on identification, UK and foreign birding areas and taxonomic issues designed to appeal to experienced birders. Also contains news, readers' letters, product reviews and summaries of British bird sightings.
Editor: Dominic Mitchell
Contact details: Solo Publishing Ltd, 3D/F Leroy House, 436 Essex Road, Islington, London N1 3QP. Tel: 020 7704 9495.
Web-site: www.birdwatch.co.uk

Bird Watching

 Britain's best-selling monthly bird magazine available from all leading newsagents and on subscription. This A4 full-colour title caters for all active birdwatchers with articles to help beginners as well as the more experienced.
Every issue contains articles on garden birds and identification, plus news, readers' letters, leading columnists such as John Gooders and Ian Wallace, and the *Go Birding* pull-out guide to bird walks and reserves. The UK Bird Sightings section is the world's largest monthly round-up of bird news. Individual product reviews, complement surveys of leading optical products. The annual travel supplement *Destinations* appears with the November issue.
Editor: David Cromack
Contact details: Emap Active Ltd, Bretton Court, Peterborough PE3 8DZ. Tel: 01733 282 601. E-mail: david.cromack@emap.com

British Birds

A long-established subscription-only journal of record that aims to publish material on behaviour, conservation, distribution, ecology, identification, status and taxonomy for birders throughout the Western Palearctic. Organises both the *BB Bird Illustrator of the Year* and *BB Bird Photograph of the Year* competitions. Publishes the annual report of the British Birds Rarities Committee.
Editor: Roger Riddington
Contact details: BB 2000 Ltd, Chapel Cottage, Dunrossness, Shetland ZE2 9JH.
Tel: 01950 460 080.
E-mail: editor@britishbirds.co.uk

World Birdwatch

This is the long-established quarterly subscription-only magazine from BirdLife International that seeks to promote its global conservation activities. An extensive round-up of world bird-related news is supported with features such as Sites To Save and Country Fact File, plus articles on education, habitat protection and events.
Editor: Richard Thomas
Contact details: BirdLife International, Wellbrook Court, Girton Road, Cambridge CB3 0NA. E-mail: birdlife@birdlife.org.uk

FINLAND

Alula

Started in 1995, *Alula* is an independent journal for people interested in birds and bird identification. Regular topics include ID papers by field experts, articles about birding sites, tests of optical equipment, literature reviews, competitions and current birding issues. In order to widen its sales appeal, this high-quality quarterly A4 magazine is now available in an English-language edition as well as Finnish.
Editor: Antero Topp
Contact details: Alula Oy, Eestinkalliontie 16D, FIN-02280 Espoo, Finland.
E-mail: antero.topp@alula.fi
Web-site: www.alula.fi

HOLLAND

Dutch Birding

Many of the articles in this long-established monthly journal that caters for serious birders and twitchers are published in English, and the Dutch pieces generally have an English summary. Regular topics include ID papers by field experts, extensive coverage of scarcer birds in Holland and the Western Paearctic generally, literature reviews, competitions and current birding issues.
Editor: Arnoud van den Berg
Contact details: Dutch Birding, Postbus 116, 2080 AC Santpoort-Zuid, Netherlands.
E-mail: editors@dutchbirding.nl
www.dutchbirding.nl

SOUTH AFRICA

Africa Birds & Birding

This award-winning glossy A4 bi-monthly colour magazine enjoys support from BirdLife South Africa but remains totally independent. It strives to foster an awareness of the continent's birdlife and encourages birdwatching as a pastime and for its ecotourism potential. High quality photographic features are included along with articles on sites, book and product reviews, news and letters.
Editor-in-Chief/Publisher: Peter Borchert
Contact details: Black Eagle Publishing, PO Box 44223, Claremont 7735, Cape Town, South Africa.
E-mail: wildmags@blackeaglemedia.co.za
Web-site: www.africa-geographic.com

USA

Birder's World

A popular title for American birdwatchers of all experience levels, this A4 all-colour monthly magazine carries features on garden birds, profiles of individual bird species, guides to top birding locations in the US, conservation issues, bird behaviour, book and optics

BIRDWATCHING AND RELATED COURSES

reviews. In addition to readers' letters, there is usually a section devoted to answering reader questions and a photo-quiz. Copies can be found in larger branches of leading British newsagents.

Editor: Charles J Hagner.

Contact details: Klambach Publishing Co, Birder's World editorial dept, PO Box 1612, Waukesha, WI 53187-1612, USA.

E-mail: mail@birder'sworld.com

Birding

Issued exclusively to members six times a year by the American Birders Association, a not-for-profit organisation that aims to help field birders develop their knowledge, skills and enjoyment of wild birds. The organisation (membership open to all birdwatchers) also encourages the conservation of birds and their habitats. In practice this means the magazine carries full-colour features on bird-finding in the USA and Canada, in-depth ID articles, book and product reviews, photo quizzes, fieldcraft, taxonomy and conservation articles.

Editor: Paul J Baicich

Contact details: American Birding Association, 720 W Monument Street, Colorado Springs, Colorado 80904-3624, USA.

Web-site: www.americanbirding.org

Birdwatcher's Digest

This pocket-sized full-colour bi-monthly magazine is unashamedly populist in its approach and features a high proportion of articles about backyard birding and readers' birding tales as well as helpful advice on ID and fieldcraft. Top birding areas in the USA are spotlighted and Book Notes covers the latest publications.

Editor: William H Thompson.

Contact details: Birdwatcher's Digest, PO Box 110, Marietta, Ohio 45750, USA.

E-mail: editor@birdwatchersdigest.com

Web-site: www.birdwatchersdigest.com

BIRDWATCHING AND RELATED COURSES FOR 2003

MANY birdwatchers, both beginners and the more experienced, find that they can increase their knowledge and skills significantly by attending one of the many courses that are available for birdwatching. We have geographically listed a selection here, which we hope readers will find useful. If you attend a course from this list, don't forget to tell the organisers that you found the information in *The Birdwatcher's Yearbook*.

ALSTON HALL
Longridge, Preston, Lancs
01772 784 661

Winter Farmland Birds	Mar-29
Spring Migration	Apr-26
Contact college for details of courses later in 2003	

BURTON MANOR COLLEGE
Burton, S.Wirral, Cheshire
01513 365172

| Seabird Summer | Apr 23-25 |
| Another course to be arranged for July | |

FIELD STUDIES COUNCIL (see contact details in National Directory)

Blencathra, Keswick, Cumbria
01768 779601

| Introduction to Birds | May 30 - Jun 1 |
| What's that Bird? | Oct 23-26 |

Epping Forest, Loughton, Essex
020 8508 7714

| Winter Birds at Lea Valley | Feb 1 |
| Minsmere Birds in May | May 11 |

BIRDWATCHING AND RELATED COURSES

Flatford Mill, East Bergholt, Suffolk
01206 298283

Mid Winter Birdwatching Weekend	Jan 24-26
Late Winter Birdwatching Weekend	Feb 21-23
Spring Birdwatching Weekend	Apr 25-27
Bird Songs and Calls for Beginners	May 2-4
Bird Songs and Calls for Improvers	May 9-11
Mid Summer Birdwatching Weekend	Jun 13-15
Introducing Bird Ringing	Aug 29-31
Early Autumn Birdwatching: Birds on Migration	Sep 12-14
Late Autumn Birdwatching Weekend	Nov 21-23
Autumn Birdwatching Weekend	Oct 10-12
Training for BTO Bird Ringers	Oct 24-26

Juniper Hall, Dorking, Surrey, 0845 458 3507

Spring Birds and their Songs	May 16-18
Winter Birdwatching: Waders and Wildfowl	Nov 21-23

Malham Tarn, Settle, N.Yorks
01729 830331

Birdwatching in the Dales	May 16-18

Nettlecombe Court, Taunton, Somerset
01984 640320

February Birds	Feb 21-24
Bird Song	Apr 18-20
Birds and Butterflies in High Summer	Aug 4-11

Orielton, Pembrokeshire
01646 661225

Spring Birds	May 8-12

Preston Montford, Shrewsbury, Shropshire
01743 850380

Discovering Birds	Apr 11-13
In Search of the Red Kite and Other Birds	Jul 4-6
Birds: Sight and Sound in Early Summer	May 23-27

Rhyd-y-Creuau, Betws-y-Coed, Conwy, 01690 710494

Autumn Birds of Snowdonia and the North Wales Coast	Sep 5-12

Slapton Ley, Kingsbridge, Devon

South Devon Birds: Sights and Sounds of Spring	May 2-6
Wintering Wildfowl and Waders of South Devon	Jan 16-18 2004

HIGHAM HALL, Bassenthwaite Lake, Cumbria
01768 776276

Beginners' Guide to Ornithology	Jan 10-12
Winter Birds on the Solway	Feb 7-9
Wildlife through the Camera	Mar 7-9
Lakeland Birds	Jun 8-13

LOSEHILL HALL, Castleton Derbyshire
01433 620373

RSPB/Losehill Hall Structured course	
Getting to Know Birds- part 1	Nov 22-26 2002
Getting to Know Birds- part 2	May 9-13
Peak Birds (TBC)	30 May- 3 Jun

NORTH NOTTS RINGING GROUP
Based at Western Burton power station

North Notts Ringing and training course (See County Directory for contact details)	Aug 2-9

SCOTTISH FIELD STUDIES ASSOCIATION
Kindrogan Field Centre, Perthshire
01250 881286

Spring Birds for Beginners	May 16-18
Spring Birds	May 23-25
Autumn Birds	Oct 17-24
Birds for Beginners	Oct 24-26
How do birds weather the weather?	Oct 3-5

WANSFELL COLLEGE
Theydon Bois, Epping, Essex.6
01992 813286

Winter Birds	Jan 21-24
What's that Bird?	Apr 22-24

36

EVENTS DIARY 2003

JANUARY

25-26th Big Garden Birdwatch
contact Richard Bashford, RSPB.
e-mail:
richard.bashford@rspb.org.uk

FEBRUARY

**8-9th The Great West
Bird Fair**
WWT, Slimbridge, Glos.
Contact WWT.

**22nd South-East England
Regional Members Conference**
Didcot Civic Hall, Oxfordshire.
Contact: Dawn Balmer at BTO or
Peter Abbott.
e-mail: dawn.balmer@bto.org or
peterabbott@waitrose.com.

22nd-23rd Lee Valley Bird Fair
Lee Valley Park Farms, nr Fishers
Green, Essex. 01992 702200.
www.leavalleypark.org.uk

**26th Glasgow RSPB Member's
Group, 30th Anniversary
Lecture.**
Stuart Housden, Director RSPB,
Scotland, Woodside Halls,
Glasgow.

MARCH

**1st West Midlands Regional
Ringing Conference.**
Hosted by Chelmarsh Ringing
Group. Contact Dawn Balmer at
BTO or Dave Fulton.
e-mail: dawn.balmer@bto.org or
DaveBirder@aol.com

**15th Sheffield BTO
Conference**
University of Sheffield Students
Union Auditorium. Organised by
Chris Falshaw. Theme: Woodland
Birds. Speakers include David
Jardine, Rob Fuller, Andy Wilson,
Keith Clarkson and Ben Hatchwell.
E-mail: chris.falsh@virgin.net or
dawn.balmer@bto.org.

**15th North-West England
Regional Ringing Conference**
hosted by North Lancashire
Ringing Group. To be held at
Leighton Moss, Lancashire.
Contact John Wilson, 40 Church

Hill Avenue, Warton, Carnforth,
Lancashire, LA5 9NU e-mail:
johnwilsonpanurus@callnetuk.com.

**21th – April 6th National
Exhibition of Wildlife Art**
Road Range Gallery, Liverpool.
Contact NEWA, e-mail:
newa@mtuffrey.freeserve.co.uk

**28-30th RSPB members
weekend in York**
Contact RSPB. e-mail:
carol.roddy@rspb.org.uk

APRIL

**11-16th Long Term Studies Of
Birds**
BOU Annual Conference and AGM
University of Oxford, Oxfordshire,
UK. Held jointly with the Edward
Grey Institute.

MAY

**18-25th The VIth World
Conference on Birds of Prey
and Owls**
Hosted by BirdLife Hungary in
Budapest. All enquiries should be
addressed to: WWGBP, PO Box 52,
Towcester, NN12 7ZW, Tel & Fax:
01604 86 23 31.
e-mail: WWGBP@aol.com &
robin.chancellor@virgin.net,
www.Raptors-International.de.

**24-30th Wake up to Birds
Week**
Carole McCormick, 01767 680551.
e-mail:
carole.mccormick@rspb.org.uk

SE Bird Fair
(date to be confirmed)
WWT, Arundel.
01903 883355.

JUNE

Wildlife Photo and Bird Fair
(date and venue to be confirmed)
Alan Richards, 0152 785 2357.
www.birder.co.uk

AUGUST

**15-17th The British
Birdwatching Fair**
Rutland Water. www.birdfair.org.uk

**30th – 31th The Scottish
Wildlife and Countryside Fair**
Vane Farm,
Contact the RSPB Scotland.

SEPTEMBER

**9-11th British Ecological
Society Annual Meeting.**
Manchester Metropolitan
University. Abstract submission
deadline May 2003. Details from
British Ecological Society, 26
Blades Court, Deodar Rd, Putney,
London, SW15 2NU, Tel: 020 8871
9797, Fax: 020 8871 9779.
e-mail: general@
ecology.demon.co.uk,
www.demon.co.uk/bes

**24th - 5th October SWLA annual
exhibition.**
Mall Galleries, London.
Contact SWLA.

OCTOBER

4th RSPB AGM
Queen Elizabeth II Conference
Centre, London,
Contact Carol Roddy, RSPB,
e-mail: carol.roddy@rspb.org.uk

24-27th Time for Birds
Contact Carole McCormick, 01767
680551. e-mail:
carole.mccormick@rspb.org.uk

Norfolk Bird Fair
Date to be confirmed (Autumn
half-term weekend)
Titchwell, Norfolk.
01485 210779.

NOVEMBER

15-17th NW Bird Fair
WWT, Martin Mere
01704 895181.

DECEMBER

**5-7th The BTO's Members'
Weekend.**
(date to be confirmed)
Hayes Conference Centre,
Swanwick, Derbyshire.
Contact Nick Carter, BTO.

Full contact details for the clubs and organisations listed here can be found under their entries in the County,
National and International directories.

DIARY - JANUARY 2003

1	Wed	*New Year's Day*
2	Thu	*Holiday (Scotland)*
3	Fri	
4	Sat	
5	Sun	
6	Mon	
7	Tue	
8	Wed	
9	Thu	
10	Fri	
11	Sat	
12	Sun	
13	Mon	
14	Tue	
15	Wed	
16	Thu	
17	Fri	
18	Sat	
19	Sun	
20	Mon	
21	Tue	
22	Wed	
23	Thu	
24	Fri	
25	Sat	
26	Sun	
27	Mon	
28	Tue	
29	Wed	
30	Thu	
31	Fri	

DIARY 2003

DIARY - FEBRUARY 2003

1	Sat	
2	Sun	
3	Mon	
4	Tue	
5	Wed	
6	Thu	
7	Fri	
8	Sat	
9	Sun	
10	Mon	
11	Tue	
12	Wed	
13	Thu	
14	Fri	
15	Sat	
16	Sun	
17	Mon	
18	Tue	
19	Wed	
20	Thu	
21	Fri	
22	Sat	
23	Sun	
24	Mon	
25	Tue	
26	Wed	
27	Thu	
28	Fri	

DIARY - MARCH 2003

1	Sat	
2	Sun	
3	Mon	
4	Tue	
5	Wed	
6	Thu	
7	Fri	
8	Sat	
9	Sun	
10	Mon	
11	Tue	
12	Wed	
13	Thu	
14	Fri	
15	Sat	
16	Sun	
17	Mon	
18	Tue	
19	Wed	
20	Thu	
21	Fri	
22	Sat	
23	Sun	
24	Mon	
25	Tue	
26	Wed	
27	Thu	
28	Fri	
29	Sat	
30	Sun	*Mothering Sunday* *British Summertime begins*
31	Mon	

BIRD NOTES - MARCH 2003

DIARY - APRIL 2003

1	Tue	
2	Wed	
3	Thu	
4	Fri	
5	Sat	
6	Sun	
7	Mon	
8	Tue	
9	Wed	
10	Thu	
11	Fri	
12	Sat	
13	Sun	
14	Mon	
15	Tue	
16	Wed	
17	Thu	
18	Fri	*Good Friday*
19	Sat	
20	Sun	*Easter Sunday*
21	Mon	*Easter Monday*
22	Tue	
23	Wed	
24	Thu	
25	Fri	
26	Sat	
27	Sun	
28	Mon	
29	Tue	
30	Wed	

DIARY - MAY 2003

1 Thu		
2 Fri		
3 Sat		
4 Sun		
5 Mon		*May Day*
6 Tue		
7 Wed		
8 Thu		
9 Fri		
10 Sat		
11 Sun		
12 Mon		
13 Tue		
14 Wed		
15 Thu		
16 Fri		
17 Sat		
18 Sun		
19 Mon		
20 Tue		
21 Wed		
22 Thu		
23 Fri		
24 Sat		
25 Sun		
26 Mon		*Spring Bank Holiday*
27 Tue		
28 Wed		
29 Thu		
30 Fri		
31 Sat		

DIARY - JUNE 2003

1	Sun
2	Mon
3	Tue
4	Wed
5	Thu
6	Fri
7	Sat
8	Sun
9	Mon
10	Tue
11	Wed
12	Thu
13	Fri
14	Sat
15	Sun
16	Mon
17	Tue
18	Wed
19	Thu
20	Fri
21	Sat
22	Sun
23	Mon
24	Tue
25	Wed
26	Thu
27	Fri
28	Sat
29	Sun
30	Mon

48

DIARY - JULY 2003

1	Tue
2	Wed
3	Thu
4	Fri
5	Sat
6	Sun
7	Mon
8	Tue
9	Wed
10	Thu
11	Fri
12	Sat
13	Sun
14	Mon
15	Tue
16	Wed
17	Thu
18	Fri
19	Sat
20	Sun
21	Mon
22	Tue
23	Wed
24	Thu
25	Fri
26	Sat
27	Sun
28	Mon
29	Tue
30	Wed
31	Thu

BIRD NOTES -JULY 2003

DIARY - AUGUST 2003

1 Fri	
2 Sat	
3 Sun	
4 Mon	
5 Tue	
6 Wed	
7 Thu	
8 Fri	
9 Sat	
10 Sun	
11 Mon	
12 Tue	
13 Wed	
14 Thu	
15 Fri	
16 Sat	
17 Sun	
18 Mon	
19 Tue	
20 Wed	
21 Thu	
22 Fri	
23 Sat	
24 Sun	
25 Mon	*Late Summer Holiday*
26 Tue	
27 Wed	
28 Thu	
29 Fri	
30 Sat	
31 Sun	

BIRD NOTES AUGUST 2003

DIARY - SEPTEMBER 2003

1	Mon
2	Tue
3	Wed
4	Thu
5	Fri
6	Sat
7	Sun
8	Mon
9	Tue
10	Wed
11	Thu
12	Fri
13	Sat
14	Sun
15	Mon
16	Tue
17	Wed
18	Thu
19	Fri
20	Sat
21	Sun
22	Mon
23	Tue
24	Wed
25	Thu
26	Fri
27	Sat
28	Sun
29	Mon
30	Tue

DIARY - OCTOBER 2003

1 Wed	
2 Thu	
3 Fri	
4 Sat	
5 Sun	
6 Mon	
7 Tue	
8 Wed	
9 Thu	
10 Fri	
11 Sat	
12 Sun	
13 Mon	
14 Tue	
15 Wed	
16 Thu	
17 Fri	
18 Sat	
19 Sun	
20 Mon	
21 Tue	
22 Wed	
23 Thu	
24 Fri	
25 Sat	
26 Sun	*British Summertime ends*
27 Mon	
28 Tue	
29 Wed	
30 Thu	
31 Fri	

DIARY 2003

DIARY - NOVEMBER 2003

1	Sat	
2	Sun	
3	Mon	
4	Tue	
5	Wed	
6	Thu	
7	Fri	
8	Sat	
9	Sun	*Rememberance Sunday*
10	Mon	
11	Tue	
12	Wed	
13	Thu	
14	Fri	
15	Sat	
16	Sun	
17	Mon	
18	Tue	
19	Wed	
20	Thu	
21	Fri	
22	Sat	
23	Sun	
24	Mon	
25	Tue	
26	Wed	
27	Thu	
28	Fri	
29	Sat	
30	Sun	

DIARY - DECEMBER 2003

1	Mon	
2	Tue	
3	Wed	
4	Thu	
5	Fri	
6	Sat	
7	Sun	
8	Mon	
9	Tue	
10	Wed	
11	Thu	
12	Fri	
13	Sat	
14	Sun	
15	Mon	
16	Tue	
17	Wed	
18	Thu	
19	Fri	
20	Sat	
21	Sun	
22	Mon	
23	Tue	
24	Wed	
25	Thu	*Christmas Day*
26	Fri	*Boxing Day*
27	Sat	
28	Sun	
29	Mon	
30	Tue	
31	Wed	

BIRD NOTES -DECEMBER 2003

YEAR PLANNER 2004

January

February

March

April

May

June

July

August

September

October

November

December

LOG CHARTS

A pair of Avocets, drawn by Marco Preziosi, for the 2002 BB
illustration competition.

SPECIES, CATEGORIES, CODES AND GUIDE TO USE

Species list

The charts include all species on the British List and is based on the 1992 *BOU Checklist of Birds of Britain and Ireland* and the various BOURC reports published up to September 2002, when a major revision of taxonomic order was announced by the BOU.

The current list is augmented by birds which breed or occur regularly in Europe - almost 600 species altogether. Vagrants which are not on the British List, but which may have occurred in other parts of the British Isles, are not included. Readers who wish to record such species may use the extra rows provided on the last page. In this connection it should be noted that separate lists exist for Northern Ireland (kept by the Northern Ireland Birdwatchers' Association) and the Isle of Man (kept by the Manx Ornithological Society), and that Irish records are assessed by the Irish Rare Birds Committee.

There was insufficient time to implement the taxonomic changes introduced this year so species remain arranged in Voous order; their names are those most widely used in the current field guides (with some proposed changes shown in parentheses); each is followed by its scientific name, printed in italics. We welcome reader feedback to help us decide whether to adopt the new taxonomic order for future editions.

Species categories

The following categories are those assigned by the British Ornithologists' Union.

A Species which have been recorded in an apparently natural state at least once since January 1, 1950.

B Species which would otherwise be in Category A but have not been recorded since December 31, 1949.

C Species that, although originally introduced by man, either deliberately or accidentally, have established breeding populations derived from introduced stock that maintain themselves without necessary recourse to further introduction. (This category has been subdivided to differentiate between various groups of naturalised species, but these subdivisions are outside the purpose of the log charts).

D Species that would otherwise appear in Categories A or B except that there is reasonable doubt that they have ever occurred in a natural state. (Species in this category are included in the log charts, though they do not qualify for inclusion in the British List, which comprises species in Categories A, B and C only. One of the objects of Category D is to note records of species which are not yet full additions, so that they are not overlooked if acceptable records subsequently occur. Bird report editors are encouraged to include records of species in Category D as appendices to their systematic lists).

E Species that have been recorded as introductions, transportees or escapees from captivity, and whose populations (if any) are thought not to be self-sustaining. They do not form part of the British List and are not included in the log charts.

EU Species not on the British List, or in Category D, but which either breed or occur regularly elsewhere in Europe.

LOG CHARTS

Life list

Ticks made in the 'Life List' column suffice for keeping a running personal total of species. However, added benefit can be obtained by replacing ticks with a note of the year of first occurrence. To take an example: one's first-ever Marsh Sandpiper, seen on April 14, 2003, would be logged with '03' in the Life List and '14' in the April column (as well as a tick in the 2003 column). As Life List entries are carried forward annually, in years to come it would be a simple matter to relocate this record.

First and last dates of migrants

Arrivals of migrants can be recorded by inserting dates instead of ticks in the relevant month columns. For example, a Common Sandpiper on March 11 would be recorded by inserting '11' against Common Sandpiper in the March column. The same applies to departures, though dates of last sightings can only be entered at the end of the year after checking one's field notebook.

Unheaded columns

The three unheaded columns at the right hand end of each chart are for special (personal) use. This may be, for example, a, second holiday, a particular county or a 'local patch'. Another use could be to indicate species on, for example, the Northern Ireland List or the Isle of Man List.

BTO species codes

British Trust for Ornithology two-letter species codes are shown in brackets in the fourth column from the right. They exist for many species, races and hybrids recorded in recent surveys. Readers should refer to the BTO if more codes are needed. In addition to those given in the charts, the following are available for some well-marked races or forms - Whistling Swan (WZ), European White-fronted Goose (EW), Greenland White-fronted Goose (NW), dark-bellied Brent Goose (DB), pale-bellied Brent Goose (PB), Black Brant (BB), Green-winged Teal (TA), Yellow-legged Gull (YG), Kumlien's Gull (KG), Feral Pigeon (FP), White Wagtail (WB), Black-bellied Dipper (DJ), Hooded Crow (HC), intermediate crow (HB).

Rarities

Rarities are indicated by a capital letter 'R' immediately preceding the 'Euring No.' column.

EURING species numbers

EURING species numbers are given in the last column. As they are taken from the full Holarctic bird list there are many apparent gaps. It is important that these are not filled arbitrarily by observers wishing to record species not listed in the charts, as this would compromise the integrity of the scheme. Similarly, the addition of a further digit to indicate sub-species is to be avoided, since EURING has already assigned numbers for this purpose. The numbering follows the Voous order of species.

Rare breeding birds

Species monitored by the Rare Breeding Birds Panel (see National Directory) comprise all those on Schedule 1 of the Wildlife and Countryside Act 1981 (see Quick Reference) together with all escaped or introduced species breeding in small numbers. The following annotations in the charts (third column from the right) reflect the RBBP's categories:

(b)[A]   Rare species. All breeding details requested.

(b)[B]   Less scarce species. Totals requested from counties with more than 10 pairs or localities; elsewhere all details requested.

(b)[C]   Less scarce species (specifically Barn Owl, Kingfisher, Crossbill). County summaries requested.

(b)[D]   Escaped or introduced species. Treated as less scarce species.

DIVERS, GREBES, ALBATROSS, FULMAR, PETRELS, SHEARWATERS.

	Species	Scientific name	Life list	2003 list	24 hr	Garden	Holiday	Jan	Feb	Mar	Apr	May	Jun	Jul	Aug	Sep	Oct	Nov	Dec	BTO	RBBP	Bou	EU No
A	Red-throated Diver	Gavia stellata																		(RH)	(b)B		0002
A	Black-throated Diver	G. arctica																		(BV)	(b)A		0003
A	Great Northern Diver	G. immer																		(ND)			0004
A	White-(Yellow)billed Diver	G. adamsii																		(IW)		R	0005
A	Pied-billed Grebe	Podilymbus podiceps																		(PJ)		R	0006
A	Little Grebe	Tachybaptus ruficollis																		(LG)			0007
A	Great Crested Grebe	Podiceps cristatus																		(GG)			0009
A	Red-necked Grebe	P. grisegena																		(RX)	(b)A		0010
A	Slavonian Grebe	P. auritus																		(SZ)	(b)A		0011
A	Black-necked Grebe	P. nigricollis																		(BN)	(b)A		0012
A	Black-browed Albatross	Thalassarche melanophris																		(AA)		R	0014
A	Fulmar	Fulmarus glacialis																		(F)			0020
A	*'Soft-plumaged Petrel	'Pterodroma mollis/madeira/feae																				R	0026
B	Capped Petrel	Pterodroma hasitata																				R	0029
B	Bulwer's Petrel	Bulweria bulwerii																				R	0034
A	Cory's Shearwater	Calonectris diomedea																		(CQ)			0036
A	Great Shearwater	Puffinus gravis																		(GQ)			0040
A	Sooty Shearwater	P. griseus																		(OT)			0043
A	Manx Shearwater	P. puffinus																		(MX)			0046
A	Mediterranean Shearwater	P. mauretanicus																					0046
A	Little Shearwater	P. assimilis																				R	0048
A	Wilson's Petrel	Oceanites oceanicus																				R	0050
B	White-faced Petrel	Pelagodroma marina																				R	0051
A	Storm Petrel	Hydrobates pelagicus																		(TM)			0052

Sub-total

*Alternative sub-species

66

PETRELS, cont. GANNET, CORMORANTS, PELICANS, BITTERNS, HERONS, STORKS

	Species	Scientific name	Life list	2003 list	24 hr	Garden	Holiday	Jan	Feb	Mar	Apr	May	Jun	Jul	Aug	Sep	Oct	Nov	Dec	BTO	RBBP	Bou	EU No
A	Leach's Petrel	Oceanodroma leucorhoa																		(TL)	(b)B		0055
A	Swinhoe's Petrel	O. monorhis																				R	0056
B	Madeiran Petrel	O. castro																				R	0058
A	Red-billed Tropicbird	Phaethon aethereus																					
A	Gannet	Morus bassanus																		(GX)			0071
A	Cormorant	Phalacrocorax carbo																		(CA)			0072
A	Double-crested Cormorant	P. auritus																				R	0078
A	Shag	P. aristotelis																		(SA)			0080
EU	Pygmy Cormorant	P. pygmeus																					0082
D	Great White Pelican	Pelecanus onocrotalus																		(YP)		R	0088
EU	Dalmatian Pelican	P. crispus																					0089
A	Magnificent Frigatebird	Fregata magnificens																				R	0093
A	Bittern	Botaurus stellaris																		(BI)	(b)A		0095
A	American Bittern	B. lentiginosus																		(AM)		R	0096
A	Little Bittern	Ixobrychus minutus																		(LL)		R	0098
A	Night Heron	Nycticorax nycticorax																		(NT)	(b)AD	R	0104
A	Green Heron	Butorides virescens																		(HR)		R	0107
A	Squacco Heron	Ardeola ralloides																		(QH)		R	0108
A	Cattle Egret	Bubulcus ibis																		(EC)		R	0111
A	Little Egret	Egretta garzetta																		(ET)	(b)A		0119
A	Great White Egret	Ardea alba																		(HW)		R	0121
A	Grey Heron	A. cinerea																		(H)			0122
A	Purple Heron	A. purpurea																		(UR)			0124
A	Black Stork	Ciconia nigra																		(OS)		R	0131
	Sub-total																						

67

IBIS, SPOONBILL, FLAMINGO, SWANS, GEESE, DUCKS

	Name	Scientific name	Life list	2003 list	24 hr	Garden	Holiday	Jan	Feb	Mar	Apr	May	Jun	Jul	Aug	Sep	Oct	Nov	Dec	BTO	RBBP	Bou	EU No
A	White Stork	C. ciconia																		(OR)			0134
A	Glossy Ibis	Plegadis falcinellus																		(IB)			0136
A	Spoonbill	Platalea leucorodia																		(NB)	(b)A		0144
D	Greater Flamingo	Phoenicopterus roseus																		(FL)		R	0147
AC	Mute Swan	Cygnus olor																		(MS)			0152
A	Bewick's (Tundra) Swan	C. columbianus																		(BS)			0153
A	Whooper Swan	C. cygnus																		(WS)	(b)AD		0154
A	Bean Goose	Anser fabalis																		(BE)	(b)D		0157
A	Pink-footed Goose	A. brachyrhynchus																		(PG)	(b)AD		0158
A	White-fronted Goose	A. albifrons																		(WG)	(b)D		0159
A	Lesser White-fr Goose	A. erythropus																		(LC)	(b)B	R	0160
AC	Greylag Goose	A. anser																		(GJ)			0161
A	Snow Goose	A. caerulescens																		(SJ)	(b)D		0163
AC	Canada Goose	Branta canadensis																		(CG)			0166
A	Barnacle Goose	B. leucopsis																		(BY)	(b)D		0167
A	Brent Goose	B. bernicla																		(BG)	(b)D		0168
A	Red-breasted Goose	B. ruficollis																		(EB)	(b)B	R	0169
C	Egyptian Goose	Alopochen aegyptiacus																		(EG)	(b)D		0170
B	Ruddy Shelduck	Tadorna ferruginea																		(UD)	(b)D		0171
A	Shelduck	T. tadorna																		(SU)			0173
C	Mandarin Duck	Aix galericulata																		(MN)			0178
A	Wigeon	Anas penelope																		(WN)	(b)B		0179
A	American Wigeon	A. americana																		(AW)		R	0180
D	Falcated Duck	A. falcata																		(FT)		R	0181

Sub-total

68

DUCKS continued

	Common name	Scientific name	Life list	2003 list	24 hr	Garden	Holiday	Jan	Feb	Mar	Apr	May	Jun	Jul	Aug	Sep	Oct	Nov	Dec	BTO	RBBP	BoU	EU No
AC	Gadwall	A. strepera																		(GA)	(b)B		0182
D	Baikal Teal	A. formosa																		(IK)		R	0183
A	Eurasian Teal	A. crecca																		(T)			0184
A	Green-winged Teal	A. carolinensis																					
AC	Mallard	A. platyrhynchos																		(MA)			0186
A	American Black Duck	A. rubripes																		(BD)		R	0187
A	Pintail	A. acuta																		(PT)	(b)A		0189
A	Garganey	A. querquedula																		(GY)	(b)A		0191
A	Blue-winged Teal	A. discors																		(TB)	(b)B	R	0192
A	Shoveler	A. clypeata																		(SV)			0194
D	Marbled Duck	Marmaronetta angustirostris																				R	0195
A	Red-crested Pochard	Netta rufina																		(RQ)	(b)D		0196
A	Canvasback	Aythya valisineria																				R	0197
A	Pochard	A. ferina																		(PO)	(b)B		0198
A	Redhead	A. americana																		(AZ)		R	0199
A	Ring-necked Duck	A. collaris																		(NG)			0200
A	Ferruginous Duck	A. nyroca																		(ED)			0202
A	Tufted Duck	A. fuligula																		(TU)			0203
A	Scaup	A. marila																		(SP)	(b)A		0204
A	Lesser Scaup	A. affinis																		(AY)		R	0205
A	Eider	Somateria mollissima																		(E)			0206
A	King Eider	S. spectabilis																		(KE)		R	0207
A	Steller's Eider	Polysticta stelleri																		(ES)		R	0209
A	Harlequin	Histrionicus histrionicus																		(HQ)		R	0211

Sub-total

DUCKS continued, RAPTORS

	Species	Scientific name	Life list	2003 list	24 hr	Garden	Holiday	Jan	Feb	Mar	Apr	May	Jun	Jul	Aug	Sep	Oct	Nov	Dec	BTO	RBBP	Bou	EU No
A	Long-tailed Duck	Clangula hyemalis																		(LN)	(b)A		0212
A	Common Scoter	Melanitta nigra																		(CX)	(b)A		0213
A	Surf Scoter	M. perspicillata																		(FS)			0214
A	Velvet Scoter	M. fusca																		(VS)			0215
A	Bufflehead	Bucephala albeola																		(VH)		R	0216
A	Barrow's Goldeneye	B. islandica																				R	0217
A	Goldeneye	B. clangula																		(GN)	(b)AD		0218
A	Smew	Mergellus albellus																		(SY)			0220
A	Red-breasted Merganser	Mergus serrator																		(RM)			0221
A	Goosander	M. merganser																		(GD)			0223
C	Ruddy Duck	Oxyura jamaicensis																		(BY)			0225
EU	White-headed Duck	O. Leucocephala																		(WQ)			0226
A	Honey Buzzard	Pernis apivorus																		(HZ)	(b)A		0231
EU	Black-winged Kite	Elanus caeruleus																					0235
A	Black Kite	Milvus migrans																		(KB)		R	0238
AC	Red Kite	M. milvus																		(KT)	(b)A		0239
A	White-tailed Eagle	Haliaeetus albicilla																		(WE)	(b)A		0243
D	Bald Eagle	H. leucocephalus																				R	0244
EU	Lammergeier	Gypaetus barbatus																					0246
BD	Egyptian Vulture	Neophron percnopterus																				R	0247
D	Black (Monk) Vulture	Aegypius monachus																				R	0255
A	Short-toed Eagle	Circaetus gallicus																					0256
A	Marsh Harrier	Circus aeruginosus																		(MR)	(b)A		0260
A	Hen Harrier	C. cyaneus																		(HH)	(b)B		0261

Sub-total

RAPTORS continued

Cat	Species	Scientific name	Life list	2003 list	24 hr	Garden	Holiday	Jan	Feb	Mar	Apr	May	Jun	Jul	Aug	Sep	Oct	Nov	Dec	BTO	RBBP	Bou	EU No
A	Pallid Harrier	C. macrourus																		(MO)	(b)A	R	0262
A	Montagu's Harrier	C. pygargus																		(GI)	(b)B		0263
AC	Goshawk	Accipiter gentilis																					0267
A	Sparrowhawk	A. nisus																		(SH)			0269
EU	Levant Sparrowhawk	A. brevipes																					0273
A	Buzzard	Buteo buteo																		(BZ)			0287
EU	Long-legged Buzzard	B. rufinus																					0288
A	Rough-legged Buzzard	B. lagopus																		(RF)			0290
EU	Lesser Spotted Eagle	Aquila pomarina																					0292
B	Greater Spotted Eagle	A. clanga																				R	0293
EU	Imperial Eagle	A. heliaca																					0295
A	Golden Eagle	A. chrysaetos																		(EA)	(b)B		0296
EU	Booted Eagle	Hieraaetus pennatus																					0298
EU	Bonelli's Eagle	H. fasciatus																					0299
A	Osprey	Pandion haliaetus																		(OP)	(b)A		0301
A	Lesser Kestrel	Falco naumanni																				R	0303
A	Kestrel	F. tinnunculus																		(K)			0304
A	American Kestrel	F. sparverius																				R	0305
A	Red-footed Falcon	F. vespertinus																		(FV)		R	0307
A	Merlin	F. columbarius																		(ML)	(b)B		0309
A	Hobby	F. subbuteo																		(HY)	(b)B		0310
A	Eleonora's Falcon	F. eleonorae																				R	0311
EU	Lanner	F. biarmicus																		(FB)			0314
D	Saker	F. cherrug																		(JF)		R	0316
	Sub-total																						

RAPTORS cont. GAMEBIRDS, RAILS, CRAKES, GALLINULES

	English name	Scientific name	Life list	2003 list	24 hr	Garden	Holiday	Jan	Feb	Mar	Apr	May	Jun	Jul	Aug	Sep	Oct	Nov	Dec	BTO	RBBP	Bou	EU No
A	Gyrfalcon	F. rusticolus																		(YF)		R	0318
A	Peregrine	F. peregrinus																		(PE)	(b)B		0320
EU	Hazel Grouse	Bonasa bonasia																					0326
A	Red (Willow) Grouse	Lagopus lagopus																		(RG)			0329
A	Ptarmigan	L. mutus																		(PM)			0330
A	Black Grouse	Tetrao tetrix																		(BK)			0332
BC	Capercaillie	T. urogallus																		(CP)			0335
EU	Rock Partridge	Alectoris graeca																					0357
C	Red-legged Partridge	A. rufa																		(RL)			0358
EU	Barbary Partridge	A. barbara																					0359
AC	Grey Partridge	Perdix perdix																		(P)			0367
A	Quail	Coturnix coturnix																		(Q)	(b)B		0370
C	Pheasant	Phasianus colchicus																		(PH)			0394
C	Golden Pheasant	Chrysolophus pictus																		(GF)	(b)D		0396
C	Lady Amherst's Pheasant	C. amherstiae																		(LM)	(b)D		0397
EU	Andalusian Hemipode	Turnix sylvatica																					0400
A	Water Rail	Rallus aquaticus																		(WA)			0407
A	Spotted Crake	Porzana porzana																		(AK)	(b)A		0408
A	Sora	P. carolina																				R	0409
A	Little Crake	P. parva																		(JC)		R	0410
A	Baillon's Crake	P. pusilla																		(VC)		R	0411
A	Corncrake	Crex crex																		(CE)	(b)A		0421
A	Moorhen	Gallinula chloropus																		(MH)			0424
B	Allen's Gallinule	Porphyrula alleni																				R	0425
	Sub-total																						

GALLINULES cont. COOTS, CRANES, BUSTARDS, WADERS

	Common name	Scientific name	Life list	2003 list	24 hr	Garden	Holiday	Jan	Feb	Mar	Apr	May	Jun	Jul	Aug	Sep	Oct	Nov	Dec	BTO	RBBP	Bou	EU No
A	American Purple Gallinule	P. martinica																				R	0426
EU	Purple (Swamp-hen) Gallinule	Porphyrio porphyrio																					0427
A	Coot	Fulica atra																		(CO)			0429
A	American Coot	F. americana																				R	0430
EL	Crested Coot	F. cristata																					0431
A	Crane	Grus grus																		(AN)	(b)A		0433
A	Sandhill Crane	G. canadensis																				R	0436
A	Little Bustard	Tetrax tetrax																				R	0442
C	Houbara Bustard	Chlamydotis undulata																				R	0444
B	Macqueen's Bustard	Chlamydotis macqueenii																				R	0444
A	Oystercatcher	Haematopus ostralegus																		(OC)			0450
A	Black-winged Stilt	Himantopus himantopus																		(IT)		R	0455
A	Avocet	Recurvirostra avosetta																		(AV)	(b)A		0456
A	Stone Curlew	Burhinus oedicnemus																		(TN)	(b)A		0459
A	Cream-coloured Courser	Cursorius cursor																				R	0464
A	Collared Pratincole	Glareola pratincola																				R	0465
A	Oriental Pratincole	G. maldivarum																		(GM)		R	0466
A	Black-winged Pratincole	G. nordmanni																		(KW)		R	0467
A	Little Ringed Plover	Charadrius dubius																		(LP)	(b)B		0469
A	Ringed Plover	C. hiaticula																		(RP)			0470
A	Semipalmated Plover	C. semipalmatus																		(TV)		R	0471
A	Killdeer	C. vociferus																		(KL)		R	0474
A	Kentish Plover	C. alexandrinus																		(KP)			0477
A	Lesser Sand Plover	C. mongolus																				R	0478

Sub-total

WADERS continued

	Common Name	Scientific Name	Life list	2003 list	24 hr	Garden	Holiday	Jan	Feb	Mar	Apr	May	Jun	Jul	Aug	Sep	Oct	Nov	Dec	BTO	RBBP	Bou	EU No
FA	Greater Sand Plover	C. leschenaultii																		(DP)		R	0479
A	Caspian Plover	C. asiaticus																				R	0480
A	Dotterel	C. morinellus																		(DO)	(b)B		0482
A	American Golden Plover	Pluvialis dominica																		(ID)		R	0484
A	Pacific Golden Plover	P. fulva																		(IF)		R	0484
A	Golden Plover	P. apricaria																		(GP)			0485
A	Grey Plover	P. squatarola																		(GV)			0486
EU	Spur-winged Plover	Hoplopterus spinosus																		(UW)			0487
A	Sociable Lapwing	Vanellus gregarius																		(IP)		R	0491
A	White-tailed Lapwing	V. leucurus																				R	0492
A	Lapwing	V. vanellus																		(L)			0493
A	Great Knot	Calidris tenuirostris																		(KO)		R	0495
A	Knot	C. canutus																		(KN)			0496
A	Sanderling	C. alba																		(SS)			0497
A	Semipalmated Sandpiper	C. pusilla																		(PZ)		R	0498
A	Western Sandpiper	C. mauri																		(ER)		R	0499
A	Red-necked Stint	C. ruficollis																				R	0500
A	Little Stint	C. minuta																		(LX)			0501
A	Temminck's Stint	C. temminckii																		(TK)	(b)A		0502
A	Long-toed Stint	C. subminuta																				R	0503
A	Least Sandpiper	C. minutilla																		(EP)		R	0504
A	White-rumped Sandpiper	C. fuscicollis																		(WU)		R	0505
A	Baird's Sandpiper	C. bairdii																		(BP)		R	0506
A	Pectoral Sandpiper	C. melanotos																		(PP)			0507

Sub-total

LOG CHARTS

WADERS continued

Cat	Species	Scientific name	Life list	2003 list	24 hr	Garden	Holiday	Jan	Feb	Mar	Apr	May	Jun	Jul	Aug	Sep	Oct	Nov	Dec	BTO	RBBP	Bou	EU No
A	Sharp-tailed Sandpiper	C. acuminata																		(VV)		R	0508
A	Curlew Sandpiper	C. ferruginea																		(CV)			0509
A	Purple Sandpiper	C. maritima																		(PS)	(b)A		0510
A	Dunlin	C. alpina																		(DN)			0512
A	Broad-billed Sandpiper	Limicola falcinellus																		(OA)		R	0514
A	Stilt Sandpiper	Micropalama himantopus																		(MI)		R	0515
A	Buff-breasted Sandpiper	Tryngites subruficollis																		(BQ)			0516
A	Ruff	Philomachus pugnax																		(RU)	(b)A		0517
A	Jack Snipe	Lymnocryptes minimus																		(JS)			0518
A	Snipe	Gallinago gallinago																		(SN)			0519
A	Great Snipe	G. media																		(DS)		R	0520
A	Short-billed Dowitcher	Limnodromus griseus																					
A	Long-billed Dowitcher	L. scolopaceus																		(LD)		R	0527
A	Woodcock	Scolopax rusticola																		(WK)			0529
A	Black-tailed Godwit	Limosa limosa																		(BW)	(b)A		0532
A	Hudsonian Godwit	L. haemastica																		(HU)		R	0533
A	Bar-tailed Godwit	L. lapponica																		(BA)			0534
A	Little Whimbrel (Curlew)	N. minutus																				R	0536
B	Eskimo Curlew	N. borealis																				R	0537
A	Whimbrel	N. phaeopus																		(WM)	(b)A		0538
A	Curlew	N. arquata																		(CU)			0541
A	Upland Sandpiper	Bartramia longicauda																		(UP)		R	0544
A	Spotted Redshank	T. erythropus																		(DR)			0545
A	Redshank	T. totanus																		(RK)			0546

Sub-total

75

WADERS continued, GULLS

	Common name	Scientific name	Life list	2003 list	24 hr	Garden	Holiday	Jan	Feb	Mar	Apr	May	Jun	Jul	Aug	Sep	Oct	Nov	Dec	BTO	RBBP	Bou	EU No
A	Marsh Sandpiper	T. stagnatilis																		(MD)		R	0547
A	Greenshank	T. nebularia																		(GK)	(b)B		0548
A	Greater Yellowlegs	T. melanoleuca																		(LZ)		R	0550
A	Lesser Yellowlegs	T. flavipes																		(LY)		R	0551
A	Solitary Sandpiper	T. solitaria																		(I)		R	0552
A	Green Sandpiper	T. ochropus																		(GE)			0553
A	Wood Sandpiper	T. glareola																		(OD)	(b)A		0554
A	Terek Sandpiper	Xenus cinereus																		(TR)		R	0555
A	Common Sandpiper	Actitis hypoleucos																		(CS)			0556
A	Spotted Sandpiper	A. macularia																		(PQ)		R	0557
A	Grey-tailed Tattler	Heteroscelus brevipes																		(YT)		R	0558
A	Turnstone	Arenaria interpres																		(TT)			0561
A	Wilson's Phalarope	Phalaropus tricolor																		(WF)		R	0563
A	Red-necked Phalarope	P. lobatus																		(NK)	(b)A		0564
A	Grey Phalarope	P. fulicarius																		(PL)			0565
A	Pomarine Skua	Stercorarius pomarinus																		(PK)			0566
A	Arctic Skua	S. parasiticus																		(AC)			0567
A	Long-tailed Skua	S. longicaudus																		(OG)			0568
A	Great Skua	Catharacta skua																		(NX)			0569
B	Great Black-headed (Pallas's) Gull	L. ichthyaetus																				R	0573
A	Mediterranean Gull	L. melanocephalus																		(MU)	(b)A		0575
A	Laughing Gull	L. atricilla																		(LF)		R	0576
A	Franklin's Gull	L. pipixcan																		(FG)		R	0577
A	Little Gull	L. minutus																		(LU)			0578

Sub-total

GULLS continued, TERNS

	Common name	Scientific name	Life list	2003 list	24 hr	Garden	Holiday	Jan	Feb	Mar	Apr	May	Jun	Jul	Aug	Sep	Oct	Nov	Dec	BTO	RBBP	Bou	EU No
A	Sabine's Gull	L. sabini																		(AB)			0579
A	Bonaparte's Gull	L. philadelphia																		(ON)		R	0581
A	Black-headed Gull	L. ridibundus																		(BH)			0582
A	Slender-billed Gull	L. genei																		(EI)			0585
FU	Audouin's Gull	L. audouinii																		(IN)			0588
A	Ring-billed Gull	L. delawarensis																		(CM)			0589
A	Common (Mew) Gull	L. canus																		(CM)			0590
A	Lesser Black-backed Gull	L. fuscus																		(LB)			0591
A	Herring Gull	L. argentatus																		(HG)			0592
A	Iceland Gull	L. glaucoides																		(IG)			0598
A	Glaucous Gull	L. hyperboreus																		(GZ)			0599
A	Great Black-backed Gull	L. marinus																		(GB)			0600
A	Ross's Gull	Rhodostethia rosea																		(QG)		R	0601
A	Kittiwake	Rissa tridactyla																		(KI)			0602
A	Ivory Gull	Pagophila eburnea																		(IV)		R	0604
A	Gull-billed Tern	S.nilotica																		(TG)		R	0605
A	Caspian Tern	S.caspia																		(CJ)		R	0606
A	Royal Tern	S.maxima																		(QT)		R	0607
A	Lesser Crested Tern	S.bengalensis																		(TF)	(b)A	R	0609
A	Sandwich Tern	S.sandvicensis																		(TE)			0611
A	Roseate Tern	S.dougallii																		(RS)	(b)A		0614
A	Common Tern	S.hirundo																		(CN)			0615
A	Arctic Tern	S.paradisaea																		(AE)			0616
A	Aleutian Tern	S.aleutica																				R	0617

Sub-total

77

TERNS cont. AUKS, SANDGROUSE, DOVES/PIGEONS, PARAKEET, CUCKOOS

	Name	Scientific	Life list	2003 list	24 hr	Garden	Holiday	Jan	Feb	Mar	Apr	May	Jun	Jul	Aug	Sep	Oct	Nov	Dec	BTO	RBBP	Bou	EU No
A	Forster's Tern	S.forsteri																		(FO)		R	0618
A	Bridled Tern	S.anaethetus																				R	0622
A	Sooty Tern	S.fuscata																				R	0623
A	Little Tern	S.albifrons																		(AF)	(b)B		0624
A	Whiskered Tern	Chlidonias hybrida																		(WD)		R	0626
A	Black Tern	C. niger																		(BJ)			0627
A	White-winged Black Tern	C. leucopterus																		(WJ)		R	0628
A	Guillemot	Uria aalge																		(GU)			0634
A	Brünnich's Guillemot	U. lomvia																		(TZ)		R	0635
A	Razorbill	Alca torda																		(RA)			0636
A	Black Guillemot	Cepphus grylle																		(TY)			0638
A	Ancient Murrelet	Synthliboramphus antiquus																				R	0645
A	Little Auk	Alle alle																		(LK)			0647
A	Puffin	Fratercula arctica																		(PU)			0654
EU	Black-bellied Sandgrouse	Pterocles orientalis																					0661
EU	Pin-tailed Sandgrouse	P. alchata																					0662
A	Pallas's Sandgrouse	Syrrhaptes paradoxus																				R	0663
AC	Rock Dove	Columba livia																		(DV)			0665
A	Stock Dove	C. oenas																		(SD)			0668
A	Woodpigeon	C. palumbus																		(WP)			0670
A	Collared Dove	Streptopelia decaocto																		(CD)			0684
A	Turtle Dove	S. turtur																		(TD)			0687
A	Rufous (Oriental) Turtle Dove	S. orientalis																				R	0689
A	Mourning Dove	Zenaida macroura																				R	0695
	Sub-total																						

	CUCKOOS, OWLS, NIGHTJARS, SWIFTS		Life list	2003 list	24 hr	Garden	Holiday	Jan	Feb	Mar	Apr	May	Jun	Jul	Aug	Sep	Oct	Nov	Dec	BTO	RBBP	Bou	EU No
C	Rose-ringed Parakeet	Psittacula krameri																		(RI)	(b)D		0712
A	Great Spotted Cuckoo	Clamator glandarius																				R	0716
A	Cuckoo	Cuculus canorus																		(UK)			0724
A	Black-billed Cuckoo	Coccyzus erythrophthalmus																		(CK)		R	0727
A	Yellow-billed Cuckoo	C. americanus																				R	0728
A	Barn Owl	Tyto alba																		(BO)	(b)C		0735
A	Scops Owl	Otus scops																				R	0739
A	Eagle Owl	Bubo bubo																		(EO)	(b)D		0744
A	Snowy Owl	Nyctea scandiaca																		(SO)	(b)AR		0749
A	Hawk Owl	Surnia ulula																				R	0750
EU	Pygmy Owl	Glaucidium passerinum																					0751
C	Little Owl	Athene noctua																		(LO)			0757
A	Tawny Owl	Strix aluco																		(TO)			0761
EU	Ural Owl	S. uralensis																					0765
EU	Great Grey Owl	S. nebulosa																					0766
A	Long-eared Owl	Asio otus																		(LE)			0767
A	Short-eared Owl	A. flammeus																		(SE)			0768
A	Tengmalm's Owl	Aegolius funereus																				R	0770
A	Nightjar	Caprimulgus europaeus																		(NJ)			0778
B	Red-necked Nightjar	C. ruficollis																				R	0779
A	Egyptian Nightjar	C. aegyptius																				R	0781
A	Common Nighthawk	Chordeiles minor																				R	0786
A	Chimney Swift	Chaetura pelagica																				R	0790
A	White-throated Needletail	Hirundapus caudacutus																		(NI)		R	0792
	Sub-total																						

79

SWIFTS etc. KINGFISHERS, BEE-EATERS, ROLLER, HOOPOE, WOODPECKERS, PHOEBE, LARKS

			Life list	2003 list	24 hr	Garden	Holiday	Jan	Feb	Mar	Apr	May	Jun	Jul	Aug	Sep	Oct	Nov	Dec		BTO	RBBP	Bou	EU No
A	**Swift**	*Apus apus*																			(SI)			0795
A	**Pallid Swift**	*A. pallidus*																					R	0796
A	**Pacific Swift**	*A. pallidus*																					R	0797
A	**Alpine Swift**	*A. pacificus*																			(AI)		R	0798
EL	**White-rumped Swift**	*A. melba*																						0799
A	**Little Swift**	*A. affinis*																					R	0800
A	**Kingfisher**	*Alcedo atthis*																			(KF)	(b)C		0831
A	**Belted Kingfisher**	*Ceryle alcyon*																					R	0834
A	**Blue-checked Bee-eater**	*Merops superciliosus*																					R	0839
A	**Bee-eater**	*M. apiaster*																			(MZ)			0840
A	**Roller**	*Coracias garrulus*																					R	0841
A	**Hoopoe**	*Upupa epops*																			(HP)			0846
A	**Wryneck**	*Jynx torquilla*																			(WY)	(b)A		0848
EU	**Grey-headed Woodpecker**	*Picus canus*																						0855
A	**Green Woodpecker**	*P. viridis*																			(G)			0856
EU	**Black Woodpecker**	*Dryocopus martius*																						0863
A	**Yellow-bellied Sapsucker**	*Sphyrapicus varius*																					R	0872
A	**Great Spotted Woodpecker**	*Dendrocopos major*																			(GS)			0876
EU	**Syrian Woodpecker**	*D. syriacus*																						0878
EU	**Middle Spotted Woodpecker**	*D. medius*																						0883
EU	**White-backed Woodpecker**	*D. leucotos*																						0884
A	**Lesser Spotted Woodpecker**	*D. minor*																			(LS)			0887
EU	**Three-toed Woodpecker**	*Picoides tridactylus*																						0898
A	**Eastern Phoebe**	*Sayornis phoebe*																					R	0909
	Sub-total																							

LARKS cont. MARTINS, SWALLOWS, PIPITS

			Life list	2003 list	24 hr	Garden	Holiday	Jan	Feb	Mar	Apr	May	Jun	Jul	Aug	Sep	Oct	Nov	Dec			BTO	RBBP	Bou	EU No
EU	Dupont's Lark	Chersophilus duponti																							0959
A	Calandra Lark	Melanocorypha calandra																						R	0961
A	Bimaculated Lark	M. bimaculata																						R	0962
A	White-winged Lark	M. leucoptera																						R	0965
A	Short-toed Lark	Calandrella brachydactyla																				(VL)			0968
A	Lesser Short-toed Lark	C. rufescens																						R	0970
A	Crested Lark	Galerida cristata																						R	0972
EU	Thekla Lark	G. theklae																							0973
A	Wood Lark	Lullula arborea																				(WL)	(b)B	R	0974
A	Sky Lark	Alauda arvensis																				(S)			0976
A	Shore (Horned) Lark	Eremophila alpestris																				(SX)			0978
A	Sand Martin	Riparia riparia																				(SM)			0981
A	Tree Swallow	Tachycineta bicolor																						R	0983
A	Crag Martin	Ptyonoprogne rupestris																						R	0991
A	Swallow	Hirundo rustica																				(SL)			0992
A	Red-rumped Swallow	H. daurica																				(VR)		R	0995
A	Cliff Swallow	H. pyrrhonota																						R	0998
A	House Martin	Delichon urbica																				(HM)			1001
A	Richard's Pipit	Anthus novaeseelandiae																				(PR)			1002
A	Blyth's Pipit	A. godlewskii																						R	1004
A	Tawny Pipit	A. campestris																				(TT)			1005
A	Olive-backed Pipit	A. hodgsoni																				(OV)		R	1008
A	Tree Pipit	A. trivialis																				(TP)			1009
A	Pechora Pipit	A. gustavi																						R	1010
	Sub-total																							

PIPITS cont. WAGTAILS, WAXWINGS, DIPPER, WREN, ACCENTORS, ROBINS

Cat	Name	Scientific	Life list	2003 list	24 hr	Garden	Holiday	Jan	Feb	Mar	Apr	May	Jun	Jul	Aug	Sep	Oct	Nov	Dec	BTO	RBBP	Bou	EU No
A	Meadow Pipit	A. pratensis																		(MP)			1011
A	Red-throated Pipit	A. cervinus																		(VP)		R	1012
A	Rock Pipit	A. petrosus																		(RC)			1014
A	Water Pipit	A. spinoletta																		(WI)			1014
A	Buff-bellied Pipit	A. rubescens																				R	1014
A	Yellow Wagtail	Motacilla flava																		(YW)			1017
A	Citrine Wagtail	M. citreola																				R	1018
A	Grey Wagtail	M. cinerea																		(GL)			1019
A	Pied (White) Wagtail	M. alba																		(PW)			1020
A	Cedar Waxing	Bombycilla cedrorum																				R	1046
A	(Bohemian) Waxwing	Bombycilla garrulus																		(WX)			1048
A	Dipper	Cinclus cinclus																		(DI)			1050
A	Wren	Troglodytes troglodytes																		(WR)			1066
A	Northern Mockingbird	Mimus polyglottos																				R	1067
A	Brown Thrasher	Toxostoma rufum																				R	1069
A	Gray Catbird	Dumetella carolinensis																					1084
A	Dunnock	Prunella modularis																		(D)			1094
A	Alpine Accentor	P. collaris																				R	1095
A	Rufous-tailed Scrub Robin	Cercotrichas galactotes																				R	1099
A	Robin	Erithacus rubecula																		(R)			1103
A	Thrush Nightingale	Luscinia luscinia																		(FN)		R	1104
A	Nightingale	L. megarhynchos																		(N)			1105
A	Siberian Rubythroat	L. calliope																				R	
A	Bluethroat	L. svecica																		(BU)			1106
	Sub-total																						

82

REDSTARTS, CHATS, WHEATEARS, THRUSHES

			Life list	2003 list	24 hr	Garden	Holiday	Jan	Feb	Mar	Apr	May	Jun	Jul	Aug	Sep	Oct	Nov	Dec	BTO	RBBP	Bou	EU No
A	Siberian Blue Robin	L. cyane																					1113
A	Red-flanked Bluetail	Tarsiger cyanurus																				R	1117
A	White-throated Robin	Irania gutturalis																					1121
A	Black Redstart	Phoenicurus ochruros																		(BX)	(b)A		1121
A	Redstart	P. phoenicurus																		(RT)			1122
A	Moussier's Redstart	P. moussieri																				R	1127
A	Whinchat	Saxicola rubetra																		(WC)			1137
A	Stonechat	S. torquata																		(SC)			1139
A	Isabelline Wheatear	Oenanthe isabellina																				R	1144
A	Wheatear	O. O.																		(W)			1146
A	Pied Wheatear	O. pleschanka																		(PI)		R	1147
A	Black-eared Wheatear	O. hispanica																				R	1148
A	Desert Wheatear	O. deserti																				R	1149
A	White-crowned(-tailed) Black Wheatear O. leucopyga																							1157
EU	Black Wheatear	O. Leucura																				R	1158
A	Rock Thrush	Monticola saxatilis																		(OH)		R	1162
A	Blue Rock Thrush	M. solitarius																				R	1166
A	White's Thrush	Zoothera dauma																				R	1170
A	Siberian Thrush	Z. sibirica																				R	1171
A	Varied Thrush	Z. naevia																		(VT)		R	1172
A	Wood Thrush	Hylocichla mustelina																				R	1175
A	Hermit Thrush	Catharus guttatus																				R	1176
A	Swainson's Thrush	C. ustulatus																				R	1177
A	Grey-cheeked Thrush	C. minimus																				R	1178

Sub-total

THRUSHES continued, WARBLERS

	Name	Scientific name	Life list	2003 list	24 hr	Garden	Holiday	Jan	Feb	Mar	Apr	May	Jun	Jul	Aug	Sep	Oct	Nov	Dec	BTO	RBBP	Bou	EU No
A	Veery	C. fuscescens																		(RZ)		R	1179
A	Ring Ouzel	Turdus torquatus																		(B)			1186
A	Blackbird	T. merula																					1187
1A	Eyebrowed Thrush	T. obscurus																				R	1195
A	Dusky Thrush	T. naumanni																		(XC)		R	1196
A	Dark-throated Thrush	T. ruficollis																				R	1197
A	Fieldfare	T. pilaris																		(FF)	(b)A		1198
A	Song Thrush	T. philomelos																		(ST)			1200
A	Redwing	T. iliacus																		(RE)	(b)A		1201
A	Mistle Thrush	T. viscivorus																		(M)			1202
A	American Robin	T. migratorius																		(AR)		R	1203
A	Cetti's Warbler	Cettia cetti																		(CW)	(b)A	R	1220
A	Zitting Cisticola (Fan-tailed Warbler)	Cisticola juncidis																				R	1226
A	Pallas's Grasshopper Warbler	Locustella certhiola																				R	1233
A	Lanceolated Warbler	L.lanceolata																				R	1235
A	Grasshopper Warbler	L.naevia																		(GH)			1236
A	River Warbler	L.fluviatilis																		(VW)		R	1237
A	Savi's Warbler	L.luscinioides																		(VI)	(b)A	R	1238
A	Moustached Warbler	Acrocephalus melanopogon																				R	1241
A	Aquatic Warbler	A. paludicola																		(AQ)			1242
A	Sedge Warbler	A. schoenobaenus																		(SW)			1243
A	Paddyfield Warbler	A. agricola																		(PY)		R	1247
A	Blyth's Reed Warbler	A. dumetorum																				R	1248
A	Marsh Warbler	A. palustris																		(MW)	(b)A		1250

Sub-total

84

WARBLERS continued

		Life list	2003 list	24 hr	Garden	Holiday	Jan	Feb	Mar	Apr	May	Jun	Jul	Aug	Sep	Oct	Nov	Dec		BTO	RBBP	Bou	EU No
A	**Reed Warbler**	*A. scirpaceus*																			(RW)			1251
A	**Great Reed Warbler**	*A. arundinaceus*																			(QW)		R	1253
A	**Thick-billed Warbler**	*A. aedon*																					R	1254
A	**Eastern Olivaceous Warbler**	*Hippolais pallida*																					R	1255
A	**Western Olivaceous Warbler**	*Hippolais opaca*																					R	1256
A	**Booted Warbler**	*H. caligata*																						
A	**Syke's Warbler**	*H. rama*																						
EU	**Olive-tree Warbler**	*H. olivetorum*																						1258
A	**Icterine Warbler**	*H. icterina*																			(IC)			1259
A	**Melodious Warbler**	*H. polyglotta*																			(ME)			1260
A	**Marmora's Warbler**	*Sylvia sarda*																			(MM)			1261
A	**Dartford Warbler**	*S. undata*																			(DW)	(b)B		1262
A	**Spectacled Warbler**	*S. conspicillata*																						1264
A	**Subalpine Warbler**	*S. cantillans*																						1265
A	**Sardinian Warbler**	*S. melanocephala*																						1267
EU	**Cyprus Warbler**	*S. melanothorax*																						1268
A	**Rüppell's Warbler**	*S. rueppelli*																						1269
A	**Desert Warbler**	*S. nana*																						1270
A	**Orphean Warbler**	*S. hortensis*																						1272
A	**Barred Warbler**	*S. nisoria*																			(RR)			1273
A	**Lesser Whitethroat**	*S. curruca*																			(LW)			1274
A	**Whitethroat**	*S. communis*																			(WH)			1275
A	**Garden Warbler**	*S. borin*																			(GW)			1276
A	**Blackcap**	*S. atricapilla*																			(BC)			1277

Sub-total

85

WARBLERS continued, 'CRESTS', FLYCATCHERS, TITS

			Life list	2003 list	24 hr	Garden	Holiday	Jan	Feb	Mar	Apr	May	Jun	Jul	Aug	Sep	Oct	Nov	Dec	BTO	RBBP	Bou	EU No
A	Greenish Warbler	Phylloscopus trochiloides																		(NP)			1293
A	Arctic Warbler	P. borealis																		(AP)			1295
A	Pallas's Warbler	P. proregulus																		(PA)			1298
A	Yellow-browed Warbler	P. inornatus																		(YB)			1300
A	Hume's Leaf Warbler	P. humei																					1300
A	Radde's Warbler	P. schwarzi																					1301
A	Dusky Warbler,	P. fuscatus																		(UY)		R	1303
A	Western Bonelli's Warbler	P. bonelli																		(IW)		R	1307
A	Eastern Bonelli's Warbler	P. orientalis																				R	1307
A	Wood Warbler	P. sibilatrix																		(WO)			1308
A	Common Chiffchaff	P. collybita																		(CC)			1311
A	Iberian Chiffchaff	P. ibericus																				R	1311
A	Willow Warbler	P. trochilus																		(WW)			1312
A	Goldcrest	Regulus regulus																		(GC)			1314
A	Firecrest	R. ignicapilla																		(FC)	(b)A		1315
D	Asian Brown Flycatcher	Muscicapa dauurica																					1335
A	Spotted Flycatcher	Muscicapa striata																					1335
A	Red-breasted Flycatcher	Ficedula parva																		(FY)			1343
D	Mugimaki Flycatcher	F. mugimaki																				R	1344
EU	Semi-collared Flycatcher	F. semitorquata																					1347
A	Collared Flycatcher	F. albicollis																				R	1348
A	Pied Flycatcher	F. hypoleuca																		(PF)			1349
A	Bearded Tit	Panurus biarmicus																		(BR)	(b)B		1364
A	Long-tailed Tit	Aegithalos caudatus																		(LT)			1437
	Sub-total																						

TITS continued, NUTHATCHES, TREECREEPERS, ORIOLE, SHRIKES

	Species		Life list	2003 list	24 hr	Garden	Holiday	Jan	Feb	Mar	Apr	May	Jun	Jul	Aug	Sep	Oct	Nov	Dec	BTO	RBBP	BoU	EU No
A	Marsh Tit	Parus palustris																		(MT)			1440
EU	Sombre Tit	P. lugubris																					1441
A	Willow Tit	P. montanus																		(WT)			1442
EU	Siberian Tit	P. cinctus																					1448
A	Crested Tit	P.cristatus																		(CI)	(b)B		1454
A	Coal Tit	P. ater																		(CT)			1461
A	Blue Tit	P. caeruleus																		(BT)			1462
A	Great Tit	P. major																		(GT)			1464
EU	Krüper's Nuthatch	Sitta krueperi																					1469
EU	Corsican Nuthatch	S. whiteheadi																					1470
A	Red-breasted Nuthatch	S. canadensis																				R	1472
A	Nuthatch	S. europaea																		(NH)			1479
EU	Rock Nuthatch	S. neumayer																					1481
A	Wallcreeper	Tichodroma muraria																				R	1482
A	Treecreeper	Certhia familiaris																		(TC)			1486
A	Short-toed Treecreeper	C. brachydactyla																		(TH)		R	1487
A	Penduline Tit	Remiz pendulinus																		(DT)		R	1490
A	Golden Oriole	Oriolus oriolus																		(OL)	(b)A		1508
A	Brown Shrike	Lanius cristatus																				R	1513
A	Isabelline Shrike	L. isabellinus																		(IL)		R	1514
A	Red-backed Shrike	L. collurio																		(ED)	(b)A		1515
A	Lesser Grey Shrike	L. minor																				R	1519
A	Great Grey Shrike	L. excubitor																		(SR)			1520
A	Southern Grey Shrike	L. meridionalis																				R	1520
	Sub-total																						

CROWS, STARLINGS, SPARROWS, FINCHES

	Name	Scientific	BTO	RBBP	Bou	EU No
A	**Woodchat Shrike**	L. senator	(OO)			1523
EU	**Masked Shrike**	L. nubicus				1524
A	**Jay**	Garrulus glandarius	(J)			1539
EU	**Siberian Jay**	Perisoreus infaustus				1543
EU	**Azure-winged Magpie**	Cyanopica cyana				1547
A	**Magpie**	Pica pica	(MG)			1549
A	**Nutcracker**	Nucifraga caryocatactes	(NC)		R	1557
EU	**Alpine Chough**	Pyrrhocorax graculus				1558
A	**Chough**	P. pyrrhocorax	(CF)	(b)B		1559
A	**Jackdaw**	Corvus monedula	(JD)			1560
A	**Rook**	C. frugilegus	(RO)			1563
A	**Carrion (Hooded) Crow**	C. corone	(C)			1567
A	**Hooded Crow**	C. cornix				
A	**Raven**	C. corax	(RN)			1572
D	**Daurian Starling**	Sturnus sturninus			R	1579
A	**Starling**	S. vulgaris	(SG)			1582
EU	**Spotless Starling**	S. unicolor				1583
A	**Rose-coloured (Rosy) Starling**	Sturnus roseus	(OE)		R	1594
A	**House Sparrow**	Passer domesticus	(HS)			1591
A	**Spanish Sparrow**	P. hispaniolensis			R	1592
A	**Tree Sparrow**	P.r montanus	(TS)			1598
A	**Rock Sparrow**	Petronia petronia			R	1604
D	**Snow Finch**	Montifringilla nivalis			R	1611
A	**Yellow-throated Vireo**	Vireo flavifrons			R	1628

Sub-total

FINCHES continued, NORTH AMERICAN WARBLERS

A	Species	Scientific name	Life list	2003 list	24 hr	Garden	Holiday	Jan	Feb	Mar	Apr	May	Jun	Jul	Aug	Sep	Oct	Nov	Dec	BTO	RBBP	Bou	EU No
A	Philadelphia Vireo	*V. philadelphicus*																				R	1631
A	Red-eyed Vireo	*V.olivaceus*																		(EV)		R	1633
A	Chaffinch	*Fringilla coelebs*																		(CH)			1636
A	Brambling	*F. montifringilla*																		(BL)	(b)A		1638
A	Serin	*Serinus serinus*																		(NS)	(b)A		1640
A	Greenfinch	*Carduelis chloris*																		(GR)			1649
A	Goldfinch	*C carduelis*																		(GO)			1653
A	Siskin	*C. spinus*																		(SK)			1654
A	Linnet	*C. cannabina*																		(LI)			1660
A	Twite	*C. flavirostris*																		(TW)			1662
	Lesser Redpoll	*C. cabaret*																		(LR)			
A	Mealy Redpoll	*C. flammea*																					1663
A	Arctic Redpoll	*C. hornemanni*																		(AL)		R	1664
A	Two-barred Crossbill	*Loxia leucoptera*																		(PD)		R	1665
A	Crossbill	*L. curvirostra*																		(CR)	(b)C		1666
A	Scottish Crossbill	*L. scotica*																		(CY)	(b)B		1667
A	Parrot Crossbill	*L. pytyopsittacus*																		(PC)	(b)A	R	1668
A	Trumpeter Finch	*Bucanetes githagineus*																				R	1676
A	Common Rosefinch	*Carpodacus erythrinus*																		(SQ)	(b)A		1679
A	Pine Grosbeak	*Pinicola enucleator*																				R	1699
A	Bullfinch	*Pyrrhula pyrrhula*																		(BF)			1710
A	Hawfinch	*Coccothraustes coccothraustes*																		(HF)			1717
A	Evening Grosbeak	*Hesperiphona vespertina*																				R	1718
A	Black-and-white Warbler	*Mniotilta varia*																				R	1720

Sub-total

89

NORTH AMERICAN WARBLERS continued, NEW WORLD SPARROWS, BUNTINGS

	Species	Scientific name	Life list	2003 list	24 hr	Garden	Holiday	Jan	Feb	Mar	Apr	May	Jun	Jul	Aug	Sep	Oct	Nov	Dec	BTO	RBBP	BOU	EU No
A	Golden-winged Warbler	Vermivora chrysoptera																				R	1722
A	Tennessee Warbler	V. peregrina																				R	1724
A	Northern Parula	Parula americana																				R	1732
A	Yellow Warbler	Dendroica petechia																				R	1733
A	Chestnut-sided Warbler	D. pensylvanica																				R	1734
A	Blackburnian Warbler	D. fusca																				R	1747
A	Cape May Warbler	D. tigrina																				R	1749
A	Magnolia Warbler	D. magnolia																				R	1750
A	Yellow-rumped Warbler	D. coronata																				R	1751
D	Palm Warbler	D. palmarum																				R	1752
A	Blackpoll Warbler	D. striata																				R	1753
A	Bay-breasted Warbler	D. castanea																				R	1754
A	American Redstart	Setophaga ruticilla																		(AD)		R	1755
A	Ovenbird	Seiurus aurocapilla																				R	1756
A	Northern Waterthrush	S. noveboracensis																				R	1757
A	Yellowthroat	Geothlypis trichas																				R	1762
A	Hooded Warbler	Wilsonia citrina																				R	1771
A	Wilson's Warbler	Wilsonia pusilla																				R	1772
A	Summer Tanager	Piranga rubra																				R	1786
A	Scarlet Tanager	P. olivacea																				R	1788
A	Eastern Towhee	Pipilo erythrophthalmus																				R	1798
A	Lark Sparrow	Chondestes grammacus																				R	1824
A	Savannah Sparrow	Passerculus sandwichensis																				R	1826
A	Song Sparrow	Melospiza melodia																				R	1835
Sub-total																							

BUNTINGS continued, NORTH AMERICAN GROSBEAKS etc.

			Life list	2003 list	24 hr	Garden	Holiday	Jan	Feb	Mar	Apr	May	Jun	Jul	Aug	Sep	Oct	Nov	Dec	BTO	RBBP	Bou	EU No
A	White-crowned Sparrow	Zonotrichia leucophrys																				R	1839
A	White-throated Sparrow	Z. albicollis																				R	1840
A	Dark-eyed Junco	Junco hyemalis																		(JU)		R	1842
A	Lapland Bunting	Calcarius lapponicus																		(LA)			1847
A	Snow Bunting	Plectrophenax nivalis																		(SB)	(b)A		1850
A	Black-faced Bunting	Emberiza spodocephala																				R	1853
A	Pine Bunting	E. leucocephalos																		(EL)		R	1856
A	Yellowhammer	E. citrinella																		(Y)			1857
A	Cirl Bunting	E. cirlus																		(CL)	(b)A		1958
A	Rock Bunting	E. cia																				R	1860
EU	Cinereous Bunting	E. cineracea																					1865
A	Ortolan Bunting	E. hortulana																		(OB)			1866
A	Cretzschmar's Bunting	E. caesia																				R	1868
A	Yellow-browed Bunting	E. chrysophrys																				R	1871
A	Rustic Bunting	E. rustica																				R	1873
A	Little Bunting	E. pusilla																		(LJ)			1874
D	Chestnut Bunting	E. rutila																				R	1875
A	Yellow-breasted Bunting	E. aureola																				R	1876
A	Reed Bunting	E. schoeniclus																		(RB)			1877
A	Pallas's Bunting	E. pallasi																				R	1878
D	Red-headed Bunting	E. bruniceps																					1880
A	Black-headed Bunting	E. melanocephala																				R	1881
A	Corn Bunting	Miliaria calandra																		(CB)			1882
A	Rose-breasted Grosbeak	Pheucticus ludovicianus																				R	1887

Sub-total

NORTH AMERICAN BUNTINGS, PREVIOUSLY UNLISTED SPECIES

	Species		Life list	2003 list	24 hr	Garden	Holiday	Jan	Feb	Mar	Apr	May	Jun	Jul	Aug	Sep	Oct	Nov	Dec				BTO	RBBP	Bou	EU No
D	Blue Grosbeak	*Guiraca caerulea*																							R	1891
A	Indigo Bunting	*Passerina cyanea*																							R	1892
A	Bobolink	*Dolichonyx oryzivorus*																							R	1897
A	Brown-headed Cowbird	*Molothrus ater*																							R	1899
A	Baltimore Oriole	*Icterus galbula*																							R	1918
	Sub-total																									

DIRECTORY OF ART, PHOTOGRAPHY AND LECTURERS

Italian artist Alessandro Troisi submittted this artwork of Razorbills for the *British Birds* prize in 2002.

DIRECTORY OF
WILDLIFE ART GALLERIES

THE KITTIWAKE GALLERY AT ST ABBS HEAD
Key exhibitions for 2003:
Frederick J Watson, on-going dispay of work from Mar-Nov.
Opening times: Mar and Oct-Dec 11am-5pm (weekends only or by appointment on 018907 71588), Apr-Sept 11am-5pm daily (closed Tuesdays).
Address: The Kittiwake Gallery at St Abbs Head, St Abbs, Eymouth, TD14 5QF. 018907 71588(home), 018907 71504(work).
e-mail: derickwatson@btopenworld.com

NATURE IN ART MUSEUM AND ART GALLERY
Key exhibitions for 2003:
World's first museum dedicated to art inspired by nature. Picasso to David Shepherd, Flemish Masters to contemporary crafts. Permanent collection plus regular special exhibitions and 70 artists in residence each year. Look on our website.
Opening times: Tues-Sun (10am-5pm) and Bank holidays. Closed Dec 24-26.
Address: Wallsworth Hall, A38, Twigworth, Gloucester, GL2 9PA; 01452 731422; (Fax)01452 730937.
e-mail: ninart@globalnet.co.uk
www.nature-in-art.org.uk

OLD BREWERY STUDIOS
Key exhibitions for 2003:
Changing exhibitions of work the whole year through. Various painting and drawing courses available.
Opening times: Variable, best to telephone first.
Address; The Manor House, Kings Cliffe, Peterborough, PE8 6XB; 01780 470247; (Fax)01780 470334.
www.oldbrewerystudios.co.uk

DIRECTORY OF
WILDLIFE ARTISTS

BARRETT, Priscilla
Watercolour, pastel and mixed media studies of all wild mammals, (domesticated also!). Line drawings of behaviour a speciality. Commissions accepted. Published many books: HarperCollins, Academic Press etc.
Address: Jack of Clubs, Lode, Cambridge, CB5 9HE; 01223 812229; (Fax)01223 330869.
e-mail: gh105@cus.cam.ac.uk

BENINGTON, Michael
Original paintings of mainly Western Palearctic wildlife, in natural settings, from field sketches. Illustrations for many books, including *Breeding Birds of the Algarve* and for own articles in birding press. Commissions a specialty.
Exhibitions for 2003: Contact artist for details; Artists for Nature Foundation Algarve exhibitions and related book.
Address: Eyrie Studio, 3 The Courtyard, Tollymore Road, Newcastle, Northern Ireland, BT33 0TE:028 4372 5224.

BINNS, David SWLA, NDD, Doctor of Letters
Watercolours of British wildlife. Published work includes book illustrations, jigsaw designs for RSPB, RSNC, designs for Country Artists Ltd, Medici Society and in-house designs and limited edition prints for the Brent Gallery, run with wife Molly at 60a Keighley Rd, Cowling, BD22 0BH. Award-winning member of the SWLA. Commissions usually accepted.
Exhibitions for 2003: NEWA (Liverpool), SWLA (London), Brent Gallery (Cowling, W.Yorks), Milnethorpe (Silverdale).
Address: Holmestead, 9 Boundary Avenue, Sutton-in-Craven, Nr Keighley, Yorkshire, BD20 8BL; (Tel/Fax)01535 632774.

BROWN, Diana E. SWLA
Member of Society of Wildlife Artists since 1967. Founder member British Deer Society. Specialises in deer and British wildlife. Oils, watercolour, pen and pencil sketches. B/W book and magazine illustrations, most recent being *Carnivores* for Cambridge University Press due Autumn 2002.
Address: The Shannel, Ballogie, Aboyne, Aberdeenshire, AB34 5DR; 013398 84207. e-mail: inverchat@btinernet.com

Key: BBF = British Birdwatching Fair. NEWA = National Exhibition of Wildlife Art. SWLA = Society of Wildlife Artists.

DIRECTORY OF WILDLIFE ARTISTS

BURTON, Philip

Acrylics on canvas; current enthusiasm is seabirds. Many book illustrations e.g. in recent *Raptors of the World*. Founder member of Society of Wildlife Artists.
Exhibitions for 2003: Some at SWLA, London, annually.
Address: High Kelton, Doctors Commons Road, Berkhamsted, Herts, HP4 3DW; 01442 865020.
e-mail: pjkburton@aol.com

BUSBY, John SWLA

Illustrator of natural history books and articles, especially bird and animal behaviour. Lifelong field experience. Over 30 books illustrated, inc nine Poyser titles. Also oil and w/c landscapes. See website for examples. Studio visits by appointment.
Exhibitions for 2003: SWLA, RSA, RSW, London.
Address: Easter Haining, Ormiston Hall, Tranent, E.Lothian, EH35 5NJ; (Fax)01875 341011.
e-mail: jj.busby@lineone.net
www.johnbusby-artist.com

CALE, Steve

Steve is now a full-time professional wildlife artist and keen naturalist. Specialising in painting in acrylics, his paintings have gone as far afield as Hong Kong, USA, South Africa, Australia and New Zealand. A wide range of cards, book marks etc. based on field sketches also available.
Address: Bramble Cottage, Westwood Lane, Gt Rysburgh, Fakenham, Norfolk, NR21 7AP; 01328 829589.

COOK, David

Original paintings, drawings, paper cuts and paper sculptures of wildlife, especially waterfowl. Workshops for *Bird Watching* magazine. Publications include HarperCollins art book, three videos, RSPB and WWT greetings cards.
Exhibitions for 2003: SWLA, London. RSMA October.
Address: Holly House, 3 Lynn Road, South Runcton, King's Lynn, Norfolk, PE33 0EW; 01553 811980.

DAVIS, John SWLA

Watercolours, oils and acrylics of birds, mammals and general wildlife, including landscapes. Published illustrations in various books and magazines, including *BBC Wildlife*. Won black and white section of *Birdwatch* Artist of the Year awards 2002.
Exhibitions for 2003: NEWA (Liverpool), SWLA, London.
Address: 6 Redmoor, Birdham, Chichester, West Sussex, PO20 7HS; 01243 512351.

GREENHALF, Robert

Watercolours, oils, woodcuts and drypoints of birds in landscape. Book *Towards the Sea* published 1999 by Pica Press/A&C Black contains many examples. Commissions accepted.
Exhibitions for 2003: Regular exhibitor at Wildlife Art Gallery, Lavenham, Suffolk and Bircham Gallery, Holt, Norfolk.
Address: Romney House, Saltbarn Lane, Playden, Rye, East Sussex, TN31 7PH; 01797 222381.

HAMPTON, Michael SWLA

Watercolours of birds and mammals. John Aspinall, the late zoo owner, commissioned many paintings of his animals. Via the Federation of British Artists, he painted Arabian mammals for the Sultan of Oman in 2000. Michael's work has appeared on many magazine covers and calendars.

A busy feeding flock of Redpolls and Siskins was one of David Thelwell's BB entries.

Exhibitions for 2003: SWLA, London (Sept), WWT, Arundel (Sept 7 - Oct 14).
Address: 13 Sandy Way, Shirley, Croydon, Surrey CR0 8QT.
www.croydonartsociety.org.uk

JONES, Chris

Oils and acrylics of British, exotic and domestic species (especially poultry). Regular contributor to *Bird Watching* magazine. International Young Artist of the Year 1998. Gold Award winner TWAS 2000. Illustration work and commissions accepted.
Exhibitions for 2003: NEWA (Liverpool, Falconry Fair (Shropshire), Slimbridge (Gloucester), Marwell Zoo (Hants), Crossing Gate Gallery (Hants 01420 488912).
Address: 47 Church Lane, North Bradley, Trowbridge, Wilts, BA14 0TE; 01225 769717. e-mail:
chrisjones@eco-art.freeserve.co.uk
www.chrisjoneswildlifeart.com

KOSTER, David

Original prints – etchings, woodcuts, linocuts, lithographs – of birds, fish, flowers, insects etc. Watercolours, oils. Commissions accepted. Published work includes wood engravings for *Down to Earth* by John Collis, ink drawings for *Fellow Mortals*, an anthology of animal poetry.
Exhibitions for 2003:
Headcorn Gallery, March.
Address: 5 East Cliff Gardens, Folkestone, Kent, CT19 6AR; 01303 240544.

LEAHY, Ernest

Original watercolours and drawings of Western Palearctic birds, wildlife and country scenes. Illustrations for many publications including Poysers. Wide range of framed and unframed originals available. Commissions accepted and enquiries welcome.
Exhibitions for 2003: BBF 2003, Redbourn Exhibition, Dec 6,7 and 8, contact for details.
Address: 32 Ben Austins, Redbourn, Herts, AL3 7DR; 01582 793 144. e-mail:
ernest.leahy@ntlworld.com
www.
wildlifewatercolours.co.uk

MACKAY, Andrew

Colour and line artwork of birds and insects. Illustrations in *Concise BWP, RSPB Birds of Britain and Europe, Birds of South-east Asia* etc. Commissions for paintings and illustrations welcome.
Address: 68 Leicester Road, Markfield, Leicester, LE67 9RE:01530 243770.
e-mail:
AndrewjMackay@aol.com
www.ajm-wildlife-art.co.uk

PAIGE, John SWLA,
PAIGE, Jane Leycester
FSBA

Wildlife and wild flowers in their natural surroundings. Watercolour, oil, acrylic, collage, mono, screen and lino prints.
Exhibitions for 2003: Annual exhibitions of the SWLA and The Society of Botanical Artists.
Address: The Manor House, Kings Cliffe, Peterborough, PE8 6XB; 01780 470247; (Fax)01780 470334.
www.oldbrewerystudios.co.uk

PARTINGTON, Peter

Beloved medium is watercolour followed by oils and etching. Happiest in the field with sketchbook - favourite habitat East Anglian shoreline plus marsh. Travels widely. Many one-man shows, work widely collected. Commissions welcome. Three books: HarperCollins *Learn to Draw* series, *Farm Animals, Wildlife* and *Birds*.
Exhibitions for 2003: BBF (Aug) SWLA, London, Sept.
Address: The Hall, Kettlebaston, Suffolk, IP7 7QA; 01449 741538; (Fax)01449 744286.
e-mail: peter.partington@ kettlebaston.co.uk
www.
peter-partington.fsnet.co.uk

PEARSON. Bruce

Working in oils, watercolour and mixed media, paintings are completed either directly in the field or re-evaluated and reworked in the studio to express the natural rhythm, elemental energy and sheer excitement of 'being there'.
Exhibitions for 2003: SWLA, (Sept).
Address: The Old Plough, Caxton Road, Great Gransden, Sandy, Beds, SG19 3BE; 01767 677558. e-mail:
bep@openstudio.evesham.net
www.brucepearson.info

RIDLEY, Martin

Artist specialising in British wildlife. Original oils and watercolours of birds and animals in their natural habitat. Prints, cards and commissions. RSPB 2002 calendar, cover of 2002 *Birdwatcher's Yearbook*. Extensive website.
Exhibitions for 2003: WWT,

Slimbridge.
Address: Beinn a'Ghlo, Dalguise, Dunkeld, Scotland, PH8 0JU; 01350 727388; (Fax) by arragement.
e-mail: art@martinridley.com
www.martinridley.com

ROSE, Chris

Originals in oils and acrylics of birds and animals in landscapes. Particularly interested in painting water and its myriad effects. Limited edition prints available. Illustrated many books including *Grebes of the World* (publ. end 2002) and *Robins and Chats of the World* (in progress).
Exhibitions for 2003: SWLA, (Sept); Wildlife Art Gallery, Suffolk, (Sept). Maple Cottage, Holydean, Bowden, Melrose, Scotland, TD6 9HT; (Tel/Fax)01835 822547. e-mail: chrisroseswla@onetel.net.uk

SCOTT, Dafila

Original oil paintings of wildlife and landcape. Has illustrated articles and books and has exhibited paintings widely in UK.
Exhibitions for 2003: WWT Slimbridge (Feb/Mar), SWLA, London (Sept).
Address: White Roses, The Hythe, Reach, Cambridgeshire, CB5 0JQ; 01638 742344. e-mail: dafila@dafila.freeserve.co.uk

SHACKLETON, Keith

Original oil paintings - wildlife and marine subjects.
Exhibitions for 2003: Nature in Art: Wallsworth Hall, Gloucester - 15th Anniversary Exhibition, (June 2003).
Address: Wood Farm, Woodleigh, Kingsbridge,

Devon, TQ7 4DR; 01548 550165; (Fax)01548 550165.

SMITH, James P

Original colour and black-and-whites of British, European and Middle Eastern birds. Finished runner-up in *British Birds* 'Bird Illustrator of the Year' 1992. Commissions accepted, originals for sale.
Address: 157 Standon Rd, Sheffield, South Yorkshire, S9 1PH; (Tel/Fax)0114 2491378. e-mail: jameslotan@yahoo.com
www.birdingisrael.com

SNOW, Philip

Original paintings, sketches and illustrations of wildlife, mainly birds in landscape. Has illustrated or contributed to over 50 books, magazines etc. including *Collins Guide to Character of Birds*, 2003 and *Hebridean Wildlife and Landscape Sketch Book*, 2003.
Exhibitions for 2003: Tegfryn Gallery, Menai Bridge, Anglesey; Pensychnant Nature Centre, Conwy, N.Wales; NEWA, Liverpool.
Address: 2 Beach Cottages, Malltraeth, Anglesey, North Wales, LL62 5AT; (Tel/Fax)01407 840512. e-mail: philip@snow.swinternet.co.uk

STOCK, Andrew
SWLA, ARE

Watercolour, oil and mixed-media paintings of wildlife and landscape. Also etchings. Member of the Society of Wildlife Artists (SWLA) since 1983 (currently Hon Sec) SWLA and RE since 2001. Exhibits SWLA, Tryon Gallery, Royal Academy and locally. Commissions undertaken.
Exhibitions for 2003: SWLA,

London and local venues.
Address: The Old Schoolhouse, Ryme Intrinseca, Sherborne, Dorset, DT9 6JX; (Tel/Fax)01935 873620. e-mail: Andrewstock1@compuserve.com
www.andrewstock.co.uk

SYKES, Thelma

Artist printmaker: original linocuts, woodcuts, mainly British birds. Three linocuts for RSPB cards Christmas 2002. Illustrations in scraperboard for *New Breeding Bird Atlas, European Atlas, Birdwatcher's Yearbooks*, 1986-1996, Exhibits SWLA and National Print, London, Society of Wood Engravers touring exhibitions. Artist in residence Nature in Art, Gloucester.
Exhibitions for 2003: Solo exhibition, WWT Slimbridge, (Nov 24 2002 - Jan 7 2003). NEWA, Liverpool. SWLA, London.
Address: Blue Neb Studios, 18 Newcroft, Saughall, Chester, CH1 6EL; 01244 880209.

WALLACE, D.Ian.M.

Gouache paintings, pencil and ink drawings; "paints birds like birdwatchers see them", supplies roughs free for commissions. Many published illustrations in own/other books and a regular contributor to *Bird Watching* magazine.
Exhibitions for 2003: SWLA London (Sept).
Address: Mount Pleasant Farm, Main Road, Anslow, Burton-on-Trent, Staffs, DE13 9QE; 01283 812364.

WARREN, Michael

Original watercolour paintings of birds, all based on field observations. Books, calendars,

ART/PHOTOGRAPHY/LECTURERS

cards and commissions.
Exhibitions for 2003: Focus
Gallery, Nottingham (May),
SWLA, London, Wildlife Art
Gallery, Lavenham, (Autumn).
Address: The Laurels, The
Green, Winthorpe,
Nottinghamshire, NG24 2NR;
01636 673554; (Fax)01636
611569.
e-mail: mike.warren.birdart@
care4free.net
www.mikewarren.co.uk

WATSON, Derick
Wildlife/bird paintings in
watercolour, acriylic. Digitally
generated 'original' limited
edition prints. Illustrations in
scraperboard/pen and ink. Has
been featured in various
publications in the UK and
USA including *Artist's
Magazine* (USA), Leigh
Yawkey Woodson *Birds in Art
Catalogues* and several bird
atlases and annual bird reports.
Exhibitions for 2003:
Permanent Summer exhibition
at Kittiwake Gallery, St Abbs
Head, Art Inspired Slimbridge
(Apr 3-10), Edinburgh Zoo
(May 15 - Jun 29).
Address: The Kittiwake
Gallery at St Abbs Head, St
Abbs, Eymouth, TD14 5QF.
(H)018907 71588, (W)018907
71504. e-mail: derickwatson@
btopenworld.com

WILCZUR, Jan
Original gouache/watercolours
of birds and landscapes.
Published illustrations for
*Handbook of Birds of the
World*, *Concise Birds of the
Western Palearctic* and other
fieldguides. Cover painting for
*Best Birdwatching Sites in
Norfolk* (Buckingham Press).
Commissions accepted.
Address: 30 Dover House Rd,
London, SW15 5AU;0208 878
8925.
www.birdillustrators.com

**WILLIAMSON-BELL,
James, SWLA, HC (Paris)**
Any wildlife subject, in
watercolour and acrylics. Also
limited edition original prints.
Chinese watercolours and
woodblock prints a speciality.
Illustrated details available.
Commisions welcome.
Exhibitions for 2003: SWLA,
London.
Address: 2 Pauline Gardens,
Newcastle-upon-Tyne, NE15
7TD; (Tel/Fax)0191 274 6594.
e-mail:
autumnleaves@supanet.com

**WOODHEAD, Darren
MA(RCA), SWLA**
Original watercolours and
woodcuts of birds, butterflies,
mammals and other wildlife
subjects, as well as landscapes
and cloudscapes. All subjects
painted direct in the field.
Commissions undertaken.
Exhibitions for 2003: SWLA,
London.
Address: 44F(2F3), Millhill,
Musselburgh, East Lothian,
EH21 7RN; 0131 665 6802.
e-mail:
darren.woodhead@virgin.net

WOOLF, Colin
Beautiful original watercolour
paintings. The atmosphere of a
landscape and the character of
his subject are his hallmark,
together with a watercolour
technique that imparts a
softness to the natural subjects
he paints. Owls, birds of prey
and ducks are specialities.
Wide range of limited editions
and greetings cards, special
commissions also accepted.
Exhibitions for 2003: British
Birdwatching Fair, August.
Address: Tremallt,
Penmachno, Betws y Coed,
Conwy, LL24 0YL; +44 (0)
1690 760 308.
e-mail: colin@wildart.co.uk
www.wildart.co.uk

**Ringed
Plovers on
the shingle
was one of
Gerald
Russell's
BB entries**

DIRECTORY OF WILDLIFE PHOTOGRAPHERS

BASTON, Bill

Photographer
Subjects: East Anglian rarities and common birds, Mediterranean birds and landscapes, UK wildlife and landscapes, Florida birds and landscapes.
Formats: Prints, slides, digital, mounted/unmounted.
Address: 86 George Street, Hadleigh, Ipswich, IP7 5BU; 01473 827062.
e-mail: bill.baston@bt.com

BATES, Tony

Photographer and lecturer.
Subjects: Mainly British wildlife, landscapes and astro landscapes.
Formats: 35mm, prints (loose, mounted or framed), original handmade photo greetings cards.
Address: 22 Fir Avenue, Bourne, Lincs PE10 9RY. 01778 425137.
e-mail: mtr@masher.f9.co.uk

BORG, Les

Photographer, course leader.
Subjects: Mostly British wildlife, with some from Florida and elsewhere.
Formats: Mounted, unmounted or framed, inkjet prints or Ilfochromes if required.
Address: 17 Harwood Close, Tewin, Welwyn, Herts, AL6 0LF; 01438 717841, (Fax)01438 840459.
e-mail: les@les-borg-photography.co.uk
www.les-borg-photography.co.uk

BROADBENT, David

Professional photographer.
Subjects: UK birds and wild places.
Formats: 35mm, 6x7, CD-Roms, scans.
Address: 12 Thomas Street, Glossop, Derbyshire, SK13 8QN; 01457 862997, (W)07889 47266. e-mail: info@davidbroadbent.com
www.davidbroadbent.com

BROOKS, Richard

Wildlife photographer, writer, lecturer.
Subjects: Owls (Barn Owl especially), raptors, Kingfisher and a variety of European birds (Lesvos especially) and landscapes.
Formats: Mounted and unmounted computer prints (6x4 - A3+ size), framed pictures, surplus slides for sale.
Address: 24 Croxton Hamlet, Fulmodeston, Fakenham, Norfolk, NR21 0NP; 01328 878632. e-mail: email@richard-brooks.co.uk
www.richard-brooks.co.uk

CANIS, Robert

Professional photographer, tour leader.
Subjects: British flora and fauna, landscapes and environment of southern England, also Finland and Poland.
Formats: 35mm transparencies. Digital and conventional mounted/unmounted prints available.
Address: 26 Park Avenue, Sittingbourne, Kent, ME10 1QY; 07939 117570.
e-mail: rm.canis@msn.com

CHAPMAN, David

Natural history photographer, writer, speaker and workshop leader.
Subjects: British natural history (esp.birds) and farm animal images.
Formats: 35mm slides, mounted &/or framed photos, photo cards.
Address: 41 Bosence Road, Townshend, Cornwall, TR27 6AL; (Tel/fax) 01736 850 287.
e-mail: David@Ruralimages.freeserve.co.uk
www.Ruralimages.freeserve.co.uk

CONWAY, Wendy PSA4

Award-winning wildlife photographer.
Subjects: Birds, mammals, landscapes: UK, USA, Lesvos and Africa.
Formats: 35mm and medium format. Prints matted and unmatted.
Address: 4 Meriden Close, Winyates Green, Redditch, B98 0QN; 01527 457793.
e-mail: wendy@terry-wall.com

COOK, Garry

Photographer, birder.
Subjects: UK rarities.
Formats: Unmounted prints.
Address: Herons Flight, New Road, Blakeney, Nr Holt, Norfolk, NR25 7PA; 01263 741614.

DENNING, Paul

Wildlife photographer, lecturer.
Subjects: Birds, mammals, reptiles, butterflies and plants from UK, Europe, North and Central America.

Formats: 35mm transparencies and prints.
Address: 17 Maes Maelwg, Beddau, Pontypridd, CF38 2LD; (H)01443 202607; (W)02920 673243.
e-mail: pgdenning.naturepics@virgin.net

GARBUTT, Nick

Author, photographer, artist, tour leader.
Subjects: Madagascar (Ground rollers, Vangas, Couas, Mesites etc), East/Southern Africa, Indian subcontinent, Borneo.
Formats: Mounted 35mm and 70mm transparencies, Cibachrome prints to order.
Address: c/o 30 School Road, Wales, Sheffield, S26 5QJ; 01909 770954.
e-mail: nick@nickgarbutt.com
www.nickgarbutt.com

HARROP, Hugh

Professional wildlife guide, photographer and author.
Subjects: European birds, cetaceans, wild flowers, butterflies and dragonflies. Hugh specialises in all Shetland subjects.
Formats: 35mm transparency. Digital images on CD or via modem. Commercial enquiries only please.
Address: Longhill, Maywick, Shetland, ZE2 9JF; 01950 422483; (Fax)01950422430.
e-mail: hugh@hughharrop.com
www.hughharrop.com

HORNE, Robert

Wildlife photographer.
Subjects: Specialising in British wildlife, reserves and landscapes.
Formats: Mounted and unmounted prints and framed photographs.

Address: 5 Dalton Close, Broadfield, Crawley, West Sussex, RH11 9JR.
e-mail: robert.horne@virgin.net

KNELL, Steve

Wildlife photographer and lecturer.
Subjects: Birds, mammals, butterflies, dragonflies etc. mostly British, Lesvos, Florida, Spain and India.
Formats: 35mm slides mounted/unmounted and high class prints. Slides for lectures for sale/hire. Wildlife calendar 2003.
Address: 10 Windmill Crescent, Skelmanthorpe, Huddersfield, Yorks, HD8 9EL; 01484 860799; (W)07798 828756.

KNIGHTS, Chris

Farmer, wildlife photographer and film maker.
Subjects: British wildlife, North America, Eastern Europe, East Africa, Siberia, Lesvos and Canada.
Formats: 35mm mounted and digital prints, framed pictures and slides, copies to CD Rom.
Address: Crow Hall Farm, Gooderstone, King's Lynn, Norfolk, PE33 9DA;01366 328646. e-mail:
chris.knights@talk21.com

LANE, Mike

Wildlife photographer.
Subjects: Birds and wildlife from around the world, also landscapes and the environment.
Formats: 35mm, medium format and digital.
Address: 36 Berkeley Road, Shirley, Solihull, West Midlands, B90 2HS;

0121 744 7988.
e-mail: mikelane@nature-photography.co.uk
www.nature-photography.co.uk

LANGSBURY, Gordon FRPS

Professional wildlife photographer, lecturer, author and tour leader.
Subjects: Birds and mammals from UK, Europe, Scandinavia, N America, Gambia, Kenya, Tanzania, Morocco and Falklands.
Formats: 35mm transparencies for publication, lectures and prints.
Address: Sanderlings, 80 Shepherds Close, Hurley, Maidenhead, Berkshire, SL6 5LZ; (Tel/fax)01628 824252.
e-mail: gordonlangsbury@birdphoto.org.uk

McCARTHY, George

Professional wildlife photographer, lecturer, author and tour organiser.
Subjects: British wildlife and nature specialist, birds of Europe and USA.
Formats: Framed, mounted and un-mounted prints.
Address: 12 Searles View, Horsham, West Sussex, RH12 4FG; 01403 257917, (Fax)01403 267503.
e-mail: george.mccarthy@btinternet.com
www.georgemccarthy.com

MOCKLER, Mike

Safari guide, tour leader, writer and photographer.
Subjects: Birds and wildlife of Britain, Europe, Central America, India and several African countries.
Formats: 35mm transparencies.
Address: Gulliver's Cottage,

Chapel Rise, Avon Castle, Ringwood, Hampshire, BH24 2BL; 01425 478103. e-mail: mikemockler@lineone.net

OFFORD, Keith

Photographer, writer, tour leader, conservationist.
Subjects: Raptors, UK wildlife and scenery, birds and other wildlife of USA, Africa, Spain, Australia, India.
Formats: Conventional prints, greetings cards, framed pictures.
Address: Yew Tree Farmhouse, Craignant, Selattyn, Nr Oswestry, Shrops. SY10 7NP; 01691 718740. e-mail: keith-offord@virgin.net
www.keithofford.co.uk

OWEN, Charles

Wildlife and landscape photographer, ornithologist/ walks leader.
Subjects: Specialising in British wildlife, flora, birds, reserves and habitats.
Formats: 35mm transparencies available for publication, framed prints to order.
Address: 21 Pembroke Road, Hindley Green, Wigan, Lancashire, WN2 4TG; 01942 256163.

PARKER, Susan and Allan ARPS

Professional photographers (ASPphoto - images of nature) lecturers and tutors.
Subjects: Birds, plus other flora and fauna from the UK, Spain, Lesvos, Cyprus, Florida and Texas.
Formats: 35mm 645 medium format, slides, mounted digital prints, greetings cards and digital images on CD for reproduction (high quality scans up to A3+).

Address: Ashtree House, 51 Kiveton Lane, Todwick, Sheffield, South Yorkshire, S26 1HJ; 01909 770238. e-mail: aspaspphoto@clara.co.uk

PIKE, David

Photographer, presenter and writer.
Subjects: Wildlife, including birds from Japan, N America and Africa.
Formats: 35mm mounted. Conventional prints and digital.
Address: Uffington Manor, Main Road, Uffington, Lincs, PE9 4SN; 01780 751944;(W)01780 767711; (Fax)01780 489218. e-mail: david.pike@ ukphotographics.co.uk www. ukphotographics.co.uk.com

POWER, John
FRPS

Bird photographer.
Subjects: British birds, dragonflies, wild flowers.
Formats: Mounted, unmounted or framed prints. Cibachrome or computer prints if required.
Address: 15 Brynmor Road, Mossley Hill, Liverpool, L18 4RW; 0151 724 5004, (W)0151 729 0094,(Fax)0151 724 3667.

READ, Mike

Photographer (wildlife and landscapes), tour leader, writer.
Subjects: Birds, mammals, plants, landscapes, and some insects. UK, France, USA, Ecuador (including Galapagos).
Formats: 35mm.
Address: Claremont, Redwood Close, Ringwood, Hampshire, BH24 1PR; 01425 475008, (Fax)01425 473160. e-mail: mike@mikeread.co.uk www.mikeread.co.uk

SIMPSON, Geoff

Professional natural history and landscape photographer.
Subjects: Specialises in evocative images of Britain's wildlife and landscape.
Formats: 35mm and panoramic. Slides and CD.
Address: Camberwell, 1 Buxton Road, New Mills, High Peak, Derbyshire, SK22 3JS; 01633 743089. e-mail: info@geoffsimpson.co.uk www.geoffsimpson.co.uk

SWASH, Andy

Photographer, author, tour leader.
Subjects: Birds, habitats/ landscapes and general wildlife from all continents; photographic library currently features 1,500 bird species.
Formats: Slides for publication and duplicates for lectures. High resolution scans on CD-Rom. Conventional and digital prints, unmounted, mounted or framed.
Address: Stretton Lodge, 9 Birch Grove, West Hill, Ottery St Mary, Devon, EX11 1XP; (H&fax)01404 815383, (W)01392 822901. e-mail: andy_swash@ wildguides.co.uk www.wildguides.co.uk

TIPLING, David

Wildlife and landscape photographer, photographic tour leader, author.
Subjects: Worldwide wildlife and landscapes. Specialist areas include; UK, Antarctic, Finland and Arctic Norway, N India, Amazon, Alaska and China.
Formats: 35mm to 6x17 panoramas available as transparencies for commercial use only. Mounted prints available for sale, plus

ART/PHOTOGRAPHY/LECTURERS

greetings cards and fine art posters.
Address: 99 Noah's Ark, Kemsing, Sevenoaks, Kent, TN15 6PD; 01732 763486.
e-mail: windrushphotos@hotmail.com

WALL, Terry
ARPS EFIAP PPSA

Wildlife photographer.
Subjects: Birds, mammals, landscapes from UK, USA, Lesvos, Africa and Galapagos.
Formats: 35mm/medium. Prints matted/unmatted. 35mm scanning service and restoration and retouching service. Quality printing service. One-to-one Photoshop tuition.
Address: 4 Meriden Close, Winyates Green, Redditch, B98 0QN; 01527 457793.
e-mail: wildimages@terry-wall.com
www.terry-wall.com

WARD, Chris

Photographer.
Subjects: Birds and landscapes, plus some other wildlife. UK (mostly commoner species, some rarities), W.Palearctic, S.Africa, Florida, California, Venezuela, Argentina, Australia.
Formats: Prints and framed pictures, slide copies for lectures.
Address: 276 Bideford Green, Linslade, Leighton Buzzard, Beds, LU7 7TU; 01525 375528. e-mail: chris@chriswardphotography.co.uk

WILKES, Mike
FRPS

Professional wildlife photographer, tour leader.
Subjects: African, European and British birds.
Address: 43 Feckenham Road, Headless Cross, Redditch, Worcestershire, B97 5AS; 01527 550686.
e-mail: wilkes@photoshot.com

WILLIAMS, Nick

Photographer, lecturer, author, tour leader.
Subjects: W.Palearctic including Cape Verde Islands and Falkland Islands.
Formats: Duplicate slides, some originals, prints also available.
Address: Owl Cottage, Station Road, Rippingale, Lincs, PE10 0TA; (Tel/Fax)01778 440500.
e-mail: magick2@hotmail.co.uk
www.wildlifebreaks.co.uk

WILMSHURST, Roger

Wildlife photographer, particularly birds.
Subjects: All aspects of wildlife, particularly British and European birds, butterflies, plants, mammals etc.
Formats: 35mm, 6x6, 6x7, 6x5.
Address: Sandhill Farmhouse, Sandhill Lane, Washington, Pulborough, West Sussex, RH20 4TD; 01903 892210, (fax)01903 893376.

DIRECTORY OF LECTURERS

Lecturers who have indicated that they are willing to travel to all parts of Britain are listed first. For the remainder we have grouped them geographically in the following regions: England, Eastern; North-eastern; North-western; South-eastern; South-western; West Midlands and Wales; Scotland.

To ensure this valuable section continues strongly in the future, we would be grateful if you would mention the *Yearbook* when contacting any of the listed lecturers.

If your group has enjoyed a talk from anyone not listed here, we would appreciate receiving contact details so they might be included in the 2004 edition.

NO MILEAGE LIMITS

BATES,Tony
Photographer and lecturer. **Subjects:** Mainly British wildlife, folklore, landscapes and astro landscapes. **Fees:** £65 plus travel. **Limits:** None. **Times:** To suit. **Address:** 22 Fir Avenue, Bourne, Lincs, PE10 9RY; 01778 425137. e-mail: mtr@masher.f9.co.uk

BELL, Graham
Cruise lecturer worldwide, photographer, author. **Subjects:** Arctic, Antarctic, America, Siberia, Australia, Canada, Iceland, Seychelles, UK - identification, behaviour, seabirds, bird imitations etc. **Fees:** £35 plus travel. **Limits:** None. **Times:** Any. **Address:** Ros View, South Yearle, Wooler, Northumberland, NE71 6RB; (Tel/fax)01668 281310. e-mail: seabirds@talk21.com

BOND, Terry
Bank director, photographer, group field leader, conference speaker worldwide. **Subjects:** Eight talks (including Scilly Isles, Southern Europe, USA – shorebirds and inland birds, Birdwatching Identification – a new approach). **Fees:** By arrangement (usually only expenses). **Limits:** Most of UK. **Times:** Evenings. **Address:** 3 Lapwing Crescent, Chippenham, Wiltshire, SN14 6YF; 01249 462674. e-mail: terryebond@btopenworld.com

BROOKS, Richard
Wildlife photographer, writer, lecturer. **Subjects:** 12 talks (including Lesvos, N.Greece, Israel, Canaries, E.Anglia, Scotland, Wales, Oman). **Fees:** £65 plus petrol. **Limits:** None if accom provided. **Times:** Any. **Address:** 24 Croxton Hamlet, Fulmodeston, Fakenham, Norfolk, NR21 0NP; 01328 878632. e-mail: email@richard-brooks.co.uk www.richard-brooks.co.uk

BURROWS, Ian
Tour leader. **Subjects:** Papua New Guinea, Cape Clear Island and 'Food from the Wild'. **Fees:** £70 plus mileage over 100. **Limits:** Anything considered. **Times:** Evenings preferable but other times considered. **Address:** Well Cottage, 38 Creake Road, Sculthorpe, Fakenham, Norfolk, NR21 9NQ; 01328 856925; (Fax) 01328 862017. e-mail: Ian@sicklebill.demon.co.uk www.sicklebill.com

CANIS, Robert
Professional photographer, tour leader. **Subjects:** Illustrated talks (including British and Finnish wildlife).

Fees: £40 plus petrol. **Limits:** None. **Times:** Sept-April. **Address:** 26 Park Avenue, Sittingbourne, Kent, ME10 1QY; 07939 117570. e-mail: rm.canis@msn.com

CARRIER, Michael

Lifelong interest in natural history.
Subjects: 1) 'Birds in Cumbria', 2) 'The Solway and its Birds' and 3)'The Isle of May'.
Fees: £20. **Limits:** None but rail connection essential.
Times: Sept-March inc, afternoons or evenings.
Address: Lismore Cottage, 1 Front Street, Armathwaite, Carlisle, Cumbria, CA4 9PB; 01697 472218.

CROUCHER, Roy

Wildlife tour leader, local authority ecologist.
Subjects: Four talks (Northern France, Montenegro, Managing Britain's Habitats, Bird Song).
Fees: £50 plus petrol from Birmingham. **Limits:** Mainland Britain. **Times:** November and December.
Address: Place de L'Eglise, 53700, Averton, Mayenne, France; 0033 2430 06969.
e-mail:
roy_croucher@lineone.net

DOODY, Dee

Ornithologist, wildlife cameraman, artist, television presenter (wildlife).
Subjects: Two half-hour films and talk on Red Kite and Goshawk; birds of coasts, rivers, moorland, woodlands, estuaries, urban areas, lakes and reservoirs, reserves, farmland plus half-hour programmes on the birds of Wales.

Fees: £250-300. **Limits:** None. **Times:** Evenings, Autumn and Winter. **Address:** 2 Fan Terrace, Fan, Llanidloes, Powys, SY18 6NW: 01686 413819.

DUGGAN, Glenn

Ex-Commander Royal Navy, tour leader, researcher.
Subjects: Ten talks including, birds of paradise and bower birds, history of bird art (caveman to present day), famous Victorian bird artists (John Gould, the Birdman and John James Andubohon.
Fees: £50 plus expenses.
Limits: none with o.n accom.
Times: Any.
Address: 25 Hampton Grove, Fareham, Hampshire, PO15 5NL; 01329 845976, (M)07771 605320. e-mail: glennduggan@ cardinal-tours.com
www.cardinal-tours.com

EYRE, John

Author, photographer, conservationist and chairman Hampshire Ornithological Society.
Subjects: World birding (Europe, Africa, Australasia and the Americas), plus special Hampshire subjects (eg. Gilbert White's birds and heathland birds).
Fees: £55 plus travel. **Limits:** Any location negotiable.
Times: Any.
Address: 3 Dunmow Hill, Fleet, Hampshire, GU51 3AN; 01252 677850. e-mail: JohnEyre@compuserve.com

GALLOP, Brian

Speaker, photographer, tour leader.
Subjects: 25+ talks covering UK, Africa, India, Galapagos and Europe - All natural

history subjects.
Fees: £40 plus 20p per ml.
Limits: None - o.n acc. if over 100 mls. **Times:** Any.
Address: 13 Orchard Drive, Tonbridge, Kent, TN10 4LT; 01732 361892.

GARBUTT, Nick

Author, photographer, artist, tour leader.
Subjects: Madagascar, (mammals, birds, reptiles, frogs), India, Borneo, East and Southern Africa.
Fees: £150 plus expenses.
Limits: None. **Times:** Any.
Address: c/o 30 School Road, Wales, Sheffield, S26 5QJ; 01909 770954.
e-mail: nick@nickgarbutt.com
www.nickgarbutt.com

GARNER, David

Wildlife photographer.
Subjects: 17 live talks and audio-visual shows on all aspects of wildlife in UK and some parts of Europe - list available.
Fees: £35 plus 15p per ml.
Limits: None. **Times:** Any.
Address: 73 Needingworth Road, St Ives, Cambridgeshire, PE27 5JY; (H)01480 463194; (W)01480 463194.

GIBSON, Chris

Conservation professional, tour leader, photographer, writer, broadcaster.
Subjects: Include the wildlife, lepidoptera and botany of Essex, East Anglia and the Mediterranean.
Fees: £50 plus expenses in Essex and Suffolk, £100 plus expenses elsewhere. **Limits:** None. **Times:** Evenings.
Address: 1 Dove House Cottage, Oakley Road, Dovercourt, Essex, CO12

5DR; 01255 502960. e-mail:
gibson@dovehc.freeserve.co.uk

GUNTON, Trevor

Ex-RSPB Staff, recruitment
advisor, lecturer.
Subjects: Eight talks - Birds
and Pits, Yorkshire, NT
Reserves, UK Bird Islands,
Geese, Shetland, Garden Birds,
European Conservation.
Membership recruitement
workshops a speciality,
Fees: Variable (basic £55 plus
expenses). **Limits:** None.
Times: Anytime, anywhere.
Address: 15 St James Road,
Little Paxton, St Neots,
Cambs, PE19 6QW; 01480
473562. e-mail:
trevor.gunton@tesco.net

HARROP, Hugh

Professional wildlife guide,
photographer and author.
Subjects: 15 talks including
Shetland wildlife, Shetland
birds, polar bears, whales and
dolphins, Galapagos, seals and
sea lions, Alaska, Iceland,
general wildlife photography.
Fees: £125 plus accom at cost
and return flight from Shetland.
Limits: UK only. **Times:**
November to March.
Address: Longhill, Maywick,
Shetland, ZE2 9JF; 01950
422483; (Fax)01950422430.
e-mail: hugh@hughharrop.com
www.hughharrop.com

JAMES, David

Environmental educator,
photographer, RSPB leader.
Subjects: Five subjects
including: Antarctica, southern
S.America, Ramsey Island
(RSPB), Earthwatch
expedition. Can also do school
presentations.
Fees: £55 plus expenses.
Limits: None. **Times:** Any

(also short notice).
Address: 78 Colney Road,
Dartford, Kent, DA1
1UH:01322 274791, (M)07904
107449. e-mail:
dartdiva56@hotmail.com

KNYSTAUTAS, Algirdas

Ornithologist, photographer,
writer, tour leader.
Subjects: Birds and natural
history of Russia, Baltic States,
S America, Indonesia (six
talks).
Fees: £1 per person. £70
minimum plus £20 travelling.
Limits: None - in UK, o.n
accom needed. **Times:** Oct and
Nov.
Address: 7 Holders Hill
Gardens, London, NW4 1NP;
020 8203 4317.
e-mail: ibisbill@talk21.com

LANE, Mike

Wildlife photographer.
Subjects: Seven talks from the
UK and worldwide, mostly on
birds.
Fees: Varies. **Limits:** None.
Times: Any.
Address: 36 Berkeley Road,
Shirley, Solihull, West
Midlands, B90 2HS; 0121 744
7988. e-mail: mikelane@
nature-photography.co.uk
www.nature-photography.co.uk

LANGSBURY, Gordon FRPS

Professional wildlife
photographer, lecturer, author
and tour leader.
Subjects: 20 talks - Africa,
Europe, USA, Falklands and
UK. Full list provided.
Fees: £75 plus travel expenses.
Limits: None. **Times:** Any.
Address: Sanderlings, 80
Shepherds Close, Hurley,
Maidenhead, Berkshire, SL6
5LZ; (Tel/fax)01628 824252.

e-mail: gordonlangsbury@
birdphoto.org.uk

McCARTHY, George

Professional wildlife and nature
photographer.
Subjects: Various talks
including birds of New
Mexico, Florida and Lesvos.
Full list available by post or on
website.
Fees: £50 plus 25p per ml.
Limits: No limits (check
website). **Times:** Any during
Sept - Dec.
Address: 12 Searles View,
Horsham, West Sussex, RH12
4FG; 01403 257917,
(Fax) 01403 267503. e-mail:
george.mccarthy@btinternet.com
www.georgemccarthy.com

McKAVETT, Mike

Photographer.
Subjects: Five talks, Birds and
Wildlife of India, North and
Western Kenya and the
Gambia, Bird Migration in
North America.
Fees: £30 plus expenses.
Limits: None. **Times:** Any.
Address: 34 Rectory Road,
Churchtown, Southport, PR9
7PU; 01704 231358.

MOCKLER, Mike

Safari guide, tour leader, writer
and photographer.
Subjects: Birds and other
wildlife of: Botswana, Kenya,
Tanzania, Spain, Finland and
Norway, Costa Rica, India and
Brazil.
Fees: Negotiable. **Limits:**
None. **Times:** Evenings.
Address: Gulliver's Cottage,
Chapel Rise, Avon Castle,
Ringwood, Hampshire, BH24
2BL; 01425 478103. e-mail:
mikemockler@lineone.net

ART/PHOTOGRAPHY/LECTURERS

MOIR, Geoffrey
DFC, FRGS, FRPSL

Ret. Schoolmaster, lecturer, writer, philatelist, lived in Falkland Islands.
Subjects: Fully illustrated talks on subjects including: 'Falklands 2000', 'The Island of South Georgia with Whales and Whaling', 'The Flora of the Falkland Islands'.
Fees: £20. **Limits:** None. **Times:** Any.
Address: 37 Kingscote Road, Croydon, Surrey, CR0 7DP; Tel/fax 020 8654 9463.

OFFORD, Keith

Photographer, writer, tour leader, conservationist.
Subjects: 14 talks covering raptors, uplands, gardens, migration, woodland wildlife, Australia, Southern USA, Tanzania, Gambia, Spain, SW.Africa.
Fees: £80 plus petrol. **Limits:** None. **Times:** Sept - April.
Address: Yew Tree Farmhouse, Craignant, Selattyn, Nr Oswestry, Shropshire, SY10 7NP; 01691 718740.
e-mail: keith-offord@virgin.net
www.keithofford.co.uk

OWEN, Charles

Retired nature reserve warden, photographer, ornithologist.
Subjects: Various talks (birds, butterflies, plants, habitats and landscapes), list available.
Fees: £50 plus petrol. **Limits:** None. **Times:** Any (can fill in for cancellations).
Address: 21 Pembroke Road, Hindley Green, Wigan, Lancashire, WN2 4TG; 01942 256163.

PALMER, Phil

Tour leader for Bird Holidays.
Subjects: Mostly birds, but includes mammals, insects, reptiles, whale watching etc. Many foreign trips including Alaska, Midway Atoll, Antarctica and India. British birds - 'First for Britain' from Phil's book, the secret life of the Nightjar, twitching in the UK and bird photography.
Fees: To suit all club budgets. **Limits:** None. **Times:** Any.
Address: 72 Grove Road, Retford, Notts, DN22 7JN; 01777 709841; (W/Fax)0113 3910510. e-mail:
Phil@birdholidays.fsnet.co.uk
www.britishbirdguides.co.uk

PICKFORD, Terry

Co-ordinator NW Raptor Protection Group, advisory member to the government's raptor forum committee.
Subjects: 1) Raptor conservation/persecution NW England; 2) Home Life of the Golden Eagle in Scotland; 3) Wildlife of the Czech Republic.
Fees: £70 plus 15p per ml. **Limits:** None. **Times:** Any.
Address: Plane Tree House, 114 Pilling Lane, Preesall, Lancs,FY6 0HG; 01253 810620, (M)07977 890116. e-mail:
conservation@raptor.uk.com

RUMLEY-DAWSON, Ian

Photographer, course leader.
Subjects: 96 talks using twin dissolving projectors. Birds, mammals, insects, plants, habitats, ethology. Arctic, Antarctic, Falklands, N and S America, N.Z, Seychelles. albatrosses, penguins, Snowy Owls, polar bears etc.
Fees: £50 plus expenses. **Limits:** None. **Times:** Any.
Address: Oakhurst, Whatlington Road, Battle, East Sussex, TN33 0JN; 01424 772673.

SCOTT, Ann and Bob

Ex-RSPB staff, tour leaders, writers, lecturers, tutors, trainers.
Subjects: 16+ talks (including nature reserves, RSPB, tours, gardening, Europe, Africa, S America, after dinner talks).
Fees: £60 plus travel over 50 mls. **Limits:** None (by arrangement). **Times:** Any.
Address: 8 Woodlands, St Neots, Cambridgeshire, PE19 1UE; 01480 214904; (fax)01480 473009.
e-mail: abscott@tiscali.co.uk

SIMPSON, Geoff

Professional natural history and landscape photographer.
Subjects: 1) 'A Nature Photographer's Diary', 2) 'Wild Britain', 3) 'The Flora and Fauna of the Peak District'.
Fees: £100 plus petrol. **Limits:** Anywhere in the UK.
Times: Any.
Address: Camberwell, 1 Buxton Road, New Mills, High Peak, Derbyshire, SK22 3JS; 01633 743089. e-mail:
info@geoffsimpson.co.uk
www.geoffsimpson.co.uk

SWASH, Andy

Photographer, author, tour leader.
Subjects: Ten talks (birds and general wildlife: Brazil, Argentina, Galapagos, Antarctica, Africa, Australia, China, USA, Costa Rica, Venezuela).
Fees: £85 plus petrol. **Limits:** None. **Times:** Evenings.
Address: Stretton Lodge, 9 Birch Grove, West Hill, Ottery St Mary, Devon, EX11 1XP;

DIRECTORY OF LECTURERS

(H&fax)01404 815383,
(W)01392 822901. e-mail:
andy_swash@wildguides.co.uk
www.wildguides.co.uk

TODD, Ralph
Tour leader.
Subjects: Six talks incl.
Galapagos wildlife, Antarctica,
Pyrenees, Iceland, Osprey
wardening at Loch Garten,
Wintering in Africa.
Fees: £55 plus expenses.
Limits: None, neg over 120
mls. **Times:** Any - also short
notice.
Address: 9 Horsham Road,
Bexleyheath, Kent, DA6 7HU;
(Tel/fax)01322 528335.
e-mail: rbtodd@
todds9.fsnet.co.uk
www.users.globalnet.co.uk/
~rbtodd/todd.htm

WALLACE, D.Ian.M.
Field ornithologist, writer,
artist.
Subjects: Early birdwatching
(1930s-1960s) and other
subjects.
Fees: Negotiable plus travel.
Limits: None, overnight accom
over 150 mls. **Times:** Any.
Address: Mount Pleasant
Farm, Main Road, Anslow,
Burton on Trent, Staffordshire,
DE13 9QE; 01283 812364.

WATTS, Nicholas
Farmer, conservationist,
ornithologist, photographer.
Subjects: Farming and
Wildlife', 'Birds on my Farm'.
Fees: £40 within 40 miles.
Limits: None. Over 40 miles,
larger fee. **Times:** Evenings,
not Jun-Sep.
Address: Vine House Farm,
Deeping St Nicholas, Spalding,
PE11 3DG; 01775 630208.
e-mail:
p.n.watts@farming.co.uk

WILKES, Mike
FRPS
Professional wildlife
photographer, tour leader.
Subjects: 13 talks - natural
history - Africa, America,
South America, Europe, Gt
Britain.
Fees: According to distance on
request. **Limits:** None.
Times: Any.
Address: 43 Feckenham Road,
Headless Cross, Redditch,
Worcestershire, B97 5AS;
01527 550686.
e-mail: wilkes@photoshot.com

WILLIAMS, Nick
Photographer, lecturer, author,
tour leader.
Subjects: Several audio visual
shows (including Spain,
Camargue, Turkey, Canaries
and Cape Verde Islands,
Falklands).
Fee: £80-£99 depending on
group size and distance.
Limits: None
Times: Any
Address: Owl Cottage, Station
Road, Rippingale, Lincs, PE10
0TA; (Tel/Fax)01778 440500.
e-mail:
magick2@hotmail.co.uk
www.wildlifebreaks.co.uk

WILLOUGHBY, Paul
Tour leader for Bird Holidays.
Subjects: Extremely varied but
include many foreign locations
such as Alaska, Midway Atoll,
Galapagos, United Arab
Emirates, British birds and
Whale watching.
Fees: To suit club budgets.
Limits: None. **Times:** Any.
Address: Bird Holidays, 10
Ivegate, Yeadon, Leeds LS19
7RE. 0113 3910510(daytime).
www.birdguides.co.uk

WOODALL, Andrew
Tour leader for Bird Holidays.
Subjects: Extremely varied but
include many foreign locations
such as Alaska, Midway Atoll,
Galapagos, United Arab
Emirates, British birds and
Whale watching.
Fees: To suit club budgets.
Limits: None. **Times:** Any.
Address: Bird Holidays, 10
Ivegate, Yeadon, Leeds LS19
7RE. 0113 3910510(daytime).
www.birdguides.co.uk

WREN, Graham ARPS
Wildlife photographer, lecturer,
tour guide.
Subjects: 17 talks, birds - UK
and Scandinavia, the
environment - recent habitat
changes and effect on bird
populations, wildlife - Ohio and
Kenya.
Fees: £50-70 plus petrol.
Limits: None. **Times:** Any.
Address: The Kiln House,
Great Doward, Whitchurch,
Ross-on-Wye, Herefordshire,
HR9 6DU; 01600 890488,
(Fax)01600 890294.

WYATT, John
Tour leader, photographer,
writer, co-author of *Teach
Yourself Bird Sounds* cassette
series.
Subjects: More than 30 talks
(including birds and other
wildlife of Africa, Central
America, Europe and of
specific habitats within these
areas, bird identification by
sight and sound), general
natural history topics.
Fees: £55 plus travel. **Limits:**
England and Wales only.
Times: Any.
Address: Little Okeford,
Christchurch Road, Tring,
Hertfordshire, HP23 4EF;
01442 823356. e-mail:
wyatt@waxwing.u-net.com

ART/PHOTOGRAPHY/LECTURERS

ENGLAND

EASTERN

APPLETON, Tim

Reserve Manager, Rutland Water.
Subjects: Rutland Water, British Birdwatching Fair, Return of Ospreys to England, Trips and birds of Spain, Australia, Papua New Guinea, various African countries, Argentina and more.
Fees: Negotiable. **Limits:** Preferably within 2hrs of Rutland. **Times:** Winter preferred but can be flexible.
Address: Fishponds Cottage, Stamford Road, Oakham, Rutland, LE15 8AB; (H)01572 724101, (W)01572 770651: (Fax) 01572 755931.

BROADBENT, David

Photographer.
Subjects: UK birds and wild places. In praise of natural places.
Fees: £70 plus travel. **Limits:** 50mls without o.n accom Anywhere otherwise.
Times: Any.
Address: 12 Thomas Street, Glossop, Derbyshire, SK13 8QN; 01457 862997, (W)07889 47266. e-mail: info@davidbroadbent.com
www.davidbroadbent.com

BROOKS, David

Freelance naturalist.
Subjects: Various talks on wildlife, principally birds, in UK and overseas.
Fees: £50 plus petrol. **Limits:** 50 mls without o.n. accom 100 mls otherwise. **Times:** Any.
Address: 2 Malthouse Court, Green Lane, Thornham, Norfolk, PE36 6NW; 01485 512548. e-mail: david.g.brooks@tesco.net

CLARKE, Roger

Author of books on harriers, Phd in raptor feeding ecology.
Subjects: Harriers (overview and feeding ecology), other raptors if pressed.
Fees: £55 plus petrol. **Limits:** Negotiable. **Times:** Flexible.
Address: New Hythe House, Reach, Cambridge, CB5 0JQ; 01638 742447.

COOK, Tony MBE

35 years employed by WWT. Travelled in Europe, Africa and N. America.
Subjects: 22 talks from Birds of The Wash, garden birds to travelogues of Kenya, E and W North America, Europe (Med to North Cape).
Fees: £35 plus 15p per ml.
Limits: 100 mls. **Times:** Any.
Address: 11 Carnoustie Court, Sutton Bridge, Spalding, Lincs, PE12; 01406 350069.

COURT, John

Enthusiastic amateur naturalist and photographer.
Subjects: Seven talks (including general wildlife, butterflies, dragonflies and birdwatching.
Fees: £32 plus 20p per mile.
Limits: 100 mls. **Times:** Any (not July or August), also short notice.
Address: Cedars, Hulletts Lane, Pilgrims Hatch, Brentwood, Essex, CM15 9RX; 01277 372217.

CROMACK, David

Editor of *Bird Watching* magazine, bird tour leader.
Subjects: 1) 'Bird Magazines and the Art of Bird Photography' and 2) 'Birds of Arizona and California'.
Fees: 1) No fee - expenses only, 2) £50 plus expenses.
Limits: 175 mls. **Times:** Jan/ Feb.
Address: c/o *Bird Watching* Magazine, Bretton Court, Peterborough, PE3 8DZ. e-mail: david.cromack@.emap.com

JOHNSTONE, Leslie

Photographer.
Subjects: Several (St Kilda, Hebrides and Shetland and offbeat view of bird photography).
Fees: £45 or 45p per ml (whichever greater). **Limits:** 70 mls without o.n. accom, 200 mls otherwise. **Times:** Any.
Address: 3 Muirfield Way, Woodhall-Spa, Lincs, LN10 6WB; 01526 354696.

KNIGHTS, Chris

Farmer, conservationist, photographer.
Subjects: British wildlife, North America, Eastern Europe, East Africa, Siberia, Lesvos, Canada.
Fee: £60 plus petrol.
Limits: 60 mls without o.n. accom. **Times:** Evenings only.
Address: Crow Hall Farm, Gooderstone, King's Lynn, Norfolk, PE33 9DA; 01366 328646. e-mail: chris.knights@talk21.com

PIKE, David

Photographer, presenter and writer.
Subjects: Winter Birds of Japan.
Fees: £50.
Address: Uffington Manor, Main Road, Uffington, Lincs,

PE9 4SN; 01780 751944; (W)01780 767711; (Fax) 01780 489218. e-mail: david.pike@ukphotographics.co.uk www. ukphotographics.co.uk.com

SHERWIN, Andrew

Interests in natural history and photography.
Subjects: Ten talks including Kenya, Gambia, Israel, California, Canada, India, Lesvos, Pyrenees.
Fees: £45. **Limits:** 50 mls.
Times: Evenings only.
Address: 26 Rockingham Close, Ashgate, Chesterfield, Derbyshire, S40 1JE; 01246 221070.
e-mail: andrew.sherwin@btinternet.com

TAYLOR, Mick

Co-ordinator South Peak Raptor Group, photographer, ornithologist, writer.
Subjects: Several talks including (Merlins, Raptors, Peak District birds, Alaskan wildlife).
Fees: £50 plus petrol. **Limits:** Negotiable.
Times: Evenings preferred.
Address: 76 Hawksley Avenue, Chesterfield, Derbyshire, S40 4TL;01246 277749.

NORTH-EASTERN

DOHERTY, Paul

Video maker/photographer.
Subjects: Five talks (Birds of Prey, Waders, Wetlands, and Birdwatchers Quiz).
Fees: £60 plus petrol. **Limits:** 100 mls. **Times:** Any.
Address: 28 Carousel Walk, Sherburn in Elmet, North

Yorkshire, LS25 6LP; (Tel/fax)01977 684666.
e-mail: paul@birdimages.swinternet.co.uk

KNELL, Steve

Wildlife photographer and lecturer.
Subjects: Birds, mammals, butterflies, dragonflies, mostly from Britain (inc. Scotland), Lesvos, Florida, Spain, India.
Fees: £50 plus travel expenses.
Limits: 100 mls. **Times:** Any time outside May-Aug.
Address: 10 Windmill Crescent, Skelmanthorpe, Huddersfield, Yorks, HD8 9EL. 01484 860799; (W)07798 828756.

MATHER, John Robert

Ornithologist, writer, tour guide, lecturer.
Subjects: Birds and wildlife of: Kenya, Tanzania, Uganda, Costa Rica, Romania, India, Nepal. 'Bird on the Bench'.
Fees: £65 plus 20p per ml.
Limits: 100 mls. **Times:** Evenings.
Address: Eagle Lodge, 44 Aspin Lane, Knaresborough, North Yorkshire, HG5 8EP; 01423 862775.

PARKER, Susan and Allan ARPS

Professional photographers, (ASPphoto – Images of Nature), lecturers and tutors.
Subjects: Talks on birds and natural history, natural history photography - countries include UK, USA (Texas, Florida), Spain, Greece, Cyprus.
Fees: On application.
Limits: Up to 120 mls

without o.n accom. **Times:** Any.
Address: Ashtree House, 51 Kiveton Lane, Todwick, Sheffield, South Yorkshire, S26 1HJ; 01909 770238.
e-mail: aspaspphoto@clara.co.uk

NORTH-WESTERN

MELLOR GREENHALGH, Pauline

Photographer, writer, countryside ranger.
Subjects: Hebridean wildlife - birds, flora, insects, fauna.
Fees: £50 plus petrol. **Limits:** 100 mls from Leigh. **Times:** Evenings.
Address: 78 Firs Lane, Leigh, Lancashire, WN7 4SB; (H)01942 606576, (W)01695 625338.

POWER, John FRPS

Bird photographer.
Subjects: British birds - four talks (slides) plus photographic workshop (equipment/prints).
Fees: Negotiable. **Limits:** To be discussed. **Times:** Evenings (days poss).
Address: 15 Brynmor Road, Mossley Hill, Liverpool, L18 4RW; 0151 724 5004, (W)0151 729 0094,(Fax)0151 724 3667.

SOUTH-EASTERN

BELLIS, Gwyneth

Ex-RSPB group leader, Chair of Maple Lodge Conservation Society.
Subjects: The Secret Sanctuary' (Maple Lodge Reserve), garden birds, work of the RSPB.
Fees: £30. **Limits:** 20 mls.
Times: Afternoons/evenings.

ART/PHOTOGRAPHY/LECTURERS

109

Address: 23B Belmont Road, Bushey, Hertfordshire, WD2 2JS; 01923 230277. e-mail: gwyneth@bellis7fsnet.co.uk

BEVAN, David

Conservation officer, photographer, writer.
Subjects: Nature conservation, natural history of the garden, butterflies, wild flowers. SAE for full details.
Fees: £70 plus petrol. **Limits:** 50 miles without o.n. accom,150 mls otherwise.
Times: Evenings, days poss.
Address: 3 Queens Road, Bounds Green, London, N11 2QJ; (H)020 8889 6375, (W)020 8348 6005, Fax 020 8342 8754.
e-mail: conserving.bevan@virgin.net

BORG, Les

Photographer, course leader.
Subjects: Florida (mostly birds), nature photography (parts I, II and III), cetaceans of the Azores, images of 2001.
Fees: Negotiable. **Limits:** 150 mls without o.n accom. **Times:** Any.
Address: 17 Harwood Close, Tewin, Welwyn, Herts, AL6 0LF; 01438 717841. e-mail: les@les-borg-photography.co.uk www.les-borg-photography.co.uk

BRITTEN, John

Leader of local RSPB group.
Subjects: Birding trips to Antarctica, Caribbean, Galapagos, Australia, New Zealand.
Fees: No fee (donation to RSPB requested), petrol costs.
Limits: About an hour from Watford. **Times:** Any.
Address: Harlestone, 98

Sheepcot Lane, Garston, Hertfordshire, WD25 0EB; 01923 673205. e-mail; john.britten@btinternet.com

BUCKINGHAM, John

Lecturer, photographer, tour leader.
Subjects: 60+ titles covering birds, wildlife, botany, ecology and habitats in UK, Europe, Africa, Australia, India and the Americas.
Fees: £55 plus expenses.
Limits: Any reasonable distance. **Times:** Any.
Address: 3 Cardinal Close, Tonbridge, Kent, TN9 2EN; (Tel/fax) 01732 354970.

CLEAVE, Andrew MBE

Head of environmental education centre, author, tour leader.
Subjects: 30 talks (including Galapagos, Arctic, Mediterranean and Indian birds, dormice, woodlands). List available.
Fees: £50 plus petrol. **Limits:** 60 mls without o.n accom.
Times: Evenings, not school holidays.
Address: 31 Petersfield Close, Chineham, Basingstoke, Hampshire, RG24 8WP; (H)01256 320050, (W)01256 882094, (Fax)01256 880174. e-mail: andrew.cleave@care4free.net

COOMBER, Richard

Tour leader, photographer, writer.
Subjects: Alaska, Australia, Botswana, Namibia, Seychelles, Falklands, Galapagos, S America, USA, seabirds.
Fees: £60 plus petrol. **Limits:** 50 mls without o.n accom 150 mls otherwise. **Times:**

Afternoons or evenings.
Address: 1 Haglane Copse, Lymington, Hampshire, SO41 8DT; 01590 674471. e-mail: richard@coomber1.fsbusiness.co.uk

FURNELL, Dennis

Natural history writer, radio and television broadcaster, artist and wildlife sound recordist.
Subjects: British and European wildlife, France, Thailand and West Africa. Wildlife sound recording, wildlife and disability access issues.
Fees: 100.
Limits: 50 miles, further with o.n. accom. **Times:** Afternoons or evenings according to commitments.
Address: 19 Manscroft Road, Gadebridge, Hemel Hempstead, Hertfordshire, HP1 3HU; 01442 242915, (Fax)01442 242032. e-mail; dennis.furnell@btinternet.com www.natureman.co.uk

HAMMOND, Nicholas

Writer, wildlife trust director.
Subjects: Nine talks (including Modern Wildlife Painting, In Search of Tigers, Wildlife Artists in Extremadura, Wildlife Trusts, Island Wildlife, Carl Linnaeus).
Fees: £70 plus petrol. **Limits:** 50 mls without o.n. accom.
Times: Evenings/weekends.
Address: 30 Ivel Road, Sandy, Bedfordshire, SG19 1BA; (H)01767 680504, (W)01223 712406. e-mail: n.hammond4@ntlworld.com

HASSELL, David

Birdwatcher and photographer.
Subjects: Five talks (including Seabirds, Shetland Birds, British Birds, USA Birds).

Fees: £40 plus petrol. **Limits:** 100 mls. **Times:** Evenings. **Address:** 15 Grafton Road, Enfield, Middlesex, EN2 7EY; (H)020 8367 0308, (W)020 7587 4500. e-mail: david@ hassell99.freeserve.co.uk www.davidhassell.co.uk

MASON, Barrie

Wildlife photographer, RSPB group leader. **Subjects:** The Brilliant Kingfisher', 'The Birds of Strawberry Hill Farm', Grassholm and Skokholm, Wildlife of Scotland, trips by lorry in Peru and Africa. **Fees:** £30 plus petrol. **Limits:** 100 mls. **Times:** Evening. **Address:** 6 Landseer Walk, Bedford, MK41 7LZ; (H)01234 262280.

NOBBS, Brian

Amateur birdwatcher and photographer. **Subjects:** Wildlife of the Wild West, Israel, Mediterranean, Florida, wildlife gardening. **Fees:** £30 plus 25p per ml. **Limits:** Kent, Surrey, Sussex. **Times:** Evenings. **Address:** The Grebes, 36 Main Road, Sundridge, Sevenoaks, Kent, TN14 6EP; 01959 563530. e-mail: Brian.nobbs@tiscali.co.uk

READ, Mike

Photographer, tour leader, writer. **Subjects:** 12 talks featuring British and foreign subjects (list available on receipt of sae). **Fees:** £70 plus travel. **Limits:** 175 mls. **Times:** Any. **Address:** Claremont, Redwood Close, Ringwood, Hampshire, BH24 1PR; 01425 475008, (Fax)01425 473160.

e-mail: mike@mikeread.co.uk www.mikeread.co.uk

REVELS, Revels

Wildlife photographer and lecturer. **Subjects:** Eight slide shows about British wildlife. **Fees:** £30 plus 30p per mile. **Limits:** 60 mls without o.n accom. **Times:** Nov - Mar inclusive. **Address:** 73 London Road, Biggleswade, Bedfordshire, SG18 8EE; 01767 313065. e-mail: richard.revels@care4free.net

TREVIS, Barry

Nature reserve warden, birdringer, widely travelled birdwatcher. **Subjects:** Birding in Peru; Birds of Churchill, Manitoba; Tanzania - birds, parks and Kilimanjaro; Birding 'Downunder'; Lemford Springs Nature Reserve. **Fees:** £75. **Limits:** Up to 20mls, travel costs otherwise. **Times:** Any. **Address:** 11 Lemsford Village, Welwyn Garden City, Hertfordshire, AL8 7TN; (H)01707 335517. e-mail: trevis@unisonfree.net

WARD, Chris

Photographer. **Subjects:** 16 talks on UK and worldwide topics (W.Palearctic, Americas, Africa, Australia) - primarily birds, some other wildlife. **Fees:** £30 plus petrol. **Limits:** 100 mls. **Times:** Evenings, afternoons poss. **Address:** 276 Bideford Green, Leighton Buzzard, Bedfordshire, LU7 7TU; 01525 375528; e-mail: chris@ chriswardphotography.co.uk

WRIGHT, Barry

Biomedical scientist, widely travelled abroad. **Subjects:** Various South American countries and West Indies. 'A Year Abroad!', 'Journey across South America', 'Travels in Tibet' - all talks based on birding trips. **Fees:** £50 plus petrol. **Limits:** 60 mls without o.n accom. **Times:** Evenings. **Address:** 18 Chestnut Grove, Wilmington, Kent, DA2 7PG; (H)01322 527345, (W)01322 428100 (4895). e-mail: barry@birding98.fsnet.co.uk

SOUTH-WESTERN

CHAPMAN, David

Natural history photographer, writer, speaker and workshop leader. **Subjects:** British natural history, birds, photography, small holding wildlife. **Fees:** £30 plus travel. **Limits:** Negotiable. **Times:** Negotiable. **Address:** 41 Bosence Road, Townshend, Cornwall, TR27 6AL; (Tel/fax) 01736 850 287. e-mail: David@ Ruralimages.freeserve.co.uk www. Ruralimages.freeserve.co.uk

COUZENS, Dominic

Full-time birdwatcher, tour leader (UK and overseas), writer and lecturer. **Subjects:** The Secret Habits of Garden Birds', 'Birds Behaving Badly - the trials and Tribulations of Birds Through the Year', 'Bird Sounds - As You've Never Heard Them Before'. **Fees:** £50 plus travel. **Limits:** London and south. **Times:** Any.

ART/PHOTOGRAPHY/LECTURERS

111

Address: 3 Clifton Gardens, Ferndown, Dorset, BH22 9BE; (Tel/fax) 01202 874330. e-mail: Dominic@ birdwords.freeserve.co.uk www.birdwords.co.uk

GREEN, DR George

Author, birdguide and tour leader.
Subjects: Nine talks (including Dorset birds, African wildlife safari, wildlife of the Picos Mountains, birds of Northern India, Costa Rica, Florida, Gambia, N.Africa and Middle East.
Fees: £50 plus petrol. **Limits:** 200 mls. **Times:** Afternoons and evenings.
Address: 20 Paget Close, Wimborne, Dorset, BH21 2SW; (H)01202 886885, (W)01258 843414.

ROBINSON, Peter

Consultant ornithologist and former Scilly resident.
Subjects: Various talks on sea and land birds of Scilly and life in an island environment; Song Thrushes, Storm Petrels and Kittiwakes.
Fees: £45 plus Petrol. **Limits:** None (by arrangement). **Times:** Any.
Address: 19 Pine Park Road, Honiton, Devon, EX14 2HR; 01404 549873.
e-mail: probinson2@cs.com

WEST MIDLANDS AND WALES

CONWAY, Wendy PSA4

Award-winning wildlife photographer.

Subjects: Several talks, birds, mammals, landscapes from UK, USA, Lesvos and Africa.
Fees: £45 plus petrol. **Limits:** Over 50mls please contact.
Times: Any.
Address: 4 Meriden Close, Winyates Green, Redditch, B98 0QN; 01527 457793.
e-mail: wendy@terry-wall.com

DENNING, Paul

Wildlife photographer, lecturer.
Subjects: 15 talks, (birds, mammals, reptiles, butterflies etc, UK, western and eastern Europe, north and central America, Canaries).
Fees: £30 plus petrol. **Limits:** 80 mls. **Times:** Evenings, weekends.
Address: 17 Maes Maelwg, Beddau, Pontypridd, CF38 2LD; (H)01443 202607; (W)02920 673243.
e-mail: pgdenning.naturepics@ virgin.net

HOLT, Brayton

Photographer, writer, county recorder.
Subjects: 20 talks (world wide - all continents plus UK).
Fees: £25 plus 25p per ml.
Limits: 100 mls without o.n. accom 150 mls otherwise.
Times: Evenings.
Address: Scops Cottage, Pentre Beirdd, Welshpool, Powys, SY21 9DL; 01938 500266.

LINN, Hugh ARPS

Experienced lecturer, photographer.
Subjects: Various: location-based (UK and Europe) plus subject-based (eg. understanding birds, photography etc).

Fees: £40 plus petrol. **Limits:** 75 mls without o.n. accom 150 mls otherwise. **Times:** Flexible.
Address: 4 Stonewalls, Rosemary Lane, Burton, Rossett, Wrexham, LL12 0LG; 01244 571942.

WALL, Terry
ARPS EFIAP PPSA

Wildlife photographer.
Subjects: Several (birds, mammals, landscapes - USA, UK, Lesvos, Africa and Galapagos).
Fees: £50 plus petrol. **Limits:** Over 50 mls please contact.
Times: Any.
Address: 4 Meriden Close, Winyates Green, Redditch, B98 0QN; 01527 457793.
e-mail: wildimages@ terry-wall.com
www.terry-wall.com

SCOTLAND

WATSON, Derick

Wildlife artist and gallery owner
Subjects: Painting demonstrations with commentary. Slide talks: Birding with a Sketchbook, the Art of Birding, Seabirds of the North Sea, Citizens of the Bass, California etc.
Fees: £75 plus petrol. **Limits:** 250 mls. **Times:** All year, autumn/winter preferred.
Address: The Kittiwake Gallery at St Abbs Head, St Abbs, Eyemouth, TD14 5QF; (H)018907 71588, (W)018907 71504. e-mail: derickwatson@ btopenworld.com

TRADE DIRECTORY

STEVE GALE.02.

TRADE DIRECTORY

BIRD GARDEN SUPPLIERS

BAMFORDS TOP FLIGHT

Company ethos: Family owned manufacturing company providing good quality bird foods via a network of UK stockists or mail order. RSPB Corporate Member, BTO Business Ally, Petcare Trust Member.

Key product lines: A range of wild bird mixtures containing the revolutionary new 'Pro-tec Health Aid', developed by Bamfords, to protect and promote the welfare of wild birds. Vast array of other foods and seeds for birds.

Other services: Trade suppliers of bulk and pre-packed bird and petfoods. Custom packing/ own label if required.

Opening times: Mon to Fri (8am- 5.30pm), Sat (8am–12 noon), (Sunday 10am–12 noon, Mill Shop only).

Address; Globe Mill, Midge Hall, Leyland, Lancashire, PR26 6TN:01772 456300;(Fax) 01772 456302.
email: sales@bamfords.co.uk
www.bamfords.co.uk

CJ WILDBIRD FOODS LTD

Company ethos: High quality products, no-quibble guarantee, friendly, professional service.

Key product lines: Complete range of RSPB Birdcare feeders, food and accessories, alongside a collection of other wildlife-related products.

Other services: Mail order company, online ordering, 24hr delivery service. Free handbook.

Opening times: Mon-Fri (9am-5pm).

Address; The Rea, Upton Magna, Shrewsbury, Shropshire, SY4 4UR. 0800 731 2820; Fax; 01743 709504. e-mail:
enquiries@birdfood.co.uk
www.birdfood.co.uk

ERNEST CHARLES

Company ethos: Member of Birdcare Standards Assoc. ISO 9002 registered. Offering quality bird foods/wildlife products through a friendly mail-order service.

Key product lines: Bird foods, feeders, nest boxes and other wildlife products.

Other services: Own label work for other companies considered and trade enquiries.

Opening times: Mon to Fri (8am-5pm).

Contact: Stuart Christopher, Crediton, Devon; 01363 84842; (Fax)01363 84147. e-mail:
stuart@ernest-charles.com
www.ernest-charles.com

GARDEN BIRD SUPPLIES LTD

Company ethos: The very best for your garden birds, delivered direct to your door. Fast and friendly service. RSPB Corporate Partner. BTO Business Ally. Birdcare Standards Association founder member.

Key product lines: Huge range of high-quality wild bird foods, feeders, tables, nest boxes, birdbaths, poles, baffles, books, videos, CDs and more.

Other services: Exclusively mail order.

Opening times: Mon to Fri (8;30-5pm).

Contact: For free *Garden Bird Feeding Guide* and catalogue, Wem, Shrewsbury, Shropshire, SY4 5BF; 01939 232233;

(Fax)01939 233155.
e-mail: info@gardenbird.com
www.gardenbird.com

JACOBI JAYNE & CO.

Company ethos: To supply products of proven conservation worth and highest quality. To offer expertise and special prices to wildlife groups, schools and colleges.

Key product lines: Birdfeeders, birdfoods, nest boxes & accessories. UK distributor of Schwegler woodcrete nest boxes, Droll Yankees feeders and Jacobi Jayne wildlife foods.

Other services: *Wild Bird News* mail-order catalogue.

Opening times: 24hrs (please use websites or answering service when office is closed).

Contact: Graham Evans/Sally Haynes, Jacobi Jayne & Co, Wealden Forest Park, Canterbury, Kent, CT6 7LQ; 0800 072 0130; (Fax)01227 719235. e-mail:
enquiries@jacobijayne.com
www.jacobijayne.com
www.birdon.com
www.wildbirdnews.com

JAMIE WOOD LTD

Company ethos: Quality hand-made products at competitive prices as supplied to the RSPB, universities, film units, householders. Thirty years experience.

Key products: Hides, photographic electronics, nest boxes, feeders, bird tables, patio stands.

Other services: Mail order, delivery ex-stock, within seven days.

Opening times: Telesales, Mon to Fri (9am-9pm), Sat to Sun (10am-4pm).

Contact: Keith, Karen or Ron, Jamie Wood Ltd, Dept BYD, 1

Green Street, Old Town, Eastbourne, Sussex, BN21 1QN; Tel/Fax; 01323 727291. e-mail: Jamiewood@birdtables.com www.birdtables.com

www.thebirdtable.co.uk

Company ethos: A family business that supplies an extensive range of quality products combined with superb service. Supporters of The Essex Wildlife Trust.
Key product lines: Bird tables, bird feeders, nest boxes, bird baths and a variety of mixes and feeds for wild birds and other wildlife.
Other services: Courier service, 48 hour delivery.
Contact: Browse our website for our extensive range of products, advice, drawings and photographs; 01268 413109; (Fax)01268 419258. e-mail: enquiries@thebirdtable.co.uk www.thebirdtable.co.uk

VINE HOUSE FARM BIRD FOODS

Company ethos: Growing and selling black sunflower and other bird seed direct from the farm.
Key product lines: Full range of bird food, plus feeders and other accessories.
Other services: Open days in the winter to view all the finches and buntings feeding at our farm. Farm walks in the summer.
Opening times: Mon to Fri (8am-5pm), Sat (8am-12noon).
Contact: Nicholas Watts, Vine House Farm, Deeping St Nicholas, Spalding, PE11 3DG; 01775 630208; (Fax)01775 630244. e-mail p.n.watts@farming.co.uk

BOOK PUBLISHERS

BRITISH ORNITHOLOGISTS' UNION

Single imprint specialising in the highly acclaimed Checklists Series providing detailed avifaunas for poorly known cuontries, regions and islands around the world.
Address: The Natural History Museum, Tring, Herts, HP23 6AP; 01 442 890 080; (Fax)020 7942 6150. e-mail: sales@bou.org.uk www.bou.org.uk

BUCKINGHAM PRESS

Imprints: Single imprint company - publishers of *The Birdwatcher's Yearbook* since 1980 and *Who's Who in Ornithology* (1997).
New for 2003: *Best Birdwatching Sites in Norfolk* by Neil Glenn, *Best Birdwatching Sites in the Highlands of Scotland* by Gordon Hamlett.
Address: 55 Thorpe Park Road, Peterborough, PE3 6LJ. 01733 561739. e-mail: buck.press@btinternet.com

CHRISTOPHER HELM PUBLISHERS

Imprints: An imprint of A & C Black Publishers Ltd, incorporating Pica Press (acquired Oct 2000) and T&AD Poyser (acquired June 2002).
New for 2003: *The Migration Atlas, Birds of the Mediterranean, Birds of Venezuela, 'Howard & Moore' complete Checklist of the Birds of the World (3rd edition).*
Address: 37 Soho Square, London, W1D 3QZ; 020 7758

0200; (Fax)020 7758 0222. e-mail: ornithology@acblack.com

HARPERCOLLINS PUBLISHERS

Imprints: Collins Natural History — the leading publisher of fieldguides to the natural world.
Collins New Naturalist Series, the encyclopaedic reference for all areas of British natural history.
HarperCollins, publisher of the best illustrated books.
New for 2003: *New Naturalist: British Bats* by John Altringham; *Collins Birds by Behaviour* by Dominic Couzens, illustrated by Philip Snow, Anthony Disley, Richard Jarvis, Michael Webb and Dave Nurney; *Field Guide to Warbler Songs and Calls* by Geoff Sample; *Nature Safari: 100 Things to do in the Wild* by Geoff Sample.
Address: 77-85 Fulham Palace Rd, Hammersmith, London, W6 8JB; 020 8307 4998; (Fax)020 8307 4037. e-mail: isabel.sheehy@ harpercollins.co.uk www.fireandwater.com www.collins.co.uk

NEW HOLLAND PUBLISHERS (UK) LTD

Imprints; New Holland, illustrated bird books, general wildlife and personality-led natural history.
New for 2003: *WildlifeTrusts' Birdwatchers Guide: How to Birdwatch, Understanding Bird Behaviour, Where to Watch Birds in Britain, Nick Baker's British Wildlife, The Wildlife Pond Handbook, Birdwatchers' Pocket Field Guide, Step-by-step Bird Boxes and Feeders, Chris Packham's Wild Side of*

Town, Birdwatcher's Log Book, The Garden Bird Handbook, Whalewatchng in Britain & Europe.
Address: Garfield House, 86-88 Edgware Road, London, W2 2EA; 020 7724 7773; (Fax)020 7258 1293. e-mail: postmaster@nhpub.co.uk www. newhollandpublishers.com

OCTOPUS PUBLISHING

Imprints; Mitchell Beazley, Hamlyn, Bounty-Brimax, Phillips.
New for 2003: The Complete Guide to Birdwatching in Britain and Europe; The Birdwatcher's Guide to Britain and Europe; The Pocket Guide to Garden Birds.
Address: 2-4 Herons Quay, London, E14 4JP; 020 7531 8480; (Fax)020 7531 8534. www.mitchell-beazley.com

PRION LTD

Imprints: Birdwatchers' Guides — a series of guides providing the travelling birdwatcher with information he or she needs to make the most of a birdwatching holiday or tour. Soft-back, with maps. Titles include: Nepal, Morocco, Canary Islands, Gambia, Turkey, India, Portugal & Madeira.
New for 2003: A Birdwatchers' Guide to Trinidad and Tobago.
Address: Kings Head Cottage. Cley-next-the-Sea, Norfolk, NR25 7RX.

WILDGuides LTD

Imprints; WILDGuides — definitive natural history fieldguides. Hardback and flexicover.
OCEANGuides — definitive identification guides to marine wildlife. Flexicover.

Your Countryside Guides — regional heritage guides for walkers. Hardback and flexicover.
WILD eARTh — lavishly illustrated celebrations of wildlife and natural places. Hardback.
New for 2003: Britain's Dragonflies (WG), Whales & Dolphins of the North American Pacific (OG), The Thames Valley (YCG).
Address: Parr House, 63 Hatch Lane, Old Basing, Hants, RG24 7EB; 01256 478309; (Fax)01256 818039. e-mail: info@wildguides.co.uk www.wildguides.co.uk

BOOK SELLERS

ATROPOS/ATROPOS BOOKSHOP

Company ethos: All the latest information about butterflies, moths and dragonflies published in a lively and entertaining journal.
Key subjects: Journal suited to birdwatchers interested in butterflies, moths and dragonflies. Field guides and key books supplied.
Address: Mark Tunmore, 36 Tinker Lane, Meltham, Holmfirth, West Yorkshire, HD9 4EX; 01326 290287. e-mail: atropos@ atroposed.freeserve.co.uk www.atroposuk.co.uk

BOOKS FOR BIRDERS/ BIRDING WORLD SALES

Company ethos: Friendly and informative staff, providing a fast delivery service.
Key subjects: Ornithology, (fieldguides, site guides and monographs).
Other services: Birding World magazine. Mail-order.
Opening times: Mon-Fri (9am-

5pm), answerphone outside office hours.
Address; Stonerunner, Coast Road, Cley, Norfolk, NR25 7RZ; 01263 741139. e-mail: sales@birdingworld.co.uk

NHBS MAIL ORDER BOOKSTORE

Company ethos: A unique natural history, conservation and environmental bookstore.
Key subjects: Natural history, conservation, environmental science, zoology, habitats and ecosystems, botany, marine biology.
Other services: NHBS.com offers a searchable and browsable web catalogue with more than 85,000 titles.
Opening times: Mon-Fri (9am-5pm). Mail-order, viewing by appointment only.
Address; 2-3 Wills Road, Totnes, Devon, TQ9 5XN; 01803 865913; (Fax)01803 865280. www.nhbs.com e-mail: nhbs@nhbs.co.uk

PORTLAND OBSERVATORY BOOK SHOP

Company ethos: To meet the needs of amateur and professional naturalists.
Key subjects: Ornithology, general natural history, topography, art and local history. New and secondhand.
Other services: Mail order, discount on new books, increased discount for observatory members.
Opening times: Wed, Thur and weekends; (10am to 5pm). Other times on request.
Address; Bird Observatory, Old Lower Light, Portland Bill, Dorset, DT5 2JT; 01305 820553.
e-mail: obs@btinternet.com www.portlandbirdobs. btinternet.co.uk

CLOTHING AND EQUIPMENT SUPPLIERS

SECOND NATURE
Company ethos: Buying and selling out-of-print/secondhand/antiquarian books on natural history, topography and travel.
Key subjects: Birds, mammals and travel with a natural history interest. Very large specialist stock.
Other services; Occasional catalogues issued. Often exhibiting at bird/natural history fairs.
Opening times: Mail order only.
Address; Knapton Book Barn, Back Lane, Knapton, York, YO26 6QJ; (Tel/fax) 01904 339493. e-mail: SecondnatureYork@aol.com

SUBBUTEO BOOKS
Company ethos: Specialist knowledge on all aspects of natural history, friendly service.
Key subjects: Wildlife, natural history and travel books.
Other services: Source any natural history book from around the world. Online ordering, free catalogue.
Opening times: Mon-Fri (9am-5pm).
Address: The Rea, Upton Magna, Shrewsbury, Shropshire, SY4 4UR; 0870 010 9700; (Fax)0870 010 9699. e-mail: info@wildlifebooks.com www.wildlifebooks.com

WILDSOUNDS
Company ethos: Donates a significant portion of profit to bird conservation, committed to sound environmental practices, official bookseller to African Bird Club and Oriental Bird Club.
Key product lines: Mail order, post-free books and multi-media guides i.e. the award winning *Bird Songs & Calls of Britain and Europe* on four CDs. Field recording equipment.
New for 2003: *Bird Sounds of Europe and NW Africa* (on 10 CDs), comprehensive 2003 catalogue.
Address: Cross Street, Salthouse, Norfolk, NR25 7XH; (Tel/fax) +44(UK) (0)1263 741100. e-mail: duncan@wildsounds.com www.wildsounds.com

CLOTHING SUPPLIERS

COUNTRY INNOVATION
Company ethos: Friendly advice by well-trained staff.
Key product lines: Full range of outdoor wear: Jackets, fleeces, trousers, walking boots, poles, lightweight clothing, hats, gloves, bags and pouches. Ladies fit available.
Other services: Mail order.
Opening times; Mon-Fri (9am-5pm).
Address: The Bridge, Langford Road, Lower Langford, North Somerset, BS40 5HU; 01934 863863; (Fax)01934 863016. e-mail: sales@countryinnovation.com

EQUIPMENT and SERVICES

BirdCall
Company ethos: To provide the most cost-effective, fast, reliable and up-to-date bird news at local and national level.
Key product lines: Bird news to your mobile by SMS or to your PC by e-mail.
Service times: Mon-Sun.

Address: Paul Longley or Dr Paul Brewster. 01925 730775. e-mail: birdcall@dial.pipex.com

BIRDGUIDES LTD
Company ethos: Top quality products and services especially using new technologies such as CD-Rom, DVD, websites, plus one-stop on-line shop for books, bird food etc.
Key product lines: CD-Rom, DVD, video guides to British, European and American birds. Rare bird news services via e-mail and website.
Address: Dave Gosney, Jack House, Ewden, Sheffield, S36 4ZA; 0114 2831002; order line (freephone) 0800 919391. e-mail: sales@birdguides.com www.birdguides.com

BIRD IMAGES
Company ethos: High quality products at affordable prices.
Key product lines: Bird videos and DVDs.
New for 2003: The first in a new range of DVDs.
Address: 28 Carousel Walk, Sherburn in Elmet, N Yorks LS25 6LP. 01977 684666. www.birdvideodvd.com

EagleEye OpticZooms
Company ethos: Innovative design, quality manufacturing, custom products, expert advice on all aspects of digital photography.
Key product lines: Telephoto lenses for digital cameras/camcorders, digiscoping adapters and products, custom digital camera accessories.
New for 2003: New digiscoping eyepiece (low magnification) for use with most leading scopes. Open days and workshops (check website for details).

Opening times: Mon-Frit (9am-6pm).
Address: Carlo Bonacci, Wentshaw Lodge, Fairseat, Sevenoaks, Kent, TN15 7LR; Tel/(Fax)01474 871219.
e-mail: info@eagleeyeuk.com
www.eagleeyeuk.com

WILDLIFE WATCHING SUPPLIES

Company ethos: To bring together a comprehensive range of materials, clothing and equipment to make it easier and more comfortable for you to blend in with the environment. Quick and friendly service.
Key product lines: Hides, camouflage, bean bags, lens and camera covers, clothing etc.etc.
New for 2003: Wider range of hides and equipment. Free CD of website available.
Opening times: Mon to Fri (9am-5pm), Mail order. Visitors by appointment.
Address: Town Living Farmhouse, Puddington, Tiverton, Devon, EX16 8LW; 01884 860692(24hr); (Fax) 01884 860994.
e-mail: enquiries@ wildlifewatchingsupplies.co.uk www. wildlifewatchingsupplies.co.uk

HOLIDAY COMPANIES

AVIAN ADVENTURES

Company ethos: Quality tours, escorted by friendly, expert leaders at a relaxed pace. ATOL no 3367.
Types of tours: Birdwatching, birds and wildlife photography and wildlife safaris. Suitable for both the first-time and the more experienced traveller.
Destinations: 70 tours to Europe, Africa, Australasia, North & South America, Asia.
New for 2003: Estonia, Picos d' Europa, Öland, Sweden, Chile, Mull, Kwa-Zulu, three-centre raptor special (USA).
Brochure from: 49 Sandy Road, Norton, Stourbridge, DY8 3AJ; 01384 372013; (Fax)01384 441340. e-mail: aviantours@argonet.co.uk www.avianadventures.co.uk

BIOSPHERE EXPEDITIONS

Company ethos: Award winning, not-for-profit wildlife conservation expeditions for everyone. Birding adventures with a purpose.
Types of tours: Bird conservation and surveying.
Destinations: Black Sea, Amazon, Altai Mountains, Namibia, Norfolk Broads.
Brochure from: Sprat's Water, Nr Carlton Colville, Suffolk, NR33 8BP; 01502 583085.
e-mail: info@ www-biosphere-expeditions.org www.biosphere-expeditions.org

BIRDFINDERS

Company ethos: Good-value birding tours to see all specialities/endemics of a country/area, using top UK and local guides.
Types of tours: Birdwatching for all abilities.
Destinations: 36 tours in Europe, Africa, Asia, Australasia, North and South America and Antarctica.
New for 2003: China/Tibet, Cuba and Jamaica, Florida, Kenya, South Korea.
Brochure from: Vaughan Ashby, 18 Midleaze, Sherborne, Dorset, DT9 6DY.(Tel/fax)01935 817001
e-mail: Birdfinders@ compuserve.com www.Birdfinders.co.uk

BIRD HOLIDAYS

Company ethos: Relaxed pace, professional leaders, small groups, exciting itineraries.
Types of tours: Birdwatching for all levels, beginners to advanced.
Destinations: Worldwide (40 tours, five continents).
New for 2003: California, Denmark, Jamaica, Costa Rica, Morocco, Spanish grand tour, Galapagos, Spanish Steppes and the Picos.
Brochure from: 10 Ivegate, Yeadon, Leeds, LS19 7RE; (Tel/fax)0113 3910 510.
e-mail: pjw.birdholidays@ care4free.net

BIRDSEEKERS

Company ethos: Best value-for-money birdwatching tours, with an enviable success at finding the most sought-after species.
Types of tours: High standard birdwatching tours with an emphasis on seeing the birds and other wildlife well.
Destinations: Britain, Europe and worldwide.
New for 2003: Peru, Uganda, Madagascar, Malaysia, Trinidad and Tobago, Nepal (trek), California, Romania.
Brochure from: 19 Crabtree Close, Marshmills, Plymouth, Devon, PL3 6EL; 01752 342001; (Fax)01752 342001.
e-mail: Bird@ birdseekers.freeserve.co.uk www.birdseekers.co.uk

BIRDQUEST

Company ethos: Superb leaders and small groups are behind our worldwide reputation. ATOL no 2937.
Types of tours: Birdwatching tours, wildlife tours (including Antarctica), bird and wildlife photography.

Destinations: More than 140 different tours worldwide (more than 80 offered annually).
New for 2003: N.China Cambodia, remote Tanzania, Colorado, Central Peru, SE Brazil, Pantanal and interior Brazil.
Brochure from: Two Jays, Kemple End, Stonyhurst, Clitheroe, Lancashire, BB7 9QY; 01254 826317; (Fax)01254 826780. e-mail: birders@birdquest.co.uk www.birdquest.co.uk

BIRDWATCHING BREAKS
Company ethos: Professional guides and local experts in the countries we visit, a winning combination.
Types of tours: Birdwatching holidays.
Destinations: 40 tours in North, Central and South America, Europe, Asia and Africa.
New for 2003: Brazil, Lithuania, Malawi, Seychelles, Mauritius, Reunion & Rodrigues, Taiwan & Okinawa,
Brochure from: 26 School Lane, Herne, Kent, CT6 7AL; 01227 740799; (Fax)01227 363946.
e-mail: m.finn@ birdwatchingbreaks.com www.birdwatchingbreaks.com

CAMBRIAN BIRD HOLIDAYS
Company ethos: Friendly and personal attention. We don't twitch, our aim is to enjoy good views of those birds and other wildlife that we find.
Types of tours: Birdwatching and general natural history. Some themed holidays: Birds and Flowers, Birds and Butterflies, Birds and Geology, Birding for Beginners etc.
Destinations: West Wales and Southern Ireland.

New for 2003: A continuation of our recent and evolving programme.
Brochure from: Rhydlewis, Llandysul, Ceredigian, SA44 5SP; 01239 851758.
www.cambihols.co.uk

CARPATHIAN WILDLIFE SOCIETY
Company ethos: A non-profit organisation bringing together people with a shared interest in conservation of large mammals and birds.
Types of tours: Wildlife tours contributing to research. Tracking of wolves, bears and lynx. Birdwatching and working holidays.
Destinations: Slovakia. Five national parks, seven primeval forests and one wetland reserve.
New for 2003: New holidays to the above sites.
Brochure from: Driftwood, The Marrams, Sea Palling, Norfolk NR12 0UN.
e-mail:cws@szm.sk www.cws.szm.sk

CELTIC BIRD TOURS
Company ethos: Relaxed, bird-filled holidays suitable for all levels of birdwatching ability.
Types of tours: General birdwatching, birding for beginners, some general wildlife holidays, pelagics.
Destinations: Wales, UK, Europe, Middle East, Africa and Indian sub-continent.
New for 2003: Estonia, Turkey, Heligoland, Eastern Finland.
Brochure from: 84 Coity Road, Bridgend, CF31 1LT; 01656 645709; (mobile)07971 983227. e-mail: birds@ celtictours.org.uk www.celticbirdtours.com

CLASSIC JOURNEYS
Company ethos: Professional and friendly company, providing well organised and enjoyable birdwatching holidays.
Types of tours: General birdwatching and wildlife holidays on the Indian sub-continent.
Destinations: Nepal, India, Bhutan, Sri Lanka.
Brochure from: 33 High Street, Tibshelf, Alfreton, Derbyshire, DE55 5NX; 01773 873497; (Fax)01773 590243.
e-mail: birds@classicjourneys.co.uk www.classicjourneys.co.uk

FSC OVERSEAS
Company ethos: A selection of study tours aiming to increase environmental understanding and awareness, led by experienced tutors and open to anyone.
Types of tours: Birdwatching, natural history, photography, botany, insects, geology, mammals, ecology, art.
Destinations: Around 40 locations in all continents.
New for 2003: Namibia, Ghana, Gujarat, Brazil, Faroes, Hungary, Catalonia and more!
Brochure from: Montford Bridge, Shrewsbury, Shropshire, SY4 1HW; 01743 852150; (Fax)01743 852155.
e-mail: fsc.overseas@ukonline.co.uk www.fscOverseas.org.uk

GREAT GLEN WILDLIFE
Company ethos: Quality wildlife watching experience at a relaxed pace.
Types of tours: General wildlife watching, predominantly birds and mammals, also butterflies and wild flowers. Small groups

(eight participants), high standard accommodation.
Destinations: Full range of Scottish Highland and Island destinations, also Belarus, France, Sweden, Spain, Greece, Norway.
New for 2003: Norway (Northern lights), Hardanger area, Spain (Pyrenees and Ebro Delta), Sweden (Central mountains), N.America (Mississipi to Great Lakes).
Brochure from: Sherren, Harray, Orkney, KW17 2JU; (Tel/fax)01856 761604. e-mail: davidkent@onetel.net.uk

GULLIVERS NATURAL HISTORY HOLIDAYS

Company ethos: We are the "small company that takes care of you", we aim to fulfil your holiday dreams. ATOL 4256.
Types of tours: Relaxed, escorted, friendly, fun holidays. Birdwatching, botany, wildlife and general natural history. Singles welcome. Also no-hassle quotes and arrangements for your club/society trip.
Destinations: Worldwide.
New for 2003: Sri Lanka, New Mexico, Brazil and Bosphorus.
Brochure from: Bob Gulliver, Oak Farm (H), Stoke Hammond, Milton Keynes, MK17 9DB; 01525 270100; (Fax)01525 270777.

HEATHERLEA

Company ethos: Exciting holidays to see all the birds of Scotland. Experienced guides and comfortable award-winning hotel to give great customer service.
Types of tours: Birdwatching and other wildlife watching tours in the beautiful Scottish Highlands.

Destinations: Scottish Highlands, including holidays from our base in Nethybridge, plus Outer Hebrides, Orkney, Shetlands and more.
New for 2003: Majorca and other overseas destinations.
Brochure from: The Mountview Hotel, Nethybridge, Inverness-shire, PH25 3EB; 01479 821248; (Fax)01479 821515.
e-mail: hleabirds@aol.com
www.heatherlea.co.uk

HONEYGUIDE WILDLIFE HOLIDAYS

Company ethos: Relaxed natural history holidays with wildlife close to home. Quality accommodation, expert leaders, beginners welcome.
Types of tours: Birds, flowers and butterflies, with a varied mix depending on the location.
Destinations: Europe, including Extremadura, Spanish Pyrenees, Crete, Menorca, Camargue, Slovakia and Danube Delta.
New for 2003: Lesvos, French Pyrenees.
Brochure from: 36 Thunder Lane, Thorpe St Andrew, Norwich, Norfolk, NR7 0PX; (Tel/fax)01603 300552 (Evenings).
e-mail: honeyguide@tesco.net
www.honeyguide.co.uk

HOSKING TOURS LTD

Company ethos: The best in wildlife photographic holidays.
Types of tours: Wildlife photography for all levels of experience.
Destinations: Africa, America, Europe.
New for 2003: Ecuador, Arizona, Cyprus.
Brochure from: Pages Green House, Wetheringsett, Stowmarket, Suffolk, IP14

5QA; 01728 861113; (Fax)01728 860222.
www.hosking-tours.co.uk

IBIS EXCURSIONS

Company ethos: Providing you with the "holiday of a lifetime".
Types of tours: Tailor-made specialist. Anywhere you want to go, whenever you want. Also 'your favourite' catalogue tours.
Destinations: Tailor-made – you choose! – anywhere in the world. Catalogue tours Spain, Finland, Norway, Sweden, Denmark (Scandinavia specialist), Spitsbergen.
New for 2003: Wherever you want to - alone, with friends, local bird group etc.
Brochure from: Ganloseparken 46, 3660 Stenlose, Denmark.(UK no)01327 831225, (DK no)0045 48195940; (Fax)0045 48195945. e-mail: jeffprice@ ibis-excursions.dk
www.ibis-excursions.dk

ISLAND HOLIDAYS

Company ethos: Relaxed pace holidays with conservation and responsibility to the environment paramount.
Types of tours: Relaxed birding and natural history tours. We like to enjoy all aspects of the islands we visit, not just the birds.
Destinations: More than 20 island destinations in the UK and worldwide.
New for 2003: Susewe, S.Africa; Sao Tomé; Dominica; Trinidad and Tobago; Jamaica; Mascarene Islands; Öland, Sweden; Harris and Lewis; Hebrides and St Kilda; Barra and Uists; Inner Hebrides.
Brochure from: Drummond Street, Comrie, Perthshire,

PH6 2DS; 01764 670107;
(Fax)01764 670958. e-mail:
enquiries@islandholidays.net
www.islandholidays.net

LIMOSA HOLIDAYS

Company ethos: The very best
in birdwatching and wildlife
holidays - expertly led, fun,
friendly and full of birds. AITO
member. ATOL 2950.
Types of tours: Birdwatching
tours, plus birds and
butterflies, bears and whales.
Destinations: More than 70
holidays worldwide.
New for 2003: Argentina,
Jamaica, Taiwan and Hong
Kong, Venezuela, plus six
special tours in support of the
Wildfowl and Wetlands Trust.
Brochure from: Suffield
House, Northrepps, Norfolk,
NR27 0LZ; 01263 578143;
(Fax)01263 579251.
e-mail: limosaholidays@
compuserve.com

NATURE PHOTOGRAPHY PRO-TOURS LTD

Company ethos: Photographic
tours to Lesvos and USA.
Types of tours: Photography
tours only.
Destinations: Lesvos, Florida,
Bosque del Apache, Europe.
Brochure from: 12 Searles
View, Horsham, West Sussex,
RH12 4FG; 01403 257917,
(Fax)01403 267503.
www.georgemccarthy.com
www.lesvostravel.co.uk

NATURETREK

Company ethos: Friendly,
gentle-paced, birdwatching
holidays with broad-brush
approach. Sympathetic to other
wildlife interests, history and
local culture. ATOL no 2962.
Types of tours: Escorted
birdwatching, botanical and
natural history holidays
worldwide.

Destinations: Worldwide – see
brochure.
New for 2003: Peru and
Ecuador – bargain selection;
Turkey, Eastern China,
Holland, Belgium, Bavaria,
Azores.
Brochure from: Cheriton Mill,
Cheriton, Alresford,
Hampshire, SO24 0NG; 01962
733051; (Fax)01962 736426.
e-mail: info@naturetrek.co.uk
www.naturetrek.co.uk

NORTH WEST BIRDS

Company ethos: Friendly,
relaxed and unhurried but
targetted to scarce local birds.
Types of tours: Very small
groups (up to four) based on
large family home in South
Lakes with good home
cooking. Short breaks with
birding in local area. Butterflies
in season.
Destinations: Local to
Northwest England.
Lancashire, Morecambe Bay
and Lake District.
Brochure from: Mike
Robinson, Barn Close,
Beetham, Cumbria, LA7 7AL;
(Tel/fax)015395 63191.
e-mail: mike@nwbirds.co.uk
www.nwbirds.co.uk

ORNITHOLIDAYS AND CRUISES FOR NATURE

Company ethos: Full-time tour
leaders and a company with
more than 35 years'
experience. ABTA member.
ATOL no 0743.
Types of tours: Birdwatching
and natural history tours as
well as cruises to Antarctica
and Galapagos.
Destinations: 80 tours to all
seven continents.
New for 2003: Northern Peru,
Portugal and Finland for bears.
Brochure from: 29 Straight
Mile, Romsey, Hampshire,

SO51 9BB; 01794 519445;
(Fax)01794 523544.
e-mail: ornitholidays@
compuserve.com
www.ornitholidays.co.uk

SHETLAND WILDLIFE

Company ethos: Award-
winning small group travel with
the very best naturalist guides.
Types of tours: A unique
blend of itineraries to bring you
the very best of Shetland.
Week-long or three-day
holidays dedicated to wildlife,
photography, walking and
archaeology.
Destinations: All corners of
Shetland, including Fair Isle.
New for 2003: Fair Isle Spring
and Autumn Migration
holidays.
Brochure from: Longhill,
Maywick, Shetland, ZE2 9JF;
01950 422483; (Fax)01950
422430. e-mail; info@
shetlandwildlife.co.uk
www.shetlandwildlife.co.uk

SICKLEBILL SAFARIS LTD

Company ethos: Qualified and
very experienced, genial
leader, to show you the real
natural world. Under ATOL
4002.
Types of tours: Birdwatching
and general natural history
tours, including mammals,
insects, higher plants and
macrofungi.
Destinations: East Anglia,
Ireland, Papua New Guinea and
other South Pacific countries
we have lived in.
Brochure from: Well Cottage,
38 Creake Road, Sculthorpe,
Fakenham, Norfolk, NR21
9NQ;01328 856925; (Fax)
01328 862014. e-mail:
Ian@sicklebill.demon.co.uk
www.sicklebill.com

TRADE DIRECTORY

SPEYSIDE WILDLIFE

Company ethos: Expert leaders, personal attention and a sense of fun - it's your holiday. ATOL no 4259.
Types of tours: Experts in Scotland and leaders worldwide – birdwatching, mammals and whale watching.
Destinations: Speyside and the Scottish Islands, Scandinavia, the Arctic, Europe, Middle East, N America.
New for 2003: Costa Rica, Sea of Cortez, Trinidad and Tobago, Galapagos, Antarctica (2004).
Brochure from: Garden Office, Inverdruie House, Inverdruie, Aviemore, Inverness-shire, PH22 1QH; (Tel/fax)01479 812498. e-mail: enquiries@ speysidewildlife.co.uk www.speysidewildlife.co.uk

SUNBIRD

Company ethos: Enjoyable birdwatching tours led by full-time professional leaders. ATOL no 3003
Types of tours: Birdwatching, Birds & Music, Birds & History, Birds & Butterflies, Sunbirder events.
Destinations: Worldwide.
New for 2003: Bulgaria, Uganda, Spring Across America, Great Grouse Tour (N. America), South Africa - Kalahari to the Cape, Dominican Republic and Puerto Rico, Birds & Butterflies in the Picos, Photographic tours in Finland and Sweden.
Brochure from: PO Box 76, Sandy, Bedfordshire, SG19 1DF; 01767 682969; (Fax)01767 692481. e-mail: sunbird@sunbirdtours.co.uk www.sunbirdtours.co.uk

THE BIRD ID COMPANY

Company ethos: Expert tour guides teaching bird watchers of all levels bird identification and field craft skills.
Types of tours: Daily guided tours £25. Weekend breaks, five day migration tours, rare breeding bird tours to see Golden Oriole, Montagu's Harrier and Honey Buzzard. Personalised and customised tours UK and abroad.
Destinations: Norfolk, Britain, Europe, America, Middle East.
New for 2003: Ireland in October
Brochure from: Paul Laurie, 37 Westgate, Warham Road, Binham, Norfolk, NR21 0DQ; 01328 830617. e-mail: Paul.seethebird@virgin.net www.birdtour.co.uk

THE TRAVELLING NATURALIST

Company ethos: Friendly, easy-going, expertly-led birdwatching and wildlife tours.
Types of tours: Tours include birds and history, birds and bears, whale-watching, birds and flowers.
Destinations: Worldwide.
New for 2003: Tanzania, Mexico, Borneo, Chile.
Brochure from: PO Box 3141, Dorchester, Dorset, DT1 2XD; 01305 267994; (Fax)01305 265506.
e-mail: jamie@naturalist.co.uk www.naturalist.co.uk

WORLDWIDE JOURNEYS

Company ethos: Shared enjoyment of the natural world.
Types of tours: Relaxed wildlife and birdwatching holidays with friendly groups and Britain's most experienced leaders.

Destinations: 26 locations in Africa, Australasia, North and South America, India, Indian Ocean and Europe.
New for 2003: Bahamas, Borneo, Brazil, Florida, The Gambia, Northern Greece, Jordan, Morocco and Sri Lanka.
Brochure from: Worldwide Journeys and Expeditions, 27 Vanston Place, London, SW6 1AZ; 020 7386 4676; (Fax)020 7381 0836. e-mail: wwj@wjournex.demon.co.uk

WILDWINGS

Company ethos: Superb value holidays led by expert guides.
Types of tours: Birdwatching holidays, whale and dolphin watching holidays, wildlife cruises, ecovolunteers.
Destinations: Europe, Arctic, Asia, The Americas, Antarctica, Africa, Trinidad and Tobago.
New for 2003: Cuba and Egypt.
Brochure from: 577-579 Fishponds Road, Fishponds, Bristol, BS16 3AF; e-mail: wildinfo@wildwings.co.uk

OPTICAL MANUFACTURERS & IMPORTERS

CAPE INSTRUMENTS LTD

Company ethos: Top quality products at competitive prices, direct to the public, sold by helpful and knowledgeable staff.
Product lines: Evolution telescope with eye pieces from 35x to 150x and camera adapter.
Address: Unit 18, Dawsons Lane Enterprise Centre,

Barwell, Leics, LE9 8BE;
01455 848417; (Fax)01455
618520.
e-mail: pwise.cape@virgin.net
www.evolutiontelescope.co.uk

CARL ZEISS LTD
Company ethos: World
renowned, high quality
performance and innovative
optical products.
Product lines: Product ranges
of stabilised, Victory, Dialyt,
compacts and binoculars and
Diascope telescopes.
Address: PO Box 78,
Woodfield Road, Welwyn
Garden City, Hertfordshire,
AL7 1LU; 01707 871350;
(Fax)01707 871287.
e-mail: binos@zeiss.co.uk
www.zeiss.co.uk

INTRO2020
Company ethos: Experienced
importer of photo and optical
products.
Product lines: Summit and
Steiner (binoculars), Velbon
(tripods), Kenko (range of
telescopes).
Address: Unit 1, Priors Way,
Maidenhead, Berkshire, SL6
2HR; 01628 674411;
(Fax)01628 771055.
e-mail: jane@introphoto.co.uk
www.introphoto.co.uk

LEICA CAMERA LTD
Company ethos: Professional
advice from Leica factory-
trained staff.
Product lines: Duovid the
world's first dual magnification
binocular. Trinovid binoculars,
eight full size and six
compacts. Televid 62 and 77
spotting scopes with angled or
straight view with a choice of
five eyepieces, a photo-adapter
and a digiscope adaptor for the
Leica Digilux 1 digital camera.

Address: Leica Camera
Limited, Davy Avenue,
Knowlhill, Milton Keynes,
MK5 8LB; 01908
256400;(Fax)01908 671316.
e-mail: info@
leica-camera.co.uk
www.leica-camera.com

CT DISTRIBUTION
Company ethos: Distributor of
Manfrotto tripods and
accessories for the wildlife and
birding specialist. National
dealer network.
Product lines: Manfrotto
tripods, heads and accessories.
Available as separates or kits,
suitable for video, scope and
camera use.
Address: PO Box 3128,
Tilbrook, Milton Keynes, MK7
8JB; 01908 646444;
(Fax)01908 646434. e-mail:
sales@ctdistribution.com

MARCHWOOD
Company ethos: Quality
European optics offering
outstanding value for money.
Product lines: Kahles
binoculars from Austria,
Meopta telescopes from the
Czech Republic and
Eschenbach Optik binoculars
from Germany. Dowling and
Rowe optics for the discerning
observer.
Address: Unit 308, Cannock
Chase Enterprise Park,
Hednesford, Staffordshire,
WS15 5QU; 01543 424255;
(Fax)01543 422082.
e-mail: john@
lancashirej.freeserve.co.uk

OPTICRON
Company ethos: To provide
the highest quality, value-for-
money optics for today's
birdwatcher.

Product lines: Official
importers of Opticron
binoculars and telescopes, plus
mounting systems and
accessories.
Address: PO Box 370, Unit
21, Titan Court, Laporte Way,
Luton, LU4 8YR; 01582
726522; (Fax)01582 273559.
e-mail: info@opticron.co.uk

SWAROVSKI UK
Company ethos: Constantly
improving on what is good in
terms of products and
committed to conservation
world-wide.
Product lines: ATS 80 spotting
scope, the latest addition to a
market-leading range of
telescopes and binoculars.
Swarovski tripods also
available.
Address: Perrywood Business
Park, Salfords, Surrey, RH1
5JQ; 01737 856812;
(Fax)01737 856885. e-mail:
christine.percy@swarovski.com

VICKERS SPORTS OPTICS
Company ethos: Importers of
world renowned products from
American companies Bausch &
Lomb and Bushnell.
Product lines: High
performance Bausch & Lomb
binoculars (including compacts)
and telescopes. The extensive
Bushnell list includes market-
leading Natureview range and
Legacy Compacts. New models
in 2002 include the Legend
8x32.
Address: Unit 9, 35 Revenge
Road, Lordswood, Kent, ME5
8DW; 01634 201284;
(Fax)01634 201286.
e-mail: info@jjvickers.co.uk
www.jjvickers.co.uk

OPTICAL DEALERS

OPTICAL DEALERS

EAST MIDLANDS AND EAST ANGLIA

BIRDNET OPTICS LTD

Company ethos: To provide the birdwatcher with the best value for money on optics, books and rare bird information on pagers and mobile phones.
Viewing facilities: Clear views to distant hills for comparison of optics at long range and wide variety of textures and edges for clarity and resolution comparison.
Optical stock: Most leading binocular and telescope ranges stocked. If we do not have it in stock we will endeavour to get it for you.
Non-optical stock: Books incl. New Naturalist Series and Poysers, videos, CDs, audio tapes, tripods, hide clamps, accessories and clothing.
Opening times: Mon-Sat (9:30am-5:30pm). Sundays by appointment only.
Address: 5 London Road, Buxton, Derbyshire, SK17 9PA;01298 71844; (Fax)01298 73052.
e-mail: paulflint@birdnet.co.uk
www.birdnet.co.uk

In focus

Company ethos: The binocular and telescope specialists, offering customers informed advice at birdwatchng venues throughout the country. Main sponsor of the British Birdwatchng Fair.
Viewing facilities: Available at all shops (contact your local outlet), or at field events (10am-4pm) at bird reserves

(see *Bird Watching* magazine or website www.at-infocus.co.uk for calendar)
Optical stock: Most leading makes of binoculars and telescopes, plus own-brand Delta range of binocualrs and tripods.
Non-optical stock: Wide range of tripods, clamps and other accessories. Repair service available.
Opening times: Vary - please contact local shop or website before travelling.
NORFOLK; Main Street, Titchwell, Nr King's Lynn, Norfolk, PE31 8BB: 01485 210101.
RUTLAND; Anglian Water Birdwatching Centre, Egleton Reserve, Rutland Water, Rutland, LE15 8BT: 01572 770656.

LONDON CAMERA EXCHANGE

Company ethos: To supply good quality optical equipment at a competitive price, helped by knowlegeable staff.
Viewing facilities: In shop and at local shows. Contact local branch.
Optical stock: All leading makes of binoculars and scopes.
Non-optical stock: All main brands of photo, digital and video equipment.
Opening times: Mon-Sat (9am-5.30pm).
CHESTERFIELD: 1A South Street, Chesterfield, Derbyshire, S40 1QZ; 01246 211891; (Fax)01246 211563; e-mail: chesterfield@ lcegroup.co.uk
DERBY: 17 Sadler Gate, Derby, Derbyshire, DE1 3NH; 01332 348644; (Fax)01332 369136;
e-mail: derby@lcegroup.co.uk

LINCOLN; 6 Silver Street, Lincoln, LN2 1DY; 01522 514131; (Fax)01522 537480; e-mail: lincoln@lcegroup.co.uk
NOTTINGHAM: 7 Pelham Street, Nottingham, NG1 2EH; 0115 941 7486; (Fax)0115 952 0547; e-mail: nottingham@lcegroup.co.uk

WAREHOUSE EXPRESS

Company ethos: Mail order and website.
Viewing facilities: By appointment only.
Optical stock: All major brands including, Leica, Swarvoski, Opticron, Kowa, Zeiss, Nikon, Bushnell, Slik, Canon, Minolta etc.
Non-optical stock: All related accessories including hides, tripods and window mounts etc.
Opening times: Mon-Fri (9am-5.30pm).
Address: PO Box 659, Norwich, Norfolk, NR2 1UJ; 01603 626222; (Fax)01603 626446.
www.warehouseexpress.com

NORTHERN ENGLAND

FOCALPOINT

Company ethos: Friendly advice by well-trained staff. Competitive prices, no 'grey imports'.
Viewing facilities: Fantastic open countryside for superb viewing from the shop, plenty of wildlife. Parking for up to 20 cars.
Optical stock: All leading brands of binoculars and telescopes from stock, plus many pre-owned binoculars and telescopes available.
Non-optical stock: Bird books, outdoor clothing, boots, tripods

plus full range of Skua products etc. available from stock.

Opening times: Mon-Sat (9:30am-5pm).

Address: Marbury House Farm, Bentleys Farm Lane, Higher Whitley, Warrington, Cheshire, WA4 4QW; 01925 730399; (Fax)01925 730368.

e-mail:
focalpoint@dial.pipex.com
www.fpoint.co.uk

In focus

(see entry in Eastern England).
LANCASHIRE: WWT Martin Mere, Burscough, Ormskirk, Lancs, L40 0TA: 01704 897020.
WEST YORKSHIRE: Westleigh House Office Est. Wakefield Road, Denby Dale, West Yorks, HD8 8QJ: 01484 864729.

LONDON CAMERA EXCHANGE

(See entry in Eastern England).
CHESTER: 9 Bridge Street Row, CH1 1NW; 01244 326531.
MANCHESTER: 37 Parker Street, Picadilly, M1 4AJ; 0161 236 5819.

SHEFFIELD PHOTOGRAPHIC CENTRE

Company ethos: Quality branded goods at competitive prices. Service to match.
Viewing facilities: Urban viewing - to horizon.
Optical stock: Swarovski, Leica, Eschenbach, Opticron, Kowa, Minolta etc.
Non-optical stock: All forms of photographic equipment plus darkroom products and digital.
Opening times: Mon-Sat (9am-5.00pm).

Address: 294 Ecclesall Road, Sheffield, S11 8PE; (Tel/fax) 0114 2667077.
e-mail: john@
sheffphotocentre.demon.co.uk

SOUTH EAST ENGLAND

FORESIGHT OPTICAL

Company ethos: Personal service is our pleasure. Quality optical products - no 'grey imports'.
Viewing facilities: Showroom with viewing facilities.
Optical stock: Wide range of binoculars and telescopes, most popular brands stocked. New, secondhand and ex-demonstration stock for sale. Part exchange undertaken. Mail order available, credit cards accepted and credit facilities.
Non-optical stock: Night vision equipment, magnifiers, microscopes, tripods and accessories.
Opening times: Mon-Fri (8:30am-5:30pm).
Address: 13 New Road, Banbury, Oxon, OX16 9PN; 01295 264365.

In focus

(see entry in Eastern England).
ST ALBANS; Bowmans Farm, London Colney, St Albans, Herts, AL2 1BB: 01727 827799; (Fax)01727 827766.
SOUTH WEST LONDON: WWT The Wetland Centre, Queen Elizabeth Walk, Barnes, London, SW13 9WT: 020 8409 4433.

KAY OPTICAL

Company ethos: Unrivalled expertise, experience and service, since 1962.
Viewing facilities: At Morden. Also field-days every weekend at reserves in South.
Optical stock: All leading makes of binoculars and telescopes stocked. Also giant binoculars and astronomical.
Non-optical stock: Tripods, clamps etc.
Opening times: Mon-Sat (9am-5pm) closed (1-2pm).
Address: 89(B) London Road, Morden, Surrey, SM4 5HP: 020 8648 8822; (Fax)020 8687 2021.
e-mail: info@kayoptical.co.uk
www.kayoptical.co.uk and www.bigbinoculars.co.uk

LONDON CAMERA EXCHANGE

(See entry in Eastern England).
FAREHAM: 135 West Street, Fareham, Hampshire, PO16 0DU; 01329 236441; (Fax)01329 823294; e-mail: fareham@lcegroup.co.uk
PORTSMOUTH: 40 Kingswell Path, Cascados, Portsmouth, PO1 4RR; 023 9283 9933; (Fax)023 9283 9955; e-mail: portsmouth@lcegroup.co.uk
GUILDFORD: 8/9 Tunsgate, Guildford, Surrey, GU1 2DH; 01483 504040; (Fax)01483 538216; e-mail: guildford@lcegroup.co.uk
READING: 7 Station Road, Reading, Berkshire, RG1 1LG; 0118 959 2149; (Fax)0118 959 2197; e-mail: reading@lcegroup.co.uk
SOUTHAMPTON: 10 High Street, Southampton, Hampshire, SO14 2DH; 023 8022 1597; (Fax)023 8023 3838; e-mail: southampton@lcegroup.co.uk

TRADE DIRECTORY

STRAND, LONDON: 98 The Strand, London, WC2R 0AG; 020 7379 0200; (Fax)020 7379 6991; e-mail: strand@lcegroup.co.uk
WINCHESTER: 15 The Square, Winchester, Hampshire, SO23 9ES; 01962 866203; (Fax)01962 840978; e-mail: winchester@lcegroup.co.uk

SOUTH WEST ENGLAND

ACE CAMERAS

Company ethos: To be the best - service, price and stock.
Viewing facilities: Bird of prey at 100 yds, Leica test card to check quality.
Optical stock: All the top brands, including Questar. Official importer for Optolyth products.
Non-optical stock: All the best tripods and an array of optical related accessories.
Opening times: Mon-Sat (8:45am-6pm).
Address: 16 Green Street, Bath, BA1 2JZ; 01225 466364; (fax)01225 469761. e-mail: aceoptics@balzjz.freeserve.co.uk

LONDON CAMERA EXCHANGE

(See entry in Eastern England).
BATH: 13 Cheap Street, Bath, Avon, BA1 1NB; 01225 462234; (Fax)01225 480334. e-mail: bath@lcegroup,co.uk
BOURNEMOUTH: 95 Old Christchurch Road, Bournemouth, Dorset, BH1 1EP; 01202 556549; (Fax)01202 293288; e-mail: bournemouth@lcegroup.co.uk
BRISTOL: 53 The Horsefair, Bristol, BS1 3JP; 0117 927 6185; (Fax)0117 925 8716; e-mail: bristol.horsefair@lcegroup.co.uk
EXETER: 174 Fore Street, Exeter, Devon, EX4 3AX;01392 279024/438167; (Fax)01392 426988. e-mail: exeter@lcegroup.co.uk
PAIGNTON: 71 Hyde Road, Paingnton, Devon, TQ4 5BP;01803 553077; (Fax)01803664081. e-mail: paignton@lcegroup.co.uk
PLYMOUTH: 10 Frankfort Gate, Plymouth, Devon, PL1 1QD; 01752 668894; (Fax) 01752 604248. e-mail: plymouth@lcegroup.co.uk
SALISBURY: 6 Queen Street, Salisbury, Wiltshire, SP1 1EY; 01722 335436; (Fax)01722 411670; e-mail: salisbury@lcegroup.co.uk
TAUNTON: 6 North Street, Taunton, Somerset, TA1 1LH; 01823 259955; (Fax)01823 338001. e-mail: taunton@lcegroup.co.uk

WESTERN ENGLAND

FOCUS OPTICS

Company ethos: Friendly, expert service. Top quality instruments. No 'grey imports'.
Viewing facilities: Our own pool and nature reserve with feeding stations.
Optical stock: Full range of leading makes of binoculars and telescopes.
Non-optical stock: Waterproof clothing, fleeces, walking boots and shoes, bird food and feeders. Books, videos, walking poles.
Opening times: Mon-Sat (9am-5pm). Some Bank-holidays.
Address: Church Lane, Corley, Coventry, CV7 8BA; 01676 540501/542476; (Fax) 01676 540930. e-mail: focopt1@aol.com www.focusoptics.co.uk

In focus

(see entry in Eastern England).
GLOUCESTERSHIRE: WWT Slimbridge, Gloucestershire, GL2 7BT: 01453 890978.

LONDON CAMERA EXCHANGE

(see entry in Eastern England).
CHELTENHAM: 10-12 The Promenade, Cheltenham, Gloucestershire, GL50 1LR; 01242 519851; (Fax)01242 576771; e-mail: cheltenham@lcegroup.co.uk e-mail: derby@lcegroup.co.uk
GLOUCESTER: 12 Southgate Street, Gloucester, GL1 2DH; 01452 304513; (Fax)01452 387309; e-mail: gloucester@lcegroup.co.uk
LEAMINGTON: Clarendon Avenue, Leamington, Warwickshire, CV32 5PP; 01926 886166; (Fax)01926 887611; e-mail: leamington@lcegroup.co.uk
WORCESTER: 8 Pump Street, Worcester, WR1 2QT; 01905 22314; (Fax)01905 724585; e-mail: worcester@lcegroup.co.uk

WILD BIRD FOODS

FROM October 2002, Bamfords Top Flight Wild Bird Food blends contain **Pro-tec**, a small crumble containing a unique blend of natural ingredients to protect and promote the welfare of wild birds.

✓ Helps protect against disease and toxins, including aflatoxin
✓ Promotes and conserves energy
✓ Aids fertility and reproduction
✓ Improves general health and well-being

By giving the birds in your garden foods with **Pro-tec**, you really can improve their chances of surviving harsh winters and chronic disease. You will also contribute to their ability to reproduce their species more successfully in the spring.

Available in: **Bamfords Top Flight Wild Bird Food, Garden Gourmet, Wild Bird Feeder Seed & Winter Picnic Table Seed.**
Also in stock
PEANUTS – SUNFLOWER HEARTS – NIGERSEED
SMALL & BLACK SUNFLOWER – PEANUT GRANULES etc.
For more details of these products, our mail order system and network of UK stockists please contact:

R&E Bamford Limited.
Globe Mill, Midge Hall, Leyland, Lancashire PR26 6TN
tel: 01772 456300 fax: 01772 456302
email: sales@bamfords.co.uk web: www.bamfords.co.uk

128

BIRD RESERVES
AND
OBSERVATORIES

This picure of Woodpigeons bathing in the rain was an entry by
Andrew Mart in the BB competitions.

Bedfordshire

Key to sites:
1. Begwary Brook
2. Blow's Downs
3. Harrold Odell Country Park
4. Marston Vale Millenium Country Park
5. Priory Marina Country Park
6. Stockgrove Country Park

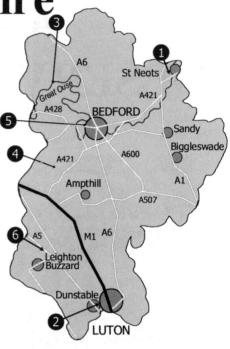

BEGWARY BROOK

The Wildlife Trust for Beds, Cambs, Northants & Peterborough.
Location: TL 169 564. S of St Neots off A428 at the A1 junction through the Wyboston Lakes complex. Follow road to car park at the reserve entrance.
Access: Open all year. Partially suitable for wheelchairs.
Facilities: None.
Public transport: None.
Habitat: Former gravel pit, small lake, marshy area.
Key birds: Wildfowl and wader species.
Contact: Trust HQ, 3B Langford Arch, London Road, Sawtry, Cambridge CB2 4EE, 01223 712400. e-mail: cambswt@cix.co.uk www.wildlifetrust.org.uk/bcnp

BLOW'S DOWNS

The Wildlife Trust for Beds, Cambs, Northants & Peterborough.
Location: TL 033 216. On the outskirts of Dunstable, W of Luton. Parking is at Skimpot roundabout, off Hatters Way on A505, and in Half Moon Lane, Dunstable.
Access: Open all year.
Facilities: None.
Public transport: None.
Habitat: Chalk downland and scrub and grassland that is a traditional resting place for incoming spring migrants.
Key birds: *Spring/summer*: Hobby, Turtle Dove, Grasshopper Warbler, Lesser Whitethroat, Cuckoo, Spotted Flycatcher, Golden Plover. *Winter*: Buzzard, winter thrushes, possible Brambling. *Passage*: Ring Ouzel, Wheatear,

Redstart. *All year*: Marsh and Willow Tits, Bullfinch, Sparrowhawk.
Contact: Trust HQ, 3B Langford Arch, London Road, Sawtry, Cambridge CB2 4EE, 01223 712400. e-mail: cambswt@cix.co.uk www.wildlifetrust.org.uk/bcnp

HARROLD ODELL COUNTRY PARK

Harrold Odell Country Park.
Location: SP 960 570. 10 miles NW of Bedford off the Harrold to Carlton road.
Access: Open at all times.
Facilities: Visitor centre. Cafe open 9am-6pm every day. Hide.
Public transport: None.
Habitat: Lakes (one with island), lagoons, osier beds, meadows adjacent River Great Ouse, woodland.
Key birds: *Summer*: Breeding Reed and Sedge Warblers, Lesser Whitethroat. Passage waders, Common and Black Terns, late summer Hobby.

NATURE RESERVES - ENGLAND

Winter: Wildfowl, Water Rail.
Contact: Bill Thwaites, Country Park, Carlton Road, Harrold, Bedford MK43 7DS. 01234 720016. www.ivelandouse.co.uk
e-mail: thwaitesbgdeed.bedfordshire.gov.uk

MARSTON VALE MILLENNIUM COUNTRY PARK

Location: SW of Bedford off A421 at Marston Moretaine. Only five mins from J13 of M1.
Contact: Forest Centre, Station Road, Marston Moretaine, Beds MK43 0PR. 01234 767037.

PRIORY MARINA COUNTRY PARK

Bedford Borough Council.
Location: TL 071 495. 1.5 miles from Bedford town centre. Signposted A428 and A421.
Access: Open at all times.
Facilities: Toilets, visitor centre, hides, nature trail. Provision for disabled visitors.
Public transport: Stagecoach bus service 103 passes Barkers Lane (main) entrance.
Habitat: Lakes, reedbeds, scrub/plantations, meadows adjoining River Great Ouse.
Key birds: *Winter*: Grebes, wildfowl, Merlin, Sparrowhawk, Water Rail, Stonechat, Chiffchaff, thrushes, corvid, finch and bunting roosts.
Summer: Terns, Hobby, woodpeckers, Kingfisher, Swift, Nightingale, warblers.
Passage: Raptors, gulls, terns, waders, hirundines, pipits, wagtails.
Contact: Errol Newman, Wardens Office, Visitor Centre, Priory CP, Barkers Lane, Bedford MK41 9SH. 01234 211182.

STOCKGROVE COUNTRY PARK

Greensand Trust on behalf of Bedfordshire and Buckinghamshire Councils.
Location: SP 920 293. From Leighton Buzzard take the Woburn Road N. Turn W at sign into Brickhill Road. Alternatively, from Flying Fox roundabout on A5 head S to Heath and Reach for 0.5 miles following signs for country park.
Access: A network of public footpaths affords good access. Park by the Visitor Centre (£1 contribution) or along the lane. Path round the lake is suitable for wheelchair users.
Facilities: Visitor Centre, disabled toilets, information and sightings boards and new restaurant.
Public transport: Arriva bus from Leighton Buzzard stops in Woburn Road, a five-minute walk from the park. Tel: 08706 082 608.
Habitat: Mixed woodland, lake, heathland.
Key birds: *Spring*: Mandarin Duck, Goshawk, Buzzard, Tawny Owl, Lesser Spotted Woodpecker, Wood Lark, Marsh Tit, Nuthatch, Siskin, Redpoll, Crossbill. *Summer*: Woodcock, Hobby, Turtle Dove, Cuckoo, Spotted Flycatcher, Tree Pipit, warblers, Linnet, Yellowhammer.
Contact: The Site Manager, Stockgrove Country Park, Brickhill Road, Heath and Reach, Leighton Buzzard, Bedfordshire LU7 0BA, 01525 237760. e-mail: rangers@stockgrove.co.uk

Berkshire

BAYNES AND BOWDEN

Berks, Bucks & Oxon Wildlife Trust.
Location: SU 551 651 and SU 501 655. From Newbury travel S on the A34 to roundabout turn off to Greenham. Follow Bury's Bank Road for 1.5 miles to a small gravel track on L. This is marked Footpath - No Vehicular Access. Go down this track to the car park on the R. Alternatively, follow Bury's Bank Road for one mile to a L turn to Jack and Jill Nursery. The Baynes car park is one mile down the track. From A4 at Thatcham take the unclassified road S past Thatcham Station over the canal. Take a narrow R turn onto Bury's Bank Road. After one mile look for the signs as described before. Parking is also available at the Old Bomb Site at the West Berkshire Council's car park.
Access: Open all year. Only guide dogs allowed.
Facilities: Car park.
Public transport: None.
Habitat: Ancient woodland, heath, acid grassland.
Key birds: *Spring/summer*: Spotted Flycatcher, Woodcock. *All year*: Song Thrush, all three woodpeckers, Sparrowhawk. Slow-worms, grass snakes, adders, good for butterflies.
Contact: Trust HQ, 1 Armstrong Road, Littlemore, Oxford OX4 4XT, 01865 775476. e-mail: bbowt@cix.co.uk
www.wildlifetrust.org.uk/berksbucksoxon

131

Berkshire

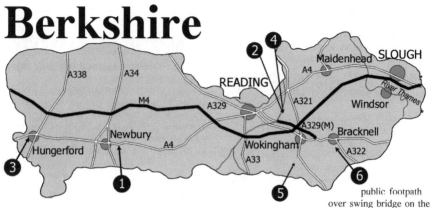

Key to sites:
1. Baynes and Bowdown
2. Dinton Pastures CP
3. Hungerford Marsh
4. Lavell's Lake
5. Moor Green Lakes
6. Wildmoor Heath

DINTON PASTURES COUNTRY PARK

Wokingham District Council.
Location: SU 784 718. E of Reading off B3030 between Hurst and Winnersh.
Access: Open all year, dawn to dusk.
Facilities: Hides, information centre, car park, café, toilets. Suitable for wheelchairs.
Public transport: Information not available.
Habitat: Mature gravel pits and banks of River Loddon.
Key birds: Kingfisher, Water Rail, Little Ringed Plover, Common Tern, Nightingale. *Winter*: Wildfowl (inc. Goldeneye, Wigeon, Teal, Gadwall).
Contact: Dave Webster, Ranger, Dinton Pastures Country Park, Davis Street, Hurst, Berks. 0118 934 2016.

HUNGERFORD MARSH

Berks, Bucks & Oxon Wildlife Trust.
Location: SU 333 687. On W side of Hungerford, beside the Kennet and Avon Canal. From town centre, go along Church Street past the town hall. Turn R under the railway. Follow public footpath over swing bridge on the canal near the church. The reserve is separated from Freeman's Marsh by a line of willows and bushes.
Access: Open all year. Please keep to the footpath. Dogs on leads please.
Facilities: Car park.
Public transport: None.
Habitat: Unimproved rough grazing and reedbed.
Key birds: *Spring/summer*: Reed Warbler. *Winter*: Siskin. *All year*: Mute Swan, Mallard. Birds seen in the last ten years include Kingfisher, Yellow Wagtail, Water Rail and Grasshopper Warbler.
Contact: Trust HQ, 1 Armstrong Road, Littlemore, Oxford OX4 4XT, 01865 775476. e-mail: bbowt@cix.co.uk www.wildlifetrust.org.uk/berksbucksoxon

LAVELL'S LAKE

Location: SU 781 729. Via Sandford Lane off B3030 between Hurst and Winnersh, E of Reading.
Contact: Dave Webster, Ranger, Dinton Pastures Country Park, Davis Street, Hurst, Berks. 0118 934 2016.

MOOR GREEN LAKES

Blackwater Valley Countryside Service.
Location: SU 805 628. Main access and parking off Lower Sandhurst Road, Finchampstead. Alternatively, Rambler's car park, Mill Lane, Sandhurst (SU 820 619).
Access: Car parks open dawn-dusk. Two bird hides open to members of the Moor Green Lakes Group (contact management body for details). Dogs on leads. Site can be used by people in

wheelchairs though surface not very suitable.
Facilities: Two bird hides, footpaths around site, Blackwater Valley Long-distance Path passes through site.
Public transport: Nearest bus stop, Finchampstead (approx 1.5 miles from main entrance). Local bus companies – Stagecoach Hants & Surrey, tel 01256 464501, First Beeline & Londonlink, tel 01344 424938.
Habitat: Thirty-six hectares (90 acres) in total. Three lakes with gravel islands, beaches and scrapes. River Blackwater, grassland, surrounded by willow, ash, hazel and thorn hedgerows.
Key birds: *Spring/summer*: Redshank, Little Ringed Plover, Sand Martin, Willow Warbler, and of particular interest, a flock of Goosander. Also Whitethroat, Sedge Warbler, Common Sandpiper, Common Tern, Dunlin and Black Terns. Lapwings breed on site. Several sightings of Red Kite. *Winter*: Ruddy Duck, Wigeon, Teal, Gadwall.
Contact: Blackwater Valley Countryside Service, Ash Lock Cottage, Government Road, Aldershot, Hants GU11 2PS01276 686615. e-mail: blackwater.valley@hants.gov.uk www.blackwater-valley.org.uk

WILDMOOR HEATH

Berks, Bucks & Oxon Wildlife Trust.
Location: SU 842 627. Between Bracknell and Sandhurst. From Sandhurst shopping area, take the A321 NW towards Wokingham. Turn E at the mini-roundabout on to Crowthorne Road. Continue for about one mile through one set of traffic lights. Car park is on the R at the bottom of the hill.
Access: Open all year. No access to woodland N of Rackstraw Road at Broadmoor Bottom. Please keep dogs on a lead.
Facilities: Car park.
Public transport: None.
Habitat: Wet and dry lowland heath, bog, mixed woodland and mature Scots pine plantation.
Key birds: *Spring/summer*: Wood Lark, Nightjar, Dartford Warbler, Stonechat. Good for dragonflies.
Contact: Trust HQ, 1 Armstrong Road, Littlemore, Oxford OX4 4XT, 01865 775476. e-mail: bbowt@cix.co.uk www.wildlifetrust.org.uk/berksbucksoxon

Buckinghamshire

COLLEGE LAKE WILDLIFE CENTRE

RSPB (Central England Office).
Location: SU 972 872. Reserve lies S of M40, between village of Hedgerley and Gerrards Cross. From J2 of M40 head S on A355 to Hedgerley. Take small private track beside village pond next to the pub. Alternatively, approach from the S via B416 (Gerrards Cross to Stoke Poges).
Access: Open all year. Parking is difficult.
Facilities: Two marked paths.
Public transport: None.
Habitat: Mixed woodland.
Key birds: *Spring/summer*: Blackcap, Garden Warbler, Spotted Flycatcher, Swallow. *Winter*: Redpoll, Siskin. *Passage*: Possible Firecrest. *All year*: Marsh Tit, Willow Tit, Tree Sparrow, Nuthatch, all three woodpeckers.
Contact: RSPB, 46 The Green, South Bar, Banbury, Oxfordshire OX16 9AB, 01295 253330. www.rspb.org.uk/wildlife/reserves

COLLEGE LAKE WILDLIFE CENTRE

Berks, Bucks & Oxon Wildlife Trust with Castle Cement (Pitstone) Ltd.
Location: SP 935 139. On B488 Tring/Ivinghoe road at Bulbourne.
Access: Open daily 10am-5pm. Permits available on site or from Trust HQ.
Facilities: Hides, nature trails, visitor centre, toilets.
Public transport: None.
Habitat: Marsh area, lake, islands, shingle.
Key birds: *Spring/summer*: Breeding Lapwing, Redshank, Little Ringed Plover, Hobby, *Passage*: Waders inc. Green Sandpiper.
Contact: Graham Atkins, College Lake Wildlife Centre, Upper Icknield Way, Bulbourne, Tring, Herts HP23 5QG. H: 01296 662890.

Buckinghamshire

Key to sites:
1. Church Wood
2. College Lake
3. Foxcote & Hydelane Waters
4. Hanson Env Study Cnt
5. Stony Stratford Wildlife Conservation Area
6. Weston Turville

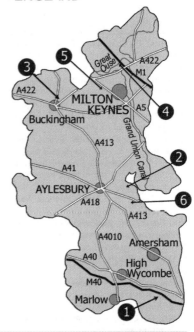

FOXCOTE AND HYDELANE WATERS

Berks, Bucks & Oxon Wildlife Trust.
Location: SP 715 364 and SP 725 348. Foxcote Reservoir is one mile NE of Buckingham, off A422 on a lane between Maids Moreton and Leckhampstead. Hydelane Lake is S of A422 opposite the entrance to Home Farm.
Access: Open all year. The hides are for BBOWT members only. View from road or follow public footpath to Foxcote Wood that runs parallel to E bank for views over the water.
Facilities: Hides.
Public transport: None.
Habitat: Open water.
Key birds: *Spring*: Common Tern, Hobby, Common Sandpiper, Corn Bunting. *Summer*: Spotted Flycatcher at Hydelane, warblers, Common Tern, ducks, Great Crested and Little Grebes. *Winter*: Duck, inc. Wigeon and Goldeneye, Goosander, Water Rail. Possible, Smew, Slavonian Grebe, winter thrushes, wild swans at Hydelane. *All year*: Sparrowhawk, Kingfisher, Little and Tawny Owls, Grey Wagtail, Green and Great Spotted Woodpeckers, Marsh Tit, Jay.
Contact: Trust HQ, The Lodge, 1 Armstrong Road, Littlemore, Oxford OX4 4XT, 01865 775476. e-mail: bbontwt@cix.co.uk

HANSON ENVIRONMENTAL STUDY CENTRE

Location: SP 842 429. Two miles N of central Milton Keynes. Entrance almost opposite Proud Perch public house on Wolverton to Newport Pagnell road.
Contact: Andrew Stevenson, Hanson Environmental Study Centre, Wolverton Road, Great Linford, Milton Keynes, Bucks MK14 5AH. 01908 604810.

STONY STRATFORD WILDLIFE CONSERVATION AREA

Berks, Bucks & Oxon Wildlife Trust.
Location: SP 786 411. Off Stony Stratford loop road (A5).
Access: Open daily.
Facilities: Public footpath. Public hide.
Public transport: None.
Habitat: Wet riverside meadow, lakes, islands.
Key birds: Summer: Breeding Redshank. Passage waders. Winter: Wildfowl.
Contact: Trust HQ, 01223 712400.

WESTON TURVILLE

Berks, Bucks & Oxon Wildlife Trust.
Location: SP 859 095. From Wendover take A413 north; turn right after one mile opp Marquis of Granby pub; park in lay-by after 600 yards and reserve is on right.
Access: Public access on perimeter path.
Facilities: Hide.
Public transport: None.
Habitat: Reservoir, large reed fen.
Key birds: Water Rail. *Summer*; Breeding waRblers. *Winter*: Wildfowl and gulls.
Contact: Trust HQ, 01223 712400.

Cambridgeshire

Key to sites:
1. Brampton Wood
2. Castor Hanglands NNR
3. Dogsthorpe Star Pit SSSI
4. Ferry Meadows CP
5. Fowlmere
6. Grafham Water
7. Hayley Wood
8. Nene Washes
9. Ouse Washes
10. Paxton Pits
11. Wicken Fen

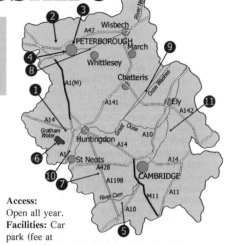

BRAMPTON WOOD

Wildlife Trust for Beds, Cambs, Northants & Peterborough.
Location: TL 185 698. Two miles E of Grafham village on N side of road to Brampton. From A14 take main road S from Ellington.
Access: Open daily.
Facilities: Car park, interpretative shelter.
Public transport: None.
Habitat: SSSI. Primarily ash and field maple with hazel coppice.
Key birds: *Summer*: Breeding Grasshopper Warbler, Nightingale, Spotted Flycatcher, Woodcock; all three woodpeckers. *Winter*: Thrushes. **Contact:** Trust HQ, 01223 712400.

DOGSTHORPE STAR PIT SSSI

Wildlife Trust for Beds, Cambs, Northants & Peterborough.
Location: TF 213 025. On NE edge of Peterborough. From A47 turn into White Post Road on Eye by-pass. No parking at reserve.
Access: Open all year. Entrance is via the Green Wheel cycle track in the disused Welland Road.
Facilities: None.
Public transport: None.
Habitat: Brackish water, scrub.
Key birds: *Winter*: Large numbers of gulls, attracted to nearby rubbish tip inc. Mediterranean, Glaucous and Yellow-legged. *Passage*: Occasional waders, inc Green Sandpiper. *All year*: Kingfisher, Green Woodpecker. *Summer*: Common warblers.
Contact: Trust HQ, 3B Langford Arch, London Road, Sawston, Cambridge CB2 4EE, 01223 712400. e-mail: cambswt@cix.co.uk www.wildlifetrust.org.uk/bcnp

FERRY MEADOWS

Nene Park Trust.
Location: TL 145 975. Three miles W of Peterborough town centre signed off A605.
Access:
Open all year.
Facilities: Car park (fee at weekends), visitor centre, toilets, café, hide.
Habitat: Lakes, scrub, small nature reserve.
Key birds: *Spring*: Common and Arctic Terns, waders, Yellow Wagtail. *Winter*: Siskin, Redpoll, Water Rail, occasional Hawfinch. *All year*: Good selection of woodland and water birds, Kingfisher.
Contact: Nene Park Trust, Ham Farm House, Orton, Peterborough PE2 5UU, 01733 234443.

FOWLMERE

RSPB (East Anglia Office).
Location: TL 407 461. Turn off A10 Cambridge to Royston road by Shepreth and follow signs.
Access: Access at all times along marked trail.
Facilities: Four hides, portable toilets.
Public transport: Shepreth railway station 3km away.
Habitat: Reedbeds, meres, woodland, scrub.
Key birds: *Summer*: Nine breeding warblers. *All year*: Water Rail, Kingfisher. *Winter*: Snipe, raptors. Corn Bunting roost.
Contact: Doug Radford, RSPB, Manor Farm, High Street, Fowlmere, Royston, Herts SG8 7SH. Tel/fax 01763 208978.

GRAFHAM WATER

Wildlife Trust for Beds, Cambs, Northants & Peterborough.
Location: TL 143 671. Follow signs for Grafham Water from A1 at Buckden or A14 at Ellington.

Nature reserve entrance is from Mander car park, W of Perry village.
Access: Open all year. Permits required for settlement lagoons only. Dogs barred in wildlife garden only, on leads elsewhere.
Facilities: Six hides in nature reserve. Two in wildlife garden accessible to wheelchairs. Cycle track accessible to wheelchairs. Visitor centre (restaurant, shop, toilets). Disabled parking. Wildlife cabin open weekends in summer.
Public transport: None.
Habitat: Open water, ancient and plantation woodland, grassland.
Key birds: *Winter*: Wildfowl, gulls. *Spring/summer*: Breeding Nightingale, Reed, Willow and Sedge Warblers, Common and Black Terns. *Autumn*: Passage waders.
Contact: Jo Calvert, c/o The Lodge, West Perry, Huntingdon, Cambs PE28 0BX. 01480 811075.
e-mail: grafham@cix.co.uk
www.wildlifetrust.org.uk/bcnp

HAYLEY WOOD

Wildlife Trust for Beds, Cambs, Northants & Peterborough.
Location: TL 292 529. Between Cambridge and Sandy. Take B1046 W out of Longstowe for one and a half miles and park opposite water tower. Walk up old track to wood.
Access: Open at all times.
Facilities: Interpretative centre.
Public transport: None.
Habitat: Ancient semi-natural woodland. Active coppice cycle and derelict coppice.
Key birds: Woodland species inc. Nightingale, Blackcap, Garden Warbler, Nuthatch, Treecreeper, Marsh Tit, Woodcock, woodpeckers.
Contact: Trust HQ, 01223 712400

NENE WASHES

RSPB (East Anglia Office).
Location: TL 290 995. Six miles E of Peterborough, off B1040 to Thorney, one mile N of Whittlesey.
Access: Open at all times on droves and south barrier bank. Group visits by arrangement. No access to fields.
Facilities: None.
Public transport: Bus and trains to Whittlesey.
Habitat: Wet grassland with ditches. Frequently flooded.
Key birds: *Spring/early summer*: Breeding

waders, including Black-tailed Godwit, duck, including Garganey, Marsh Harrier and Hobby. *Winter*: Waterfowl including Bewick's Swan and Pintail, Barn Owl, Hen Harrier.
Contact: Charlie Kitchin, RSPB Nene Washes, 21a East Delph, Whittlesey, Cambs PE7 1RH. 01733 205140.

OUSE WASHES

RSPB (East Anglia Office).
Location: TL 471 861. Between Chatteris and March on A141, take B1093 to Manea. Reserve signposted from Manea. Reserve office and visitor centre located off Welches Dam. Approximately ten miles from March or Chatteris.
Contact: Cliff Carson, (Site Manager), Ouse Washes Reserve, Welches Dam, Manea, March, Cambs PE15 0NF. 01354 680212.
e-mail: cliff.carson@rspb.org.uk

PAXTON PITS

Huntingdonshire District Council.
Location: TL 197 629. Access from A1 at Little Paxton, two miles N of St Neots.
Access: District Council site – no charge. Open 24 hours. Visitor centre manned at weekends. Dogs allowed under control. Heron trail suitable for wheelchairs during summer.
Facilities: Toilets available most days 9am-5pm (including disabled), two bird hides (always open), marked nature trails.
Public transport: Stagecoach X46. Runs between Huntingdon-Bedford. Tel 0870 608 2608.
Habitat: Grassland, scrub, lakes.
Key birds: *Spring/summer*: Nightingale, Kingfisher, Common Tern, Sparrowhawk, Hobby, Grasshopper, Sedge and Reed Warblers, Lesser Whitethroat. *Winter*: Smew, Goldeneye, Goosander, Gadwall, Pochard.
Contact: Ron Elloway, Ranger, The Visitor Centre, High Street, Little Paxton, St Neots, Cambs PE19 6ET. 01480 406795.
e-mail: tony@howfreeserve.co.uk
www.paxton-pits.org.uk

WICKEN FEN

Location: TL 563 705. Lies ten miles S of Ely. From A10 drive E along A1123.
Contact: Martin Lester, Lode Lane, Wicken, Cambs CB7 5XP. 01353 720274.
www.wicken.org.uk
e-mail: awnmdl@smtp.ntrust.org.uk

Cheshire

1. Fiddlers Ferry
2. Gayton Sands
3. Marbury Reedbed
4. Moore Nature Reserve
5. Rostherne Mere
6. Rudheath Woods
7. Sandbach Flashes
8. Tatton Park
9. Woolston Eyes

FIDDLERS FERRY

Location: SJ 552 853. Off A562 between Warrington and Widnes.
Access: Parking at main gate of power station. Summer (8am-8pm); winter (8am-5pm). For free permit apply in advance with sae to Manager, Fiddlers Ferry Power Station, Warrington WA5 2UT.
Facilities: Hide, nature trail.
Public transport: Arriva bus 110 every 20 minutes.
Habitat: Ash and water lagoons, tidal and non-tidal marshes with phragmites and great reedmace, meadow grassland with small wooded areas.
Key birds: *Summer*: Breeding Oystercatcher, Ringed and Little Ringed Plovers, Raven and Jay. *Winter*: Glaucous, Iceland and Yellow-legged Gulls, Short-eared Owl, Peregrine, Jack Snipe. *Recent rarities*: Black-necked Grebe, Little Egret, Goshawk, Rough-legged Buzzard, Marsh Harrier, Hen Harrier, Osprey, Hobby, Little Crake, Red-necked Phalarope, Pectoral and Wood Sandpiper, Hoopoe, Greenish and Yellow-browed Warbler.
Contact: Keith Massey, 4 Hall Terrace, Great Sankey, Warrington WA5 3EZ. 01925 721382.

GAYTON SANDS

RSPB (North West England Office).
Location: SJ 275 785. On W side of Wirral, S of Birkenhead. View high tide activity from the Old Baths car park near the Boathouse public house, Parkgate.
Access: Open at all times. Viewing from public footpaths and car parks overlooking saltmarsh. Please do not walk on the saltmarsh, the tides are dangerous.

Facilities: Car park, picnic area, group bookings, guided walks, special events, wheelchair access. Toilets at Parkgate village opposite the Square.
Public transport: Bus – Parkgate every hour. Rail – Neston, two miles.
Habitat: Estuary – saltmarsh, pools, mud and sandflats.
Key birds: *Spring/summer/autumn*: Greenshank, Spotted Redshank, Curlew Sandpiper. *Winter*: Shelduck, Teal, Wigeon, Pintail, Oystercatcher, Black-tailed Godwit, Curlew, Redshank, Merlin, Peregrine, Water Rail, Short-eared Owl.
Contact: Colin E Wells, Burton Point Farm, Station Road, Burton, Nr Neston, Cheshire CH64 5SB. 0151 3367681.

MARBURY REEDBEDS NATURE RESERVE

Location: SJ 651 768. North of Northwich.
Contact: Cheshire Wildlife Trust HQ, 01270 610180.

MOORE NATURE RESERVE

Location: SJ 577 854. Located SW of Warrington. Take A56 towards Chester. At Higher Walton follow signs for Moore village into Moore Lane. Cross swing bridge and park beyond crossroads.
Contact: Miss Estelle Linney, c/o Arpley Landfill Site, Forest Way, Sankey Bridge, Warrington WA4 6YZ. 01925 444 689.
e-mail: Estelle.Linney@wrg.co.uk

ROSTHERNE MERE

English Nature.
Location: SJ 744 843. Lies N of Knutsford and S of M56 (junction 8).
Access: View from Rostherne churchyard and lanes; no public access, except to A W Boyd Observatory (permits from D A Clarke, 1 Hart Avenue, Sale M33 2JY, tel 0161 973 7122).
Facilities: None.
Public transport: None.
Habitat: Deep lake, woodland, willow bed, pasture.
Key birds: *Winter*: Good range of duck (inc Ruddy Duck and Pintail), gull roost (inc. occasional Iceland and Glaucous). Passage Black Terns.
Contact: Tim Coleshaw, (Site Manager), English Nature, Attingham Park, Shrewsbury SY4 4TW. 01743 282000; fax 01743 709303; e-mail tim.coleshaw@english-nature.org.uk.

RUDHEATH WOODS NATURE RESERVE

Cheshire Wildlife Trust.
Location: SJ 740 700. Located five miles S of Knutsford, at Allostock. From A50, turn W on to Wash Lane. Park in an unmade track which heads S after 0.25 miles. The track continues as a bridle path along the reserve, which is accessed over stiles and along various paths.
Access: Open all year.
Facilities: None.
Public transport: None.
Habitat: Heathland, wet woodland.
Key birds: *Spring/summer*: Chiffchaff, other warblers, possible Hobby. *Autumn*: Waders, possible Greenshank, Green Sandpiper. *Winter*: Siskin, Redpoll, Snipe. *All year*: All three woodpeckers, Willow Tit.
Contact: Trust HQ, Reaseheath, Nantwich, Cheshire CS5 6DG, 01270 610180. www.wildlifetrust.org.uk/cheshire

SANDBACH FLASHES

Management Committee.
Location: SJ 720 590. Leave M6 at junction 17 for Sandbach.
Access: Elton Hall Flash from new road at SJ 716 595; Foden's Flash from road at SJ 730 614; Watch Lane Flash from car park at SJ 728 608.
Facilities: None.
Public transport: None.

Habitat: Fresh and brackish water, reedbed, carr woodland, inland saltmarsh.
Key birds: Passage waders; nesting and wintering wildfowl; many rarities occur.
Contact: Patrick Whalley, 3 Barracks Lane, Ravensmoor, Nantwich, Cheshire CW5 8PR (please enclose SAE if writing). 01270 624420.

TATTON PARK

National Trust/Cheshire County Council.
Location: SJ 738 816. Lies 2.5 miles NW of Knutsford. Leave M56 (J8) via A556 for Knutsford or M6 (J19) via A556 for Altrincham. Follow signs from Swan Hotel at Bucklow Hill.
Access: Open all year except Christmas Day.
Facilities: Toilets, café, garden, hall, suitable for the disabled.
Public transport: None.
Habitat: Parkland, farmland, ornamental gardens, lakes.
Key birds: *Spring/summer*: Woodcock, Grasshopper Warbler, Whitethroat, Stonechat, Whinchat. *Winter*: Snipe, possible Smew, wildfowl. *All year*: Ruddy Duck, usual woodland species.
Contact: National Trust HQ. www.nationaltrust.org.uk

WOOLSTON EYES

Woolston Eyes Conservation Group.
Location: SJ 654 888. E of Warrington between the River Mersey and Manchester Ship Canal. Off Manchester Road down Weir Lane or from Latchford to end of Thelwall Lane.
Access: Open all year. Permits required from Chairman, £6 each, £12 per family (see address below).
Facilities: No toilets or visitor centre but good hides and elevated hides.
Public transport: Buses along A57 nearest stop to Weir Lane.
Habitat: Wetland, marsh, scrubland, wildflower meadow areas.
Key birds: Breeding Black-necked Grebe, warblers, all raptors (inc. Merlin, Peregrine, Marsh Harrier). SSSI for wintering wildfowl, many duck species breed.
Contact: B R Ankers, Chairman, 9 Lynton Gardens, Appleton, Cheshire WA4 5ED. 01925 267355.
http://home.clara.net/nortonw/

Cornwall

BRENEY COMMON

Cornwall Wildlife Trust.
Location: SX 054 610. Three miles S of Bodmin.
Take minor road off A390 one mile W of
Lostwithiel to Lowertown.
Access: Open at all times but please keep to
paths. Disabled access.
Facilities: Wilderness trail.
Public transport: None.
Habitat: Wetland, heath and scrub.
Key birds: Willow Tit, Nightjar, Tree Pipit,
Sparrowhawk, Lesser Whitethroat, Curlew.
Contact: Eric Higgs, Crift Farm, Lanlivery,
Bodmin PL30 5DE. 01208 872702.

BUDE MARSHES

Location: SS 208 057. By public footpath beside
Bude Canal.
Contact: R Braund, 36 Killerton Road, Bude,
Cornwall EX23 8EN. 01288 353906.

DRIFT RESERVOIR

South West Lakes Trust/Cornwall BWPS.
Location: Three miles W of Penzance on A30
(signposted).
Access: No restrictions (not suitable for
disabled).
Facilities: Walk round S side of reserve to the
unlocked hide.
Public transport: None.
Habitat: Reservoir, fresh water with muddy
margins.
Key birds: *Autumn*: Gulls, ducks, waders plus
regular rarities.
Contact: Graham Hobin, Lower Drift
Farmhouse, Buryas Bridge, Drift, Penzance.
01736 362206

GOLITHA NATIONAL NATURE RESERVE

Cornwall Wildlife Trust.
Location: SX 227 690. Golitha is three miles
NW of Liskeard in E Cornwall. Take minor roads
N for 2.5 miles from Dobwalls on A38.
Access: Various paths from 0.5 mile to four
miles. Can be muddy after rain. Limited disabled
access.
Facilities: Toilets.
Public transport: None.

Habitat: Ancient woodland, deep granite gorge.
Key birds: *All year*: Sparrowhawk, Buzzard,
Kingfisher, all three woodpeckers, Jay, Grey
Wagtail, Dipper, Marsh Tit, Treecreeper,
Nuthatch. *Summer*: Redstart, Wood Warbler,
Pied Flycatcher.
Contact: Trust HQ, Five Acres, Allet, Truro,
Cornwall TR4 9DJ. 01872 273939.
e-mail: cornwt@cix.co.uk
www.wildlifetrust.org.uk/cornwall

HAYLE ESTUARY

RSPB (South West England Office).
Location: SW 550 370. In town of Hayle.
Follow signs to Hayle from A30.
Access: Open at all times. No permits required.
No admission charges. Dogs on leads please.
Facilities: Eric Grace Memorial Hide at Ryan's
Field has disabled parking and viewing. Nearest
disabled toilets at Wyevale Garden centre, Lelant,
600 yards W, just off the roundabout. No visitor
centre but information board at hide.
Public transport: Buses and trains at Hayle.
Habitat: Intertidal mudflats, saltmarsh, lagoon
and islands, sandy beaches and sand dunes.
Key birds: *Winter*: Wildfowl, gulls, Kingfisher,
Ring-billed Gull, Great Northern Diver. *Spring/
summer*: Migrant waders, breeding Shelduck.
Autumn: Rare waders, often from N America!
Terns, gulls.
Contact: Dave Flumm, RSPB, The Manor
Office, Marazion, Cornwall TR17 0EF. Tel/fax;
01736 711682.

LOVENY RESERVE - COLLIFORD RESERVOIR

Cornwall Birdwatching & Preservation Society.
Location: SX183744. By foot from SW Water
Deweymeads car park, A30 E of Bodmin.
Access: Open at all times; access restricted to SW
edge of reserve.
Facilities: None.
Public transport: None.
Habitat: Wetlands, moorland.
Key birds: Wildfowl (inc. Shoveler, Wigeon,
Smew); passage waders can inc. N American
species.
Contact: David Conway, Tregenna, Cooksland,
Bodmin, Cornwall PL31 2AR. 01208 77686.

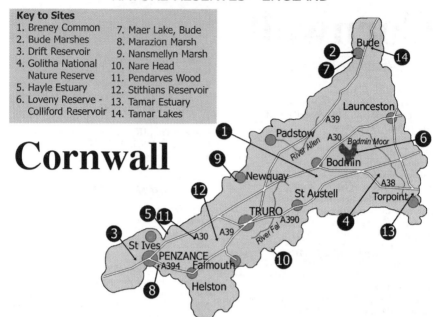

Key to Sites
1. Breney Common
2. Bude Marshes
3. Drift Reservoir
4. Golitha National Nature Reserve
5. Hayle Estuary
6. Loveny Reserve - Colliford Reservoir
7. Maer Lake, Bude
8. Marazion Marsh
9. Nansmellyn Marsh
10. Nare Head
11. Pendarves Wood
12. Stithians Reservoir
13. Tamar Estuary
14. Tamar Lakes

Cornwall

MAER LAKE, BUDE

Location: SS 208 075. View from private road next to Maer Lodge Hotel, heading N.
Contact: As Loveny Reserve.

MARAZION MARSH

RSPB (South West England Office).
Location: SW 510 315. Reserve is one mile E of Penzance, 500 yards W of Marazion. Entrance off seafront road near Marazion.
Access: Open at all times. No permits required. No admission charges. Dogs on leads please.
Facilities: One hide. No toilets. No visitor centre. Nearest toilets in Marazion and seafront car park.
Public transport: Bus from Penzance.
Habitat: Wet reedbed, willow carr.
Key birds: *Winter*: Wildfowl, Snipe, occasional Bittern. *Spring/summer*: Breeding Reed, Sedge and Cetti's Warblers, herons, swans. *Autumn*: Occasional Aquatic Warbler, Spotted Crake. Large roost of swallows and martins in reedbeds, migrant warblers and waders.
Contact: Dave Flumm, RSPB, The Manor Office, Marazion, Cornwall TR17 0EF. Tel/fax; 01736 711682.

NANSMELLYN MARSH

Cornwall Wildlife Trust.
Location: SW 762 541. Access from Perranzabuloe Sports Club car park, off the road to Goonhavern, just E of Perranporth.
Access: Open at all times with access suitable for disabled. Dogs on leads.
Facilities: Bird hide and circular path/boardwalk.
Public transport: None.
Habitat: Four and a half hectares of reedbed with willow carr.
Key birds: Cetti's Warbler, Grasshopper Warbler, Willow Warbler, Sedge Warbler, Snipe, Water Rail, Reed Bunting.
Contact: Stuart Hutchings, 5 Acres, Allet, Cornwall TR4 9DJ. 01827 273939.
e-mail stuart@cornwt.demon.co.uk
www.wildlifetrust.org.uk/cornwall

NARE HEAD

National Trust.
Location: Approx ten miles SE of Truro. from A390 head S on A307 to two miles S of Tregony just past the garage. Follow signs to Veryan then L signposted to Carne. Go straight over at crossroad, following Carne and Pendower. Turn L on a bend following NT signs for Nare Head.

Bearing R, cross over a cattle grid to the car park. From the garage, Nare Head is about four miles.
Access: Open all year.
Facilities: Car park.
Public transport: None.
Habitat: Headland.
Key birds: *Spring/summer*: Razorbill, Guillemot, Sandwich, Common and Arctic Terns, possible Whimbrel, Fulmar. *Winter*: Black-throated and Great Northern Divers. Red-throated Diver possible, Scoter, Velvet Scoter, Slavonian, Black-necked and Red-necked Grebes.
Contact: National Trust, Lanhydrock House, Lanhydrock, Cornwall PL30 4DE. 01208 432691.

PENDARVES WOOD

Location: SW 640 376. From the B3303, two miles S of Camborne. Entrance on left.
Contact: Malcolm Perry, 7 Relistian Park, Reawla, Gwinear, Hayle TR27 5HF. 01736 850612.

STITHIANS RESERVOIR

Cornwall Birdwatching & Preservation Society.
Location: SS 715 365. From B3297 S of Redruth.
Access: Good viewing from causeway. Hides accessible to members only.
Facilities: None.
Public transport: None.
Habitat: Open water, marshland.
Key birds: Wildfowl and waders (inc. rarities, eg. Pectoral and Semipalmated Sandpipers, Lesser Yellowlegs).
Contact: See Loveny Reserve.

TAMAR ESTUARY

Cornwall Wildlife Trust.
Location: SX 434 631 (Northern Boundary). SX 421 604 (Southern Boundary). From Plymouth head W on A38. Access parking at Cargreen and Landulph from minor roads off A388.
Access: Open at all times.
Facilities: Information boards at Cargreen and Landulph.
Public transport: None.
Habitat: Tidal mudflat with some saltmarsh.
Key birds: *Winter*: Avocet, Snipe, Black-tailed Godwit, Redshank, Dunlin, Curlew, Whimbrel, Spotted Redshank, Green Sandpiper, Golden Plover, Kingfisher.
Contact: Stuart Hutchings, 5 Acres, Allet, Cornwall TR4 9DJ. 01827 273939.
e-mail: stuart@cornwt.demon.co.uk
www.wildlifetrust.org.uk/cornwall

TAMAR LAKES

Tamar Lakes Country Park.
Location: SS 295 115. Leave A39 at Kilkhampton. Take minor road E to Thardon, car park off minor road running between upper and lower lakes.
Access: Open all year.
Facilities: Hide open all year round. New birdwatching centre on lower Tamar. Cafe, toilets (Apr-Sep).
Public transport: None.
Habitat: Two large bodies of water.
Key birds: Migrant waders (inc. North American vagrants). *Spring*: Black Tern. *Winter*: Wildfowl (inc. Goldeneye, Wigeon, Pochard).
Contact: Ranger, Tamar Lakes Water Park, Kilkhampton, N Cornwall, 01288 321262.

Cumbria

CAMPFIELD MARSH

RSPB (North of England Office).
Location: NY 207 620. On S shore of Solway estuary, W of Bowness-on-Solway. Follow signs from B5307 from Carlisle.
Access: Open at all times, no charge. Views of high-tide roosts from roadside lay-bys (suitable for disabled).
Facilities: Viewing screens overlooking wetland areas, along nature trail (1.5 miles). No toilets or visitor centre.
Public transport: Nearest railway station – Carlisle (13 miles). Infrequent bus service.
Habitat: Saltmarsh/intertidal areas, open water, peat bog, wet grassland.
Key birds: *Winter*: Waders and wildfowl include Barnacle Goose, Shoveler, Scaup, Grey Plover. *Spring/summer*: Breeding Lapwing, Redshank, Snipe, Tree Sparrow and warblers. *Autumn*: Passage waders.

Cumbria

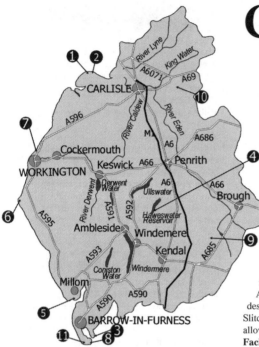

Key to sites:
1. Campfield Marsh
2. Drumburgh Moss NNR
3. Foulney Island
4. Haweswater
5. Hodbarrow
6. St Bees Head
7. Siddick Pond
8. South Walney
9. Smardale Gill NNR
10. Talkin Tarn Country Park
11. Walney Bird Observatory

Contact: Norman Holton, North Plain Farm, Bowness-on-Solway, Wigton, Cumbria CA7 5AG. e-mail: norman.holton@rspb.org.uk www.rspb.org.uk

DRUMBURGH MOSS NNR

Cumbria Wildlife Trust.
Location: NY 255 568. From Carlisle City Centre head W on B5307 to Kirkbride. After one mile turn R to Burgh by Sands. Follow road for 7.5 miles to Drumburgh Village. In the village, turn L by the Post Office. Continue down the track and park on the right past Moss Cottage.
Access: Open all year.
Facilities: None.
Public transport: None.
Habitat: Raised bog, woodland, grassland.
Key birds: *Summer*: Curlew, Grasshopper Warbler, Red Grouse. Large heath butterfly, adder.
Contact: Trust HQ, Plumgarths, Crook Road, Kendal LA8 8LX. 01539 816300.
e-mail: cumbriawt@cix.co.uk www.cumbriawildlifetrust.org.uk

FOULNEY ISLAND

Cumbria Wildlife Trust.
Location: SD 246 640. Three miles SE of Barrow town centre on the A5087 from Barrow or Ulverston. At a roundabout 2.5 miles S of Barrow take a minor road through Rampside to Roa Island. Turn L into reserve car park. The main island is reached by walking along the stone causeway.
Access: Open all year. Access restricted to designated paths during bird breeding season. Slitch Ridge is closed at this time. No dogs allowed during bird breeding season.
Facilities: None.
Public transport: Bus: regular service from Barrow to Roa Island.
Habitat: Shingle, sand, grassland.
Key birds: *Summer*: Arctic and Little Terns, Oystercatcher, Ringed Plover, Eider Duck. *Winter*: Brent Goose, Redshank, Dunlin, Sanderling. **Contact:** Trust HQ.

HAWESWATER

RSPB and United Utilities.
Location: NY 470 108. Off A6 at Shap, follow signs to Bampton and turn L in village; car park at S end of reservoir.
Access: Access at all times.
Facilities: Golden Eagle viewpoint, telescopes available Apr-end Aug (10am-5pm).
Public transport: None.
Habitat: Fells with rocky streams, steep oak and birch woodlands.
Key birds: Upland breeders: Golden Eagle, Peregrine, Raven, Ring Ouzel, Curlew, Redshank, Snipe. Woodlands: Pied Flycatcher, Wood Warbler, Tree Pipit, Redstart, Buzzard, Sparrowhawk.

Contact: Bill Kenmir, 7 Naddlegate, Burn Banks, Penrith, Cumbria CA10 2RL.

HODBARROW

RSPB (North of England Office).
Location: SD 174 791. Lying beside Duddon Estuary on the outskirts of Millom. Follow signs via Mainsgate Road.
Access: Open at all times, no charge.
Facilities: One hide overlooking island. Public toilets in Millom (two miles). Nature trail around the lagoon.
Public transport: Nearest railway station is in Millom (two miles).
Habitat: Brackish coastal lagoon bordered by limestone scrub and grassland.
Key birds: *Winter*: Waders and wildfowl includes Redshank, Dunlin, Goldeneye, Red-breasted Merganser. *Spring/summer*: Breeding gulls and terns, Eider, grebes, Lapwing. *Autumn*: Passage waders.
Contact: Norman Holton, (Site Manager), see Camfield Marsh.

ST BEES HEAD

RSPB (North of England Office).
Location: NX 962 118. S of Whitehaven via the B5345 road to St Bees village.
Access: Open at all times, no charge. Access via coast to coast footpath. The walk to the viewpoints is long and steep in parts.
Facilities: Three viewpoints overlooking seabird colony. Public toilets in St Bee's beach car park at entrance to reserve.
Public transport: Nearest railway station in St Bees (0.5 mile).
Habitat: Three miles of sandstone cliffs up to 300 ft high.
Key birds: *Summer*: Largest seabird colony on W coast of England: Guillemot, Razorbill, Puffin, Kittiwake, Fulmar and England's only breeding Black Guillemot.
Contact: Norman Holton, (Site Manager),See Campfield Marsh.

SIDDICK POND

Location: NY 001 305. One mile N of Workington, adjacent to A596.
Contact: Patrick Joyce, Technical Officer Leisure Services, Parks Development Officer, Allerdale BC, Allerdale House, Workington, Cumbria CA14 3YJ. 01900 326324; (fax)01900 326346.

SMARDALE GILL

Cumbria Wildlife Trust.
Location: NY 727 070. Six miles SW of Brough, approx 2.5 miles W of Ravenstonedale on A685 or 0.5 miles S of Kirkby Stephen station take turning signed to Smardale. Cross over the railway and turn L to junction ignoring the turn to Waitby. Cross over the railway and turn L at junction ignoring sign for Smardale. Cross disused railway and turn L immediately and L again to car park.
Access: Railway line is open to members and non-members but non-members should obtain a permit before visiting other parts of the reserve.
Facilities: None.
Public transport: Train: nearest station Kirkby Stephen.
Habitat: Limestone grassland, river, ancient semi-natural woodland, quarry.
Key birds: *Summer*: Pied Flycatcher, Wood Warbler. *All year*: usual woodland birds. Red squirrels, butterflies.
Contact: Trust HQ. 01539 816300.

SOUTH WALNEY

Cumbria Wildlife Trust.
Location: SD 215 620. Six miles S of Barrow-in-Furness.
Access: Open daily (10am-5pm) plus Bank Holidays. No dogs except assistance dogs. Small charge for day permits but Cumbria Wildlife Trust members free.
Facilities: Toilets, nature trails, six hides (one of which is wheelchair accessible), cottage available to rent.
Public transport: None.
Habitat: Shingle, lagoon, sand dune, saltmarsh.
Key birds: *Spring/autumn*: Passage migrants. *Summer*: Breeding Eider, Herring and Lesser Black-backed Gulls, Shelduck. *Winter*: Teal, Wigeon, Redshank, Oystercatcher, Knot, Twite.
Contact: Mick Venters, No 1 Coastguard Cottages, South Walney Nature Reserve, Walney Island, Barrow-in-Furness, Cumbria LA14 3YQ.
e-mail: cumbriawt@cix.co.uk
www.cumbriawildlifetrust.org.uk

TALKIN TARN COUNTRY PARK

Cumbria County Council.
Location: NY544 591. Twelve miles E of Carlisle. From A69 E at Brampton, head S on

B6413 for two miles. Talkin Tarn is on the E just after a level crossing.
Access: All year. Wheelchair access restricted by ten kissing gates.
Facilities: Toilets and restaurant open Easter-Oct (11am-4pm). Dogs allowed.
Public transport: Bus: infrequent. Tel: 0870 608 2608. Train: nearest station is Brampton Junction. Tel: 0845 748 4950.
Habitat: Natural tarn, mature woodland.
Key birds: *Spring/summer*: Pied Flycatcher, Spotted Flycatcher, Redstart, Chiffchaff, Wood Warbler. *Winter*: Grebes, Smew, Long-tailed Duck, Goosander, Gadwall.
Contact: Talkin Tarn Country Park, Brampton, Cumbria CA8 1HN. 01697 741050.
e-mail: ccs@cumbriacc.gov.uk
www.ccs-cumbria.com

WALNEY BIRD OBSERVATORY

For bookings write to Walney Bird Observatory, South End, Walney Island, Barrow-in-Furness, Cumbria LA14 3YQ.
Contact: As South Walney.

Derbyshire

DRAKELOW WILDFOWL RESERVE

Powergen PLC.
Location: SK 22 72 07. Drakelow Power Station, one mile NE of Walton-on-Trent.
Access: Permit by post from Drakelow Power Station, Burton-on-Trent. Open daily 9:30am-dusk (closed to 11am for wildfowl count on Sun once a month. Date in hide). Closed Jun. No dogs. Unsuitable in parts for disabled. Parties by special arrangement, limit ten.
Facilities: Seven hides, no other facilities
Public transport: Not known.
Habitat: Disused flooded gravel pits with wooded islands and reedbeds.
Key birds: *Summer*: Breeding Reed and Sedge Warblers. Water Rail, Hobby. *Winter*: Wildfowl (Goldeneye, Gadwall, Smew), Merlin. Regular sightings of Peregrine in Station area. Recent rarities include Little Egret, Cetti's Warbler and Golden Oriole. Excellent for dragonflies and butterflies.
Contact: Tom Cockburn, Hon, Warden, 1 Dickens Drive, Swadlincote, Derbys DE11 0DX. 01283 217146.

OGSTON RESERVOIR

Severn Trent Water Plc.
Location: From Matlock, take A615 E to B6014. From Chesterfield take A61 S of Clay Cross onto B6014 .
Access: View from roads, car parks or hides
Facilities: Four hides (three for Ogston BC members, one public), toilets. Information pack on request.
Public transport: None.

Habitat: Open water, pasture, mixed woodland.
Key birds: All three woodpeckers, Little and Tawny Owls, Kingfisher, Grey Wagtail, warblers. Passage raptors (inc. Osprey), terns and waders. *Winter*: Gull roost, wildfowl, tit and finch flocks.
Contact: Malcolm Hill, Manager,Ogston Bird Club, c/o 2 Sycamore Avenue, Glapwell, Chesterfield, S44 5LH. 01623 812159
www.ogstonbirdclub.co.uk

PADLEY GORGE SSSI

The National Trust (Yorkshire & North East).
Location: From Sheffield, take the A625. After eight miles, turn L on B6521 to Nether Padley. Grindleford Station is just off the B6521 (NW of Nether Padley) and one mile NE of Grindleford.
Access: All year. Not suitable for disabled or those unused to steep climbs. Some of the paths are rocky. No dogs allowed.
Facilities: Café and toilets at Grindleford Station.
Public transport: Bus: from Sheffield to Bakewell stops at Grindleford/Nether Padley. Tel: 01709 566 000. Train: from Sheffield to Manchester Piccadilly stops at Grindleford Station. Tel: 0161 228 2141.
Habitat: A steep-sided valley containing the largest area of sessile oak woodland in the south Pennines.
Key birds: *Summer*: Pied Flycatcher, Spotted Flycatcher, Redstart, Wheatear, Whinchat, Wood Warbler, Tree Pipit.
Contact: The National Trust Regional Offices for Yorkshire & North East, Goddards, 27 Tadcaster Road, Dringhouses, York YO24 1GG, 01904 702021. www.nationaltrust.org.uk

Devon

Key to sites:
1. Aylesbeare Common
2. Bowling Green Marsh
3. Burrator Reservoir
4. Chapel Wood
5. Dart Valley
6. Dawlish Warren NNR
7. Exminster Marshes
8. Haldon Woods
9. Old Sludge Beds
10. Otter Estuary
11. Plymbridge Wood
12. Prawle Point
13. Rackenford and Knowstone Moors
14. South Milton Ley
15. Stover Lake and Woods
16. Yarner Wood

AYLESBEARE COMMON

RSPB (South West Office).
Location: SY 058 897. Five miles E of J30 of the M5 at Exeter, 0.5 miles past the Halfway Inn on the B3052. Turn R to Hawkerland. The reserve is on the opposite side of the main road.
Access: Open all year. One track suitable for wheelchairs and pushchairs.
Facilities: Car park, picnic area, group bookings, guided walks and special events. Disabled access via metalled track to private farm
Public transport: None.
Habitat: Heathland, wood fringes, streams and ponds.
Key birds: *Spring/summer*: Nightjar, Stonechat. *All year*: Dartford Warbler, Buzzard. *Winter*: possible Hen Harrier.
Contact: Toby Taylor, Hawkerland Brake Barn, Exmouth Road, Aylesbeare, Nr Exeter, Devon, Nr Exeter, Devon EX5 2JS. 01395 233655.

BOWLING GREEN MARSH

RSPB (South West England Office).
Location: SX 972 876. On the E side of River Exe, four miles SE of Exeter, 0.5 miles SE of Topsham.
Access: Open at all times. Please park at the public car parks in Topsham, not in the lane by the reserve.
Facilities: One hide suitable for wheelchair access. Viewing platform overlooking estuary reached by steps from track. No toilets. No visitor centre.
Public transport: Exeter to Exmouth railway has regular (every 30 mins) service to Topsham station (half a mile from reserve). Stagecoach Devon – T bus has frequent service (every 10-20 mins) from Exeter to Topsham.
Habitat: Coastal grassland, open water/marsh, hedgerows.
Key birds: *Winter:* Wigeon, Shoveler, Teal, Black-tailed Godwit, Curlew, Golden Plover. *Spring*: Shelduck, passage waders – Whimbrel, passage Garganey and Yellow Wagtail. *Summer:* Gull/tern roosts, high tide wader roosts contain many passage birds. *Autumn:* Wildfowl, Peregrine, wader roosts.
Contact: RSPB, Unit 3, Lions Rest Estate, Station Road, Exminster, Exeter EX6 8DZ. 01392 824614. www.rspb.org.uk

BURRATOR RESERVOIR

South West Lakes Trust.
Location: SX 551 681. Lies 10 miles NE of Plymouth, off A386 (Tavistock road). At Yelverton take B3212 towards Princeton. Turn R at Burrator Inn and follow signs to reservoir.
Access: Open all year. Numerous free parking areas around reservoir. Main route is suitable for disabled but is also used by motorists and

cyclists. There are about 25 stiles around the reservoir.

Facilities: Toilets (not suitable for wheelchairs). Snacks and ice-creams available during summer. Notice board with walk details and local facts.

Public transport: Bus: daily from Plymouth to Dousland (a short walk from the reservoir). No 82 Western National or No 48 (Sun). Tel: 01752 402 060. Train: nearest station is Plymouth. Tel: 08457 484 950.

Habitat: Pine forests, wooded streams, open moorland scrub.

Key birds: *Winter:* Goosander, Dipper, Grey Wagtail, Green Sandpiper, Brambling, Crossbill, Siskin, Redpoll. *All year:* All three woodpeckers, Buzzard, Sparrowhawk, Kestrel, Barn Owl, Tree Sparrow.

Contact: South West Lakes Trust, Higher Coombepark, Lewdown, Okehampton, Devon EX20 4QT. 01837 871565. www.swlakestrust.org.uk

CHAPEL WOOD

Location: SS 483 413. Off minor road to Georgeham, W of A361 two miles N of Braunton.

Contact: Alan Worth, 65 Chanters Hill, Barnstaple, North Devon EX32 8DE.

DART VALLEY

Location: SX 680 727. On Dartmoor nine miles NW from Ashburton. From A38 'Peartree Cross' near Ashburton, follow signs towards Princetown. Access from National Park car parks at New Bridge (S) or Dartmeet (N).

Contact: Devon Wildlife Trust HQ.

DAWLISH WARREN NNR

Teignbridge District Council.

Location: SX 983 788. At Dawlish Warren on S side of Exe estuary mouth. Turn off A379 at sign to Warren Golf Club, between Cockwood and Dawlish. Turn into car park adjacent to Lea Cliff Holiday Park. Park at far end of car park and pass through two pedestrian gates.

Access: Open public access but avoid mudflats and beach beyond groyne nine at high tide due to roosting birds. Parking charges apply. Restricted access for dogs.

Facilities: Visitor centre (tel 01626 863980) open most weekends all year (10.30am-1pm and 2pm-5pm) also most Summer weekdays, but can be closed if warden on site. Toilets at entrance

tunnel and in resort area only. Hide open at all times – best around high tide.

Public transport: Train station at site, also regular bus service operated by Stagecoach.

Habitat: High tide roost site for wildfowl and waders of Exe estuary on mudflats and shore. Dunes, dune grassland, woodland, scrub, ponds.

Key birds: *Winter:* Waders and wildfowl – large numbers, plus divers and Slavonian Grebe off shore. *Summer:* Good for terns. Excellent variety all year, especially on migration.

Contact: Keri Walsh/Andrew Buckley/Philip Chambers, Countryside Management Section, Teignbridge District Council, Forde House, Brunel Road, Newton Abbot, Devon TQ12 4XX. Visitor centre: 01626 863980. Teignbridge District Council: 01626 361101 (Ext 5754).

EXMINSTER MARSHES

RSPB (South West England Office).

Location: SX 954 872. Five miles S of Exeter on W bank of River Exe, at Exminster.

Access: Open at all times.

Facilities: No toilets or visitor centre. Information in RSPB car park and marked footpaths across reserve.

Public transport: Stagecoach Devon (01392 427711). Exeter to Newton Abbot/Torquay buses – stops are 400 yds from car park.

Habitat: Coastal grazing marsh with freshwater ditches and pools, reed and scrub-flanked canal.

Key birds: *Winter:* Brent Goose, Wigeon, Water Rail, Short-eared Owl. *Spring:* Lapwing, Redshank and wildfowl breed, Cetti's Warbler on canal banks. *Summer:* Gull roosts, passage waders. *Autumn:* Peregrine, winter wildfowl.

Contact: RSPB, Unit 3, Lions Rest Estate, Station Road, Exminster, Exeter, Devon EX6 8DZ. 01392 824614. www.rspb.org.uk

HALDON WOODS
BIRD OF PREY VIEWPOINT

Forest Enterprise.

Location: Five miles W of Exeter. Follow signs for the racecourse. At A38 junction take the underpass road N towards Dunchideock. Continue N until you reach an open hillside on the L with extensive views. There is a car park L signed 'Bird of Prey Viewpoint'. Park at the bottom. Follow signs to the viewing point.

Access: Open all year.

Facilities: Viewing point with benches. Path suitable for wheelchair access.

Public transport: None.
Habitat: Plantations, clearings.
Key birds: *Spring/summer*: Wood, Grasshopper and other warblers, Redstart, Whinchat, possible Honey Buzzard, Cuckoo, Hobby, Nightjar, Turtle Dove, Tree Pipit, Woodcock. *All year*: Goshawk, Sparrowhawk, Great and Lesser Spotted Woodpecker, Stonechat, Willow Tit, Crossbill, Siskin, Redpoll.
Contact: Forest Enterprise, Bullers Hill, Kennford, Exeter, Devon EX6 7XR. 01392 832262.

OLD SLUDGE BEDS

Location: SX 952 888. Located on S edge of Exeter. Park at University boathouse car park at entrance to SWW sewage treatment works off A379 towards Dawlish. Walk along canal past sewage works to reach reserve.
Contact: Devon Trust HQ.

OTTER ESTUARY

Location: SY 076 822. Lies on E edge of Budleigh Salterton. Park at Lime Kiln car park at eastern end of seafront. Public footpath runs alongside reserve from here.
Contact: Devon Wildlife Trust HQ.

PLYMBRIDGE WOOD

National Trust/Forest Enterprise.
Location: From Plymouth, take A386 N to Estover roundabout, (near Wrigley factory), take Plymbridge Road on R. Park at bridge area at bottom of hill.
Access: Open all year.
Facilities: Car park, woodland paths, picnic area.
Public transport: None.
Habitat: Mixed woodland inc. conifers, river.
Key birds: *Spring/summer*: Cuckoo, Wood Warbler, Redstart, Blackcap, possible Nightjar, Crossbill. *Winter*: Woodcock, Snipe, Fieldfare, Redwing, Brambling, Siskin, Redpoll, possible Crossbill. *All year*: Mandarin Duck, Sparrowhawk, Buzzard, Kestrel, Tawny Owl, all three woodpeckers, Kingfisher, Grey Wagtail, Dipper, Goldcrest, Marsh Tit, Raven.
Contact: National Trust, Lanhydrock House, Lanhydrock, Cornwall PL30 4DE. 01208 432691.

PRAWLE POINT

Location: SE of Salcombe. Two acres by NT car park & two small plots in Pigs Nose Valley.
Access: Devon Birdwatching & Preservation Society members only.
Contact: See contact in County Directory.

RACKENFORD AND KNOWSTONE MOOR

Location: SS 858 211. Approx nine miles W of Tiverton along A361 (North Devon link road) to Barnstaple. Turn off at Moortown Cross junction to access reserve.
Contact: Devon Wildlife Trust HQ.

SOUTH MILTON LEY

Location: South coast near Thurlestone. W of Kingsbridge.
Access: Strictly DBW&PS members only, but can be overlooked from public footpath.
Contact: See contact in County Directory.

STOVER LAKE AND WOODS

Devon County Council.
Location: Two miles N of Newton Abbott off A38 Exeter-Plymouth road. Follow the A382 L at Drumbridges roundabout, signed to Newton Abbot. After 0.25 miles follow the brown tourist sign L into the car park (fee payable).
Access: Open all year.
Facilities: Car park, information centre, hide with feeding station.
Public transport: None.
Habitat: Mixed woodland, lake.
Key birds: *Spring/summer*: Sand Martin, Chiffchaff, Willow Warbler, Wood Warbler, Spotted Flycatcher, Nightjar. *Winter*: Water Rail, Marsh Tit, Snipe. *All year*: Woodpeckers, Jay, Siskin, Crossbill, Kingfisher.
Contact: Rangers Office, Devon County Council, Stover Country Park, Stover, Newton Abbot, Devon TQ12 6QG. 01626 835236.

YARNER WOOD

Location: SX 778 787. Part of East Dartmoor Woods and Heaths NNR. Two miles from Bovey Tracey on the road to Becky Falls and Manaton.
Contact: Site Manager, Yarner Wood, Bovey Tracey, Devon TW13 9LJ. 01626 832330. www.english-nature.org.uk

Dorset

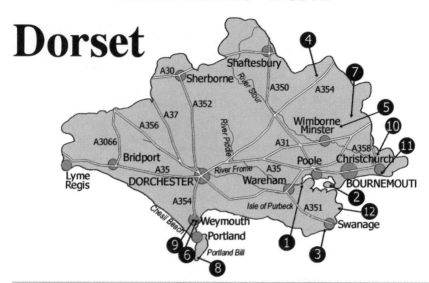

Key to sites:

1. Arne
2. Brownsea Island
3. Durlston Country Park
4. Garston Wood
5. Holt Heath
6. Lodmoor
7. Moors Valley CP and Ringwood Forest
8. Portland Bird Observatory
9. Radipole Lake
10. Sopley Common
11. Stanpit Marsh SSSI, LNR
12. Studland & Godlingston Heaths

ARNE

RSPB (South West England Office).
Location: SY 973 882. Four miles SE of Wareham, turn off A351 at Stoborough.
Access: Shipstal Point and hide open all year, with access from car park. Coaches and escorted parties by prior arrangement.
Facilities: Toilets in car park. Bird hide at Shipstal. Various footpaths. Reception hut (open end-May-early Sept).
Public transport: None.
Habitat: Lowland heath, woodland reedbed and saltmarsh leading to extensive mudflats of Poole Harbour.
Key birds: *All year*: Dartford Warbler, Little Egret, Stonechat. *Winter*: Hen Harrier, Red-breasted Merganser, Black-tailed Godwit. *Summer*: Nightjar, warblers. *Passage*: Spotted Redshank, Whimbrel, Greenshank, Osprey.
Contact: Neil Gartshore, (Senior Warden),Syldata, Arne, Wareham, Dorset BH20 5BJ01929 553360.
e-mail: neil.gartshore@rspb.org.uk
www.rspb.org.uk

BROWNSEA ISLAND

Dorset Wildlife Trust.
Location: SZ 026 883. Half hour boat ride from Poole Quay. Ten minutes from Sandbanks Quay (next to Studland chain-ferry).
Access: Apr, May, Jun, Sept and Oct. Access by self-guided nature trail. Costs £2 adults, £1 children. Jul, Aug access by afternoon guided tour (2.00pm daily, duration 105 minutes). Costs £2 adults, £1 children.
Facilities: Toilets, information centre, five hides, nature trail.
Public transport: Poole Rail/bus station for access to Poole Quay and boats.
Habitat: Saline lagoon, reedbed, lakes, coniferous and mixed woodland.
Key birds: *Spring*: Avocet, Black-tailed Godwit, waders, gulls and wildfowl. *Summer*: Common and Sandwich Terns, Yellow-legged Gull, Little Egret, Little Grebe, Golden Pheasant. *Autumn*: Curlew Sandpiper, Little Stint.
Contact: Chris Thain, The Villa, Brownsea Island, Poole, Dorset BH13 7EE01202 709445.
e-mail: dorsetwtisland@cix.co.uk
www.wildlifetrust.org.uk/dorset

NATURE RESERVES - ENGLAND

DURLSTON COUNTRY PARK

Dorset County Council.
Location: SZ 032 774. One mile S of Swanage (signposted).
Access: Visitor centre in car park open weekends during winter and daily in other seasons (phone for times).
Facilities: Guided walks.
Public transport: 2 buses per day except Sundays and Bank Holidays.
Habitat: Grassland, hedges, cliff.
Key birds: Cliff-nesting seabird colonies; good variety of scrub and woodland breeding species; spring and autumn migrants; seawatching esp. Apr/May & Aug/Nov.
Contact: The Ranger, Durlston Country Park, Swanage, Dorset BH19 2JL. 01929 424443. www.durlston.co.uk

GARSTON WOOD

Location: SU 004 194. Small car park on Sixpenny Handley to Bowerchalke minor road, off B3081 midway between Salisbury and Blandford Forum.
Contact: Warden: Jack Edwards c/o Arne, above,

HOLT HEATH

English Nature (Dorset Team).
Location: SU 047 036 (Whitesheet car park). Located W of Ringwood and four miles NE of Wimborne Minster. From A31, two miles E of Wimborne, take minor road N to Broomhill and Holt. After two miles, turn right at Broomhill crossroads. From there, 1.5 miles to Whitesheet car park.
Access: Open access on foot. Dogs to be kept under close control.
Facilities: None.
Public transport: Buses to Colehill about three miles away – Wilts & Dorset.
Habitat: Heathland, woodland.
Key birds: *Spring/summer*: Dartford Warbler, Stonechat, Nightjar, Tree Pipit. *Winter*: Hen Harrier, Merlin.
Contact: Ian Nicol, (Site Manager),English Nature, Slepe Farm, Arne, Wareham, Dorset BH20 5BN01202 841026.
e-mail: ian.nicol@english-nature.org.uk

LODMOOR

RSPB (South West England Office).
Location: SY 686 807. Adjacent Lodmoor Country Park, in Weymouth, off A353 to Wareham.
Access: Open all times.
Facilities: One viewing shelter, network of paths.
Public transport: Local bus service.
Habitat: Marsh, shallow pools, reeds and scrub, remnant saltmarsh.
Key birds: *Spring/summer*: Breeding Common Tern, warblers (including Reed, Sedge, Grasshopper and Cetti's), Bearded Tit. *Winter*: Wildfowl and waders. Passage waders and other migrants.
Contact: Keith Ballard, RSPB Visitor Centre, Swannery Car Park, Weymouth DT4 7TZ01305 778313. www.rspb.org.uk

MOORS VALLEY COUNTRY PARK AND RINGWOOD FOREST

East Dorset District Council/Forest Enterprise.
Location: Two miles W of Ringwood, well-signposted from the Horton Road between Ashley Heath and Woolsbridge.
Access: Open every day (except Christmas Day) 7am-dusk.
Facilities: Car parks (9.30am-4.30pm), visitor centre.
Public transport: None.
Habitat: River, wet meadow, lakes, scrub, broad-leaved woodland, coniferous forest, golf course.
Key birds: *Spring/summer*: Hobby, Cuckoo, Nightjar, Sand Martin, Tree Pipit, Lesser Whitethroat. *Winter*: Teal, Pochard, Gadwall, Snipe, Redpoll, occasional Brambling. *Passage*: Whimbrel, Common Sandpiper, waders. *All year*: Buzzard, Lapwing, Woodcock, Little Owl, Grey Wagtail, Dartford Warbler, Crossbill, usual woodland species.
Contact: Moors Valley Country Park, Horton Road, Ashley Heath, Nr Ringwood, Dorset BH24 2ET, 01425 470721. www.moors-valley.co.uk e-mail: moorsvalley@eastdorset.gov.uk

PORTLAND BIRD OBSERVATORY

Portland Bird Observatory (independent registered charity).
Location: SY 681 690. Six miles S of Weymouth beside the road to Portland Bill.
Access: Open at all times. Parking only for

members of Portland Bird Observatory. Self-catering accommodation for up to 20. Take own towels, sheets, sleeping bags.
Facilities: Displays and information, toilets, natural history bookshop, equipped kitchen, laboratory.
Public transport: Bus service from Weymouth (First Dorset Transit Route 1).
Habitat: Scrub and ponds.
Key birds: *Spring/autumn*: Migrants including many rarities. *Summer*: Breeding auks, Fulmar, Kittiwake.
Contact: Martin Cade, Old Lower Light, Portland Bill, Dorset DT5 2JT
e-mail: obs@btinternet.com
www.portlandbirdobs.btinternet.co.uk

RADIPOLE LAKE

RSPB (South West England Office).
Location: SY 677 796. In Weymouth. Enter from Swannery car park on footpaths.
Access: Visitor centre and nature trail open every day, summer (9am-5pm), winter (9am-4pm). Hide open (8.30am-4.30pm). Permit available from visitor centre required by non-RSPB members.
Facilities: Network of paths, one hide, one viewing shelter.
Public transport: Close to train station which serves London and Bristol.
Habitat: Lake, reedbeds.
Key birds: *Winter*: Wildfowl. *Summer*: Breeding reedbed warblers (including Cetti's), Bearded Tit, passage waders and other migrants. Garganey regular in Spring. Good for rarer gulls.
Contact: Keith Ballard, RSPB Visitor Centre, Swannery Car Park, Weymouth DT4 7TZ01305 778313. www.rspb.org.uk

SOPLEY COMMON

Dorset Wildlife Trust.
Location: SZ 132 975. Four miles NW of Christchurch near Hurn village.
Access: Open at all times. Permits required for surveying and group visits. Dogs allowed under close control. Limited access for disabled.
Facilities: None.
Public transport: None.
Habitat: Lowland heath (dry and wet) and deciduous woodland.
Key birds: *Summer*: Breeding Dartford Warbler, Nightjar, Woodlark, Stonechat. Also Hobby.

Winter: Snipe.
Contact: Rob Brunt, Dorset Wildlife Trust, Brooklands Farm, Forston, Dorchester, Dorset DT2 7AA01305 264620.
e-mail: rbrunt@dorsetwt.cix.co.uk
www.wildlifetrust.org.uk/dorset

STANPIT MARSH

Stanpit Marsh Advisory Panel, Community Services, Christchurch Borough Council.
Location: SZ 167 924.
Access: Public open space.
Facilities: Information centre.
Public transport: Wilts & Dorset bus no 123 (tel 01202 673555) Stanpit recreation ground stop. Bournemouth Yellow Buses no 20 (tel 01202 636000) Purewell Cross roundabout stop.
Habitat: Salt, fresh, brackish marsh, sand dune and scrub.
Key birds: *Estuarine*: Waders, winter wildfowl, migrants. Reedbed: Bearded Tit, Cetti's Warbler. *Scrub*: Sedge Warbler, Reed Warbler. River/streams/bankside: Kingfisher. Feeding and roosting site.
Contact: Peter Holloway, Christchurch Countryside Service, Steamer Point Nature Reserve, Highcliffe, Christchurch, Dorset BH23 4XX. 01425 272479.
e-mail: countrysideservice@christchurch.gov.uk

STUDLAND & GODLINGSTON HEATHS

English Nature (Dorset Team).
Location: SZ 030 846. From Ferry Road N of Studland village.
Access: Open all year.
Facilities: Hides, nature trails.
Public transport: None.
Habitat: Woodland, heath, dunes, inter-tidal mudflats, saltings, freshwater lake, reedbeds, carr.
Key birds: Water Rail, Reed and Dartford Warblers, Nightjar, Stonechat. *Winter*: Wildfowl. Studland Bay, outside the reserve, has winter Black-necked and Slavonian Grebes, Scoter, Eider.
Contact: English Nature, Slepe Farm, Arne, Wareham, Dorset BH19 3AX. 01929 450259.

Durham

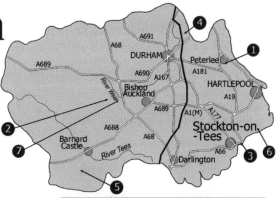

Key to sites:
1. Castle Eden Dene
2. Hamsterley Forest
3. Maze Hill and Portrack Marsh
4. Rainton Meadows
5. Stang Forest and Hope Moor
6. Teesmouth
7. Witton-Le-Wear (Low Barns)

CASTLE EDEN DENE

English Nature (Northumbria Team).
Location: NZ 435 397. Adjacent to Peterlee, signposted from A19 and Peterlee town centre.
Access: Open from 8am-8pm or sunset if earlier. Car park. Dogs under tight control please.
Facilities: Car parking at Oakerside Dene Lodge. 12 miles of footpath, two waymarked trails.
Public transport: Bus to Peterlee town centre.
Habitat: Yew/oak/sycamore woodland, paramaritime, limestone grassland.
Key birds: More than 170 recorded, 50 regular breeding species, typical woodland species.
Contact: Rob Lamboll, Oakerside Dene Lodge, Stanhope Chase, Peterlee, Co Durham SR8 1NJ 0191 586 0004.

HAMSTERLEY FOREST

Forest Enterprise.
Location: NZ 093 315. Eight miles NW of Bishop Auckland. Main entrance is five miles from A68, S of Witton-le-Wear and signposted through Hamsterley village and Bedburn.
Access: Open all year. Toll charge. Vehicles should not be left unattended after dark.
Facilities: Visitor Centre, toilets, shop, access for disabled. Please do not enter fenced farmland.
Public transport: None.
Habitat: Commercial woodland, mixed and broadleaved trees.
Key birds: *Spring/summer*: Willow Warbler, Chiffchaff, Wood Warbler, Redstart, Pied Flycatcher. *Winter*: Crossbill, Redwing, Fieldfare. *All year*: Jay, Dipper, Green Woodpecker.
Contact: Forest Enterprise, Eels Burn, Bellingham, Hexham, Northumberland NE48 2AJ, 01434 220242.
e-mail: pippa.kirkham@forestry.gsi.gov.uk

MAZE PARK AND PORTRACK MARSH

Tees Valley Wildlife Trust.
Location: NZ 463 190. Located midway between Middlesbrough and Stockton. Access from A66 at Tees Barrage. Sites are located on opposite banks to the River Tees, E of the barrage.
Access: No permits required. National cycle route passes through Maze Park. Surfaced paths at both sites. Hide suitable for disabled users at Portrack Marsh. Please keep to rights of way.
Facilities: Hide at Portrack Marsh. No toilets or visitor centre.
Public transport: Regular buses between Middlesbrough and Stockton stop at the Tees Barrage (Arriva, tel 0870 6082608). Thornaby Station one mile. Frequent trains from Darlington and Middlesbrough.
Habitat: Freshwater marsh, scrub, post-industrial grassland, riverside.
Key birds: *Winter*: Ducks, passage waders, Redshank, Snipe, Lapwing, Grey Heron, Sky Lark, Grey Partridge, Sand Martin, occasional Kingfisher and Grasshopper Warbler.
Contact: Bill Ashton-Wickett, Bellamy Pavilion, Kirkleatham Old Hall, Kirkleatham, Redcar TS10 5NW. 01642 759900.
e-mail: teesvaleywt@cix.co.uk
www.wildlifetrust.org.uk/teesvalley

RAINTON MEADOWS

Durham Wildlife Trust, the City of Sunderland and RJB Mining (UK) Ltd.
Location: NZ 326 486. Located W of A690 between Durham and Sunderland. Just S of Houghton-le-Spring turn onto B1284, signposted to Fence Houses and Hetton-le-Hole. Head W

towards Fence Houses and turn L at the first roundabout after 0.5 miles into Rye Hill Site.
Access: Park at Visitor Centre (entrance gate locked at 4.30pm) or Mallard Way. Paths generally wheelchair-accessible but there are some muddy areas. Main circular walk.
Facilities: Visitor Centre, toilets, café, log book, shop, wildlife display. Dogs on lead.
Public transport: Buses from Sunderland and Durham (222 and 220) stop at Mill Inn. Reserve is reached via B1284 passing under A690. Bus from Chester-le-Street (231) stops at Fencehouses Station. Walk E along B1284. Tel: Traveline 0870 608 2608.
Habitat: Reedbed, ponds, young tree plantation.
Key birds: *Spring/summer*: Great Crested Grebe, Ruddy Duck, Cuckoo, Whinchat, Reed Warbler. *Winter*: Water Rail, Kingfisher, Peregrine, Merlin, Long and Short-eared Owls. *Passage*: waders.
Contact: Trust HQ, Rainton Meadows, Chilton Moor, Houghton-le-Spring, Tyne & Wear DH4 6PU, 0191 5843112.
e-mail: durhamwt@cix.co.uk
www.wildlifetrust.org.uk/durham

STANG FOREST AND HOPE MOOR

Forest Enterprise.
Location: NZ 022 075. The wood is six miles S of Barnard Castle. On A66 follow signs for Reeth after the turn-of to Barnard Castle on the W-bound carriageway. Stang is then about 3.5 miles from the A66 (car park for Hope Edge Walk).
Access: Open all year. Road dangerous in frost.
Facilities: Number of parking lay-bys and forest trails. Best for birdwatchers heads E and then N to Hope Edge.
Public transport: None.
Habitat: Woodland, moorland.
Key birds: *Spring/summer*: Whinchat, Wheatear, Cuckoo. *All year*: Red Grouse, Crossbill.
Contact: Forest Enterprise, Eels Burn, Bellingham, Hexham, Northumberland NE48 2AJ, 01434 220242.

TEESMOUTH

English Nature (Northumbria).
Location: Two components, centred on NZ 535 276 and NZ 530 260, three and five miles S of Hartlepool, E of A178. Access to northern component from car park at NZ 534 282, 0.5 miles E of A178. Access to southern compartment from A178 bridge over Greatham Creek at NZ 510 254.
Access: Open at all times. In northern component, no restrictions over most of dunes and North Gare Sands (avoid golf course, dogs must be kept under close control). In southern component, disabled access path to public hides at NZ 516 255 and NZ 516 252 (no other access).
Facilities: Nearest toilets at Seaton Carew, one mile to the N. Disabled access path and hides (see above), interpretive panels and leaflet. Teesmouth Field Centre (Tel: 01429 264912).
Public transport: Hourly bus service operates Mon-Sat between Middlesbrough and Hartlepool, along A178 (service X9, Stagecoach Hartlepool, Tel: 01429 267082).
Habitat: Grazing marsh, sand dune, intertidal flats.
Key birds: Passage and winter wildfowl and waders. Passage terns and skuas in late summer. Scarce passerine migrants and rarities. *Winter*: Merlin, Peregrine, Snow Bunting, Twite, divers, grebes.
Contact: Mike Leakey, English Nature, c/o British Energy, Tees Road, Hartlepool TS25 2BZ01429 853325. www.english-nature.org.uk
e-mail: northumbria@english-nature.org.uk

WITTON-LE-WEAR (Low Barns)

Durham Wildlife Trust.
Location: NZ 160 315. Off unclassified road between Witton-le-Wear (signposted on A68) and High Grange.
Access: Open all year.
Facilities: Three hides two with disabled access), observation tower above visitor centre (manned), nature trail.
Public transport: None.
Habitat: Former gravel workings, lake, ponds, riverbank.
Key birds: *All Year*: Greylag Geese, Kingfisher. *Summer*: Goosander, Grey Wagtail, Redpoll have bred. *Winter*: Wildfowl (inc. Goldeneye, Shoveler).
Contact: Visitor Centre Manager, Low Barns Nature Reserve, Witton-le-Wear, Bishop Auckland, Co Durham DL14 0AG. 01388 488728.

Essex

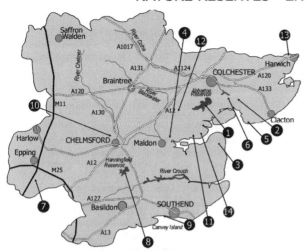

Key to sites:
1. Abberton Reservoir
2. Alexander Reserve
3. Bradwell Bird Observatory
4. Chigborough Lakes
5. Colne Point
6. Fingringhoe Wick
7. Hainault Forest
8. Hanningfield Reservoir
9. Leigh
10. Little Waltham Meadows
11. Old Hall Marshes
12. Oxley Meadow
13. Stour Estuary
14. Tollesbury Wick NR

ABBERTON RESERVOIR

Location: TL 963 185. Six miles SW of Colchester on B1026. Follow signs from Layer-de-la-Haye.
Contact: Centre Manager, Essex Wildlife Trust, Abberton Reservoir Visitor Centre, Layer-de-la-Haye, Colchester CO2 0EU. 01206 738172.
e-mail: abberton@essexwt.org.uk

ALEXANDER RESERVE

Essex Wildlife Trust.
Location: GR 079 208. Mid-way between Clacton and Colchester off B1027 at the bottom of Tenpenny Hill, Thorrington, on the Thorrington/Alresford border.
Access: Awaiting installation of footbridge.
Facilities: None.
Public transport: Bus: roughly hourly from Colchester. Stop, opposite and at the bottom of Tenpenny Hill.
Habitat: Freshwater marsh and grassland.
Key birds: *Spring/summer*: Warblers, Bullfinch, Kingfisher. *Winter*: Grey Wagtail, Snipe, Siskin, all three woodpeckers.
Contact: Trust HQ, Abbotts Hall Farm, Great Wigborough, Colchester, Essex CO5 7RT, 01621 862960. e-mail: admin@essexwt.org.uk
www.essexwt.org.uk

BRADWELL BIRD OBSERVATORY

Essex Birdwatching Society
Location: 100 yards S of St Peter's Chapel,

Bradwell-on-Sea. Mouth of Blackwater estuary, between Maldon and Foulness.
Access: Open all year.
Facilities: Accommodation for eight in hut; two rooms each with four bunks; blankets, cutlery, etc. supplied.
Public transport: None.
Habitat: Mudflats, saltmarsh.
Key birds: *Winter*: Wildfowl (inc. Brent Geese, Red-throated Diver, Red-breasted Merganser), large numbers of waders; small numbers of Twite, Snow Bunting and occasional Shore Lark on beaches, also Hen Harrier, Merlin and Peregrine. Good passage of migrants usual in spring and autumn. *Summer*: Small breeding population of terns and other estuarine species.
Contact: Graham Smith, 48 The Meads, Ingatestone, Essex CM4 0AE. 01277 354034.

CHIGBOROUGH LAKES

Essex Wildlife Trust.
Location: GR 877 086. Lies NE of Maldon, about one mile from Heybridge on B1026 towards Tolleshunt d'Arcy. In Chigborough Road, go past fishery entrance and Chigborough Farm buildings to entrance gate to Chigborough Quarry. The reserve entrance on L.
Access: Open all year. Please take care not to obstruct the gravel pit entrance.
Facilities: None.
Public transport: Bus: Colchester to Maldon Leisure Centre along the B1026.
Habitat: Flooded gravel pits, small ponds, willow carr, grassland, scrub.

Key birds: *Spring/summer*: Sedge and Reed Warblers, Whitethroat, Reed Bunting, Willow Warbler, Great Crested and Little Grebes, Kingfisher, Water Rail. *Passage*: Waders including Greenshank. Grass snakes and common lizards, common blue, small copper and ringlet butterflies and various dragonflies.
Contact: Trust HQ, Abbotts Hall Farm, Great Wigborough, Colchester, Essex CO5 7RT, warden: 01621 853 969, Trust office 01621 862960. e-mail: admin@essexwt.org.uk www.essexwt.org.uk

COLNE POINT

Location: TM 108 125. W of Clacton, via B1027 to St Osyth then Lee Wick Lane. Car park just inside reserve on seaward side of sea wall (liable to flood at very high tides).
Contact: Essex Trust HQ.

FINGRINGHOE WICK

Essex Wildlife Trust.
Location: TM 046 197. Colchester five miles. The reserve is signposted from B1025 to Mersea Island, S of Colchester.
Access: Open six days per week (not Mon or Christmas or Boxing Day). No permits needed. Donations invited. Centre/reserve open (9am-5pm). Dogs must be on a lead.
Facilities: Visitor centre – toilets, shop, light refreshments, car park, displays. Reserve – seven bird hides, two nature trails, plus one for disabled visitors.
Public transport: The reserve is best reached by car, coach.
Habitat: Old gravel pit, large lake, many ponds, sallow/birch thickets, young scrub, reedbeds, saltmarsh, gorse heathland.
Key birds: *Autumn/winter*: Brent Goose, waders, Hen Harriers, Little Egrets. *Spring*: 40 male Nightingales. Good variety of warblers in scrub, thickets, reedbeds and Turtle Doves, Green/Great Spotted Woodpeckers. *Winter*: Dabchicks, Mute Swans, Teal, Wigeon, Shoveler, Gadwall on lake.
Contact: Laurie Forsyth, Wick Farm, South Green Road, Fingringhoe, Colchester, Essex CO5 7DN. e-mail: admin@essexwt.org.uk www.essexwt.org.uk

HAINAULT FOREST

Redbridge Council.
Location: GR 473 924. On NE outskirts of London, between M11 and Romford. Main

entrance at Foxburrows Road is off Romford Road (A1112) about one mile S of Chigwell Row, reached from S from A12 (London-Chelmsford) and the N from the A113 (Woodford-Chelmsford).
Access: Open all year. The car park at Foxburrows Road is open from 7am-dusk, the other car parks are always open.
Facilities: Visitor Centre, toilets, café.
Public transport: Bus: from Romford, Chadwell Heath and Barkingside. Train: nearest station Ilford (Liverpool St line) and Hainault (Central Line tube).
Habitat: Grassland, scrub, ancient woodland, heathland, lake.
Key birds: *All year*: Woodland birds, including all three woodpeckers, numbers increasing in spring when migrants, including Spotted Flycatchers arrive for summer. Area very good for bats in summer.
Contact: Hainault Forest CP. 0208 500 7353.

HANNINGFIELD RESERVOIR

Essex Wildlife Trust.
Location: TQ 725 972. Three miles N of Wickford. Exit off A130 at Rettendon onto South Hanningfield Road. Follow this for two miles until reaching the T-junction with Hawkswood Road. Turn right and the entrance to the Visitor Centre and reserve is one mile on the right.
Access: Open Tue-Sun (9am-5pm) plus Bank Holiday Mon. Disabled parking, toilets, and adapted birdwatching hide. No dogs. No cycling.
Facilities: Visitor centre, gift shop, optics, refreshments, toilets, four bird hides, picnic area, coach parking, education room.
Public transport: Chelmsford to Wickford bus no 14 to Downham village and walk half mile down Crowsheath Lane.
Habitat: One hundred acre mixed woodland with grassy glades and rides, adjoining the 870 acre Hanningfield Reservoir, designated an SSSI due to its high numbers of wildfowl.
Key birds: *Spring*: Good numbers and mix of woodland warblers. *Summer*: Vast numbers of Swifts, Swallows and martins feeding over the water. Hobby and Osprey. *Winter*: Good numbers and mix of waterfowl. Large gull roost.
Contact: Chris Scott, Hanningfield Reservoir Visitor Centre, Hawkswood Road, Downham, Billericay CM11 1WT. 01268 711001. www.essexwt.org.uk

LEIGH

Location: TQ 824 852. Two Tree Island, approached from Leigh on Sea.
Contact: Essex Wildlife Trust HQ.

LITTLE WALTHAM MEADOWS

Essex Wildlife Trust.
Location: GR 713 119. Reserve lies N of Chelmsford about one mile W of A130 (Essex Regiment Way), just S of Little Waltham. Access is via Back Lane, Little Waltham. Park on the wide verge at the end of the bridleway.
Access: Open all year.
Facilities: None.
Public transport: Bus: from Chelmsford to Little Waltham via Broomfield to W and Essex Regiment Way to E.
Habitat: Old flood meadows, dry meadows, alder carr woodland, river.
Key birds: *All year*: Green Woodpecker, Tawny Owl, Kestrel, Kingfisher.
Contact: Trust HQ. 01621 862960.

OLD HALL MARSHES

RSPB (East Anglia Office).
Location: TL 97 51 25. Approx eight miles S of Colchester. From A12 take B1023, via Tiptree, to Tolleshunt D'Arcy. Then take Chapel Road (back road to Tollesbury), after one mile turn left into Old Hall Lane. Continue up Old Hall Lane, over speed ramp and through iron gates to cattle grid, then follow signs to car park.
Access: Permit only in advance from Warden. Open 9am-9pm or dusk, closed Tue.
Facilities: Two trails – one of three miles and one of 6.5 miles. Two viewing screens at E end of reserve. No visitor centre or toilets.
Public transport: None.
Habitat: Coastal grazing marsh, reedbed, saline lagoon, saltmarsh and mudflat.
Key birds: *Summer*: Breeding Avocet, Redshank, Lapwing, Pochard, Shoveler, Gadwall, Garganey, Barn Owl. *Winter*: Brent Goose, Wigeon, Teal Shoveler, Goldeneye, Red-breasted Merganser, all the expected waders, Hen Harrier, Merlin, Short-eared Owl and Twite. *Passage*: All expected waders (particularly Spotted Redshank, Green Sandpiper and Whimbrel), Yellow Wagtail, Whinchat and Wheatear.
Contact: Paul Charlton, Site Manager, c/o 1 Old Hall Lane, Tolleshunt D'Arcy, Maldon, Essex CM9 8TP. 01621 869015.
e-mail: paul.charlton@rspb.org.uk

OXLEY MEADOW

Essex Wildlife Trust.
Location: GR 918 149. Lies SW of Colchester. Leave A12 at Kelvedon exit following the B1023 towards Tiptree. Pass through village down Factory Hill to a Y junction and turn L towards Mersea. Take first L down Park Lane just after the telephone box. The reserve entrance is 2nd L. Limited parking for about six cars.
Access: Open all year.
Facilities: None.
Public transport: Bus: regular Colchester-Maldon buses to Tiptree. The reserve is then one mile along footpaths.
Habitat: Two flower-rich meadows, hedgerows, trees.
Key birds: *Spring/summer*: Lesser Whitethroat, usual woodland species.
Contact: Trust HQ. 01621 862960.

STOUR ESTUARY

RSPB (East Anglia Office).
Location: TM 191 310. Car park – by B1352 Harwich-Manningtree Road, five miles W of Harwich, 0.5 miles E of Wrabness.
Contact: Rick Vonk, 80 California Road, Mistley, Essex, CO11 1JN. 1603 661662.
e-mail: rick.vonk@RSPB.org.uk

TOLLESBURY WICK

Essex Wildlife Trust.
Location: GR 970 104. On Blackwater Estuary eight miles E of Maldon. Follow B1023 to Tollesbury via Tiptree, leaving A12 at Kelvedon. Then follow Woodrolfe Road S towards the marina. Use car park at Woodrolfe Green.
Access: Open all times along public footpath on top of sea wall.
Facilities: Toilets at Woodrolfe Green car park.
Public transport: Bus services run to Tollesbury from Maldon, Colchester and Witham.
Habitat: Estuary with fringing saltmarsh and mudflats with some shingle. Extensive freshwater grazing marsh.
Key birds: *Winter*: Wildfowl and waders, Short-eared Owl, Hen Harrier. *Summer*: Breeding Avocet, Redshank, Lapwing, occasional Little Tern, Reed and Sedge Warblers, Reed, Corn Bunting, Barn Owl.
Contact: Jonathan Smith, Tollesbury, Maldon, Essex CM9 8RJ. 01621 868628.
e-mail: jonathans@essexwt.org.uk

Gloucestershire

Key to sites:
1. Ashleworth Ham and Meerend Thicket
2. Coombe Hill Meadows
3. Cotswold Water Park
4. Highnam Woods
5. Nagshead
6. Slimbridge
7. Symond's Yat
8. Whelford Pools
9. Woorgreens Lake and Marsh

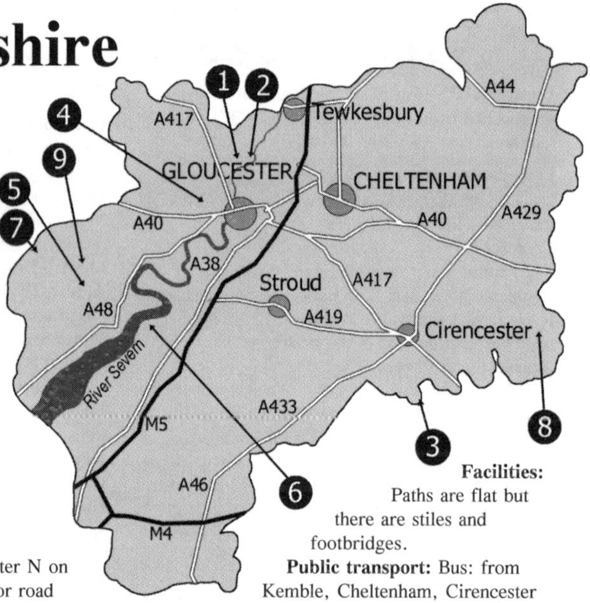

(Map of Gloucestershire with numbered site markers, showing towns Tewkesbury, Gloucester, Cheltenham, Stroud, Cirencester, roads A44, A417, A40, A429, A38, A48, A433, A419, A46, M5, M4, and River Severn)

ASHLEWORTH HAM & MEEREND THICKET

Gloucestershire Wildlife Trust.
Location: SO830265. Leave Gloucester N on A417; R at Hartpury and follow minor road through Ashleworth towards Hasfield.
Contact: Trust HQ, 01452 383333.

COOMBE HILL MEADOWS

Gloucestershire Wildlife Trust.
Location: SO 887 272. NNE of Gloucester. W of A38 between Apperley and The Leigh.
Access: Open at all times.
Facilities: None.
Public transport: None.
Habitat: Disused canal and adjacent flood meadows. Enlarged in 2001 with 140 acres for wetland restoration. Scrapes due to be excavated in Sept 2002, hides and circular walk in Sept 2003.
Key birds: *Winter:* Wildfowl (large numbers of Wigeon and Teal; also Bewick's Swan, Pintail, Gadwall, Goldeneye). Good range of migrant warblers.
Contact: Trust HQ, 01452 383333.

COTSWOLD WATER PARK

Cotswold Water Park Society.
Location: SU 028 953. From Cirencester, take the A419 SE. Turn L after three miles onto B4696. Take fourth turning on R to Keynes Country Park (Spratsgate Lane). The Nature Reserve car park is on R.
Access: Open all year.

Facilities: Paths are flat but there are stiles and footbridges.
Public transport: Bus: from Kemble, Cheltenham, Cirencester and Swindon. Tel: 08457 090 899. Train: nearest station is four miles away at Kemble. Tel: 08457 484 950.
Habitat: Gravel extraction which has created 130 lakes, set to become one of the largest man-made wetland sites in Europe.
Key birds: *Winter:* Common wildfowl, Smew, Red-crested Pochard. *Summer:* warblers, Nightingale, Hobby.
Contact: Cotswold Water Park Society, Keynes Country Park, Shorncote, Cirencester, Glos GL7 6DF, 01285 862777.

HIGHNAM WOODS

RSPB (Central England Office).
Location: SO 778 190. Signed on A40 three miles W of Gloucester.
Access: Open at all times, no permit required. Disabled access to a hide 120 yards from car park. The nature trails can be very muddy. Dogs allowed on leads.
Facilities: One nature trail (approx 1.5 miles), one birdwatching hide with winter bird-feeding programme.
Public transport: Contact Glos. CC public transport information line. Tel: 01452 425543.
Habitat: Ancient woodland in the Severn Vale with areas of coppice and scrub.
Key birds: *Spring/summer:* The reserve has Gloucestershire's main concentration of

NATURE RESERVES - ENGLAND

Nightingales – about 20 pairs. Resident birds include all three woodpeckers, Buzzard and Sparrowhawk. Ravens are frequently seen.
Contact: Ivan Proctor, The Puffins, Parkend, Lydney, Glos GL15 4JA. 01594 562852.
e-mail: ivan.proctor@rspb.org.uk
www.rspb.org.uk

NAGSHEAD

RSPB (Central England Office).
Location: SO 097 085. In Forest of Dean, N of Lydney. Signed immediately W of Parkend village on the road to Coleford.
Access: Open at all times, no permit required. The reserve is hilly and there are some stiles to negotiate on the nature trails. Dogs must be kept under close control.
Facilities: There are two nature trails (one mile and 2.25 miles). Information centre open at weekends mid-Apr to end Aug.
Public transport: Contact Glos. County Council public transport information line, 01452 425543.
Habitat: Much of the reserve is 200-year-old oak plantations, grazed in some areas by sheep. The rest of the reserve is a mixture of open areas and conifer/mixed woodland.
Key birds: *Spring*: Pied Flycatcher, Wood Warbler, Redstart, warblers. *Summer*: Siskin, Crossbill in some years. *All year*: Buzzard, Raven, all three woodpeckers.
Contact: Ivan Proctor, The Puffins, Parkend, Lydney, Glos GL15 4JA. 01594 562852.
e-mail: ivan.proctor@rspb.org.uk
www.rspb.org.uk

SLIMBRIDGE

The Wildfowl & Wetlands Trust.
Location: SO 723 048. Signposted from M5 (exit 13 or 14).
Access: Open daily except Christmas Day, (9am-5.30pm, 5pm in winter).
Facilities: Hides, observatory, observation tower, Hanson Discovery Centre, wildlife art gallery, tropical house, facilities for disabled, worldwide collection of wildfowl species.
Public transport: None.
Habitat: Reedbed, saltmarsh, freshwater pools, mudflats.
Key birds: Kingfisher, waders, raptors. *Winter*; Wildfowl esp. Bewick's Swans, White-fronted Geese, Wigeon, Teal.
Contact: Jane Allen, Marketing Manager, The Wildfowl & Wetlands Trust, Slimbridge, Gloucester GL2 7BT. 01453 890333.

SYMONDS YAT

RSPB/Forest Enterprise.
Location: Hill-top site on the edge of Forest of Dean, three miles N of Coleford on the B4432 signposted from the Forest Enterprise car park. Also signposted from A40 S of Ross-on-Wye.
Access: Daily Apr-Aug only.
Facilities: Car park, toilets with adapted facilities for disabled visitors, picnic area, drinks and light snacks, environmental education programmes available, enquire at reserve for details.
Public transport: None.
Habitat: Cliff above the River Wye and woodland.
Key birds: *Summer*: Peregrine, nuthatch and other woodland species.
Contact: The Puffins, Parkend, Lydney, Gloucestershire GL15 4JA, 01594 562852.

WHELFORD POOLS

Gloucestershire Wildlife Trust.
Location: SU 174 995. SE of Fairford. Leave Fairford E on A417, turn towards Whelford and reserve is on left (just before Whelford sign).
Access: Open at all times.
Facilities: Two hides, one with wheelchair access.
Public transport: None.
Habitat: Flooded gravel pits in eastern section of Cotswold Water Park.
Key birds: On main passage flight route (Yellow Wagtail, Black Tern, Osprey, waders). *Summer:* Breeding Common Tern, Hobby. *Winter:* Wildfowl.
Contact: Trust HQ, 01452 383333.

WOORGREENS LAKE AND MARSH

Gloucestershire Wildlife Trust.
Location: SO 630 127. Forest of Dean, W of Cinderford, N of B4226 Cannop road.
Access: Open at all times.
Facilities: None.
Public transport: None.
Habitat: Marsh, lake, heath on reclaimed opencast coalmine.
Key birds: Stonechat, Tree Pipit, Nightjar; birds of prey (inc, Buzzard, Goshawk, occasional Hobby). Passage waders (inc. Greenshank, Spotted Redshank, Green Sandpiper).
Contact: Trust HQ, 01452 383333.

Hampshire

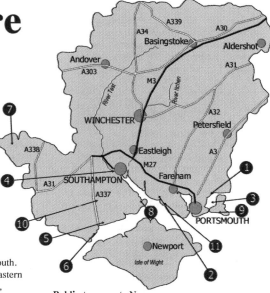

Key to sites:
1. Farlington Marshes
2. Hook-With-Warsash LNR
3. Langstone Harbour
4. Lower Test
5. Lymington Reedbeds
6. Lymington-Keyhaven NNR
7. Martin Down
8. North Solent
9. Pilsey Island
10. Roydon Woods
11. Titchfield Haven NNR

FARLINGTON MARSHES

Hampshire Wildlife Trust.
Location: SU 685 045. E side of Portsmouth.
Entrance of roundabout at junc A2030 (Eastern
Road) and A27, or from Harts Farm Way,
Broadmarsh, Havant (S side of A27).
Access: Open at all times, no charge or permits,
but donations welcome. Dogs on leads only. Not
presently suitable for disabled. Groups please
book to avoid clash of dates.
Facilities: Information at entrance and in shelter
area of building. No toilets.
Public transport: None.
Habitat: Coastal grazing marsh with pools and
reedbed within reserve. Views over intertidal
mudflats/saltmarshes of Langstone Harbour.
Key birds: *Autumn to spring:* Waders and
wildfowl. *Winter:* Brent Goose, Wigeon, Pintail
etc and waders (Dunlin, Grey Plover etc). On
migration wide range of waders including rarities.
Reedbeds with Bearded Tit, Water Rail etc, scrub
areas attract small migrants (Redstart, Wryneck,
warblers etc).
Contact: Bob Chapman, c/o Hampshire Wildlife
Trust, Woodside House, Woodside Road,
Eastleigh, Hants SO50 4ET. 013 9221 4683.
www.hwt.org.uk

HOOK-WITH-WARSASH LNR

Hampshire County Council.
Location: SU 490 050. W of Fareham. Car parks
by foreshore at Warsash. Reserve includes Hook
Lake.
Access: Open all year.
Facilities: Public footpaths.

Public transport: None.
Habitat: Shingle beach, saltings, marsh, reedbed,
scrape.
Key birds: *Winter:* Brent Geese on Hamble
estuary. Waders. Stonechat, Cetti's Warbler.
Contact: Barry Duffin, Haven House Visitor
Centre, Cliff Road, Hill Head, Fareham, Hants
PO14 3JT. 01329 662145; fax 01329 667113.

LANGSTONE HARBOUR

RSPB (South East England Office).
Location: SU 695 035. Harbour lies E of
Portsmouth, one mile S of Havant. Car parks at
Broadmarsh (SE of A27/A3(M) junction) and
West Hayling LNR (first right on A2030 after
Esso garage).
Access: Restricted access. Good views from West
Hayling LNR, Broadmarsh and Farlington
Marshes LNR (qv). Winter boat trips may be
booked from the nearby Portsmouth Outdoor
Centre.
Facilities: None.
Public transport: Mainline trains all stop at
Havant. Local bus service to W Hayling LNR.
Habitat: Intertidal mud, saltmarsh, shingle
islands.
Key birds: *Summer:* Breeding waders and
seabirds inc. Mediterranean Gull and Little Tern.
Passage/winter: Waterfowl, (inc. Black-necked
Grebe, c500 dark-bellied Brent Geese, Shelduck,

Shoveler, Goldeneye and Red-breasted Merganser). Waders inc. (Oystercatcher, Ringed and Grey Plover, Dunlin, Black and Bar-tailed Godwit and Greenshank). Peregrine, Merlin and Short-eared Owl.
Contact: Chris Cockburn (Warden), 20 Childe Square, Stamshaw, Portsmouth, Hants PO2 8PL. 023 9265 0672.
e-mail: chris.cockburn@rspb.org.uk

LOWER TEST

Hampshire Wildlife Trust.
Location: SU 364 150. M271 S to Redbridge, three miles from Southampton city centre.
Access: Open at all times, no dogs except guide dogs.
Facilities: Three hides, one suitable for disabled (access by arrangement with the warden).
Public transport: Totton train station and bus stops within easy walking distance.
Habitat: Saltmarsh, brackish grassland, wet meadows, reedbed, scrapes and meres.
Key birds: *Summer*: Breeding Little, Sandwich and Common Terns, Black-headed and Mediterranean Gulls, waders. *Passage/winter*: Waders. *Autumn/winter:* Waders (inc. Black-tailed and Bar-tailed Godwits, Oystercatcher, Ringed and Grey Plover, Dunlin). Wildfowl (inc. Shelduck Shoveler, Goldeneye, Merganser and c7000 dark-bellied Brent Geese). Black-necked Grebe, Short-eared Owl, Peregrine.
Contact: Jess Pain, Hampshire Wildlife Trust, Woodside House, Woodside Road, Eastleigh, Hants SO50 4ET. 023 8066 7919.
e-mail: jessp@hwt.org.uk www.hwt.org.uk

LYMINGTON REEDBED

Hampshire Wildlife Trust.
Location: SZ 324 965. From Lyndhurst in New Forest take A337 to Lymington. Turn L after railway bridge into Marsh Lane. Park in the lay-by next to allotments. The reserve entrance is on opposite side, to R of the house and over railway crossing. The footpath exits the reserve near the Old Ampress Words, leading to a minor road between the A337 and Boldre.
Access: Open all year. The best viewpoint over the reedbeds is from Bridge Road or from the Undershore leading from the B3054.
Facilities: None.
Public transport: Bus: at either end of the footpath through the site, Marshal Lane and on the A337 (route 112). Five minutes walk from train station.
Habitat: One of largest reedbeds on S coast, fringed by alder and willow woodland.
Key birds: One of highest concentrations of Water Rail in the country; resident but most evident in winter. *Spring/summer*: Cetti's Warbler, Bearded Tit, Yellow Wagtail, Swallows, martins, Reed Warbler. *Passage*: Snipe, ducks. Otters are in the area.
Contact: Michael Boxall, Hampshire and Isle of Wight Wildlife Trust, Woodside House, Hampshire SO50 4ET. 01590 622708. e-mail: feedback@hwt.org.uk www.hwt.org.uk

LYMINGTON-KEYHAVEN

Hampshire County Council.
Location: SZ 315 920. S of Lymington along seawall footpath; car parks at Bath Road, Lymington and at Keyhaven Harbour.
Access: Open all year
Facilities: None.
Public transport: None.
Habitat: Coastal marshland and lagoons.
Key birds: *Spring*: Passage waders (inc. Knot, Sanderling, Bar-tailed and Black-tailed Godwits, Whimbrel, Spotted Redshank), Pomarine and Great Skuas. Breeding Oystercatcher, Ringed Plover, and Sandwich, Common and Little Terns. *Autumn*: Passage raptors, waders and passerines. *Winter*: Wildfowl (inc. Brent Geese, Wigeon, Pintail, Red-breasted Merganser), waders (inc. Golden Plover), Little Egret, gulls.
Contact: Hampshire County Council, Mottisfont Court, High Street, Winchester, Hants SO23 8ZF.

MARTIN DOWN

English Nature (Wiltshire Team).
Location: SY 05 19. Nine miles SW of Salisbury, car park on A354.
Access: Open access, organised groups should book in advance.
Facilities: Two car parks, interpretative boards and leaflets.
Public transport: One bus Salisbury/Blandford.
Habitat: Chalk downland.
Key birds: *Spring/summer*: Grey Partridge, warblers, Nightingale, Stone Curlew. *Winter*: Merlin, Hen Harrier.
Contact: David Burton, Parsonage Down NNR, Cherry Lodge, Shrewton, Nr Salisbury, Wilts, 01980 620485.
e-mail: david.burton@english-nature.org.uk

NORTH SOLENT

English Nature (Hampshire and Isle of Wight Team).
Location: 1. Beaulieu Estate. SZ 420 975. Fifteen miles Southampton – minor roads from Beaulieu.
2. Cadland Estate. SU 460 015. Minor roads from Hythe/Fawley.
Access: 1. Permits available from Beaulieu Estate (tel 01590 614621). No dogs, designated parts only. No public right of way at Needs Ore. Public footpath along Beaulieu River (Beaulieu-Bucklers Hard).
2. Public rights of way only.
Facilities: 1. Hides (one with disabled access).
2. None.
Public transport: 1. None.
2. Southampton to Blackfield/Fawley bus.
Habitat: 1. Coastal – saltmarsh/estuary, grazing marsh, reedbed.
2. Heathland, river valleys.
Key birds: 1. Coastal-seabirds/waders all year and woodland species.
2. Heathland/woodland species.
Contact: Bob Lord, Sites Manager,English Nature, 1 Southampton Road, Lyndhurst SO43 7BU023802 86428.
e-mail: bob.lord@english-nature.org.uk
www.english-nature.org.uk

PILSEY ISLAND

RSPB (South East England Office).
Location: SU 770 006. Approach via coastal footpath around Thorney Island, (E of Portsmouth).
Access: No access on to island but good views from surrounding areas at low tide.
Facilities: None.
Public transport: Mainline trains stop at Havant. Local train service to Emsworth.
Habitat: Saltmarsh and sand/shingle islands.
Key birds: *Winter/passage:* Major wader roost for Chichester harbour.
Contact: Langstone Harbour (see above).

ROYDON WOODS

Hampshire & Isle of Wight Wildlife Trust.
Location: SU 315 009. Roydon is one mile SE of Brockenhurst. For N Roydon, head S on A337 from Brockenhurst. Take the second L after the level crossing. Go past church and park in Church Lane. Take the track S leading to the reserve. For S Roydon, head S on the A337 and turn L past the Filly Inn. There are two parking areas down the road.
Access: Open all year.
Facilities: Car park. Several bridlepaths are surfaced but the smaller ones are not and can get muddy.
Public transport: Bus: From Brockenhurst to Setley, routes 56 and 56A, past the Filly Inn.
Habitat: Ancient woodland, pastures, ponds, heath, river.
Key birds: *Spring/summer:* Redstart, warblers, Nightjar. *All year:* Usual woodland species, all three woodpeckers.
Contact: Trust HQ, Woodside Road, Eastleigh, Hampshire SO50 4ET, 0238 0613636.
e-mail: feedback@hwt.org.uk www.hwt.org.uk

TITCHFIELD HAVEN NNR

Hampshire County Council.
Location: SU 535 025. From A27 W of Fareham; public footpath follows derelict canal along W of reserve and road skirts S edge.
Access: Open Wed-Sun all year, plus Bank Hols.
Facilities: Centre has information desk, toilets, tea room and shop. Guided tours (book in advance). Hides.
Public transport: None.
Habitat: Reedbeds, freshwater scrapes, wet grazing meadows.
Key birds: *Spring/summer:* Bearded Tit, waders (inc. Black-tailed Godwit, Ruff), wildfowl, Common Tern, breeding Cetti's Warbler, Water Rail. *Winter:* Bittern.
Contact: Barry Duffin, Haven House Visitor Centre, Cliff Road, Hill Head, Fareham, Hants PO14 3JT. 01329 662145; fax 01329 667113.

Hertfordshire

Key to sites:
1. Amwell NR
2. Broad Colney Lakes
3. Hill End Pit
4. Lemsford Springs
5. Meads, The
6. Rye House Marsh and Meads
7. Stocker's Lake
8. Stanborough Reed Marsh
9. Tring Reservoirs

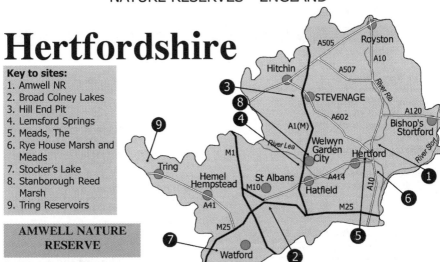

AMWELL NATURE RESERVE

St Albans Sand & Gravel.
Location: TL 375 128. Site lies between Hoddesdon and Ware, on the back road to Stanstead Abbotts near Great Amwell village.
Access: Open all year.
Facilities: Public hide and viewing area.
Public transport: None.
Habitat: Disused gravel pit with reedbeds and woodland.
Key birds: *Spring/summer*: Ringed Plover, Little Ringed Plover. *Winter*: Smew, ducks, Bittern. In process of becoming SSSI for wintering Gadwall and Shoveler.

BROAD COLNEY LAKES

Herts & Middlesex Wildlife Trust.
Location: TL 177 034. Lies S of M25 and SE of St Abans. Exit M25 at Junction 22 to Shenley on the B5378. Turn L into car park just before the British Legion huts.
Access: Open all year. Pathway and viewing area over lakes suitable for wheelchairs.
Facilities: None.
Public transport: Bus: to High Street, London Colney. Train: nearest station St Albans.
Habitat: Gravel pit, three lakes, marshy woodland, grassland.
Key birds: *Winter*: Siskin and Redpoll in alders, tits including Willow Tit, common water birds.
Contact: Trust HQ, Grebe House, St Michael's Street, St Albans, Herts AL3 4SN, 01727 858 901. e-mail: hertswt@cix.co.uk
www.wildlifetrust.org.uk/herts

HILL END PIT

Herts & Middlesex Wildlife Trust.
Location: TL 198 239. From Hitchin, head S on B651 to St Paul's Walden and onto minor roads towards Codicote. Look out for Hitch Wood where there is a car park. The reserve is on the other side of the road.
Access: Open all year.
Facilities: None.
Public transport: Bus: nearest stop is in Whitwell.
Habitat: Small chalk pit, grassland and scrub.
Key birds: *Summer*: Chiffchaff, Whitethroat, Lesser Whitethroat, Garden Warbler, Blackcap. *All year*: Tits, finches, all three woodpeckers.
Contact: Trust HQ, Grebe House, St Michael's Street, St Albans, Herts AL3 4SN, 01727 858901. e-mail: hertswt@cix.co.uk
www.wildlifetrust.org.uk/herts

LEMSFORD SPRINGS

Herts & Middlesex Wildlife Trust.
Location: TL 223 123. Lies 1.5 miles W of Welwyn Garden City town centre, off roundabout leading to Lemsford village on B197, W of A1(M).
Contact: Barry Trevis, 11 Lemsford Village, Welwyn Garden City, Herts AL8 7TN. 01707 335517. e-mail: hertswt@cix.co.uk
www.wildlifetrust.org.uk/herts

MEADS, THE

Herts & Middlesex Wildlife Trust/Thames Water/
Glaxo Wellcome/East Herts District Council.
Location: Between Hertford and Ware, lying
alongside A119 Ware Road. Park in Priory Street
and Broadmeads (Ware) and streets in Hertford.
Access: Open all year.
Facilities: None.
Public transport: None.
Habitat: Largest remaining area of grazed
riverside flood meadow in Hertfordshire.
Key birds: *Summer*: Sky Lark, Reed Warbler,
Reed Bunting, Sedge Warbler, Yellow Wagtail.
Winter/spring: Gadwall, Shoveler, Wigeon, Teal,
Snipe, gulls, waders.
Contact: Trust HQ, Grebe House, St Michael's
Street, St Albans, Herts AL3 4SN, 01727
858901. www.wildlifetrust.org.uk/herts

RYE HOUSE MARSH AND MEADS

RSPB/Hertfordshire & Middlesex Wildlife Trust.
Location: TL 387 099. E of Hoddesdon, near
Rye House railway station.
Access: Open all year. Charge for non-RSPB
members.
Facilities: Nature trails, hides. RSPB reserve has
close circuit CCTV on Kingfisher and Common
Terns.
Public transport: None.
Habitat: Two adjoining reserves of marshland.
Key birds: *Spring/summer*: Common Tern,
warblers, Kingfisher, Snipe. *Winter*: Bittern,
Water Rail, Jack Snipe, wildfowl.
Contact: Trust HQ, Grebe House, St Michael's
Street, St Albans, Herts AL3 4SN, 01727
858901. e-mail: hertswt@cix.co.uk
www.wildlifetrust.org.uk/herts

STOCKER'S LAKE

Herts & Middlesex Wildlife Trust.
Location: TQ 044 931. Rickmansworth, off
A412 into Springwell Lane (TQ043932) L after
bridge, or via Bury Lake Aquadrome (parking).
Contact: Trust HQ, 01727 858901.

STANBOROUGH REED MARSH

Herts & Middlesex Wildlife Trust.
Location: TL 230 105. Leave the A1M at J4 on
A6129 Stanborough Road. At next small
roundabout, turn R to Welwyn Garden City town
centre. Continue past lakes to next roundabout.
Take a U turn and then turn L into reserve car
park. Follow path between river and lake into
reserve.
Access: Open all year. No access into reedbed.
Circular walk.
Facilities: None.
Public transport: Bus: stops on Stanborough
Road. Train: nearest station Welwyn Garden Cty.
Habitat: Willow woodland, river, reed marsh.
Key birds: *Summer*: good numbers of Reed and
Sedge Warblers. *Winter*: Water Rail and Corn
Bunting roost.
Contact: Herts & Middlesex Wildlife Trust,
Grebe House, St Michael's Street, St Albans,
Herts AL3 4SN, 01727 858901.
e-mail: hertswt@cix.co.uk
www.wildlifetrust.org.uk/herts

TRING RESERVOIRS

Wilstone Reservoir – Herts & Middlesex Wildlife
Trust; other reservoirs – British Waterways and
Friends of Tring Res.
Location: Wilstone Reservoir SP90 51 34. Other
reservoirs SP 92 01 35. WTW Lagoon SP 92 31
34 adjacent to Marsworth Reservoir. Reservoirs
1.5 miles due N of Tring, all accessible from
B489 which leaves A41 at Aston Clinton.
Access: Reservoirs – open at all times. WTW
Lagoon: open at all times by permit from FOTR.
Facilities: Café and public house adjacent to
Startops Reservoir car park. Also disabled trail
from here. Public house also in Wilstone village
about 800 metres from reservoir. Hides with
disabled access at Startops/Marsworth Reservoir
& WTW Lagoon. Also other hides.
Public transport: Buses are available to and from
Aylesbury & Tring including a weekend service,
tel. 0870 6082608. Tring Station is 2½ miles
away via canal towpath.
Habitat: Four reservoirs with surrounding
woodland, scrub and meadows. Two of the
reservoirs with extensive reedbeds. WTW lagoon
with islands, surrounding hedgerows and scrub.
Key birds: *Spring/summer*: Breeding warblers,
regular Hobby, occasional Black Tern, Marsh
Harrier, Osprey. *Autumn*: Passage waders and
wildfowl. *Winter*: Gull roost, large wildfowl
flocks, bunting roosts, occasional Bittern.
Contact: Trust HQ, FOTR: see Peter Hearn in
Bucks BTO entry, British Waterways, Watery
Lane, Marsworth, Tring HP23 4LZ. 01442
825938. www.tringreservoirs.btinternet.co.uk

Kent

RSPB BLEAN WOODS

RSPB (South East England Office).
Location: TR 126 592. From Rough Common (off A290, one and a half miles NW of Canterbury).
Access: Open 8am-9pm.
Facilities: Public footpaths and five waymarked trails.
Public transport: 24 and 24a buses from Canterbury to Rough Common.
Habitat: Woodland (mainly oak and sweet chestnut), relics of heath.
Key birds: Nightingale, Nightjar, three species of woodpecker.
Contact: Michael Walter, 11 Garden Close, Rough Common, Canterbury, Kent CT2 9BP. 01227 455972.

BLEAN WOODS

English Nature (Kent Team).
Location: TR 120 609. NW of Canterbury on A290. Road opposite Chapel Lane at Blean.
Access: Keep to paths.
Facilities: None.
Public transport: Buses every 15mins (between Canterbury and Whitstable) pass close to reserve.
Habitat: Mixed coppice with standard sessile oak, glades, rides.
Key birds: *Summer:* Some 70 breeding species, inc. Woodcock, all three woodpeckers, Tree Pipit, Redstart, Nightingale, Wood Warbler, Hawfinch.
Contact: David Maylam, Colharbour Farm, Wye, Ashford, Kent TN25 5DB, 01233 812525.

BOUGH BEECH RESERVOIR

Kent Wildlife Trust.
Location: TQ49 64 89. Bough Beech is situated 3.5 miles S of Ide Hill, signposted off B2042.
Contact: Dave Hutton, Kent Wildlife Trust, Tyland Barn, Sandling, Maidstone, Kent ME14 3BD. 01622 662012.

BURHAM MARSHES

Kent Wildlife Trust.
Location: TQ 71 46 15. On E bank of the River Medway to the W of Burham Village. 4.5 miles from J3 (M2) S or J6 (M20) N.
Contact: Dave Hutton (as above).

DUNGENESS

RSPB (South East England Office).
Location: TR 063 196. SE of Lydd.
Access: Open daily 9am-9pm or sunset when earlier. Visitor centre open (10am-5pm, 4pm Nov-Feb). Parties over 20 by prior arrangement.
Facilities: Visitor centre, toilets (including disabled access), five hides, nature trail, wheelchair access to visitor centre and four hides.
Public transport: Service 12 from Lydd or Folkestone stops at reserve entrance on request – one mile walk to visitor centre.
Habitat: Shingle, flooded gravel pits, sallow scrub, reedbed, wet grassland.
Key birds: Resident Corn Bunting. *Winter:* Wildfowl (including Wigeon, Goldeneye, Goosander, Smew), divers and grebes. Migrant waders, landfall for passerines. *Summer:* Breeding Lapwing, Redshank, wildfowl, terns and gulls.
Contact: Christine Hawkins/Simon Busuttil, Boulderwall Farm, Dungeness Road, Lydd, Romney Marsh, Kent TN29 9PN. 01797 320588.

DUNGENESS BIRD OBSERVATORY

Dungeness Bird Observatory Trust.
Location: TR 085 173. Three miles SE of Lydd. Turn south off Dungeness Road at TR 087 185 and continue to end of road.
Access: Observatory open throughout the year.
Facilities: Accommodation available. Bring own sleeping bag/sheets and toiletries. Shared facilities including fully-equipped kitchen.
Public transport: Bus service between Rye and Folkestone, numbers 11, 12, 711, 712. Alight at the Pilot Inn, Lydd-on-Sea. Tel 01227 472082.
Habitat: Shingle promontory with scrub and gravel pits. RSPB reserve nearby.
Key birds: Breeding birds include Wheatear and Black Redstart and seabirds on RSPB Reserve. Important migration site.
Contact: David Walker, Dungeness Bird Observatory, 11 RNSSS, Dungeness, Kent TN29 9NA. 01797 321309

ELMLEY MARSHES

RSPB (South East England Office).
Location: TQ 93 86 80. Isle-of-Sheppey signposted from A249, one mile beyond Kingsferry Bridge. Reserve car park is two miles from the main road.
Access: Open every day except Tue, Christmas

Key to sites:
1. RSPB Blean Woods
2. Blean Woods
3. Bough Beech Reservoir
4. Burham Marshes
5. Dungeness
6. Dungeness Bird Observatory
7. Elmley Marshes
8. Hamstreet Woods
9. Jeffery Harrison Reserve, Sevenoaks
10. Nor Marsh
11. Northward Hill
12. Oare Marshes
13. Oldbury Hill And Styant's Wood
14. Riverside Country Park
15. Sandwich and Pegwell Bay
16. Sandwich Bay Bird Observatory
17. Stodmarsh National
18. Tudeley Woods
19. Wye
20. Yockletts Bank

Kent

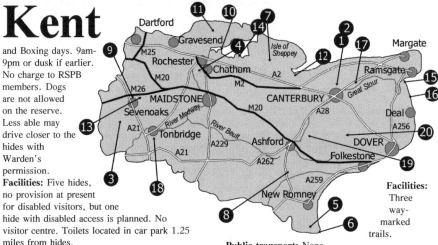

and Boxing days. 9am-9pm or dusk if earlier. No charge to RSPB members. Dogs are not allowed on the reserve. Less able may drive closer to the hides with Warden's permission.

Facilities: Five hides, no provision at present for disabled visitors, but one hide with disabled access is planned. No visitor centre. Toilets located in car park 1.25 miles from hides.

Public transport: Swale Halt, a request stop is nearest railway station on Sittingbourne to Sheerness line. From there it is a three mile walk to reserve

Habitat: Coastal grazing marsh, ditches and pools alongside the Swale Esturay with extensive intertidal mudflats and saltmarsh

Key birds: *Spring/summer:* Breeding waders – Redshank, Lapwing, Avocet, Yellow Wagtail, passage waders, Hobby. *Autumn:* Passage waders. *Winter:* Spectacular numbers of wildfowl especially Wigeon and White-fronted Goose. Waders. Hunting raptors – Peregrine, Merlin, Hen Harrier and Short-eared Owl.

Contact: Bob Gomes, Elmley RSPB Reserve, Kingshill Farm, Elmley, Sheerness, Kent ME12 3RW. 01795 665969.

HAMSTREET WOODS

English Nature (Kent Team).
Location: TR 003 337. E on B2067 from Hamstreet, car park first L at green.
Access: Keep to paths.

Public transport: None.
Habitat: Damp oak woodland, coppice/standards.
Key birds: Over 90 species recorded. Woodcock, Great and Lesser Spotted Woodpeckers, Nightingale, Redstart, warblers, Hawfinch; Hoopoe regular summer visitor.
Contact: David Maylam, Coldharbour Farm, Wye, Ashford, Kent TN25 5DB. 01233 812525.

JEFFERY HARRISON RESERVE, SEVENOAKS

Jeffery Harrison Memorial Trust.
Location: TQ 519 568. From A25 immediately N of Sevenoaks.
Access: Wed, Sat, Sun 10am-5pm (or dusk if earlier).
Facilities: Visitor centre, nature trail, hides.
Public transport: Ten minutes walk from Bat & Ball station, 15 minutes from Sevenoaks station.
Habitat: Flooded gravel pits.
Key birds: Wintering wildfowl, waders, woodland birds.
Contact: John Tyler, Tadorna, Bradbourne Vale

Facilities: Three way-marked trails.

Road, Sevenoaks, Kent TN13 3DH.
01732 456407.

NOR MARSH

RSPB (South East England Office).
Location: TQ 810 700. One mile NE of
Gillingham in the Medway Estuary.
Contact: Michael Ellison, Bromhey Farm,
Eastborough, Cooling, Rochester, Kent ME3
8DS. 01634 222480.

NORTHWARD HILL

RSPB (South East England Office).
Location: TQ 780 765. Adjacent to village of
High Halstow, off A228, approx six miles N of
Rochester.
Contact: Michael Ellison, (see Nor Marsh).

OARE MARSHES LNR

Kent Wildlife Trust.
Location: TR 01 36 48 (car park). Two miles N
of Faversham. From A2 follow signs to Oare and
Harty Ferry.
Contact: Tony Swandale, Kent Wildlife Trust,
Tyland Barn, Sandling, Maidstone, Kent ME14
3BD. 01622 662012.

OLDBURY HILL AND STYANT'S WOOD

National Trust/Kent County Council.
Location: 578 559. Lies between Sevenoaks and
Brough Green, alongside A25 three miles E of
Sevenoaks. Car park is on the L of Styant's
Bottom Road.
Access: Open all year to walkers. Not suitable for
wheelchairs.
Facilities: Two waymarked routes. Picnic tables.
Full facilities at Crown Point Inn 400m from car
park on A25.
Public transport: Bus: from Sevenoaks to
Borough Green Mon-Sat. Tel: 01732 743 040.
Train: nearest station is Kemsing (1.5 miles) on
London-Maidstone East line Mon-Sat. Tel: 08457
484 950.
Habitat: Coppiced woodland, mostly oak, but
beech, Scots pine, hazel and ash included.
Key birds: *Spring/summer*: warblers, Spotted
Flycatcher, Willow Warbler, Wood Warbler. *All
year:* Nuthatch, Treecreeper, tits and other
woodland species.
Contact: National Trust Regional Office,
Polesden Lacey, Dorking, Surrey RH5 6BD,
01372 453401. www.nationaltrust.org.uk

RIVERSIDE COUNTRY PARK

Medway County Council.
Location: TQ 808 683. From Rochester, take the
A2 E into Gillingham and turn L onto A289.
After one mile, turn R onto the B2004 at Grange.
After one mile, the visitor centre is on the L
overlooking River Medway.
Access: Open all year, free access from 8.30am-
4.30pm (winter) or 8.30am-8.30pm or dusk
(summer).
Facilities: Visitor Centre with restaurant and
toilets open every day except Dec 25 from 10am-
5pm summer (4pm winter). Large car park and
smaller one at Rainham Dock.
Public transport: Bus: contact Arriva tel: 08706
082 608. Train: nearest stations at Rainham and
Gillingham. Cycle racks at visitor centre and a
Sustrans cycle route.
Habitat: Mudflats, saltmarsh, ponds, reedbeds,
grassland and scrub.
Key birds: *Winter*: Dunlin, Redshank, Grey
Plover, Avocet, Brent Goose, Teal, Pintail,
Goldeneye, Wigeon, Shelduck, Peregrine, Hen
Harrier, thrushes, Brambling, Merlin, Short-eared
Owl, Mediterranean Gull, Water Rail, Rock Pipit.
Contact: Riverside Country Park, Lower
Rainham Road, Gillingham, Kent ME7 2XH,
01634 378987.

SANDWICH & PEGWELL BAY

Kent Wildlife Trust.
Location: TR 34 26 35. Main carpark is off
A256 Sandwich – Ramsgate road at Pegwell Bay.
Access: Open 7.30am-8.00pm or dusk whichever
is earlier.
Facilities: Toilets, hide, car parking and trails
Public transport: Bus stop within 400m
(Stagecoach). Sustrans National Bike Route
passes along the edge of the reserve.
Habitat: Saltmarsh, mudflats, sand dunes and
coastal scrub.
Key birds: Good range of wetland birds
throughout the year.
Contact: Pete Forrest, Kent Wildlife Trust,
Tyland Barn, Sandling, Maidstone, Kent ME14
3BD. 01622 662012.

SANDWICH BAY BIRD OBSERVATORY

Sandwich Bay Bird Observatory Trust.
Location: TR 355 575. 2.5 miles from Sandwich,
five miles from Deal, 15 miles from Canterbury.

A256 to Sandwich from Dover or Ramsgate. Follow signs to Sandwich Station and then Sandwich Bay.
Access: Open daily. Disabled access.
Facilities: New Field Study Centre. Visitor centre, toilets, refreshments, hostel-type accommodation.
Public transport: Sandwich train station two miles from Observatory. No public transport, but within walking distance.
Habitat: Coastal, dune land, farmland, marsh, small scrape.
Key birds: *Spring/autumn passage*: Good variety of migrants and waders, specially Corn Bunting. Annual Golden Oriole. *Winter*: Golden Plover.
Contact: Gaynor Cross, Sandwich Bay Bird Observatory, Guildford Road, Sandwich Bay, Sandwich, Kent CT13 9PF. 01304 617341.

STODMARSH

English Nature (Kent Team).
Location: TR 222 618. Lies alongside River Stone and A28, five miles NE of Canterbury.
Access: Open at all times. Many paths and viewing areas are fully accessible. Keep to reserve paths and keep dogs under control.
Facilities: Fully accessible toilets are available at the Stodmarsh entrance car park. Four hides (one fully accessible), easy access nature trail, footpaths and information panels. Car park, picnic area and toilets adjoining the Grove Ferry entrance with easily accessible path, viewing mound and two hides.
Public transport: There is a regular bus service from Canterbury to Margate/Ramsgate. Alight at Upstreet for Grove Ferry. Hourly on Sun.
Habitat: Open water, reedbeds, wet meadows, dry meadows, woodland.
Key birds: *Spring/summer*: Breeding Bearded Tit, Cetti's Warbler, Garganey, Reed, Sedge and Willow Warblers, Nightingale. Migrant Black Tern, Hobby, Osprey, Little Egret. *Winter*: Wildfowl. Hen Harrier, Bittern.
Contact: David Feast, English Nature, Coldharbour Farm, Wye, Ashford, Kent TN25 5DB. 01233 812525 or 07767 321058 (mobile).

TUDDLEY WOODS

RSPB (South East England Office).
Location: TQ 618 434. Beside A21, one mile S of Tonbridge. Take minor road to Capel on left immediately before Fairthorne Garage. Car park 0.25 miles on left.

Access: Open every day except Christmas Day. No dogs. No disabled facilities.
Facilities: Leaflet, two nature trails.
Public transport: None.
Habitat: Semi-natural ancient woodland, lowland heathland (restored), pasture.
Key birds: *Spring/summer*: Willow Warbler, Garden Warbler, Blackcap, Turtle Dove, Spotted Flycatcher, Nightingale, Tree Pipit, Wood Lark, Nightjar, Hobby, Whitethroat. *All year*: Marsh Tit, Willow Tit, Nuthatch, three woodpecker species, Yellowhammer, Treecreeper.
Contact: Martin Allison, 12 The Grove, Crowborough, East Sussex TN6 1NY. 01273 775333 (South East Regional Office).

WYE

English Nature (Kent Team).
Location: TR 079 454. From Wye up hill towards Hastingleigh, car park at roadside.
Access: Open daily except Christmas Day. No dogs. Keep to paths.
Facilities: One nature trail.
Public transport: None.
Habitat: Downland, scrub, woodlands, grazing meadows.
Key birds: *Summer*: Breeding Sparrowhawk, Tawny Owl, Nightingale, Spotted Flycatcher, Lesser Whitethroat, Hawfinch.
Contact: David Maylam, Coldharbour Farm, Wye, Ashford, Kent TN25 5DB. 01233 812525.

YOCKLETTS BANK SSSI

Kent Wildlife Trust.
Location: TR 125 477. Lies NE of Ashford, two miles S of Petham, one mile W of the Canterbury-Hythe road (B2068). Park at the side of the road at the bottom of the hill, near Yockletts Farm.
Access: Open all year. Please keep to the paths. The reserve car park is normally open only at weekends during the main orchid-flowering period for parties booked in advance.
Facilities: None.
Public transport: None.
Habitat: Mixed woodland, grassland.
Key birds: *Spring/summer*: Nightingale, warblers. *All year*: Usual woodland species, Green and Great Spotted Woodpeckers. Good for plants.
Contact: Kent Wildlife Trust, Tyland Barn, Sandling, Maidstone, Kent ME14 3BD, 01622 662012.

Lancashire

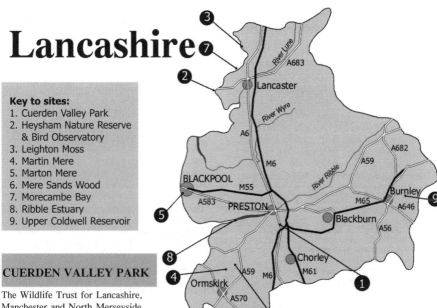

Key to sites:
1. Cuerden Valley Park
2. Heysham Nature Reserve & Bird Observatory
3. Leighton Moss
4. Martin Mere
5. Marton Mere
6. Mere Sands Wood
7. Morecambe Bay
8. Ribble Estuary
9. Upper Coldwell Reservoir

CUERDEN VALLEY PARK

The Wildlife Trust for Lancashire, Manchester and North Merseyside
Location: SD 565 238. S of Preston on A6, close to junction of M6 and M62. Easy access from J28 and J28 of M6 and J8 and J9 on M62.
Access: Open all year.
Facilities: Paths.
Public transport: None.
Habitat: Woodland, river, pond, agricultural grassland.
Key birds: *All year*: Kingfisher, Dipper, Great Spotted Woodpecker, Goldcrest, usual woodland birds.
Contact: Trust HQ, Cuerden Park Wildlife Centre, Shady Lane, Bamber Bridge, Preston, Lancs PR5 6AU, 01772 324129.
e-mail: lancswt@cix.co.uk

HEYSHAM NATURE RESERVE AND BIRD OBSERVATORY

The Wildlife Trust for Lancashire, Manchester and North Merseyside in conjunction with British Energy Estates.
Location: The main reserve is at SD 404 596. A683 to Heysham port. Turn left at traffic lights by Duke of Rothersay pub, then first right after 300m.
Access: Gate to reserve car park usually open 9.30am-6pm (longer in summer and shorter in winter). Pedestrian access at all times. Dogs on lead. Disabled access to the reserve circuit, please phone security at 01524 863911.
Facilities: Hide overlooking Power Station outfalls. Map giving access details at the reserve car park. No manned visitor centre or toilet access but someone usually in reserve office, next to the main car park, in the morning. Latest sightings board can be viewed through the window if office closed.
Public transport: Train services connect with nearby Isle of Man and Belfast ferries. Plenty of buses from various Heysham sites within walking distance to Lancaster (ask for nearest stop to the harbour).
Habitat: Varied: wetland, acid grassland, alkaline grassland, foreshore.
Key birds: Passerine migrants in the correct conditions. Good passage of seabirds in spring, especially Arctic Tern. Storm Petrel and Leach's Petrel during strong onshore (SW-WWNW) winds in midsummer and autumn respectively. Good variety of breeding birds (e.g. eight species of warbler on the reserve itself). Two-three scarce land birds each year, most frequent being Yellow-browed Warbler. Notable area for dragonflies, including scarce migrants.

Contact: Pete Marsh, 17 Albion Street, Lancaster LA1 1DY. 01524 66775.
e-mail: pbmarsh@btopenworld.com
(observatory). Annual report from Leighton Moss RSPB reserve shop.

LEIGHTON MOSS

RSPB (North West England Office).
Location: SD 478 750. Four miles NW of Carnforth. Signposted from A6 N of Carnforth.
Access: Reserve open daily 9am-dusk. Visitor centre open daily 10am-5pm (except Christmas Day). No dogs. No charge to RSPB members.
Facilities: Visitor centre, shop, tea-room and toilets. Nature trails and five hides (four have wheelchair access).
Public transport: Silverdale Train Station 150 metres from reserve. Tel: 08457 484950.
Habitat: Reedbed, shallow meres and surrounding woodland.
Key birds: *All year*: Bittern, Bearded Tit, Water Rail, Pochard and Shoveler. *Summer*: Marsh Harrier, Reed and Sedge Warblers.
Contact: Robin Horner, Leighton Moss RSPB Nature Reserve, Myers Farm, Silverdale, Carnforth, Lancashire LA 0SW. 01524 701601. www.RSPB.org.uk

MARTIN MERE

The Wildfowl & Wetlands Trust.
Location: SD 428 145. Six miles N of Ormskirk via Burscough Bridge (A59), 20 miles from Liverpool and Preston.
Access: Opening times: 9.30am-5.00pm (Nov-Feb), 9.30am-5.30pm (rest of year). Special dawn and evening events. Guide dogs only allowed. Admission charge. No charge for members. Fully accessible to disabled.
Facilities: Visitor centre with toilets, gift shop, restaurant, education centre, play area, nature reserve and nature trails, hides, waterfowl collection and sustainable garden. Provision for disabled visitors.
Public transport: Bus service to WWT Martin Mere from Ormskirk. Train to Burscough Bridge or New Lane Stations (both 1.5 miles from reserve).
Habitat: Open water, wet grassland, moss, copses, reedbed, parkland.
Key birds: *Winter*: Whooper and Bewick's Swans, Pink-footed Goose, various duck, Ruff, Black-tailed Godwit, Peregrine, Hen Harrier, Tree Sparrow. *Spring*: Ruff, Shelduck, Little

Ringed and Ringed Plover, Lapwing, Redshank. *Summer*: Marsh Harrier, Garganey, hirundines, Tree Sparrow. *Autumn*: Pink-footed Goose, waders on passage.
Contact: Patrick Wisniewski, WWT Martin Mere, Fish Lane, Burscough, Lancs L40 0TA. 01704 895181.
e-mail: info@wwt.org.uk
www.wwt.org.uk

MARTON MERE

Blackpool Borough Council.
Location: SD 345 352. Signposted from Blackpool Zoo car park (free) and De Veres Hotel car park.
Access: Open at all times. Dogs on lead.
Facilities: Hides.
Public transport: None.
Habitat: Open water surrounded by patchwork of grassland, scrub and reedbed.
Key birds: *Summer*: Breeding warblers. Migrant waders (inc. Little Ringed Plover, Jack Snipe), Black Tern. *Winter*: Good range of duck, also Bittern annual. Regular Mediterranean and Little Gulls.
Contact: David McGrath, Community & Tourism Services, c/o Blackpool Zoo, East Park Drive, Blackpool FY3 8PP,

MERE SANDS WOOD

Wildlife Trust for Lancashire, Manchester and North Merseyside.
Location: SD 44 71 57. Four miles inland of Southport, 0.5 miles off A59 Preston – Liverpool road, in Rufford along B5246 (Holmeswood Road).
Access: Visitor centre open 9am-5pm daily except Christmas Day. Car park open until 8pm in summer. 750m of wheelchair-accessible path, leading to two hides and viewpoint.
Facilities: Visitor centre with toilets (disabled), seven hides, two trails, exhibition room, latest sightings board. Feeding stations
Public transport: Bus: Southport-Chorley 347 stops in Rufford, ½ mile walk. Train: Preston-Ormskirk train stops at Rufford station, one mile walk.
Habitat: Freshwater lakes, mixed woodland, sandy grassland/heath. 105h.
Key birds: *Winter*: Nationally important for Teal and Gadwall, good range of waterfowl, Kingfisher. Feeding stations attract Tree Sparrow, Bullfinch, Reed Bunting. Woodland: Treecreeper.

Summer: Little Ringed Plover, Kingfisher, Lesser Spotted Woodpecker. *Passage*: Most years, Osprey, Crossbill, Green Sandpiper, Greenshank, Wood Warbler, Turtle Dove.
Contact: Dominic Rigby, Warden,Mere Sands Wood Nature Reserve, Holmeswood Road, Rufford, Ormskirk, Lancs L40 1TG. 01704 821809. e-mail: lancswtmsw@cix.co.uk www.wildlifetrust.org/lancashire

MORECAMBE BAY

RSPB (North West England Office).
Location: SD 468 667. Two miles N of Morecambe at Hest Bank.
Access: Open at all times. Do not venture onto saltmarsh or intertidal area, there are dangerous channels and quicksands.
Facilities: Viewpoint at car park.
Public transport: No 5 bus runs between Carnforth and Morecambe. Tel: 0870 608 2608.
Habitat: Saltmarsh, estuary.
Key birds: *Winter*: Wildfowl (Pintail, Shelduck, Wigeon) and waders – important high tide roost for Oystercatcher, Curlew, Redshank, Dunlin, Bar-tailed Godwit.
Contact: Robin Horner, Leighton Moss & Morecambe Bay RSPB Reserves, Myers Farm, Silverdale, Carnforth, Lancashire LA5 0SW. 01524 701601. www.rspb.org.uk

RIBBLE ESTUARY

English Nature (Cheshire to Lancashire team).
Location: SD 380 240.
Access: Open at all times.

Facilities: No formal visiting facilities.
Public transport: None.
Habitat: Saltmarsh, mudflats.
Key birds: High water wader roosts (of Knot, Dunlin, Black-tailed Godwit, Oystercatcher and Grey Plover) are best viewed from Southport, Marshside, Lytham and St Annes. Pink-footed Geese and wintering swans are present in large numbers from Oct-Feb on Banks Marsh and along River Douglas respectively. The large flocks of Wigeon, for which the site is renowned, can be seen on high tides from Marshside but feed on saltmarsh areas at night. Good numbers of raptors also present in winter.
Contact: Site Manager, Old Hollow, Marsh Road, Banks, Southport PR9 8EA. 01704 225624.

UPPER COLDWELL

The Wildlife Trust for Lancashire, Manchester and North Merseyside
Location: SD 905 360. Three miles SE of Nelson. Enter from junction 13 of M65, then take minor road towards Hebden Bridge.
Access: Public footpath along N perimeter wall. Access to reserve area by permit.
Facilities: None.
Public transport: None.
Habitat: Upland reservoir, coniferous woodland, moorland.
Key birds: Breeding Tufted Duck, Little Ringed Plover, Whinchat; moors have Twite, Short-eared Owl, Golden Plover.
Contact: Trust HQ, 01772 324129.

Leicestershire and Rutland

BEACON HILL COUNTRY PARK

Leicestershire County Council.
Location: SK 522 149. From Loughborough, take the A512 SW for 2.5 miles. Turn L onto Breakback Road and follow it for 2.5 miles through Nanpantan. Park in the car park on the left in Woodhouse Lane.
Access: Open all year 8am-dusk. If opening times are different, these will be clearly displayed at the park. A permissive path is followed from Deans

Lane to Woodhouse Lane which is occasionally closed during the year. Please check first.
Facilities: Two pay and display car parks, easy-to-follow, well waymarked tracks and woodland paths. Several climbs to hill tops. Rocky outcrops slippy after rain. Information boards. Toilets at lower car park, the Outwoods car park and Woodhouse Eaves. Wheelchair access along park paths but no access to summit. Refreshments at Bull's Head, Woodhouse Eaves.
Public transport: Bus: No 123 Leicester to Shepshed calls at Woodhouse Eaves. Tel: 0870

Leicestershire and Rutland

608 2608. Train: from Loughborough and Leicester.

Habitat: Forest, one of the oldest geological outcrops in England and the second highest point in Leicestershire.

Key birds: *All year*: Treecreeper, Nuthatch, Lesser Spotted and Green Woodpeckers, Great and Coal Tits, Little Owl, wagtails. *Summer*: Pied Flycatcher, Whitethroat, Blackcap, Whinchat, Garden Warbler, Stonechat.

Contact: Beacon Hill Estate Office, Broombriggs Farm, Beacon Road, Woodhouse Eaves, Loughborough, Leics. LE12 8SR, 01509 890048.

BURBAGE COMMON AND WOOD

Hinckley and Bosworth Borough Council.

Location: SK 447 954. Lies E of Hinckley. From J2 of M69, take B590 to park entrance in Burbage Common Road.

Access: Open access to all areas. Dogs on lead. No wheelchair access.

Facilities: Visitor Centre open all week (not all day). Toilets, picnic areas. For information tel: 01455 633 712. Small hide in Burbage Wood. Refreshments at Wood House Farm, large parties should book. Tel: 01455 634 459.

Public transport: Bus: Arriva buses pass frequently from Hinckley and Leicester. Tel: 0870 608 2608. Train: Good train service to Hinckley from Leicester and Nuneaton. Tel: 0845 748 4950.

Habitat: Woodland, scrub and grassland.

Key birds: *Spring/summer*: Peregrine, Cuckoo, Lesser Whitethroat, Whitethroat, Garden and Willow Warblers, occasional Grasshopper Warbler. *Winter*: Lapwing, Redstart, Wheatear, Firecrest, Brambling, Siskin, Twite, Redpoll, Redwing, Fieldfare and occasional Merlin.

Contact: Hinckley & Bosworth Borough Council, Argents Mead, Hinckley, Leicestershire LE10 1BZ, 01455 238141.

EYEBROOK RESERVOIR

Corby & District Water Co.

Location: SP 853 964. Reservoir built 1940. S of Uppingham, from unclassified road W of A6003 at Stoke Dry.

Access: Access to 150 acres private grounds granted to members of Leics and Rutland Ornithological Society, and Rutland Nat Hist Soc. Organised groups with written permission (from Corby Water Co, PO Box 101, Weldon Road, Corby NN17 5UA).

Facilities: SSSI since 1955. Good viewing from public roads. Trout fishery season Apr-Oct.

Public transport: None.

Habitat: Open water, plantations and pasture.

Key birds: *Summer*: Good populations of breeding birds, sightings of Ospreys. Passage waders and Black Tern. *Winter*: Wildfowl (inc. Goldeneye, Goosander, Bewick's Swan) and waders.

Contact: Corby Water Co. www.eyebrook.org.uk

RUTLAND WATER

Leics and Rutland Wildlife Trust.

Location: SK 866 6760 72. 1. Egleton Reserve: from Egleton village off A6003 S of Oakham. 2. Lyndon Reserve: south shore E of Manton village off A6003 S of Oakham.

Access: 1. Open daily 9am-5pm. 2. Open winter (Sat, Sun 10am-4pm), summer daily except Mon (10am-4pm). Day permits available for both reserves.

Facilities: 1: Anglian Water Birdwatching Centre, now enlarged. Toilets and disabled access to 10 hides, electric buggies, conference facilities. 2: Interpretive centre.

Public transport: None.

Habitat: Reservoir, lagoons, scrapes, woods, meadows, plantations.

Key birds: *Spring/autumn*: Outstanding wader passage. Also harriers, owls, passerine flocks, terns (Black, Arctic, breeding Common, occasional Little and Sandwich). *Winter*: Wildfowl (inc Goldeneye, Smew, Goosander, rare grebes, all divers), Ruff flock. *Summer*: Breeding Ospreys.

Contact: Tim Appleton, Fishponds Cottage, Stamford Road, Oakham, Rutland LE15 8AB. 01572 770651; fax 01572 755931; e-mail awbc@rutlandwater.org.uk; www.rutlandwater.org.uk www.ospreys.org.uk www.birdfair.org.uk.

Lincolnshire

DONNA NOOK-SALTFLEETBY

Lincolnshire Wildlife Trust.
Location: TF 422 998. Near North Somercotes, off A1031 coast road, S of Grimsby.
Access: Donna Nook beach is frequently closed as this is an active bombing range, but dunes remain open. Dogs on leads. Some disabled access.
Facilities: No toilets or visitor centre. Interpretation boards and paths.
Public transport: None.
Habitat: Dunes, slacks and intertidal areas, seashore, mudflats, sandflats.
Key birds: *Summer*: Little Tern, Ringed Plover, Oystercatcher. *Winter*: Brent Goose, Shelduck, Twite, Lapland Bunting, Shore Lark, Linnet.
Contact: c/o Lincolnshire Wildlife Trust, Banavallum House, Manor House Street, Horncastle, Lincs LN9 5HF. 01507 526667.
e-mail: lincstrust@cix.co.uk
www.lincstrust.co.uk

FAR INGS

Lincolnshire Wildlife Trust.
Location: TA 011 229 and TA 023 230. Off Far Ings Lane, W of Barton-on-Humber, the last turn off before the Humber Bridge.
Contact: Lionel Grooby, Far Ings Visitor Centre, Far Ings Road, Barton on Humber DN18 5RG. 01652 634507. www.lincstrust.co.uk
e-mail: farings@lincstrust.co.uk

FRAMPTON MARSH

RSPB (East Anglia Office).
Location: TR 36 43 85. Four miles SE of Boston. From A16 follow signs to Frampton then Frampton Marsh.
Access: Open at all times. Free.
Facilities: Footpaths, bench, car park, Free information leaflets available (please contact the office), guided walks programme.
Public transport: None.
Habitat: Saltmarsh.
Key birds: *Summer*: Breeding Redshank, passage waders (inc Greenshank, Ruff and Black-tailed Godwit) and Hobby. *Winter*: Hen Harrier, Short-eared Owl, Merlin, dark-bellied Brent Goose, Twite, Golden Plover.
Contact: John Badley, RSPB Lincolnshire Wash

Office, 61 Horseshoe Lane, Kirton, Kirton, Boston, Lincs PE20 1LW. 01205 724678.
e-mail: john.badley@rspb.org.uk
www.rspb.org.uk

FREISTON SHORE

RSPB (East Anglia Office).
Location: TF 39 74 24. Four miles E of Boston. From A52 at Haltoft End follow signs to Freiston Shore.
Access: Open at all times, free.
Facilities: Footpaths, two car parks, bird hide. Free information leaflets available (please contact the office), guided walks programme.
Public transport: None.
Habitat: Saltmarsh, saline lagoon, mudflats.
Key birds: *Summer*: Breeding waders including Avocet, Little Ringed Plover and Oystercatcher, Corn Bunting and Tree Sparrow. *Winter*: Lapland Bunting, Twite, Dark-bellied Brent Goose, wildfowl, waders, birds of prey including Short-eared Owl and Hen Harrier. *Passage*: Waders, including Curlew Sandpiper and Little Stint. *Autumn:* Occasional seabirds including Arctic and Great Skuas.
Contact: John Badley, RSPB Lincolnshire Wash Office, 61 Horseshoe Lane, Kirton, Boston, Lincs PE20 1LW. 01205 724678.
e-mail: john.badley@rspb.org.uk
www.rspb.org.uk

GIBRALTAR POINT NNR AND BIRD OBSERVATORY

Lincolnshire Wildlife Trust.
Location: TF 556 580. Three miles S of Skegness on the N edge of The Wash. Signposted from Skegness town centre.
Access: Reserve is open dawn-dusk all year. Seasonal charges for car parking. Free admission to reserve, visitor centre and toilets. Some access restrictions to sensitive sites at S end, open access to N. Dogs on leads at all times – no dogs on beach during summer. Visitor centre and toilets suitable for wheelchairs, also network of surfaced foot paths. Bird observatory and four hides suitable for wheelchairs. Day visit groups must be booked in advance. Contact Gibralter Point Field Station for residential or day visits.
Facilities: Site also location of Wash Study Centre and Bird Observatory. Field centre is an

Lincolnshire

Key to sites:
1. Donna Nook-Saltfleetby
2. Far Ings
3. Frampton Marsh
4. Freiston Shore
5. Gibraltar Point
6. Messingham Sand Quarry
7. Rigsby Wood
8. Saltfleetby-Theddlethorpe Dunes
9. Snipe Dales
10. Tetney Marshes
11. Whisby Nature Park

waders and wildfowl.
Contact: Kev Wilson, (Site Manager), Gibraltar Point Field Centre, Gibraltar Road, Skegness, Lincs PE24 4SU. 01754 762677.
e-mail:
lincstrust@gibpoint.freeserve.co.uk
www.lincstrust.co.uk

ideal base for birdwatching/natural history groups in spring, summer and autumn. Visitor centre and gift shop open daily (May-Oct) and weekends for remainder of the year. Toilets open daily.
Network of foot paths bisect all major habitats. Public hides overlook freshwater and brackish lagoons. Wash viewpoint overlooks saltmarsh and mudflats.
Public transport: Bus service from Skegness runs in occasional years but summer service only. Otherwise taxi/car from Skegness. Cycle route from Skegness.
Habitat: Sand dune grassland and scrub, saltmarshes and mudflats, freshwater marsh and lagoons.
Key birds: Large migration visible during spring and autumn passage – hirundines, chats, pipits, larks, thrushes and occasional rarities. Large numbers of waterfowl including internationally important populations of non-breeding waders. Sept-May impressive wader roosts on high tides. *Summer*: Little Tern and good assemblage of breeding warblers. *Winter*: Shore Lark, raptors,

MESSINGHAM SAND QUARRY

Lincolnshire Wildlife Trust.
Location: SK 908 032. Lies SE of Scunthorpe.
Access: Open all year. Permit required.
Facilities: Waymarked route, hide.
Public transport: None.
Habitat: Lagoons, heath, woodland, marsh.
Key birds: *Spring/summer*: Great Crested Grebe, warblers, woodpeckers, tits. *Autumn/winter*: Ducks, Bewick's Swan occasionally, Goldcrest.
Contact: Trust HQ, Banovallum House, Manor House Street, Horncastle, Lincs LN9 5HF, 01507 526 667.

RIGSBY WOOD

Lincolnshire Wildlife Trust.
Location: TF 421 762. Site lies SE of Louth. From there take A16 to A1104 (Ulceby Cross to Alford road). Turn N to South Thoresby. Wood is about two miles on the L. Park on the road. Entrance is down a track from the road.
Access: Open all year.
Facilities: Waymarked route.

Public transport: None.
Habitat: Ancient woodland.
Key birds: *Spring/summer*: Chiffchaff, Garden Warbler, Blackcap, Whitethroat, Cuckoo, Great-spotted Woodpecker, Treecreeper, Tawny Owl. *Autumn/winter*: Woodcock, Redpoll.
Contact: Trust HQ, Banovallum House, Manor House Street, Horncastle, Lincs LN9 5HF, 01507 526 667.

SALTFLEETBY-THEDDLETHORPE DUNES

English Nature (East Midlands Team).
Location: TF 46 59 24-TF 49 08 83. Approx two miles N of Mablethorpe. All the following car parks may be accessed from the A1031: Crook Bank, Brickyard Lane, Churchill Lane, Rimac, Sea View
Access: Open all year at all times. Dogs on leads. A purpose-built easy access trail suitable for wheelchair users starts adjacent to Rimac car park, just over 0.5 miles long meanders past ponds. Includes pond-viewing platform and saltmarsh-viewing platform.
Facilities: Toilets, including wheelchair suitability at Rimac car park (next to trail) May to end of Sept.
Public transport: Grayscroft coaches (01507 473236) and Lincolnshire Roadcar (01522 532424). Both run services past Rimac entrance (Louth to Mablethorpe service). Lincs Roadcar can connect with trains at Lincoln. Applebys Coaches (01507 357900). Grimsby to Saltfleet bus connects with Grimsby train service.
Habitat: 13th Century dunes, freshwater marsh, new dune ridge with large areas of sea blackthorn, saltmarsh, shingle ridge and foreshore.
Key birds: *Summer*: Small breeding colony of Little Terns. Breeding birds in scrub include Nightingale, Grasshopper Warbler, Whitethroat, Lesser Whitethroat, Redpoll. *Winter*: Large flocks of Brent Goose, Shelduck, Teal and Wigeon. Wintering Short-eared Owl, Hen Harrier.
Contact: Simon Smith, English Nature, The Maltings, Wharf Road, Grantham, Lincs NG31 6BH. 01205 311674.
e-mail: simonb.smith@english-nature.org.uk

SNIPE DALES NATURE

Lincolnshire Wildlife Trust.
Location: TF 319 683 (nature reserve) and TF 330 682 (country park). Well signposted off the A158 Skegness-Lincoln Road and from the B1195 Horncastle-Spilsby road.
Contact: Peter Graves, Snipe Dales Country Park, Lusby, Spilsby PE23 4JB. 01507 588401. www.lincstrust.co.uk

TETNEY MARSHES

RSPB (North of England Office).
Location: TA 345 025. Near Cleethorpes. Via gate or river bank E of Tetney Lock, which is two miles E of A1031 at Tetney, or through Humberston Fithes.
Access: Access at all times. Visitors are asked to keep to the seawalls, especially during the breeding season (Apr-Aug).
Facilities: None.
Public transport: None.
Habitat: Saltmarsh, sand-dunes and inter-tidal sandflats.
Key birds: *Summer*: Breeding Little Tern, Redshank, Shelduck. *Winter*: Brent Goose, Common Scoter, Wigeon, Bar-tailed Godwit, Knot, Grey and Golden Plovers. All three harriers recorded on passage. Migrant Whimbrel.
Contact: RSPB, 4 Benton Terrace, Sandyford Road, Newcastle-upon-Tyne NE2 1QU.

WHISBY NATURE PARK

Lincolnshire Wildlife Trust.
Location: SK 914 661. W of Lincoln off A46 southern end of Lincoln relief road. Brown tourist signs.
Access: Nature Park open dawn to dusk. Consult notice board at entrance. Car park closed out of hours. Free entry. Natural World Visitor Centre open (10am-5pm), free entry. Some special exhibitions will have a charge. Disabled access. Dogs on leads.
Facilities: Toilets, visitor centre, café, education centre, waymarked routes, interpretation signs, leaflets.
Public transport: No. 65 bus Mon-Sat from Lincoln to Thorpe-on-the-Hill (1/4 mile away).
Habitat: Flooded sand and gravel pits.
Key birds: *Summer*: Common Tern on specially-built rafts, Nightingale, Whitethroat, Lesser Whitethroat, Tree Sparrow. *Winter*: Wigeon, Teal, Pochard, Tufted Duck, Goldeneye.
Contact: Phil Porter, Whisby Nature Park, Moor Lane, Thorpe-on-the-Hill, Lincoln LN6 9BW. 01522 500676. www.lincstrust.co.uk
e-mail: whisby@cix.co.uk

London, Greater

BEDFONT LAKES COUNTRY PARK

Ecology and Countryside Parks Service.
Location: TQ 080 728. OS map sheet 176 (west London). 0.5 miles from Ashford, Middx, 0.5 miles S of A30, Clockhouse Roundabout, on B3003 (Clockhouse Lane).
Access: Open 7.30am-9pm or dusk whichever is earlier, all days except Christmas Day. Disabled friendly. Dogs on leads. Main nature reserve area only open Sun (2pm-4pm).
Facilities: Toilets, information centre, several hides, nature trail, free parking, up-to-date information.
Public transport: Train to Feltham and Ashford. Bus – H26 and 116 from Hounslow.
Habitat: Lakes, wildflower meadows, woodland, scrub.
Key birds: *Winter*: Water Rail, Bittern, Smew and other wildfowl, Meadow Pipit. *Summer*: Common Tern, Willow, Garden, Reed and Sedge Warblers, Whitethroat, Lesser Whitethroat, hirundines, Hobby, Blackcap, Chiffchaff, Skylark. *Passage*: Wheatear, Wood Warbler, Spotted Flycatcher, Ring Ouzel, Redstart, Yellow Wagtail.
Contact: Paul Morgan (Ecology Ranger), BLCP, Clockhouse Lane, Bedfont, Middx TW14 8QA. 01784 423556; Fax:01784 423451. e-mail: bedfont-lakes@cip.org.uk

CAMLEY STREET NATURAL PARK

London Wildlife Trust.
Location: From Kings Cross Station travel up Pancras Road between Kings Cross and St Pancras Stations. At the junction under a railway bridge turn R into Goods Way. Turn L into Camley Street and follow the telegraph pole fence to the large wrought-iron gates.
Access: Weekdays (9am-5pm), weekends (11am-5pm). Closed Fri.
Facilities: Path.
Public transport: Nearest train/tube: Kings Cross, St Pancras.
Habitat: Woodland scrub, reedbeds, meadow, pond.
Key birds: *Spring/summer*: Warblers. *All year*: Mallard, Tufted Duck, Moorhen, Grey Heron. *Winter*: Siskin, Reed Warbler. *All year*: Sparrowhawk. Good for dragonflies.

Contact: London Wildlife Trust, Harling House, 47-51 Great Suffolk Street, London SE1 0BS, 0207 2610447.
e-mail: enquiries@wildlondon.org.uk
www.wildlondon.org.uk

THE CHASE NNR

London Wildlife Trust.
Location: TQ 515 860. Lies in the Dagenham Corridor, an area of green belt between the London Boroughs of Barking & Dagenham and Havering.
Access: Open throughout the year and at all times. Reserve not suitable for wheelchair access. Eastbrookend Country Park which borders The Chase LNR has surfaced footpaths which are easily accessible for wheelchair use.
Facilities: Millennium visitor centre, toilets, ample car parking, Timberland Trail walk.
Public transport: Rail Dagenham East (District Line) 15 minute walk. Bus 174 from Romford five minute walk.
Habitat: Shallow wetlands, reedbeds, horse-grazed pasture, scrub and wetland. These harbour an impressive range of animals and plants including the nationally rare black poplar tree. This site is a haven for birds, with approx 190 different species recorded here over the years.
Key birds: *Summer*: Breeding Reed Warbler, Lapwing, Water Rail, Lesser Whitethroat and Little Ringed Plover. *Winter*: Significant numbers of Teal, Shoveler, Redwing, Fieldfare and Snipe dominate the scene. *Spring/autumn migration*: Yellow Wagtail, Wheatear, Ruff, Wood Sandpiper, Sand Martin and Hobby regularly seen.
Contact: Gareth Winn/Ian Holt, Project Manager/Project Officer,The Millennium Centre, The Chase, Off Dagenham Road, Rush Green, Romford, Essex RM7 0SS. 020 8593 8096. e-mail: lwtchase@cix.co.uk
www.wildlifetrust.org.uk/london/

RIPPLE NATURE RESERVE

London Wildlife Trust/Thames Water.
Location: TQ 167 757. About eight miles from the centre of London, next to Thamesmead Park City Farm on the Thames Road/Renwick.
Access: Open all year.

Facilities: None
Public transport: Bus: to the end of route in Thames View Estate. Tube: Barking/District Line.
Habitat: Meadow, roughland, reeds, copse, water.
Key birds: *Spring/summer*: Warblers inc Reed Warbler, migrants. *All year*: Kingfisher, Chaffinch, woodpeckers, usual woodland species.
Contact: London Wildlife Trust, Harling House, 47-51 Great Suffolk Street, London SE1 0BS, 0207 2610447. www.wildlondon.org.uk
e-mail: enquiries@wildlondon.org.uk

SYDENHAM HILL WOOD

London Wildlife Trust.
Location: TQ 335 722. SE London, SE26, between Forest Hill and Crystal Palace, just off South Circular (A205).
Access: Open at all times, no permits required. Some steep slopes which makes disabled access limited
Facilities: Nature trail, no toilets.
Public transport: Train – Sydenham Hill, Forest Hill. Bus – 63, 202, 356, 185, 312, 176.
Habitat: Oak and hornbeam woodland, small pond, meadow and glades.
Key birds: *Resident*: Kestrel, Sparrowhawk, Tawny Owl, all three woodpeckers, Treecreeper, Nuthatch, Song Thrush. *Summer*: Chiffchaff, Blackcap. *Winter*: Redwing, Fieldfare.
Contact: The Warden, London Wildlife Trust, Horniman Museum, 100 London Road, London SE23 3PQ. 020 8699 5698.
e-mail: lwtsydenham@cix.co.uk

THE WETLAND CENTRE

The Wildfowl & Wetlands Trust.
Location: TQ 228 770. In London, Zone 2, one mile from Hammersmith.
Access: Winter (9.30am-5pm: last admission 4pm), summer (9.30am-6pm: last admission 5pm). Charge for admission.
Facilities: Visitor centre, hides, nature trails, art gallery, discovery restaurant (hot and cold food), cinema, shop, observatory centre, seven hides (one with a lift for wheelchair access), three interpretive buildings.
Public transport: Train: Barnes. Tube: hammersmith then Duckbus 283 (comes into centre). Bus from Hammersmith – 283, 33, 72, 209. Bus from Richmond 33, 72.
Habitat: Main lake, reedbeds, wetland, wader scrape, mudflats, open water lakes, grazing marsh.
Key birds: Nationally important numbers of wintering waterfowl including Gadwall and Shoveler. Important numbers of wetland breeding birds including grebes, swans, a range of duck species, such as Pochard plus Lapwing, Little Ringed Plover, Redshank, warblers and Reed Bunting.
Contact: John Arbon (Grounds and Facilities Manager), Stephanie Fudge (Manager), The Wetland Centre, Queen Elizabeth Walk, Barnes, London SW13 9WT. 0208 409 4400.
e-mail: info@wetlandcentre.org.uk
www.wetlandcentre.co.uk

Manchester, Greater

ASTLEY MOSS

The Wildlife Trust for Lancashire, Manchester and North Merseyside
Location: Lancs WT SJ692975. S of A580 at Astley; follow Higher Green Lane to Rindle Farm.
Contact: Dave Woodward, 54 Windermere Road, Leigh, Lancs WN7 1UZ,

AUDENSHAW RESERVOIRS

United Utilities, Bottoms Office.
Location: NW Water SJ915965. Access and parking on Audenshaw Road B6390 at N end of site.
Access: No disabled access.
Facilities: Hide (contact R Travis on 0161 330 2607). Permit (free) from D Tomes, UU Bottoms Office, Woodhead Road, Tintwistle, Glossop SK13 1HS.
Public transport: None.
Habitat: Reservoir.
Key birds: Major migration point; *Winter*: Notable gull roost inc. regular Mediterranean Gull; large Goosander roost; many rarities.

Manchester, Greater

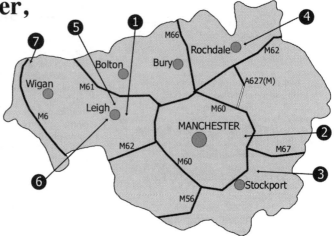

Key to sites:
1. Astley Moss
2. Audenshaw Reservoirs
3. Etherow Country Park
4. Hollingworth Lake Country Park
5. Hope Carr Nature Reserve
6. Pennington Flash Country Park
7. Wigan Flashes

ETHEROW COUNTRY PARK

Stockport Metropolitan Borough Council.
Location: SJ 965 908. B6104 into Compstall near Romiley, Stockport.
Contact: John Rowland, Etherow Country Park, Compstall, Stockport, Cheshire SK6 5JD. 0161 427 6937; fax 0161 427 3643.

HOLLINGWORTH LAKE

Hollingworth Lake Country Park – Rochdale MBC.
Location: SD 939 153 (visitor centre). Four miles NE of Rochdale, signed from A58 Halifax Road. Near J21 of M62 – B6225 to Littleborough.
Access: Access open to lake and surroundings at all times.
Facilities: Cafes, hide, trails and education service, car parks. Visitor centre open 10.30am-6pm (Mon-Fri), 10.30am-7pm (Sat & Sun) in summer, 11am-4pm (Mon-Fri), 10.30am-5pm (Sat & Sun) in winter.
Public transport: Bus Nos 452, 450. Train to Littleborough or Smithy Bridge.
Habitat: Lake (116 acres 47 ha includes 20 acre nature reserve), woodland, streams, marsh, willow scrub.
Key birds: *All year*: Great Crested Grebe, Kingfisher, Lapwing, Little Owl, Bullfinch, Cormorant. Occasional Peregrine Falcon, Sedge Warbler, Water Rail, Snipe. *Spring/autumn*: passage waders, wildfowl, Kittiwake. *Summer*: Reed Bunting, Dipper, Common Sandpiper,

Curlew, Oystercatcher, Black Tern, 'Commic' Tern, Grey Partridge, Blackcap. *Winter*: Goosander, Goldeneye, Siskin, Redpoll, Golden Plover.
Contact: The Ranger, Hollingworth Lake Visitor Centre, Rakewood Road, Littleborough OL15 0AQ01706 373421.
e-mail: holl.lakecp@rochdale.gov.uk

HOPE CARR NATURE RESERVE

NW Water.
Location: SJ 664 986. In Leigh, W of Salford. From A580 E Lancs Road turn N at Greyhound Motel roundabout, L at first lights, first L at mini roundabout.
Contact: Joe Grima, Leigh Environmental, Education Centre, Hope Carr, Hope Carr Lane, Leigh WN7 3XB. 01942 269027; fax 01942 269028; mobile 0790 9996272.

PENNINGTON FLASH

Wigan Council (Leisure & Cultural Services Department).
Location: SJ 640 990. One mile from Leigh town centre. Main entrance on A572 (St Helens Road).
Access: Park is signposted from A580 (East Lancs Road) and is permanently open. Four largest hides, toilets and information point open 9am-dusk (except Christmas Day). Main paths flat and suitable for disabled.
Facilities: Toilets including disabled toilet and information point. Total of seven bird hides. Site leaflet available and Rangers based on site. Group

visits welcome, guided tours or a site introduction can be arranged subject to staff availability.
Public transport: None.
Habitat: Lowland lake, ponds and scrapes, fringed with reeds, rough grassland, scrub and young woodland.
Key birds: Waterfowl all year, waders mainly passage spring and autumn (14-plus species). Breeding Common Tern and Little Ringed Plover. Feeding station attracts Willow Tit and Bullfinch all year.
Contact: Peter Alker, Pennington Flash Country Park, St Helens Road, Leigh WN7 3PA. 01942 605253 (also fax number).

WIGAN FLASHES

Lancashire Wildlife Trust/Wigan Council/RSPB.

Location: SD 580 035. One mile from J25 of M6.
Access: Free access, open at all times. Areas suitable for disabled but some motor cycle barriers with gates. Paths being upgraded.
Facilities: None.
Public transport: 610 bus (Hawkley Hall Circular).
Habitat: Wetland with reedbed.
Key birds: Black Tern on migration. *Summer*: Nationally important for Reed Warbler and breeding Common Tern. Willow Tit, Grasshopper Warbler, Kingfisher. *Winter*: Wildfowl especially diving duck and Gadwall. Bittern (especially winter).
Contact: Mark Champion, 225 Poolstock Lane, Wigan, Lancs WN3 5JE. 01942 236337. e-mail: mark@championx.freeserve.co.uk

Merseyside

AINSDALE AND BIRKDALE

Sefton Council.
Location: SD 300 115. SD 310 138. Lies on coast between Formby and Southport. Leave the A565 at Arnsdale just N of Formby and car parking areas are off the unnumbered coastal road.

Access: Track from Ainsdale or Southport along the shore. Wheelchair access across boardwalks at Ainsdale Sands Lake Nature Trail and the Queen's Jubilee Nature Trail, opposite Weld Road.
Facilities: Ainsdale Visitor Centre open summer. Toilets (Easter-Oct).
Public transport: Ainsdale and Southport stations 20 minute walk. Hillside Station is a 30 minute walk across the Birkdale Sandhills to beach.
Habitat: Foreshore, dune scrub and pine woodland.
Key birds: *Spring/summer*: Grasshopper Warbler, Chiffchaff, waders. *Winter*: Blackcap, Stonechat, Redwing, Fieldfare, waders and wildfowl. *All year*: Sky Lark, Grey Partridge.
Contact: Sefton Council, Southport Town Hall, Lord Street, Southport PR8 1DA, www.sefton.gov.uk

Key to sites:
1. Ainsdale & Birkdale LNR
2. Dee Estuary
3. Hilbre Islands LNR
4. Marshside
5. Seaforth Nature Reserve

DEE ESTUARY

Wirral Country Park Centre (Metropolitan Borough of Wirral).
Location: SJ 255 815. Leave A540 Chester to Hoylake road at Heswall and head downhill (one mile) to the free car park at the shore end of Banks Road. Heswall is 30 minutes from South Liverpool and Chester by car.
Access: Open at all times. Best viewpoint 600 yards along shore N of Banks Road. No disabled access along shore, but good birdwatching from bottom of Banks Road. Arrive 2.5 hours before high tide.
Facilities: Toilets in car park and information board. Wirral Country Park Centre three miles N off A540 has toilets, hide, café, kiosk (all accessible to wheelchairs). Birdwatching events programme available from visitor centre.
Public transport: Bus service to Banks Road car park from Heswall bus station. Contact Mersey Travel (tel 0151 236 7676).
Habitat: Saltmarsh and mudflats.
Key birds: *Autumn/winter:* Large passage and winter wader roosts – Redshank, Curlew, Black-tailed Godwit, Oystercatcher, Golden Plover, Knot, Shelduck, Teal, Red-breasted Merganser, Peregrine, Merlin, Hen Harrier, Short-eared Owl. Smaller numbers of Pintail, Wigeon, Bar-tailed Godwit, Greenshank, Spotted Redshank, Grey and Ringed Plovers, Whimbrel, Curlew Sandpiper, Little Stint, occasional Scaup and Little Egret.
Contact: Martyn Jamieson, Head Ranger, Wirral Country Park Centre, Station Road, Thurstaston, Wirral, CH61 0HN. 0151 648 4371/3884. e-mail: wirralcountrypark@wirral.gov.uk www.wirral.gov.uk/leisure/ranger

HILBRE ISLAND

Location: SJ 184 880. Three tidal islands in the mouth of the Dee Estuary. Park in West Kirby which is on the A540 Chester-to-Hoylake road – 30 minutes from Liverpool, 45 minutes from Chester. Follow the brown Marine Lake signs to Dee Lane pay and display car park.
Contact: Martyn Jamieson, Head Ranger, Wirral Country Park Centre, Station Road, Thurstaston, Wirral, Merseyside CH61 0HN0151 648 4371/3884. e-mail: wirralcountrypark@wirral.gov.uk www.wirral.gov.uk/leisure/ranger

MARSHSIDE

RSPB (North West England Office).
Location: SD 355 202. On south shore of Ribble Estuary, one mile north of Southport centre on Marine Drive.
Access: Open 8.30am-5pm all year. No toilets. No dogs please. Coach parties please book in advance. No charges but donations welcomed.
Facilities: Two hides and trails accessible to wheelchairs.
Public transport: Bus service to Elswick Road/Marshside Road half-hourly, bus No 44. Contact Southport Buses (01704 536137).
Habitat: Coastal grazing marsh and lagoons.
Key birds: *Winter:* Pink-footed Goose, wildfowl, waders, raptors. *Spring:* Breeding waders and wildfowl, Garganey, migrants. *Autumn:* Migrants. *All year:* Black-tailed Godwit.
Contact: Tony Baker, RSPB, Beechwood, Cat Tail Lane, Scarisbrick, Southport PR8 5LW. 01704 233003.
e-mail: tony.baker@rspb.org.uk

SEAFORTH NATURE RESERVE

The Wildlife Trust for Lancashire, Manchester and North Merseyside
Location: SJ 315 970. Five miles from Liverpool city centre. From M57/M58 take A5036 to docks.
Access: Open dawn-dusk daily. £1 donation expected. No dogs. Wheelchairs possible but difficult.
Facilities: Toilets when visitor centre open, three hides.
Public transport: Train to Waterloo or Seaforth stations from Liverpool. Buses to dock gates from Liverpool.
Habitat: Saltwater and freshwater lagoons, scrub grassland.
Key birds: Little Gull on passage (Apr) plus Roseate, Little and Black Terns. Breeding and passage Common Tern (Apr-Sept) plus Roseate, Little and Black Terns on passage. Passage and winter waders and gulls. Passage passerines, especially White Wagtail, pipits and Wheatear.
Contact: Steve White, Seaforth Nature Reserve, Port of Liverpool L21 1JD. 0151 9203769.
e-mail: lwildlife@cix.co.uk

Norfolk

BERNEY MARSHES

Location: TG 465 055. W of Great Yarmouth. In the Halvergate Marshes.
Contact: Chris Gregory, Warden, Ashtree Farm, Goodchild Marine, Butt Lane, Burgh Castle, Great Yarmouth, Norfolk NR31 9PE,

BLAKENEY POINT

Location: TG 000 465. Famous sand and shingle spit N of Morston and Blakeney off A149 road.
Contact: Joe Reed, Property Manager, 35 The Cornfield, Langham, Holt, Norfolk NR25 7DQ. 01263 740241.
e-mail: abyjrx@smtp.ntrust.org.uk

BUCKENHAM MARSHES

Location: TG 352 056. Located N of River Yare, SE of Norwich. From A47 take minor road S to Strumpshaw and Buckenham. Park at Buckenham Station.
Contact: Mark Smart, Staithe Cottage, Low Road, Strumpshaw, Norwich, Norfolk NR13 4HS. 01603 715191. www.rspb.org.uk
e-mail strumpshaw@rspb.org.uk

CLEY MARSHES

Norfolk Wildlife Trust.
Location: TG 054 441. NWT Cley Marshes is situated three miles N of Holt on A149 coast road, half a mile E of Cley-next-the-Sea.
Access: Open all year round (closed Mon – except Bank Holidays). Visitor centre open Apr-Oct (10am-5pm daily), Nov-mid Dec (10am-4pm Wed-Sun). Cost: adults £3.50, children under 16 free. NWT members free.
Facilities: Hides, gift shop, refreshments, toilets, coach and car parking, disabled access to centre, boardwalk and hides and toilets, groups welcome.
Public transport: Bus service from Norwich, Fakenham and Holt Mon-Sat. The Coasthopper service stops outside daily. Connections for train and bus services at Sheringham. Special discounts to visitors arriving by bus.
Habitat: Reedbeds, salt and freshwater marshes, scrapes and shingle ridge with international reputation.
Key birds: *Feb:* Brent Goose, warblers, Wigeon, Teal, Shoveler, Pintail. *Spring*: Wheatear,

Sandwich Tern, Reed and Sedge Warblers, Ruff, Black-tailed Godwit. *Jun*: Spoonbill, Avocet, Bittern, Bearded Tit. *Autumn*: Common and rare waders.
Contact: Dick Bagnall, Oakeley Centre, NWT Cley Marshes, Cley, Holt, Norfolk NR25 7RZ. 01263 740008. e-mail BernardB@nwt.cix.co.uk www.wildlifetrust.org.uk.Norfolk

EAST WRETHAM HEATH

Location: TL 913 887. Site lies in the centre of Breckland N of Thetford. From A11 take A1075 to Watton. Travel over level crossing and pass the lay-by to L. Car park and entrance to reserve are by the first house on L.
Contact: Bev Nichols, The Wardens' House, East Wretham Heath, Thetford Road, Wretham, Thetford IP24 1RU. 01953 498339.
e-mail: BevN@nwt.cix.co.uk
www.wildlifetrust.org.uk/Norfolk

FOXLEY WOOD

Location: TG 049 229. Foxley Wood is situated 12 miles NW of Norwich on A1067, signposted at Foxley village from main road.
Contact: Norfolk Wildlife Trust HQ.

HICKLING BROAD

Norfolk Wildlife Trust.
Location: TG 428 222. Approx four miles SE of Stalham, just off A149 Yarmouth Road. From Hickling village, follow the brown 'duck' tourist signs into Stubb Road at the Greyhound Inn. Take first turning left to follow Stubb Road for another mile. Turn right for nature reserve.
Access: Open all year. Visitor centre open Apr-Sept (10am-5pm daily). Cost: adults £2.50, children under 16 free. NWT members free.
Facilities: Visitor centre, boardwalk trail, hides, gift shop, refreshments, picnic site, toilets, coach and car parking, disabled access to broad, boardwalk and toilets. Groups welcome. Water trail (additional charge – booking essential).
Public transport: Morning bus service only Mon-Fri from Norwich (Neaves Coaches) Cromer to North Walsham (Sanders). Buses stop in Hickling village, a 20 minute walk away.
Habitat: The largest and wildest of the Norfolk Broads with reedbeds and grazing marshes.
Key birds: Marsh Harriers, Bittern. Swallowtail

Key to sites:
1. Berney Marshes
2. Blakeney Point
3. Buckenham Marshes
4. Cley Marshes
5. East Wretham Heath
6. Foxley Wood
7. Hickling Broad
8. Holkham
9. Holme Bird Observatory
10. Nunnery Lakes
11. Ranworth Broad
12. Redwell Marsh
13. Scolt Head Island
14. Snettisham
15. Strumpshaw Fen
16. Surlingham Church Marsh
17. Titchwell Marsh
18. Walsey Hills
19. The Wash NNR
20. Weeting Heath
21. Welney

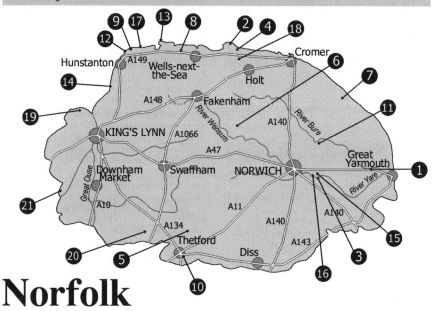

Norfolk

butterfly, Norfolk hawker (rare dragonfly).
Contact: John Blackburn, Hickling Broad Visitor Centre, Stubb Road, Hickling NR12 0BN,
e-mail johnb@nwt.cix.co.uk
www.wildlifetrust.org.uk/norfolk

HOLKHAM

Location: TF 890 450. From Holkham village turn N off A149 down Lady Ann's Drive; parking.
Contact: R Harold, Hill Farm Offices, Main Road, Holkham, Wells-next-the-Sea NR23 1AB. 01328 711183; fax 01328 711893.

HOLME BIRD OBSERVATORY

Norfolk Ornithologist's Association (NOA).
Location: TF 717 450. E of Hunstanton, signposted from A149. Access from Broadwater Road.
Access: Reserve open daily to members dawn to

dusk; non-members (9am-5pm) by permit from the Observatory. Please keep dogs on leads in the reserve. Parties by prior arrangement.
Facilities: Visitor centre, car park and several hides (seawatch hide reserved for NOA members) together with access to beach and coastal path.
Public transport: Coastal bus service runs from Hunstanton to Sheringham roughly every 30 mins but is seasonal and times may vary. Phone Norfolk Green Bus, 01553 776 980.
Habitat: In 10 acres of diverse habitat: sand dunes, Corsican pines, scrub and reed-fringed lagoon make this a migration hotspot.
Key birds: Species list over 320. Ringed species over 150. Recent rarities have included Pallas' and Yellow-browed Warbler, Red-breasted Flycatcher, Tawny Pipit and Bee-eater.
Contact: Jed Andrews, Holme Bird Observatory, Broadwater Road, Holme, Hunstanton, Norfolk PE36 6LQ. 01485 525406. www.noa.org.uk
e-mail: jedandrews@shrike4.freeserve.co.uk

Please note: Holme Bird Observatory, Redwell Marsh and Walsey Hills are run by the Norfolk Ornithologist's Association. They were incorrectly named as Norfolk Wildlife Trust reserves in the 2002 edition of *The Birdwatcher's Yearbook*. We apologise for any confusion this may have caused.

NUNNERY LAKES

Location: TL 873 815. On the S edge of Thetford, adjacent to the BTO's headquarters at The Nunnery, off Nun's Bridges Road. Main access point is about 60 yards upriver of Nun's Bridges car park (TL 874 825) on the opposite side of the River Little Ouse.
Contact: Chris Gregory, The British Trust for Ornithology, The Nunnery, Thetford, Norfolk IP24 2PU. 01842 750050. www.bto.org

RANWORTH BROAD

Location: TG 357 149. Ranworth is approx four miles SE of Wroxham, signposted on the B1140 Norwich to Acle road at South Walsham. At Ranworth village look out for the signs to the centre and the Norfolk Wildlife Trust car park.
Contact: Norfolk Wildlife Trust HQ.

REDWELL MARSH

Norfolk Ornithologist's Association (NOA).
Location: TF 702 436. In Holme, off A149, E of Hunstanton. Access from Broadwater road.
Contact: Jed Andrews, Holme Bird Observatory, see details above.

SNETTISHAM

RSPB (East Anglia Office).
Location: TF 630 310. Car park two miles along Beach road, signposted off A149 King's Lynn to Hunstanton, opposite Snettisham village.
Access: Open at all times. £2 car parking fee for non-members. Dogs to be kept on leads. Two hides are suitable for wheelchairs. Disabled access is across a private road. Please phone office number for permission and directions.
Facilities: Four birdwatching hides, connected by reserve footpath. No toilets on site.
Public transport: Nearest over two miles away.
Habitat: Intertidal mudflats, saltmarsh, shingle beach, brackish lagoons, and unimproved grassland/scrub. Best visited on a high tide.
Key birds: *Autumn/winter/spring*: Waders (particularly Knot, Bar and Black-tailed Godwits, Dunlin, Grey Plover), wildfowl (particularly Pink-footed and Brent Geese, Wigeon, Gadwall, Goldeneye), Peregrine, Hen Harrier, Merlin, owls. Migrants in season. *Summer*: Breeding Ringed Plover, Redshank, Avocet, Common Tern. Marsh Harrier regular.

Contact: Jim Scott, RSPB, 43 Lynn Road, Snettisham, King's Lynn, Norfolk PE31 7LR. 01485 542689.

STRUMPSHAW FEN

RSPB (East Anglia Office).
Location: TG 33 06. Seven miles ESE of Norwich. Follow signposts. Entrance across level-crossing from car park, reached by turning sharp right and right again into Low Road from Brundall, off A47 to Great Yarmouth.
Access: Open dawn-dusk. RSPB members free, adults £2.50, children 50p, family £5. Guide dogs only. Viewing platform for wheelchair users.
Facilities: Toilets, reception hide and two other hides, two walks, five miles of trails.
Public transport: Brundall train station about one mile. Bus stop half a mile – contact NORBIC (0845 300 6116).
Habitat: Reedbed and reedfen, wet grassland and woodland.
Key birds: *Summer*: Bittern, Bearded Tit, Marsh Harrier, Cetti's Warbler and other reedbed birds. *Winter*: Bean and White-fronted Geese, Hen Harrier. Swallowtails in Jun.
Contact: Tim Strudwick, Staithe Cottage, Low Road, Strumpshaw, Norwich, Norfolk NR13 4HS. 01603 715191.
e-mail: strumpshaw@rspb.org.uk
www.rspb.org.uk

SURLINGHAM CHURCH MARSH

RSPB (East Anglia Office).
Location: TG 304 066. Six miles E of Norwich, S of River Yare, N of A146 Norwich to Lowestoft road.
Contact: Tim Strudwick, see above.

TITCHWELL MARSH

RSPB (East Anglia Office).
Location: TF 749 436. Near Hunstanton. Footpath along sea wall from A149 between Thornham and Titchwell.
Access: Fen and meadow trails are new additions allowing further access to the reserve. Reserve and hides open at all times.
Facilities: Visitor centre, shop and servery open every day as follows: summer (BST) Mon-Fri (10am-5pm), Sat-Sun (9.30am-5pm), winter Mon-Fri (10am-4pm), Sat-Sun (9.30am-5pm). Closed Christmas and Boxing Days.

Public transport: Phone Norfolk Green Bus 01553 776980.
Habitat: Reedbed, brackish & freshwater pools, saltmarsh, dunes, shingle.
Key birds: *Spring/summer*: Nesting Avocet, Bearded Tit, Water Rail, Marsh Harrier, Reed and Sedge Warblers. *Autumn*: Knot. *Winter*: Brent Geese, Goldeneye, Scoter, Eider, Hen Harrier roost, Snow Bunting and Shorelark.
Contact: Warden, Titchwell Marsh Reserve, King's Lynn, Norfolk PE31 8BB. Tel/fax 01485 210779.

WALSEY HILLS

Norfolk Ornithologist's Association (NOA).
Location: TG 062 441. Up footpath and steps from A149 at Cley.
Access: Open daily throughout year.
Facilities: Wardened visitor centre providing up-to-date birding information. Short walk through scrub. Excellent views across adjoining reserves between Cley and Salthouse. Important migration watch point.
Public transport: Phone Norfolk Green Bus 01553 776980.
Habitat: Scrub.
Key birds: Recent sightings include Bittern, White Stork, Rough-legged Buzzard, Osprey, Merlin, Crane, Red-necked Phalarope, Wryneck, Marsh Warbler, Bluethroat, Rustic Bunting.
Contact: Tom Fletcher, 01263 740875.

THE WASH NNR

English Nature East Midlands Team.
Location: TR 49 22 57. 7.5 miles West of King's Lynn. From A17, follow road along East bank of River Nene at Sutton Bridge.
Access: Open access, remain on public footpaths along seabank and keep dogs under control.
Contact: English Nature East Midlands, The Maltings, Wharf Road, Grantham, Lincs NG31 6BH. 01205 311674. www.english-nature.org.uk e-mail: simonb.smith@english-nature.org.uk

WEETING HEATH

Norfolk Wildlife Trust.
Location: TL 756 881. Weeting Heath is signposted from the Weeting-Hockwold road, two miles W of Weeting near to Brandon in Suffolk. Nature reserve can be reached via B1112 at Hockwold or B1106 at Weeting.
Access: Open daily from Apr-Aug. Cost: adults £2.00, children free. NWT members free. Disabled access to visitor centre only.
Facilities: Visitor centre, birdwatching hides, wildlife gift shop, refreshments, toilets, coach parking, car park, groups welcome (book first).
Public transport: Train services to Brandon and bus connections from Brandon High Street.
Habitat: Breckland.
Key birds: Stone Curlew, migrant passerines.
Contact: Bev Nichols, (see East Wretham Heath). 01842 827615.

WELNEY

Location: TL 546 944. Ten miles N of Ely, signposted from A10 and A1101.
Contact: Carl Mitchell, WWT, Hundred Foot Bank, Welney, Nr Wisbech PE14 9TN. 01353 860711. e-mail: welney@wwt.org.uk www.wwt.org.uk

Northants

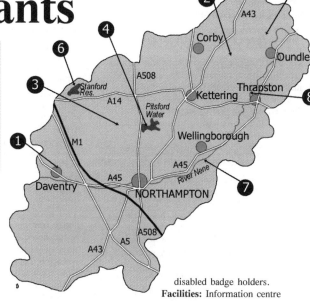

Key to sites:
1. Daventry Reservoir CP
2. Fermyn Woods CP
3. Hollowell Reservoir
4. Pitsford Reservoir
5. Short Wood
6. Stanford Reservoir
7. Summer Leys LNR
8. Thrapston Gravel Pits &
   Titchmarsh LNR

DAVENTRY RESERVOIR

Daventry District Council .
Location: SP 577 642. Signposted from B4036
Daventry to Welton road.
Access: Open at all times
Facilities: Two hides open all year, cafe, visitor
centre.
Public transport: None.
Habitat: Open water, wetlands, reed, meadows,
woodland.
Key birds: *Autumn*: Passage waders inc. Dunlin,
Ruff, Greenshank, Green Sandpiper; nesting
Common Tern, Arctic and sometimes Black
Tern on passage; gull roost; rare species inc.
Pacific Swift, Baird's Sandpiper, Wilson's
Phalarope, Sabine's Gull Honey Buzzard. Over
180 species recorded; 60 have bred.
Contact: Dewi Morris, Daventry Country Park,
Reservoir Cottage, Northern Way, Daventry,
Northants NN11 5JB. 01327 877193;
e-mail countrysideservices@daventrydc.gov.uk.

FERMYN WOODS COUNTRY PARK

Northamptonshire County Council.
Location: SP 952 849. Lies SE of Corby off
A6116 at Brigstock.
Access: Open all year. Toilets open (9am-5pm
except Christmas Day), car parking fee, free to
disabled badge holders.
Facilities: Information centre
with toilets, including disabled.
Rangers present at weekends and school
holidays. Refreshments available. Picnic tables,
children's play area, feeding station for birds.
Dogs allowed on leads. Park paths are hard
packed and suitable for wheelchairs, but some in
the nearby woodland can get muddy.
Public transport: Bus: leave from Kettering at
8.50am, arriving Brigstock village 9.11am.
Several link to Corby and Peterborough. Tel:
01604 676 060.
Habitat: Undulating meadow, scrub, freshwater
ponds, ancient woodland.
Key birds: *Summer*: Turtle Dove, Nightingale.
All year: Red Kite, woodpeckers, Jay. *Winter*:
Hawfinch, but numbers fluctuate wildly. Finches,
buntings, thrushes.
Contact: Fermyn Woods Country Park, Lyveden
Road, Brigstock, Kettering, Northamptonshire
NN14 3HS, 01536 373625.

HOLLOWELL RESERVOIR

Anglian Water.
Location: SP 683 738. From Northampton, take
the A5199 NW. After eight miles, turn L. The
car park is on the L.
Access: Open all year. Permit required. Keep
dogs on lead.

Facilities: None.
Public transport: Bus: No 60 from Northampton, first one arriving at 8.58am. Tel: 01604 676 060.
Habitat: Grass, mature, mixed and conifer plantations.
Key birds: *Autumn/winter*: Dunlin, Greenshank, Redshank, Green Sandpiper, Mediterranean Gull, ducks. Crossbill occurs in invasion years. Bearded Tit and Dartford Warbler occasional.
Contact: Anglian Water, Anglian House, Ambury Road, Huntingdon, Cambs PE29 3NZ, 01480 323000.

PITSFORD RESERVOIR

Beds, Cambs & Northants Wildlife Trust.
Location: SP 787 702. Five miles N of Northampton. On A43 take turn to Holcot and Brixworth. On A508 take turn to Brixworth and Holcot.
Contact: Dave Francis, Pitsford Water Lodge, Brixworth Road, Holcot, Northampton NN6 9SJ. 01604 780148.
e-mail: pitsford@cix.compulink.co.uk

SHORT WOOD

Beds, Cambs & Northants Wildlife Trust.
Location: TL 015 913. Via bridle path from minor road between Glapthorn and Southwick, NW of Oundle. Park on roadside verge.
Access: Open all year.
Facilities: None.
Public transport: Not known.
Habitat: Primary and secondary mixed woodland (oak, ash, field maple, hazel), coppiced.
Key birds: Woodcock, Marsh Tit, warblers, Redpoll.
Contact: Trust HQ, 01604 405285.

STANFORD RESERVOIR

Severn Trent Water/Northants Wildlife Trust.
Location: SP 600 805. One mile SW of South Kilworth off Kilworth/Stanford-on-Avon road.
Access: Daytime, permits from Northants Wildlife Trust. No dogs. Limited access for disabled.
Facilities: Toilets (inc disabled). Two hides, perimeter track. Disabled parking.
Public transport: None.
Habitat: Reservoir with willow, reed and hedgerow edges.
Key birds: *Winter*: Wildfowl, especially Ruddy

Duck. *Spring*: migratory terns and warblers. *Late summer*: Terns, Hobby, waders.
Contact: Northants Wildlife Trust, Ling House, Billing Lings, Northampton NN3 8BE. 01604 405285.

SUMMER LEYS

Northamptonshire County Council.
Location: SP 886 634. Three miles from Wellingborough, accessible from A45 and A509, situated on Great Doddington to Wollaston Road.
Access: Open 24 hours a day, 365 days a year, no permits required. Dogs welcome but must be kept on leads at all times. 40 space car park, small tarmaced circular route suitable for wheelchairs.
Facilities: Three hides, one feeding station. No toilets, nearest are at Irchester Country Park on A509 towards Wellingborough.
Public transport: Nearest main station is Wellingborough. No direct bus service, though buses run regularly to Great Doddington and Wollaston, both about a mile away. Tel: 01604 236712 (24 hrs) for copies of timetables.
Habitat: Scrape, two ponds, lake, scrub, grassland, hedgerow.
Key birds: Hobby, Lapwing, Golden Plover, Ruff, Gadwall, Garganey, Pintail, Shelduck, Shoveler, Little Ringed Plover, Tree Sparrow, Redshank, Green Sandpiper, Oystercatcher, Black-headed Gull colony, terns.
Contact: Chris Haines, Countryside and Tourism Northamptonshire Council, PO Box 163, County Hall, Northampton NN1 1AX. 01604 237227 – please ring for a leaflet about the reserve.
e-mail: countryside@northamptonshire.gov.uk

THRAPSTON GRAVEL PITS & TITCHMARSH

Beds, Cambs & Northants Wildlife Trust.
Location: TL 008 804.
Access: Public footpath from layby on A605 N of Thrapston.
Facilities: Two hides.
Public transport: Bus service to Thrapston.
Habitat: Alder/birch/willow wood; old duck decoy, series of water-filled gravel pits.
Key birds: *Summer*: Breeding Grey Heron (no access to Heronry), Common Tern, Little Ringed Plover; warblers. Migrants, inc. Red-necked and Slavonian Grebes, Bittern and Marsh Harrier.
Contact: Trust HQ, 01604 405285.

Northumberland

ARNOLD RESERVE, CRASTER

Northumberland Wildlife Trust.
Location: NU 255 197. Lies NE of Alnwick and SW of Craster village.
Access: Public footpath from car park in disused quarry.
Facilities: Information centre open in Summer. Toilets (incl disabled) and picnic site in quarry.
Public transport: Ariva Northumberland nos. 501 and 401.
Habitat: Semi-natural woodland and scrub.
Key birds: Good site for migrant passerines to rest and feed. Look for Bluethroat, Red-breasted Flycatcher, Barred and Icterine Warblers, Wryneck; moulting site for Lesser Redpoll.
Summer: Breeding warblers.
Contact: Trust HQ, 0191 284 6884.

BRIARWOOD BANKS

Northumberland Wildlife Trust.
Location: NY 791 620. From Haydon Bridge, take minor road from A686 to Plankey Mill, three miles away at junction of Kingswood Burn and River Allen.
Access: Footpaths open to public. One steep route may be impassable after heavy rain.
Facilities: Parking at Plankey Mill. Picnic site and toilets at NT carpark at Allenbanks.
Public transport: None.
Habitat: Ancient woodland along steep valley.
Key birds: Pied Flycatcher, Wood Warbler, Redstart, Dipper, Woodcock, Treecreeper, Nuthatch.
Contact: Trust HQ, 0191 284 6884.

COCKLAWBURN DUNES

Location: NU 033 481. SE of Scremerston off A1, four miles S of Berwick.
Contact: Northumberland Wildlife Trust.

Key to sites:
1. Arnold Reserve
2. Briarwood Banks
3. Cocklawburn Dunes
4. Coquet Island
5. Druridge Bay
6. Farne Islands
7. Grindon Lough
8. Holywell Pond
9. Lindisfarne NNR
10. Newton Pool Nature Reserve

COQUET ISLAND

Location: NU 294 046. Small island E of Amble. Take A1068 SE from Alnwick.
Contact: RSPB Warden, c/o RSPB North of England Office.

DRURIDGE BAY RESERVES

Northumberland Wildlife Trust.
Location: 1. NU 285 023. S of Amble. Hauxley (67a) approached by track from road midway between High and Low Hauxley. 2. Druridge Pools NZ 272 965. 3. Cresswell Pond NZ 283 945. Half mile N of Cresswell.
Access: Day permits for all three reserves.
Facilities: 1. Visitor centre, five hides (one suitable for disabled). Disabled toilet. Lake with islands behind dunes. 2. Three hides. 3. Hide.
Public transport: None.
Habitat: 2. Deep lake and wet meadows with pools behind dunes.
3. Shallow brackish lagoon behind

185

dunes fringed by saltmarsh and reedbed, some mudflats.

Key birds: 1. *Spring and autumn*: Good for passage birds (inc. divers, skuas). *Summer*: Coastal birds, esp. terns (inc. Roseate).
2. Especially good in spring. Winter and breeding wildfowl; passage and breeding waders.
3. Good for waders, esp. on passage.

Contact: Jim Martin, Hauxley Nature Reserve, Low Hauxley, Amble, Morpeth, Northumberland. 01665 711578.

FARNE ISLANDS

The National Trust.

Location: NU 230 370. Access by boat from Seahouses Harbour. Access from A1.

Access: Apr, Aug-Sept: Inner Farne and Staple 10.30am-6pm (majority of boats land at Inner Farne). May-Jul: Staple Island 10.30am-1.30pm, Inner Farne: 1.30pm-5pm. Disabled access possible on Inner Farne, telephone Property Manager for details. Dogs allowed on boats – not on islands.

Facilities: Toilets on Inner Farne.

Public transport: Nearest rail stations at Alnmouth and Berwick.

Habitat: Maritime islands, 15-28 depending on state of tide.

Key birds: 18 species of seabirds/waders, four species of tern (including Roseate), 34,000-plus pairs of Puffin, Rock Pipit, Pied Wagtail, Starling, 1,200 Eider etc.

Contact: John Walton, 8 St Aidans,Seahouses, Northumberland NE68 7SR. 01665 720651

GRINDON LOUGH

Location: NY 806 677. View from unclassified road W of Grindon Hill, three miles NW of Haydon Bridge.

Contact: Northumberland Wildlife Trust HQ.

HOLYWELL POND

Northumberland Wildlife Trust.

Location: NZ 319 752. N of Holywell near Seaton Delaval on A192.

Access: Open all year.

Facilities: Public hide (suitable for disabled) accessed from public footpath leading from housing estate.

Public transport: Ariva Northumberland buses to Seton Delaval and Holywell.

Habitat: Pond and reedbed.

Key birds: Good for winter wildfowl (inc. Goldeneye, Greylag Geese) and passage species.

Contact: Trust HQ, 0191 284 6884.

LINDISFARNE

English Nature (Northumbria Team).

Location: NU 090 430. Island lying two miles E of A1 at Beal, eight miles S of Berwick-on-Tweed.

Access: Open all hours. Some restricted access (refuges).

Facilities: Toilets, visitor centre in village. Hide on island (new hide with disabled access at Fareham-le-Moor). Nature trail on island.

Public transport: Irregular bus service to Holy Island, mainly in summer. Bus route follows mainland boundary of site north-south.

Habitat: Dunes, sand and mudflats.

Key birds: *Passage and winter*: Wildfowl and waders, including pale-bellied Brent Goose, Long-tailed Duck and Whooper Swan. Rare migrants.

Contact: Phil Davey, Site Manager, Beal Station, Berwick-on-Tweed TD15 2PB. 01289 381470.

NEWTON POOL NATURE RESERVE

National Trust (North East).

Location: NU 243 240. From Alnwick, head N on B1340. After 8 miles, follow signs to High Newton N of Embleton at the junction of B1339 and B1340. In village, follow signs to Low Newton. Just before village is a car park which must be used as no public parking is available further on. A National Trust sign in village square shows way to bird hide along Craster footpath (about a five minute walk).

Access: Open all year. From May to mid-August parts of the beach may be cordoned off to avoid disturbing nesting birds.

Facilities: Car park, hide.

Public transport: None.

Habitat: Dunes, tidal flats, beach, freshwater pool with artificial islands, scrub.

Key birds: *Spring/summer*: Grasshopper Warbler, Water Rail, Little Grebe, Whitethroat, Yellow Wagtail, Whinchat, Stonechat, Corn Bunting, terns, gulls. *Winter*: waders, gulls.

Contact: National Trust (North East), Scots' Gap, Morpeth, Northumberland NE61 4EG, 01670 774691.

Nottinghamshire

ATTENBOROUGH GRAVEL PITS

Nottinghamshire Wildlife Trust.
Location: SK 523 343. On A6005, seven miles SW of Nottingham alongside River Trent. Signed from main road.
Access: Open at all times. Dogs on leads. Paths suitable for disabled access.
Facilities: Nature trail (leaflet from Notts WT), one hide (key £2.50 from Notts WT).
Public transport: Railway station at Attenborough, several buses pass close to reserve (Rainbow 525A from Nottingham every ten minutes).
Habitat: Disused, flooded gravel workings with associated marginal and wetland vegetation.
Key birds: *Spring/summer*: Breeding Common Tern (40-plus pairs), Reed Warbler, Black Tern regular (bred once). *Winter*: Wildfowl (Bittern has wintered for last two years), Grey Heron colony, adjacent Cormorant roost.
Contact: Notts WT Office, The Old Ragged School, Brook Street, Nottingham NG1 1EA. 0115 958 8242. e-mail: nottswt@cix.co.uk www.wildlifetrust.org.uk/nottinghamshire

BESTHORPE NATURE RESERVE

Nottinghamshire Wildlife Trust.
Location: SK 817 640 and SK813 646 (access points). Take A1133 N of Newark. Turn into Trent Lane S of Besthorpe village, reserve entrances second turn on left and right turn at end of lane (at River Trent).
Access: Open access to two hides (one with disabled access from car park at present). Open access to SSSI meadows. Limited access to areas grazed with sheep. Dogs on leads.
Facilities: No toilets (pubs etc in Besthorpe village), two hides, paths, nature trail (northern part).

Public transport: Buses (numbers 22, 67, 68, 6, S7L) run by Marshalls, Lincs, Road Car and Travel Wright along A1133 to Besthorpe village (0.75 mile away). Tel: 0115 924 0000 or 01777 710550 for information.
Habitat: Gravel pit with islands, SSSI neutral grasslands, hedges, reedbed, etc.
Key birds: *Spring/summer*: Breeding Grey Heron, Cormorant, Little Ringed Plover, Kingfisher, Grasshopper Warbler. *Winter*: Large numbers of ducks (Pochard, Tufted Duck, Pintail, Wigeon) and Peregrine.
Contact: Contact Notts WT Office, Nottinghamshire Wildlife Trust, The Old Ragged School, Brook Street, Nottingham NG1 1EA. 0115 958 9242. e-mail: nottswt@cix.co.uk www.wildlifetrust.org.uk/nottinghamshire

COLWICK COUNTRY PARK

Nottingham City Council .
Location: SK 610 395. Off A612 three miles E of Nottingham city centre.
Access: Open at all times, but no vehicle access after dusk or before 7am.
Facilities: Nature trails. Sightings log book in Fishing Lodge.
Public transport: Call park office for advice.
Habitat: Lakes, pools, woodlands, grasslands, new plantations, River Trent.
Key birds: *Summer*: Warblers, Hobby, Common Tern (15+ pairs). *Winter*: Wildfowl and gulls. Passage migrants.
Contact: Mark Dennis, The Fishing Lodge, Colwick, Country Park, River Road, Colwick, Nottingham NG4 2DW. 0115 987 0785.
www.colwick2000.freeserve.co.uk

DUKE'S WOOD NATURE RESERVE

Nottinghamshire Wildlife Trust/BP Petroleum Development Ltd.
Location: 675 603. From Mansfield head E on A617. After 10 miles take minor road N to Eakring. The entrance to the reserve is off the minor road to Eakring, which leaves the A617 near Kirklington.
Access: Open all year. School parties are particularly welcome. Please contact the Trust office.
Facilities: None.
Public transport: None.
Habitat: Mixed deciduous woodland, industrial archaeological site.
Key birds: *Spring/summer*: Blackcap, Garden Warbler, Spotted Flycatcher. *All year*: Great Spotted Woodpecker, Jay, usual woodland species. Hawfinch possible.
Contact: Trust HQ, The Old Ragged School, Brook Street, Nottingham NG1 1EA, 0115 958 8242. e-mail: nottswt@cix.co.uk
www.wildlifetrust.org.uk/nottinghamshire

LOUND WATERFOWL RESERVE

Tarmac, ARC, Nottinghamshire Wildlife Trust.
Location: SK 690 856. Two miles N of Retford off A638 adjacent to Sutton and Lound villages.
Access: Open at all times. Use public rights of way only.
Facilities: Public viewing platform/screen off Chainbridge Lane (overlooking Chainbridge NR. Scrape).
Public transport: Buses from Bawtry (Church Street), Retford bus station and Worksop (Hardy Street) on services 27/27A/83/83A/84 to Lound Village crossroads (Chainbridge Lane).
Habitat: Working gravel quarries, fish ponds, river valley, infilled and disused fly ash tanks, farmland, scrub, open water.
Key birds: *Summer*: Gulls and terns. Passage waders and raptors. *Winter*: Wildfowl, rarities inc. Ring-billed Gull, Caspian and White-winged Black Terns, Lesser Scaup, Richard's Pipit, Baird's Sandpiper, Long-billed Dowitcher, Buff-breasted Sandpiper, Pectoral Sandpiper, Spoonbill, White Stork, Red-footed Falcon, Blue-winged Teal, Great Skua.
Contact: Lound Bird Club, Paul Hobson (Secretary), 6 St Mary's Crescent, Tickhill, Doncaster South Yorks. 0794 0428326 (after 4pm).

WILWELL FARM

Nottinghamshire Wildlife Trust/Rushcliffe Borough Council.
Location: Situated on the southern outskirts of Nottingham between Ruddington and Wilford. Leave A60 at Ruddington on B680.
Access: Open all year.
Facilities: None.
Public transport: None.
Habitat: Abandoned railway cutting, neutral grassland, limestone, track bed, acid fen and scrub woodland.
Key birds: *All year*: Green Woodpecker, Sparrowhawk, usual woodland species, Tawny Owl. 91 species have been recorded on the reserve.
Contact: Trust HQ, The Old Ragged School, Brook Street, Nottingham NG1 1EA, 0115 958 8242.
e-mail: nottswt@cix.co.uk
www.wildlifetrust.org.uk/nottinghamshire

Oxfordshire

ASTON ROWANT

English Nature (Thames & Chiltern Team).
Location: SU 731 966. From the M40 at the
Lewknor interchange at J6, travel NE for a short
distance and turn R onto the A40. After 1.5 miles
at the top of the hill, turn R and R again into a
narrow, metalled lane. Drive to the end of this
road to the car park.
ontact: English Nature, Aston Rowant Reserve
Office, Aston Hill, Lewknor, Watlington OX9
5SG. 01844 351833. www.english-nature.org.uk

CHIMNEY MEADOWS

Berkshire, Buckinghamshire & Oxfordshire
Wildlife Trust/English Nature.
Location: SP 352 000. Head SE from Oxford on
A420. Turn R into an unclassified road. Park in
the lay-by on the roadside just N of Tadpole
Bridge. Walk along the Thames Path on the N
side of the Thames heading back towards Oxford.
Access: Open all year but only view from the
Thames Path due to the sensitive nature of the
breeding and wintering waders. Please do not let
dogs run into the meadows.
Facilities: Car park.
Public transport: None.
Habitat: Six meadows next to the River Thames.
Key birds: *Spring/summer*: Whitethroat, Willow
Warbler, Chiffchaff, Sedge Warbler, Curlew,
Snipe, Redshank. *Winter*: Waders.
Contact: Trust HQ, The Lodge, 1 Armstrong
Road, Littlemore, Oxford OX4 4XT, 01865
775476. e-mail: bbowt@cix.co.uk
www.wildlifetrust.org.uk/berksbucksoxon

OTMOOR NATURE RESERVE

RSPB (Central England).
Location: SP 570 126. Car park seven miles NE
of Oxford city centre. From B4027, take turn to
Horton-cum-Studley, then first left to Beckley.
After 0.67 miles at the bottom of a short hill turn
(before the Abingdon Arms public house). After
200 yards, turn left into Otmoor Lane. Reserve
car park is at the end of the lane (approx one
mile).
Access: Open dawn-dusk. No permits or fees. No
dogs allowed on the reserve visitor trail (except
public rights of way). In wet conditions, the
public bridleway (which forms part of the visitor
trail) can become virtually impassable and
wellington boots are essential.
Facilities: Limited. Small car park with cycle
racks, visitor trail (4.5km round trip) and two
screened viewpoints. The reserve is not accessible
by coach and is unsuitable for large groups.
Public transport: None.
Habitat: Wet grassland and open water lagoons.
The lagoons are in the process of being converted
into a reedbed.
Key birds: *Summer*: Breeding birds include
Lapwing, Redshank, Curlew, Snipe, Yellow
Wagtail, Shoveler, Gadwall, Pochard, Tufted
Duck, Little Grebe, Great Crested Grebe. Hobby
breeds locally. *Winter*: Wigeon, Teal, Shoveler,
Pintail, Gadwall, Pochard, Tufted Duck,
Lapwing, Golden Plover, Hen Harrier, Peregrine,
Merlin. *Autumn and spring passage*: Marsh
Harrier, Short-eared Owl, Greenshank, Green
Sandpiper, Common Sandpiper, Spotted
Redshank and occasional Black Tern.
Contact: Neil Lambert, Site Manager, RSPB , c/
o Lower Farm, Noke, Oxford OX3 9TX. 01865
848385. www.rspb.org.uk

THE WARBURG RESERVE

Berkshire, Buckinghamshire & Oxfordshire
Wildlife Trust.
Location: SU 720 879. Leave Henley-on-Thames
NW on the A4130. Turn R at end of Fair Mile
onto B480. Take second L just N of Middle
Assendon and follow road for two miles. Soon
after the road becomes a track, the reserve is
reached with the car park on the R. Please close
the gate after you enter the car park.
Access: Open all year. Please keep dogs on a
lead. In some areas, only guide dogs allowed.
Facilities: Visitor Centre, car park, hide with
disabled access, nature trail, leaflets. Visitors
with disabilities and groups wishing to visit
should contact the warden.
Public transport: None.
Habitat: Scrub, mixed woodland, grassland,
ponds.
Key birds: *Spring/summer*: Whitethroat, Lesser
Whitethroat, Woodcock. *All year*: Sparrowhawk,
all three woodpeckers, Treecreeper, Nuthatch,
Tawny Owl. Good for butterflies and mammals.
Contact: Warburg Reserve, Bix Bottom, Henley-
on-Thames, Oxfordshire, 01491 642001.
e-mail: bbowtwarburg@cix.co.uk

189

Shropshire

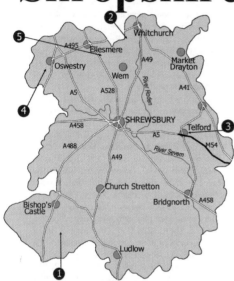

Key to sites:
1. Clunton Coppice
2. Fenn's, Whixall and Bettisfield Mosses NNR
3. Granville Nature Reserve
4. Llynclys Hill
5. Wood Lane

entrances, and a large car park at Manor House.
Access: Permit required. Disabled access by prior arrangement along the railway line.
Facilities: There are panels at all of the main entrances to the site, and leaflets are available when permits are applied for.
Public transport: Bus passes nearby.
Habitat: Peatland meres and mosses.
Key birds: *Spring/summer*: Nightjar, Tree Sparrow. *All year*: Sky Lark, Linnet. Water vole, brown hare.
Contact: English Nature, Attingham Park, Shrewsbury, Shropshire SY4 4TW, 01743 282000.
e-mail: north.mercia@english-nature.org.uk

CLUNTON COPPICE

Shropshire Wildlife Trust.
Location: SO 343 806. Take B4385 S from Bishop's Castle. After two miles take road to Brockton, Lower Down and Clunton. Park in Clunton village and walk S into the woodland.
Access: Open at all times. Access along road and public rights of way only.
Facilities: Limited parking in small quarry entrance on R, or opposite The Crown pub.
Public transport: Not known.
Habitat: Oak coppice. Good for ferns, mosses and fungi.
Key birds: Buzzard and Raven regular. *Spring/summer*: Wide range of woodland birds, inc. Redstart, Wood Warbler and Pied Flycatcher.
Contact: Trust HQ, 01743 284280.

FENN'S WHIXALL AND BETTISFIELD MOSSES NNR

English Nature (North Mercia Team).
Location: The reserve is located four miles SW of Whitchurch, ten miles SW of Wrexham, S of A495 between Fenn's bank, Whixall and Bettisfield. There is parking at roadside

GRANVILLE NATURE RESERVE

Shropshire Wildlife Trust.
Location: The reserve is located in Granville Country Park on NE edge of Telford. From M54 (J4), join A5 to Priorslee. Go straight over at the Limekiln Bank roundabout on the B5060. Turn R at the next roundabout and the park is on the L.
Access: Open all year.
Facilities: None.
Public transport: None.
Habitat: Open water, meadow, scrub, woodland, wetland.
Key birds: *Spring/summer*: Warblers, passage waders. *All year*: Good variety of woodland birds.
Contact: Trust HQ, 193 Abbey Foregate, Shrewsbury SY2 6AH, 01743 284280.
e-mail: shropshirewt@cix.co.uk
www.swt-granville.org.uk.

LLYNCLYS HILL

Shropshire Wildlife Trust.
Location: SJ 273 237. SSW of Oswestry. Park in layby on A495 at SJ 277 242 and walk up Turner's Lane.
Access: Open at all times.
Facilities: None.
Public transport: None.

Habitat: Old mixed limestone sward with some woodland and scrub, small pond.
Key birds: Sparrowhawk, Green Woodpecker, Goldcrest, large warbler population. Occasional Peregrine, Buzzard. Eight species of orchid.
Contact: Trust HQ, 01743 284280.

WOOD LANE

Shropshire Wildlife Trust.
Location: SJ 425 327. Turn off A528 at Spurnhill near Ellesmere.
Access: Open at all times.
Facilities: Car parks. Hides (access by permit).
Public transport: None.
Habitat: Gravel pit.
Key birds: *Summer*: Breeding Sand Martins. Popular staging post for waders (inc. Redshank, Greenshank, Ruff, Dunlin, Little Stint, Green and Wood Sandpiper). *Winter*: Lapwing and Curlew.
Contact: Trust HQ, 01743 284280.

Somerset

AVONMOUTH SEWAGE WORKS

Location: ST 533 797. Lane connecting Kings Weston and Lawrence Weston Lanes near Avonmouth.
Contact: Avon Wildlife Trust HQ, 0117 9177270.

BRANDON HILL NATURE PARK

Bristol City Council/Avon Wildlife Trust.
Location: 578 728. The reserve is in the centre of Bristol, in the SW corner of Brandon Hill Park which overlooks Jacobs Wells Road. Metered parking available in the nearby roads - Great George Street, Berkeley Square, NCP car park on Jacobs Wells Road.
Access: Open all year. Wheelchair access from Great George Street and Berkeley Square only.
Facilities: Woodland walk, butterfly garden, picnic area.
Public transport: None.
Habitat: Wildflower meadow, woodland.
Key birds: *Spring/summer*: Blackcap, warblers. *All year*: Jay, Bullfinch, usual woodland species.
Contact: Avon Wildlife Trust, The Wildlife Centre, 32 Jacob's Wells Road, Bristol BS8 1DR, 0117 917 7270.
e-mail: mail@avonwildlifetrust.co.uk
www.avonwildlifetrust.co.uk

BRIDGWATER BAY

English Nature (Somerset & Gloucestershire Team).
Location: ST 270 470. Nine miles N of Bridgwater. Take J23 or 24 off M5. Turn N off A39 at Cannington.
Access: Hides open every day except Christmas Day. Permits needed for Steart Island (by boat only). Dogs on leads – grazing animals/nesting birds. Disabled access to hides by arrangement, other areas accessible.
Facilities: Car park at Steart. Footpath approx 0.5 miles to tower and hides.
Public transport: None.
Habitat: Estuary, intertidal mudflats, saltmarsh.
Key birds: *Winter*: Wildfowl and waders, birds of prey. *Spring/autumn*: passage migrants.
Contact: Robin Prowse, Dowells Farm, Steart, Bridgwater, Somerset TA5 2PX. 01278 652426.
www.english-nature.org.uk

CATCOTT LOWS

Somerset Wildlife Trust.
Location: ST 400 415. Approx one mile N of Catcott village (off A39 from J23 of M5).
Access: Open at all times.
Facilities: Two hides, one with ramp, one with steps. Car park by ramped hide at ST 400 416. No toilets.
Public transport: None.
Habitat: Wet meadows with winter flooding and summer grazing.
Key birds: *Winter*: Wigeon, Teal, Pintail, Shoveler, Gadwall, Bewick's Swan, Peregrine. *Spring*: Little Egret, passage waders, breeding Lapwing, Snipe, Redshank, Yellow Wagtail.
Contact: David Reid, SWT, Fyne Court, Broomfield, Bridgwater, Somerset TA5 2EQ. 01823 451587.

191

CHEW VALLEY LAKE

Avon Wildlife Trust, Bristol Water Plc.
Location: ST 570 600. Reservoir (partly a Trust reserve) between Chew Stoke and West Harptree, crossed by A368 and B3114, nine miles S of Bristol.
Access: Permit for access to hides (five at Chew, two at Blagdon). Best roadside viewing from causeways at Herriott's Bridge (nature reserve) and Herons Green Bay. Day, half-year and year permits from Bristol Water, Recreation Department, Woodford Lodge, Chew Stoke, Bristol BS18 8SH. Tel/fax 01275 332339.
Facilities: Hides.
Public transport: Travel line, 0870 6082608.
Habitat: Reservoir.
Key birds: *Autumn/winter*: Concentrations of wildfowl (inc. Bewick's Swan, Goldeneye, Smew, Ruddy Duck), gull roost (inc. regular Mediterranean, occasional Ring-billed). Migrant waders and terns (inc. Black). Recent rarities inc. Blue-winged Teal, Spoonbill, Alpine Swift, Citrine Wagtail, Little Bunting, Ring-necked Duck, Kumlien's Gull.
Contact: Trust HQ, 0117 9177270.

CLAPTON MOOR

Avon Wildlife Trust.
Location: ST 457 736. NW of Bristol. From J19 of M5 take A369 W towards Portishead. Turn SW on B3124 then SE towards Clapton in Gordon then SE at T-junction into Clapton Lane. Reserve is to N off this lane.
Access: Open access to hide via Clapton Lane. Permit access to rest of site (members only).
Facilities: Hide (with wheelchair access). Leaflet available.
Public transport: Travel line, 0870 6082608.
Habitat: Peat and clay moors. Species-rich grassland, hedges, rhynes (ditches).
Key birds: *All year*: Lapwing, Redshank, Snipe, Buzzard, Mallard, Teal. *Summer migrants*: Hobby, Yellow Wagtail, Whinchat, Stonechat, Redstart, Spotted Flycatcher.
Contact: Trust HQ, 0117 9177270.

EBBOR GORGE

English Nature (Somerset Team).
Location: ST 521 484. Approx two miles from the centre of Wells. Access via Wookey Hole from A39, A371 or via Priddy village from B3135.
Contact: Bob Corns, English Nature, Rough Moor, Bishops Hull, Taunton, Somerset TA1 5AA. 01823 283211.

HURSCOMBE-WIMBLEBALL LAKE

Location: SS 974 317. Four miles NE of Dulverton.
Contact: Miss Joan Loraine,

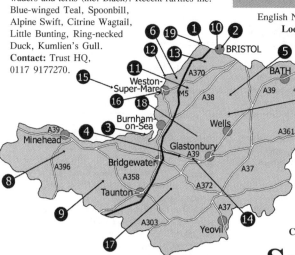

Somerset

Greencombe, Porlock, Minehead, Somerset
TA24 8NU. 01643 862363.

LANGFORD HEATHFIELD

Somerset Wildlife Trust.
Location: ST 106 227. From Taunton take A38
SW to Wellington. Turn W to Langford
Budville. Reserve lies NW from the village
Contact: Trust HQ, 01823 451587.

LEIGH WOODS

National Trust (Bristol).
Location: ST 560 736. Two miles W from centre
of Bristol. Pedestrian access from North Road,
Leigh Woods or via Forestry Commission car
park at end of Coronation Avenue, Abbots
Leigh. Access to both roads is from A369 which
goes from Bristol to J19 of M5.
Access: Open all year. A good network of paths
around the plateau. The paths down to the
towpath are steep and uneven.
Facilities: Two waymarked trails from Forestry
Commission car park: purple trail (1.75 miles)
on level ground, red trail (2.5 miles) more
undulating.
Public transport: Bristol-Portishead. Bus service
(358/658 and 359/659) goes along A369. Leaves
Bristol generally at 20 and 50 minutes past the
hour. More details from First Badgerline. Tel:
0117 955 3231.
Habitat: Ancient woodland, former wood
pasture, two grassland areas, calcareous
grassland and scree by towpath.
Key birds: *Summer*: Peregrine, Blackcap,
Chiffchaff, Spotted Flycatcher. *Winter*: Great
Spotted and Green Woodpeckers, Song Thrush,
Long-tailed, Marsh and common tits.
Contact: Bill Morris, Reserve Office, Valley
Road, Leigh Woods, Bristol, 01936 429336.
e-mail: wlwbgm@smtp.ntrust.org.uk

PUXTON MOOR

Avon Wildlife Trust.
Location: ST 414 634. Lies E of Weston-super-
Mare. Leave M5 at J21, heading E on A370.
Turn S on minor road to Puxton.
Access: Open access via Dolemoor Lane,
Puxton.
Facilities: None.
Public transport: Travel line, 0870 6082608.
Habitat: Alluvial clay levels, improved to semi-
improved grassland, hedges and rhynes (ditches).
Key birds: *All year*: Tree Sparrow, Reed

Bunting, Linnet, Sky Lark, Buzzard, Kestrel,
Raven. *Summer migrants*: Yellow Wagtail,
Whinchat, Stonechat, Whimbrel, Hobby,
Redstart.
Contact: Trust HQ, 0117 9177270.

SAND POINT/MIDDLE HOPE

National Trust (North Somerset).
Location: ST 290 590. 182 map. Five miles N of
Burnham on Sea. J22 of M5, head for Weston
Super Mare on A370 and then head for Brean at
Lympsham.
Contact: The National Trust, Barton Rocks,
Barton, Winscombe, North Somerset BS25 1DU.
01934 844518.

NETCOTT'S MEADOW

Avon Wildlife Trust.
Location: 476 696. From the A370 Bristol-
Congresbury Road, when in Backwell turn R at
traffic lights to Nailsea. Go under the railway
bridge and turn L into car part. Walk around
Buckland's Pool. Climb the stile to the reserve
entrance which is in the lane on the R.
Access: Open all year. No wheelchair access.
Please keep to mown paths. No access along
Bucklands End.
Facilities: None.
Public transport: None.
Habitat: Damp grassland, hedges, scrub.
Key birds: *All year*: Green Woodpecker, Tawny
Owl, Redpoll.
Contact: Avon Wildlife Trust, The Wildlife
Centre, 32 Jacob's Wells Road, Bristol BS8 1DR,
0117 917 7270. www.avonwildlifetrust.co.uk
e-mail: mail@avonwildlifetrust.co.uk

SHAPWICK HEATH NNR

English Nature (Somerset & Gloucester Team).
Location: Shapwick is on A39, W of
Glastonbury. Nearest car park is at the Willows
garden centre, Westhay, reached by minor road
heading N.
Access: Open all year. Disabled access to
displays, hides.
Facilities: Network of paths, hides. Toilets,
leaflets and refreshments available at the garden
centre.
Public transport: None.
Habitat: Traditionally managed herb-rich
grassland, ferny wet woodland, fen, scrub,
ditches, open water, reedswamp and reedbed.
Key birds: *All year*: Ducks, waders.

Contact: English Nature, Roughmoor, Bishop's Hull, Taunton, Somerset TA1 5AA, 01823 283211. e-mail: somerset@english-nature.org.uk

STEEP HOLM ISLAND

Kenneth Allsop Memorial Trust.
Location: ST 229 607. Small island in Severn River, five miles from Weston-super-Mare harbour.
Access: Scheduled service depending on tides, via ferry. Advance booking advisable. No animals allowed. Not suitable for disabled.
Facilities: Visitor centre, toilets, trails, basic refreshments and sales counter, postal service.
Public transport: None.
Habitat: Limestone grassland, scrub, rare flora, small sycamore wood.
Key birds: Important breeding station for Greater and Lesser Black-backed and Herring Gulls, largest colony of Cormorants in south-west of England. On migration routes.
Contact: Mrs Joan Rendell, Stonedale, 11 Fairfield Close, Milton, Weston-super-Mare BS22 8EA. 01934 632307.
www.steepholm.org.uk

WALBOROUGH

Avon Wildlife Trust.
Location: ST 315 579. On S edge of Weston-super-Mare at mouth of River Axe.
Access: Access from Uphill boatyard. Special access trail suitable for less able visitors.
Facilities: None.
Public transport: Travel line, 0870 6082608.
Habitat: Limestone grassland, scrub, saltmarsh, estuary.
Key birds: The Axe Estuary holds good numbers of migrant and wintering wildfowl (inc. Teal, Shelduck) and waders (inc. Black-tailed Godwit, Lapwing, Golden Plover, Dunlin, Redshank). Other migrants inc. Little Stint, Curlew Sandpiper, Ruff. Little Egret occurs each year, mostly in late summer.
Contact: Trust HQ, 0117 9177270.

WEST SEDGEMOOR

RSPB (South West England Office).
Location: ST 361 238. Entrance down by-road off A378 Taunton-Langport road, one mile E of Fivehead.
Access: Access at all times to woodland car park and both hides.

Facilities: Heronry hide, nature trail and moorland hide.
Public transport: Bus from Taunton to Fivehead.
Habitat: Semi-natural ancient oak woodland and wet grassland. Part of the Somerset Levels and Moors.
Key birds: *Spring/summer*: Breeding Grey Heron, Curlew, Lapwing, Redshank, Snipe, Buzzard, Sedge Warbler, Nightingale. Passage Whimbrel and Hobby. *Winter*: Large flocks of waders and wildfowl (including Lapwing, Golden Plover, Shoveler, Teal and Wigeon).
Contact: The Warden, Dewlands Farm, Redhill, Curry Rivel, Langport, Somerset TA10 0PH. 01458 252805, fax 01458 252184.
e-mail: sally.brown@rspb.org.uk

WESTHAY MOOR

Somerset Wildlife Trust.
Location: ST 458 438. From Glastonbury, take B3151 to site approx one mile NW of Westhay village on minor road to Godney.
Access: Open at all times.
Facilities: Hides and viewing screens, no toilets. Hides have disabled access.
Public transport: None.
Habitat: Open water and reedbeds.
Key birds: *Winter*: Bittern and wildfowl, Red-breasted Merganser, Water Rail, Goosander. *Summer*: Hobby, Reed, Sedge and Cetti's Warblers, Whitethroat.
Contact: David Reid, SWT, Fyne Court, Broomfield, Bridgwater, Somerset TA5 2EQ. 01823 451587.

WILLSBRIDGE MILL

Avon Wildlife Trust.
Location: ST 665 708. Turn N off A431 at Longwell Green along Long Beach Road, park after quarter mile in car park overlooking valley.
Access: Unrestricted access
Facilities: Visitor centre, nature trail.
Public transport: None.
Habitat: Broadleaved woodland, grassland, scrub, stream, pond.
Key birds: High densities of birds of woodland and scrub. *Winter*: Kingfisher and Dipper regular.
Contact: Ruth Worsley, Willsbridge Mill, Willsbridge Hill, Bristol BS30 6EX. 0117 932 6885; fax 0117 932 9440.
e-mail wtwmill@cix.co.uk

Staffordshire

Key to sites:
1. Allimore Green Common
2. Belvide Reservoir
3. Black Brook
4. Blithfield Reservoir
5. Branston Water Park
6. Burnt Wood
7. Castern Wood
8. Coombes Valley
9. Doxey Marshes
10. Longsdon Woods
11. Swineholes Wood

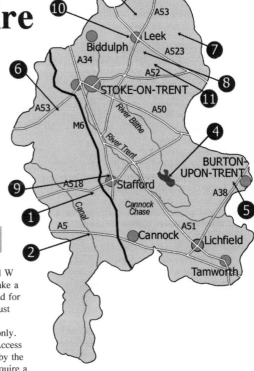

ALLIMORE GREEN COMMON

Staffordshire Wildlife Trust.
Location: SJ 858 193. From Stafford head W on A518 towards Newport. In Haughton take a minor road S to Church Eaton. Follow road for about one mile to reserve, which is on L just before Allimore Green.
Access: Open all year. Roadside parking only. Please park with care and consideration. Access is via a stile at the N end of the Common by the road. Groups of more than eight people require a permit available from the Trust.
Facilities: Interpretation board.
Public transport: None.
Habitat: Woodland, scrub, wet pasture, ditch.
Key birds: *Spring/summer*: Whitethroat, Willow Tit, Willow Warbler. *Winter*: Siskin.
Contact: Trust HQ, Coutts House, Sandon, Stafford ST18 0DN, 01889 508534.
e-mail: staffswt@cix.co.uk
www.wildlifetrust.org.uk/staffs

BELVIDE RESERVOIR

British Waterways Board and West Midland Bird Club.
Location: SJ865102. Near Brewood, 7 miles NW of Wolverhampton.
Access: Access only by permit from the West Midland Bird Club.
Facilities: Hides.
Public transport: Not known.
Habitat: Canal feeder reservoir with marshy margins and gravel islands.
Key birds: Important breeding, moulting and wintering ground for wildfowl, (including Ruddy Duck, Goldeneye and Goosander), passage terns and waders. Night roost for gulls.
Contact: Miss M Surman, 6 Lloyd Square, 12 Niall Close, Edgbaston, Birmingham B15 3LX.

BLACK BROOK

Staffordshire Wildlife Trust.
Location: SK 020 645. N of Leek, W of A53. West of road from Royal Cottage to Gib Tor.
Access: Access is via public footpath from Gib Tor to Newstone Farm; this first passes through a conifer plantation which is outside the reserve.
Facilities: None.
Public transport: None.
Habitat: Heather and bilberry moorland, and upland acidic grassland.
Key birds: Merlin, Kestrel, Red Grouse, Golden Plover, Snipe, Curlew, Dipper, Wheatear, Whinchat, Twite.

Contact: Trust HQ, 01889 508534.
e-mail: staffswt@cix.co.uk
www.wildlifetrust.org.uk/staffs

BLITHFIELD RESERVOIR

South Staffs Waterworks Co.
Location: SK 058 237. View from causeway on
B5013 (Rugeley/Uttoxeter).
Access: Access to reservoir and hides by permit
from West Midland Bird Club.
Facilities: None.
Public transport: None.
Habitat: Large reservoir.
Key birds: *Winter*: Good populations of wildfowl
(inc. Bewick's Swan, Goosander, Goldeneye,
Ruddy Duck), large gull roost (can inc.
Glaucous, Iceland). Passage terns (Common,
Arctic, Black) and waders, esp. in autumn (Little
Stint, Curlew Sandpiper, Spotted Redshank
regular).
Contact: Miss M Surman, 6 Lloyd Square, 12
Niall Close, Edgbaston, Birmingham B15 3LX.

BRANSTON WATER PARK

Staffordshire Wildlife Trust.
Location: SK 217 207. From Litchfield, follow
brown tourist sign from A38 N. No access from
the S – head to the Barton-under-Needwood exit
and return N. The park is 0.5 miles S of the
A5121 Burton-upon-Trent exit.
Access: Open all year. Paths flat and generally
dry.
Facilities: Toilets, picnic benches.
Public transport: Call trust for details.
Habitat: Reedbed, willow carr woodland, scrub.
Key birds: *Spring/summer*: Reed Warbler,
Cuckoo, Reed Bunting. Important roost for
Swallow and Sand Martin. *Winter*: waders, Little
Ringed Plover occasionally, Pied Wagtail roost.
Contact: Trust HQ, Coutts House, Sandon,
Stafford ST18 0DN, 01889 508534.
e-mail: staffswt@cix.co.uk
www.wildlifetrust.org.uk/staffs

BURNT WOOD

Staffordshire Wildlife Trust.
Location: SJ 736 355. From Newcastle take A53
SE to Market Drayton. At Loggerheads, where
main road crosses B5026 turn into Kestrel Drive
and then Pheasant Drive. Access also possible
from the B5026 Eccleshall Road 0.3 miles from
the A53.

Access: Open all year. Parking is difficult for this
reserve.
Facilities: None.
Public transport: None.
Habitat: Ancient oak woodland, pond.
Key birds: *All year*: Goshawk, Raven,
Woodcock, all three woodpeckers. Good for
butterflies and moths, adder, grass snake, slow
worm and common lizard
Contact: Trust HQ, Coutts House, Sandon,
Stafford ST18 0DN, 01889 508534.
e-mail: staffswt@cix.co.uk
www.wildlifetrust.org.uk/staffs

CASTERN WOOD

Staffordshire Wildlife Trust.
Location: SK 119 537. E of Leek. Unclassified
road SE of Wetton, seven miles NW of
Ashbourne.
Access: Use parking area at end of minor road
running due SE from Wetton.
Facilities: None.
Public transport: None.
Habitat: Limestone grassland and woodland,
spoil heaps from former lead mines.
Key birds: All three woodpeckers, warblers, Pied
Flycatcher, Redstart, Sparrowhawk, Tawny Owl.
Contact: Trust HQ, Coutts House, Sandon,
Stafford ST18 0DN. 01889 508534.
e-mail: staffswt@cix.co.uk
www.wildlifetrust.org.uk/staffs

COOMBES VALLEY

RSPB (North West England Office).
Location: SK 005 530. Four miles from Leek
along A523 between Leek and Ashbourne and 0.5
miles down unclassified road – signposted.
Access: No dogs allowed. Most of the trails are
unsuitable for disabled. Open daily – no charge.
Facilities: Visitor centre, toilets, two miles of
nature trail, one hide. Events and guided walks.
Public transport: None.
Habitat: Sessile oak woodland, unimproved
pasture and meadow.
Key birds: *Spring*: Pied Flycatcher, Redstart,
Wood Warbler. *Jan-Mar*: Displaying birds of
prey.
Contact: Nick Chambers, Six Oaks Farm,
Bradnop, Leek, Staffs ST13 7EU. 01438 384017.
e-mail: nick.chambers@RSPB.org.uk
www.RSPB.org.uk

DOXEY MARSHES

Staffordshire Wildlife Trust.
Location: SJ 903 250. In Stafford. Parking 0.25 miles off M6 J14/A5013 or walk from town centre.
Access: Open at all times. Dogs on leads. Disabled access being improved 2001.
Facilities: Two hides – accessible to wheelchairs.
Public transport: Walk from town centre via Sainsbury's.
Habitat: Marsh, pools, reedbeds, hedgerows, reed sweet-grass swamp.
Key birds: *Spring/summer*: Breeding Snipe, Lapwing, Redshank, buntings, Skylark, Water Rail. *Winter*: Snipe, wildfowl, thrushes, Short-eared Owl. Passage waders, vagrants.
Contact: Trust HQ, Coutts House, Sandon, Stafford ST18 0DN. 01889 508534.
e-mail: staffswt@cix.co.uk
www.wildlifetrust.org.uk/staffs

LONGSDON WOODS

Staffordshire Wildlife Trust.
Location: SK 965 555. Reserve lies off A53 Leek road. Can be approached from Ladderedge near Leek; City Lane, Longsdon; or Rudyard Station.
Access: Public rights of way only.
Facilities: None.
Public transport: None.

Habitat: Woodland and wet grassland.
Key birds: Heronry, Sparrowhawk, Curlew, Snipe, Jack Snipe, Woodcock, Little and Tawny Owls, all three woodpeckers, Redstart, Blackcap, Garden Warbler.
Contact: Trust HQ, Coutts House, Sandon, Stafford ST18 0DN. 01889 508534.
e-mail: staffswt@cix.co.uk
www.wildlifetrust.org.uk/staffs

SWINEHOLES WOOD

Staffordshire Wildlife Trust.
Location: SK 046 503. From Stoke-on-Trent, head E on A52, taking B5053 N at Froghall. Drive 0.75 miles N of Ipstones to a crossroads. Turn R into minor road for 1.25 miles to a radio mast where there is a small lay-by on the R opposite the reserve. Please park carefully.
Access: Open all year. Tussocky ground so walking can be difficult.
Facilities: None.
Public transport: None.
Habitat: Lowland heath, upland moorland, woodland.
Key birds: *Spring/summer*: Roding Woodcock at dawn and dusk. *All year*: good range of woodland birds.
Contact: Trust HQ, Coutts House, Sandon, Stafford ST18 0DN, 01889 508534.
e-mail: staffswt@cix.co.uk
www.wildlifetrust.org.uk/staffs

Suffolk

BONNY WOOD

Suffolk Wildlife Trust.
Location: TM 076 520. From Ipswich head NW on A14 to junction with B1078. Head W from Needham Market about 0.5 miles to Barking.
Access: Open all year. Dogs on leads at all times. Park at the village hall for access to this SSSI.
Facilities: Nature trail.
Public transport: None.
Habitat: Ancient, semi-natural woodland.
Key birds: *Spring/summer*: Nightingale, Blackcap, Willow Warbler, Woodcock. *All year*: All three woodpeckers, Treecreeper, Tawny Owl, usual woodland birds.
Contact: Trust HQ, Brook House, Ashbocking,

Ipswich IP6 9JY, 01473 890089.
e-mail: suffolkwildlife@cix.co.uk
www.wildlifetrust.org.uk/suffolk

BRADFIELD WOODS

Location: TL 935 581. Seven miles SE of Bury St Edmunds.
Contact: Peter Fordham, Felsham Road, Bradfield St George, Bury St Edmunds, Suffolk IP30 0HU. 01449 737996.

CARLTON MARSHES

Suffolk Wildlife Trust.
Location: TM 508 920. SW of Lowestoft, at W end of Oulton Broad. Take A146 towards Beccles

Suffolk

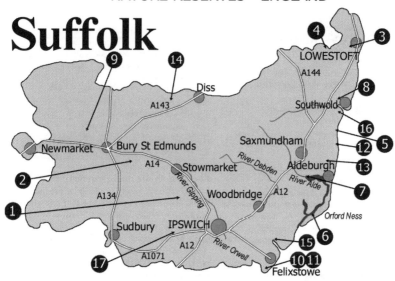

Key to sites:

1. Bonny Wood	6. Havergate Island	11. Landguard Bird OBS
2. Bradfield Woods	7. Hazelwood Marshes	12. Minsmere
3. Carlton Marshes	8. Hen Reedbed National	13. North Warren & Aldringham Walks
4. Castle Marshes	Nature Reserve	14. Redgrave And Lopham Fens
5. Dingle Marshes,	9. Lackford Wildfowl	15. Trimley Marshes
Dunwich	Reserve	16. Walberswick
	10. Landguard	17. Wolves Wood RSPB Reserve

and turn R after Tesco.
Access: Open during daylight hours. Keep to marked paths. Dogs only allowed in some areas, on leads at all times.
Facilities: Information centre and shop. Snacks available.
Public transport: None.
Habitat: 100 acres of grazing marsh, peat pools and fen.
Key birds: Wide range of wetland and Broadland birds, including Marsh Harrier.
Contact: Catriona Finlayson, Suffolk Broads Wildlife Centre, Carlton Colville, Lowestoft, Suffolk NR33 8HU. 01502 564250.

CASTLE MARSHES

Suffolk Wildlife Trust.
Location: TM 471 904. From Beccles head E on A146. Take the first L turn after Three Horseshoes pub. Continue on minor road which bends round to the R. Carry straight on - the road bends to the R again. The car park is on the L just after White Gables house.

Access: Public right of way. Unsuitable for wheelchairs. Stiles where path leaves the reserve. Unmanned level crossing is gated.
Facilities: None.
Public transport: Bus: nearest bus route is on the A146 Lowestoft to Beccles road. Tel: 0845 958 3358. Train: Beccles and Oulton Broad South on the Ipswich to Lowestoft line.
Habitat: Grazing marshes, riverbank.
Key birds: *Spring/summer:* Marsh Harrier, Cetti's Warbler, occasional Grasshopper Warbler. *Winter:* Hen Harrier, wildfowl, Snipe.
Contact: Trust HQ, Brook House, Ashbocking, Ipswich IP6 9JY, 01473 890089.
e-mail: suffolkwildlife@cix.co.uk
www.wildlifetrust.org.uk/suffolk

DINGLE MARSHES, DUNWICH

Location: TM 48 07 20. Eight miles from Saxmundham. Follow brown signs from A12 to Minsmere and continue to Dunwich. Forest carpark (hide) – TM 46 77 10. Beach carpark – TM 479 707.

Contact: Alan Miller, Suffolk Wildlife Trust, 9 Valley Terrace, Valley Road, Leiston, Suffolk IP16 4AP. 01728 833405.
e-mail: alanm@suffolkwildife.cix.co.uk

HAVERGATE ISLAND

RSPB (East Anglia Office).
Location: TM 425 496. Part of the Orfordness NNR at the mouth of the River Alde.
Access: Open Apr-Aug (1st & 3rd weekends and every Thu), Sep-Mar (1st Sat every month). Book in advance, in writing. Park in Orford.
Facilities: None.
Public transport: Boat trips from Orford (one mile)
Habitat: Shallow brackish water, lagoons with islands, saltmarsh, shingle beaches.
Key birds: *Summer*: Breeding Arctic, Common and Sandwich Terns, migrants. Leading site for Avocet. *Winter*: Wildfowl.
Contact: John Partridge, Manager, 30 Mundays Lane, Orford, Woodbridge, Suffolk IP12 2LX. 01394 450732.

HAZELWOOD MARSHES

Location: TM 435 575. Four miles W of Aldeburgh. Small car park on A1094. Mile walk down sandy track.
Contact: Rodney West, Flint Cottage, Stone Common, Blaxhall, Woodbridge, Suffolk IP12 2DP. 01728 689171; fax 01728 688044;
e-mail: rodwest@ndirect.co.uk.

HEN REEDBED NNR

Suffolk Wildlife Trust.
Location: TM 470 770. Just E of Southwold off A1095 from Southwold to Lowestoft.
Access: Park in the lay-by on the A1095. Open all year. Dogs on leads, but not allowed in the hide.
Facilities: Hide, viewing platform, trail.
Public transport: None.
Habitat: Reedbed,dykes, fens, pools.
Key birds: *Spring/summer*: Marsh Harrier, Bearded Tit, Hobby, waders, wildfowl.
Contact: Trust HQ, Brook House, Ashbocking, Ipswich IP6 9JY, 01473 890089.
e-mail: suffolkwildlife@cix.co.uk
www.wildlifetrust.org.uk/suffolk

LACKFORD WILDFOWL RESERVE

Suffolk Wildlife Trust and Atlas Aggregates.
Location: TL 803 708. Via track off N side of A1101 (Bury St Edmunds to Mildenhall road), between Lackford and Flempton. Five miles from Bury.
Access: Open daytime. Access to hides and visitor hut only. No dogs.
Facilities: Eight hides, visitor hut.
Public transport: None.
Habitat: Restored gravel pit with open water, lagoons, islands, willow scrub.
Key birds: *Winter*: Large gull roost. Wide range of waders and wildfowl (inc. Goosander, Pochard, Tufted Duck, Shoveler. No1 hide excellent for Kingfisher). *Spring/autumn*: Migrants, inc. raptors. Breeding Shelduck, Little Ringed Plover and reed warblers.
Contact: Joe Davis, Lackford Lakes Centre, Lackford, Bury St Edmunds, Suffolk. 01284 728541.

LANDGUARD

Location: TM 285 315. Take A154 S from Felixtowe town centre.
Contact: Malte Iden, Landguard Bird Observatory, see below.

LANDGUARD BIRD OBSERVATORY

Location: TM 283 317. Road S of Felixstowe to Landguard Nature Reserve and Fort.
Access: Visiting by appointment.
Facilities: Migration watch point and ringing station.
Public transport: Call for advice.
Habitat: Close grazed turf, raised banks with holm oak, tamarisk, etc.
Key birds: Unusual species and common migrants. Seabirds.
Contact: Malte Iden, Landguard Bird Observatory, View Point Road, Felixstowe, Suffolk IP11 8TW. 01394 673782.

MINSMERE

RSPB (East Anglia Office).
Location: TM 452 680. Six miles NE of Samundham. From A12 head for Westleton, N of Yoxford. Access from Westleton (follow the brown tourist signs).
Access: Open every day, except Tue, Christmas Day and Boxing Day (9am-9pm or dusk if

earlier). Visitor centre open 9am-5pm (9am-4pm Nov-Jan). Tea-room 10.30am-4.30pm (10am-4pm Nov-Jan). Free to RSPB members, otherwise £5 adults, £1.50 children, £3 concession.
Facilities: Toilets, visitor centre, hides, nature trails.
Public transport: Train to Saxmundham then taxi.
Habitat: Woodland, wetland – reedbed and grazing marsh, heathland, dunes and beach, farmland – arable conversion to heath, coastal lagoons, 'the scrape'.
Key birds: *Summer*: Avocet, Bittern, Marsh Harrier, Bearded Tit, Redstart, Nightingale, Nightjar. *Winter*: Wigeon, White-fronted Goose, Bewick's Swan. *Autumn/spring*: Passage migrants, waders etc.
Contact: Geoff Welch, Minsmere RSPB Reserve, Westleton, Saxmundham, Suffolk IP17 3BY01728 648281. www.rspb.org.uk

NORTH WARREN & ADRINGHAM WALKS

RSPB (East Anglia Office).
Location: TM 468 575. Directly N of Aldeburgh on Suffolk coast. Use signposted main car park on beach.
Access: Open at all times. Please keep dogs under close control. Beach area suitable for disabled.
Facilities: Three nature trails, leaflet available from TIC Aldeburgh or Minsmere RSPB. Toilets in Aldeburgh and Thorpeness.
Public transport: Bus service to Aldeburgh. First Eastern Counties (08456 020121).
Habitat: Grazing marsh, lowland heath, reedbed, woodland.
Key birds: *Winter*: White-fronted Goose, Tundra Bean Goose, Wigeon, Shoveler, Teal, Gadwall, Pintail, Snow Bunting. *Spring/summer*: Breeding Bittern, Garganey, Marsh Harrier, Hobby, Nightjar, Wood Lark, Nightingale, Dartford Warbler.
Contact: Rob Macklin, Racewalk, Priory Road, Snape, Suffolk IP17 1SD. 01728 688481.
e-mail: rob.macklin@tesco.net

REDGRAVE & LOPHAM FENS

Suffolk Wildlife Trust.
Location: TM 05 07 97. Five miles from Diss, signposted and easily accessed from A1066 and A143 roads.
Access: Open all year, dogs strictly on leads

only. Visitor centre open all year at weekends, call for details on 01379 688333.
Facilities: Visitor centre with coffee shop, toilets, including disabled toilets, disabled/wheelchair accessible boardwalk and viewing platform. Other general circular trails (not wheelchair access).
Public transport: Buses and trains to Diss town – Simonds coaches to local villages of Redgrave and South Lopham from Diss.
Habitat: Calcareous fen, wet acid heath, scrub and woodland
Key birds: *All year*: Water Rail, Snipe, Teal, Woodcock, Sparrowhawk, Kestrel, all three woodpeckers, Tawny and Little Owls, Shelduck. *Summer*: Reed, Sedge and Grasshopper Warblers, other leaf and *Sylvia* warblers, Hobby plus large Swallow and Starling roosts. *Winter/ occasionals on passage*: Bearded Tit, Marsh Harrier, Greenshank, Green Sandpiper, Shoveler, Gadwall, Pintail, Garganey.
Contact: Andrew Excell, Redgrave and Lopham Fens, Low Common Road, South Lopham, Diss, Norfolk IP22 2HX. 01379 687618.
e-mail: redgrave@suffolkwildlife.cix.co.uk

TRIMLEY MARSHES

Location: TM 260 352. Main Road A14 – Felixstowe two miles – Ipswich ten miles. Parking at top of Cordy's Lane, Trimley St Mary one mile from reserve.
Contact: Mick Wright, 15 Avondale Road, Ipswich, Suffolk IP3 9JT. 01473 710032.
e-mail: mickwright@btinternet.com
www.wildlifetrust.org.uk/suffolk

WALBERSWICK

English Nature (Suffolk Team).
Location: TM 475 733. Good views from B1387 and from lane running W from Walberswick towards Westwood Lodge; elsewhere keep to public footpaths or shingle beach.
Access: Parties and coach parking by prior arrangement.
Facilities: Hide on S side of Blyth estuary, E of A12.
Public transport: Call for advice.
Habitat: Tidal estuary, fen, freshwater marsh and reedbeds, heath, mixed woodland, carr.
Key birds: *Spring/summer*: Marsh Harrier, Bearded Tit, Water Rail, Bittern, Nightjar. *Passage/winter*: Wildfowl, waders and raptors.
Contact: Adam Burrows, English Nature, Regent

House, 110 Northgate Street, Bury St Edmunds IP33 1HP. 01502 676171.

WOLVES WOOD RSPB RESERVE

RSPB (East Anglia).
Location: Two miles E of Hadleigh on the A1071 to Ipswich.
Access: Open all year. Wellington boots advisable between Sept-May. Charge for non-members.
Facilities: Car park for fifteen cars (no coaches)

off A1071. Group bookings, guided walks and special events, no dogs except guide dogs.
Public transport: Bus: Hadleigh (two miles). Train: nearest station Harling Road station.
Habitat: Ancient woodland.
Key birds: *Spring/summer:* Traditional top site for Nightingale, three woodpecker species, usual woodland species.
Contact: RSPB Stour Estuary Nature Reserve, 24 Orchard Close, Great Oakley, Harwich, Essex CO12 5AX, 01255 886043.

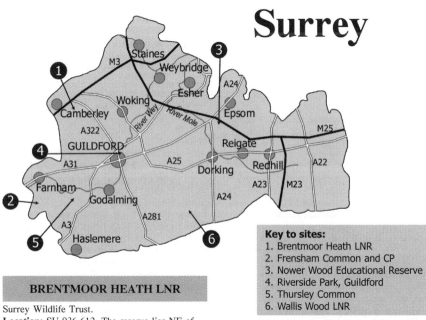

Surrey

Key to sites:
1. Brentmoor Heath LNR
2. Frensham Common and CP
3. Nower Wood Educational Reserve
4. Riverside Park, Guildford
5. Thursley Common
6. Wallis Wood LNR

BRENTMOOR HEATH LNR

Surrey Wildlife Trust.
Location: SU 936 612. The reserve lies NE of Camberley alongside the A322 (Guildford to Bagshot road), at the intersection with A319/B311. Best access is by Brentmoor Road, which runs W from West End past Donkey Town.
Access: Open all year.
Facilities: None.
Public transport: None.
Habitat: Heathland, woodland, grassland, ponds.
Key birds: *Spring/summer:* Stonechat, Nightjar, Hobby. *All year:* Usual woodland birds.
Contact: Trust HQ, School Lane, Pirbright, Woking, Surrey GU24 0JN, 01483 488055.
e-mail: surreywt@cix.co.uk
www.wildlifetrust.org.uk/surrey

FRENSHAM COMMON

Waverley BC and National Trust.
Location: SU 855 405. Common lies on either side of A287 between Farnham and Hindhead.
Access: Open at all times. Car park (locked 9pm-9am). Keep to paths.
Facilities: Information rooms, toilets and refreshment kiosk at Great Pond.
Public transport: Call Trust for advice.
Habitat: Dry and humid heath, woodland, two large ponds, reedbeds.
Key birds: *Summer:* Dartford Warbler, Wood Lark, Hobby, Nightjar, Stonechat. *Winter:*

Wildfowl (inc. occasional Smew), Bittern, Great Grey Shrike.
Contact: Mike Coates, Rangers Office, Bacon Lane, Churt, Surrey GU10 2QB. 01252 792416.

NOWER WOOD EDUCATIONAL RESERVE

Surrey Wildlife Trust.
Location: TQ 193 546. B2033 Leatherhead to Headley road.
Access: Open days Apr-Oct (call for dates and times).
Facilities: Refreshments. Hide, nature trail, visitor centre.
Public transport: None.
Habitat: Ancient deciduous woodland with ponds.
Key birds: *Summer*: 35 breeding species include, Sparrowhawk, all three woodpeckers, Tawny Owl, Spotted Flycatcher, Woodcock, common warblers, Mandarin Duck.
Contact: Education Department, Surrey Wildlife Trust, Nower Wood, Mill Way, Leatherhead KT22 8QA. 01372 379509; fax 01372 363964.

RIVERSIDE PARK

Guildford Borough Council.
Location: TQ 005515 (Guildford BC). From car park at Bowers Lane, Burpham (TQ 011 527). Three miles from town centre.
Access: Open at all times. Follow marked paths. Access to far side of lake and marshland area via boardwalk.
Facilities: Boardwalk.
Public transport: Guildford town centre to Burpham (Sainsburys) No 36 Bus (Arriva timetable information. Tel 0870 608 2608).
Habitat: Wetland, lake, meadow, woodland.
Key birds: *Summer*: Sedge, Reed and Garden Warblers, Common Tern, Lesser Whitethroat, Hobby. *Winter*: Jack Snipe, Chiffchaff, Water Rail. *Passage*: Common Sandpiper, Whinchat,

Water Pipit (up to 12 most years).
Contact: Parks Helpdesk, Guildford Borough Council, Millmead House, Millmead, Guildford, Surrey GO2 5BB. 01483 444715.
e-mail: parks@guildford.gov.uk
www.guildfordborough.co.uk/pages/leisure/parks/parks.htm

THURSLEY COMMON

English Nature (Sussex & Surrey Team).
Location: SU 900 417. From Guildford, take A3 SW to B3001 (Elstead/Churt road). Use the Moat car park.
Access: Open access. Parties must obtain prior permission.
Facilities: Boardwalk in wetter areas.
Public transport: None.
Habitat: Wet and dry heathland, woodland, bog.
Key birds: *Winter*: Hen Harrier and Great Grey Shrike. *Summer*: Hobby, Woodlark, Dartford Warbler, Stonechat, Curlew, Snipe, Nightjar.
Contact: Simon Nobes, English Nature, Uplands Stud, Brook, Godalming, Surrey GU8 5LA. 01428 685878.

WALLIS WOOD LOCAL NATURE RESERVE

Surrey Wildlife Trust.
Location: TQ 121 388. Wallis wood village is about 5 miles NW of Horsham, on minor roads from A29. The reserve is 0.5 miles N of the village, on the E side of Walliswood Green Road to Forest Green.
Access: Open all year.
Facilities: None.
Public transport: None.
Habitat: Oak/hazel coppice woodland, stream, small pond.
Key birds: *All year*: usual woodland species.
Contact: Trust HQ, School Lane, Pirbright, Woking, Surrey GU24 0JN, 01483 488055.
e-mail: surreywt@cix.co.uk
www.wildlifetrust.org.uk/surrey

Sussex, East

BEWL WATER

Sussex Wildlife Trust/Southern Water.
Location: TQ 674 320. Lies SE of Tunbridge Wells. Take A267 and B2099 to Wadhurst and then minor roads N.
Access: Open all year.
Facilities: Car park, hide. Footpath round reservoir. Southern Water Visitor Centre on the N side (from A21 at Bewlbridge) but the reserve cannot be viewed from there. Call 01892 890661.
Public transport: None.
Habitat: Reservoir, woodland, plantation.
Key birds: *Spring/summer*: Chiffchaff, other warblers, terns. *Passage*: Osprey, Common Sandpiper, Green Sandpiper, Greenshank, stints. *All year*: Pochard, Wigeon, Teal, Gadwall.
Contact: Trust HQ, Woods Mill, Shoreham Road, Henfield, West Sussex BN5 9SD, 01273 492630. e-mail: sussexwt@cix.co.uk www.wildlifetrust.org.uk/sussex

FORE WOOD

RSPB (South East England Office).
Location: TQ 758 123. From the A2100 (Battle/Hastings) take lane to Crowhurst at Crowhurst Park Caravan Park. Park at Crowhurst village hall and walk back up Forwood Lane for 0.5 miles. Entrance to reserve on left at top of hill.
Access: Open all year. Closed Christmas Day. No disabled facilities. No dogs.
Facilities: Two nature trails.
Public transport: Station at Crowhurst, about 0.5 mile walk. Charing Cross/Hastings line.
Habitat: Semi-natural ancient woodland.
Key birds: Three species woodpecker, Nuthatch, Treecreeper, Sparrowhawk, Marsh Tit. *Spring/Summer*: Blackcap, Nightingale, Spotted Flycatcher.
Contact: Martin Allison, 12 The Grove, Crowborough, East Sussex TN6 1NY01273 775333 (South East Regional Office). e-mail: martin.allison@rspb.org.uk www.rspb.org.uk

LULLINGTON HEATH

English Nature (Sussex & Surrey Team).
Location: TQ 525 026. W of Eastbourne, after six miles on A259 turn N on minor road to Lullington Court for parking, then one mile up hill (bridleway).
Access: Permit only off rights of way
Facilities: None.

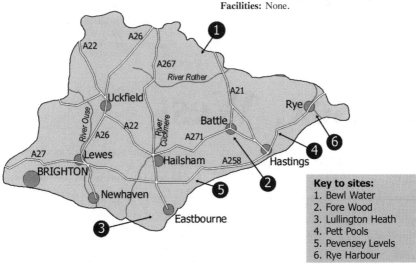

Key to sites:
1. Bewl Water
2. Fore Wood
3. Lullington Heath
4. Pett Pools
5. Pevensey Levels
6. Rye Harbour

Public transport: None.
Habitat: Chalk downland and heath, dense woodland scrub and areas of gorse.
Key birds: *Summer*: Breeding Nightingale, Nightjar and Grasshopper Warbler, Turtle Dove. *Winter*: Raptors (inc. Hen Harrier), Woodcock.
Contact: Malcolm Emery, English Nature, Phoenix House, 32-33 North Street, Lewes, E Sussex BN7 2PH. 01273 476595; fax 01273 483063;
e-mail sussex.surrey@english-nature.org.uk; www.english-nature.org.uk.

PETT POOL

Sussex Wildlife Trust.
Location: TQ 903 145. NE of Hastings on A259.
Access: Good views from Rye/Hastings coast road.
Facilities: None.
Public transport: Call Trust for advice.
Habitat: Man-made shallow pools.
Key birds: *Autumn*: Good wader passage. *Winter*: Bearded Tit.
Contact: Trust HQ, 01273 492630.

PEVENSEY LEVELS

English Nature (Sussex & Surrey Team).
Location: TQ 665 054. NE of Eastbourne. S of A259, one mile along minor road from Pevensey E to Norman's Bay.
Access: Good views from road.
Facilities: None.
Public transport: Call for advice.
Habitat: Freshwater grazing marsh, subject to light flooding after rains.
Key birds: *Summer*: Breeding Reed and Sedge Warblers, Yellow Wagtail, Snipe, Redshank,

Lapwing. *Winter*: Large numbers of wildfowl (inc. some Bewick's and Whooper Swans) and waders (inc. Golden Plover). Birds of prey (inc. Merlin, Peregrine, Hobby, Short-eared Owl).
Contact: Malcolm Emery, English Nature, Phoenix House, 32-33 North Street, Lewes, E Sussex BN7 2PH. 01273 476595; fax 01273 483063;
e-mail sussex.surrey@english-nature.org.uk; www.english-nature.org.uk.

RYE HARBOUR

Rye Harbour Local Nature Reserve Management Committee.
Location: TQ 941 188. One mile from Rye off A259 signed Rye Harbour. From J10 of M20 take A2070 until it joins A259.
Access: Open at all times by footpaths. Organised groups please book.
Facilities: Car park in Rye Harbour village. Information kiosk in car park. Toilets and disabled facilities near car park, four hides (one with wheelchair access), information centre open at weekends.
Public transport: Train (tel: 08457 484950), bus (tel: 0870 608 2608), Rye tourist information (tel: 01797 226696).
Habitat: Sea, sand, shingle, pits and grassland.
Key birds: *Spring*: Passage waders, especially roosting Whimbrel. *Summer*: Breeding terns, waders, Wheatear, Yellow Wagtail, Tree Sparrow. *Winter*: Wildfowl, Water Rail, Bittern.
Contact: Barry Yates, (Manager),2 Watch Cottages, Winchelsea, East Sussex TN36 4LU. 01797 223862. e-mail: yates@clara.net www.natureserve.ryeharbour.org

Sussex, West

ADUR ESTUARY

RSPB (South East England Office).
Location: TQ211050. On W side of Shoreham-on-Sea.
Access: Good views from riverside paths between footbridge in Shoreham town centre and A259 Norfolk bridge (car park).
Facilities: None.

Public transport: Call RSPB for advice.
Habitat: Mudflats and saltmarsh.
Key birds: Small area but good for easy viewing of waders.
Contact: RSPB office, 01273 775333.

ARUNDEL

The Wildfowl and Wetlands Trust.
Location: TQ 020 081. Clearly signposted from

Sussex, West

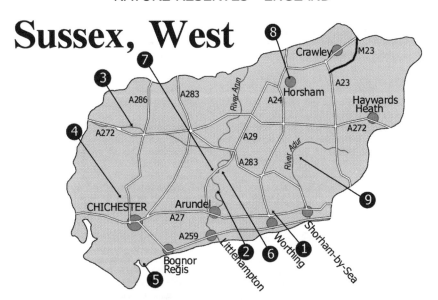

Key to sites:
1. Adur Estuary
2. Arundel
3. Iping And Stedham Commons LNR
4. Kingley Vale
5. Pagham Harbour
6. Pulborough Brooks
7. Waltham Brooks
8. Warnham Nature Reserve
9. Woods Mill

Arundel, just N of A27.
Access: Summer (9.30am-5.30pm) winter (9.30am-4.30pm). Closed Christmas Day. Approx 1.5 miles of level footpaths, suitable for wheelchairs. No dogs except guide dogs.
Facilities: Visitor centre, restaurant, shop, hides, picnic area, seasonal nature trails. Eye of The Wind Wildlife Gallery. Corporate hire facilities.
Public transport: Arundel station, 15-20 minute walk. Tel: 01903 882131.
Habitat: Lakes, wader scrapes, reedbed.
Key birds: *Summer*: Nesting Redshank, Lapwing, Oystercatcher, Common Tern, Sedge, Reed and Cetti's Warblers, Peregrine, Hobby. *Winter*: Teal, Wigeon, roosting Bewick's Swan, Water Rail, Cetti's Warbler.
Contact: James Sharpe, Mill Road, Arundel, West Sussex BN18 9PB01903 883355.
e-mail: wwt.arundel@virgin.org.uk
www.wwt.org.uk

IPING ANDSTEDHAM COMMONS LOCAL NATURE RESERVE

Sussex Wildlife Trust/Sussex Downs Conservation Board.
Location: Head E from Petersfield on A272 to 2.5 miles W of Midhurst. The car park is 0.5 miles down road to Elsted on R.
Access: Open all year. Height barrier to prevent tall vehicles entering.
Facilities: Car park, paths.
Public transport: None.
Habitat: Heathland, coniferous plantations, woodland.
Key birds: *Spring/summer*: Willow Warbler, Tree Pipit, Whitethroat, Yellowhammer, Turtle Dove, Nightjar, Woodcock. *Winter*: possible Hen Harrier, finches, Siskin, Redpoll. *All year*: Sparrowhawk, Green and Great Spotted Woodpeckers, Goldcrest, Marsh Tit.
Contact: Trust HQ, Woods Mill, Shoreham Road, Henfield, West Sussex BN5 9SD, 01273 492630. e-mail: sussexwt@cix.co.uk
www.wildlifetrust.org.uk/sussex

KINGLEY VALE

English Nature (Sussex & Surrey Team).
Location: SU 825 088. West Stoke car park. Approx three miles NW of Chichester town

205

centre (as the crow flies). Travel W along B2178 from Chichester, approx three miles, to East Ashling. Immediately after village turn right (on sharp left hand bend). After approx 0.5 miles turn left (off sharp right hand bend) and car park is on the right.

Access: Always open, no permits, no disabled access, no toilets. Dogs on a lead please.

Facilities: There is a nature trail (posts 1-24) and an unmanned information centre – no toilets, plenty of trees and bushes!

Public transport: Nearest railway station approx four miles walking distance. Nearest main bus route just over one mile on A286 at Mid Lavant.

Habitat: Greatest yew forest in Europe (more than 30,000 trees). Chalk grassland, mixed oak/ash woodland and scrub. Chalk heath.

Key birds: *Spring/summer*: Nightingale, Golden Pheasant, Whitethroat, Blackcap, Lesser Whitethroat. *Autumn/winter*: Hen Harrier, Buzzard, Hobby on migration, Red Kite.

Contact: Simon Nobes, English Nature, Game Keeper's Lodge, West Stoke House Farm, Downs Road, West Stoke, Chichester, West Sussex PO18 9BN. 01243 575353.

PAGHAM HARBOUR

West Sussex County Council.

Location: SZ 857 966. Five miles S of Chichester on B2145 towards Selsey.

Access: Open at all times, dogs must be on leads, disabled trail with accessible hide.

Facilities: Visitor centre open at weekends (10am-4pm), toilets (including disabled), three hides, one nature trail.

Public transport: Bus stop by visitor centre.

Habitat: Intertidal saltmarsh, shingle beaches, lagoons and farmland.

Key birds: *Spring*: Passage migrants. *Autumn*: Passage waders, other migrants. *Winter*: Brent Goose, Slavonian Grebe, wildfowl. *All year*: Little Egret.

Contact: Sarah Patton, Pagham Harbour LNR, Selsey Road, Sidlesham, Chichester, West Sussex PO20 7NE. 01243 641508.
e-mail: pagham.nr@westsussex.gov.uk

PULBOROUGH BROOKS

RSPB (South East England Office).

Location: TQ 054 170. Signposted on A283 between Pulborough (via A29) and Storrington (via A24). Two miles SE of Pulborough.

Access: Open daily. Visitor centre 10am-5pm (Tea-room 4.45pm, 4pm Mon-Fri in winter), closed Christmas Day and Boxing Day. Nature trail and hides (9am-9pm or sunset), closed Christmas Day. Admission fee for nature trail (free to RSPB members). No dogs. All four hides accessible to wheelchair users, although a strong helper is needed.

Facilities: Visitor centre (incl RSPB shop, tea room with terrace, displays, toilets). Nature trail and four hides and two viewpoints. Large car park. Play and picnic areas. A mobility buggy is available for free hire.

Public transport: Two miles from Pulborough train station. Connecting bus service regularly passes reserve entrance (not Suns). Compass Travel (01903 233767). Cycle stands.

Habitat: Lowland wet grassland (wet meadows and ditches). Hedgerows and woodland.

Key birds: *Winter*: Wintering waterbirds, Bewick's Swan. *Spring*: Breeding wading birds and songbirds (incl Lapwing and Nightingale). *Summer*: Butterflies and dragonflies, warblers. *Autumn*: Passage wading birds, Redstart, Whinchat.

Contact: Tim Callaway, Site Manager, Upperton's Barn, Wiggonholt, Pulborough, West Sussex RH20 2EL. 01798 875851.
e-mail: pulborough.brooks@rspb.org.uk

WALTHAM BROOKS

Sussex Wildlife Trust.

Location: TQ 026 159. SW of Pulborough. On S side of minor road E of Coldwaltham on A29.

Access: Park at Greatham Bridge car park, not on roadside. Permit only.

Facilities: None.

Public transport: None.

Habitat: Wet grassland with muddy pools in spring, flooded meadows in winter.

Key birds: *Winter:* Waders, wildfowl (inc. Bewick's Swan, Shoveler, Teal, Wigeon). *Spring/summer:* Redshank, Lapwing, Gadwall and Shelduck.

Contact: Trust HQ, 01273 492630.

WARNHAM NATURE RESERVE

Horsham District Council.

Location: TQ 167 324. One mile from Horsham Town Centre. Reserve located off A24 at the 'Robin Hood' roundabout, on B2237.

Access: Open Thu-Sun throughout the year and

Bank Holidays (10am-6pm or dusk). Free access over part of reserve, permits required for some areas (small charge day or annual permits). No dogs allowed. Hide nearest visitor centre has good disabled access, otherwise no hardstanding paths.
Facilities: Visitor centre and café open Sat and Sun in summer, Sun only in winter. Toilets (including disabled) available, two hides, nature reserve leaflets available to lead you round.
Public transport: From Horsham Railway Station it is a mile walk along Hurst Road, with a right turn onto Warnham Road. A bus from the 'Carfax' in Horsham Centre can take you to within 150 yards of the reserve. Travel line, 0870 608 2608.
Habitat: Millpond with reedbeds, marsh, meadow and woodland (broadleaf and coniferous).
Key birds: Heronry, Great Crested Grebe, Kingfisher. *Summer*: Swift, Swallow, House Martin, Sedge Warbler, Reed Warbler, Garden Warbler, Willow Warbler, Whitethroat, Blackcap, Chiffchaff, Spotted Flycatcher. *Winter*: Cormorant, Teal, Pochard, Tufted Duck, Black-headed Gull, Meadow Pipit, Siskin.
Contact: Julia Hargreaves, Leisure Services, Park House Lodge, North Street , Horsham, W Sussex RH12 1RL. 01403 256890

WOODS MILL

Sussex Wildlife Trust.
Location: TQ 218 138. Located NW of Brighton, one mile S of Henfield on A2037.
Access: Nature trail – every day except Christmas week (9am-5pm). Muddy in winter, access by wheelchair in summer. Headquarters of Sussex Wildlife Trust.
Facilities: Toilets, hide, nature trail, car park. Events programme.
Public transport: From Henfield hourly. Compass Travel 01903 233767.
Habitat: Woodland, reedbeds, wet meadow, lake.
Key birds: General woodland birds and Kingfisher all year. *Summer*: Warblers (Reed, Blackcap, Garden, Whitethroat, Lesser Whitethroat) and Nightingale.
Contact: Steve Tillman, Woods Mill, Henfield, West Sussex BN5 9SD01273 492630.

Tyne & Wear

BIG WATERS

Location: NZ 227 734. S along track off Wide Open/Dinnington road.
Contact: Northumberland Wildlife Trust HQ, 0191 284 6884.

BOLDON FLATS

Location: NZ 377 614. Take A184 N from Sunderland to Boldon.
Contact: South Tyneside Metropolitan Council.

DERWENT WALK

Gateshead Council.
Location: NZ 178 604. Along River Derwent, four miles SW of Newcastle and Gateshead. Several car parks along A614.
Access: Site open all times. Thornley visitor centre open weekends and Bank Holidays (12-5pm). Keys for hides available from Thornley Woodlands Centre (£2).
Facilities: Toilets at Thornley visitor centre. Toilets at Swalwell visitor centre. Hides at Far Pasture Ponds and Thornley feeding station.
Public transport: 45, 46, 46A, M20 and 611 buses from Newcastle/Gateshead to Swalwell/Rowlands Gill. Bus stop Thornley Woodlands Centre. (Regular bus service from Newcastle). Information from News Travel Line. Tel: 0191 2325325.
Habitat: Mixed woodland, river, ponds, meadows.
Key birds: *Summer*: Wood Warbler, Pied Flycatcher, Green Sandpiper, Kingfisher, Dipper, Great Spotted and Green Woodpeckers, Blackcap, Garden Warbler, Nuthatch. *Winter*: Brambling, Marsh Tit, Willow Tit, Bullfinch, Great Spotted Woodpecker, Nuthatch, Goosander, Kingfisher.
Contact: Stephen Westerberg, Thornley Woodlands Centre, Rowlands Gill, Tyne & Wear

Tyne & Wear

Key to sites:
1. Big Waters
2. Boldon Flats
3. Derwent Walk CP
4. Ryton Willows
5. Shibdon Pond

6. Tyne Riverside CP and Throckley Pond Nature Reserve
7. Wallsend Swallow Pond

8. Washington
9. Watergate Forest Park/ Washingwell Wood
10. Whitburn Bird Observatory

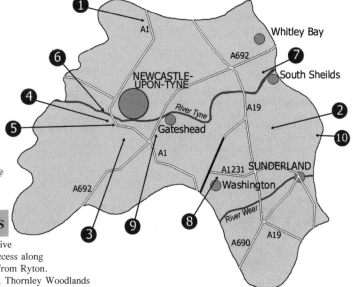

NE39 1AU. 01207 545212. e-mail: thornleywoodlandscentre@unisonFree.net www.gateshead.gov.uk

RYTON WILLOWS

Location: NZ 155 650. Five miles W of Newcastle. Access along several tracks running N from Ryton.
Contact: Andrew McLay, Thornley Woodlands Centre (see above).

SHIBDON POND

Gateshead Council.
Location: NZ 192 628. E of Blaydon, S of Scotswood Bridge, close to A1. Car park at Blaydon swimming baths. Open access from B6317 (Shibdon Road).
Access: Open at all times. Disabled access to hide. Key for hide available from Thornley Woodlands Centre (£2).
Facilities: Hide in SW corner of pond. Free leaflet available.
Public transport: At least six buses per hour from Newcastle/Gateshead to Blaydon (bus stop Shibdon Road). Information from Nexus Travel Line (0191 232 5325).
Habitat: Pond, marsh, scrub and damp grassland.
Key birds: *Winter*: Wildfowl, Water Rail, white-winged gulls. *Summer*: Reed Warbler, Sedge Warbler, Lesser Whitethroat, Grasshopper Warbler, Water Rail. *Autumn*: Passage waders and wildfowl, Kingfisher.
Contact: Brian Pollinger, Thornley Woodlands Centre, Rowlands Gill, Tyne & Wear NE39 1AU. 01209 545212.
www.gateshead.gov.uk
e-mail: thornleywoodlandscentre@unisonFree.net

TYNE RIVERSIDE COUNTRY PARK AND THROCKLEY POND

Newcastle City Council/Northumberland Wildlife Trust.
Location: NZ 158 658. On W edge of Newcastle S of A69(T). Take A6085 into Newburn. The park is signposted along road to Blaydon. 0.25 miles after this junction, turn due W (the Newburn Hotel is on the corner) and after 0.5 miles the parking and information area is signed just beyond the Newburn Leisure Centre.
Access: Open all year.
Facilities: Car park. Leaflets and walk details available.
Public transport: None.
Habitat: River, pond with reed and willow stands, mixed woodland, open grassland.
Key birds: *Spring/summer*: Swift, Swallow, Whitethroat, Lesser Whitethroat. *Winter*: Sparrowhawk, Kingfisher, Little Grebe, finches, Siskin, Fieldfare, Redwing, duck, Goosander and other wildfowl. *All year*: Grey Partridge, Green and Great Spotted Woodpecker, Bullfinch, Yellowhammer.
Contact: Trust HQ, The Garden House, St Nicholas Park, Jubilee Road, Newcastle upon Tyne NE3 3XT, 0191 284 6884.
e-mail: northwildlife@cix.co.uk
www.wildlifetrust.org.uk/northumberland

WALLSEND SWALLOW POND

Location: NZ 301 693. Halfway between Whitley Bay and Gosforth in the Rising Sun Country Park. S off A191 by garden centre.
Contact: Trust HQ, 0191 284 6884.

WASHINGTON

The Wildfowl & Wetlands Trust.
Location: NZ 331 566. In Washington. On N bank of River Wear, W of Sunderland. Signposted from A195, A19, A1231 and A182.
Access: Open 9.30am-5pm (summer), 9.30am-4pm (winter). Free to WWT members. Admission charge for non-members. No dogs except guide dogs. Good access for people with disabilities.
Facilities: Visitor centre, toilets, parent and baby room, range of hides. Shop and café.
Public transport: Buses to Waterview Park (250 yards walk) from Washington, from Sunderland,

Newcastle-upon-Tyne, Durham and South Shields. Tel: 0845 6060260 for details.
Habitat: Wetlands and woodland.
Key birds: *Spring/summer*: Nesting colony of Grey Heron, other breeders include Common Tern, Oystercatcher, Lapwing. *Winter*: Bird-feeding station visited by Great Spotted Woodpecker, Bullfinch, Jay and Sparrowhawk. Goldeneye and other ducks.
Contact: Andrew Donnison, (Grounds Manager),Wildfowl & Wetlands Trust, District 15, Washington NE38 8LE. 0191 4165454 ext 222. e-mail: wetlands@euphony.net
www.wwt.org.uk

WASHINGWELL WOOD WATERGATE PARK

Gateshead Council.
Location: NZ 229 606. Two miles SW of Newcastle.
Access: Open at all times. Access for all on several paths.
Facilities: Nature trails.
Public transport: Regular bus service to Lobley Hill from Newcastle/Gateshead. Information from Nexus Travel Line 0191 232 5325.
Habitat: Lake, conifer wood, grassland (young tree planting areas).
Key birds: *Winter*: Wildfowl, Siskin, finches. *Summer*: Wildfowl, Common Sandpiper, Skylark, Linnet.
Contact: Melanie Bowden, Thornley Woodlands Centre, Rowlands Gill, Tyne & Wear NE39 1AU. 01207 545212.
www.gateshead.gov.uk
e-mail: thornleywoodlandscentre@unisonFree.net

WHITBURN BIRD OBSERVATORY

National Trust/Durham Bird Club.
Location: NZ 414 633.
Access: Access details from Recorder.
Facilities: None.
Public transport: None.
Habitat: Cliff top location.
Key birds: Esp. seawatching but also passerine migrants inc. rarities.
Contact: Tony Armstrong, 39 Western Hill, Durham City DH1 4RJ. 0191 386 1519; e-mail ope@globalnet.co.uk.

Warwickshire

ALVECOTE POOLS

Warwickshire Wildlife Trust.
Location: SK 253 034. Located alongside River Anker E of Tamworth. Access via Robey's Lane (off B5000) just past Alvecote Priory car park. Also along towpath via Pooley Hall visitor centre.
Access: Some paths accessible to disabled. Parking Alvecote Priory car park.
Facilities: Nature trail.
Public transport: None.
Habitat: Marsh, pools (open and reedbeds) and woodland.
Key birds: *Spring/summer*: Breeding Oystercatcher, Common Tern and Little Ringed Plover. Important for wintering, passage and breeding wetland birds.
Contact: Alan Preece, Brandon Marsh Nature Centre, Brandon Lane, Brandon, Coventry CV3 3GW 01276 308993.
e-mail: apreece@warkswt.cix.co.uk
www.warwickshire-wildlife-trust.org.uk

BRANDON MARSH

Warwickshire Wildlife Trust.
Location: SP 386 762. Three miles SE of Coventry, 200 yards SE of A45/A46 junction (Tollbar End). Turn E off A45 into Brandon Lane. Reserve entrance 1.25 miles on right.
Access: Open weekdays (9am-5pm), weekends (10am-4.30pm). Entrance £2.50 (free to Trust members). Wheelchair access to nature trail and Wright hide. No dogs.
Facilities: Visitor centre, toilets, tea-rooms (open at above times), nature trail, six hides.
Public transport: Bus service from Coventry to Tollbar End then 1.25 mile walk. Tel Travel West Midlands 02476 817032 for bus times.
Habitat: Ten pools, together with marsh, reedbeds, willow carr, scrub and small mixed woodland in 260 acres.
Key birds: *Spring/summer*: Migrant warblers inc. Grasshopper, Hobby, Little Ringed Plover, Whinchat, Wheatear. *Autumn/winter*: Dunlin, Ruff, Snipe, Greenshank, Green and Common Sandpipers, wildfowl, Siskin, Redpoll. *All year*: Cetti's Warbler, Kingfisher, Water Rail.
Contact: Ken Bond, Hon. Sec. Brandon Marsh Voluntary Conservation Team, 54 Wiclif Way, Stockingford, Nuneaton, Warwickshire CV10 8NF. 02476 328785.

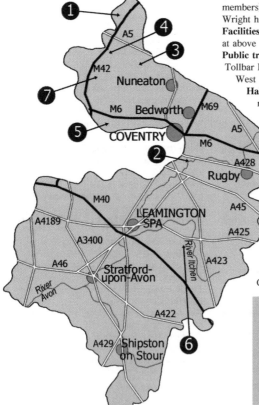

Key to sites:
1. Alvecote Pools
2. Brandon Marsh
3. Hartshill Hayes Country Park
4. Kingsbury Water Park
5. Marsh Lane Nature Reserve
6. Ufton Fields
7. Whitacre Heath

HARTSHILL HAYES

Location: SP 317 943. Signposted as 'Country Park' from B4114 W of Nuneaton.
Contact: Country Park Manager's Office, Kingsbury Water Park, Bodymoor Heath Lane, Sutton Coldfield, West Midlands B76 0DY. 01827 872660;
e-mail: parks@warwickshire.gov.uk.

KINGSBURY WATER PARK

Warwickshire County Council.
Location: SP 203 960. Signposted 'Water Park' from J9 M42, A4097 NE of Birmingham.
Access: Open all year except Christmas Day.
Facilities: Four hides, one with wheelchair access. Miles of flat surfaced footpaths, free loan scheme for mobility scooters. Cafes, information centre with gift shop.
Public transport: Call for advice.
Habitat: Open water; numerous small pools, some with gravel islands, rough areas and grassland.
Key birds: *Summer*: Breeding warblers (nine species), Little Ringed Plover, Great Crested and Little Grebes. Shoveler, Shelduck and a thriving Common Tern colony. Passage waders (esp. spring). *Winter*: Wildfowl, Short-eared Owl.
Contact: Country Park Manager's Office, Kingsbury Water Park, Bodymoor Heath Lane, Sutton Coldfield, West Midlands B76 0DY. 01827 872660;
e-mail: parks@warwickshire.gov.uk.

MARSH LANE

Packington Estate Enterprises Limited.
Location: SP 217 804. Equidistant between Birmingham and Coventry, off A452 between A45 and Balsall Common. Turn right into Marsh Lane and immediately right onto Old Kenilworth Road (now a public footpath), to locked gate. Key required for access.
Access: Site suitable for disabled. Day or year permit only. Membership rates: annual – adult £20, OAP £15, children (under 16) £10. Day permit adult £3, OAP £2.50, children (under 16) £2 obtained from Golf Professional Shop, Stonebridge Golf Centre, Somers Road, off Hampton Lane, Meriden, nr Coventry CV7 7PL (tel 01676 522442) only three to four minutes car

journey from site. Open Mon-Sun (7am-7pm). £10 deposit required for key for access. Only guide dogs allowed.
Facilities: Four hides and hard tracks between hides. Car park behind locked gates. Stonebridge Golf Centre open to non-members. Visitors can obtain drinks and meals on site
Public transport: Hampton-in-Arden railway station within walking distance on footpath loop. Bus no 194 stops at N end of Old Kenilworth Road one mile from reserve gate.
Habitat: Two large pools with islands, three small areas of woodland, five acre field set aside for arable growth for finches and buntings as winter feed.
Key birds: 152 species. *Summer:* Breeding birds include Little Ringed Plover, Common Tern, most species of warbler including Grasshopper. Good passage of waders in Apr, May, Aug and Sept. Hobby and Buzzard breed locally.
Contact: Nicholas P Barlow, Packington Hall, Packington Park, Meriden, Nr Coventry CV7 7HF. 01676 522020 www.packingtonestate.net

UFTON FIELDS

Location: SP 378 615. Located SE of Leamington Spa off A425. At South Ufton village, take B4452.
Contact: Alan Preece, Brandon Marsh Nature Centre (see above).

WHITACRE HEATH

Warwickshire Wildlife Trust.
Location: SP 209 931. Three miles N of Coleshill, just W of Whitacre Heath village.
Access: Trust members only.
Facilities: Three hides.
Public transport: None.
Habitat: Pools, wet woodland and grassland.
Key birds: *Summer:* Sedge Warbler, Reed Warbler, Lesser Whitethroat, Whitethroat, Garden Warbler, Willow Warbler and Blackcap. Migrant Curlew, Whinchat. Also Snipe, Water Rail and Kingfisher.
Contact: Alan Preece, Brandon Marsh Nature Centre, Brandon Lane, Brandon, Coventry CV3 3GW. 01276 308993.
e-mail: apreece@warkswt.cix.co.uk
www.warwickshire-wildlife-trust.org.uk

West Midlands

LICKEY HILLS COUNTRY PARK

Birmingham County Council.
Location: Eleven miles SW of Birmingham City
Centre on A38. Take B4120 S from Rednal or
B4096 from M42(J1).
Access: Open all year.
Facilities: Car park, visitor centre with
wheelchair pathway with viewing gallery, picnic
site, toilets, café, shop.
Public transport: Bus: West Midlands 62 Rednal
(20 mins walk to visitor centre. Rail: Barnt Green
(25 mins walk through woods to the centre).
Habitat: Hills covered with mixed deciduous
woodland, conifer plantations and heathland.
Key birds: *Spring/summer*: Warblers, Tree Pipit,
Redstart. *Winter*: Redwing, Fieldfare. *All year*:
Common woodland species.
Contact: The Visitor Centre, Lickey Hills
Country Park, Warren Lane, Rednal, Birmingham
B45 8ER, 0121 4477106.
e-mail: visitorcentre@lickeyhills.fsnet.co.uk

SANDWELL VALLEY (1)

Metropolitan Borough Council.
Location: SP 012 918 & SP 028 992.
Access: Access and car park from Dagger Lane
or Forge Lane, West Bromwich.
Facilities: Mainly public open space.
Public transport: Call for advice.
Habitat: Nature reserve, lakes, woods and
farmland.
Key birds: *Summer*: Breeding Lapwing, Little
Ringed Plover, Sparrowhawk. All three
woodpeckers, Tawny Owl, Reed Warbler.
Passage waders.
Contact: Senior Ranger, Sandwell Valley
Country Park, Salters Lane, West Bromwich, W
Midlands B71 4BG. 0121 553 0220 or 2147.

SANDWELL VALLEY (2)

RSPB (Central England).
Location: SP 035 928. Great Barr, Birmingham.

Follow signs S from M6 (J7) via A34. Take right
at first junction onto A4041. Take fourth left onto
Hamstead Road (B4167), then right at first mini
roundabout onto Tanhouse Avenue.
Access: 800 metres of wheelchair accessible paths
around reserve, centre fully accessible.
Facilities: Visitor Centre and car park (open Tue-
Sun 9.30am-5pm) with viewing area, small shop
and hot drinks, four viewing screens.
Public transport: Bus: 16 from Colmore Row,
Birmingham City Centre (ask for Tanhouse
Avenue). Train: Hamstead Station, then 16 bus
for one mile towards West Bromwich from
Hamstead (ask for Tanhouse Avenue).
Habitat: Open water, wet grassland, reedbed, dry
grassland and scrub.
Key birds: *Summer*: Lapwing, Reed Warbler,
Willow Tit. *Passage*: Waders, Yellow Wagtail,
chats, Common Tern. *Winter*: Water Rail, Snipe,
Jack Snipe, Goosander, Bullfinch, woodpeckers,
Goosander and other wildfowl.
Contact: Colin Horne, RSPB, 20 Tanhouse
Avenue, Great Barr, Birmingham B43 5AG, 0121
3577395.

SMESTOW VALLEY

Wolverhampton Council.
Location: SJ 895 005. Main entrance at
Henwood Road, Tettenhall near junction of A41
and A454, W of Wolverhampton.
Access: Open at all times.
Facilities: None.
Public transport: None.
Habitat: Woodland, meadowland, canal.
Key birds: *Summer*: Breeding Nuthatch, Great
Spotted and Green Woodpeckers, Treecreeper,
Reed Bunting, Sky Lark, warblers (seven
species). *Winter*: Little Grebe, Siskin, Redwing,
Fieldfare, Snipe, Water Rail.
Contact: Chris Jones, (Leisure Services), 01902
555133.

Wiltshire

FYFIELD DOWNS

Wiltshire Wildlife Trust.
Location: On the Marlborough Downs. From A345 at the N end of Marlborough, a minor road signed Broad Hinton, bisects the downs, dipping steeply at Hackpen Hill to the A361 just before Broad Hinton. From Hackpen Hill walk S to Fyfield Down.
Access: Open all year but avoid the racing gallops. Keep dogs on leads.
Facilities: Car park.
Public transport: None.
Habitat: Downland.
Key birds: *Spring*: Ring Ouzel possible on passage, Wheatear, Cuckoo, Redstart, common warblers. *Summer*: Possible Quail. *Winter*: Occasional Hen Harrier, possible Merlin, Golden Plover, Short-eared Owl, thrushes. *All year*: Sparrowhawk, Buzzard, Kestrel, partridges, Green and Great Spotted Woodpeckers, Goldfinch, Corn Bunting.
Contact: Trust HQ, Elm Tree Court, Long Street, Devizes, Wiltshire SN10 1NJ, 01380 725670. e-mail: admin@wiltshirewildlife.org www.wiltshirewildlife.org

JONES'S MILL NATURE RESERVE

Wiltshire Wildlife Trust.
Location: SU 170 611. From Pewsey, follow the B3087 for 0.5 miles toward Burbage. Turn L at the crossroads into Dursden Lane. Continue along the lane and over a railway bridge. Parking is limited on the left-hand verge. Walk a short distance along the lane to the reserve entrance, a sunken track just before the 1st house on the L.
Access: Open all year as long as the habitat is not damaged.
Facilities: None.
Public transport: None.
Habitat: River, former water meadows, fen carr, pond.
Key birds: *Spring/summer*: Warblers. *All year*: Kingfisher, Little Grebe, Bullfinch, Snipe, other common species.
Contact: Trust HQ, Elm Tree Court, Long Street, Devizes, Wiltshire SN10 1NJ, 01380 725670. e-mail: admin@wiltshirewildlife.org www.wiltshirewildlife.org

SAVERNAKE FOREST

Forest Enterprise.
Location: From Marlborough the A4 Hungerford road runs along the N side of the forst. Two pillars mark the Forest Hill entrance 1.5 miles E of the A346/A4 junction. The Grand Avenue leads straight through the middle of the woodland to join a minor road from Stibb Gree on the A346 N of Burbage to the A4 W of Froxfield.
Access: Open all year.
Facilities: Car park, picnic site at NW end by A346. Fenced-off areas should not be entered unless there is a footpath.
Public transport: None.
Habitat: Ancient woodland.
Key birds: *Spring/summer*: Garden Warbler, Blackcap, Willow Warbler, Chiffchaff, Wood Warbler, Redstart, occasional Nightingale, Tree Pipit, Spotted Flycatcher. *Winter*: Finch flocks possibly inc Siskin Redpoll, Brambling. *All year*: Sparrowhawk, Buzzard, Woodcock, owls, all three woodpeckers, Marsh, Tit, Willow Tit, Jay and other woodland birds.
Contact: Forest Enterprise, 340 Bristol Business Park, Coldharbour Lane, Bristol BS16 1EJ, 0117 906 6000.

SWILLBROOK LAKES

Wiltshire Wildlife Trust.
Location: SU 018 934. NW of Swindon, one mile S of Somerford Keynes on Cotswold Water Park spine road; turn off down Minety Lane (parking).
Access: Open at all times.
Facilities: Footpath along N and E sides of lakes.
Public transport: None.
Habitat: Gravel pits with shallow pools, rough grassland and scrub around edges.
Key birds: *Winter*: Wildfowl (inc. Gadwall, Pochard, Smew, Goosander). *Summer*: Breeding Reed and Sedge Warblers; best site for Hobby in Cotswold Water Park.
Contact: Trust HQ, 01380 725670.

Worcestershire

KNAPP AND PAPERMILL

Worcestershire Wildlife Trust.
Location: SO 749 522. Take A4103 SW from
Worcester; R at Bransford roundabout then L
towards Suckley and reserve is approx three miles
(do not turn off for Alfrick). Park at Bridges
Stone layby (SO 751 522), cross road and follow
path to the Knapp House.
Access: Open daily exc Christmas Day. Large
parties should contact Warden
Facilities: Hide, nature trail, small visitor centre,
wildlife garden.
Public transport: None.
Habitat: Broadleaved woodland, unimproved
grassland, fast stream, old orchard in Leigh
Brook Valley.
Key birds: *Summer*: Breeding Grey Wagtail,
Kingfisher, Pied Flycatcher, all three
woodpeckers. Buzzard, Sparrowhawk and
Redstart also occur. Also otter.
Contact: Warden, Regional Reserves Manager,
The Knapp, Alfrick, Worcester WR6 5HR. 01886
832065.

MONKWOOD NATURE RESERVE

Worcestershire Wildlife Trust.
Location: SO 804 607. The reserve is
about five miles NW of Worcester. On
the A443 Worcester to Holt Heath
road, take any of the minor roads
N of Hallow to Sinton Green. At
the village green, take the road
to Monkwood by the side of
the New Inn pub. About a
mile down the road there is a
car park on the R.
Access: Open all year.
Facilities: Two nature trails.
Public transport: None.

Key to sites:
1. Knapp And Papermill
2. Monkwood Nature Reserve
3. Tiddesley Wood Nature Reserve
4. Trench Wood
5. Upton Warren
6. Wyre Forest

Habitat: Ancient woodland.
Key birds: *Spring/summer*: Garden Warbler,
Lesser Whitethroat, Cuckoo, Blackcap,
Woodcock. *All year*: Tawny Owl, Sparrowhawk,
Jay. Good for butterflies.
Contact: Trust HQ, Lower Smite Farm, Smite
Hill, Hindlip, Worcester WR3 8SZ, 01905
754919. e-mail: worcswt@cix.co.uk
www.worcswildlifetrust.co.uk

TIDDESLEY WOOD

Worcestershire Wildlife Trust.
Location: SO 929 462. From Pershore head NW
towards Worcester on A44. Turn L near town
boundary just before the summit of the hill
towards Besford and Croome. The entrance to the
reserve is on the L after about 0.75 miles.
Access: Open all year except Christmas Day.
Cycles and horses only allowed on the bridleway.
Please keep dogs fully under control. As there is
a military firing range at the SW corner of the
wood, do not enter the area marked by red flags.
The NE plot is private property do not enter. Not
suitable for the disabled.
Facilities: Information board. Numbered posts
around the reserve described in an old leaflet.

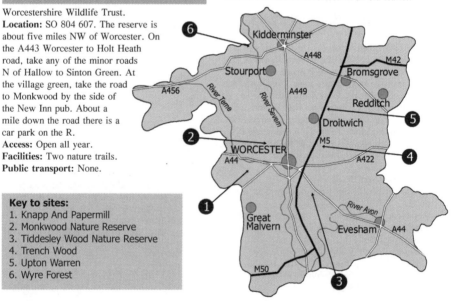

Public transport: None.
Habitat: Ancient woodland, conifers.
Key birds: *Spring*: Chiffchaff, Blackcap, Cuckoo, occasional Nightingale. *All year*: Crossbill, Coal Tit, Goldcrest, Sparrowhawk, Willow Tit, Marsh Tit. *Winter*: Redwing, Fieldfare.
Contact: Worcestershire Wildlife Trust, Lower Smite Farm, Smite Hill, Hindlip, Worcester WR3 8SZ, 01905 754919. e-mail: worcswt@cix.co.uk www.worcswildlifetrust.co.uk

TRENCH WOOD

Location: SO 931 585. NE of Worcester.
Contact: Worcestershire Wildlife Trust HQ.

UPTON WARREN

Worcestershire Wildlife Trust.
Location: SO 936 675. Two miles S of Bromsgrove on A38.
Access: Always open except Christmas Day. Trust membership gives access, or day permit from sailing centre. Disabled access to west hide at moors only. Dogs on leads.
Facilities: Seven hides, maps at entrances, can be very muddy.
Public transport: Birmingham/Worcester bus passes reserve entrance.

Habitat: Fresh and saline pools with muddy islands, some woodland and scrub.
Key birds: *Winter*: Wildfowl. *Spring/autumn*: Passage waders, Common Tern, Cetti's Warbler, Oystercatcher and Little Ringed Plover, many breeding warblers.
Contact: A F Jacobs, 3 The Beeches, Upton Warren, Bromsgrove, Worcs B61 7EL. 01527 861370.

WYRE FOREST

English Nature/Worcs Wildlife Trust.
Location: SO 750 760. A456 out of Bewdley.
Access: Observe reserve signs and keep to paths. Forestry Commission visitor centre at Callow Hill. Fred Dale Reserve is reached by footpath W of B4194 (parking at SO 776 763).
Facilities: Facilities for disabled (entry by car) if Warden telephoned in advance.
Public transport: None.
Habitat: Oak forest, conifer areas, birch heath, stream.
Key birds: Buzzard, Pied Flycatcher, Wood Warbler, Redstart, all three woodpeckers, Woodcock, Crossbill, Siskin, Hawfinch, Kingfisher, Dipper, Grey Wagtail, Tree Pipit.
Contact: Michael Taylor, Lodge Hill Farm, Bewdley, Worcs DY12 2LY. 01299 400686.

Yorkshire, East

BEMPTON CLIFFS

RSPB (North of England Office).
Location: TA 197 738. Near Bridlington. Take cliff road N from Bempton Village off B1229 to car park and visitor centre
Access: Visitor centre open Mar-Nov and weekends in Dec and Feb. Public footpath along cliff top with observation points. Four miles of chalk cliffs, highest in the county.
Facilities: Visitor centre, toilets. Viewing platforms. Picnic area.
Public transport: Railway 1.5 miles - irregular bus service to village 1.25 miles.
Habitat: Seabird nesting cliffs, farmland, scrub.
Key birds: Best to visit May to mid-July for eg Puffin, Gannet (only colony on English

mainland), Fulmar, Kittiwake; also nesting Tree Sparrow, Corn Bunting; good migration watchpoint for skuas, shearwaters and terns.
Contact: Site Manager, RSPB Visitor Centre, Cliff Lane, Bempton, Bridlington, E Yorks YO15 1JF. 01262 851179.

BLACKTOFT SANDS

RSPB (North of England Office).
Location: SE 843 232. Eight miles E of Goole on minor road between Ousefleet and Adlingfleet.
Access: Open 9am-9pm or dusk if earlier. RSPB members free, £3 permit for non-members, £2 concessionary, £1 children, £6 family.
Facilities: Car park, toilets, visitor centre, six

Yorkshire, East

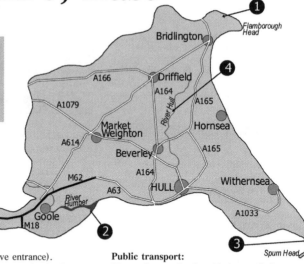

Key to sites:
1. Bempton Cliffs
2. Blacktoft Sands
3. Spurn NNR
4. Tophill Low Nature Reserve

hides, footpaths suitable for wheelchairs.
Public transport: Goole/ Scunthorpe bus (Sweynes' Coaches stops outside reserve entrance).
Habitat: Reedbed, saline lagoons, lowland wet grassland, willow scrub.
Key birds: *Summer*: Breeding Avocet, Marsh Harrier, Bearded Tit, passage waders (exceptional list inc many rarities). *Winter*: Hen Harrier, Merlin, Peregrine, wildfowl.
Contact: Pete Short (Warden) & Simon Wellock (Asst Warden), Hillcrest, Whitgift, Nr Goole, E Yorks DN14 8HL. 01405 704665.
e-mail: simonwellock@RSPB.org
peteshort@RSPB.org.uk   www.rspb.org

SPURN BIRD OBSERVATORY

Yorkshire Wildlife Trust.
Location: Entrance Gate TA 417 151. 26 miles from Hull. Take A1033 from Hull to Patrington (via Hedon) then B1445 from Patrington to Easington and unclassed roads on to Kilnsea and Spurn Head.
Access: Normally open at all times. Vehicle admission fee (at present £2.50 from Apr 1-Oct 31 and £1.50 from Nov 1-Mar 31). No charge for pedestrians. No dogs allowed under any circumstances, not even in cars. Coaches by permit only (must be in advance).
Facilities: Chemical portaloos next to information centre. Information centre open weekends, Bank Holidays, school holidays, but not Fri (10am-5pm). Two hides.

Public transport:
Nearest bus service is at Easington (3.5 miles away).
Habitat: Sand dunes with marram and sea buckthorn scrub. Mudflats around Humber Estuary.
Key birds: *Spring*: Many migrants on passage and often rare birds such as Red-backed Shrike, Bluethroat etc. *Autumn*: Passage migrants and rarities like Wryneck, Pallas's Warbler. *Winter*: Waders and Brent Goose.
Contact: The Warden, Spurn NNR, Kilnsea, Hull HU12 0UG.

TOPHILL LOW

Yorkshire Water.
Location: TA 071 482. Nine miles SE of Driffield and ten miles NE of Beverley. Signposted from village of Watton on A164.
Access: Open Wed-Sun and Bank Holiday Mon. Apr-Oct (9am-6pm). Nov-Mar (9am-4pm). Charges: £2.50 per person. £1 concessions. No dogs allowed. Provision for disabled visitors (paths, ramps, hides, toilet etc).
Facilities: Visitor Centre with toilets, CCTV camera, displays etc. 13 hides (five with access for wheelchairs). Nature trails.
Public transport: None.
Habitat: Open water (two reservoirs), marshes, wader scrapes, woodland and thorn scrub.

Key birds: *Winter*: Wildfowl, gulls, Water Rail, Kingfisher. *Spring/early summer*: Passage Black-necked Grebe and Black Tern. Breeding Pochard, Kingfisher and Grasshopper Warbler. *Late*

Summer/autumn: up to 20 species of passage wader.
Contact: Peter Izzard, Tophill Low Nature Reserve, Watton Carrs, Driffield, East Yorkshire YO25 9RH. 01377 270690.

Yorkshire, North

BOLTON ON SWALE LAKE

Location: SE 248 987. From A1 follow signs for Catterick on A6136. At Brompton-on-Swale take the B6271 E. Turn R in Scorton staying on the B6271. Pass through Bolton-on-Swale and turn into Back Lane after 0.5 miles where there is a car park.
Contact: Yorkshire Wildlife Trust HQ.

BURTON RIGGS
LOCAL NATURE RESERVE

Yorkshire Wildlife Trust/North Yorkshire County Council.
Location: 032 832. The reserve is at the E end of the Vale of Pickering, close to the village of Seamer on the outskirts of Scarborough. Park off the roundabout on the A64, opposite Morrisons supermarket and the industrial estate.
Access: Open all year.
Facilities: Waymarked trail.
Public transport: None.
Habitat: Old gravel pits, freshwater lakes, shingle, scrub, woodland.
Key birds: *Spring/summer*: Little Grebe, possible Little Ringed Plover. Yellow Wagtail, Whitethroat, Lesser Whitethroat, Kingfisher, Sand Martin.
Contact: Yorkshire Wildlife Trust, 10 Toft Green, York YO1 6JT, 01904 659579.
e-mail: yorkshirewt.@cix.co.uk

COATHAM MARSH

Tees Valley Wildlife Trust.
Location: NZ 585 250. Located on W edge of Redcar. Access from minor road to Warrenby from A1085/A1042.
Access: Reserve is open throughout daylight hours. Please keep to permissive footpaths only.
Facilities: Two hides. Key required for one of these – available to Tees Valley Wildlife Trust

members for £10 deposit. No toilets or visitor centre.
Public transport: Very frequent bus service between Middlesbrough and Redcar. Nearest stops are in Coatham 0.25 mile from reserve (Arriva tel 0870 6082608). Redcar Central Station one mile from site. Frequent trains from Middlesbrough and Darlington.
Habitat: Freshwater wetlands, lakes, reedbeds.
Key birds: *Spring/autumn*: Wader passage (including Wood Sandpiper and Greenshank). *Summer:* Passerines (including Sedge Warbler, Yellow Wagtail). *Winter:* Ducks (including Smew). Occasional rarities, Water Rail, Great White Egret, Avocet.
Contact: Mark Fishpool, Tees Valley Wildlife Trust, Bellamy Pavilion, Kirkleatham, Redcar TS50 5NW. 01642 759900.
e-mail: teesvalleywt@cix.co.uk
www.wildlifetrust.org.uk/teesvalley

DUNCOMBE PARK

Duncombe Park Estate.
Location: Set in the grounds of Duncombe Park on the S edge of Helmsley on the A170 Thirsk-Pickering road. Coming from Thirsk, enter Helmsley. Cross bridge just inside the town and turn L into the estate. Good for family birdwatching.
Access: Open all year except Christmas Day. Entry fee into Park, separate from entrance to house and gardens.
Facilities: Car park, toilets, shop, restaurant.
Public transport: None.
Habitat: Ancient woodland, parkland, conifer plantations, river, lake.
Key birds: *Spring/summer*: Curlew, Common Sandpiper, Cuckoo. Swift, Sky Lark, Swallow, House Martin, Sand Martin, Yellow Wagtail, Redstart, Pied Flycatcher, Spotted Flycatcher. *Winter*: Goosander, Fieldfare, Redwing, Brambling, Siskin. *All year*: Good range of birds

Yorkshire, North

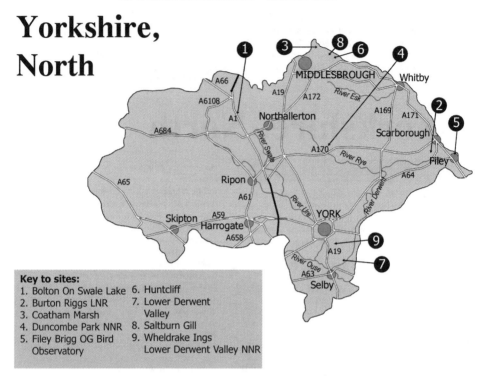

Key to sites:
1. Bolton On Swale Lake
2. Burton Riggs LNR
3. Coatham Marsh
4. Duncombe Park NNR
5. Filey Brigg OG Bird Observatory
6. Huntcliff
7. Lower Derwent Valley
8. Saltburn Gill
9. Wheldrake Ings Lower Derwent Valley NNR

inc. Lesser Spotted Woodpecker, Marsh Tit, Hawfinch, Little Owl.
Contact: Duncombe Park Estate, Helmsley, North Yorkshire, 01439 770213.

FILEY BRIGG BIRD OBSERVATORY

Location: TA 10 68 07. Two access roads into Filey from A165 (Scarborough to Bridlington road). Filey is ten miles N of Bridlington and eight miles S of Scarborough.
Contact: Lez Gillard, Recorder,12 Sycamore Avenue, Filey, N Yorks YO14 9NU. 01723 516383. e-mail: lez.gillard@talk21.com www.fbog.co.uk

HUNTCLIFF

Location: NZ 674 215. Along Cleveland Way footpath from Saltburn or Skinningrove.
Contact: Tees Valley Wildlife Trust HQ.

LOWER DERWENT VALLEY

English Nature (North & East Yorks).
Location: SE 691 447. Six miles SE of York, stretching 12 miles S along the River Derwent from Newton-on-Derwent to Wressle and along the Pocklington Canal. Visitor facilities at Bank Island, Wheldrake Ings YWT (SE 691 444), Thorganby (SE 693 422) and North Duffield Carrs (SE 698 366).
Access: Open all year. No dogs. Disabled access at North Duffield Carrs (two hides and car park). 600 yard path.
Facilities: North Duffield Carrs – two hides, wheelchair access. Wheldrake Ings (YWT) – five hides. Bank Island – two hides, viewing tower. Thorganby – viewing platform.
Public transport: Bus from York/Selby – contact Rider York (01904 435600). Bicycle stands provided in car parks at Bank Island and North Duffield Carrs.
Habitat: Hay meadow and pasture, swamp, open water and alder carr woodland.

Key birds: *Spring/summer:* Breeding wildfowl and waders including Garganey and Ruff. Barn Owl and warblers. *Winter:* 20,000-plus waterfowl including Whooper Swan, Bewick's Swan, wild geese and Wigeon. Large gull roost including white-winged gulls. Also passage waders including Whimbrel.
Contact: Site Manager, English Nature, Genesis 1, Heslington Road, York YO10 5ZQ. 01904 435500. e-mail: york@english-nature.org.uk

SALTBURN GILL

Tees Valley Wildlife Trust.
Location: NZ 674 2O5. From Middlesbrough take A174 to Saltburn-by-the-Sea. Access from the Cat Nab Car Park on the seafront.
Access: Public footpaths through the site, therefore open at all times. Paths can be muddy after rain. Some steep gradients.
Facilities: No visitor centre or hides. Parking at Cat Nab Car Park, Saltburn (charges). Toilets in car park.
Public transport: Bus – frequent buses to Saltburn town centre from Middlesbrough. 0.75 mile walk to site. The hourly 62 bus from Middlesbrough to Loftus stops at the seafront (Arriva tel 0870 6082608). Train – frequent services to Saltburn from Middlesbrough and Darlington. Reserve is 0.75 mile walk from station.
Habitat: Semi-natural deciduous woodland. Some grassland and scrub, stream.
Key birds: Typical woodland species, Marsh Tit, Woodcock, Grey Wagtail.

Contact: Bill Ashton-Wickett, Bellamy Pavilion, Kirkleatham Old Hall, Kirkleatham, Redcar TS10 5NW. 01642 759900.
e-mail: teesvalleywt@cix.co.uk
www.wildlifetrust.org.uk/teesvalley

WHELDRAKE INGS/ LOWER DERWENT VALLEY NNR

Yorkshire Wildlife Trust.
Location: From York travel S down A19 towards Selby. After one mile turn L to Wheldrake. After 3.5 miles pass through Wheldrake and continue towards Thorganby. 200 yards after a small wastewater treatment plant on left, turn L into Ings Lane. Look for two old stone gateposts with pointed tops. The car park is about 0.25 miles down the track. To reach the reserve, cross the bridge over the river and turn R over a stile.
Access: Open all year. Please keep to the riverside path. From Apr-Sept, access is restricted to YWT members only.
Facilities: Car park, four hides.
Public transport: None.
Habitat: Water meadows, river, scrub, open water.
Key birds: *Spring/summer*: Wildfowl, Grey Partridge, Turtle Dove, some waders, Spotted Flycatcher, warblers. *Winter*: Occasional divers and scarce grebes. wildfowl inc. Pintail, Pochard, Goshawk, Hen Harrier, Water Rail, Short-eared Owl, thrushes, good mix of other birds.
Contact: Trust HQ, 10 Toft Green, York YO1 6JT, 01904 659579.
e-mail: yorkshirewt.@cix.co.uk

Yorkshire, South & West

ANGLERS COUNTRY PARK

Wakefield Metropolitan Borough Council.
Location: SE 380 160. SE of Wakefield. Leave A638 at signpost for Crofton. Turn left in village on road to Ryhill, turning just past Anglers pub in Wintersett hamlet.
Access: Open at all times.
Facilities: Two hides.
Public transport: Bus service from Wakefield no 197 to Newstead.
Habitat: Three lakes.
Key birds: *Winter*: Black-necked and Slavonian

Grebes, Wildfowl (inc. Wigeon, Goosander), large gull roost with regular Iceland, Glaucous, Mediterranean. Passage waders and passerines. *Spring/summer*: Breeding Little Ringed Plover, Lapwing, and warblers (inc. Grasshopper and Lesser Whitethroat).

BRETTON COUNTRY PARK / OXLEY BANK WOOD

English Nature (Humber to Pennines Team)/ Yorkshire Wildlife Trust.
Location: SE 295 125. Lies E of Huddersfield, close to M1. Leave the motorway at J38. Take

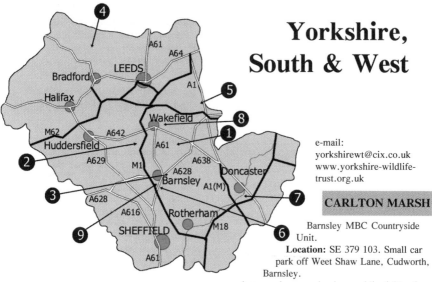

Yorkshire, South & West

e-mail:
yorkshirewt@cix.co.uk
www.yorkshire-wildlife-
trust.org.uk

CARLTON MARSH

Barnsley MBC Countryside Unit.
Location: SE 379 103. Small car park off Weet Shaw Lane, Cudworth, Barnsley.
Access: Access only along public rights of way and disused railway.
Facilities: Two hides.
Public transport: None.
Habitat: Marsh with reed and sedge, some open water.
Key birds: *Summer*: Breeding Water Rail, Little Ringed Plover, Sedge, Reed and Grasshopper Warblers. *Autumn*: Swallow roost; Barn Owl, Jack Snipe.
Contact: Nigel Labdon, Planning and transportation,Central Offices, Toendlay Street, Barnsley, S Yorks S70 2TW. 01226 772142; fax 01226 773599.
e-mail nigellabdon@barnsley.gov.uk

DENSO MARSTON

Denso Marston.
Location: SE 167 389. Two miles from Shipley on Otley Road, entrance through kissing gate past end of factory.
Access: Open at all times.
Facilities: None.
Public transport: Bus from Bradford and Leeds 655, 652, 755.
Habitat: Two pools, woodland areas, meadow areas, site next to River Aire.
Key birds: *Summer*: Garden Warbler, Blackcap, Whitethroat. Good selection of insects such as common blue and brimstone butterflies and common hawker, migrant hawker, four-spotted

Key to sites:
1. Anglers Country Park
2. Bretton Country Park and Sculpture Park/Oxley Bank Wood
3. Carlton Marsh
4. Denso Marston Nature Reserve
5. Fairburn Ings
6. Old Moor Wetland Centre
7. Potteric Carr
8. Pugneys Country Park
9. Worsbrough Country Park

the A637 Huddersfield road to the N. After 0.5 miles the entrance to the Park is on the L.
Access: Open all year. Permit required for the Yorkshire Wildlife Trust area.
Facilities: Car par, visitor centre, information leaflets.
Public transport: None.
Habitat: Landscaped park, mature woodland, two lakes.
Key birds: *Spring/summer*: Cuckoo, warblers, Spotted Flycatcher, Sand Martin, Swallow. *Winter*: Fieldfare, Redwing, Brambling, Redpoll, Siskin, Hawfinch. *All year*: Kingfisher, all three woodpeckers, Little and Tawny Owls, Linnet, Bullfinch, Yellowhammer, usual woodland birds.
Contact: Trust HQ, 10 Toft Green, York YO1 6JT, 01904 659570.

chaser dragonflies. *Winter*: Lesser Redpoll, Siskin, Water Rail.
Contact: Andrew Clarke, Denso Marston, Otley Road, Baildon, Shipley, West Yorkshire BD17 7UR. 01274 582266.

FAIRBURN INGS

RSPB (North West England Office).
Location: SE 452 277. 12.5 miles from Leeds, six miles from Pontefract, 3.5 miles from Castleford situated next to A1 at Fairburn turnoff.
Access: Reserve and hides open every day (9am-dusk). Centre with shop open weekdays (11am-4pm) and weekends (10am-5pm) and Bank Holidays. Hot and cold drinks available. Dogs on leads at all times. Boardwalk leading to Pickup Pool and feeding station and paths to centre wheelchair-friendly.
Facilities: Reserve hides include three open at all times with one locked at dusk. Toilets open when centre open or 9am-5pm. Disabled access to toilets. All nature trails follow public paths and are open at all times.
Public transport: Nearest train stations are Castleford or Pontefract. Buses approx every hour from Pontefract and Tadcaster. Infrequent from Castleford and Selby.
Habitat: Open water due to mining subsidence, wet grassland, marsh and willow scrub, reclaimed colliery spoil heaps.
Key birds: *Winter*: A herd of Whooper Swan usually roost. Normally up to five Smew including male, Wigeon, Gadwall, Goosander, Goldeney. Spring: Osprey, Wheatear, Little Gull and five species of tern pass through. *Summer*: Breeding birds include Reed and Sedge Warblers, Shoveler, Gadwall, Cormorant.
Contact: Chris Drake, Information Warden, Fairburn Ings Visitor Centre, Newton Lane, Fairburn, Castleford WF10 2BH. 01977 603796.

OLD MOOR WETLAND CENTRE

Barnsley MBC Countryside Unit.
Location: SE 422 011. From M1 J36, then A6195. From A1 J37, then A635 and A6195 – follow brown signs.
Contact: Debra Bushby, Old Moor Wetland Centre, Off Manvers Way, Broomhill, Wombwell, Barnsley, South Yorkshire S73 0YF. 01226 751593. Fax: 01226 751617.
e-mail: oldmoor@barnsley.gov.uk
www.barnsley.gov.uk

POTTERIC CARR

Location: SE 589 007. From M18 junction 3 take A6182 (Doncaster) and at first roundabout take third exit; entrance and car park are on R after 50m.
Contact: Yorkshire Wildlife Trust HQ.

PUGNEYS COUNTRY PARK

Wakefield Metropolitan Borough Council.
Location: SE 330 180. Leave M1 at J29 towards Wakefield; reserve signposted from first roundabout.
Access: Open daily 9am to one hour before sunset.
Facilities: Two hides.
Public transport: Bus service from Wakefield no 443.
Habitat: Three lakes, one of which is in reserve area.
Key birds: *Winter*: Large gull roost, Bittern, good range of wildfowl (inc. Smew), Grebes, Short-eared Owl. *Summer*: Breeding Common Tern, Sedge and Reed Warblers. Passage waders.
Contact: 01924 302360.

WORSBROUGH

Barnsley MBC Countryside Unit.
Location: SE 345 034. South of Barnsley, N of Junction 36 of M1. CP car park is off A61.
Access: Open access at all times.
Facilities: Hide, toilets.
Public transport: None.
Habitat: Open water, willow carr, phragmites and typha reedbed, deciduous wood and meadow land.
Key birds: *Summer*: Breeding Ruddy Duck, Sparrowhawk, Sedge and Reed Warblers, Kingfisher, Common Tern. *Autumn*: Swallow roost. *Winter*: Gulls.
Contact: Cultural Services, Worsborough Mill, Barnsley, S Yorks S70 5LJ. 01226 774527.

SCOTLAND

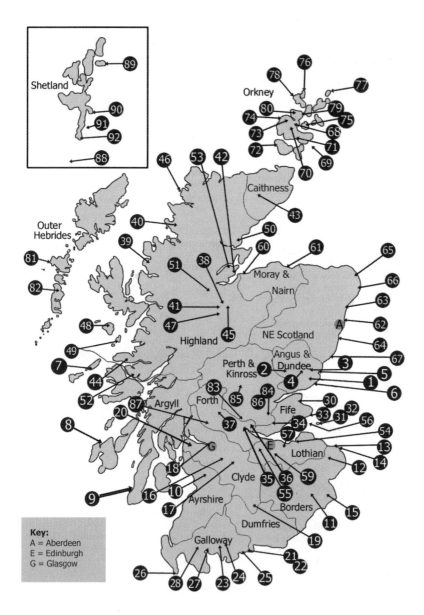

NB: Reserves in Scotland have been listed alphabetically by region (following the arrangement of the Scottish recording areas as set out by the Scottish Ornithologist's Club).

Key to sites:

Angus and Dundee
1. Balgavies Loch
2. Killiecrankie
3. Loch Of Kinnordy
4. Loch Of Lintrathen
5. Montrose Basin
6. Seaton Cliffs

Argyll
7. Coll RSPB Reserve
8. Loch Gruinart, Islay
9. Machrihanish Seabird Observatory

Ayrshire
10. Ayr Gorge Woodlands

Borders
11. Bemersyde Moss
12. Duns Castle
13. Pease Dean
14. St Abb's Head
15. Yetholm Loch

Clyde
16. Barons Haugh
17. Falls Of Clyde
18. Hogganfield Park
19. Knockshinnock Lagoons
20. Lochwinnoch

Dumfries and Galloway
21. Caerlaverock SNH
22. Caerlaverock WWT

23. Carstramon Wood
24. Ken/Dee Marshes
25. Mersehead
26. Mull Of Galloway
27. Wigtown Bay
28. Wood Of Cree

Fife
29. Cameron Reservoir
30. Eden Estuary
31. Isle Of May NNR
32. Isle Of May Bird Observatory
33. Kilminning Coast
34. Lochore Meadows

Forth
35. Cambus Pools
36. Gartmorn Dam
37. Inversnaid
87. Queen Elizabeth Forest Park

Highland & Caithness
38. Abernethy Forest – Loch Garten
39. Beinn Eighe
40. Ben More Coigach
41. Cairngorm NNR
42. Fairy Glen
43. Forsinard
44. Glenborrodale

45. Glenmore Forest Park
46. Handa
47. Insh Marshes
48. Isle Of Eigg
49. Isle Of Rum
50. Loch Fleet
51. Loch Ruthven
52. Rahoy Hills
53. Udale Bay

Lothian
54. Aberlady Bay
55. Almondell & Calderwood
56. Bass Rock
57. Bawsinch & Duddingston Loch
58. Calder Wood
59. Gladhouse Reservoir

Moray & Nairn
60. Culbin Sands
61. Lein (The), Spey Bay

NE Scotland
62. Cullaloe
63. Forvie
64. Fowlsheugh
65. Loch Of Strathbeg
66. Longhaven Cliffs
67. St Cyrus

Orkney
68. Birsay Moors
69. Copinsay
70. Cottascarth & Rendall Moss
71. Hobbister
72. Hoy
73. Loons (The)
74. Marwick Head
75. Mill Dam
76. North Hill, Papa Westray
77. North Ronaldsay Bird Observatory
78. Noup Cliffs, Westray
79. Onziebust, Egilsay
80. Trumland, Rousay

Outer Hebrides
81. Balranald
82. Loch Druidibeg

Perth & Kinross
83. Doune Ponds
84. Loch Leven
85. Loch Of The Lowes
86. Vane Farm

Shetland
88. Fair Isle Bird Observatory
89. Fetlar
90. Isle Of Noss
91. Mousa
92. Sumburgh Head

Angus & Dundee

BALGAVIES LOCH

Location: Scottish WT NO523 516. From car park on A932, four miles E of Forfar.
Contact: Montrose Basin Wildlife Centre, 01674 676336.

KILLIECRANKIE

RSPB (East Scotland).
Location: NN 907 627. W of A9 Pitlochry-Blair Atholl road, B8079 to Killiecrankie, then minor road SW to reserve.
Access: Open dawn to dusk, no dogs. £1 non-member – donations cairn. Not suitable for disabled.
Facilities: None.
Public transport: Train occasionally stops at Blair Atholl and Pitlochry.
Habitat: Upland birch wood, crags, moorland and larch.
Key birds: Buzzard, Crossbill, Wood Warbler, Redstart, Tree Pipit; Black Grouse and Whinchat on moorland fringe; occasional Golden Eagle, Peregrine, Raven.
Contact: Alan Leitch, 1 Atholl Crescent, Perth PH1 5NG. 01738 630783.
e-mail: alan.leitch@RSPB.org.uk
www.RSPB.org.uk

LOCH OF KINNORDY

RSPB (East Scotland).
Location: NO 351 539. Car park on B951 one mile W of Kirriemuir. Perth 45 minutes drive, Dundee 30 minutes drive, Aberdeen one hour drive.
Access: Open dawn-dusk. Disabled access to two hides via short trails.
Facilities: Three birdwatching hides.
Public transport: Nearest centre is Kirriemuir.
Habitat: Freshwater loch, fen, carr, marsh.
Key birds: *Spring/summer*: Osprey, Black-necked Grebe, Blacked-headed Gull. *Winter*: Wildfowl including Goosander, Goldeneye and Whooper Swan.
Contact: Alan Leitch, RSPB, 1 Atholl Crescent, Perth PH1 5NG. 01738 639783.
e-mail: alan.leitch@RSPB.org
www.RSPB.org

LOCH OF LINTRATHEN

Scottish Wildlife Trust.
Location: NO 27 54. Seven miles W of Kirriemuir. Take B951 and choose circular route on unclassified roads round loch.
Contact: Rick Goater, SWT, Annat House, South Anag, Ferryden, Montrose, Angus DD10 9UT. 01674 676555. e-mail: swtnero@cix.co.uk

MONTROSE BASIN

Scottish Wildlife Trust on behalf of Angus Council.
Location: NO 690 580 Centre of Basin. NO 702 565 Wildlife SWT Centre on A92. 1.5 miles from centre of Montrose.
Access: Apr 1-Oct 31 (10.30am-5pm). Nov 1-Mar 31, weekends only (10.30am-4pm).
Facilities: Visitor centre, shop, vending machine, toilets, disabled access to centre, two hides on western half of reserve.
Public transport: Train 1.5 miles in Montrose. Buses same as above.
Habitat: Estuary, saltmarsh, reedbeds, farmland.
Key birds: Pink-footed Goose – up to 35,000 arrive Oct. Wintering wildfowl and waders. Breeding Eider Ducks.
Contact: Karen Spalding, Scottish Wildlife Trust, Montrose Basin Wildlife Centre, Rossie Braes, Montrose DD10 9TJ. 01674 676336. e-mail: montrosebasin@swt.org.uk www.swt.org.uk

SEATON CLIFFS

Scottish Wildlife Trust.
Location: NO 667 416. 30 acre cliff reserve, less than a mile from Arbroath town centre. Car parking at N end of promenade at Arbroath.
Contact: Trust HQ,

Argyll

COLL RSPB RESERVE

RSPB (South and West Scotland Office).
Location: NM 154 546. By ferry from Oban. Take the B8070 S from Aringour for six miles. Turn L at Arileod. Continue for about 0.5 miles, keep R at the turn-off to the Castle. Park just beyond the next cattle grid. Reception point at Totronald.

Access: Open all year. Please avoid walking through fields and crops.
Facilities: Car park, information bothy at Totronald, guided walks in summer.
Public transport: None.
Habitat: Sand dunes, beaches, machair grassland.
Key birds: *Spring/summer*: Corncrake, Redshank, Lapwing, Snipe. *Winter*: Barnacle and Greenland White-fronted Geese.
Contact: RSPB Coll Nature Reserve, Totronald, Isle of Coll, Argyll PA78 6TB, 01879 230301.

LOCH GRUINART, ISLAY

Location: Sea loch on N coast, seven miles NW from Bridgend.
Contact: Yvonne Brown, RSPB, Bushmills Cottage, Gruinart, Isle of Islay PH44 7PR. 01496 850505. e-mail yvonne.brown@RSPB.org.uk www.RSPB.org.uk

MACHRIHANISH SEABIRD OBSERVATORY

Eddie Maguire and John McGlynn.
Location: NR 628 209. Six miles W of Campbeltown on A83 then B843.
Access: Daily May-Oct. Wheelchair access. Dogs welcome. Parking for three cars.
Facilities: Seawatching hide, toilets in nearby village.
Public transport: Regular buses from Campbeltown (West Coast Motors, tel 01586 552319).
Habitat: Marine, rocky shore and upland habitats.
Key birds: *Summer:* Golden Eagle, Peregrine and Twite. *Autumn:* Passage seabirds and waders. Gales often produce inshore movements of Leach's Petrel and other scarce seabirds including Balearic Shearwater and Grey Phalarope. *Winter:* Great Northern Diver.
Contact: Eddie Maguire, 25B Albyn Avenue, Campbeltown, Argyll PA28 6LX07979 395269. www.mso.1c24.net

Ayrshire

AYR GORGE WOODLANDS

Scottish Wildlife Trust.
Location: NS 457 249. From Ayr take the A719

NE for about three miles to the A77. Go straight over the roundabout onto the B473 and continue to Failford. Park in the lay-by in the village.
Access: Open all year. Access by well-maintained path along west bank of River Ayr.
Facilities: Footpaths, interpretation boards, leaflets.
Public transport: None.
Habitat: Heathland, wood fringes, streams and ponds.
Key birds: *Spring/summer*: Nightjar, Stonechat. *All year*: Dartford Warbler, Buzzard. *Winter*: possible Hen Harrier.
Contact: Scottish Wildlife Trust, Cramond House, Kirk Cramond, Cramond Glebe Road, Edinburgh EH4 6NS, 0131 3127765. e-mail: scottishwt@cix.co.uk

Borders

BEMERSYDE MOSS

Scottish Wildlife Trust.
Location: NT 614 340. Four miles E of Melrose on minor road. Between Melrose and Smailholm.
Access: Permit required.
Facilities: Hide with parking nearby.
Public transport: None.
Habitat: Shallow loch and marsh.
Key birds: *Summer*: Large Black-headed Gull colony, Black-necked Grebe, Grasshopper Warbler. *Winter:* Wildfowl, waders on migration, raptors.
Contact: Trust HQ, 0131 312 7765.

DUNS CASTLE

Scottish Wildlife Trust.
Location: NT 778 550. Located N of the centre of Duns (W of Berwick upon Tweed).
Contact: Trust HQ, 0131 312 7765.

PEASE DEAN

Location: NT 790 705. W of St Abb's Head. Park at Pease Bay Caravan Park off A1107.
Contact: Trust HQ, 0131 312 7765.

ST ABB'S HEAD

Location: NT 914 693. Lies five miles N of Eyemouth. Follow A1107 from A1.
Access: Reserve open all year. Keep dogs on lead. Cliff path is not suitable for disabled.
Facilities: Visitor centre and toilets open daily Apr-Oct.
Public transport: Nearest rail station is Berwick-upon-Tweed. Bus service from Berwick, tel 018907 81533.
Habitat: Cliffs, coastal grasslands and freshwater loch.
Key birds: *Apr-Aug*: Seabird colonies with large numbers of Kittiwake, auks, Shag, Fulmar. *Apr-May and Sept-Oct*: Good autumn seawatching.
Contact: Kevin Rideout, Rangers Cottage, Northfield, St Abbs, Borders TD14 5QF. 018907 71443. e-mail: krideout@nts.org.uk www.nts.org.uk

YETHOLM LOCH

Scottish Wildlife Trust.
Location: NT 803 279. Six miles SE of Kelso. Off B6352, turning to Lochtower (unmetalled road).
Access: No access to marsh during breeding season.
Facilities: Hide. Car park along rough track.
Public transport: None.
Habitat: Marshland and loch.
Key birds: *Summer:* Breeding wildfowl (including Great Crested Grebe, Shoveler and Teal). *Winter:* Whooper Swan, Pink-footed Goose and wide range of ducks.
Contact: Trust HQ, 0131 312 7765

Clyde

BARONS HAUGH

Location: RSPB NS 755 552. On SW edge of Motherwell, overlooking River Clyde. Via Adele Street, then lane off North Lodge Avenue.
Contact: RSPB office, Lochwinnoch,

FALLS OF CLYDE

Scottish Wildlife Trust.
Location: NS 88 34 14. Approx one mile S of Lanark. Directions from Glasgow – travel S on M74 until J7 then along A72, following signs for Lanark and New Lanark.
Access: Open daylight hours all year. Partial disabled access.
Facilities: Visitor centre open 11am-5pm all year. Toilets and cafeteria on site. Seasonal viewing facility for Peregrines. Numerous

walkways and ranger service offers comprehensive guided walks programme.
Public transport: Scotrail trains run to Lanark (0845 7484950). Local bus service from Lanark to New Lanark.
Habitat: River Clyde gorge, waterfalls, mixed riparian/conifer woodlands, meadow, pond.
Key birds: More than 100 species of bird recorded on the reserve including unrivalled views of breeding Peregrine. Others include Goshawk, Barn Owl, Kingfisher, Dipper, Lapwing, Pied Flycatcher and Skylark.
Contact: Dr Stuart Glen, The Scottish Wildlife Trust Visitor Centre, The Falls of Clyde Reserve, New Lanark, South Lanark ML11 9DB. 01555 665262. e-mail: fallsofclyde@cix.co.uk www.swt.org.uk

HOGGANFIELD PARK

Glasgow City Council (LNR).
Location: Free car park at entrance on Cumbernauld Road (A80), three miles NE of Glasgow city centre.
Contact: Iain Gibson, 0141 287 5665; e-mail iain.gibson@land.glasgow.gov.uk.

KNOCKSHINNOCK LAGOONS

Scottish Wildlife Trust.
Location: NS 776 113. Car park off B741 (New Cumnock to Dalmellington road), or from Kirkbrae in New Cumnock.
Contact: Trust HQ, 0131 312 7765.

LOCHWINNOCH

Location: NS 358 582. 18 miles SW of Glasgow, adjacent to A760.
Access: Open every day except Christmas and Boxing Day, Jan 1 and Jan 2. (10am-5pm).
Facilities: Special facilities for schools and disabled. Refreshments available. Visitor centre, hides.
Public transport: Rail station adjacent, bus services nearby.
Habitat: Shallow lochs, marsh, mixed woodland.
Key birds: *Winter*: Wildfowl (esp. Whooper Swan, Greylag, Goosander, Goldeneye). Occasional passage migrants inc. Whimbrel, Greenshank. *Summer*: Breeding Great Crested Grebe, Water Rail, Sedge and Grasshopper Warblers.
Contact: RSPB Nature Centre, Largs Road, Lochwinnoch, Renfrewshire PA12 4JF.

01505 842663; fax 01505 843026; e-mail lochwinnoch@RSPB.org.uk.

Dumfries & Galloway

CAERLAVEROCK SNH

SNH (Dumfries & Galloway Area Office).
Location: NY 040 645. From B725 and Caerlaverock Castle.
Access: Open all year. Visitors may enter most of the reserve, except sanctuary area. The saltmarsh (local: merse) can be dangerous at high tides; visitors should consult the Reserve Manager for advice. No permit, but organised groups should apply to Reserve Manager well in advance. Research and surveys require approval of SNH Area Manager.
Facilities: Woodland walks
Public transport: Buses from Dumfries.
Habitat: Saltmarsh, grassland.
Key birds: *Winter*: Barnacle, Pink-footed and Greylag Geese, Whooper and Bewick's Swans, ducks, waders and raptors.
Contact: Wally Wright, SNH Reserve Office, Hollands Farm Road, Caerlaverock, Dumfries DG1 4RS. 01387 770275.

CAERLAVEROCK WWT

The Wildfowl & Wetlands Trust.
Location: NY 051 656. From Dumfries take B725 at Bankend.
Access: Open daily except Christmas Day.
Facilities: 20 hides, heated observatory, three towers, sheltered picnic area. Self-catering accommodation and camping facilities. Nature trails in summer.
Public transport: Buses from Dumfries.
Habitat: Saltmarsh, grassland.
Key birds: *Winter*: Wildfowl esp. Barnacle Geese (max 13,700), Whooper and Bewick's Swans.
Contact: John Doherty, Centre Manager, The WWT, Eastpark Farm, Caerlaverock, Dumfries DG1 4RS. 01387 770200.

CARSTROMON WOOD

Scottish Wildlife Trust.
Location: NT 592 605. Take A75 from Castle Douglas. Reserve is two miles N of Gatehouse of Fleet on minor road off B796.

Access: Open all year.
Facilities: Car parking alongside road. Network of paths. Information boards. Leaflet from tourist office in gatehouse.
Public transport: None.
Habitat: Ancient deciduous oak woodland.
Key birds: Typical woodland birds (inc. Pied Flycatcher, Redstart, Green Woodpecker, Wood Warbler and Tree Pipit).
Contact: Trust HQ.

KEN/DEE MARSHES

RSPB (South and West Scotland Office).
Location: NX 699 684. Six miles from Castle Douglas – good views from A762 and A713 roads to New Galloway.
Contact: Paul Collin, Gairland, Old Edinburgh Road, Minnigaff, Newton Stewart DG8 6PL. 01671 402861.

MERSEHEAD

RSPB (South & West Scotland Office).
Location: NX 925 560. From Dalbeattie, take B793 or A710 to Caulkerbush.
Access: Open at all times.
Facilities: Hide, nature trails, information centre and toilets.
Public transport: None.
Habitat: Wet grassland, arable farmland, saltmarsh, inter-tidal mudflats.
Key birds: *Winter*: Up to 9,500 Barnacle Geese, 4,000 Teal, 2,000 Wigeon, 1,000 Pintail, waders (inc. Dunlin, Knot, Oystercatcher). *Summer:* Breeding birds include Lapwing, Redshank, Skylark.
Contact: Eric Nielson, Mersehead, Southwick, Mersehead, Dumfries DG2 8AH. 01387 780298

MULL OF GALLOWAY

RSPB (South and West Scotland Office).
Location: NX 156 304. Most southerly tip of Scotland – five miles from village of Drummore, S of Stranraer.
Contact: Paul Collin, Gairland, Old Edinburgh Road, Minnigaff, Newton Stewart DG8 6PL. 01671 402851.

WIGTOWN BAY

Dumfries & Galloway Council.
Location: NX 465 545. Between Wigtown and Creetown. It is the largest LNR in Britain at 2845 ha. The A75 runs along the east side with the A714 S to Wigtown and B7004 providing superb views of the LNR.
Contact: Elizabeth Tindal, County Buildings, Wigtown DG8 9JH. 01988 402 401, mobile 07702 212 728.
e-mail: elizabeth.tindal@dumgal.gov.uk

WOOD OF CREE

RSPB (South and West Scotland Office).
Location: NX 382 708. Four miles N of Newton Stewart on minor road from Minnigaff, parallel to A714.
Contact: Paul Collin, Gairland, Old Edinburgh Road, Minnigaff, Newton Stewart DG8 6PL. 01671 402861.

Fife

CAMERON RESERVOIR

Location: NO 478 115. Four miles SSW of St Andrews. Off A915.
Contact: Ian Cumming, 11 Canongate, St Andrews, Fife, 01334 473773.

EDEN ESTUARY

Fife Council.
Location: NO 470 195. The reserve can be accessed from Guardbridge, St Andrews (one mile) on A91, and from Leuchars via Tentsmuir Forest off A919 (four miles).
Access: The Eden Estuary Centre is open (9am-5pm) every day except Christmas Day, New Year's Day and the day of the Leuchars airshow. Reserve is open all year but a permit (from Ranger service) is required to access the N shore.
Facilities: Visitor centre at Guardbridge.
Public transport: Leuchars train station. Regular buses Cupar-Dundee-St Andrews. Tel: 01334 474238.
Habitat: Saltmarsh, river, tidal flats, sand dunes.
Key birds: *Winter*: Main interest is wildfowl and waders, best place in Scotland to see Black-tailed Godwit. Other species include Grey Plover, Shelduck, Bar-tailed Godwit. Offshore Common and Velvet Scoter occur and Surf Scoter is regularly seen. Peregrine, Merlin and Short-eared Owl occur in winter.
Contact: Les Hatton, Fife Ranger Service, Silverburn House, Largo Road, By Leven, Fife KY8 5PU. 01333 429785/07939 169291(m).
e-mail: refrs@craigtoun.freserve.co.uk

227

ISLE OF MAY

Scottish Natural Heritage.
Location: NT 655 995. This small island lying six miles off Fife Ness in the Firth of Forth is a National Nature Reserve.
Access: Contact boatman for day trips: J Reaper tel 01333 310103. Keep to paths. Fishing boat from Anstruther, arranged by the Observatory. Rock landings mean that delays are possible, both arriving and leaving, because of weather. For bookings contact, Mike Martin, Hon. Booking Secretary, 1 Manse Park, Uphall, West Lothian, EH52 6NX. 01506 855285,
Facilities: No dogs; no camping; no fires. Prior permission required if scientific work is to be carried out.
Public transport: None.
Habitat: Sea cliffs, rocky shoreline.
Key birds: *Summer*: Breeding auks and terns, Kittiwake, Shag, Eider, Fulmar. *Autumn/spring*: Weather-related migrations include rarities each year.
Contact: Caroline Gallacher, SNH, 46 Crossgate, Cupar, Fife KY15 5HS.

KILMINNING COAST

Scottish Wildlife Trust.
Location: NO 633 090. Take A917 from St Andews SE towards Crail. Off minor road 1.5 NE of Crail; turn R past disused airfield. Park next to coast at NO 43.20 88.
Contact: Trust HQ.

ISLE OF MAY BIRD OBSERVATORY

Facilities: Hostel accommodation in ex-lighthouse (the Low Light) for up to six, Apr-Oct; usual stay is one week. No supplies on island; visitors must take own food and sleeping bag. Five Heligoland traps used for ringing migrants when qualified personnel present. SNH Warden usually resident Apr-Sep.
Bookings: Mike Martin, 2 Manse Park, Uphall, W Lothian EH52 6NX. 01506 855285; e-mail: mwa.martin@virgin.net,

LOCHORE MEADOWS

Fife Ranger Service.
Location: NT165 958. Site lies S of Loch Leven. Exit the M90 at J4. Drive E through Kelty on A909. Turning N onto B996 Cowdenbeath-Kinross road after one mile and take first R to a car park.

Access: Open all year.
Facilities: Car park, hide. Suitable for wheelchairs.
Public transport: Bus: from Cowdenbeath/ Dunfermline to Kelty.
Habitat: Loch, meadows.
Key birds: *Spring/summer*: Pintail, other ducks, Green Woodpecker, Grasshopper Warbler, Wood Warbler, Whinchat, Common Sandpiper, Redshank, hirundines. *Winter*: Whooper Swan, Redwing, Fieldfare, Redpoll, Siskin.
Contact: Fife Ranger Service, Lochore Meadows Country Park, Crosshill, Lochgelly, Fife, 01592 860086.

Forth

CAMBUS POOL

Scottish Wildlife Trust.
Location: NS 846 937. ENE of Alloa on A907. Park by river in Cambus village.
Access: Cross River Devon by bridge at NS853940 and walk down stream on R bank past bonded warehouses. Open all year.
Facilities: None.
Public transport: None.
Habitat: Wet grassland and pools.
Key birds: Used extensively by migrants, inc. wildfowl and waders.
Contact: Trust HQ, 0131 312 7765.

GARTMORN DAM

Clackmannanshire Council.
Location: NS 912 940. Approx one mile NE of Alloa, signposted from A908 in Sauchie.
Access: Open at all times. No charge.
Facilities: Visitor centre with toilets. Open 8.30am-8.30pm daily (Apr-Sept) inclusive and 1pm-4pm (weekends only Oct-Mar). One hide, key obtainable from visitor centre. Provision for disabled.
Public transport: Bus service to Sauchie. First Bus, 01324 613777. Stirling Bus Station, 01786 446 474.
Habitat: Open water (with island), woodland – deciduous and coniferous, farmland.
Key birds: *Summer*: Great Crested Grebe, breeding Sedge and Reed Warblers. *Autumn*: Migrant waders. *Winter*: Wildfowl (regionally important site), Kingfisher, Water Rail.
Contact: Clackmannanshire Ranger Service,

Lime Tree House, Alloa, Clackmannanshire FK10 1EX. 01259 450000. www.clacksweb.org.uk e-mail: rangers@clacks.gov.uk

INVERSNAID

RSPB (South & West Scotland Office).
Location: NN 337 088. On E side of Loch Lomond. Via B829 W from Aberfoyle, then along minor road to car park by Inversnaid Hotel.
Access: Open all year.
Facilities: None.
Public transport: None.
Habitat: Deciduous woodland rises to craggy ridge and moorland.
Key birds: *Summer*: Breeding Buzzard, Blackcock, Grey Wagtail, Dipper, Wood Warbler, Redstart, Pied Flycatcher, Tree Pipit. The loch is on a migration route, especially for wildfowl and waders.
Contact: RSPB, 0141 576 4100.

QUEEN ELIZABETH FOREST PARK

Forestry Commission (Forest Enterprise).
Location: NN 521 015. From Glasgow head N on A81 to Aberfoyle. Park is off the Duke's Pass on the A821.
Access: Open all year.
Facilities: Visitor Centre, car park, trails.
Public transport: None.
Habitat: Mountain, moorland, forest, river, lochs.
Key birds: Wide range of habitats means excellent bird watching. *Spring/summer*: Pied Flycatcher, Redstart, Wood Warbler, Tree Pipit. *All year*: Dipper, Grey Wagtail, Goosander, and other wildfowl species.
Contact: Forest Enterprise, 231 Corstorphine Road, Edinburgh EH12 7AT, 0131 334 0303.

Highland & Caithness

ABERNETHY FOREST RESERVE - LOCH GARTEN

RSPB (North Scotland Office).
Location: NH 981 184. 2.5 miles from Boat of Garten, eight miles from Aviemore. Off B970, follow 'RSPB Ospreys' road signs (between Apr - Aug only).

Access: Osprey Centre open daily 10am-6pm (Apr to end Aug). Disabled access. No dogs (guide dogs only). No charge to RSPB members. Non-members: adults £2.50, senior citizens £1.50, children 50p.
Facilities: Osprey Centre overlooking nesting Ospreys, toilets, optics and CCTV live pictures.
Public transport: Bus service to Boat of Garten from Aviemore, 2.5 mile footpath to Osprey Centre. Steam railway to Boat of Garten from Aviemore.
Habitat: Caledonian pine wood.
Key birds: Ospreys nesting from Apr to Aug, Crested Tit, Crossbill, red squirrel. In 2001 hide provided views of lekking Capercaillies.
Contact: R W Thaxton, RSPB, Grinian, Tulloch, Nethybridge, Inverness-shire PH25 3EF. 01479 831694.

BEINN EIGHE

Scottish Natural Heritage.
Location: NG 990 620. By Kinlochewe, Wester Ross, 50 miles from Inverness and 20 miles from Gairloch on A832.
Access: Reserve open at all times, no charge. Visitor centre open Easter-Oct (10am-5pm).
Facilities: Visitor centre, toilets, woodland trail and mountain trail – self-guided with leaflets. Trails suitable for all abilities.
Public transport: Very limited.
Habitat: Caledonian pine forest, dwarf shrub heath, mountain tops, freshwater loch shore.
Key birds: Golden Eagle, Scottish Crossbill, Ptarmigan, Red Grouse, Siskin. *Summer*: Black-throated Diver, Redwing, Snow Bunting.
Contact: David Miller, Reserve Manager, Scottish Natural Heritage, Anancaun, Kinlochewe, Ross-shire IV22 2PD. 01445 760254. e-mail: david.miller@snh.gov.uk

BEN MORE COIGACH

Scottish Wildlife Trust.
Location: NC 075 065. 10 miles N of Ullapool, W of A835.
Contact: John Smith, North Keanchullish, Ullapool, Wester Ross IV26 2TW. 01854 612531.

CAIRNGORM NNR

SNH (East Highland Area).
Location: NJ 010 010. Largest NNR in Britain, SE of Aviemore.
Access: Unrestricted but certain areas out of

bounds during deer cull season.
Facilities: Visitor centre open all year.
Public transport: Call tourist office for advice.
Habitat: Mountain, moorland, pine woodland
and lochs.
Key birds: Goosander, Crested Tit, Siskin,
Redstart, Crossbill, Capercaillie, Black Grouse,
Ptarmigan, Dotterel, Golden Eagle.
Contact: SNH, Achantoul, Aviemore, Inverness-
shire PH22 1QD. 01479 810477; fax 01479
811363.

FAIRY GLEN RSPB RESERVE

RSPB (North Scotland Office).
Location: On the Black Isle, N of Inverness, by
Rosemarkie on A832. Car park on a corner
opposite some houses.
Access: Open all year.
Facilities: None.
Public transport: None.
Habitat: Broadleaved woodland in a steep-sided
valley, stream, waterfalls.
Key birds: *All year*: Dipper, Buzzard, Grey
Wagtail, usual woodland species.
Contact: RSPB Ross-shire and Moray Firth
Office, Littleburn, Munlochy, Ross-shire IV8
8NN, 01463 811186.

FORSINARD

RSPB (North Scotland Office).
Location: NC 89 04 25. 30 miles SW of Thurso
on A897. Turn off A9 at Helmsdale from the
South (24 miles) or A836 at Melvich from the N
coast road (14 miles).
Access: Open at all times. Contact visitor centre
during breeding season (mid-Apr to end Jun) and
during deerstalking season (Jul 1-Feb 15) for
advice. Self-guided trail open all year, no dogs,
not suitable for wheelchairs.
Facilities: Visitor centre open Apr 1-Oct (9am-
6pm), seven days per week. Static and AV
displays, live CCTV and webcam link to Hen
Harrier nest in breeding season. Wheelchair
access to centre and toilet. Guided walks Tue and
Thu, May-Aug. Tea-room nearby.
Public transport: Train from Inverness and
Thurso (0845 484950) visitor centre in Forsinard
Station building.
Habitat: Blanket bog, upland hill farm.
Key birds: Golden Plover, Greenshank, Dunlin,
Hen Harrier, Merlin, Short-eared Owl.
Contact: Norrie Russell, RSPB Forsinard,
Forsinard, Sutherland KW13 6YT. 01641
571225. e-mail: forsinard@RSPB.org.uk

GLENBORRODALE RSPB RESERVE

RSPB (North Scotland Office).
Location: Coastal site, one mile W of
Glenborrodale on the B8007 W of Fort William.
Access: Open all year.
Facilities: One nature trail.
Public transport: None.
Habitat: Ancient oak wood, loch.
Key birds: *Spring/summer*: Wood Warbler,
Redstart, Spotted Flycatcher. *All year*: usual
woodland species. Seals, possible otter.
Contact: RSPB, Beechwood Park, Inverness-
shire IV2 3BW, 01463 715000.

GLENMORE

Scottish Wildlife Trust/Forest Enterprise.
Location: NH 998 104. Park at Glenmore seven
miles E of Aviemore, opposite campsite.
Contact: Scottish Trust HQ,

HANDA

Scottish Wildlife Trust.
Location: NC 138 480. Accessible by boat from
Tarbet, near Scourie - follow A894 N from
Ullapool 40 miles. Continue another three miles,
turn left down single track road another three
miles to Tarbet.
Access: Open April-Sept. Boats leave 9.30am-
2pm (last boat back 5pm). Dogs not allowed.
Visitors are asked for a contribution of £1.50
towards costs. Not suitable for disabled due to
uneven terrain.
Facilities: Three mile circular path, shelter (no
toilets on island - use those in Tarbet car park).
Visitors are given introductory talk and a leaflet
with map on arrival.
Public transport: Post bus to Scourie (tel 01549
402357 Lairg Post Office). Train to Lairg (tel
0845 484950 National Train enquiries). No
connecting public transport between Scourie and
Tarbet.
Habitat: Sea cliffs, blanket bog.
Key birds: *Spring/summer*: Biggest Guillemot
and Razorbill colony in Britain and Ireland. Also
nationally important for Kittiwakes, Arctic and
Great Skuas. Puffin, Shag, Fulmar and Common
and Arctic Terns also present.
Contact: Mark Foxwell, Conservation Manager
Unit 4A, 3 Carsegate Road North, Inverness IV3
8PU.
e-mail: mfoxwell@swt.org.uk

www.swt.org.uk.
Charles Thomson (Boatman) 01463 714746/
01971 502347.

INSH MARSHES

RSPB (North Scotland Office).
Location: NN 775 999. In Spey Valley, two
miles NE of Kingussie on B970 minor road.
Access: Open at all times. No disabled access.
Facilities: Information viewpoint, two hides,
three nature trails. Not suitable for disabled. No
toilets.
Public transport: Nearest rail station Kingussie
(two miles). Bus from Kingussie on Tue only!
Habitat: Marshes, woodland, river, open water.
Key birds: *Spring/summer:* Waders (Lapwing,
Curlew, Redshank, Snipe), wildfowl (including
Goldeneye and Wigeon), Spotted Crake, Wood
Warbler, Redstart, Tree Pipit. *Winter:* Hen
Harrier, Whooper Swan, other wildfowl.
Contact: Pete Moore, Ivy Cottage, Insh,
Kingussie, Inverness-shire PH21 1NT. 01540
661518. e-mail: petemoore@RSPB.org.uk
www.kincraig.com/RSPB.htn

ISLE OF EIGG

Scottish Wildlife Trust.
Location: NM 38 48. Small island S of Skye,
reached by ferry from Maillaig or Arisaig (approx
12 miles).
Access: Ferries seven days per week (weather
permitting) during summer. Four days per week
(weather permitting) Sept-Apr.
Facilities: Pier centre – shops/Post Office, tea-
room, craftshop, toilets.
Public transport: Caledonian MacBrayne Ferries
NE from Mallaig (tel: 01687 462403), *MV
Shearwater* from Arisaig (tel: 01678 450 224).
Habitat: Moorland (leading to sgurr pitchstone
ridge), wood and scrub, hay fields, shoreline.
Marsh and bog.
Key birds: Red-throated Diver, Golden Eagle,
Buzzard, Raven. *Summer:* Manx Shearwater,
Arctic Tern, various warblers, Twite, etc.
Contact: John Chester, Millers Cottage, Isle of
Eigg, Small Isles PH42 4RL. 01687 482477.
www.isleofeigg.org

ISLE OF RUM

SNH (North West Region).
Location: NM 370 970. Island lying S of Skye.
Passenger ferry from Mallaig, take A830 from
Fort William.

Access: Contact Reserve Office for details of
special access arrangements relating to breeding
birds, deer stalking and deer research.
Facilities: Prior booking needed to stay
overnight. General store and Post Office (01687
462744). Self-guided trails.
Public transport: Passenger ferry to island.
Habitat: Coast, moorland, woodland restoration,
montane.
Key birds: *Summer:* Large Manx Shearwater
colonies on hill tops; breeding auks (inc. Black
Guillemot), Kittiwake, Fulmar, Eider, Golden
Plover, Merlin, Red-throated Diver, Golden
Eagle.
Contact: SNH Reserve Office, Isle of Rum PH43
4RR, 01687 462026; fax 01687 462805.

LOCH FLEET

Scottish Wildlife Trust.
Location: NH 794 965. Site lies two miles S of
Golspie on the A9 and five miles N of Dornoch.
View across tidal basin from A9 or unclassified
road to Skelbo.
Access: Park at Little Ferry or in lay-bys around
the basin.
Facilities: Guided walks in Summer. Interpretive
centre.
Public transport: None.
Habitat: Tidal basin, sand dunes, shingle,
woodland, marshes.
Key birds: *Winter:* Important feeding place for
ducks and waders. The sea off the mouth of Loch
Fleet is a major wintering area for Long-tailed
Duck, Common and Velvet Scoters, Eider Duck.
Pinewood off minor road S from Golspie to Little
Ferry, with Crossbill, occasional Crested Tit.
Contact: Trust HQ.

LOCH RUTHVEN

RSPB (North Scotland Office).
Location: H 638 281. From Inverness, take A9
SE to junction with B851. Head SW until the
minor road NE at Croachy; car park one mile.
Access: Open at all times.
Facilities: None.
Public transport: None.
Habitat: Freshwater loch and woodland.
Key birds: Best breeding site in Britain for
Slavonian Grebe. Teal, Wigeon and other
wildfowl breed. Peregrine, Hen Harrier and
Osprey often seen.
Contact: RSPB North Scotland Office.

RAHOY HILLS RESERVE

Scottish Wildlife Trust.
Location: NM 690 530. S of Ardnamurchan peninsula. Take A 861 to Strontion, heading s on A884 as rar as Acharn. Reserve is N of Loch Arienas.
Access: Open all year. Permit required.
Facilities: None.
Public transport: None.
Habitat: Mountain, oak woods, hill lochans.
Key birds: *Spring/summer*: Golden Eagle, Common Sandpiper, Pied Flycatcher, woodland birds. Pine marten and wildcat in the area.
Contact: Scottish Wildlife Trust, Cramond House, Kirk Cramond, Cramond Glebe Road, Edinburgh EH4 6NS, 0131 3127765.
e-mail: scottishwt@cix.co.uk www.swt.org.uk

UDALE BAY RSPB RESERVE

RSPB (North Scotland Office).
Location: Tidal bay on N coast of Black Isle, N of Inverness. One mile W of Jemimaville on B9163.
Access: Open all year.
Facilities: Hide, large lay-by.
Public transport: None.
Habitat: Mudflat, saltmarsh and wet grassland.
Key birds: *Spring/summer*: Wildfowl, Oystercatcher, Redshank, other waders. Possible Osprey fishing. *Autumn/winter*: Large flocks of Pink-footed and Greylag Geese, Whooper Swans, ducks and waders.
Contact: RSPB Ross-shire and Moray Firth Office, Littleburn, Munlochy, Ross-shire IV8 8NN, 01463 811186.

Lothian

ABERLADY BAY

East Lothian Council (LNR).
Location: NT 472 806. From Edinburgh take A198 E to Aberlady. Reserve is 1.5 miles E of Aberlady village.
Access: Open at all times. Please stay on footpaths to avoid disturbance. Disabled access from reserve car park. No dogs.
Facilities: Small car park and toilets. Notice board with recent sightings at end of footbridge.
Public transport: Edinburgh to N Berwick bus

service stops at reserve (request), service no 124. Railway 4 miles away at Longniddry.
Habitat: Tidal mudflats, saltmarsh, freshwater marsh, dune grassland, scrub, open sea.
Key birds: *Summer*: Breeding birds include Shelduck, Eider, Reed Bunting and up to eight species of warbler. Passage waders inc. Green, Wood and Curlew Sandpipers, Little Stint, Greenshank, Whimbrel, Black-tailed Godwit. *Winter*: Divers (esp. Red-throated), Red-necked and Slavonian grebes and geese (large numbers of Pink-footed roost); sea-ducks, waders.
Contact: Ian Thomson, 4 Craigielaw, Longniddry, East Lothian EH32 0PY. 01875 870588.

ALMONDELL AND CALDERWOOD

West Lothian Council.
Location: NT 077 670. Lies between M8 and River Almond, E of Livingston. Several entrances but this is closest to the visitor centre - signposted off the A89, two miles S of Broxburn.
Access: Open all year. Parking available off Bank Street in Mid Calder. Walk down the footpath beside the Masonic Hall or park in the lay-by on the A71 between the two shale bings, then along the roadside to the crash barrier and in.
Facilities: Car park, café, picnic area, toilets, pushchair access, partial access for wheelchairs, visitor centre (open Sat-Thu), shop, countryside ranger service.
Public transport: None.
Habitat: Woodland, marshland.
Key birds: *Spring/summer*: Woodcock, Tawny Owl, Grasshopper Warbler, Yellowhammer, Blackcap, Garden Warbler. *Winter*: Goldcrest, Redpoll, Willow Tit. *All year*: Dipper, Grey Wagtail, Sparrowhawk.
Contact: Almondell and Calderwood Country Park, Visitor Centre, Broxburn, West Lothian EH52 5PE, 01506 882254.

BASS ROCK

Location: NT602873. Island in Firth of Forth, lying E of North Berwick.
Access: Private property. Regular daily sailings from N Berwick around Rock; local boatman has owner's permission to land individuals or parties by prior arrangement. For details contact Fred Marr, N Berwick on 01620 892838.
Facilities: None.
Public transport: None.
Habitat: Sea cliffs.
Key birds: The spectacular cliffs hold a large

Gannet colony, (up to 9000 pairs), plus auks, Kittiwake, Shag and Fulmer.

BAWSINCH & DUDDINGSTON LOCH

Scottish Wildlife Trust.
Location: NT 003 631. Centre of Edinburgh below Arthur's Seat. Car park on Duddingston Road West for Bawsinch or by Holyrood Park Gate for views across loch.
Contact: Trust HQ.

GLADHOUSE RESERVOIR

Scottish Water.
Location: NT 295 535. Fifteen miles S of Edinburgh. Head to Penicuik on A701, then take B6372 past Mount Lothian and minor road S to Water.
Access: Open all year though there is no access to the reservoir itself. Most viewing can be done from the road (telescope required).
Facilities: None.
Public transport: None.
Habitat: Reservoir, grassland, farmland.
Key birds: *Spring/summer*: Oystercatcher, Lapwing, Curlew. Possible Black Grouse. *Winter*: Geese, including Pinkfeet, Twite, Brambling, Hen Harrier.
Contact: Scottish Water, PO Box 8855, Edinburgh EH10 6YQ, 0131 4456462. e-mail: customer.service@scottishwater.co.uk www.esw.co.uk

Moray & Nairn

CULBIN SANDS

RSPB (North Scotland Office).
Location: NH 900 580. Approx ½ mile from Nairn. Access to parking at East Beach car park, signed off A96.
Access: Open at all times. Not suitable for wheelchairs.
Facilities: Toilets at car park. Track along dunes and saltmarsh.
Public transport: Buses stop in Nairn, half mile W of site. Train station in Nairn three-quarters mile W of reserve.
Habitat: Saltmarsh, sandflats, dunes.
Key birds: *Winter*: Flocks of Common Scoter, Long-tailed Duck, Knot, Bar-tailed Godwit, Red-breasted Merganser. Rapters like Peregrine,

Merlin and Hen Harrier attracted by wader flocks. Roosting geese. *Summer*: Breeding Ringed Plover, Oystercatcher and Common Tern.
Contact: RSPB North Scotland Office, Etive House, Beechwood Park, Inverness IV2 3BW. 01463 715000. e-mail: nsro@RSPB.org.uk www.RSPB.org.uk

LEIN, SPEY BAY

Scottish Wildlife Trust.
Location: NJ 325 657. Eight miles NE of Elgin. From Elgin take A96 and B9015 to Kingston. Reserve is immediately E of village. Car parks at Kingston and Tugnet.
Access: Open all year.
Facilities: Wildlife centre.
Public transport: None.
Habitat: Shingle, rivermouth and coastal habitats.
Key birds: *Summer*: Osprey, waders, wildfowl. *Winter*: Seaduck and divers offshore (esp. Long-tailed Duck, Common and Velvet Scoters, Red-throated Diver).
Contact: Trust HQ,

NE Scotland

CULLALOE

Scottish Wildlife Trust.
Location: NT 188 877. On loop of B9157 just N of Aberdeen. Car parking at the disused filter beds below the old dam.
Contact: Trust HQ.

FORVIE

Scottish Natural Heritage.
Location: NK 034 289. N of Aberdeen. Take A90 N then A975 NE to Colleiston. Turn E on B9003, reserve is off this road.
Access: Dogs on leads only. Reserve open at all times but ternery closed Apr 1-end of Aug annually. Stevenson Forvie Centre open every day (Apr-Sept) and when staff are available outside those months.
Facilities: Interpretive display and toilets in Stevenson Forvie Centre. Bird hide, waymarked trail.
Public transport: Bluebird No 263 to Cruden Bay. Ask for the Newburgh or Collieston Crossroads stop. Tel: 01224 591381.
Habitat: Estuary, dunes, coastal heath.

Key birds: *Spring/summer*: Eider and terns nesting. *Winter*: Waders and wildfowl on estuary.
Contact: Alison Matheson (Area Officer), Scottish Natural Heritage, Stevenson Forvie Centre, Little Collieston Croft, Collieston, Aberdeenshire AB41 8RU. 01358 751330. www.snh.org.uk

FOWLSHEUGH

RSPB (East Scotland).
Location: NO 879 80. Cliff top path N from Crawton, signposted from A92, three miles S of Stonehaven.
Access: Unrestricted. Boat trips (May-Jul) from Stonehaven Harbour. Booking essential. Contact East Scotland regional office. Tel: 01224 624824.
Facilities: New car park (council) with limited number of spaces 200 yards from reserve (replaced following the storm damage of 1999).
Public transport: None.
Habitat: Sea cliffs.
Key birds: Spectacular seabird colony, mainly Kittiwake and auks.
Contact: The Warden, Starnafin, Crimond, Fraserburgh AB43 8QN. 01346 532017.
e-mail: esro@RSPB.org.uk www.RSPB.org.uk

LOCH OF STRATHBEG

RSPB (East Scotland).
Location: NK 057 581. Near Crimond on the A90, nine miles S of Fraserburgh.
Access: Starnafin visitor centre open at all times dawn-dusk. Loch hides, access restricted to between 8.00am and 4.00pm daily. No dogs except guide dogs please. One hide with wheelchair access. Visitor centre not fully accessible to wheelchairs and disabled visitors.
Facilities: Visitor centre at Starnafin Farm, four hides, toilets (with disabled access), car parking.
Public transport: Access to whole of reserve is difficult without a vehicle. Bus service runs between Fraserburgh and Peterhead, stopping at Crimond just over one mile from visitor centre.
Habitat: Dune loch with surrounding marshes, reedbeds, grasslands, dunes and agricultural land.
Key birds: *Winter*: Whooper Swan, Pink-footed and Barnacle Geese, large numbers of winter duck including Smew. *Spring/summer*: Lowland waders, Sandwich Tern, Water Rail, Corn Bunting, Skylark all breeding. Passage birds, *Spring/autumn*: Curlew Sandpiper, Marsh Harrier, Spotted Redshank.
Contact: RSPB Warden, Starnafin, Crimond,

Fraserburgh, Aberdeenshire, 01346 532017.
e-mail: esro@RSPB.org.uk www.RSPB.org.uk

LONGHAVEN CLIFFS

Scottish Wildlife Trust.
Location: NK 116 394. Two miles S of Peterhead. Take A952 S from Peterhead and then A975 to Bullers of Buchan (gorge).
Contact: Trust HQ.

ST CYRUS

Scottish Natural Heritage.
Location: NO 764 650. Three miles N of Montrose, follow the sign saying 'Beach' from the main coast road.
Access: The whole reserve is accessible from Sept-Mar. From Apr-Aug the south of the reserve is closed for breeding birds. Disabled access limited to visitor centre and boardwalk. Dogs on leads during the breeding season, but can be let off on the beach.
Facilities: Visitor centre and toilets.
Public transport: None to reserve. Buses to the village of St Cyrus. Walk down the cliff path from there.
Habitat: Narrow dune system, calcareous grassland and cliffs.
Key birds: *Summer*: Grasshopper Warbler, Whitethroat, Willow Warbler. Terns feeding and roosting by river mouth. Nesting Peregrine.
Contact: Andrew Turner, Scottish Natural Heritage, Old Lifeboat Station, Nether, Warberton, St Cyrus DD10 0DG. 01674 430736. www.snh.org.uk

Orkney

BIRSAY MOORS

RSPB (East Scotland).
Location: Now part of separate reserve. Separate access to hide at Burgar Hill, signposted from A966 at Evie (HY 346 247). Birsay Moors viewed from B9057 NW of Dounby.
Access: Open access all year round.
Facilities: One hide at Burgar Hill very good for watching Red-throated Divers.
Public transport: Orkney Coaches. Service within 0.5 mile of reserve. Tel: 01856 877500.
Habitat: Diverse example of Orkney moorland - wet and dry heath, bog, mire, scrub and some farmland.

Key birds: *Spring/summer*: Nesting Hen Harrier, Merlin, Great and Arctic Skuas, Short-eared Owl, Golden Plover, Curlew, Red-throated Diver. *Winter*: Hen Harrier roost.
Contact: The Warden, 12/14 North End Road, Stromness, Orkney KW16 3HG. 01856 850176.
e-mail: orkney@RSPB.org.uk
www.RSPB.co.uk

COPINSAY

RSPB (East Scotland).
Location: HY 610 010. Access by private boat or hire boat from mainland Orkney.
Access: Open all year round.
Facilities: House on island open to visitors. No toilets or hides.
Public transport: None.
Habitat: Sea cliffs, farmland.
Key birds: *Summer*: Stunning seabird-cliffs with breeding Kittiwake, Guillemot, Black Guillemot, Puffin, Razorbill, Shag, Fulmar, Rock Dove, Eider, Twite, Raven and Greater Black-backed Gull. Passage migrants esp. during periods of E winds.
Contact: The Warden, 12/14 North End Road, Stromness, Orkney KW16 3AG. 01856 850176.
e-mail: orkney@RSPB.org.uk
www.RSPB.co.uk
S Foubisher (boatman) 01856 741252 - will not sail if wind is in the east.

COTTESCARTH AND RENDALL MOSS

RSPB (East Scotland).
Location: HY 360 200. Orkney reserve off A966, three miles N of Finstown.
Access: Open all year. Hide open all year. Not suitable for dogs.
Facilities: Hide (ideal for watching raptors in the Spring) and car park.
Public transport: Orkney Coaches. Tel: 01856 877500.
Habitat: Heather moorland, areas of rushes and wet grassland.
Key birds: *Summer*: Breeding Hen Harrier, Merlin, Redshank, Oystercatcher, Curlew, Reed Bunting.
Contact: The Warden, 12/14 North End Road, Stromness, Orkney KW16 3AG. 01856 850176.
e-mail: orkney@RSPB.org.uk
www.RSPB.co.uk

HOBBISTER

RSPB (East Scotland).
Location: HY 396 070 or HY 381 068. Near Kirkwall.
Contact: The Warden, 12/14 North End Road, Stromness, Orkney KW16 3AG. 01856 850176.
e-mail: orkney@RSPB.org.uk
www.RSPB.co.uk

HOY

RSPB (East Scotland).
Location: HY 210 025. Located in NW of Hoy, a large island S of mainland Orkney. Car ferry from Houten to Lyness.
Access: Open all year round. Keep dogs on lead. Unsuitable for disabled people – rough terrain.
Facilities: Toilet facilities at Moaness Pier and at Rackwick. Nature trail – circular route from Moaness Pier to Old Man of Hoy via Old Rackwick Post Road. Leaflets available from 2003.
Public transport: Foot passenger ferry service from Stromness to Moaness Pier. Minibus taxis.
Habitat: Coastal heath, moorland, fellfield, woodland and cliffs.
Key birds: *Spring/summer:* Red-throated Diver, Merlin, Peregrine, Golden Plover, Dunlin, Great Skua, Arctic Skua, Short-eared Owl, Guillemot, Razorbill, Puffin, Fulmar, Kittiwake, Stonechat, Wheatear. *Autumn/winter:* Redwing, Fieldfare, Snow Bunting. *Migration species:* Whimbrel, Brambling plus almost anything is possible.
Contact: 1. The Warden, 01856 791298.
2. Ley House, Hoy, Orkney KW16 3NJ.
www.RSPB.org.uk

LOONS (THE)

RSPB (East Scotland).
Location: HY 246 242. Access to hide (only) via minor road from A986, three miles N of Dounby.
Access: Hide open all year.
Contact: The Warden, 12/14 North End Road, Stromness, Orkney KW16 3AG01856 850176.
e-mail: orkney@RSPB.org.uk
www.RSPB.co.uk

MARWICK HEAD

RSPB (East Scotland).
Location: HY 229 242. On W coast of mainland Orkney, near Dounby. Path N from Marwick Bay, or from car park at Cumlaquoy at HY 232 252.

Contact: The Warden, 12/14 North End Road, Stromness, Orkney KW16 3AG. 01856 850176. e-mail: orkney@RSPB.org.uk www.RSPB.co.uk

MILL DAM

RSPB (East Scotland).
Location: HY 483 178. On Shapinsay near Balfour.
Access: Hide open all year.
Facilities: None.
Public transport: Vehicular ferry from Kirkwall to Shapinsay, 1/2 hour walk from ferry. (Orkney Ferries 01856 872044).
Habitat: Wetland. A little gem affording great views from the hide of ducks and waders in spring, autumn and winter.
Key birds: *All year:* Shoveler, Pintail, Gadwall, Ruddy Duck, gulls. *Winter:* Whooper Swans, Wigeon, Teal, Shoveler
Contact: The Warden, 12/14 North End Road, Stromness, Orkney KW16 3AG. 01856 850176. e-mail: orkney@RSPB.org.uk www.RSPB.co.uk S Foubisher (boatman) 01856 741252 - will not sail if wind is in the east.

NORTH HILL, PAPA WESTRAY

RSPB (East Scotland).
Location: HY 496 538. Small island lying NE of Westray, reserve at N end of island's main road.
Access: Access at all times. During breeding season report to summer warden at Rose Cottage, 650 yards S of reserve entrance (Tel 01857 644240.) or use trail guide.
Facilities: Nature trails, hide/info hut.
Public transport: Orkney Ferries (01856 872044), Logemair Ferries (01856 872454).
Habitat: Sea cliffs, maritime heath.
Key birds: *Summer:* Close views of colony of Puffin, Guillemot, Razorbill and Kittiwake. Black Guillemot nest under flagstones around reserve's coastline. One of UK's largest colonies of Arctic Tern, also Arctic Skua.
Contact: Apr-Aug, The Warden at Rose Cottage, Papay Westray DW17 2BU. 01857 644240.,
2. RSPB Orkney Office 12/14 North End Road, Stromness, Orkney KW16 3AG. 01856 850176. e-mail: orkney@RSPB.org.uk www.RSPB.co.uk

NORTH RONALDSAY BIRD OBSERVATORY

Location: HY 64 52. 35 miles from Kirkwall, Orkney mainland.

Access: Open all year except Christmas.
Facilities: Accommodation, display room, meals, snacks etc for non-residents, fully licenced, toilets, croft walk.
Public transport: Twice daily (Mon-Sat) subsidised flights from Kirkwall (Loganair 01856 872494). Sunday flights in Summer. Once weekly ferry from Kirkwall (Fri or Sat), some Sun sailings in summer (Orkney Ferries Ltd 01856 872044).
Habitat: Crofting island with a number of eutrophic and oligotrophic wetlands. Coastline has both sandy bays and rocky shore. Walled gardens concentrate passerines.
Key birds: Prime migration site in *Spring/ Autumn* including regular BBRC species. Wide variety of breeding seabirds, wildfowl and waders. *Winter:* Waders and wildfowl include Whooper Swan and hard weather movements occur.
Contact: Alison Duncan, North Ronaldsay Bird Observatory, Twingness, North Ronaldsay, Orkney KW17 2BE. 01857 633200. e-mail: alison@nrbo.prestel.co.uk www.nrbo.f2s.com

NOUP CLIFFS WESTRAY

RSPB (East Scotland).
Location: HY 392 500. Westray lies NE of Mainland and Rousay. Take minor road to Pierowall and Noup Farm then track NW to lighthouse.
Access: No dogs, even on a lead.
Facilities: None.
Public transport: Flights from Kirkwall daily (Loganair 01856 872494). Daily ferry (Orkney Ferries 01856 872044).
Habitat: 1.5 miles of sandstone cliffs.
Key birds: *Summer:* May-Jul best. Huge seabird colony, breeding Rock Dove, Raven, Shag, auks, Rock Pipit.
Contact: RSPB Orkney Office, 12/14 North End Road, Stromness, Orkney KW16 3EQ. 01856 850176. e-mail: orkney@RSPB.org.uk www.RSPB.co.uk

ONZIEBUST, EGILSAY

RSPB (East Scotland).
Location: HY 472 282. On small island of Egilsay E of Rousay.
Access: Open at all times, use trail guide.
Facilities: Trail guide.
Public transport: Ferry from Tingwall via Rousay and Wyre to Egilsay.

Habitat: Wetland, farmland, sandy/rocky shore.
Key birds: *Summer:* Redshank, Snipe, Lapwing,
Sky Lark, Corncrake, Spotted Crake.
Contact: The Warden. Onziebust, Egilsay,
Orkney KW17 2QD. 01856 821395.

TRUMLAND, ROUSAY

RSPB (East Scotland).
Location: HY 427 276. Ferry from Tingwall in
NE Mainland to Rousay.
Access: Reserve and nature trail (access at all
times) from entrance to Taversoe Tuick Cairn.
Facilities: Nature trail.
Public transport: Orkney Ferries to Rousay from
Tingwall Pier Tel: 01856 751360.
Habitat: Moorland.
Key birds: *Summer:* Breeding Hen Harrier,
Merlin, Short-eared Owl, Red-throated Diver,
Golden Plover, Great and Arctic Skuas, Common
Gull.
Contact: Egilsay Warden. 01856 821395.
e-mail: orkney@RSPB.org.uk
www.RSPB.co.uk

Outer Hebrides

BALRANALD

RSPB (North Scotland Office).
Location: NF 705 707. From Skye take ferry to
Lochmaddy, North Uist. Drive W on A867 for
20 miles to reserve. Turn off main road three
miles NW of Bayhead at signpost to Houghharry.
Access: Open at all times, no charge. Dogs on
leads. Disabled access.
Facilities: Visitor Centre and toilets – disabled
access. Marked nature trail.
Public transport: Bus service (tel 01876
560244).
Habitat: Freshwater loch, machair, coast and
croft lands.
Key birds: *Summer:* Corncrake, Corn Bunting,
Lapwing, Oystercatcher, Dunlin, Ringed Plover,
Redshank, Snipe. *Winter:* Twite, Greylag Goose,
Wigeon, Teal Shoveler. *Passage:* Barnacle
Goose, Pomarine Skua, Long-tailed Skua.
Contact: Jamie Boyle, 9 Grenitote, Isle of North
Uist H56 5BP. 01876 560287.
e-mail: james.boyle3@btinternet.com

LOCH DRUIDIBEG

SNH (North West Region).
Location: NF 782 378. South Uist.
Access: Restricted access during breeding season.
Facilities: None.
Public transport: None.
Habitat: Loch, machair, coast.
Key birds: *Summer:* Breeding Greylag, waders.
Contact: SNH Area Officer, Stilligarry, South
Uist HS8 5RS. 01870 620238; fax 01870
620350.

Perth & Kinross

DOUNE PONDS

Stirling District Council.
Location: NN 726 019. Take the A820 Dunblane
road E from the junction with the A84 Callander-
Stirling road. Turn L onto Moray Street just
before Doune Church.
Access: Open all year.
Facilities: Information board, nature trail, hides.
Obtain keys for the hides from the Spar shop, 36
Main Street, Doune. Wheelchair access to E hide.
No access round the N pond. Leaflet from local
tourist information offices.
Public transport: Bus: from Stirling and
Callander to Doune.
Habitat: Pools, scrape, plantations.
Key birds: *All year:* Grey Heron, Buzzard,
Snipe, Goldcrest, Siskin. Possible Hawfinch.
Spring/summer: Common Sandpiper,
Whitethroat, warblers.
Contact: Stirling District Council Countryside
Ranger Service, Beechwood House, St Ninian's
Road, Stirling FK8 2AD.

LOCH LEVEN

SNH, Loch Leven Laboratory.
Location: NO 150 010. Head S from Perth and
leave M90 at exit 6, S of Kinross.
Access: Public access restricted to three short
stretches of shoreline. Most birdwatchers visiting
the reserve go to the RSPB nature centre at Vane
Farm (qv) overlooking the loch.
Facilities: Extensive ornithological research
programme.
Public transport: Bus from Perth or Edinburgh
to Kinross section of shoreline.

Habitat: Lowland loch with islands.
Key birds: *Winter*: Flocks of geese (over 20,000 Pinkfeet), ducks, Whooper Swan. *Summer*: Greatest concentration of breeding ducks in Britain (10 species) and grebes. *Passage*: Waders (Golden Plover flocks up to 500).
Contact: Paul Brooks, SNH, Loch Leven Laboratory, The Pier, Kinross KY13 8UF. 01577 864439.

LOCH OF LOWES

Scottish Wildlife Trust.
Location: NO 042 435. Sixteen miles N of Perth, two miles NE of Dunkeld – just off A923 (signposted).
Access: Visitor centre open Apr-Sept inclusive (10am-5pm), mid-Jul to mid-Aug (10am-6pm). Observation hide open all year – daylight hours. No dogs allowed. Partial access for wheelchairs.
Facilities: Visitor centre with toilets, observation hide.
Public transport: Railway station – Birnam/Dunkeld – three miles from reserve. Bus from Dunkeld – two miles from reserve.
Habitat: Freshwater loch with fringing woodland.
Key birds: Breeding Ospreys (Apr-end Aug). Nest in view, 200 metres from hide. Wildfowl and woodland birds. Greylag roost (Oct-Mar).
Contact: Mr Uwe Stoneman, (Manager), Scottish Wildlife Trust, Loch of the Lowes Visitor Centre, Dunkeld, Perthshire PH8 0HH. 01350 727337.

VANE FARM

RSPB (East Scotland).
Location: NT 160 993. By Loch Leven. Take exit 5 from M90 onto B9097.
Access: Open daily (10am-5pm) except Christmas Day, Boxing Day, Jan 1 and Jan 2. Cost £3 adults, £2 concessions, 50p children, £6 family. Free to members. No dogs except guide dogs. Disabled access to shop, coffee shop, observation room and toilets.
Facilities: Shop, coffee shop and observation room overlooking Loch Leven and the reserve. There is a 1.25 mile hill trail through woodland and moorland. Wetland trail with three observation hides. Toilets, including disabled.
Public transport: Nearest train station Cowdenbeath (nine miles away). Nearest bus station Kinross at Green Hotel (five miles away).
Habitat: Wet grassland and flooded areas by Loch Leven. Arable farmland. Native woodland

and heath moorland.
Key birds: *Spring/summer*: Breeding and passage waders (including Lapwing, Redshank, Snipe, Curlew). Farmland birds (including Sky Lark and Yellowhammer). *Winter*: Whooper Swan, Bewick's Swan, Pink-footed Goose.
Contact: Ken Shaw, Senior Site Manager, Vane Farm Nature Centre, Kinross, Tayside KY13 9LX. 01577 862355.
e-mail: vanefarm@RSPB.co.uk

Shetland

FAIR ISLE
BIRD OBSERVATORY

Fair Isle Bird Observatory.
Location: HZ 2172.
Access: Open from end Apr-end Oct. Free to roam everywhere except one croft (Lower Leogh).
Facilities: Public toilets at Airstrip and Stackhoull Stores (shop). Accommodation at Fair Isle Bird Observatory (phone/e-mail: for brochure/details). Guests can be involved in observatory work and get to see birds in the hand. Slide shows, guided walks through Ranger Service.
Public transport: Tue, Thurs, Sat – ferry (12 passengers) from Grutness, Shetland. Tel: Jimmy or Florrie Stout 01595 760222. Mon, Wed, Fri, Sat – air (7 seater) from Tingwall, Shetland. Tel: Loganair 01595 840246.
Habitat: Heather moor and lowland pasture/crofting land. Cliffs.
Key birds: Large breeding seabird colonies (auks, Gannet, Arctic Tern, Arctic Skua and Great Skua). Many common and rare migrants Apr/May/early Jun, late Aug-Nov.
Contact: Deryk Shaw (Warden), Hollie Shaw (Administrator), Fair Isle Bird Observatory, Fair Isle, Shetland ZE2 9JU. 01595 760258.
e-mail: fairisle.birdobs@zetnet.co.uk
www.fairislebirdobs.co.uk

FETLAR

RSPB (East Scotland).
Location: HU 603 917. Lies W of Yell. Take car ferry from Gutcher, N Yell. Booking advised. Tel: 01957 722259.
Access: Part of RSPB reserve (Vord Hill) closed

mid-May-end Jul. Entry during this period is only by arrangement with warden.

Facilities: Hide at Mires of Funzie. Displays etc at interpretive centre, Houbie. Toilets at ferry terminal, shop and interpretive centre.

Public transport: None.

Habitat: Serpentine heath, rough hill lane, upland mire.

Key birds: *Summer*: Breeding Red-throated Diver, Eider, Shag, Whimbrel, Golden Plover, Dunlin, skuas, Manx Shearwater, Storm Petrel. Red-necked Phalarope on Loch of Funzie (HU 655 899) viewed from road or RSPB hide overlooking Mires of Funzie.

Contact: RSPB North Isles Officer, Bealance, Fetlar, Shetland ZE2 9DJTel/Fax: 01957 733246. e-mail: malcolm.smith@RSPB.org.uk

ISLE OF NOSS

Scottish Natural Heritage (Shetland Office).

Location: HU 531 410. Four miles by car ferry and road to the E of Lerwick. Take ferry to Bressay and follow signs for Noss. Park at end of road and walk to shore (600 yards) where ferry to island will collect you (if red flag is flying, island is closed due to sea conditions).

Access: Access (Tue, Wed, Fri, Sat, Sun) 10am-5pm, late May-late Aug. Access by zodiac inflatable so unsuitable for disabled. No dogs allowed.

Facilities: Visitor centre, toilets.

Public transport: None.

Habitat: Dune grassland, moorland, blanket bog, sea cliffs.

Key birds: *Spring/summer:* Fulmar, Shag, Gannet, Arctic Tern, Kittiwake, Great Black-backed Gull, Great Skua, Arctic Skua, Guillemot, Razorbill, Puffin, Black Guillemot, Eider.

Contact: Simon Smith, Scottish Natural Heritage, Stewart Building, Alexandra Wharf, Lerwick, Shetland ZE1 0LL. 01595 693345. e-mail: simon.smith@snh.gov.uk

MOUSA

RSPB (Shetland Office).

Location: HU 460240. Small uninhabited island east of Sandwick in South Mainland of Shetland.

Access: By ferry from Leebitton Pier, Sandwick, Shetland – mid-Apr–mid-Sept.

Facilities: The Mousa Broch is the best preserved Iron Age tower in the world (World Heritage Site).

Public transport: Buses run to Sandwick from Lerwick. Details of ferry available from Tom Jamieson (01950 431367) or his web site (www.mousaboattrips.co.uk.).

Habitat: A small uninhabited island with maritime grassland and a small area of shell sand.

Key birds: *Summer*: Storm Petrels can be seen on the special night trips run by Tom Jamieson. Arctic Tern, Arctic and Great Skuas, Black Guillemot and Puffin.

Contact: Tom Jamieson, RSPB Shetland Office, East House, Sumburgh Head Lighthouse, Virkie, Shetland ZE3 9JN. 01950 460800.

SUMBURGH HEAD

RSPB (Shetland Office).

Location: HU 407 079. S tip of mainland Shetland.

Access: Open all year, but seabirds best May-mid Aug.

Facilities: View points.

Public transport: None.

Habitat: Sea cliffs.

Key birds: Breeding Puffin, Guillemot, Razorbill, Kittiwake, Shag, also minke and killer whales. Humpback whale seen occasionally.

Contact: RSPB Shetland Office, East House, Sumburgh Head Lighthouse, Virkie, Shetland ZE3 9JN. 01950 460 800.

East Wales

Key to sites:
1. Bailey Einon LNR
2. Brechfa Pool
3. Bwlchcoediog NR
4. Coed Pengugwm
5. Cwm-Y-Wydden
6. Dolydd Hafren
7. Elan Valley
8. Gilfach
9. Glaslyn, Plynlimon
10. Llangorse Lake
11. Llyn Coed Y Dinas
12. Llyn Mawr
13. Nant Irfon NNR
14. Pwll-Y-Wrach
15. Pwll Penarth
16. Roundton Hill
17. Severn Farm Pond
18. Talybont Reservoir
19. Ty Brith Meadows
20. Vyrnwy (Lake)

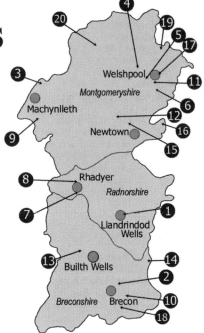

BAILEY EINON

Radnorshire Wildlife Trust.
Location: SO 083 613. From Llandrindod Wells, take the Craig Road leading to Cefnllys Lane. Down this road is Shaky Bridge with a car park and picnic site. A kissing-gate downstream from the picnic site marks the reserve entrance.
Access: Open all year. Please do not park in front of the kissing-gate.
Facilities: Car park, picnic site, waymarked trail.
Public transport: None.
Habitat: Woodland, river.
Key birds: *Spring/summer*: Pied Flycatcher, Redstart, Wood Warbler. *All year*: Great Spotted Woodpecker, Buzzard, usual woodland birds.
Contact: Trust HQ, Warwick House, High Street, Llandrindod Wells, Powys LD1 6AG, 01597 823298.
e-mail: radnorshirewt@cix.co.uk
www.waleswildlife.co.uk

BRECHFA POOL

Brecknock Wildlife Trust.
Location: SO 118 377. Travelling NE from Brecon look for lane off A470, 1.5 miles SW of

Llyswen; on Brechfa Common, pool is on right after cattle grid.
Access: Open dawn to dusk.
Facilities: None.
Public transport: None.
Habitat: Marshy grassland, large shallow pool.
Key birds: Teal, Wigeon, Bewick's Swan, Redshank, Lapwing, Dunlin
Contact: Trust HQ, 01874 625708.

BWLCHCOEDIOG

Location: SH 878 149. From Machynlleth take A489 NE for 14 miles. Half mile east of Mallwyd, turn left into Cwm Cewydd, then 1.25 miles up the valley. Park at Bwlchcoediog House.
Contact: W K and Mrs J Evans, Bwlchcoediog Isaf, Cwm Cewydd, Mallwyd, Machynlleth, Powys SY20 9EE. 01650 531243.

COED PENGUGWM

Montgomeryshire Wildlife Trust.
Location: SJ 103 142. From Welshpool head NW on A490 to Llanfyllin. Then head SW on B4393 and minor roads towards Llanfihangel. Park on the reserve cark park down a short but steep track

opposite Pendugwm Farm.
Access: Open all year.
Facilities: Footpaths.
Public transport: None.
Habitat: Broadleaved woodland, stream.
Key birds: *Spring/summer*: Pied Flycatcher,
Redstart. *All year*: Buzzard, Sparrowhawk,
woodpeckers, usual woodland species. Good for
mammals.
Contact: Trust HQ, Collot House, 20 Severn
Street, Welshpool, Powys SY21 7AD, 01938
555654. e-mail: montwt@cix.co.uk
www.wildlifetrust.org.uk/montgomeryshire

CWM-Y-WYDDEN

Montgomeryshire Wildlife Trust.
Location: SJ 136 025. The reserve is SW of
Welshpool, lying about four miles W of Berriew
and two miles E of Manafon, S of the B4390.
Park by the crossroads at the lane to Dinnant.
Walk down the lane and cross the river. Turn L
in front of the farmhouse and follow the footpath
to the stile into the wood.
Access: Open all year.
Facilities: None.
Public transport: None.
Habitat: Sessile oak woodland.
Key birds: *Spring/summer*: Redstart, usual
woodland species.
Contact: Trust HQ, Collot House, 20 Severn
Street, Welshpool, Powys SY21 7AD, 01938
555654. e-mail: montwt@cix.co.uk
www.wildlifetrust.org.uk/montgomeryshire

DOLYDD HAFREN

Location: SJ 208 005. W of B4388. Go through
Forden village and on about 1.5 miles. Turn right
at sharp left bend at Gaer Farm and down farm
track to car park at the other end.
Contact: Al Parrot, c/o Montgomeryshire
Wildlife Trust, Collot House, 20 Severn Street,
Welshpool, Powys SY21 7AD. 01938 555654.
e-mail: montwt@cixcompulink.co.uk
www.wildlifetrust.org.uk/montwt

ELAN VALLEY

Dwr Cymm/Welsh Water & Elan Valley Trust.
Location: SN 928 646 (visitor centre). Three
miles SW of Rhayader, off B4518.
Access: Mostly open access.
Facilities: Visitor centre and toilets (open mid

Mar-end Oct), nature trails all year and hide at
SN 905 617.
Public transport: Post bus from Rhayader and
Llandrindod Wells.
Habitat: Seventy square miles of moorland,
woodland, river and reservoir.
Key birds: *Spring/summer*: Birds of prey, upland
birds including Golden Plover and Dunlin.
Woodland birds include Redstart and Pied
Flycatcher.
Contact: Pete Jennings, Rangers Office, Elan
Valley Visitor Centre, Rhayader, Powys LD6
5HP. 01597 810880. www.elanvalley.org.uk
e-mail: pete@elanvalley.org.uk

GILFACH

Radnorshire Wildlife Trust.
Location: SN 952 714. Two miles NW from
Rhayader/Rhaeadr-Gwy. Take minor road to St
Harmon from A470 at Marteg Bridge.
Access: Visitor centre Easter-Sept 31 (10am-
5pm). Apr (every day). May/Jun (Fri-Mon). Jul/
Aug (every day). Sept (Fri-Mon). Reserve open
every day all year. Dogs on leads only. Disabled
access and trail.
Facilities: Visitor centre – open as above. Way-
marked trails.
Public transport: None.
Habitat: Upland hill farm, river, oak woods,
meadows, hill-land.
Key birds: *Spring/summer*: Pied Flycatcher,
Redstart. *All year*: Dipper, Red Kite.
Contact: Tim Thompson, Gilfach, St Harmon,
Rhaeadr-Gwy, Powys CD6 5LF. 01597 870 301.
e-mail: tim@ratgilfoelfisnet.co.uk
http//westwales.co.uk/gilfach.htm

GLASLYN, PLYNLIMON

Montgomeryshire Wildlife Trust.
Location: SN 826 941. Nine miles SE of
Machynlleth. Off minor road between the B4518
near Staylittle and the A489 at Machynlleth. Go
down the track for about a mile.
Access: Open at all times – dogs on a lead at all
times.
Facilities: Footpath.
Public transport: None.
Habitat: Heather moorland and upland lake.
Key birds: Red Grouse, Short-eared Owl,
Meadow Pipit, Sky Lark, Wheatear and Ring
Ouzel, Red Kite, Merlin, Peregrine. Goldeneye –
occasional. *Winter*: Greenland White-fronted
Goose.

Contact: Montgomeryshire Wildlife Trust, Collot House, 20 Severn Street, Welshpool, Powys SY21 7AD. 01938 555654.
e-mail: montwt@cix.compulink.co.uk
www.wildlifetrust.org.uk/montwt

LLANGORSE LAKE

Brecknock Wildlife Trust
Location: Lies SE of Brecon, off A40. At Bwlch, turn N onto B4560 and take minor road from Cathedine to S shore. Access to the N shore is at Llangorse village.
Access: Open all year. A footpath from the parking area near Llangorse only goes along the W and S shore to Llangasty-Talyllyn.
Facilities: None.
Public transport: Train from Cardiff to Merthyr Tydfil then bus to Brecon. Only one post bus per day to Llangorse.
Habitat: The second largest natural lake in Wales.
Key birds: *Winter*: Wildfowl, Cormorant, Snipe, Jack Snipe, occasional Bittern. *Passage*: Oystercatcher, Ringed Plover, Dunlin, Black-tailed Godwit, Whimbrel, Greenshank, Green Sandpiper, Little Gull, terns.
Contact: Trust HQ, Lion House, Bethel Square, Brecon, Powys LD3 7AY, 01874 625708.
e-mail: brecknockwt@cix.co.uk
www.wildlifetrust.org.uk/brecknock

LLYN COED Y DINAS

Location: SJ 223 052. On A490, one mile S of Welshpool, just before roundabout at Welshpool by-pass (A483).
Contact: Glyn Roberts, Montgomeryshire Wildlife Trust,Collot House, 20 Severn Street, Welshpool, Powys SY21 7AD. 01938 555654.
e-mail: montwt@cix.compulink.co.uk
www.wildlifetrust.org.uk/montwt

LLYN MAWR

Montgomeryshire Wildlife Trust.
Location: SO 009 971. From Newtown, head NW on A470 and then take minor 'no through' road N of Clatter. Stay close to shore.
Access: Permit required.
Facilities: None.
Public transport: None.
Habitat: Upland lake, wetland, scrub.
Key birds: *Summer*: Breeding Great Crested Grebe, Black-headed Gull, Snipe, Curlew,

Whinchat. *Winter*: occasional Goldeneye, Goosander, Whooper Swan.
Contact: Trust HQ, 01938 555654.

NANT IRFON

Countryside Council for Wales.
Location: SN 840 550. Thirteen miles W of Builth Wells. Leave the A483 in Llanwrtyd Wells by the unclassified road signed to Abergwesyn.
Access: Open all year. Forest Enterprise picnic sites are all around.
Facilities: Car park.
Public transport: None.
Habitat: Valley, woodland, uplands.
Key birds: *Spring/summer*: Golden Plover, Dunlin, Common Sandpiper, Ring Ouzel, Redstart, Whinchat, Snipe, Cuckoo, Pied Flycatcher. *Winter*: Red Kite visiting the nearby feeding station. *All year*: Buzzard, Goshawk, grouse, Peregrine, Raven, Siskin, Redpoll.
Contact: CCW, Eden House, Ithon Road, Llandrindod Wells, Powys LD1 6AS, 01597 827400. e-mail: llandrindo@ccw.gov.uk
www.ccw.gov.uk

PWLL-Y-WRACH

Brecknock Wildlife Trust.
Location: SO 165 327. Between Hay-on-Wye and Brecon at foot of Black Mountains. Half mile SE of Talgarth, access is from the minor road.
Access: Limited car parking. In Talgarth use Pentent Road, go over river and follow lane 250 yards, past hospital.
Facilities: Keep to public footpaths (inc. one for disabled).
Public transport: None.
Habitat: Steep valley woodland, stream and waterfall.
Key birds: Dipper, Grey Wagtail, woodland species (inc. Pied Flycatcher, Wood Warbler). Dormouse colony.
Contact: Trust HQ, 01874 625708.

PWLL PENARTH

Montgomeryshire Wildlife Trust.
Location: SO 137 926. Take B4568 from Newtown to Llanllwchaiarn, turn down by the church and follow lane for a mile to sewage works gates.
Access: Open at all times. Disabled access via Severn Trent sewage works between 9am-4pm, Mon-Fri only. Dogs to be kept on lead at all times.

Facilities: Two hides.
Public transport: None.
Habitat: Lake, Sand Martin bank, arable crops.
Key birds: *Late spring/summer*: Sand Martin, Lapwing, Sky Lark, Grey Wagtail. *Winter*: buntings, finches. *All year*: Kingfisher, Mallard, Coot, Canada Goose, Ruddy Duck.
Contact: Mike Green, Montgomeryshire Wildlife Trust, Collot House, 20 Severn Street, Welshpool, Powys SY21 7AD. 01938 555654.
e-mail: montwt@cix.compulink.co.uk
www.wildlifetrust.org.uk/montwt

ROUNDTON HILL

Montgomeryshire Wildlife Trust.
Location: SO 293 947. SE of Montgomery. From Churchstoke on A489, take minor road to Old Churchstoke, R at phone box, then first R.
Access: Open access. Tracks rough in places.
Facilities: Car park. Waymarked trails.
Public transport: None.
Habitat: Ancient hill grassland, woodland, streamside wet flushes, scree, rock outcrops.
Key birds: Buzzard, Raven, Wheatear, all three woodpeckers, Tawny Owl, Redstart, Linnet, Goldfinch.
Contact: Trust HQ, 01938 555654.

SEVERN FARM POND

Montgomeryshire Wildlife Trust.
Location: SJ 228 068. From the centre of Welshpool take the B4381 (Leighton road) over the railway. Reserve is signposted from there. Reserve is between the railway and the factories on the Severn Farm Industrial Estate.
Access: Open all year. This is the Trust's first urban educational reserve.
Facilities: Footpath suitable for wheelchair, hide, dipping pond, picnic tables.
Public transport: None.
Habitat: Meadow, pond.
Key birds: *Spring/summer*: Swallow, House Martin. *All year*: Reed Bunting, Mute Swan, Moorhen, Coot, Ruddy Duck.
Contact: Trust HQ, Collot House, 20 Severn Street, Welshpool, Powys SY21 7AD, 01938 555654. e-mail: montwt@cix.co.uk
www.wildlifetrust.org.uk/montgomeryshire

TALYBONT RESERVOIR

Brecknock Wildlife Trust.
Location: SO 100 190. Take minor road off B4558 S of Talybont, SE of Brecon.

Access: No access to reservoir area, view from road.
Facilities: Displays at the Glyn Collwm information centre at Aber, between the reservoir and Talybont.
Public transport: None.
Habitat: Reservoir, woodland.
Key birds: *Winter*: Wildfowl (inc. Goldeneye, Goosander, Whooper Swan), Redpoll, Siskin. Migrant waders.
Contact: Trust HQ, 01874 625708.

TY BRITH MEADOWS

Montgomeryshire Wildlife Trust.
Location: SJ 244 178. From Oswestry, head S on A483 and A495. The reserve is about two miles W of Four Crosses, adjacent to a minor road that runs W off the B4393. Reserve is accessed through the signed field gate off a metalled road.
Access: Open all year.
Facilities: Public footpath.
Public transport: None.
Habitat: Meadows, stream.
Key birds: *Spring/summer*: Lapwing. Excellent for flora. Best in early summer.
Contact: Trust HQ, Collot House, 20 Severn Street, Welshpool, Powys SY21 7AD, 01938 555654. e-mail: montwt@cix.co.uk
www.wildlifetrust.org.uk/montgomeryshire

VYRNWY (LAKE)

RSPB (North Wales Office).
Location: SJ 020 193. Located WSW of Oswestry. Nearest village is Llanfyllin on A490. Take B4393 to lake.
Access: Reserve open all year. Visitor centre open Apr-Dec (10.30am-4.30pm), Dec-Apr weekends only (10.30am-4.30pm).
Facilities: Toilets, visitor centre, hides, nature trails, coffee shop, RSPB shop, craft workshops.
Public transport: Train and bus Welshpool (25 miles away).
Habitat: Heather moorland, woodland, meadows, rocky streams and large reservoir.
Key birds: Dipper, Kingfisher, Pied Flycatcher, Wood Warbler, Redstart, Peregrine and Buzzard.
Contact: Jo Morris, Centre Manager, RSPB Lake Vyrnwy Reserve, Bryn Awel, Llanwddyn, Oswestry, Salop SY10 0LZ. 01691 870278. e-mail: lake.vyrnwy@rspb.org.uk

North Wales

Key to sites:
1. Bardsey Bird Obs
2. Cadair Idris
3. Ceiriog Forest
4. Cemlyn
5. Coedydd Aber
6. Coedydd Maentwrog
7. Connahs Quay
8. Conwy
9. Cwm Idwal
10. Gors Maen Llwyd
11. Loggerheads CP
12. Llyn Alaw
13. Llyn Cefni
14. Marford LNR
15. Mawddach Valley
16. Morfa Harlech NNR
17. Newborough Warren
18. Pehnros Coastal Park
19. Point Of Air
20. South Stack Cliffs
21. Spinnies
22. Traeth Lafan
23. Valley Lakes

BARDSEY BIRD OBSERVATORY

Bardsey Bird Observatory.
Location: SH 11 21. Private 444 acre island.
One hour boat journey from Pwllheli (18 miles
SW of Bangor).
Access: Mar-Nov. No dogs. Visitor
accommodation in 150-year-old farmhouse –
contact Alicia Normand (01626 773908,
e-mail: bob&lis@solfach.freeserve.co.uk). Day
visitors by Bardsey Island Trust (tel Simon Glyn
01758 730326).
Facilities: Public toilets available for day visitors.
Three hides, one on small bay, two seawatching.
Public transport: Trains from Birmingham to
Pwllheli. Tel: 0345 484950. Arriva bus from
Bangor to Pwllheli. Tel: 0870 6082608.
Habitat: Sea-birds cliffs viewable from boat
only. Farm and scrubland, Spruce plantation,
willow copses and gorse-covered hillside.
Key birds: *All Year*: Chough, Peregrine. *Spring/
summer*: Manx Shearwaters 7,500 pairs, other
seabirds. Migrant warblers, chats, Redstart,
thrushes. *Autumn*: Many rarities.
Contact: Steven Stansfield, Cristen, Ynys Enlli
(Bardsey), off Aberaron, via Pwllheil, Gwynedd
LL53 8DE07855 264151. www.bbfo.org.uk
e-mail: steve@bbfo.freeserve.co.uk

CADAIR IDRIS

Location: SH 728 116. Three miles SW of
Dolgellau. Take A487 SE to junction with
B4405.
Contact: CCW North West Area, Tel/fax 01766
780868; mobile 07771 925885.

CERIOG FOREST

Forest Enterprise.
Location: SJ 166 384. Lies S of Llangollen. Take
minor road S to Glyn Ceiriog and Nantyr. Turn R
at a white cottage called Bryn Awel, through a
gate marked Glyndyfrdwy into the forest.
Access: Open all year. Park at the Forest
Enterprise picnic site. Long walk on metalled
track.
Facilities: None.
Public transport: None.
Habitat: Heather moor, woodland.
Key birds: *Spring/summer*: Redstart, Pied
Flycatcher, Wood Warbler, Whinchat, Tree Pipit,

Ring Ouzel, Wheatear. *All year*: Black Grouse, Dipper, Grey wagtail, Red Grouse, Raven, Chaffinch, Redpoll, Siskin, Crossbill, all three woodpeckers, Sparrowhawk, Buzzard.
Contact: Forest Enterprise Wales, Victoria Terrace, Aberystwyth, Ceredigion SY23 2DQ, 01970 612367.

CEMLYN

Location: SH 337 932. Ten miles from Holyhead, Anglesey, minor roads from A5025 at Tregele.
Contact: Chris Wynne, North Wales Wildlife Trust, 376 High Street, Bangor, Gwynedd LL57 1YE. 01248 351541. e-mail: nwwt@cix.co.uk www.wildlifetrust.org.uk/northwales

COEDYDD ABER

CCW (North West Area).
Location: SH 660 710. E of Bangor.
Access: From car park at Bont Newydd, SE of Aber Falls. Permit required for places away from designated routes.
Facilities: Small visitor centre. Leaflets.
Public transport: None.
Habitat: Upland valley, deciduous woodland, river and spectacular waterfall.
Key birds: *All year*: Dipper, Grey Wagtail, Buzzard, Raven, woodland birds. *Summer*: Warblers and Ring Ouzel.
Contact: Duncan Brown, Tel/fax 01286 650547; mobile 0421 869263.

COEDYDD MAENTWROG

Location: SH 667 416. Smallest of three woodland blocks high above Vale of Festiniog.
Contact: Doug Oliver, Tel/fax 01766 530461; mobile 07771 925888.

CONNAHS QUAY

Location: SJ 275 715. NW of Chester. Take B5129 from Queensferry for two miles towards Flint.
Contact: R A Roberts, 38 Kelsterton Road, Connahs Quay, Flints CH5 4BJ.

CONWY

RSPB (North Wales Office).
Location: SH 799 771. On E bank of Conwy Estuary. Access from A55 at exit signed to Conwy and Deganwy.
Access: Open daily (10am-5pm) or dusk if earlier. Closed for Christmas Day.
Facilities: Visitor centre, toilets including disabled. Two hides, all accessible to wheelchairs. Trails firm and level, though a little rough in places. Two further hides accessible to pedestrians.
Public transport: Train service to Llandudno Junction. Bus service to Tesco supermarket, Llandudno Junction. Tel: 08706 082 608.
Habitat: Open water, islands, reedbeds, grassland, estuary.
Key birds: *Spring/summer*: Breeding Reed and Sedge Warblers, Lapwing, Redshank, Sky Lark, Reed Bunting and rarities. *Autumn*: Passage waders and rarities. *Winter*: Kingfisher, Goldeneye, Red-breasted Merganser, wildfowl.
Contact: Ian Higginson, Conwy RSPB Nature Reserve, Llandudno Junction, Conwy, North Wales LL33 9XZ. 01492 584091.

CWM IDWAL

Location: SH 648 603. Head for the Snowdonia National Park car park on A5 between Bethesda and Capel Curig.
Contact: Hywel Roberts, Tel/fax 01248 362312; mobile 0468 918573.

GORS MAEN LLWYD

North Wales Wildlife Trust.
Location: SH 975 580. Follow A5 to Cerrigydrudion (seven miles S of site), then take B4501 and go past the Llyn Brennig Visitor Centre. Approx two miles beyond centre, turn right (still on B4501). First car park on right approx 300 yards after the cattle grid.
Access: Open all the time. Dogs on leads. Keep to the paths. Rare breeding birds on the heather so keep to paths.
Facilities: In second car park by lake shore there are toilets and short walk to bird hide. Paths are waymarked, but can be very wet and muddy in poor weather.
Public transport: None.
Habitat: Heathland. Heather and grass overlooking large lake.
Key birds: *Summer*: Red and Black Grouse, Hen Harrier, Merlin, Sky Lark, Curlew. *Winter*: Wildfowl on lake.
Contact: Neil Griffiths, Reserves Officer, NWWT, 376 High Street, Bangor, Gwynedd LL57 1YE. 01248 351541. e-mail: nwwt@cix.co.uk www.wildlifetrust.org.uk/northwales

NATURE RESERVES - WALES

LOGGERHEADS COUNTRY PARK

Location: From Mold, take A494 W. Reserve is reached via minor road after Cadole.
Access: Open all year.
Facilities: Large car park, visitor centre, café, leaflet.
Public transport: None.
Habitat: Limestone woodland, river.
Key birds: *Spring/summer*: Pied and Spotted Flycatchers, Redstart, Garden Warbler, Blackcap, Wood Warbler, Chiffchaff. *All year*: All three woodpeckers, Tawny Owl, Sparrowhawk, Nuthatch, Treecreeper, Goldcrest, Redpoll, Hawfinch. Occasional Crossbill.
Contact: Loggerheads Country Park, Loggerheads, Mold, Denbighsire CH5 5LH.

LLYN ALAW

Welsh Water/Hamdden Ltd.
Location: SH 390 865. Large lake five miles from Amlwch in northern part of Anglesey. Signposted from A55/A5/B5112/B5111/B5109.
Access: Open all year. No dogs to hides or sanctuary area but dogs allowed (maximum two per adult) other areas.
Facilities: Toilets (including disabled), two hides, two nature trails, information centre, car parks, network of mapped walks, picnic sites, information boards.
Public transport: Not to within a mile.
Habitat: Large area of standing water, shallow reedy bays, hedges, scrub, woodland, marsh, grassland.
Key birds: *Summer*: Lesser Whitethroat, Sedge and Grasshopper Warblers, Little and Great Crested Grebes, Tawny Owl, Barn Owl, Buzzard. *Winter*: Whooper Swan, Goldeneye, Hen Harrier, Short-eared Owl, Redwing, Fieldfare, Peregrine, Raven. *All year*: Bullfinch, Siskin, Redpoll, Goldfinch, Stonechat. *Passage waders*: Ruff, Spotted Redshank, Curlew Sandpiper, Green Sandpiper.
Contact: Jim Clark, Llyn Alaw, Llantrisant, Holyhead LL65 4TW. 01407 730762.
e-mail: llynalaw@amserve.net

LLYN CEFNI

Location: SH 440 775. A reservoir located two miles NW of Llangefni, in central Anglesey. Follow B5111 or B5109 from the village. coniferous woodland, carr, scrub.
Contact: Jim Clark, Llyn Alaw, Llantrisant,

Holyhead LL65 4TW. 01407 730762.
e-mail: llynalaw@amserve.net

MARFORD LNR

North Wales Wildlife Trust.
Location: SJ 357 560. Eight miles SW of Chester off A483. Turn E onto B5445 to Gresford and Marford. At Marford turn L into Springfield Lane, just past the Trevor Arms Hotel. The reserve entrance is on L just before the railway bridge. Park either side of the bridge.
Access: Open all year.
Facilities: Path.
Public transport: None.
Habitat: Disused sand and gravel pit, cliff face, grassland, scrub, woodland, pool.
Key birds: *Spring/summer*: Spotted Flycatcher, Wood Warbler, good range of migrant birds. *All year*: Woodpeckers inc. Lesser Spotted, Linnet, Yellowhammer, woodland birds.
Contact: Trust HQ, 376 High Street, Bangor, Gwynedd LL57 1YE, 01248 351541.
e-mail: nwwt@cix.co.uk
www.wildlifetrust.org.uk/northwales

MAWDDACH VALLEY

RSPB (North Wales Office).
Location: SH 696 185 (information centre). Two miles W of Dolgellau on A493. Next to toll bridge at Penmaenpool.
Access: Reserve open at all times. Information centre open daily during Easter week and from Whitsun to first weekend of Sept (11am-5pm). Between Easter week and Whitsun, weekends only (noon-4pm).
Facilities: Toilets and car park at information centre.
Public transport: Buses run along A493. Morfa Mawddach railway halt four miles from information centre.
Habitat: Oak woodlands of Coed Garth Gell and willow/alder scrub at Arthog Bog SSSI.
Key birds: *Spring/summer*: Pied Flycatcher, Redstart and Tree Pipit. *Winter*: Raven, roving flocks of Siskin, Redpoll with Goosander and Goldeneye on the estuary.
Contact: The Warden, Mawddach Valley Nature Reserves, Abergwynant Lodge, Penmaenpool, Dolgellau, Gwynedd LL40 1YF. 01341 422071.
e-mail: mawddach@rspb.org.uk
www.rspb.org.uk

NATURE RESERVES - WALES

MORFA HARLECH

Countryside Council for Wales.
Location: SH 574 317. On the A496 Harlech coastal road, S of Porthmadog.
Access: Open all year.
Facilities: Car park.
Public transport: None.
Habitat: Shingle, coast, marsh, dunes.
Key birds: *Spring/summer*: Whitethroat, Spotted Flycatcher, Grasshopper Warbler, other migrants. *Passage*: waders, Manx Shearwater, ducks. *Winter*: Divers, Whooper Swan, Pintail, Scaup, Common Scoter, Hen Harrier, Merlin, Peregrine, Short-eared Owl, Snow Bunting, Twite. *All year*: Red-breasted Merganser, Kestrel, Oystercatcher, Ringed Plover, Curlew, gulls.
Contact: CCW (NW Wales), Maes y Ffynnon, Ffordd, Bangor, Gwynedd LL57 2DN, 0845 1306229. www.ccw.gov.uk
e-mail: enquiries@ccw.gov.uk

NEWBOROUGH WARREN

CCW (North West Area).
Location: SH 406 670/430 630. In SE corner of Anglesey. From Menai Bridge head SW on A4080 to Niwbwrch or Malltraeth.
Access: Permit required for places away from designated routes.
Facilities: None.
Public transport: None.
Habitat: Sandhills, estuaries, saltmarshes, dune grasslands, rocky headlands.
Key birds: Wildfowl and waders at Malltraeth Pool (visible from road), Braint and Cefni estuaries (licensed winter shoot on marked areas of Cefni estuary administered by CCW); waterfowl at Llyn Rhosddu (public hide).
Contact: W Sandison, CCW North West Area, Tel/fax 01248 716422; mobile 0468 918572.

PEHNROS COASTAL PARK

Location: SH 275 805. Signposted from A55, J2. Take A5 to Holyhead and follow signs to Park.
Access: Five mile walk of good, easy-to-follow paths with some inclines but nothing steep. Wheelchair access with good views from the car park.
Facilities: Café, information board and toilets.
Public transport: Bus: contact Arriva 0870 608 2608. Train: Holyhead within walking distance from Morawelon.

Habitat: Woodland, farmland, rocky coast, beaches, mudflats.
Key birds: *Spring*: Winter waders, duck and geese. Wimbrel, Whitethroat and Lesser Whitethroat, Sedge Warbler, Shelduck, Oystercatcher. Treecreeper, Goldcrest, Redpoll, Sparrowhawk and Buzzard.

POINT OF AIR

RSPB (North Wales Office).
Location: SJ 140 840. At mouth of the Dee Estuary. Three miles E of Prestatyn. Access from A548 coast road to Talacre village. Park at end of Station Road.
Access: Open at all times.
Facilities: Car park, public hide overlooking saltmarsh and mudflats, accessible to wheelchairs. No visitor centre. Toilets in Talacre village. Group bookings, guided walks and events.
Public transport: Bus – not known. Rail – Prestatyn.
Habitat: Intertidal mud/sand, saltmarsh, shingle.
Key birds: *Spring/summer*: Breeding Sky Lark, Meadow Pipit, Reed Bunting. *Late summer*: Pre-migratory roost of Sandwich and Common Terns. *Autumn*: Passage waders. *Winter*: Roosting waterfowl (eg Shelduck, Pintail), Oystercatcher, Curlew, Redshank, Merlin, Peregrine, Short-eared Owl. Rarities have occurred.
Contact: Gareth Stamp, Burton Point Farm, Station Road, Burton, Nr Neston, Cheshire CH64 5SB0151 3367681.
e-mail: colin.wells@rspb.org.uk

SOUTH STACK CLIFFS

RSPB (North Wales Office).
Location: SH 205 823. W of Holyhead, Anglesey. Take A5 to Tyn-y-nant.
Access: No restrictions.
Facilities: Car parks. Information centre (Ellin's Tower) with windows overlooking main auk colony open daily (11am-5pm Easter-Sep), with live TV of the seabirds. Public footpaths.
Public transport: None.
Habitat: Sea cliffs, maritime heath.
Key birds: Peregrine, Chough, Fulmar, Puffin, Guillemot, Razorbill, Kittiwake, Shag, migrant warblers. Seabirds on passage.
Contact: Alastair Moralee, Plas Nico, South Stack, Holyhead, Anglesey LL65 1YH. 01407 764973.

SPINNIES

North Wales Wildlife Trust.
Location: SH 613 721. Three miles from Bangor, Gwynedd. Use minor roads from A5122 or A55.
Access: Open all the time. Dogs on leads. Main path suitable for wheelchair users.
Facilities: Two hides, one suitable for wheelchair users.
Public transport: None.
Habitat: Woodland, tidal pool.
Key birds: Waders and passage species, woodland birds, Kingfisher, Little Egret.
Contact: Chris Wynne, Trust HQ, 01248 351541.

TRAETH LAFAN

Gwynedd Council.
Location: NE of Bangor, stretching to Penmaenmawr. 1) Minor road from old A55 near Tal-y-Bont (SH 610 710) to Aber Ogwen car park by coast (SH 614 723). 2) Also access from minor road from Aber village to Morfa Aber LNR (SH 646 731) 3) track to Morfa Madryn LNR (SH 667 743), and 4) Llanfairfechan promenade (SH 679 754).
Access: Open access from 1,2, 3 and 4.
Facilities: Public paths. 2) Car park and hide. 3) Hides. 4) Toilets and cafés.
Habitat: Intertidal sands and mudflats, wetlands, streams. SPA and SSSI.

Key birds: Third most important area in Wales for wintering waders; of national importance for moulting Great Crested Grebe and Red-breasted Merganser; internationally important for Oystercatcher and Curlew; passage waders; winter concentrations of Goldeneye and Greenshank, and of regional significance for wintering populations of Black-throated, Red-throated & Great Northern Divers and Black-necked & Slavonian Grebes.
Contact: Planning and Economic, Development Dept, Gwynedd Council, Council Offices, Caernarfon LL55 1SH. 01286 679381; fax 01286 673324; e-mail ruralservices@gwynedd.gov.uk.

VALLEY LAKES

Location: On W side of Anglesey, two miles S of Caergeilliog. Take minor road from A5.
Access: Open all year.
Facilities: Nature trail.
Public transport: Bus: Meas Awyr/RAF Valley daily from Bangor and Holyhead. Train: Valley (four miles)/Rhosneigr (seven miles).
Habitat: Reed-fringed lakes, small rocky outcrops.
Key birds: *Summer*: Cetti's Warbler. *All year*: Wildfowl, waterfowl.
Contact: RSPB, Maes Y Ffynnon, Penrhosgarnedd, Bangor, Gwynedd, 01248 363800.

South Wales

ABERTHAW SALTMARSH

The Wildlife Trust for South and West Wales.
Location: ST 045 657. E of Aberthaw Power Station, W of Barry.
Access: Open access. Use main road lay-by.
Facilities: None.
Public transport: Call Trust for advice.
Habitat: Lias limestone cliffs, saltmarsh (very mobile), pebble beach.
Key birds: *Spring*: Whimbrel. *Autumn*: Migrant waders and passerines. *Winter*: Peregrine in winter. Good seawatching.
Contact: Trust HQ, 01656 724100.

CLEDDON SHOOTS RESERVE

Gwent Wildlife Trust.
Location: SO 520 040. Lies in Wye Valley, S of Monmouth. From crossroads at S end of Trelleck village (B4293) take Cleddon road E. Fork L after one mile. Reserve car park is straight ahead. Alternatively, in Llandogo village (A466) turn up hill between village shop and garage. The Trust sign can be seen about 0.25 mile where road crosses stream.
Access: Open all year.
Facilities: Pathways and tracks.
Public transport: None.
Habitat: Ancient beech and oak woodland in a steep valley.

Key to sites:
1. Aberthaw Saltmarsh
2. Cleddon Shoots Reserve
3. Cosmeston Lakes CP
4. Croes Robert Reserve
5. Cwm Clydach
6. Cwm Col-Huw
7. Kenfig NNR
8. Lavernock Point
9. Llyn Fach
10. Magor Marsh
11. Magor Pill To Coldharbour Pill
12. Melincwrt Waterfalls
13. Oxwich
14. Parc Slip Nature Park
15. Priory Wood SSSI
16. Peterstone Wentlooge
17. Silent Valley Reserve
18. Strawberry Cottage Wood

South Wales

Key birds: *Spring/summer*: Flycatchers and warblers. *All year*: Woodpeckers, Nuthatch, Sparrowhawk.
Contact: Trust HQ, 16 White Swan Court, Church Street, Monmouth, Gwent NP25 3NY, 01600 715501. e-mail: gwentwildlife@cix.co.uk www.wildlifetrust.org.uk/gwent

COMESTON LAKES

Vale of Glamorgan Council.
Location: ST 179 692. Site lies S of Penarth and Cardiff. From J33 on M4, head S on A4243 and A4231 towards Barry. Head E on B4267 through Sully. The park is on W of Cosmeston, signposted from road.
Access: Open all year. Most of the footpath system suitable for wheelchairs.
Facilities: Visitor Centre open daily (not Dec 25), summer (10am-6pm), winter (10am-4pm). Café, shop and toilets.
Public transport: Bus: regular from Penarth to Barry stops outside the main entrance. Train: main line train to Cardiff, then to Penarth (1.5 miles from the lakes). Public transport information, tel: 08706 082 608.
Habitat: Former limestone quarry workings, ponds, paddock.
Key birds: *Spring/summer*: Buzzard, Tawny Owl, Sedge and Reed Warblers, Lesser Whitethroat, Garden Warbler, Marsh Tit. *Winter*: Little Grebe, Wigeon, Gadwall, Pochard, Water Rail, Kingfisher.
Contact: Cosmeston Lakes Country Park, Sully, Penarth, Glamorgan, 02920 701678.
e-mail: cosmestonlakes@valeofglamorgan.gov.uk

CROES ROBERT RESERVE

Gwent Wildlife Trust.
Location: SO 475 060. Leave Monmouth on the B4293 towards Trellech. Turn R past Trellech School to Cwmcarvan. After 1.25 miles turn R and the reserve and car park will be on the R.
Access: Open all year.
Facilities: None.
Public transport: None.
Habitat: Broadleaved woodland, springs, wet flushes.
Key birds: *Spring/summer*: Nightingale, Grasshopper Warbler, warblers, Woodcock. *All year*: Great Spotted Woodpecker, Bullfinch, Long-tailed Tit.
Contact: Gwent Wildlife Trust, 16 White Swan Court, Church Street, Monmouth, Gwent NP25 3NY, 01600 715501.
e-mail: gwentwildlife@cix.co.uk www.wildlifetrust.org.uk/gwent

CWM CLYDACH

RSPB (South Wales Office).
Location: SN 584 026. Three miles N of J45 on M4, through the village of Clydach on B4291.
Access: Open at all times along public footpaths and waymarked trails.
Facilities: Nature trails, car park, information boards.
Public transport: Buses from Swansea stop at

reserve entrance. Nearest railway station is eight miles away in Swansea.
Habitat: Oak woodland on steep slopes lining the banks of the fast-flowing Lower Clydach River.
Key birds: *Spring/summer*: Nesting Buzzard, Sparrowhawk and Raven. Nestboxes are used by Pied Flycatcher, Redstart and tits while Wood Warbler, all three species of woodpecker, Nuthatch, Treecreeper and Tawny Owl also nest. Dipper and Grey Wagtail frequent the river.
Contact: Martin Humphreys, 2 Tyn y Berllan, Craig Cefn Par, Clydach, Swansea SA6 5TL. 01792 842927.

CWM COL-HUW

Location: SS 957 674. On site of 2700-year-old Iron Age fort, overlooking Bristol Channel. From Bridgeend take B4265 S to Llanwit Major. Follow beach road from village.
Contact: Trust HQ, 01656 724100.

KENFIG NNR

Bridgend County Borough Council.
Location: SS 802 811. Seven miles W of Bridgend. From J37 on M4, drive towards Porthcawl, then North Cornelly, then follow signs.
Access: Open at all times.
Facilities: Toilets, hides, free car parking and nature trail for visually impaired. Visitor centre open weekends and holidays (10am-4.30pm), weekdays (2pm-4.30pm).
Public transport: None.
Habitat: Sand dunes, dune slacks, Kenfig Pool, Sker Beach.
Key birds: *Summer*: Warblers including Cetti's, Grasshopper, Sedge, Reed, Willow and Whitethroat. One of the UK's best sites for orchids. *Winter*: Wildfowl, Water Rail, Bittern, grebes.
Contact: David Carrington, Ton Kenfig, Bridgend CF33 4PT. 01656 743386.
e-mail: carridg@bridgend.gov.uk

LAVERNOCK POINT

The Wildlife Trust for South and West Wales.
Location: ST 182 680. Public footpaths S of B4267 between Barry & Penarth.
Contact: Glamorgan Trust HQ, 01656 724100.

LLYN FACH

Location: SN 905 038. From Merthyr Tydfil take A465 W to Hirwaun, then head S on A4061 to car park 1.8 miles away.
Contact: Trust HQ, 01656 724100.

MAGOR MARSH

Gwent Wildlife Trust.
Location: ST 425 867. Leave M4 at exit 23, turning R onto B4245. S of Magor village, look for gate on Whitewall Common on E side of reserve.
Access: Keep to path. Parties give advance notice.
Facilities: Hide. Information centre.
Public transport: None.
Habitat: Last remnant of fenland on Gwent levels, including marsh, reeds, pond, willow and alders, scrub.
Key birds: Waterfowl (inc. breeding Garganey); reedbed warblers; Water Rail, Kingfisher. *Winter:* Teal and raptors.
Contact: Derek Upton, 14 Westfield, Caldicot, Newport, Gwent NP6 4HE. 01291 420137.

MAGOR PILL TO COLDHARBOUR PILL

Gwent Wildlife Trust.
Location: ST 437 847. Overlooks River Severn, E of Newport.
Access: Access from Magor Pill Farm track down to sea wall.
Facilities: None.
Public transport: None.
Habitat: Foreshore, intertidal mudflats.
Key birds: Passage and winter waders.
Contact: Derek Upton, 14 Westfield, Caldicot, Newport, Gwent NP6 4HE. 01291 420137.

MELINCWRT WATERFALLS

The Wildlife Trust for South and West Wales.
Location: SN 825 017. Signposted from A465(T) road, five miles NE of Neath. Car park is on W side of B4434, S of Resolven. The reserve entrance is on the opposite side of the road via a public footpath.
Access: Open all year.
Facilities: Car park, path.
Habitat: Narrow gorge with oak woodland, 80 foot high waterfall.
Key birds: *Spring/summer*: Pied Flycatcher, Redstart, warblers. *All year*: Dipper, Grey Wagtail, usual woodland birds.
Contact: Trust HQ, Welsh Wildlife Centre, Cilgerran, Cardigan, Ceredigion SA43 2TB. 01239 621212.

NATURE RESERVES - WALES

OXWICH

CCW (Swansea Office).
Location: SS 872 773. 12 miles SW from Swansea, off A4118.
Access: NNR open at all times. No permit required for access to foreshore. Dunes, woodlands and facilities.
Facilities: Private car park, summer only. Toilets summer only. Bird hide, marsh boardwalk and marsh lookout. No visitor centre, no facilities for disabled visitors.
Public transport: Bus service Swansea/Oxwich. First Cymru, tel 01792 580580.
Habitat: Freshwater marsh, saltmarsh, foreshore, dunes, woodlands.
Key birds: *Summer*: Breeding Reed, Sedge and Cetti's Warblers, Treecreeper, Nuthatch, woodpeckers. *Winter*: Wildfowl.
Contact: Countryside Council for Wales, RVB House, Llys Felin Newydd, Phoenix Way, Swansea SA7 9FG. 01792 763500.

PARC SLIP NATURE PARK

The Wildlife Trust for South and West Wales.
Location: SS 880 840. Tondu, half mile W of Aberkenfig. From Bridgend take A4063 N, turning L onto B4281 after passing M4. Reserve is signposted from this road.
Access: Open dawn to dusk.
Facilities: Three hides, nature trail, interpretation centre.
Public transport: None.
Habitat: Restored opencast mining site, wader scrape, lagoons.
Key birds: *Summer*: Breeding Tufted Duck, Lapwing, Sky Lark. Migrant waders (inc. Little Ringed Plover, Green Sandpiper), Little Gull. Kingfisher, Green Woodpecker. Badgers on site.
Contact: Trust HQ, 01656 724100.

PRIORY WOOD SSSI

Gwent Wildlife Trust.
Location: SO 352 058. N of the Usk near Chain Bridge.
Access: Open all year. Very limited parking.
Facilities: None.
Public transport: None.
Habitat: Varied broadleaved woodland with cherry trees.
Key birds: *Spring/summer*: Pied Flycatcher, warblers. *All year*: Great Spotted Woodpecker, usual woodland species. *Winter*: Hawfinch.

Contact: Gwent Wildlife Trust, 16 White Swan Court, Church Street, Monmouth, Gwent NP25 3NY, 01600 715501.
e-mail: gwentwildlife@cix.co.uk
www.wildlifetrust.org.uk/gwent

PETERSTONE WENTLOOGE

Gwent Wildlife Trust.
Location: ST 269 800. Reserve over looks River Severn, between Newport and Cardiff.
Access: Public footpaths to sea wall, use B4239.
Facilities: None.
Public transport: None.
Habitat: Foreshore, inter-tidal mudflats, grazing.
Key birds: Passage waders and winter wildfowl.
Contact: Trust HQ, 01600 715501.

SILENT VALLEY RESERVE

Gwent Wildlife Trust.
Location: SO 187 062. Head for Cwm 2.5 miles S of Ebbw Vale, on A4046. Enter one-way system N side and take the second R by a corner shop. Park in the car park about 0.3 miles by Cwm Cemetery. Walk N across a flat grass playing area and along a path to the reserve entrance.
Access: Open all year.
Facilities: None.
Public transport: None.
Habitat: One of the most westerly and highest natural beech woods in Britain.
Key birds: *Spring/summer*: Pied Flycatcher, Redstart. *Winter*: Siskin, Redpoll, tits. *All year*: Usual woodland species, Great Spotted Woodpecker.
Contact: Trust HQ, 01600 715501.

STRAWBERRY COTTAGE WOOD

Gwent Wildlife Trust.
Location: SO 315 214. N of Abergavenny. Leave A465 at Llanvihangel Crucorney on minor road to Llanthony, about 1.25 miles.
Access: Open at all times. Keep to waymarked trail.
Facilities: None.
Habitat: Mixed woodland on valley side.
Key birds: Buzzard, Redstart, Pied Flycatcher, Wood Warbler.
Contact: Jerry Lewis, Y Bwthyn Gwyn, Coldbrook, Abergavenny, Monmouthshire NP7 9TD. 01873 855091.

West Wales

Key to sites:
1. Castle Woods
2. Cors Caron
3. Dinas & Gwenffrwd
4. Dyfi
5. Llanelli
6. Llyn Eiddwen LNR
7. Pengelli Forest
8. Ramsey Island
9. Skokholm Island
10. Skomer Island
11. Welsh Wildlife Centre
12. Westfield Pills LNR
13. Ynys-Hir

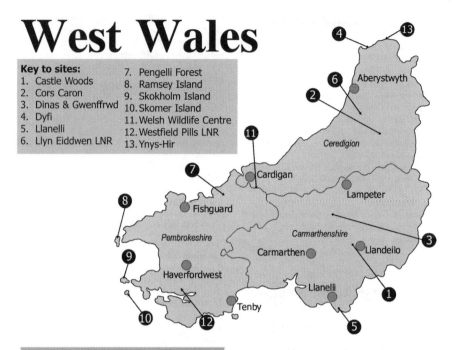

CASTLE WOODS

The Wildlife Trust for South and West Wales.
Location: SN 615 217. About 60 acres of wodland overlooking River Tywi, W of Llandeilo town centre.
Contact: Steve Lucas, Area Officer, 35 Maesquarre Road, Betws, Ammanford, Carmarthenshire SA18 2LF. 01269 594293.

CORS CARON

CCW (West Wales Area).
Location: SN 697 632 (car park). Reached from B4343 N of Tregaron.
Access: Old railway walk open all year. Access to rest of the reserve by permit. Dogs on lead.
Facilities: Observation tower on railway walk.
Public transport: None.
Habitat: Raised bog, river, fen, wet grassland, willow woodland, reedbed.
Key birds: *Summer:* Lapwing, Redshank, Curlew, Red Kite, Grasshopper Warbler, Whinchat. *Winter:* Teal, Wigeon, Whooper Swan, Hen Harrier, Red Kite.
Contact: Paul Culyer, CCW, Neuaddlas, Tregaron, Ceredigion, 01974 298480.
e-mail: p.culyer@ccw.gov.uk www.ccw.gov.uk

DINAS & GWENFFRWD

RSPB (South Wales Office).
Location: SN 788 472. Dinas car park off B road to Llyn Brianne Reservoir. Gwenffrwd (SN 749 460) off minor road to Rhandirmwyn from Llandovery or Pumpsaint, approx ten miles N of Llandovery.
Access: Public nature trail at Dinas open at all times. Access to Gwenfrwd trails for RSPB members only (Good Fri to Aug). Obtain details at Dinas car park. Some steep and rugged paths requiring particular care when wet.
Facilities: Office at Dinas.
Public transport: Nearest station at Llandovery.
Habitat: Hillside oakwoods, streams, bracken slopes and moorland.
Key birds: Buzzard, Pied Flycatcher, Redstart, Wood Warbler, Tree Pipit, Red Kite and Peregrine in area. Dipper, Goosander, Raven.
Contact: c/o RSPB (South Wales Office), Sutherland House, Castlebridge, Cowbridge Road East, Cardiff CF11 9AB. 02920 353000.

NATURE RESERVES - WALES

DYFI

CCW (West Wales Area).
Location: SN 610 942. Large estuary area W of Machyalleth. Public footpaths off A493 E of Aberdyfi, and off B4353 (S of river); minor road from B4353 at Ynyslas to dunes and parking area.
Access: Ynyslas dunes and the estuary have unrestricted access. No access to Cors Fochno (raised bog) for casual birdwatching; permit required for study and research purposes. Good views over the bog and Aberleri marshes from W bank of Afon Leri.
Facilities: Public hide overlooking marshes beside footpath at SN 611 911.
Public transport: None.
Habitat: Sandflats, mudflats, saltmarsh, creeks, dunes, raised bog, grazing marsh.
Key birds: *Winter:* Greenland White-fronted Goose, wildfowl, waders and raptors. *Summer:* Breeding wildfowl and waders (inc. Teal, Shoveler, Merganser, Lapwing, Curlew, Redshank).
Contact: Mike Bailey, CCW Warden, Plas Gogerddan, Aberystwyth, Ceredigion SY23 3EE. 01970 821100.

LLANELLI

The Wildfowl & Wetlands Trust.
Location: SS 533 984. Leave M4 at junction 47. Signposted from A484, E of Llanelli.
Access: Open daily (9.30am-5.30am summer, earlier in winter) except Chirstmas Eve and Christmas Day.
Facilities: Visitor centre, restaurant, hides, education facilities, disabled access. Overlooks Burry Inlet.
Public transport: None.
Habitat: Inter-tidal mudflats, reedbeds, pools, marsh, waterfowl collection.
Key birds: Large flocks of Curlew, Oystercatcher, Redshank on saltmarsh. *Winter:* Pintail, Wigeon, Teal. Also Little Egret, Short-eared Owl, Peregrine
Contact: Dr Geoff Proffitt, Centre Manager, The Wildfowl & Wetlands Trust, Penclacwydd, Llwynhendy, Llanelli SA14 9SH. 01554 741087.

LLYN EIDDWEN LNR

The Wildlife Trust for South and West Wales.
Location: SN 607 674. Lies 15 miles S of Aberystwyth. From Aberystwyth, take A487 and then A485 S towards Tregaron. Turn R onto B4576 at Abermad and follow road to Llangwyryfon. Turn L and head S on a narrow unclassified road through Trefenter and over the Hafod Ithel. There are several parking places.
Access: Open all year.
Facilities: None.
Public transport: None.
Habitat: Lake, grassland, small bog.
Key birds: *Winter:* Whooper Swan, wildfowl.
Contact: Trust HQ, Nature Centre, Fountain Road, Tondu, Mid Glamorgan CF32 0EH, 01656 724100. e-mail: glamorganwt@cix.co.uk www.wildlifetrust.org.uk/wtsww

PENGELLI FOREST

The Wildlife Trust for South and West Wales.
Location: SN 123 396. Between Fishguard and Cardigan. Take minor road off A487 from Felindre Farchog/Eglwyswrw.
Contact: Trust HQ, 01656 724100.

RAMSEY ISLAND

RSPB (South Wales Office).
Location: SM 706237. One mile offshore St Justinians, slipway, two miles W of St Davids.
Access: Open every day, except Fri, Apr 1-Oct 31.
Facilities: Toilets, small RSPB shop, tuck shop, hot drinks and snacks, self-guiding trail.
Public transport: Trains to Haverfordwest Station. Hourly buses to St Davids, taxi to St Justinians.
Habitat: Acid grassland, maritime heath, seacliffs.
Key birds: *Spring/summer:* Cliff-nesting auks (Guillemot, Razorbill). Kittiwake, Lesser, Great Black-backed, Herring Gulls, Shag, Peregrine, Raven, Chough, Lapwing, Wheatear, Stonechat.
Contact: Ian Bullock, Tegfan, Caerbwdi, St Davids, Pembs SA62 6QP. 07836 535733. www.rspb.org.uk

SKOKHOLM ISLAND

The Wildlife Trust for South and West Wales.
Location: SM 738 037. Island lying S of Skomer.
Access: Day visits, Mon only Jun-Aug from Martinshaven. Weekly accomm. Apr-Sep, tel 01437 765462 for details and booking.
Facilities: Call for details.
Public transport: None.

Habitat: Cliffs, bays and inlets.
Key birds: *Summer*: Large colonies of Razorbill, Puffin, Guillemot, Manx Shearwater, Storm Petrel, Lesser Black-backed Gull. Migrants inc. rare species.
Contact: Trust HQ, 01656 724100.

SKOMER ISLAND

The Wildlife Trust for South and West Wales.
Location: SM 725 095. Fifteen miles from Haverfordwest. Take B4327 turn-off for Marloes, embarkation point at Martin's Haven, two miles past village.
Access: Apr 1-Oct 31. Boats sail at 10am, 11am and noon every day except Mon (Bank Holidays excluded). Closed four days beginning of Jun for seabird counts. Not suitable for infirm (steep landing steps and rough ground).
Facilities: Information centre, toilets, two hides, wardens, booklets, guides, nature trails.
Public transport: None.
Habitat: Maritime cliff, bracken, bluebells and red campion, heathland, freshwater ponds.
Key birds: Largest colony of Manx Shearwater in the world (overnight). Puffin, Guillemot, Razorbill (Apr-end Jul). Kittiwake (until end Aug), Fulmar (absent Oct), Short-eared Owl (during day Jun and Jul), Chough, Peregrine, Buzzard (all year), migrants.
Contact: Juan Brown, Skomer Island, Marloes, Pembs SA63 2BJ. 07971 114302.
e-mail: skomer@wtww.co.uk

WELSH WILDLIFE CENTRE

The Wildlife Trust for South and West Wales.
Location: SN 188 451. Two miles SE of Cardigan. River Teifi is N boundary. Sign posted from Cardigan to Fishguard Road.
Access: Open 10am-5pm all year. Free parking for WTWW members, £5 non-members. Dogs welcome – on a lead. Disabled access to visitor centre, paths, four hides.
Facilities: Visitor centre, restaurant, network of paths and seven hides.
Public transport: Train station, Haverfordwest (23 miles). Bus station in Cardigan. Access on foot from Cardigan centre, ten mins.
Habitat: Wetlands, marsh, swamp, reedbed, open water, creek (tidal), river, saltmarsh, woodland.
Key birds: Cetti's Warbler, Kingfisher, Water Rail, Greater Spotted Woodpecker, Dipper, gulls, Marsh Harrier, Sand Martin, Hobby, Redstart, occasional Bittern.

Contact: Chris Lawrence, Welsh Wildlife Centre, Cillgerran, Ceredigion SA43 2TB. 01239 621212. e-mail: chris@wtww.co.uk
www.wildlife@wtww.co.uk

WESTFIELD PILLS LNR

The Wildlife Trust of South and West Wales.
Location: SM 958 073. N of Pembroke Dock. Take A477 N. turn N at first roundabout after toll bridge, towards Rosemarket. Reserve is to R at first crossroads.
Access: Open all year.
Facilities: Car park.
Public transport: None.
Habitat: Pool, disused railway embankment, scrub, woodland margins.
Key birds: *Spring/summer*: Hirundines, Whitethroat, Blackcap, Spotted Flycatcher. *Passage*: Waders. *Winter*: Merlin, Peregrine, Water Rail, Woodcock, Fieldfare, Redwing, Firecrest possible, Siskin, Redpoll. *All year*: Sparrowhawk, Kingfisher, Tawny Owl, Grey Wagtail, Dunnock, Raven, Bullfinch.
Contact: Trust HQ, Nature Centre, Fountain Road, Tondu, Mid Glamorgan CF32 0EH, 01656 724100. e-mail: glamorganwt@cix.co.uk
www.wildlifetrust.org.uk/wtsww

YNYS-HIR

RSPB (CYMRU).
Location: SN 68 29 63. Off A487 Aberystwyth - Machynlleth road in Eglwys-faxh village. Six miles SW of Machynlleth.
Access: Open every day (9am-9pm or dusk if earlier). Visitor centre open daily Apr-Oct (10am-5pm), weekends only Nov-Mar (10am-4pm).
Facilities: Visitor centre and toilets, both with disabled access. Numerous trails and seven hides.
Public transport: Bus service to Eglwys-fach from either Machynlleth or Aberystwyth, tel. 01970 617951. Rail service to Machynlleth.
Habitat: Estuary, freshwater pools, woodland and wet grassland.
Key birds: *Winter*: Greenland White-fronted Goose, Wigeon, Hen Harrier, Barnacle Goose. *Spring/summer*: Wood Warbler, Redstart, Pied Flycatcher. *All year*: Peregrine, Red Kite, Buzzard, Goshawk.
Contact: Dick Squires, Ynys-Hir RSPB Nature Reserve, Eglwys-fach, Machynlleth, Powys SY20 8TA. 01654 781265.
e-mail: dick.squires@rspb.org.uk

Channel Islands

COLIN McCATHIE RESERVE (VALE POND)

La Société Guernesiaise.
Location: Perry's Island Guide (page 6 B5).
Access: Open at all times.
Facilities: Hide on road to Vale Church must be used.
Public transport: Hourly bus service 7/7A (island circular), tel: 01481 720210.
Habitat: Brackish tidal pond, reed fringes.
Key birds: Passage waders. *Summer*: Breeding Reed Warbler, Moorhen, Coot. *Winter*: Wildfowl, Water Rail, Little Egret, Snipe, Kingfisher.
Contact: Vic Froome (Section Secretary), La Cloture, Courtil de Bas Lane, St Sampson's, Guernsey GY2 4XJ. 01481 254841.

LA CLAIRE MARE

La Société Guernesiaise.
Location: Perry's Island Guide (page 12 C5).
Access: Open at all times.
Facilities: Hide down concrete track off the Rue de la Rocque Road then boardwalk to second hide.
Public transport: Hourly bus service 7/7A (island circular), tel: 01481 720210.
Habitat: Reedbeds, pasture, willow thickets, scrape.
Key birds: Passage waders and passerines. *Summer*: Breeding Reed Warbler, Moorhen, Coot, Kestrel. *Winter*: Wildfowl, Water Rail, Snipe, Kingfisher.
Contact: Vic Froome (Section Secretary), La Cloture, Courtil de Bas Lane, St Sampson's, Guernsey GY2 4XJ. 01481 254841.

PLEINMONT

La Société Guernesiaise.
Location: Perry's Island Guide (Page 32 B3).
Access: Open at all times.
Facilities: Public footpath around reserve.
Public transport: Hourly bus service 7/7A (island circular) 0.5 miles from Imperial Hotel, tel 01481 720210.
Habitat: Cliff-top headland of scrub, remnant heathland and small fields.
Key birds: Passage passerines. *Summer*: Breeding Dartford Warbler, Whitethroat, Stonechat and Linnet.
Contact: Vic Froome, Section Secretary,La Cloture, Courtil Le Bas Lane, St Sampson's, Guernsey GY2 4XT. 01481 254841.

Isle of Man

BREAGLE GLEN

Manx Wildlife Trust/Castletown Town Commissioners Habitats.
Location: SC 196 688. In Port Erin from St Georges Crescent, which forms the whole N and W boundary.
Access: Open all year.
Facilities: None.
Public transport: None.
Habitat: Small woodland area, shrubs.
Key birds: *Passage*: Yellow-browed Warbler, Barred Warbler, Firecrest, Red-breasted Flycatcher have been recorded as well as common woodland species.
Contact: Trust HQ, Tynwald Mills, St Johns, Isle of Man IM4 3AE, 01624 801985.
e-mail: manxwt@cix.co.uk
www.wildlifetrust.org.uk/manxwt

CALF OF MAN BIRD OBSERVATORY

Administration Department, Manx National Heritage.
Location: SC 15 65. Small island off the SW tip of the Isle of Man. Local boat from Port Erin or Port St Mary.
Access: Apr-Oct. No dogs, fires or camping.
Facilities: Accommodation for eight people in three bedrooms at Observatory Apr-Oct. Bookings: Administration Department (address below).
Public transport: Local boat from Port Erin or Port St Mary.
Habitat: Heather/bracken moor and seabird cliffs.
Key birds: *All year*: Hen Harrier, Peregrine and

Chough. *Summer*: Breeding seabirds (nine species including Storm Petrel, Manx Shearwater). Excellent spring and autumn migration, seabird migration best in autumn.
Contact: Tim Bagworth, (Warden),Manx National Heritage, Manx Museum, Douglas, Isle of Man IM1 3LY.

CLOSE SARTFIELD

Manx Wildlife Trust.
Location: SC 361 956. From Ramsey drive W on A3. Turn on to B9, take third right and follow this road for nearly a mile. Reserve entrance is on right.
Access: Open all year round. No dogs. Path and boardwalk suitable for wheelchairs from car park through wildflower meadow and willow scrub to hide.
Facilities: Car park, hide, reserve leaflet (50p, available from office) outlines circular walk.
Public transport: None.
Habitat: Wildflower-rich hay meadow, marshy grassland, willow scrub/developing birch woodland, bog.
Key birds: *Winter*: Large roost of Hen Harrier. *Summer*: Corncrake (breeding 1999 and 2000 after 11 years' absence), Curlew, warblers.
Contact: Tricia Sayle, Reserves Officer,Manx Wildlife Trust, Tynwald Mills, St John's, Isle of Man IM4 3AE01624 801985.
e-mail: tricia@manxwt.cix.co.uk

COOILDARRY

Manx Wildlife Trust.
Location: SC 319 896. Entrance approximately one mile S of Kirk Michael village, left of A3.
Access: Open all year round. Not suitable for disabled. Dogs to be kept on a lead.
Facilities: Well-maintained paths throughout. Leaflet (50p) available from office. Nearest toilets in Kirk Michael village.
Public transport: Buses run regularly past the lower entrance off A4.
Habitat: Woodland.
Key birds: Raven, Sparrowhawk.
Contact: Trust HQ.

CRONK Y BING

Manx Wildlife Trust.
Location: NX 381 017. Take A10 coast road N from Jurby. Approx two miles along there is a sharp right hand turn over a bridge. Before the bridge there is a track to the left. A parking area is available at the end of the track.
Access: Open all year round. Dogs to be kept on a lead. Not suitable for the disabled.
Facilities: None.
Public transport: None.
Habitat: Open dune and dune grassland.
Key birds: *Summer*: Terns. *Winter*: Divers, grebes, skuas, gulls.
Contact: Trust HQ.

CURRAGH KIONDROGHAD

Manx Wildlife Trust.
Location: Turn into Church Road from the A2 near Onchan. Park on the L as the road dips. To reach the reserve cross a piece of land on the L owned by Onchan Commissioners.
Access: Open all year.
Facilities: None.
Public transport: None.
Habitat: Wetland, trees, neutral grassland, swamp.
Key birds: *Spring/summer*: Woodcock, Grey Wagtail, Chiffchaff. *Winter*: Hen Harrier.
Contact: Trust HQ

DALBY MOUNTAIN

Manx Wildlife Trust.
Location: SC 233769. Approx two miles S of Dalby village, lying adjacent to the A27.
Access: Open all year round. Dogs to be kept on a lead. Not suitable for wheelchairs.
Facilities: None.
Public transport: None.
Habitat: Heathland.
Key birds: Hen Harrier, Red Grouse.
Contact: Tricia Sayle, Reserves Officer,Manx Wildlife Trust, Tynwald Mills, St John's, Isle of Man IM4 3AE. 01624 810985.
e-mail: tricia@manxwt.cix.co.uk

COUNTY DIRECTORY

Richard Johnson submitted this illustration of a Waxwing
for the 2002 *British Birds* competition.

ENGLAND

THE INFORMATION in the directory has been obtained either from the persons listed or from the appropriate national or other bodies. In some cases, where it has not proved possible to verify the details directly, alternative responsible sources have been relied upon. When no satisfactory record was available, previously included entries have sometimes had to be deleted. Readers are requested to advise the editor of any errors or omissions.

In a change from previous years, the *Yearbook* is no longer listing the Wetland Bird Survey Organisers. There have been an increasing number of approaches to them from developers and consultants trying to access data on wetland sites. The WeBS partners are concerned that any approach should come through the central organisation so that they can be aware of any potential threat to sites and can control the data that is released.

While we regret the loss of this listing, Buckingham Press respect the concerns that the WeBS partners have raised and do not wish to publish any information that may further threaten our vulnerable wetland sites.

We are very grateful for the support and information that the WeBS Organisers have given us over the years and wish the project every success for the future. Please let us know if you have any concerns about the withdrawal of this listing or contact the WeBS Secretariat (see National Projects).

BEDFORDSHIRE

Bird Atlas/Avifauna
An Atlas of the Breeding Birds of Bedfordshire 1988-92 by R A Dazley and P Trodd (Bedfordshire Natural History Society, 1994).

Bird Recorders
Dave Odell, The Hobby, 74 The Links, Kempston, Bedford, MK42 7LT. 01234 857149.

Bedfordshire Bird Club Records & Research Committee, Phil Cannings, 30 Graham Gardens, Luton, LU3 1NQ. H:01582 400394; W:01234 842220;
e-mail: philcannings@ntlworld.com

Bird Report
BEDFORDSHIRE BIRD REPORT (1946-), from Gill Dickens, 9 Ullswater Road, Dunstable, Beds, LU6 3PX. 01582 609864.

BTO Regional Representative & Regional Development Officer
RR, Phil Cannings, 30 Graham Gardens, Luton, Beds, LU3 1NQ. H:01582 400394; W:01234 842220; e-mail: philcannings@ntlworld.com

RDO, Judith Knight, 381 Bideford Green, Linslade, Leighton Buzzard, Beds, LU7 2TY. Home 01525 378161;
e-mail: judy.knight@tinyonline.co.uk

Club
BEDFORDSHIRE BIRD CLUB, (1992; 242). Miss Sheila Alliez, Flat 61 Adamson Court, Hillgrounds Road, Kempston, Bedford, MK42 8QZ.
www.bedsbirdclub.org.uk

Ringing Groups
IVEL RG, Errol Newman, 29 Norse Road, Goldington, Bedford, MK41 0NR. 01234 343119; e-mail: lew.n@virgin.net

RSPB, Dr A D Evans, 6 Jennings Close, Potton, Sandy, Beds, SG19 2SE.

RSPB Local Groups
BEDFORD, (1970; 80). Barrie Mason, 6 Landseer Walk, Bedford, MK41 7LZ. 01234 262280.

EAST BEDFORDSHIRE, (1973; 75). Terence C Park, 8 Back Street, Biggleswade, Beds, SG18 8JA. 01767 221363.

SOUTH BEDFORDSHIRE, (1973; 150). Mick Price, 120 Common Road, Kensworth, Beds LU6 3RG. 01582 873268.

Wildlife Trust
See Cambridgeshire.

BERKSHIRE

Bird Atlas/Avifauna
The Birds of Berkshire by P E Standley et al

ENGLAND

(Berkshire Atlas Group/Reading Ornithological Club, 1996).

Bird Recorder
Peter Standley, Siskins, 7 Llanvair Drive, South Ascot, Berks, SL5 9HS. 01344 623502.

Bird Reports
BERKSHIRE BIRD BULLETIN (Monthly, 1986-), from Brian Clews, 118 Broomhill, Cookham, Berks, SL6 9LQ. 01628 525314.

BIRDS OF BERKSHIRE (1974-), from Recorder.

BIRDS OF THE THEALE AREA (1988-), from Secretary, Theale Area Bird Conservation Group.

NEWBURY DISTRICT BIRD REPORT (1959-), from Secretary, Newbury District Ornithological Club.

BTO Regional Representative & Regional Development Officer
RR, Chris Robinson, 2 Beckfords, Upper Basildon, Reading, RG8 8PB. 01491 671420;
e-mail: chris.robinson@hp.com

Clubs
BERKSHIRE BIRD BULLETIN GROUP, (1986; 100). Berkshire Bird Bulletin Group, PO Box 680, Maidenhead, Berks, SL6 9ST. 01628 525314.

NEWBURY DISTRICT ORNITHOLOGICAL CLUB, (1959; 120). Trevor Maynard, 15 Kempton Close, Newbury, Berks, RG14 7RS. 01635 36752.

READING ORNITHOLOGICAL CLUB, (1945; 200). John Hannan, Robin Cottage, Turners Green, Upper Bucklebury, Reading RG7 6RE.
www.roc.care4free.net

THEALE AREA BIRD CONSERVATION GROUP, (1988; 75). Brian Uttley, 60 Omers Rise, Burghfield Common, Reading RG7 3HH. 0118 9832894. email: msmith8741@aol.com
www.bramblingphotos.com/tabcgweb/

Ringing Groups
NEWBURY RG, J Legg, 1 Malvern Court, Old Newtown Road, Newbury, Berks, RG14 7DR. e-mail: janlegg@talk21.com

RUNNYMEDE RG, D G Harris, 22 Blossom Waye, Hounslow, TW5 9HD. e-mail: daveharris@tinyonline.co.uk

RSPB Local Groups
EAST BERKSHIRE, (1974; 200). Ken Panchen, 7 Knottocks End, Beaconsfield, Bucks, HP9 2AN. 01494 675779.

READING, (1986; 80). Carl Feltham, 39 Moriston Close, Reading, RG30 2PW. 0118 941 1713.

WOKINGHAM & BRACKNELL, (1979; 200). Patrick Crowley, 56 Ellis Road, Crowthorne, Berks, RG45 6PT. 01344 776473; www.wbrspb.btinternet.co.uk e-mail: patrick.crowley@btinternet.com

Wildlife Hospitals
KESTREL LODGE, D J Chandler, 101 Sheridan Avenue, Caversham, Reading, RG4 7QB. 01189 477107; Birds of prey, ground feeding birds, waterbirds, seabirds. Temporary homes for all except large birds of prey. Veterinary support. Small charge.

SWAN LIFELINE, Chairman, Swan Treatment Centre, Cuckoo Weir Island, South Meadow Lane, Eton, Windsor, Berks, SL4 6SS. 01753 859397; fax 01753 622709;
Registered charity. Thames Valley 24-hour swan rescue and treatment service. Veterinary support and hospital unit. Operates membership scheme. www.swanlifeline.org.uk

Wildlife Trust
Director, See Oxfordshire.

BUCKINGHAMSHIRE

Bird Atlas/Avifauna
The Birds of Buckinghamshire ed by P Lack and D Ferguson (Buckinghamshire Bird Club, 1993).

Bird Recorder
Andy Harding, 15 Jubilee Terrace, Stony Stratford, Milton Keynes, MK11 1DU. H:01908 565896; W:01908 653328;
e-mail: a.v.harding@open.ac.uk.

Bird Reports
AMERSHAM BIRDWATCHING CLUB ANNUAL REPORT (1975-), from Secretary.

BUCKINGHAMSHIRE BIRD REPORT (1980-), from Rosie Hamilton, 56 Church Hill, Cheddington, Leighton Buzzard, Beds, LU7 0SY.

NORTH BUCKS BIRD REPORT (10 pa), from Recorder.

BTO Regional Representative & Regional Development Officer
RR, Mick A'Court, 6 Chalkshire Cottages, Shalshire Road, Butlers Cross, Bucks HP17 0TW. H:01296 623610; W:01494 462246; e-mail: a.arundinaceous@virgin.net

RDO, Peter Hearn, 160 High Street, Aylesbury, Bucks, HP20 1RE. Home & fax 01296 581520; Work 01296 424145.

Clubs
AMERSHAM BIRDWATCHING CLUB, (1973; 70). Mary Mackay, 26A Highfield Close, Amersham, Bucks, HP6 3HG. 07980 503879.

BUCKINGHAMSHIRE BIRD CLUB, (1981; 300). Roger S Warren, Bakery Lodge, Skirmett, Henley on Thames, Oxon, RG9 6TD. 01491 638544.

NORTH BUCKS BIRDERS, (1977; 50). Andy Harding, 15 Jubilee Terrace, Stony Stratford, Milton Keynes, MK11 1DU. H:01908 565896; W:01908 653328.

Ringing Groups
HUGHENDEN RG, Peter Edwards, 8 The Brackens, Warren Wood, High Wycombe, Bucks, HP11 1EB. 01494 535125.

RSPB Local Groups
See also Herts: Chorleywood.

AYLESBURY, (1981; 220). Barry Oxley, 3 Swan Close, Station Road, Blackthorn, Bicester, Oxon, OX25 1TU. 01869 247780.

NORTH BUCKINGHAMSHIRE, (1976; 400). Jim Parsons, 8 The Mount, Aspley Guise, Milton Keynes, MK17 8EA. 01908 582450.

Wildlife Hospitals
MILTON KEYNES WILDLIFE HOSPITAL, Mr & Mrs V Seaton, 150 Bradwell Common Boulevard, Milton Keynes, MK13 8BE. 01908 604198; www-tec.open,ac.uk/staff/robert/robert.html Registered charity. All species of British birds and mammals. Veterinary support.

WILDLIFE HOSPITAL TRUST, St Tiggywinkles, Aston Road, Haddenham, Aylesbury, Bucks, HP17 8AF. 01844 292292; fax 01844 292640; e-mail: mail@sttiggywinkles.org.uk www.sttiggywinkles.org.uk Registered charity. All species. Veterinary referrals and helpline for vets and others on wild bird treatments. Full veterinary unit and staff. Pub: *Bright Eyes* (free to members - sae).

Wildlife Trust
Director, See Oxfordshire.

CAMBRIDGESHIRE

Bird Atlas/Avifauna
An Atlas of the Breeding Birds of Cambridgeshire (VC 29) P M M Bircham et al (Cambridge Bird Club, 1994).

The Birds of Cambridgeshire: checklist 2000 (Cambridge Bird Club).

Bird Recorders
CAMBRIDGESHIRE, John Oates, 7 Fassage Close, Lode, Cambridge, CB5 9EH. 01223 812546, (M)07860 132708. e-mail: joates9151@aol.com

HUNTINGDON & PETERBOROUGH, John Clark, 7 Westbrook, Hilton, Huntingdon, Cambs, PE28 9NW. 01480 830472.

Bird Reports
CAMBRIDGESHIRE BIRD REPORT (1925-), from Secretary. Cambridge Bird Club.

PAXTON PITS BIRD REPORT (1994-), from Trevor Gunton, 15 St James Road, Little Paxton, Cambs, PE19 6QW. (Tel/fax)01480 473562.

PETERBOROUGH BIRD CLUB REPORT (1999-), from Secretary, Peterborough Bird Club.

BTO Regional Representatives
CAMBRIDGESHIRE, John Le Gassick, 17 Acacia Avenue, St Ives, Cambs, PE27 6TN. 01480 391991; e-mail: john.legassick@ntlworld.com

HUNTINGDON & PETERBOROUGH, vacant.

Clubs
CAMBRIDGESHIRE BIRD CLUB, (1925; 270). Bruce Martin, 178 Nuns Way, Cambridge, CB4 2NS. 01223 700656; e-mail: bruce.s.martin@ntlworld.com www. cambridgeshirebirdclub.org.uk

GREATER PETERBOROUGH ORNITHOLOGICAL GROUP, (1983; 20). Martin Coates, 63 Primrose Way, Stamford, PE9 4BU. 01780 755016; e-mail: martin.shelagh@virgin.net

PETERBOROUGH BIRD CLUB, (1999; 190). Jane Williams, The Old Rectory, Church St, Market Deeping, Lincs, 01778 345711; e-mail: jane@oldrectory.screaming.net www.peterboroughbirdclub.org.uk

ST NEOTS BIRD & WILDLIFE CLUB, (1993; 150).

Tim Watling, 39 Shakespeare Road, Eaton Socon, St Neots, Cambs, PE19 8HG. 01480 212763; www.paxton-pits.org.uk e-mail: tim@watling2000.fsnet.co.uk

Ringing Group
WICKEN FEN RG, Dr C J R Thorne, Norden House, 17 The Footpath, Coton, Cambs, CB3 7PX. 01954 210566; e-mail: cjrt@cam.ac.uk

RSPB Local Groups
CAMBRIDGE, (1977; 200). Colin Kirtland, 22 Montgomery Road, Cambridge, CB4 2EQ. 01223 363092.

HUNTINGDONSHIRE, (1982; 200). Pam Peacock, Old Post Office, Warboys Road, Pidley, Huntingdon, Cambs, PE28 3DA. 01487 840615; e-mail: pam.peacock@care4free.net www.huntsrspb.co.uk

Wildlife Trust
BEDS, CAMBS, NORTHANTS & PETERBOROUGH WILDLIFE TRUST, (1990; 12,500). 3B Langford Arch, London Road, Sawston, Cambridge, CB2 4EE. 01223 712400; fax 01223 712412; e-mail: cambswt@cix.co.uk www.wildtrust.org.uk/bcnp

CHESHIRE

Bird Atlas/Avifauna
The Birds of Sandbach Flashes 1935-1999 by Andrew Goodwin and Colin Lythgoe (The Printing House, Crewe, 2000).

Bird Recorder (inc Wirral)
Tony Broome, 4 Larchwood Drive, Wilmslow, Cheshire, SK9 2NU. 01625 540434.

Bird Report
CHESHIRE & WIRRAL BIRD REPORT (1969-), from David Cogger, 113 Nantwich Road, Middlewich, Cheshire, CW10 9HD. 01606 832517; e-mail: memsec@cawos.org www.cawos.org

SOUTH EAST CHESHIRE ORNITHOLOGICAL SOCIETY BIRD REPORT (1985-), from secretary, South East Cheshire Ornithol Soc.

BTO Regional Representatives & Regional Development Officer
MID RR, Position vacant.

NORTH & EAST RR, David B Jones, 8 Wey Gates Drive, Hale Barns, Cheshire, WA15 0BW. 0161 980 5273; e-mail: d.b.jones@lineone.net

SOUTH RR & RDO, Charles Hull, Edleston Cottage, Edleston Hall Lane, Nantwich, Cheshire, CW5 8PL. 01270 628194; e-mail: edleston@yahoo.co.uk

Clubs
CHESHIRE & WIRRAL ORNITHOLOGICAL SOCIETY, (1988; 355). David Cogger, 113 Nantwich Road, Middlewich, Cheshire, CW10 9HD. 01606 832517; e-mail: memsec@cawos.org www.cawos.org

CHESTER & DISTRICT ORNITHOLOGICAL SOCIETY, (1967; 50). David King, 13 Bennett Close, Willaston, South Wirral, CH64 2XF. 0151 327 7212.

KNUTSFORD ORNITHOLOGICAL SOCIETY, (1974; 45). Roy Bircumshaw, 267 Longridge, Knutsford, Cheshire, WA16 8PH. 01565 634193. www.10x50.com

LANCASHIRE & CHESHIRE FAUNA SOCIETY, (1914; 140). Dave Bickerton, 64 Petre Crescent, Rishton, Lancs, BB1 4RB. 01254 886257; e-mail: bickertond@aol.com

LYMM ORNITHOLOGY GROUP, (1975; 65). Mrs Ann Ledden, 4 Hill View, Widnes, WA8 9AL. 0151 424 0441.

MID-CHESHIRE ORNITHOLOGICAL SOCIETY, (1963; 80). Les Goulding, 7 Summerville Gardens, Grappenhall, Warrington, WA4 2EG. 01925 265578; www.hems.u-net.com e-mail: les@goulding7.fsnet.co.uk

NANTWICH NATURAL HISTORY SOCIETY, (1972; 45). Mike Holmes, 114 Merlin Way, Coppenhall, Crewe, Cheshire, CW1 3RZ.01270 216890; e-mail: mike@mimprove.com www.crewe25.freeserve.co.uk

SOUTH EAST CHESHIRE ORNITHOLOGICAL SOCIETY, (1964; 105). Colin Lythgoe, 11 Waterloo Road, Haslington, Crewe, CW1 5TF. 01270 582642.

WILMSLOW GUILD ORNITHOLOGICAL SOCIETY, (1965; 60). Tom Gibbons, Chestnut Cottage, 37 Strawberry Lane, Wilmslow, Cheshire, SK9 6AQ. 01625 520317.

Ringing Groups
MERSEYSIDE RG, P Slater, 45 Greenway Road, Speke, Liverpool, L24 7RY.

SOUTH MANCHESTER RG, C M Richards, Fairhaven, 13 The Green, Handforth, Wilmslow,

Cheshire, SK9 3AG. 01625 524527;
e-mail: cliveandkay.richards@care4free.net

RSPB Local Groups
CHESTER, (1987; 350). Bernard Wright, Carden
Smithy, Clutton, Chester, CH3 9EP. 01829 782243;
e-mail: knoydart@globalnet.co.uk

MACCLESFIELD, (1979; 358). Peter Kirk, Field
Rise, Dumbah Lane, Bollington, Macclesfield,
Cheshire, SK10 5AB. 01625 829119;
email: peter@kirk199.freeserve.co.uk
www.macclesfieldrspb.org.uk

NORTH CHESHIRE, (1976; 100). Steve Davidson,
11 Morton Close, Old Hall, Warrington, WA5 8QH.
01925 635967.

Wildlife Hospitals
RSPCA STAPELEY GRANGE WILDLIFE HOSPITAL,
London Road, Stapeley, Nantwich, Cheshire, CW5
7JW. 0870 442 7102. All wild birds. Oiled bird
wash facilities and pools. Veterinary support.

SWAN SANCTUARY, Mrs C Clements, 24 St David's
Drive, Callands, Warrington, WA5 5SB. 01925
636245. Veterinary support.

Wildlife Trust
CHESHIRE WILDLIFE TRUST, (1962; 4,500). Grebe
House, Reaseheath, Nantwich, Cheshire, CW5
6DG. 01270 610180; fax 01270 610430;
e-mail: cheshirewt@cix.co.uk
www.wildlifetrust.org.uk/cheshire

CORNWALL

Bird Recorders
CORNWALL, K Wilson, No.1 Tol-pedn House,
School Hill Road, St Levan, Penzance, Cornwall,
TR19 6LP. 01736 871800;
e-mail: kesteraw@yahoo.co.uk

ISLES OF SCILLY, Paul Stancliffe, 1 Heydor Flats,
Garrison Lane, St Mary's, Isles of Scilly, TR21 0JD.
e-mail: paulnabby@supanet.com

Bird Reports
BIRDS IN CORNWALL (1931-), from Colin Boyd, 4
Henliston Drive, Helston, Cornwall, TR13 8BW.

*ISLES OF SCILLY BIRD REPORT and NATURAL
HISTORY REVIEW 2000 (1969-),* from club
secretary, Isles of Scilly Bird Group.

**BTO Regional Representatives & Regional
Development Officers**
CORNWALL RR & RDO, John Woodland (acting),
Glebe Cottage, Dunsford, Exeter, EX6 7AA. Tel/fax

01647 252494;
e-mail: jwoodland@btodv.fsnet.co.uk

ISLES OF SCILLY RR & RDO, Will Wagstaff, 42 Sally
Port, St Mary's, Isles of Scilly, TR21 0JE. 01720
422212; e-mail: william.wagstaff@virgin.net

Clubs
CORNWALL BIRDWATCHING & PRESERVATION
SOCIETY, (1931; 990). Steve Rogers, Roseland,
Cyril Road, Truro, TR1 3TA.
e-mail: steve@swoptics.co.uk.

CORNWALL WILDLIFE TRUST PHOTOGRAPHIC
GROUP (1970; 40). David Chapman, 41 Bosence
Road, Townshend, nr Hayle, Cornwall, TR27 6AL.
01736 850287.
e-mail: david@ruralimages.freeserve.co.uk
www.ruralimages.freeserve.co.uk

ISLES OF SCILLY BIRD GROUP, (2000; 20). Nigel
Hudson, Post Office Flat, St Mary's, Isles of Scilly;
TR21 0LL01720 422267;
e-mail: nig_hudson@lineone.net

Ringing Group
SCILLONIA SEABIRD GROUP, Peter Robinson, 19
Pine Park Road, Honiton, Devon, EX14 2HR. 01404
549873; e-mail: pjrobinson2@cs.com

RSPB Local Group
CORNWALL, (1972; 550). Michael Lord, Gue
Gassel, Church Cove, The Lizard, Cornwall, TR12
7PH. 01326 290981.

Wildlife Hospital
MOUSEHOLE WILD BIRD HOSPITAL & SANCTUARY
ASSOCIATION LTD, Raginnis Hill, Mousehole,
Penzance, Cornwall, TR19 6SR. 01736 731386. All
species. No ringing.

Wildlife Trust
CORNWALL WILDLIFE TRUST, (1962; 8,500). Five
Acres, Allet, Truro, Cornwall, TR4 9DJ. 01872
273939; fax 01872 225476;
e-mail: cornwt@cix.co.uk
www.wildlifetrust.org.uk/cornwall

CUMBRIA

Bird Atlas/Avifauna
The Breeding Birds of Cumbria by Stoff, Callion,
Kinley, Raven and Roberts (Cumbria Bird Club,
2002).

Bird Recorders
COUNTY, Colin Raven, 18 Seathwaite Road,
Barrow-in-Furness, Cumbria, LA14 4LX.

NORTH EAST (Carlisle & Eden), Michael F Carrier, Lismore Cottage, 1 Front Street, Armathwaite, Cumbria, CA4 9PB. 01697 472218.

NORTH WEST (Allerdale & Copeland), J K Manson, Fell Beck, East Road, Egremont, Cumbria, CA22 2ED. 01946 822947;
e-mail: jake@jakemanson.freeserve.co.uk

SOUTH (South Lakeland & Furness), Ronnie Irving, 24 Birchwood Close, Kendal, Cumbria, LA9 5BJ. 01539 727523;
e-mail: ronald.irving@virginnet.co.uk

Bird Reports
BIRDS AND WILDLIFE IN CUMBRIA (1970-), from D Clarke, Tullie House Museum, Castle Street, Carlisle, Cumbria, CA3 8TP.
e-mail: DavidC@carlisle-city.gov.uk

WALNEY BIRD OBSERVATORY REPORT, from Warden, see Reserves.

BTO Regional Representatives
NORTH RR, John Callion, The Cherries, 2 Scawfield, Scaw Road, High Harrington, Workington, Cumbria, CA14 4LZ. H:01946 830651; W:01946 830694.

SOUTH RR, Stephen Dunstan, 29 Greenfinch Court, Herons Reach, Blackpool, FY3 8FG. 01253 301009; e-mail: stephen@greenfinch.fslife.co.uk

Clubs
ARNSIDE & DISTRICT NATURAL HISTORY SOCIETY, (1967; 221). Mrs GM Smith, West Wind, Orchard Road, Arnside, via Carnforth, Cumbria, LA5 0DP. 01524 762522.

CUMBRIA BIRD CLUB, (1989; 230). Peter Ullrich, 25 Arlecdon Parks Road, Arlecdon, Frizington, Cumbria, CA26 3XG. 01946 861376;
www.cumbriabirdclub.freeserve.co.uk.

 CUMBRIA RAPTOR STUDY GROUP, (1992). P N Davies, Snowhill Cottage, Caldbeck, Wigton, Cumbria, CA7 8HL. 016973 712249;
e-mail:
pete.caldbeck@virgin.net

Ringing Groups
EDEN RG, G Longrigg, Mere Bank, Bleatarn, Warcop, Appleby, Cumbria, CA16 6PX.

MORECAMBE BAY WADER RG, J Sheldon, 415 West Shore Park, Barrow-in-Furness, Cumbria, LA14 3XZ. 01229 473102.

WALNEY BIRD OBSERVATORY, K Parkes, 176

Harrogate Street, Barrow-in-Furness, Cumbria, LA14 5NA. 01229 824219.

RSPB Local Groups
CARLISLE, (1974; 400). Alistair Leslie, 15 High Garth Meadows, Ivegill, Carlisle, CA4 0PA. 01697 473138.

SOUTH LAKELAND, (1973; 350). Ms Kathleen Atkinson, 2 Langdale Crescent, Windermere, Cumbria, LA23 2HE. 01539 444254.

WEST CUMBRIA, (1986; 230). Neil Hutchin, Orchard House, Main Street, Greysouthen, Cockermouth, Cumbria, CA13 0UG. 01900 825231; e-mail: neil@hutchin50.fsnet.co.uk

Wildlife Trust
CUMBRIA WILDLIFE TRUST, (1962; 8,000). Plumgarths, Crook Road, Kendal, LA8 8LX. 01539 816300; (fax)01539 816301;
e-mail: cumbriawt@cix.co.uk
www.wildlifetrust.org.uk/cumbria

DERBYSHIRE

Bird Recorders
1. Rare breeding records, Roy A Frost, 66 St Lawrence Road, North Wingfield, Chesterfield, Derbyshire, S42 5LL. 01246 850037.

2. Records Committee & rarity records, Rodney W Key, 3 Farningham Close, Spondon, Derby, DE21 7DZ. 01332 678571; e-mail: rod.key@talk21.co.uk

3. Annual Report editor, Richard M R James, 10 Eastbrae Road, Littleover, Derby, DE23 1WA. 01332 771787.

Bird Reports
BENNERLEY MARSH WILDLIFE GROUP ANNUAL REPORT, from Secretary.

CARSINGTON BIRD CLUB ANNUAL REPORT, from Secretary.

DERBYSHIRE BIRD REPORT (1954-), from Andrew Hattersley, 104 Longedge Lane, Wingerworth, Chesterfield, S42 6PQ. 01246 230522.

OGSTON BIRD CLUB REPORT (1970-), from Secretary.

BTO Regional Representatives
NORTH RR, Dave Budworth, 121 Wood Lane, Newhall, Swadlincote, Derbys, DE11 0LX. 01283 215188; e-mail: dbud01@aol.com

SOUTH RR, Dave Budworth, 121 Wood Lane, Newhall, Swadlincote, Derbys, DE11 0LX. 01283 215188; e-mail: dbud01@aol.com

Clubs

BENNERLEY MARSH WILDLIFE GROUP, (1995; 135). Mr R Davis, 3 Windrush Close, Bramcote, Nottingham, NG9 3LN. 0115 9228547.

BAKEWELL & DISTRICT BIRD STUDY GROUP, (1987; 70). Ann Wrench, Longstone Byre, Little Longstone, Nr Bakewell, Derbys, DE45 1NN. e-mail: ann.wrench@btinternet.com

BUXTON FIELD CLUB, (1946; 78). B Aries, 1 Horsefair Avenue, Chapel-en-le-Frith, High Peak, Derbys, SK23 9SQ. 01298 815291.

CARSINGTON BIRD CLUB, (1992; 257). Mrs Dorothy Evans, 41 Belvedere Avenue, Walton, Chesterfield, Derbys, S40 3HY. 01246 238421.

 **Derbyshire Ornithological Society**

DERBYSHIRE ORNITHOLOGICAL SOCIETY, (1954; 550). Steve Shaw, 84 Moorland View Road, Walton, Chesterfield, Derbys, S40 3DF. 01246 236090; e-mail: steveshaw@ornsoc.freeserve.co.uk

OGSTON BIRD CLUB, (1969; 710). Mrs Ann Hunt, 2 Sycamore Avenue, Glapwell, Chesterfield, S44 5LH. 01623 812159. www.ogstonbirdclub.co.uk

SOUTH PEAK RAPTOR STUDY GROUP, (1998; 12). M E Taylor, 76 Hawksley Avenue, Newbold, Chesterfield, Derbys, S40 4TL. 01246 277749.

Ringing Groups

DARK PEAK RG, W M Underwood, 56 Bank Street, Hadfield, Glossop, Derbys, SK13 1BB. e-mail: w.m.underwood@talk21.com

SORBY-BRECK RG, Geoff P Mawson, Moonpenny Farm, Farwater Lane, Dronfield, Sheffield, S18 1RA. 01246 415097; e-mail: gpmawson@hotmail.com

SOUDER RG, Dave Budworth, 121 Wood Lane, Newhall, Swadlincote, Derbys, DE11 0LX. 0121 6953384.

RSPB Local Groups

CHESTERFIELD, (1987; 274). Tony Atkinson. 01246 233840. e-mail: TAA@care4free.net

DERBY, (1973; 3,800). Brian Myring, 74 The Bancroft, Etwall, Derby, DE65 6NF. 01283 734851.

HIGH PEAK, (1974; 220). Peter Griffiths, 17 Clifton Drive, Marple, Stockport SK6 6PP. 0161 427 5325.

Wildlife Trust

DERBYSHIRE WILDLIFE TRUST, (1962; 5,000). Elvaston Castle, Derby, DE72 3EP. 01773 881188; (fax)01332 758872; e-mail: derbywt@cix.co.uk www.wildlifetrust.org.uk/derbyshire

DEVON

Bird Atlas/Avifauna

Tetrad Atlas of Breeding Birds of Devon by H P Sitters (Devon Birdwatching & Preservation Society, 1988).

Bird Recorder

Mike Langman, 38 Brantwood Drive, Paignton, Devon, TQ4 5HZ. 01803 528008; e-mail: mikelangman38@aol.com

Bird Reports

DEVON BIRD REPORT (1928-), from H Kendall, 33 Victoria Road, Bude, Cornwall, EX23 8RJ. 01288 353818; e-mail: harvey.kendall@btopenworld.com.

LUNDY FIELD SOCIETY ANNUAL REPORT (1946-), from Secretary. Index to Report is on Society's website.

BTO Regional Representative & Regional Development Officer

John Woodland, Glebe Cottage, Dunsford, Exeter, EX6 7AA. Tel/fax 01647 252494; e-mail: jwoodland@btodv.fsnet.co.uk

Clubs

DEVON BIRDWATCHING & PRESERVATION SOCIETY, (1928; 1400). Mrs Joy Vaughan, 28 Fern Meadow, Okehampton, Devon, EX20 1PB. 01837 53360.

KINGSBRIDGE & DISTRICT NATURAL HISTORY SOCIETY, (1989; 130). Martin Catt, Migrants Rest, East Prawle, Kingsbridge, Devon, TQ7 2DB. 01548 511443; e-mail: martin.catt@btinternet.com

LUNDY FIELD SOCIETY, (1946; 450). Chris Webster, 38 Greenway Avenue, Taunton, Somerset, TA2 6HY. 01823 282889; e-mail: chris@webster5.demon.co.uk www.lundy.org.uk

TOPSHAM BIRDWATCHING & NATURALISTS' SOCIETY, (1969; 90). Mrs Janice Vining, 2 The Maltings, Fore Street, Topsham, Exeter, EX3 0HF. 01392 873514; e-mail: tbns@talk21.com

Ringing Groups

DEVON & CORNWALL WADER RG, R C Swinfen, 72 Dunraven Drive, Derriford, Plymouth, PL6 6AT. 01752 704184.

LUNDY FIELD SOCIETY, A M Taylor, 26 High Street, Spetisbury, Blandford, Dorset, DT11 9DJ. 01258 857336.

SLAPTON BIRD OBSERVATORY, Peter Ellicott, 10 Chapel Road, Alphington, Exeter, EX2 8TB. 01392 277387.

RSPB Local Groups

EXETER & DISTRICT, (1974; 466). Allan Hancock, Pineta, Sand Down Lane, Newton St Cyres, Exeter, EX5 5DE. 01392 851744;
e-mail: allan.h@care4free.net

NORTH DEVON, (1970; 96). David Gayton, 29 Merrythorne Road, Fremington, Barnstaple, Devon, EX31 3AL. 01271 371092.
e-mail: HEVDAV@aol.com

PLYMOUTH, (1974; 850). Mrs Eileen Willey, 11 Beverstone Way, Roborough, Plymouth, PL6 7DY. 01752 208996.

Wildlife Hospitals

BIRD OF PREY CASUALTY CENTRE, Mrs J E L Vinson, Crooked Meadow, Stidston Lane, South Brent, Devon, TQ10 9JS. 01364 72174. Birds of prey, with emergency advice on other species. Aviaries, releasing pen. Veterinary support.

BONDLEIGH BIRD HOSPITAL, Manager, Samantha Hart, North Tawton, Devon, EX20 2AJ. 01837 82328. All species. 14 aviaries, 2 aquapens. Veterinary support available, if requested, with payment of full charges.

CATT, Martin, Migrants Rest, East Prawle, Kingsbridge, Devon, TQ7 2DB. 01548 511443;
e-mail: martin.catt@btinternet.com
Collects and records oiled birds and gives initial treatment before forwarding to cleaning station.

HURRELL, Dr L H, 201 Outland Road, Peverell, Plymouth, PL2 3PF. 01752 771838.
Birds of prey only. Veterinary support.

TORBAY WILDLIFE RESCUE CENTRE, Malcolm Higgs, 6A Gerston Place, Paignton, S Devon, TQ3 3DX. 01803 557624. ww.twrs.fsnet.co.uk
All wild birds, inc. oiled. Pools, aviaries, intensive care, washing facilities. Open at all times. 24-hr veterinary support. Holding areas off limits to public as all wildlife must be returned to the wild.

Wildlife Trust

DEVON WILDLIFE TRUST, (1962; 16,000). Shirehampton House, 35-37 St David's Hill, Exeter, EX4 4DA. 01392 279244; fax 01392 433221;
e-mail: devonwt@cix.co.uk
www.devonwildlifetrust.org

DORSET

Bird Atlas/Avifauna
Dorset Breeding Bird Atlas (working title). In preparation.

Bird Recorder
Neil Gartshore, 54 Corfe Road, Stoborough, Wareham, Dorset, BH20 5AF. 01929 552560;
e-mail: neil&yuki@onaga54.freeserve.co.uk

Bird Reports
DORSET BIRDS (1987-), from Miss J W Adams, 16 Sherford Drive, Wareham, Dorset, BH20 4EN. 01929 552299.

THE BIRDS OF CHRISTCHURCH HARBOUR (1959-), from General Secretary, Christchurch Harbour, Ornithological Group.

PORTLAND BIRD OBSERVATORY REPORT, from Warden, see Reserves.

BTO Regional Representatives
Catherine and Graham Whitby, 2 Helston Close, Portesham, Weymouth, Dorset, DT3 4EY. 01305 871301; e-mail:
catherineandgraham@portisham2.fsnet.co.uk

Clubs
CHRISTCHURCH HARBOUR ORNITHOLOGICAL GROUP, (1956; 150). John Hall, 15 Kingsbere Gardens, Haslemere Avenue, Highcliffe, Dorset, BH23 5BQ. 01425 275610.

DORSET BIRD CLUB, (1987; 550). Mrs Eileen Bowman, 53 Lonnen Road, Colehill, Wimborne, Dorset, BH21 7AT. 01202 884788.

DORSET NATURAL HISTORY & ARCHAEOLOGICAL SOCIETY, (1845; 2,188). Kate Hebditch, Dorset County Museum, High West Street, Dorchester, Dorset, DT1 1XA. 01305 262735; e-mail:
dorsetcountymuseum@dor-mus.demon.co.uk
www.dorsetcountymuseum.co.uk

Ringing Groups
CHRISTCHURCH HARBOUR RS, E C Brett, 3 Whitfield Park, St Ives, Ringwood, Hants, BH24 2DX.

PORTLAND BIRD OBSERVATORY, Martin Cade, Old Lower Light, Portland Bill, Dorset, DT5 2JT. 01305 820553; e-mail: obs@btinternet.com
www.portlandbirdobs.btinternet.co.uk

STOUR RG, R Gifford, 62 Beacon Park Road, Upton, Poole, Dorset, BH16 5PE.

RSPB Local Groups

BLACKMOOR VALE, (1981; 120). Mrs Margaret Marris, 15 Burges Close, Marnhull, Sturminster Newton, Dorset, DT10 1QQ. 01258 820091.

EAST DORSET, (1974; 310). Tony Long, 93 Wimborne Road, Corfe Mullen, Wimborne, BH21 3DS. 01202 880508.

POOLE, (1982; 305). John Derricott, 51 Dacombe Drive, Upton, Poole, Dorset, BH16 5JJ. 01202 776312.

SOUTH DORSET, (1976; 400). Marion Perriss, Old Barn Cottage, Affpuddle, Dorchester, Dorset, DT2 7HH. 01305 848268.

Wildlife Hospital

SWAN RESCUE SANCTUARY, Ken and Judy Merriman, The Wigeon, Crooked Withies, Holt, Wimborne, Dorset, BH21 7LB. 01202 828166; mobile 0385 917457; www.swan-rescue.co.uk e-mail: ken@swan-rescue.fsnet.co.uk Swans. Hospital unit with indoor ponds and recovery pens. Outdoors: 35 ponds and lakes, and recovery pens. 24-hr veterinary support. Viewing by appointment only.

Wildlife Trust

DORSET WILDLIFE TRUST, (1961; 10,000). Brooklands Farm, Forston, Dorchester, Dorset, DT2 7AA. 01305 264620; fax 01305 251120; e-mail: dorsetwt@cix.co.uk; www.wildlifetrust.org.uk/dorset

DURHAM

Bird Atlas/Avifauna

A Summer Atlas of Breeding Birds of County Durham by Stephen Westerberg/Kieth Bowey. (Durham Bird Club, 2000).

Bird Recorders

Tony Armstrong, 39 Western Hill, Durham City, DH1 4RJ. 0191 386 1519; e-mail: ope@globalnet.co.uk

CLEVELAND, Graeme Joynt, 3 Brigandine Close, Warrior Park, Seaton Carew, Hartlepool, TS25 1ES. 01429 289968.

Bird Reports

BIRDS IN DURHAM (1971-), from D Sowerbutts, 9 Prebends Fields, Gilesgate, Durham, DH1 1HH.

CLEVELAND BIRD REPORT (1974-), from Mr J Sharp, 10 Glendale, Pinehills, Guisborough, TS14 8JF. 01287 633976.

BTO Regional Representatives

David L Sowerbutts, 9 Prebends Field, Gilesgate Moor, Durham, DH1 1HH. H:0191 386 7201; W:0191 374 3011; e-mail: d.l.sowerbutts@durham.ac.uk

CLEVELAND RR, Russell McAndrew, 5 Thornhill Gardens, Hartlepool, TS26 0HX. 01429 277291.

Clubs

DURHAM BIRD CLUB, (1975; 263). Kevin Spindloe, 31 Comrie Road, Hartlepool, TS25 4JQ. 01429 867550. www.durhambirdclub.org.uk

 SUMMERHILL (HARTLEPOOL) BIRD CLUB, (2000; 75). Kevin Spindloe, 31 Comrie Road, Hartlepool, TS25 4JQ. 1430 867550.

TEESMOUTH BIRD CLUB, (1960; 220). Chris Sharp, 20 Auckland Way, Hartlepool, TS26 0AN. 01429 865163.

Ringing Groups

DURHAM RG, S Westerberg, 32 Manor Road, Medomsley, Consett, Co Durham, DH8 6QW. 01207 563862.

DURHAM DALES RG, J R Hawes, Fairways, 5 Raby Terrace, Willington, Crook, Durham, DL15 0HR.

RSPB Local Group

DURHAM, (1974; 100). Lo Brown, 4 Ann's Place, Langley Moor, Durham, DH7 8JY.

Wildlife Trust

DURHAM WILDLIFE TRUST, (1971; 3500). Rainton Meadows, Chilton Moor, Houghton-le-Spring, Tyne & Wear, DH4 6PU. 0191 5843112; fax 0191 584 3934; e-mail: durhamwt@cix.co.uk www.wildlifetrust.org.uk/durham

ESSEX

Bird Atlas/Avifauna

Birds of Essex (provisional title) by Simon Woods (Essex Birdwatching Society, date to be announced).

The Breeding Birds of Essex by M K Dennis (Essex Birdwatching Society, 1996). New county avifauna, edited by Simon Wood.

Bird Recorder
Howard Vaughan, 68 Leigh Road East, London E6 2AS;
e-mail: howardebs@vaughanh.fsnet.co.uk

Mike Dennis, 173 Collier Row Lane, Romford, RM5 3ED. 01708 761865.

Bird Report
ESSEX BIRD REPORT (inc Bradwell Bird Obs records) (1950-), from Brian Cooper, 4 Helston Road, Chelmsford, Essex, CM1 6JE. 01245 251353.

BTO Regional Representatives & Regional Development Officer
NORTH-EAST RR & RDO, Peter Dwyer, 48 Churchill Avenue, Halstead, Essex, CO9 2BE. Tel/fax 01787 476524; e-mail: petedwyer@aol.com
or pete@northessex.co.uk

NORTH-WEST RR, Roy Ledgerton, 25 Bunyan Road, Braintree, Essex, CM7 2PL. 01376 326103; e-mail: r.ledgerton@virgin.net

SOUTH RR, Jean Stone, Topcroft, 8 Hillview Road, Rayleigh, Essex, SS6 7HX. 01268 775328.

Club
ESSEX BIRDWATCHING SOCIETY, (1949; 750). Roy Ledgerton, 25 Bunyan Road, Braintree, Essex, CM7 2PL. 01376 326103;
e-mail: r.ledgerton@virgin.net

LEE VALLEY NATURE PHOTOGRAPHERS (1994). Hon. Secretary; Les Borg. 01438 717841.
www.lvnaturephotographers.org.uk
e-mail: les@les-borg-photography.co.uk

Ringing Groups
ABBERTON RG, C P Harris, Wylandotte, Seamer Road, Southminster, Essex, CM0 7BX.

BASILDON RG, B J Manton, 72 Leighcliff Road, Leigh-on-Sea, Essex, SS9 1DN. 01702 475183;
e-mail: bjmanton@lineone.net

BRADWELL BIRD OBSERVATORY, C P Harris, Wyandotte, Seamer Road, Southminster, Essex, CM0 7BX.

RSPB Local Groups
CHELMSFORD, (1976; 5500). Mike Logan Wood, Highwood, Ishams Chase, Wickham Bishops, Essex, CM8 3LG. 01621 892045.

COLCHESTER, (1981; 250). Graham Brown, Oakdene, Inworth Lane, Wakes Colne, Colchester, CO6 2BE. 01787 227629.

SOUTHEND, (1983; 250). Peter D Hirst, 61 Symons Avenue, Eastwood, Leigh on Sea, Essex SS9 5QD. 01702 527069;
www.southendrspb.co.uk

Wildlife Trust
ESSEX WILDLIFE TRUST, (1959; 15,500). Visitor Centre, Abbotts Hall Farm, Great Wigborough, Colchester, Essex CO5 7RZ. 01621 862960; (fax)01621 862990;
e-mail: admin@essexwt.org.uk
www.essexwt.org.uk

GLOUCESTERSHIRE

Bird Atlas/Avifauna
Atlas of Breeding Birds of the North Cotswolds. (North Cotswold Ornithological Society, 1990).

Bird Recorder
Gordon Avery, 12 Hemmingsdale Road, Hempsted, Gloucester, GL2 5HN.
e-mail: gravery@hembirds.freeserve.co.uk

Bird Reports
CHELTENHAM BIRD CLUB BIRD REPORT (1998-), from Secretary.

GLOUCESTERSHIRE BIRD REPORT (1953-), from Peter Jones, 2 Beech Close, Highnam, Gloucester, GL2 8EG. 01452 413561;
e-mail: peter@joneshighnam.freeserve.co.uk

NORTH COTSWOLD ORNITHOLOGICAL SOCIETY ANNUAL REPORT (1983-), from Secretary.

BTO Regional Representative
Mike Smart, 143 Cheltenham Road, Gloucester, GL2 0JH. Home/work 01452 421131;
e-mail: smartmike@smartmike.fsnet.co.uk

Clubs
CHELTENHAM BIRD CLUB, (1976; 93). Mrs Frances Meredith, 14 Greatfield Drive, Charlton Kings, Cheltenham, GL53 9BU. 01242 516393;
e-mail: chelt.birds@virgin.net
www.beehive.thisisgloucestershire.co.uk/
cheltbirdclub

DURSLEY BIRDWATCHING & PRESERVATION SOCIETY, (1952; 450). Maurice Bullen, 20 South Street, Uley, Dursley, Glos, GL11 5SP. 01453 860004. email:
dursleybirdwatch@hotmail.com
or
maurice.bullen@care4free.net
http://beehive.thisisgoloucestershire.co.uk/dbwps.

ENGLAND

GLOUCESTERSHIRE NATURALISTS' SOCIETY, (1948; 600). John McLellan, 15 Charlton Road, Tetbury, Glos, GL8 8DX. 01666 504757; e-mail: johnmclellan.birds@virgin.net (for membership info) glosnats@blueyonder.co.uk

NORTH COTSWOLD ORNITHOLOGICAL SOCIETY, (1982; 60). T Hutton, 15 Green Close, Childswickham, Broadway, Worcs, WR12 7JJ. 01386 858511.

Ringing Groups
SEVERN ESTUARY GULL GROUP, M E Durham, 6 Glebe Close, Frampton-on-Severn, Glos, GL2 7EL. 01452 741312.

SEVERN VALE RG, R Hearn, Wildfowl & Wetlands Trust, Slimbridge, Glos, GL2 7BT. 01453 891900 ext 185; e-mail: richard.hearn@wwt.org.uk

WILDFOWL & WETLANDS TRUST, R Hearn, Wildfowl & Wetlands Trust, Slimbridge, Glos, GL2 7BT. 01453 891900 ext 185; e-mail: richard.hearn@wwt.org.uk

RSPB Local Group
GLOUCESTERSHIRE, (1972; 787). David Cramp, 2 Ellenor, Alderton, Tewkesbury, GL20 8NZ. 01242 620281.

Wildlife Hospital
GLOUCESTER WILDLIFE RESCUE CENTRE, Alan and Louise Brockbank, 2 Home Farm, Hartpury, Glos, GL19 3DE. 01452 700038; e-mail: louise.brockbank@lineone.net http://beehive.thisisgloucestershire.co.uk/gloswildliferescue
Intensive care, treatment and rehabilitation facilities. Vetinary support. No restrictions or conditions.

VALE WILDLIFE RESCUE - WILDLIFE HOSPITAL & REHABILITATION CENTRE, Ms Caroline Gould, Station Road, Beckford, Tewkesbury, Glos, GL20 7AN. 01386 882288; (Fax)01386 882299; e-mail: info@vwr.org.uk
www.vwr.org.uk
All wild birds. Intensive care. Registered charity. Veterinary support.

Wildlife Trust
GLOUCESTERSHIRE WILDLIFE TRUST, (1961; 6,200). Dulverton Building, Robinswood Hill Country Park, Reservoir Road, Gloucester, GL4 6SX. 01452 383333; (fax)01452 383334; e-mail: info@gloucesterwildlifetrust.co.uk
www.gloucesterwildlife.co.uk

HAMPSHIRE

Bird Atlas/Avifauna
Birds of Hampshire by J M Clark and J A Eyre (Hampshire Ornithological Society, 1993).

Bird Recorder
John Clark, 4 Cygnet Court, Old Cove Road, Fleet, Hants, GU51 2RL. Tel/fax 01252 623397; e-mail: johnclark@cygnetcourt.demon.co.uk

Bird Reports
HAMPSHIRE BIRD REPORT (1955-), from Mrs Margaret Boswell, 5 Clarence Road, Lyndhurst, Hants, SO43 7AL. 023 8028 2105; e-mail: maq.bos@btinternet.com

HANTS/SURREY BORDER BIRD REPORT (1971-), from Recorder.

BTO Regional Representative & Regional Development Officer
Glynne C Evans, Waverley, Station Road, Chilbolton, Stockbridge, Hants, SO20 6AL. H:01264 860697; W:01962 847435; e-mail: hantsbto@hotmail.com

Clubs
HAMPSHIRE ORNITHOLOGICAL SOCIETY, (1979; 955). Peter Dudley, 3 Copsewood Road, Hythe, Southampton, SO45 5DX. 02380 847149; e-mail: peter.dudley@lineone.net

SOUTHAMPTON & DISTRICT BIRD GROUP, (1994; 100). Les Stride, 196 Calmore Road, Calmore, Southampton, SO40 2RA. 023 8086 8058; e-mail: lestri@compuserve.com

Ringing Groups
FARLINGTON RG, D A Bell, 38 Holly Grove, Fareham, Hants, PO16 7UP.

ITCHEN RG, W F Simcox, 10 Holdaway Close, Kingsworthy, Winchester, SO23 7QH.

LOWER TEST RG, J Pain, Owlery Holt, Nations Hill, Kingsworthy, Winchester, SO23 7QY. 023 8066 7919; e-mail: jessp@hwt.org.uk

RSPB Local Groups
BASINGSTOKE, (1979; 90). Peter Hutchins, 35

ENGLAND

Woodlands, Overton, Whitchurch, RG25 3HN. 01256 770831.

NORTH EAST HAMPSHIRE, (1976; 350). Graham Dumbleton, 28 Castle Street, Fleet, Hants, GU52 7ST. 01252 622699.

PORTSMOUTH, (1974; 205). Gordon Humby, 19 Charlesworth Gardens, Waterlooville, Hants, PO7 6AU. 02392 353949.

WINCHESTER & DISTRICT, (1974; 152). Maurice Walker, Jesmond, 1 Compton Way, Olivers Battery, Winchester, SO22 4EY. 01962 854033.

Wildlife Hospital
NEW FOREST OWL SANCTUARY, Bruce Berry, New Forest Owl Sanctuary, Crow Lane, Crow, Ringwood, Hants, BH24 1EA. 01425 476487; A selection of owls, hawks and falcons from around the world with flying demonstrations at set times throughout the day. An opportunity to observe birds of prey at close range, an enjoyable day for the whole family. Open daily from Feb to Nov.
e-mail: nfosowls@aol.com
www.owlsanctuary.co.uk

Wildlife Trust
HAMPSHIRE AND ISLE OF WIGHT WILDLIFE TRUST, (1960; 11,295). Woodside House, Woodside Road, Eastleigh, Hampshire SO50 4ET. 023 80613636; (Fax)023 80688900;
e-mail: feedback@hwt.org.uk
www.hwt.org.uk

2 High Street, Newport, Isle of Wight, PO30 1SS. Tel/Fax: 01983 533 180
e-mail: feedback@hwt.org.uk

HEREFORDSHIRE

Bird Recorder
Steve Coney, Lion's Den, Bredwardine, Hereford, HR3 6DE. 01981 500236;
e-mail: coney@bluecarrots.com

Bird Report
HEREFORDSHIRE ORNITHOLOGICAL CLUB ANNUAL REPORT (1951-), from Mr I Evans, 12 Brockington Drive, Tupsley, Hereford , HR1 1TA. 01432 265509; e-mail: iforelaine@care4free.net.

BTO Regional Representative
Steve Coney, Lion's Den, Bredwardine, Hereford, HR3 6DE. 01981 500236;
e-mail: coney@bluecarrots.com

Club
HEREFORDSHIRE ORNITHOLOGICAL CLUB, (1950;

407). TM Weale, Foxholes, Bringsty Common, Worcester, WR6 5UN. 01886 821368.
www.herefordshirebirding.net

Ringing Group
LLANCILLO RG, Dr G R Geen, 6 The Copse, Bannister Green, Felsted, Dunmow, Essex, CM6 3NP. 01371 820189; e-mail: thegeens@aol.com

Wildlife Hospital
ATHENE BIRD SANCTUARY, B N Bayliss, 61 Chartwell Road, Hereford, HR1 2TU. 01432 273259. Birds of prey, ducks and waders, seabirds, pigeons and doves. Heated cages, small pond. Veterinary support.

Wildlife Trust
HEREFORDSHIRE NATURE TRUST, (1962; 1,700). Lower House Farm, Ledbury Road, Tupsley, Hereford, HR1 1UT. 01432 356872; fax 01432 275489; e-mail: herefordwt@cix.co.uk
www.wildlifetrust.org.uk/hereford

HERTFORDSHIRE

Bird Atlas/Avifauna
Birds at Tring Reservoirs by R Young et al (Hertfordshire Natural History Society, 1996).

Mammals, Amphibians and Reptiles of Hertfordshire by Hertfordshire NHS in association with Training Publications Ltd, 3 Finway Court, Whippendell Road, Watford WD18 7EN, (2001).

The Breeding Birds of Hertfordshire by K W Smith et al (Herts NHS, 1993).

Bird Recorder
Mike Ilett, 14 Cowper Crescent, Bengeo, Hertford, Herts, SG14 3DY.
e-mail: michael.ilett@uk.tesco.com

Bird Report
HERTFORDSHIRE BIRD REPORT (1908-1998), from Hon Secretary, Herts Bird Club, 46 Manor Way, Boreham Wood, Herts, WD6 1QY.

BTO Regional Representative & Regional Development Officer
Chris Dee, 26 Broadleaf Avenue, Thorley Park, Bishop's Stortford, Herts, CM23 4JY. H:01279 755637; e-mail: chris_w_dee@hotmail.com

Clubs
FRIENDS OF TRING RESERVOIRS, (1993; 350). Judith Knight, 381 Bideford Green, Linslade, Leighton Buzzard, Beds, LU7 2TY. 01525 378161. www.tringreservoirs.btinternet.co.uk

269

ENGLAND

HERTFORDSHIRE BIRD CLUB, (1971; 290). Jim Terry, 46 Manor Way, Borehamwood, Herts, WD6 1QY. 020 8905 1461;
e-mail: jim@jayjoy.fsnet.co.uk

Ringing Groups
AYLESBURY VALE RG (main activity at Marsworth), S M Downhill, 12 Millfield, Berkhamsted, Herts, HP4 2PB. 01442 865821;
e-mail: smdjbd@waitrose.com

MAPLE CROSS RG, P Delaloye, 34 Watford Road, Croxley Green, Herts, WD3 3BJ. 01923 442182;
e-mail: delaloye34@lineone.net

RYE MEADS RG, D G Baggott, 86 Fordwich Rise, Hertford, SG14 2DE. www.rmrg.care4free.net

TRING RG, Mick A'Court, 6 Chalkshire Cottages, Chalkshire Road, Butlers Cross, Bucks ,HP17 0TW. H:01296 623610; W:01494 462246;
e-mail: mick@focusrite.com

RSPB Local Groups
CHORLEYWOOD & DISTRICT, (1977; 128). Sam Thomas, 01923 449917.

HARPENDEN, (1974; 1,000). Peter Thomley, 10 Lea Road, Harpenden, Herts, AL5 4PG. 01582 620755.

HEMEL HEMPSTEAD, (1973; 130). Paul Green, 207 Northridge Way, Hemel Hempstead, Herts, HP1 2AU. 01442 266637;
e-mail: paul@310nrwhh.freeserve.co.uk.

HITCHIN & LETCHWORTH, (1973; 106). Ms Jean Crystal, Amadeus House, Charlton, Hitchin, Herts, SG4 7TE. 01462 433912;
e-mail: jeanlcrystal@aol.com
http://uk.geocities.com/hitchin_letchworth_rspb

POTTERS BAR & BARNET, (1977; 1,800). Stan Bailey, 23 Bowmans Close, Potters Bar, Herts, EN6 5NN. 01707 646073.

ST ALBANS, (1979; 1,550). John Maxfield, 46 Gladeside, Jersey Farm, St Albans, Herts, AL4 9JA. 01727 832688; www.antram.demon.co.uk/
e-mail: peterantram@antram.demon.co.uk

SOUTH EAST HERTS, (1971; 2,001). Phil Blatcher, 3 Churchfields, Broxbourne, Herts, EN10 7JU. 01992 441024;
e-mail: SE_Herts_RSPB@hotmail.com

STEVENAGE, (1982; 1,300). Mrs Ann Collis, 16 Stevenage Road, Walkern, Herts, 01438 861547.

WATFORD, (1974; 522). John Britten, Harlestone, 98 Sheepcot Lane, Garston, Watford, WD25 0EB. 01923 673205;
e-mail: john.britten@btinternet.com;
http://members.tripod.co.uk/watford_rspb/

Wildlife Hospital
SWAN CARE, Secretary, Swan Care, 14 Moorland Road, Boxmoor, Hemel Hempstead, Herts, HP1 1NH. 01442 251961. Swans. Sanctuary and treatment centre. Veterinary support.

Wildlife Trust
HERTS & MIDDLESEX WILDLIFE TRUST, (1964; 8500). Grebe House, St Michael's Street, St Albans, Herts, AL3 4SN. 01727 858901; fax 01727 854542; e-mail: info@hmwt.org
www.wildlifetrust.org.uk/herts

ISLE OF WIGHT

Bird Recorder
G Sparshott, Leopards Farm, Main Road, Havenstreet, Isle of Wight, PO33 4DR. 01983 882549.

Bird Reports
ISLE OF WIGHT BIRD REPORT (1986-) (Pre-1986 not available), from DJ Hunnybun, 40 Churchill Road, Cowes, Isle of Wight, PO31 8HH.

BTO Regional Representative
James C Gloyn, 3 School Close, Newchurch, Isle of Wight, PO36 0NL. 01983 865567;
e-mail: gloynjc@yahoo.com

Clubs
ISLE OF WIGHT NATURAL HISTORY & ARCHAEOLOGICAL SOCIETY, (1919; 500). Dr Margaret Jackson, The Fruitery, Brook Hill, Brook, Newport, Isle of Wight, PO30 6EP. 01983 740015.

ISLE OF WIGHT ORNITHOLOGICAL GROUP, (1986; 135). DJ Hunnybun, 40 Churchill Road, Cowes, Isle of Wight, PO31 8HH. 01983 882549.

RSPB Local Group
ISLE OF WIGHT, (1979; 206). John Cole, 12 Monterey Road, Ryde, Isle of Wight, PO33 3JR. 01983 611797.

Wildlife Trust
Director, See Hampshire.

KENT

Bird Atlas/Avifauna
The Birds of Kent by D W Taylor et al (Kent Ornithological Society, 1981).

Kent Ornithological Society Winter Bird Survey by N Tardivel (KOS, 1984).

Bird Recorder
Don Taylor, 1 Rose Cottages, Old Loose Hill, Loose, Maidstone, Kent, ME15 0BN. 01622 745641; e-mail: Don.Taylor@care4free.net

Bird Reports
DUNGENESS BIRD OBSERVATORY REPORT (1989-), from Warden, see Reserves,

KENT BIRD REPORT (1952-), from Dave Sutton, 61 Alpha Road, Birchington, Kent, CT7 9ED. 01843 842541; e-mail: dave@sutton8.freeserve.co.uk

SANDWICH BAY BIRD OBSERVATORY REPORT, from Warden, see Reserves.

BTO Regional Representative & Regional Development Officer
RR, Martin Coath, 77 Oakhill Road, Sevenoaks, Kent, TN13 1NU. 01732 460710; e-mail: mcoath@waitrose.com

Club
KENT ORNITHOLOGICAL SOCIETY, (1952; 720). Dr Grant Hazlehurst, PO Box 1211, London, NW1 1AE. 020 8650 7063.

Ringing Groups
DARTFORD RG, P E Jones, Sheppards Barn, Hurst Green, Oxted, Surrey, RH8 9BS.

DUNGENESS BIRD OBSERVATORY, David Walker, Dungeness Bird Observatory, Dungeness, Romney Marsh, Kent, TN29 9NA. 01797 321309; e-mail: dungeness.obs@tinyonline.co.uk www.dungenessbirdobs.org.uk

RECULVER RG, Chris Hindle, 42 Glenbervie Drive, Herne Bay, Kent, CT6 6QL. 01227 373070; e-mail: christopherhindle@hotmail.com

SANDWICH BAY BIRD OBSERVATORY, K J Webb, Sandwich Bay Bird Observatory, Guilford Road, Sandwich, Kent, CT13 9PF. 01304 617341; e-mail: kevwebb88@hotmail.com

SWALE WADER GROUP, Rod Smith, 67 York Avenue, Chatham, Kent, ME5 9ES. 01634 865863; e-mail: rod.Smith@care4free.net

RSPB Local Groups
CANTERBURY, (1973; 230). Jean Bomber, St Heliers, 30a Castle Road, Tankerton, Whitstable, Kent, CT5 2DY. 01227 277725.

GRAVESEND & DISTRICT, (1977; 250). Peter Heathcote, 9 Greenfinches, New Barn, Kent, DA3 7ND. 01474 702498:

e-mail: peter@heathcote100.freeserve.co.uk www.gravesend-rspb.freeserve.co.uk

MAIDSTONE, (1973; 250). Dick Marchese, 11 Bathurst Road, Staplehurst, Tonbridge, Kent, TN12 0LG. 01580 892458.

MEDWAY, (1974; 230). Sue Carter, 31 Ufton Lane, Sittingbourne, ME10 1JB. 01795 427854 www.medway-rspb.pwp.blueyonder.co.uk

SEVENOAKS, (1974; 350). Bernard Morris, New House Farm, Kilkhampton, Bude, Cornwall, EX23 9RZ. 01288 321727; or 07967 564699;(Fax)01288 321838; e-mail: bernard@amorris32.freeserve.co.uk

SOUTH EAST KENT, (1981; 260). Keith Shepherd, 23 Barton Road, Dover, Kent, CT16 9NF. 01304 225757.

THANET, (1976; 200). Paul Hale, 2 Shutler Road, Broadstairs, Kent, CT10 1HD. 01843 601482; e-mail: paul.hale@care4free.net

TONBRIDGE, (1975; 1,700). Ms Gabrielle Sutcliffe, 1 Postern Heath Cottages, Postern Lane, Tonbridge, Kent, TN11 0QU. 01732 365583.

Wildlife Hospital
RAPTOR CENTRE, Eddie Hare, Ivy Cottage, Groombridge Place, Groombridge, Tunbridge Wells, Kent, TN3 9QG. 01892 861175; fax 01892 863761. www.raptorcentre.co.uk
Birds of prey. Veterinary support.

Wildlife Trust
KENT WILDLIFE TRUST, (1958; 17,000). Tyland Barn, Sandling, Maidstone, Kent, ME14 3BD. 01622 662012; (fax)01622 671390; e-mail: kentwildlife@cix.co.uk www.wildlifetrust.org.uk/kent

LANCASHIRE

Bird Atlas/Avifauna
An Atlas of Breeding Birds of Lancaster and District by Ken Harrison (Lancaster & District Birdwatching Society, 1995).

Breeding Birds of Lancashire and North Merseyside (2001), sponsored by North West Water. Contact: Bob Pyefinch, 12 Bannistre Court, Tarleton, Preston PR4 6HA.

Bird Recorder
(See also Manchester),

Inc North Merseyside, Steve White, 102 Minster Court, Crown Street, Liverpool, L7 3QD. 0151 707 2744; e-mail: lwildlife@cix.co.uk

Bird Reports

BIRDS OF LANCASTER & DISTRICT (1959-), from Secretary. Lancaster & District BWS.

EAST LANCASHIRE ORNITHOLOGISTS' CLUB BIRD REPORT (1982-), from Secretary.

BLACKBURN & DISTRICT BIRD CLUB ANNUAL REPORT (1992-), from Doreen Bonner, 6 Winston Road, Blackburn, BB1 8BJ. Tel/fax;01254 261480; www.blackburnbirds.freeuk.com.

FYLDE BIRD REPORT (1983-), from Secretary Fylde Bird Club.

LANCASHIRE BIRD REPORT (1914-), from Secretary. Lancs & Cheshire Fauna Soc.

BTO Regional Representatives & Regional Development Officer

EAST RR, Tony Cooper, 28 Peel Park Avenue, Clitheroe, Lancs, BB7 1ET. 01200 424577; e-mail: tonycooper@beeb.net

NORTH & WEST RR & RDO, Dave Sharpe, 17 Greenwood Avenue, Bolton-le-Sands, Carnforth, Lancs, LA5 8AN. H:01524 822492; e-mail: dave.s@airtime.co.uk

SOUTH RR, Philip Shearwood, Netherside, Green Lane, Whitestake, Preston, PR4 4AH. 01772 745488; e-mail: phil.shearwood@virgin.net

Clubs

BLACKBURN & DISTRICT BIRD CLUB, (1991; 134). Jim Bonner, 6 Winston Road, Blackburn, BB1 8BJ. Tel/fax;01254 261480.

CHORLEY & DISTRICT NATURAL HISTORY SOCIETY, (1979; 170). Phil Kirk, Millend, Dawbers Lane, Euxton, Chorley, Lancs, PR7 6EB. 01257 266783; e-mail: philkirk@clara.net www.philkirk.clara.net/cdnhs/

EAST LANCASHIRE ORNITHOLOGISTS' CLUB, (1955; 45). Doug Windle, 39 Stone Edge Road, Barrowford, Nelson, Lancs, BB9 6BB. 01282 617401; e-mail: doug.windle@care4free.net

FYLDE BIRD CLUB, (1982; 60). Paul Ellis, 18 Staining Rise, Blackpool, FY3 0BU. 01253 891281; e-mail: kinta.beaver@man.ac.uk or paulellis@fyldebirdclub.freeuk.com www.fyldebirdclub.freeuk.com

FYLDE NATURALISTS' SOCIETY, (1946; 120). Gerry Stephen, 10 Birch Way, Poulton-le-Fylde, Blackpool, FY6 7SF. 01253 895195.

LANCASHIRE & CHESHIRE FAUNA SOCIETY, (1914; 140). Dave Bickerton, 64 Petre Crescent, Rishton, Lancs, BB1 4RB. 01254 886257; e-mail: bickertond@aol.com

LANCASHIRE BIRD CLUB, (1996). Dave Bickerton, 64 Petre Crescent, Rishton, Lancs, BB1 4RB. 01254 886257; e-mail: bickertond@aol.com

LANCASTER & DISTRICT BIRD WATCHING SOCIETY, (1959; 200). Andrew Cadman, 57 Greenways, Over Kellet, Carnforth, Lancs, LA6 1DE. 01524 734462; e-mail: andrewokuk@yahoo.co.uk.

ROSSENDALE ORNITHOLOGISTS' CLUB, (1976; 35). Ian Brady, 25 Church St, Newchurch, Rossendale, Lancs, BB4 9EX. 01706 222120.

Ringing Groups

FYLDE RG, G Barnes, 17 Lomond Avenue, Marton, Blackpool, FY3 9QL.

MORECAMBE BAY WADER RG, J Sheldon, 415 West Shore Park, Barrow-in-Furness, Cumbria, LA14 3XZ. 01229 473102.

NORTH LANCS RG, John Wilson BEM, 40 Church Hill Avenue, Warton, Carnforth, Lancs, LA5 9NU.

SOUTH WEST LANCASHIRE RG, J D Fletcher, 4 Hawksworth Drive, Freshfield, Formby, Merseyside, L37 7EZ. 01704 877837.

RSPB Local Groups

BLACKPOOL, (1983; 170). Alan Stamford, 6 Kensington Road, Cleveleys, FY5 1EP. 01253 859662.

LANCASTER, (1972; 210). John Wilson BEM, 40 Church Hill Avenue, Warton, Carnforth, Lancs, LA5 9NU.

Wildlife Trust

THE WILDLIFE TRUST FOR LANCASHIRE, MANCHESTER AND NORTH MERSEYSIDE, (1962; 8,800). Cuerden Park Wildlife Centre, Shady Lane, Bamber Bridge, Preston, PR5 6AU. 01772 324129; fax: 01772 628849; e-mail: lancswt@cix.co.uk www.wildlifetrust.org.uk/lancashire

LEICESTERSHIRE & RUTLAND

Bird Recorder

(Lancashire and Rutland) Rob Fray, 5 New Park Road, Aylestone, Leicester, LE2 8AW. 0116 223 8491; e-mail: robfray@fray-r.freeserve.co.uk www.lros.org.uk

Bird Reports

LEICESTERSHIRE & RUTLAND BIRD REPORT (1941-), from Mrs S Graham, 5 Brading Road, Leicester, LE3 9BG. 0116 262 5505; e-mail: jsgraham83@aol.com

RUTLAND NAT HIST SOC ANNUAL REPORT (1965-), from Secretary.

BTO Regional Representative

LEICESTER & RUTLAND, Jim Graham, 5 Brading Road, Leicester, LE3 9BG. H:0116 262 5505; e-mail: jsgraham83@aol.com

Clubs

BIRSTALL BIRDWATCHING CLUB, (1976; 50). Ken J Goodrich, 6 Riversdale Close, Birstall, Leicester, LE4 4EH. 0116 267 4813.

LEICESTERSHIRE & RUTLAND ORNITHOLOGICAL SOCIETY, (1941; 462). Mrs Marion Vincent, 48 Templar Way, Rothley, Leicester, LE7 7RB. 0116 230 3405. www.lros.org.uk

MARKET HARBOROUGH & DISTRICT NATURAL HISTORY SOCIETY, (1971; 40). Mrs Sue Allibone, 20 Smyth Close, Market Harborough, Leics, LE16 7NS. 01858 410385.

RUTLAND NATURAL HISTORY SOCIETY, (1964; 256). Mrs L Worrall, 6 Redland Close, Barrowden, Oakham, Rutland, LE15 8ES. 01572 747302.

Ringing Groups

RUTLAND WATER RG, D Roizer, 38 Kestrel Road, Oakham, Rutland, LE15 6BU.

STANFORD RG, M J Townsend, 87 Dunton Road, Broughton Astley, Leics, LE9 6NA.

RSPB Local Groups

LEICESTER, (1969; 400). Chris Woolass, 136 Braunstone Lane, Leicester, LE3 2RW. 0116 2990078; e-mail: chris@jclwoolass.freeserve.co.uk

LOUGHBOROUGH, (1970; 300). Robert Orton, 12 Avon Road, Barrow-on-Soar, Leics, LE12 8LE. 1509 413936.

Wildlife Trust

LEICESTERSHIRE & RUTLAND WILDLIFE TRUST, (1956; 3,000). Longfellow Road, Knighton Fields, Leicester, LE2 6BT. 0116 270 2999; (fax)0116 270 9555; e-mail: leicswt@cix.co.uk

LINCOLNSHIRE

Bird Recorders

NORTH, Position vacant.

SOUTH, Position vacant.

Bird Reports

LINCOLNSHIRE BIRD REPORT inc Gibraltar Point Bird Obs (1979-), from RK Watson, 8 High Street, Skegness, Lincs, PE25 3NW. 01754 763481.

SCUNTHORPE & NORTH WEST LINCOLNSHIRE BIRD REPORT (1973-), from Secretary, Scunthorpe Museum Society, Ornithological Section.

BTO Regional Representatives & Regional Development Officer

EAST RR, Position vacant.

NORTH RR, Position vacant.

SOUTH RR, Richard & Kay Heath, 56 Pennytoft Lane, Pinchbeck, Spalding, Lincs, PE11 3PQ. 01775 767055; e-mail: heathsrk@ecossetel.com

WEST RR, Peter Overton, Hilltop Farm, Welbourn, Lincoln, LN5 0QH. Work 01400 273323; e-mail: nyika@biosearch.org.uk

RDO, Nicholas Watts, Vine House Farm, Deeping St Nicholas, Spalding, Lincs, PE11 3DG. 01775 630208.

Club

LINCOLNSHIRE BIRD CLUB, (1979; 220). M Harrison, Sherbrooke, Holme Road, Kirton Holme, Boston, Lincs, PE20 1SY. 01205 290575.

SCUNTHORPE MUSEUM SOCIETY (Ornithological Section), (1973; 50). Craig Nimick, 115 Grange Lane South, Scunthorpe, N Lincs, DN16 3BW. 01724 339659.

Ringing Groups

GIBRALTAR POINT BIRD OBSERVATORY, Adrian Blackburn, Suleska, 1 Richmond Road, Retford, Notts, DN22 6SJ. 01777 706516; (M)07718 766873; e-mail: blackburns@suleska.freeserve.co.uk.

MID LINCOLNSHIRE RG, J Mawer, 18 Standish Lane, Immingham, Lincs, DN40 2HA. 01469 518549.

WASH WADER RG, P L Ireland, 27 Hainfield Drive, Solihull, W Midlands, B91 2PL. 0121 704 1168; e-mail: phil_ireland@bigfoot.com

RSPB Local Groups

GRIMSBY AND CLEETHORPES DISTRICT, (1986; 2200). Brian Sykes, 93 Humberstone Road, Grimsby, Lincs, 01472 320418
e-mail: brian.sykes3@ntlworld.com
www.rspb.members.easyspace.com

LINCOLN, (1974; 250). Peter Skelson, 26 Parksgate Avenue, Lincoln, LN6 7HP. 01522 695747; e-mail: peterskelson@hotmail.com
www.lincoln.rspb.care4free.net

SOUTH LINCOLNSHIRE, (1987; 350). Barry Hancock, The Limes, Meer Booth Road, Antons Gowt, Boston, Lincs, PE22 7BG. 01205 280057.

Wildlife Hospital

FEATHERED FRIENDS WILD BIRD RESCUE, Colin Riches, 5 Blacksmith Lane, Thorpe-on-the-Hill, Lincoln, LN6 9BQ. 01522 684874.
All species. Purpose-built hospital unit. Heated cages, etc. Membership and adoption scheme available. Quarterly newsletter. Veterinary support.

Wildlife Trust

LINCOLNSHIRE WILDLIFE TRUST, (1948; 17,000). Banovallum House, Manor House Street, Horncastle, Lincs, LN9 5HF. 01507 526667; (fax)01507 525732; e-mail: info@lincstrust.co.uk
www.lincstrust.co.uk

LONDON, GREATER

Bird Atlas/Avifauna

New Atlas of Breeding Birds of the London Area by Keith Betton (London Natural History Society, in preparation).

Bird Recorder see also Surrey

Andrew Self, 16 Harp Island Close, Neasden, London, NW10 0DF.
e-mail: andrewself@lineone.net
www.users.globalnet.co.uk/~lnhsweb

Bird Report

CROYDON BIRD SURVEY (1995), from Secretary, Croydon RSPB Group, 020 8777 9370.

LONDON BIRD REPORT (20-mile radius of St Paul's Cath) (1936-), from Catherine Schmitt, 4 Falkland Avenue, London, N3 1QR.

BTO Regional Representative & Regional Development Officer

LONDON & MIDDLESEX RR, Derek Coleman, 23c Park Hill, Carshalton, Surrey, SM5 3SA. 020 8669 7421.

Clubs

LONDON NATURAL HISTORY SOCIETY (Ornithology Section), (1858; 1,100). Ms N Duckworth, 9 Abbey Court, Cerne Abbas, Dorchester, Dorset, DT2 7JH. 01300 341 195.

MARYLEBONE BIRDWATCHING SOCIETY, (1981; 100). Judy Powell, 7 Rochester Terrace, London, NW1 9JN. 020 7485 0863;
e-mail: birdsmbs@yahoo.co.uk
www.geocities.com/birdsmbs

Ringing Groups

LONDON GULL STUDY GROUP, Mark Fletcher, 24 The Gowans, Sutton-on-the-Forest, York, YO61 1DJ. e-mail: m.fletcher@col.gov.uk

RUNNYMEDE RG, D G Harris, 22 Blossom Waye, Hounslow, TW5 9HD.
e-mail: daveharris@tinyonline.co.uk

RSPB Local Groups

BEXLEY, (1979; 3,500). David James, 78 Colney Road, Dartford, DA1 1UH. 01322 274791;
e-mail: dartdiva56@hotmail.com

BROMLEY, (1972; 273). Bob Francis, 2 Perry Rise, Forest Hill, London, SE23 2QL. 020 8669 9325.
www.bromleyrspb.org.uk

CENTRAL LONDON, (1970; 370). Miss Annette Warrick, 12 Tredegar Sq, London, E3 5AD. 020 8981 9624;
e-mail: annette@warricka.freeserve.co.uk
www.janja@dircon.co.uk/rspb

CROYDON, (1973; 4,000). Sheila Mason, 5 Freshfields, Shirley, Croydon, CR0 7QS. 020 8777 9370. www.croydon-rspb.org.uk

ENFIELD, (1971; 2,700). Norman G Hudson, 125 Morley Hill, Enfield, Middx, EN2 0BQ. 020 8363 1431.

HAVERING, (1972; 270). Eric Hammond, 33 Canterbury Avenue, Upminster, Essex, RM14 3LD. 01708 222230.

NORTH LONDON, (1974; 3,000). John Parsons, 65 Rutland Gardens, Harringay, London, N4 1JW. 020 8802 9537.

NORTH WEST LONDON, (1983; 800). Bob Husband, The Firs, 49 Carson Road, Cockfosters, Barnet, Herts, EN4 9EN. 020 8441 8742.

PINNER & DISTRICT, (1972; 300). Dennis Bristow, 118 Crofts Road, Harrow, Middx, HA1 2PJ. 020 8863 5026.

RICHMOND & TWICKENHAM, (1979; 2,300). Steve Harrington, 93 Shaftesbury Way, Twickenham, TW2 5RW. 020 8898 4539.

WEST LONDON, (1973; 400). Alan Bender, 6 Allenby Road, Southall, Middx, UB1 2HQ. 020 8571 0285.

Wildlife Hospitals
WILDLIFE RESCUE & AMBULANCE SERVICE, Barry and June Smitherman, 19 Chesterfield Road, Enfield, Middx, EN3 6BE. 020 8292 5377.
All categories of wild birds. Emergency ambulance with full rescue equipment, boats, ladders etc. Own treatment centre and aviaries. Veterinary support. Essential to telephone first.

Wildlife Trust
LONDON WILDLIFE TRUST, (1981; 7,500). Harling House, 47-51 Great Suffolk Street, London, SE1 0BS. 0207 261 0447; fax 0207 261 0538; e-mail: enquiries@wildlondon.org.uk www.wildlifetrust.org.uk/london

MANCHESTER, GREATER

Bird Atlas/Avifauna
Breeding Birds in Greater Manchester by Philip Holland et al (1984).

Bird Recorder
Mrs A Judith Smith, 12 Edge Green Street, Ashton-in-Makerfield, Wigan, WN4 8SL. 01942 712615; www.gmbirds.freeserve.co.uk e-mail: judith@gmbirds.freeserve.co.uk

Bird Reports
BIRDS IN GREATER MANCHESTER (1976-), from Mrs M McCormick, 91 Sinderland Road, Altrincham WA14 5JJ (only editions up to year 2000. Year 2001 onwards from County Recorder).

LEIGH ORNITHOLOGICAL SOCIETY BIRD REPORT (1971-), from J Critchley, 2 Albany Grove, Tyldesley, Manchester, M29 7NE. 01942 884644.

BTO Regional Representative & Regional Development Officer
RR, Mrs A Judith Smith, 12 Edge Green Street, Ashton-in-Makerfield, Wigan, WN4 8SL. 01942 712615; www.gmbirds.freeserve.co.uk e-mail: judith@gmbirds.freeserve.co.uk

RDO, Jim Jeffery, 20 Church Lane, Romiley, Stockport, Cheshire, SK6 4AA. H:0161 494 5367; W:01625 522107 ext 112; e-mail: j.jeffery@kudos-idd.com

Clubs
GREATER MANCHESTER BIRD CLUB, (1954; 60). Dr R Sandling, 17 Range Road, Stalybridge, Cheshire, SK15 Z44.

GREATER MANCHESTER BIRD RECORDING GROUP (2002 ; 40), (restricted to contributors to the county bird report). Mrs A Judith Smith. www.gmbirds.freeserve.co.uk e-mail: judith@gmbirds.freeserve.co.uk

HALE ORNITHOLOGISTS, (1968; 58). Ms Diana Grellier, 8 Apsley Grove, Bowdon, Altrincham, Cheshire, WA14 3AH. 0161 928 9165.

LEIGH ORNITHOLOGICAL SOCIETY, (1971; 150). Mr D Shallcross, 10 Holden Brook Close, Leigh, Lancs, WN7 2HL. 01942 260161 www.leighos.org.uk

ROCHDALE FIELD NATURALISTS' SOCIETY, (1970; 90). Mrs J P Wood, 196 Castleton Road, Thornham, Royton, Oldham, OL2 6UP. 0161 345 2012; www.rochdaleonline.org (listed under societies and events).

STOCKPORT BIRDWATCHING SOCIETY, (1972; 80). Dave Evans, 36 Tatton Road South, Stockport, Cheshire, SK4 4LU. 0161 432 9513; e-mail: evans@36tatton.freeserve.co.uk

Ringing Groups
LEIGH RG, A J Gramauskas, 21 Elliot Avenue, Golborne, Warrington, WA3 3DU. 0151 929215.

SOUTH MANCHESTER RG, C M Richards, Fairhaven, 13 The Green, Handforth, Wilmslow, Cheshire, SK9 3AG. 01625 524527; e-mail: cliveandray.richards@care4free.net

RSPB Local Groups
BOLTON, (1978; 550). Peter Young, 83 Church Street, Blackrod, Bolton, BL6 5EE. 01204 692213; email: pfyoung@tiscali.co.uk

MANCHESTER, (2000). Peter Wolstenholme, 31 South Park Road, Gatley, Cheshire, SK8 4AL. 0161 428 2175.

STOCKPORT, (1979; 250). Brian Hallworth, 69 Talbot Street, Hazel Grove, Stockport, SK7 4BJ. 0161 456 5328; e-mail: bwh.hgsmgm@freeserve.co.uk

WIGAN, (1973; 80). Allan Rimmer, 206 Hodges Street, Wigan, Lancs, WN6 7JG. 01942 241402.

Wildlife Hospital
THREE OWLS BIRD SANCTUARY AND RESERVE, Trustee, Nigel Fowler, Wolstenholme Fold, Norden,

Rochdale, OL11 5UD. 01706 642162; 24-hr
helpline 07973 819389; www.threeowls.co.uk
e-mail: info@threeowls.co.uk
Registered charity. All species of wild bird.
Rehabilitation and release on Sanctuary Reserve.
Open every Sunday 12pm-5pm, otherwise visitors
welcome by appointment. Bi-monthly newsletter.
Veterinary support.

Wildlife Trust
Director, See Lancashire.

MERSEYSIDE & WIRRAL

Bird Atlas see Cheshire.

Bird Recorders see Cheshire; Lancashire

Bird Reports see also Cheshire
HILBRE BIRD OBSERVATORY REPORT, from
Warden, see Reserves,

NORTHWESTERN BIRD REPORT (1938- irregular),
from Secretaries, Merseyside Naturalists' Assoc.

BTO Regional Representatives
MERSEYSIDE RR, Bob Harris, 2 Dulas Road,
Wavertree Green, Liverpool, L15 6UA. Work 0151
706 4311; e-mail: harris@liv.ac.uk

WIRRAL RR, Kelvin Britton, 9B Kingsmead Road
South, Prenton, Birkenhead, Merseyside, CH43
6TA. 0151 653 9751;
e-mail: staff.kmb@birkenhead.wirral.sch.uk

Clubs
LIVERPOOL ORNITHOLOGISTS' CLUB
(membership by invitation), (1953; 40). Mrs V
McFarland, The Cedars, Quakers Lane, Heswall,
Wirral, CH60 6RD.

MERSEYSIDE NATURALISTS'
ASSOCIATION, (1938; 260).
Steven Cross, 58 Kingswood
Avenue, Waterloo, Liverpool, L22
4RL.

WIRRAL BIRD CLUB, (1977; 150).
Mrs Hilda Truesdale, Cader, 8 Park
Road, Meols, Wirral, CH47 7BG. 0151 632 2705.

Ringing Groups
MERSEYSIDE RG, P Slater, 45 Greenway Road,
Speke, Liverpool, L24 7RY.

SOUTH WEST LANCASHIRE RG, J D Fletcher, 4
Hawksworth Drive, Freshfield, Formby, Merseyside,
L37 7EZ. 01704 877837.

RSPB Local Groups
LIVERPOOL, (1966; 162). Chris Tynan, 10 Barker
Close, Huyton, Liverpool, L36 0XU. 0151 480
7938; e-mail: christtynan@aol.com
www.livbird.pwp.blueyonder.co.uk

SEFTON COAST, (1980; 199). Peter Taylor, 26
Tilston Road, Walton, Liverpool, L9 6AJ. 0151 524
1905; e-mail: ptaylor@liv.ac.uk.

SOUTHPORT, (1974; 250). Group Leader, 01704
872421.

WIRRAL, (1982; 120). Steve Woolfall, 85
Ridgemere Road, Pensby, Wirral, Merseyside,
CH61 8RR. 0151 648 6007;
e-mail: swoolfall@btinternet.com
http://website.lineone.net/~dave.jowitt/

Wildlife Trust
Director, See Lancashire.

NORFOLK

Bird Atlas/Avifauna
The Birds of Norfolk by Moss Taylor, Michael
Seago, Peter Allard & Don Dorling (Pica Press,
1999).

Bird Recorder
Giles Dunmore, 49 Nelson Road, Sheringham,
Norfolk, NR26 8DA. 01263 822550.

Bird Reports
*CLEY BIRD CLUB 10-KM SQUARE BIRD REPORT
(1987-)*, from Secretary.

*NAR VALLEY ORNITHOLOGICAL SOCIETY ANNUAL
REPORT (1976-)*, from Secretary.

NORFOLK BIRD & MAMMAL REPORT (1953-), from
Secretary, Norfolk and Norwich Naturalists Society,
Castle Museum, Norwich, NR1 3JU.

*NORFOLK ORNITHOLOGISTS' ASSOC ANNUAL
REPORT (1961-)*, from Secretary.

BTO Regional Representatives
NORTH-EAST RR, Chris Hudson, Cornerstones,
Ringland Road, Taverham, Norwich, NR8 6TG.
01603 868805.

NORTH-WEST RR, Nick Gallichan, Walnut Cottage,
High Road, Tilney cum Islington, King's Lynn, PE34
3BN. 01553 617310;
e-mail: nick@strange-brew.freeserve.co.uk

SOUTH-EAST RR, Graham Coxall, 4 Shirley Close,
Frettenham, Norwich, NR12 7LW. 01603 737486.

SOUTH-WEST RR, Vince Matthews, Rose's Cottage, The Green, Merton, Thetford, Norfolk, IP25 6QU. 01953 884125; e-mail: yam@yamatthews.u-net.com

Clubs
CLEY BIRD CLUB, (1986; 300). Peter Gooden, 45 Charles Road, Holt, Norfolk, NR25 6DA. 01263 712368.

GREAT YARMOUTH BIRD CLUB, (1989; 79). Keith R Dye, 104 Wolseley Road, Great Yarmouth, Norfolk, NR31 0EJ. 01493 600705.

NAR VALLEY ORNITHOLOGICAL SOCIETY, (1976; 125). Ian Black, Three Chimneys, Tumbler Hill, Swaffham, Norfolk, PE37 7JG. 01760 724092; e-mail: ian_a_black@hotmail.com

NORFOLK & NORWICH NATURALISTS' SOCIETY, (1869; 490). Dr Tony Leech, 3 Eccles Road, Holt, Norfolk, NR25 6HJ. 01263 712282; e-mail: leecha@dialstart.net

NORFOLK BIRD CLUB, (1992; 350). Vernon Eve, Pebble House, The Street, Syderstone, King's Lynn, Norfolk, PE31 8SD. 01485 578121.

NORFOLK ORNITHOLOGISTS' ASSOCIATION, (1962; 1,100). Jed Andrews, Broadwater Road, Holme-next-Sea, Hunstanton, Norfolk, PE36 6LQ. 01485 525406.

Ringing Groups
BTO NUNNERY RG, Dawn Balmer, 39 Station Road, Thetford, Norfolk, IP24 1AW. e-mail: dawn.balmer@bto.org www.nunnery-ringing.org.uk

HOLME BIRD OBSERVATORY, J M Reed, 21 Hardings, Panshanger, Welwyn Garden City, Herts, AL7 2EQ. 01707 336351.

NORTH WEST NORFOLK RG, J M Reed, 21 Hardings, Panshanger, Welwyn Garden City, Herts, AL7 2EQ. 01707 336351.

SHERINGHAM RG, D Sadler, Denver House, 25 Holt Road, Sheringham, Norfolk, NR26 8NB. 01263 821904; e-mail: dhsadler@onetel.net.uk

UEA RG, D Thomas, 15 Grant Street, Norwich, NR2 4HA.

WASH WADER RG, P L Ireland, 27 Hainfield Drive, Solihull, W Midlands, B91 2PL. 0121 704 1168; e-mail: phil_ireland@bigfoot.com

WISSEY RG, Dr S J Browne, End Cottage, 24 Westgate Street, Hilborough, Norfolk, IP26 5BN. e-mail: sjbathome@aol.com

RSPB Local Groups
NORWICH, (1971; 330). Charles Seagrave, 2 Riverside Cottages, Barford, Norwich, NR9 4BE. 01603 759752; e-mail: seagrave@connectfree.co.uk www.NorwichRSPB.org.uk

WEST NORFOLK, (1977; 247). David Lake, 194B Wootton Road, King's Lynn, Norfolk, PE30 3BQ. 01553 673873; e-mail: davidnesta@hotmail.com http://freespace.virgin.net/ralph.bateman/index.html.

Wildlife Trust
NORFOLK WILDLIFE TRUST, (1926; 17,500). Bewick House, 22 Thorpe Road, Norwich, Norfolk NR1 1RY. 01603 625540; (fax)01603 598300. e-mail: admin@norfolkwildlifetrust.org.uk www.wildlifetrust.org.uk/norfolk

NORTHAMPTONSHIRE

Bird Recorder
Paul Gosling, 23 Newtown Road, Little Irchester, Northants, NN8 2DX. 01933 227709; e-mail: paul_gosling@lineone.net

Bird Report
NORTHAMPTONSHIRE BIRD REPORT (1969-), from Recorder.

BTO Regional Representative & Regional Development Officer
RR, Bill Metcalfe, Blendon, Rockingham Hills, Oundle, Peterborough, PE8 4QA. 01832 274797.

RDO, Bill Metcalfe, Blendon, Rockingham Hills, Oundle, Peterborough, PE8 4QA. 01832 274797.

Clubs
DAVENTRY NATURAL HISTORY SOCIETY, (1970; 18). Leslie G Tooby, The Elms, Leamington Road, Long Itchington, Southam, Warks, CV47 9PL. 0192 681 2269.

NORTHAMPTONSHIRE BIRD CLUB, (1973; 100). Mrs Eleanor McMahon, Oriole House, 5 The Croft, Hanging Houghton, Northants, NN6 9HW. 01604 880009.

Ringing Group
NORTHANTS RG, D M Francis, 2 Brittons Drive, Billing Lane, Northampton, NN3 5DP.

RSPB Local Groups
MID NENE, (1975; 350). Michael Ridout, Melrose, 140 Northampton Road, Rushden, Northants, NN10 6AN. 01933 355544.

NORTHAMPTON, (1978; 3,000). Liz Wicks, 6 Waypost Court, Lings, Northampton, NN3 8LN. 01604 513991.

Wildlife Trust
Director, See Cambridgeshire.

NORTHUMBERLAND

Bird Atlas/Avifauna
The Atlas of Breeding Birds in Northumbria edited by J C Day et al (Northumberland and Tyneside Bird Club, 1995).

Bird Recorder
Ian Fisher, 74 Benton Park Road, Newcastle upon Tyne, NE7 7NB. 0191 266 7900;
e-mail: ian@hauxley.freeserve.co.uk
www.ntbc.org.uk

Bird Reports
BIRDS IN NORTHUMBRIA (1970-), from Muriel Cadwallender, 22 South View, Lesbury, NE66 3PZ. 01665 830884;
e-mail: tmcadwallender@lineone.net

BIRDS ON THE FARNE ISLANDS (1971-), from Secretary, Natural History Society of Northumbria.

BTO Regional Representative & Regional Development Officer
RR, Tom Cadwallender, 22 South View, Lesbury, Alnwick, Northumberland, NE66 3PZ. H:01665 830884; W:01670 533039;
e-mail: tmcadwallender@lineone.net

RDO, Muriel Cadwallender, 22 South View, Lesbury, Alnwick, Northumberland, NE66 3PZ. 01665 830884; e-mail: tmcadwallender@lineone.net

Clubs

NATURAL HISTORY SOCIETY OF NORTHUMBRIA, (1829; 900). David C Noble-Rollin, Hancock Museum, Barras Bridge, Newcastle upon Tyne, NE2 4PT. 0191 232 6386; e-mail: nhsn@ncl.ac.uk www.nhsn.ncl.ac.uk

NORTH NORTHUMBERLAND BIRD CLUB, (1984; 210). David Welch, 26 Armstrong Cottages, Bamburgh, Northumberland, NE69 7BA. 01668 214403.

NORTHUMBERLAND & TYNESIDE BIRD CLUB, (1958; 270). Sarah Barratt, 18 Frances Ville, Scotland Gate, Northumberland, NE62 5ST. 01670 827465: e-mail: sarah.barratt@btopenworld.com

Ringing Groups
BAMBURGH RS, Mike S Hodgson, 31 Uplands, Monkseaton, Whitley Bay, Tyne & Wear, NE25 9AG. 0191 252 0511.

NATURAL HISTORY SOCIETY OF NORTHUMBRIA, Dr C P F Redfern, Westfield House, Acomb, Hexham, Northumberland, NE46 4RJ.

NORTHUMBRIA RG. Secretary, B Galloway, 34 West Meadows, Stamfordham Road, Westerhope, Newcastle upon Tyne, NE5 1LS. 0191 286 4850.

Wildlife Hospitals
BERWICK SWAN & WILDLIFE TRUST, M L Allport, Keld, 4 Ryecroft Park, Wooler, Northumberland, NE71 6AS. 01668 281249;
e-mail: mail@swan-trust.org.uk
Registered charity. All categories of birds. Pools for swans and other waterfowl. Veterinary support.

WILDLIFE IN NEED SANCTUARY, Mrs Lisa Bolton, Shepherds Cottage, Chatton, Alnwick, Northumberland, NE66 5PX. 01668 215281.
All categories of birds. Number of gulls restricted. Oiled birds sent to Swan & Wildlife Trust, Berwick. Heated bird room. Aviaries. Veterinary support. Visiting strictly by appointment.

Wildlife Trust
NORTHUMBERLAND WILDLIFE TRUST, (1962; 5,000). The Garden House, St Nicholas Park, Jubilee Road, Newcastle upon Tyne, NE3 3XT. 0191 284 6884; fax 0191 284 6794;
e-mail: mail@northwt.org.uk
www.wildlifetrust.org.uk/northumberland

NOTTINGHAMSHIRE

Bird Recorders
Steve Keller, 17 Suffolk Avenue, Beeston Rylands, Notts, NG9 1NN. 0115 917 1452;
e-mail: s.keller@ntlworld.com

Bird Reports
LOUND BIRD REPORT (1990-), from Mr G Hobson, 11 Sherwood Road, Harworth, Doncaster, DN11 8HY. 01302 743654.

BIRDS OF NOTTINGHAMSHIRE (1943-), from Reg Davis, 3 Windrush Close, Bramcote View, Nottingham, NG9 3LN. 0115 922 8547;
e-mail: prlg@talk21.com

BTO Regional Representative & Regional Development Officer
RR, Mrs Lynda Milner, 6 Kirton Park, Kirton, Newark, Notts, NG22 9LR. 01623 862025; e-mail: lyndamilner@hotmail.com

Clubs
COLWICK PARK WILDLIFE GROUP, (1994; 150). Michael Walker, 14 Ramblers Close, Colwick, Nottingham, NG4 2DN. 0115 961 5494. www.colwick2000.freeserve.co.uk

LOUND BIRD CLUB, (1991; 50). P Hobson, 6 St Mary's Crescent, Tickhill, Doncaster, DN11 9JW. 07940 428326; e-mail: tichodroma@btinternet.com

NETHERFIELD WILDLIFE GROUP, (1999; 100). Philip Burnham, c/o 6 Cogenhoe Walk, Arnold, Nottingham, NG5 8LF.

NOTTINGHAMSHIRE BIRDWATCHERS, (1935; 420). Ms Jenny Swindels, 21 Chaworth Road, West Bridgeford, Nottingham. 0115 9812432.

WOLLATON NATURAL HISTORY SOCIETY, (1976; 99). Mrs P Price, 33 Coatsby Road, Hollycroft, Kimberley, Nottingham, NG16 2TH. 0115 938 4965.

Ringing Groups
BIRKLANDS RG, A D Lowe, 12 Midhurst Way, Clifton Estate, Nottingham, NG11 8DY. e-mail: birklandsringinggroup@lineone.net

NORTH NOTTS RG, Adrian Blackburn, Suleska, 1 Richmond Road, Retford, Notts, DN22 6SJ. 01777 706516; (M)07718 766873: e-mail: blackburns@suleska.freeserve.co.uk.

SOUTH WEST NOTTINGHAMSHIRE RG, K J Hemsley, 8 Grange Farm Close, Toton, Beeston, Notts, NG9 6EB. e-mail: k.hemsley@ntlworld.com

TRESWELL WOOD INTEGRATED POPULATION MONITORING GROUP, Chris du Feu, 66 High Street, Beckingham, Notts, DN10 4PF. e-mail: chris@beckingham0.demon.co.uk

RSPB Local Groups
MANSFIELD AND DISTRICT, (1986; 205). Chris Watkinson, 9 Ash Ford Rise, Sutton-in-Ashfield, Notts, NG17 2BB. 01623 403669.

NOTTINGHAM, (1974; 514). Andrew Griffin, Hawthorn Cottage, Thoroton, Notts, NG13 9DS. 01949 851426; www.notts-rspb.org.uk e-mail: andrew@thoroton.f.sworld.co.uk

Wildlife Trust
NOTTINGHAMSHIRE WILDLIFE TRUST, (1963; 6,000). The Old Ragged School, Brook Street, Nottingham, NG1 1EA. 0115 958 8242; fax 0115 924 3175; e-mail: nottswt@cix.co.uk www.wildlifetrust.org.uk/nottinghamshire

OXFORDSHIRE

Bird Atlas/Avifauna
Birds of Oxfordshire by J W Brucker et al (Oxford, Pisces, 1992).

The New Birds of the Banbury Area by T G Easterbrook (Banbury Ornithological Society, 1995).

Bird Recorder
Ian Lewington, 119 Brasenose Road, Didcot, Oxon, OX11 7BP. 01235 819792; e-mail: ian@recorder.fsnet.co.uk

Bird Reports
BIRDS OF OXFORDSHIRE (1920-), from Roy Overall, 30 Hunsdon Road, Iffley, Oxford, OX4 4JE. 01865 775632.

BANBURY ORNITHOLOGICAL SOCIETY ANNUAL REPORT (1952-), from A Turner, 33 Newcombe Close, Milcombe, Nr Banbury, Oxon, OX15 4RN. 01295 720938.

BTO Regional Representatives & Regional Development Officer
NORTH, Frances Marks, 15 Insall Road, Chipping Norton, Oxon, OX7 5LF. 01608 644425.

SOUTH RR & RDO, Peter Abbott, The Mallards, 109 Brook Street, Benson, Oxon, OX10 6LJ. 01491 837529.

Clubs
BANBURY ORNITHOLOGICAL SOCIETY, (1952; 100). Tony Clark, 11 Rye Close, Banbury, Oxon, OX16 7XG. 01295 268900.

OXFORD ORNITHOLOGICAL SOCIETY, (1921; 315). David Hawkins, The Long House, Park Lane, Long Hanborough, Oxon, OX29 8RD. 01993 880027; e-mail: dhawkins@dircon.co.uk www.oos.org.uk

Ringing Group
EDWARD GREY INSTITUTE, Dr A G Gosler, c/o Edward Grey Institute, Department of Zoology, South Parks Road, Oxford, OX1 3PS. 01865 271158.

RSPB Local Groups
OXFORD, (1977; 100). Ian Kilshaw, 6 Queens Court, Bicester, Oxon, OX26 6JX. Tel 01869 601901; (fax) 01869 600565; e-mail: ian.kilshaw@ntlworld.com www.rspb-oxford.org.uk

VALE OF WHITE HORSE, (1977; 250). Margaret Meardon, 7 Tavistock Avenue, Didcot, Oxon, OX11 8NA. 01235 210525.

Wildlife Trust
THE WILDLIFE TRUST FOR BERKS, BUCKS AND OXON. (1959; 11,000). The Lodge, 1 Armstrong Road, Littlemore, Oxford, OX4 4XT. 01865 775476; fax 01865 711301; e-mail: bbowt@cix.co.uk www.wildlifetrust.org.uk/berksbucksoxon

SHROPSHIRE

Bird Atlas/Avifauna
Atlas of the Breeding Birds of Shropshire (Shropshire Ornithological Society, 1995).

Bird Recorder
Geoff Holmes, 22 Tenbury Drive, Telford Estate, Shrewsbury, SY2 5YF. 01743 364621.

Bird Report
SHROPSHIRE BIRD REPORT (1956-) Annual, from Secretary. Shropshire, Ornithological Society.

BTO Regional Representative
Allan Dawes, Rosedale, Chapel Lane, Trefonen, Oswestry, Shrops, SY10 9DX. 01691 654245; e-mail: dawes.rosedale@talk21.com

Club
SHROPSHIRE ORNITHOLOGICAL SOCIETY, (1955; 750). John Turner, 1 Brookside Gardens, Yockleton, Shrewsbury, SY5 9PR. 01743 821678; e-mail: peregrineleada@aol.com

RSPB Local Group
SHROPSHIRE, (1992; 240). Roger M Evans, 31 The Wheatlands, Bridgnorth, WV16 5BD.

Wildlife Trust
SHROPSHIRE WILDLIFE TRUST, (1962; 2,000). 193 Abbey Foregate, Shrewsbury, SY2 6AH. 01743 284280; (fax)01743 284281; e-mail: shropshirewt@cix.co.uk www.shropshirewildlifetrust.org.uk

SOMERSET & BRISTOL

Bird Atlas/Avifauna
Atlas of Breeding Birds in Avon 1988-91 by R L Bland and John Tully (John Tully, 6 Falcondale Walk, Westbury-on-Trym, Bristol BS9 3JG, 1992).

Bird Recorders
Brian D Gibbs, 23 Lyngford Road, Taunton, Somerset, TA2 7EE. 01823 274887; e-mail: brian.gibbs@virgin.net www.somornithosoc.freeserve.co.uk

BATH, NE SOMERSET, BRISTOL, S GLOS, Harvey Rose, 12 Birbeck Road, Bristol, BS9 1BD. H:0117 968 1638; W:0117 928 7992; e-mail: h.c.rose@bris.ac.uk

Bird Reports
AVON BIRD REPORT (1977-), from Harvey Rose, 12 Birbeck Road, Bristol, BS9 1BD. H:0117 968 1638; W:0117 928 7992; e-mail: h.e.rose@bris.ac.uk

EXMOOR NATURALIST (1974-), from Secretary, Exmoor Natural History Society.

SOMERSET BIRDS (1912-), from David Ballance, Flat 2, Dunboyne, Bratton Lane, Minehead, Somerset, TA24 8SQ. 01643 706820; (fax)01643 706820(eve).

BTO Regional Representatives, Development Officer & Secretary
AVON RR, Richard L Bland, 11 Percival Road, Bristol, BS8 3LN. Home/W:01179 734828; e-mail: richardbland@blueyonder.co.uk

AVON REGIONAL SECRETARY, John Tully, 6 Falcondale Walk, Westbury-on-Trym, Bristol, BS9 3JG. 0117 950 0992; e-mail: johntully4@aol.com

SOMERSET RR, Eve Tigwell, Hawthorne Cottage, 3 Friggle Street, Frome, Somerset, BA11 5LP. 01373 451630; e-mail: evetigwell@aol.com

Clubs
BRISTOL NATURALISTS' SOCIETY (Ornithological Section), (1862; 550). Dr Mary Hill, 15 Montrose Avenue, Redland, Bristol, BS6 6EH. 0117 942 2193; www.bristolnats.org.uk e-mail: terry@jhill15.fsnet.co.uk

 BRISTOL ORNITHOLOGICAL CLUB, (1966; 690). Mrs Judy Copeland, 19 St George's Hill, Easton-in-Gordano, North Somerset, BS20 0PS. 01275 373554.

www.bristolorniclub.org.uk
e-mail: judy.copeland@ukgateway.net

CAM VALLEY WILDLIFE GROUP, (1994:). Helena Crouch, Bronwen, Farrington Road, Paulton, Bristol, BS39 7LP. 01761 410731.
e-mail: jim-helena@supanet.com
www.camvalleywildlifegroup.org.uk

EXMOOR NATURAL HISTORY SOCIETY, (1974; 450). Miss Caroline Giddens, 12 King George Road, Minehead, Somerset, TA24 5JD. 01643 707624;
e-mail: carol.enhs@virgin.net

MID-SOMERSET NATURALISTS' SOCIETY, (1949; 20). Roy Brearly, 2 Quayside, Bridgwater, Somerset, TA6 3TA. 01278 427100.

SOMERSET ORNITHOLOGICAL SOCIETY, (1923; 350). Miss Sarah Beavis, The Old Surgery, 4 The Barton, Hatch Beauchamp, Somerset, TA3 6SG. 01823 480948.

Ringing Groups
CHEW VALLEY RS, W R White, Church View Cottage, Mead Lane, Blagdon, N Somerset, BS40 7UA. 01761 463157 (evgs);
e-mail: warwickw@architen.com

GORDANO VALLEY RG, Lyndon Roberts, 20 Glebe Road, Long Ashton, Bristol, BS41 9LH. 01275 392722; e-mail: lyndonroberts@bigfoot.com

RSPCA, S Powell, 1 Rosemill Cottage, Rosemill Lane, Ilminster, Somerset, TA19 5PR.

STEEP HOLM RS, A J Parsons, Barnfield, Tower Hill Road, Crewkerne, Somerset, TA18 8BJ. 01460 73640.

RSPB Local Groups
BATH AND DISTRICT, (1989; 265). Gordon Rich, 9 Cranwells Park, Bath, BA1 2YD. 01225 422541.

CREWKERNE & DISTRICT, (1979; 325). Denise Chamings, Daniels Farm, Lower Stratton, South Petherton, Somerset, TA13 5LP. 01460 240740;
e-mail: rspb@crewkerne.fslife.co.uk
www.crewkerne.fslife.co.uk.

TAUNTON, (1975; 148). Eric Luxton, 33 Hoveland Lane, Taunton, Somerset, TA1 2EY. 01823 283033.

WESTON-SUPER-MARE (N SOMERSET), (1976; 215). Don Hurrell, Freeways, Star, Winscombe, BS25 1PS. 01934 842717.

Wildlife Trusts
AVON WILDLIFE TRUST, (1980; 5,500). The Wildlife Centre, 32 Jacobs Wells Road, Bristol, BS8

1DR. 0117 926 8018; fax 0117 929 7273;
e-mail: mail@avonwildlifetrust.org.uk
www.avonwildlifetrust.org.uk

SOMERSET WILDLIFE TRUST, (1964; 10,000). Fyne Court, Broomfield, Bridgwater, Somerset, TA5 2EQ. 01823 451587; fax 01823 451671;
e-mail: somwt@cix.co.uk
www.wildlifetrust.org.uk/somerset

STAFFORDSHIRE

Bird Recorder
Mrs Gilly Jones, 4 The Poplars, Lichfield Road, Abbots Bromley, Rugeley, Staffs, WS15 3AA. 01283 840555.

Bird Report See West Midlands.

BTO Regional Representatives
NORTH,

SOUTH & CENTRAL, Liz Palmer, 58 Fontenaye Road, Coton Green, Tamworth, Staffs, B79 8JU. Tel/fax 01827 52715;
e-mail: LIZPALMER5@aol.com

Clubs
WEST MIDLAND BIRD CLUB (STAFFORD BRANCH), Andy Lawrence, 14 Jack Haye Lane, Light Oaks, Stoke-on-Trent, ST2 7NG. 01782 253502.

WEST MIDLAND BIRD CLUB (TAMWORTH BRANCH), (1992). Barbara Stubbs, 19 Alfred Street, Tamworth, Staffs, B79 7RL. 01827 57865.

RSPB Local Groups
BURTON-ON-TRENT, (1976; 50). Dave Lummis, 121 Wilmot Road, Swadlincote, Derbys, DE11 9EN. 01283 219902.

LICHFIELD & DISTRICT, (1977; 1,150). Ray Jennett, 12 St Margarets Road, Lichfield, Staffs, WS13 7RA. 01543 255195.

NORTH STAFFORDSHIRE, (1982; 211). John Booth, 32 St Margaret Drive, Sneyd Green, Stoke-on-Trent, ST1 6EW. 01782 262082.
www.geocities.com/nsrspb

SOUTH WEST STAFFORDSHIRE, (1972; 174). Mrs Theresa Dorrance, 39 Wilkes Road, Codsall, Wolverhampton, WV8 1RZ. 01902 847041.

Wildlife Hospitals
BRITISH WILDLIFE RESCUE CENTRE, Alfred Hardy, Amerton Working Farm, Stowe-by-Chartley, Stafford, ST18 0LA. 01889 271308.
On A518 Stafford/Uttoxeter road. All species, including imprints and permanently injured.

Hospital, large aviaries and caging. Open to the public every day. Veterinary support.

GENTLESHAW BIRD OF PREY HOSPITAL, Robert A Smith, 5 Chestall Road, Cannock Wood, Rugeley, Staffs, WS15 4RB. 01543 676372
www.gentleshawwildlife.co.uk
Registered charity. All birds of prey (inc. owls). Hospital cages and aviaries; release sites. Veterinary support. Also GENTLESHAW BIRD OF PREY AND WILDLIFE CENTRE, Fletchers Country Garden Centre, Stone Road, Eccleshall, Stafford. 01785 850379 (10am-5pm).

RAPTOR RESCUE, BIRD OF PREY REHABILITATION, J M Cunningham, 8 Harvey Road, Handsacre, Rugeley, Staffs, WS15 4HF. 01543 491712; (Nat. advice line) 0870 241 0609; e-mail: mickcunningham@btinternet.com
www.raptorrescue.org.uk
Birds of prey only. Heated hospital units. Indoor flights, secluded aviaries, hacking sites, rehabilitation aviaries/flights. Falconry rehabilitation techniques, foster birds for rearing young to avoid imprinting. Veterinary support. Reg charity no. 283733.

Wildlife Trust
STAFFORDSHIRE WILDLIFE TRUST, (1969; 4,000). Coutts House, Sandon, Stafford, ST18 0DN. 01889 508534; fax 01889 508422;
e-mail: staffswt@cix.co.uk
www.wildlifetrust.org.uk/staffs

SUFFOLK

Bird Atlas/Avifauna
Birds of Suffolk by S H Piotrowski (February 2003).

Bird Recorders
NORTH EAST, Richard Walden, 21 Kilbrack, Beccles, Suffolk, NR34 9SH. 01502 713521; e-mail: walden1@supanet.com

SOUTH EAST (inc. coastal region from Slaughden Quay southwards), Brian Thompson, email: brianhilli@aol.com

WEST (whole of Suffolk W of Stowmarket, inc. Breckland), Colin Jakes, 7 Maltward Avenue, Bury St Edmunds, Suffolk, IP33 3XN. 01284 702215; e-mail: cjjakes@supanet.com

Bird Report
SUFFOLK BIRDS (inc Landguard Bird Observatory Report) (1950-), from Ipswich Museum, High Street, Ipswich, Suffolk.

BTO Regional Representative
Mick T Wright, 15 Avondale Road, Ipswich, IP3 9JT. 01473 710032;
e-mail: micktwright@btinternet.com

Clubs
LAVENHAM BIRD CLUB, (1972; 54). Richard Michette, 7 Clopton Drive, Long Melford, Sudbury, Suffolk, CO10 9LJ. 01787 377741 (day).

SUFFOLK ORNITHOLOGISTS' GROUP, (1973; 650). Andrew M Gregory, 1 Holly Road, Ipswich, IP1 3QN. 01473 253816.

Ringing Groups
DINGLE BIRD CLUB, Dr D Pearson, 4 Lupin Close, Reydon, Southwold, Suffolk, IP18 6NW.

LACKFORD RG, Dr Peter Lack, 11 Holden Road, Lackford, Bury St Edmunds, Suffolk, IP28 6HZ. e-mail: peter.diane@tinyworld.co.uk

LANDGUARD RG, SH Piotrowski, 29 Churchfields Road, Long Stratton, Norfolk, NR15 2WH. 01508 531115.

MARKET WESTON RG, Dr R H W Langston, Walnut Tree Farm, Thorpe Street, Hinderclay, Diss, Norfolk, IP22 1HT.
e-mail: rlangston@wntfarm.demon.co.uk

RSPB Local Groups
BURY ST EDMUNDS, (1982; 150). Trevor Hart, 7 Westgart Gardens, Bury St Edmunds, Suffolk, IP33 3LB. 01284 705165.

IPSWICH, (1975; 200). PL Wright, 116 Bucklesham Rd, Ipswich, Suffolk, IP3 8TU. 01473 273737; e-mail: plwright@compuserve.com

LOWESTOFT & DISTRICT, (1976; 170). Brian Sivyer, 39 Fern Avenue, Lowestoft, Suffolk, NR32 3JF. 01502 560414;
e-mail: brian.sivyer@lineone.net

WOODBRIDGE, (1986; 350). Colin Coates, 42A Bredfield Road, Woodbridge, Suffolk, IP12 1JE. 01394 385209.

Wildlife Trust
SUFFOLK WILDLIFE TRUST, (1961; 15,000). Brooke House, The Green, Ashbocking, Ipswich, IP6 9JY. 01473 890089; fax 01473 890165;
e-mail: info@suffolkwildlifetrust.cix.co.uk
www.wildlifetrust.org.uk/suffolk

SURREY

Bird Atlas/Avifauna
Birds of Surrey (avifauna). Due 2002.

Bird Recorder
(inc London S of Thames & E to Surrey Docks) Jeffery Wheatley, 9 Copse Edge, Elstead, Godalming, Surrey, GU8 6DJ. 01252 702450;(Fax) 01252 703650.

Bird Report
SURREY BIRD REPORT (1952-), from J Gates, 90 The Street, Wrecclesham, Farnham, Surrey, GU10 4QR.

BTO Regional Representative
Hugh Evans, 31 Crescent Road, Shepperton, Middx, TW17 8BL. 01932 227781; e-mail: hugh_w_evans@lineone.net

Clubs
SURBITON & DISTRICT BIRDWATCHING SOCIETY, (1954; 200). Norman Ford, 25 Canada Road, Cobham, Surrey, KT11 1BB. 01932 863475; e-mail: birds@sdbws.ndo.co.uk
www.sdbws.ndo.co.uk

SURREY BIRD CLUB, (1957; 420). Mrs Jill Cook, Moorings, Vale Wood Drive, Lower Bourne, Farnham, Surrey, GU10 3HW. 01252 792876; e-mail: jilck@aol.com
www.surreybirdclub.org.uk

Ringing Groups
HERSHAM RG, A J Beasley, 29 Selbourne Avenue, New Haw, Weybridge, Surrey, KT15 3RB. e-mail: abeasley00@hotmail.com

RUNNYMEDE RG, D G Harris, 22 Blossom Waye, Hounslow, TW5 9HD. e-mail: daveharris@tinyonline.co.uk

RSPB Local Groups
DORKING & DISTRICT, (1982; 320). Alan Clark, 11 Maplehurst, Fetcham, Surrey, KT22 9NB. 01372 450607.

EAST SURREY, (1984; 3,000). Brian Hobley, 26 Alexandra Road, Warlingham, Surrey, CR6 9DU. 01883 625404.

EPSOM & EWELL, (1974; 168). Janet Gilbert, 78 Fairfax Avenue, Ewell, Epsom, Surrey, KT17 2QQ. 0208 394 0405.

GUILDFORD AND DISTRICT, (1971; 500). Alan Bowen, Newlands, 13 Mountside, Guildford, Surrey, GU2 4JD. 01483 567041.

NORTH WEST SURREY, (1973; 125). Ms Mary Harris, 20 Meadway Drive, New Haw, Surrey, KT15 2DT. 01932 858692; e-mail: mary.harris2@virgin.net

Wildlife Hospitals
THE SWAN SANCTUARY, See National Dir.

WILDLIFE AID, Simon Cowell, Randalls Farm House, Randalls Road, Leatherhead, Surrey, KT22 0AL. 01372 377332; 24-hr emergline 09061 800 132 (50p/min); fax 01372 375183; e-mail: wildlife@pncl.co.uk
www.wildlife-aid.org.uk/wildlife
Registered charity. Wildlife hospital and rehabilitation centre helping all native British species. Special housing for birds of prey. Membership scheme and fund raising activities. Veterinary support.

Wildlife Trust
SURREY WILDLIFE TRUST, (1959; 10,000). School Lane, Pirbright, Woking, Surrey, GU24 0JN. 01483 488055; fax 01483 486505; e-mail: surreywt@cix.co.uk
www.surreywildlifetrust.co.uk

SUSSEX

Bird Atlas/Avifauna
The Birds of Selsey Bill and the Selsey Peninsula (a checklist to year 2000), from O Mitchell, 21 Trundle View Close, Barnham, Bognor Regis, PO22 0JZ.

Birds of Sussex ed by Paul James (Sussex Ornithological Society, 1996).

Bird Recorder
John A Hobson, 23 Hillside Road, Storrington, W Sussex, RH20 3 LZ. 01903 740155; e-mail: janthobson@aol.com

Bird Reports
FRIENDS OF RYE HARBOUR NR ANNUAL REPORT (1977-), from Dr Barry Yates, see Clubs.

PAGHAM HARBOUR LOCAL NATURE RESERVE ANNUAL REPORT, from Warden, see Reserves.

SHOREHAM DISTRICT ORNITHOLOGICAL SOCIETY ANNUAL REPORT (1952-), from Secretary.

SUSSEX BIRD REPORT (1963-), from J E Trowell, Lorrimer, Main Road, Icklesham, Winchelsea, E Sussex, TN36 4BS. www.susos.org.uk
e-mail: membership@susos.org.uk

BTO Regional Representative
Dr A Barrie Watson, 83 Buckingham Road, Shoreham-by-Sea, W Sussex, BN43 5UD. 01273 452472; e-mail: abwatson@mistral.co.uk

Clubs
FRIENDS OF RYE HARBOUR NATURE RESERVE, (1973; 1500). Dr Barry Yates, 2 Watch Cottages, Nook Beach, Winchelsea, E Sussex, TN36 4LU. 01797 223862;
e-mail: yates@clara.net www.yates.clara.net

HENFIELD BIRDWATCH, (1999; 110). Mike Russell, 31 Downsview, Small Dole, Henfield, West Sussex, BN5 9YB. 01273 494311.

SHOREHAM DISTRICT ORNITHOLOGICAL SOCIETY, (1953; 120). Mrs B Reeve, The Old Rectory, Coombes, Lancing, W Sussex, BN15 0RS. 01273 452497.

SUSSEX ORNITHOLOGICAL SOCIETY, (1962; 1500). Mrs V P Bentley, Chetsford, London Road, Henfield, W Sussex, BN5 9JJ. 01273 494723.
www.susos.org.uk

Ringing Groups
BEACHY HEAD RS, R D M Edgar, 6 Turnpike Close, Ringmer, Lewes, E Sussex, BN8 5PD.

CUCKMERE RG, Tim Parmenter, 22 The Kiln, Burgess Hill, W Sussex, RH15 0LU. 01444 236526.

RYE BAY RG, S J R Rumsey, Elms Farm, Pett Lane, Icklesham, Winchelsea, E Sussex, TN36 4AH. 01797 226137;
e-mail: srumsey@europeancredit.com

STEYNING RG, B R Clay, 30 The Drive, Worthing, W Sussex, BN11 5LL.
e-mail: brclay@compuserve.com

RSPB Local Groups
BATTLE, (1973; 100). Miss Lynn Jenkins, 61 Austen Way, Guestling, Hastings, E Sussex, TN35 4JH. 01424 432076;
e-mail: battlerspb@freewire.co.uk
www.battlerspb.freewire.co.uk

BRIGHTON & DISTRICT, (1974; 550). Colin Upton, 2 Montford Close, Shoreham-by-Sea, W Sussex, BN43 6YP. 01273 593938;
e-mail: colin.upton@care4free.net

CHICHESTER & SW SUSSEX, (1979; 245). Dominic Carlton, Pipits, Park Road, Barnham, Bognor Regis, W Sussex, PO22 0AQ. 01243 552716.

CRAWLEY & HORSHAM, (1978; 148). Andrea Saxton, 104 Heath Way, Horsham, W Sussex, RH12 5XS.

EAST GRINSTEAD, (1998; 218). Nick Walker, 14 York Avenue, East Grinstead, W Sussex, RH19 4TL. 01342 315825.

EASTBOURNE & DISTRICT, (1993; 520). AM Squires, 5 Hyperion Avenue, Polegate, E Sussex, BN25 5HT. 01323 487392.

HASTINGS & ST LEONARDS, (1983; 145). Richard Prebble, 1 Wayside, 490 Sedlescombe Road North, St Leonards-on-Sea, E Sussex, TN37 7PH. 01424 751790.

HEATHFIELD, (1979; 75). Mrs Dorothy Cull, 33 Horam Park Close, Horam, E Sussex, TN21 0HW. 01435 812093.

 Wildlife Hospital
BRENT LODGE BIRD & WILDLIFE TRUST, Penny Cooper, Brent Lodge, Cow Lane, Sidlesham, Chichester, West Sussex, PO20 7LN. 01243 641672.
All species of wild birds and small mammals. Full surgical and medical facilities (inc. X-ray). Purpose-built oiled bird washing unit. Veterinary support.

Wildlife Trust
SUSSEX WILDLIFE TRUST, (1961; 13,000). Woods Mill, Shoreham Road, Henfield, W Sussex, BN5 9SD. 01273 492630; (fax)01273 494500;
e-mail: enquiries@sussexwt.co.uk
www.wildlifetrust.org.uk/sussex

TYNE & WEAR

Bird Recorders
See Durham and Northumberland.

Bird Report See Durham and Northumberland.

Clubs
NATURAL HISTORY SOCIETY OF NORTHUMBRIA, (1829; 900). David C Noble-Rollin, Hancock Museum, Barras Bridge, Newcastle upon Tyne, NE2 4PT. 0191 232 6386;
e-mail: david.noble-rollin@ncl.ac.uk

NORTHUMBERLAND & TYNESIDE BIRD CLUB, (1958; 270). Sarah Barratt, 3 Haydon Close, Red House Farm, Gosforth, Newcastle upon Tyne, NE3 2BY. 0191 213 6665.

RSPB Local Groups

NEWCASTLE UPON TYNE, (1969; 250). John Evans, 21 Beacon Drive, Brunswick Green, Wideopen, Newcastle upon Tyne, NE13 7HB. 0191 236 2369.

SUNDERLAND & SOUTH TYNESIDE, (1982; 25). Paul Metters, Almonte, 1 Bloomfield Drive, Elemore View, East Rainton, Houghton-le-Spring, Tyne & Wear, DH5 9SF. 0191 5120083.

Wildlife Trust

See Durham.

WARWICKSHIRE

Bird Recorder

Jonathan Bowley, 17 Meadow Way, Fenny Compton, Southam, Warks, CV47 2WD. 01295 770069; e-mail: bowley@tesco.net

Bird Report,

See West Midlands.

BTO Regional Representatives

WARWICKSHIRE, Joe A Hardman, Red Hill House, Red Hill, Alcester, Warks, B49 6NQ. 01789 763159; e-mail: annandjoe.hardman@lineone.net

RUGBY, Barrington Jackson, 5 Harris Drive, Rugby, Warks, CV22 6DX. 01788 814466; e-mail: jacksonbj2@aol.com

Clubs

NUNEATON & DISTRICT BIRDWATCHERS' CLUB, (1950; 76). Alvin K Burton, 23 Redruth Close, Horeston Grange, Nuneaton, Warwicks, CV11 6FG. 024 7664 1591.

WEST MIDLAND BIRD CLUB (SOLIHULL BRANCH), George Morley, 64 Cambridge Avenue, Solihull, West Midlands, B91 1QF.

Ringing Groups

ARDEN RG, Joe A Hardman, Red Hill House, Red Hill, Alcester, Warks, B49 6NQ. 01789 763159; e-mail: annandjoe.hardman@lineone.net

BRANDON RG, David Stone, Overbury, Wolverton, Stratford-on-Avon, Warks, CV37 0HG. 01789 731488.

RSPB Local Group

See West Midlands.

Wildlife Trust

WARWICKSHIRE WILDLIFE TRUST, (1970; 7,500). Brandon Marsh Nature Centre, Brandon Lane, Coventry, CV3 3GW. 024 7630 2912; (fax)024

7663 9556; e-mail: admin@warkswt.cix.co.uk www.warwickshire-wildlife-trust.org.uk

WEST MIDLANDS

Bird Atlas/Avifauna

The Birds of the West Midlands edited by Graham Harrison et al (West Midland Bird Club, 1982).

Bird Recorder

Tim Hextell, 39 Windermere Road, Handsworth, Birmingham, B21 9RQ. 0121 551 9997; www.westmidlandbirdclub.com

Bird Reports

THE BIRDS OF SMESTOW VALLEY AND DUNSTALL PARK (1988-), from Secretary, Smestow Valley Bird Group.

WEST MIDLAND BIRD REPORT (inc Staffs, Warks, Worcs and W Midlands) (1934-), from J Reeves, 9 Hintons Coppice, Knowle, Solihull, B93 9RF.

BTO Regional Representative

BIRMINGHAM & WEST MIDLANDS, Position vacant.

Clubs

SMESTOW VALLEY BIRD GROUP, (1988; 56). Frank Dickson, 11 Bow Street, Bilston, Wolverhampton, WV14 7NB. 01902 493733.

WEST MIDLAND BIRD CLUB, (1929; 2,000). Mr MJ West, 6 Woodend Road, Walsall, WS5 3BG. 01922 639931; e-mail: westwoodend@care4free.net

WEST MIDLAND BIRD CLUB (BIRMINGHAM BRANCH), (1995; 800). John N Sears, 14 Ingram Street, Malmesbury, Wilts, SN16 9BX. 01666 824417.

Ringing Groups

MERCIAN RG (Sutton Coldfield), R L Castle, 91 Maney Hill Road, Sutton Coldfield, West Midlands, B72 1JT. 0121 686 7568.

RSPB Local Groups

BIRMINGHAM, (1975; 100). John Bailey, 52 Gresham Road, Hall Green, Birmingham, B28 0HY. 0121 777 4389. www.rspb-birmingham.org.uk

COVENTRY & WARWICKSHIRE, (1969; 130). Alan King, 69 Westmorland Road, Coventry, CV2 5BO. 024 7672 7348.

SOLIHULL, (1983; 2,600). John Roberts, 115 Dovehouse Lane, Solihull, West Midlands, B91 2EQ. 0121 707 3101; e-mail: d.john.roberts@care4free.net

STOURBRIDGE, (1978; 150). Paul Banks, 4 Sandpiper Close, Wollescote, Stourbridge, DY9 8TD. 01384 898948.

SUTTON COLDFIELD, (1986; 250). Paul Hobbs, 12 Hurlingham Road, Kingstanding, Birmingham, B44 0LT. 0121 382 7154.

WALSALL, (1970; 80). Mike Pittaway, 2 Kedleston Close, Bloxwich, Walsall, WS3 3TW. 01922 710568. e-mail: chair@rspb-walsall.org.uk www.rspb-walsall.org.uk

WOLVERHAMPTON, (1974; 95). Ian Wiltshire, 25 Oakridge Drive, Willenhall, WV12 4EN. 01902 630418.

Wildlife Hospitals
KIDD, D J, 20 Parry Road, Ashmore Park, Wednesfield, Wolverhampton, WV11 2PS. 01902 863971. All birds of prey, esp. owls. Aviaries, isolation pens. Veterinary support.

REPTILE & WILDLIFE RESCUE, Warren Davis, 103 Beauchamp Road, Billesley, Birmingham, B13 0NN. 0121 444 3944; mobile 07979 370525. All species of wild birds. Full hand-rearing care. Veterinary support.

WEDNESFIELD ANIMAL SANCTUARY, Jimmy Wick, 92 Vicarage Road, Nordley, Wednesfield, Wolverhampton, WV11 1SF. 01902 823064. Birds of prey, softbills, seed-eaters. Brooders, incubators, outdoor aviaries, heated accommodation. Telephone first. Veterinary support.

Wildlife Trust
THE WILDLIFE TRUST FOR BIRMINGHAM AND BLACK COUNTRY, (1980; 4,500). 28 Harborne Road, Edgbaston, Birmingham, B15 3AA. 0121 454 1199; (fax)0121 454 6556; e-mail: urbanwt@cix.co.uk www.bbcwildlife.org.uk

WILTSHIRE

Bird Recorder
Rob Turner, 14 Ethendun, Bratton, Westbury, Wilts, BA13 4RX. 01380 830862.

Bird Report
Published in Hobby (journal of the Wiltshire OS) (1975-), from Nigel Pleass, The Curlews, 22 Ferrers Drive, Swindon, SN5 6HJ. 01793 873251; e-mail: nigelpleass@aol.com

BTO Regional Representatives
NORTH, Mark Lang, 1 Sherington Mead, Pewsham, Wilts, SN15 3TU.
e-mail: mark@marknsams.fsnet.co.uk

SOUTH, Andrew Carter, Standlynch Farm, Downton, Salisbury, SP5 3QR. 01722 710382; e-mail: standlynch@aol.com

Clubs
SALISBURY & DISTRICT NATURAL HISTORY SOCIETY, (1952; 161). J Pitman, 10 The Hardings, Devizes Road, Salisbury, SP2 9LZ. 01722 327395.

WILTSHIRE ORNITHOLOGICAL SOCIETY, (1974; 504). Mrs EM Nuttall, 11 Kingsfird Close, Bradford-on-Avon, Wilts, BA15 1AW. 01225 863816.

Ringing Group
WEST WILTSHIRE RG, Mr M.J. Hamzij, 13 Halfway Close, Trowbridge, Wilts, BA14 7HQ. e-mail: mikehamzij@halfway11.freeserve.co.uk

RSPB Local Groups
NORTH WILTSHIRE, (1973; 90). Derek Lyford, 9 Devon Road, Swindon, SN2 1PQ. 01793 520997; e-mail: derek.lyford@care4free.net

SOUTH WILTSHIRE, (1986; 820). Tony Goddard, Clovelly, Lower Road, Charlton All Saints, Salisbury, SP5 4HQ. 01725 510309.

Wildlife Hospital
CALNE WILD BIRD AND ANIMAL RESCUE CENTRE, Tom and Caroline Baker, 2 North Cote, Calne, Wilts, SN11 9DL. 01249 817893.
All species of birds. Large natural aviaries (all with ponds), release areas, incubators, heated cages. Day and night collection. Veterinary support.

Wildlife Trust
WILTSHIRE WILDLIFE TRUST, (1962; 11,000). Elm Tree Court, Long Street, Devizes, Wilts, SN10 1NJ. 01380 725670; (fax)01380 729017; e-mail: admin@wiltshirewildlife.org www.wiltshire-web.co.uk/wildlife

WORCESTERSHIRE

Bird Recorder
Position vacant.

Bird Report See West Midlands.

BTO Regional Representative
G Harry Green MBE, Windy Ridge, Pershore Road, Little Comberton, Pershore, Worcs, WR10 3EW. 01386 710377;
e-mail: harrygreen@britishlibrary.net

Ringing Group

WYCHAVON RG, J R Hodson, 15 High Green, Severn Stoke, Worcester, WR8 9JS. 01905 754919(day), 01905 371333(eve); e-mail: john.hodson@tesco.net

RSPB Local Group

WORCESTER & MALVERN, (1980; 400). Garth Lowe, Sunnymead, Old Storridge, Alfrick, Worcester, WR6 5HT. 01886 833362.

Wildlife Trust

WORCESTERSHIRE WILDLIFE TRUST, (1968; 8,000). Lower Smite Farm, Smite Hill, Hindlip, Worcester, WR3 8SZ. 01905 754919; (fax)01905 755868; e-mail: worcswt@cix.co.uk www.worcswildlifetrust.co.uk

YORKSHIRE

Bird Atlas/Avifauna

Atlas of Breeding Birds in the Leeds Area 1987-1991 by Richard Fuller et al (Leeds Birdwatchers' Club, 1994).

The Birds of Halifax by Nick Dawtrey (only 20 left), 14 Moorend Gardens, Pellon, Halifax, W Yorks, HX2 0SD.

The Birds of Yorkshire by John Mather (Croom Helm, 1986).

An Atlas of the Breeding Birds of the Huddersfield Area, 1987-1992 by Brian Armitage et al (2000).

Birds of Barnsley by Nick Addey (Pub by author, 114 Everill Gate Lane, Broomhill, Barnsley S73 0YJ, 1998).

Bird Recorders

VC61 (East Yorkshire), Geoff Dobbs, 12 Park Avenue, Hull, HU5 3ER. 01482 341524; e-mail: geoffdobbs@aol.com

VC62 (North Yorkshire East), Russell Slack, 64 Sundew Gardens, High Green, Sheffield, S35 4DU. 01142 845300.

VC63 (South & West Yorkshire), Lance Degnan, 14 Fiddlers Drive, Armthorpe, Doncaster, DN3 4TT. 01302 835094; e-mail: lance.degnan@lineone.net

VC64 (West Yorkshire)/HARROGATE & CRAVEN, Jim Pewtress, 31 Piercy End, Kirbymoorside, York, YO62 6DQ. 01751 431001; e-mail: jim@pewtress.co.uk

VC65 (North Yorkshire West), Nick Morgan, Linden, Church View, Ainderby Steeple, Northallerton, N Yorks, DL7 9PU. 01609 770168; e-mail: nick.morgan1@virgin.net

Bird Reports

BARNSLEY & DISTRICT BIRD STUDY GROUP REPORT (1971-), from Secretary.

BRADFORD NATURALISTS' SOCIETY ANNUAL REPORT, from I Hogg, 23 St Matthews Road, Bankfoot, Bradford, BD5 9AB.

BRADFORD ORNITHOLOGICAL GROUP REPORT (1987-), from Jenny Barker, 4 Chapel Fold, Slack Lane, Oakworth, Keighley, BD22 0RQ.

DONCASTER BIRD REPORT (1955-), from M Roberts, 30 St Cecillia's Road, Belle Vue, Doncaster, DN4 5EG. 01302 361731.

FILEY BRIGG BIRD REPORT (1976-), from C Court, 12 Pinewood Avenue, Filey, YO14 9NS.

FIVE TOWNS BIRD REPORT (1995-), from Secretary, Five Towns Bird Group.

HALIFAX BIRDWATCHERS' CLUB ANNUAL REPORT (1991-), from Nick C Dawtrey, 14 Moorend Gardens, Pellon, Halifax, W Yorks, HX2 0SD. 01422 364228.

HARROGATE & DISTRICT NATURALISTS' ORNITHOLOGY REPORT (1996-), from Secretary.

BIRDS IN HUDDERSFIELD (1966-), from Secretary, Huddersfield Bird Club.

LEEDS BIRDWATCHERS' CLUB ANNUAL REPORT (1949-), from Secretary.

BIRDS OF ROTHERHAM (1975-), from Secretary, Rotherham Orn Soc.

BIRDS IN THE SHEFFIELD AREA (1973-), from Tony Morris, 4A Raven Road, Sheffield, S7 1SB. e-mail: tonyjmorris@blueyonder.co.uk www.sbsg.org

THE BIRDS OF SK58 (1993-), from Secretary, SK58 Birders.

SPURN BIRD OBSERVATORY ANNUAL REPORT, from Warden, see Reserves.

TOPHILL LOW BIRD REPORT (1996-), from Recorder for VC61.

WINTERSETT AREA ANNUAL REPORT (1988-), from Steve Denny, 13 Rutland Drive, Crofton, Wakefield, WF4 1SA. 01924 864487.

YORK ORNITHOLOGICAL CLUB ANNUAL REPORT (1970-), from T Lawson, Burton Garth, Main Street, Knapton, York, YO26 6QG. 01904 795489: www.yorkbirding.org.uk e-mail: info@yorkbirding.org.uk

YORKSHIRE NATURALISTS' UNION: BIRD REPORT (1940-), RARE AND SCARCE BIRD REPORT (1998-) from John A Newbould, Stonecroft, 3 Brookmead Close, Sutton Poyntz, Weymouth, Dorset, DT3 6RS.

BTO Regional Representatives & Regional Development Officers
NORTH-EAST RR, Michael Carroll. 01751 476550.

NORTH-WEST RR, Position vacant.

SOUTH-EAST AND SOUTH-WEST RR, Chris Falshaw, 6 Den Bank Crescent, Sheffield, S10 5PD. 0114 230 3857; e-mail: chris.falsh@virgin.net

EAST RR, F X Moffatt, 102 Norwood, Beverley, E Yorks, HU17 9HL. 01482 882791; e-mail: frankie@xmofatt.freeserve.co.uk.

BRADFORD RR & RDO, Mike L Denton, 77 Hawthorne Terrace, Crosland Moor, Huddersfield, HD4 5RP. 01484 646990.

HARROGATE RR, Mike Brown, 48 Pannal Ash Drive, Harrogate, N Yorks, HG2 0HU. H:01423 567382; W:01423 507237; e-mail: mike@ppemail.co.uk

LEEDS & WAKEFIELD RR & RDO, Peter Smale, 2A Hillcrest Rise, Leeds, LS16 7DL. 0113 226 9526; e-mail: petersmale@ntlworld.com

RICHMOND RR, John Edwards, 7 Church Garth, Great Smeaton, Northallerton, N Yorks, DL6 2HW. H:01609 881476; W:01609 780780 extn 2452; e-mail: john@garthwards.fsnet.co.uk

YORK RR, Rob Chapman, 12 Moorland Road, York, YO10 4HF. 01904 633558; e-mail: robert.chapman@tinyworld.co.uk

Clubs
BARNSLEY & DISTRICT BIRD STUDY GROUP, (1970; 35). Graham Speight, 58 Locke Avenue, Barnsley, South Yorkshire, S70 1QH. 01226 321300.

BRADFORD NATURALISTS' SOCIETY, (1875; 50). D R Grant, 19 The Wheatings, Ossett, W Yorks, WF5 0QQ. 01924 273628.

BRADFORD ORNITHOLOGICAL GROUP, (1987; 200). Shaun Radcliffe, 8 Longwood Avenue, Bingley, W Yorks, BD16 2RX. 01274 770960; www.bradfordbirders.co.uk.

CASTLEFORD & DISTRICT NATURALISTS' SOCIETY, (1956; 25). Michael J Warrington, 31 Mount Avenue, Hemsworth, Pontefract, W Yorks, WF9 4QE. 01977 614954.

DONCASTER & DISTRICT ORNITHOLOGICAL SOCIETY, (1955; 40). Mrs C McKee, 14 Poplar Close, Branton, Doncaster, DN3 3QA. 01302 532454.

FILEY BRIGG ORNITHOLOGICAL GROUP, (1977; 70). Jack Whitehead, 15 The Beach, Filey, N Yorkshire, YO14 9LA. 01723 514565.

FIVE TOWNS BIRD GROUP, (1994; 20). Robert Knight, 2 Milnes Grove, Airedale, Castleford, W Yorkshire, WF10 3EZ. 01977 510761; e-mail: f.t.b.g@lineone.net

HALIFAX BIRDWATCHERS' CLUB, (1992; 33). Nick C Dawtrey, 14 Moorend Gardens, Pellon, Halifax, W Yorks, HX2 0SD. 01422 364228.

HARROGATE & DISTRICT NATURALISTS' SOCIETY, (1947; 430). Mrs J McClean, 6 Rossett Park Road, Harrogate, N Yorks, HG2 9NP. 01423 879095; e-mail: joan_mcclean@hotmail.com

HORNSEA BIRD CLUB, (1967; 40). John Eldret, 44 Rolston Road, Hornsea, HU18 1UH. 01964 532854.

HUDDERSFIELD BIRDWATCHERS' CLUB, (1966; 80). David Butterfield, 15 Dene Road, Skelmanthorpe, Huddersfield, HD8 9BU. 01484 862006; e-mail: dbutt52@hotmail.com

HULL VALLEY WILDLIFE GROUP, (1997; 175). Roy Lyon, 670 Hotham Road South, Hull HU5 5LE.

LEEDS BIRDWATCHERS' CLUB, (1949; 70). Mrs Shirley Carson, 2 Woodhall Park Gardens, Stanningley, Pudsey, W Yorks, LS28 7XQ. 0113 255 2145; e-mail: shirley.carson@care4free.net

NEW SWILLINGTON INGS BIRD GROUP, (1989; 20). Nick Smith, 40 Holmsley Lane, Woodlesford, Leeds, LS26 8RN. 0113 282 6154.

PUDSEY ORNITHOLOGY GROUP, (1989; 22). Alan Patchett, 102 Half Mile Lane, Leeds, LS13 1DB. 0113 2299038.

ROTHERHAM & DISTRICT ORNITHOLOGICAL SOCIETY, (1974; 90). Malcolm Taylor, 18 Maple Place, Chapeltown, Sheffield, S35 1QW. 0114 246 1848.

SCALBY NABS ORNITHOLOGICAL GROUP, (1993; 15). Ian Glaves, Halleykeld House, Chapel Lane, Sawdon, Scarborough, N Yorkshire, YO13 9DZ. 01723 859766.

SHEFFIELD BIRD STUDY GROUP, (1972; 170). Ron Walker, 22 Parkers Lane, Sheffield, S17 3DP. 0114 236 6150; e-mail: ronw@erod.demon.co.uk

ENGLAND

SK58 BIRDERS, (1993; 60). Andy Hirst, 15 Hunters Drive, Dinnington, Sheffield, S25 2TG. 01909 560310; e-mail: sk58birders@sk58.freeserve.co.uk Chair: Mick Clay, 2 High St, S.Anston, Sheffield. 01909 566000. www.sk58.freeserve.co.uk

SORBY NHS (ORNITHOLOGICAL SECTION), (1918; 40). Chris Falshaw, 6 Den Bank Crescent, Sheffield, S10 5PD. 0114 230 3857; e-mail: chris.falsh@virgin.net

WAKEFIELD NATURALISTS' SOCIETY, (1851; 40). Philip Harrison, 392 Dewsbury Road, Wakefield, W Yorks, WF2 9DS. 01924 373604.

YORK ORNITHOLOGICAL CLUB, (1967; 80). Ian Traynor, The Owl House, 137 Osbaldwick Lane, York, YO10 3AY. e-mail: info@yorkbirding.org.uk www.yorkbirding.org.uk

YORKSHIRE NATURALISTS' UNION (Ornithological Section), (1940; 500). W F Curtis, Farm Cottage, Atwick, Driffield, YO25 8DH. 01964 532477.

Ringing Groups
BARNSLEY RG, M C Wells, 715 Manchester Road, Stocksbridge, Sheffield, S36 1DQ. 0114 288 4211.

DONCASTER RG, D Hazard, 41 Jossey Lane, Scawthorpe, Doncaster, S Yorks, DN5 9DB. 01302 788044; e-mail: davehazard@netscapeonline.co.uk

EAST DALES RG, S P Worwood, 18 Coltsgate Hill, Ripon, N Yorks, HG4 2AB.

EAST YORKS RG, Peter J Dunn, 43 West Garth Gardens, Cayton, Scarborough, N Yorks, YO11 3SF. 01723 583149; e-mail: pjd@fbog.co.uk   www.eyrg.org

SORBY-BRECK RG, Geoff P Mawson, Moonpenny Farm, Farwater Lane, Dronfield, Sheffield, S18 1RA. 01246 415097; e-mail: gpmawson@hotmail.com

SOUTH CLEVELAND RG, W Norman, 2 Station Cottages, Grosmont, Whitby, N Yorks, YO22 5PB. 01947 895226; e-mail: wilfgros@lineone.net

SPURN BIRD OBSERVATORY, I D Walker, 31 Walton Park, Pannal, Harrogate, N Yorks, HG3 1EJ. 01423 879408.

TEES RG, E Wood, Southfields, 16 Marton Moor Road, Nunthorpe, Middlesbrough, Cleveland, TS7 0BH. 01642 323563; e-mail; redshank@ntlworld.co.uk

WINTERSETT RG, P Smith, 16 Templar Street, Wakefield, W Yorks, WF1 5HB. 01924 375082.

RSPB Local Groups
AIREDALE AND BRADFORD, (1972; 3500). Peter Sutcliffe, 10 Southfield Mount, Riddlesden, Keighley, W Yorks, BD20 5HS. 01535 600937.

CLEVELAND, (1974; 200). Mark Stokeld, 38 Ash Grove, Kirklevington, Cleveland, TS15 9NQ. 01642 783819; e-mail: mark@stokeld.demon.co.uk www.stokeld.demon.uk

CRAVEN & PENDLE, (1986; 250). Ian Cresswell, Dove House, Skyreholme, Skipton, N Yorks, BD23 6DE. 01756 720355; fax 01756 720407; e-mail: ian@cravenandpendlerspb.org www.cravenandpendlerspb.org

DONCASTER, (1984; 100). Sue Clifton, West Lodge, Wadworth Hall Lane, Wadworth, Doncaster, DN11 9BH. Tel/fax 01302 854956; e-mail: sue@westlodge53.freeserve.co.uk

EAST YORKSHIRE, (1986; 90). Keith & Sal Barrow, 17 St Aidan Road, Bridlington, E Yorks, YO16 7SP. 01262 679685; www.eymg.freeserve.co.uk e-mail: keith.barrow@btinternet.com e-mail: sal.barrow@btinternet.com

HUDDERSFIELD & HALIFAX, (1981; 200). David Hemingway, 267 Long Lane, Dalton, Huddersfield, HD5 9SH. 01484 301920.

HULL & DISTRICT, (1983; 334). Derek Spencer, The Old Brewhouse, Main Road, Burton Pidsea, Hull, HU12 9AX. 01964 670024.

LEEDS, (1975; 450). Linda Jenkinson, 112 Eden Crescent, Burley, Leeds, LS4 2TR. 0113 230 4595 www.rspb-leeds.ndo.co.uk.

SHEFFIELD, (1983; 500). John Badger, 24 Athersley Gardens, Owlthorpe, Sheffield, S20 6RW. 0114 247 6622.

WAKEFIELD, (1987; 170). Paul Disken, 6 Northfield Road, Dewsbury, W Yorks, WF13 2JX. 01924 456352.

WHITBY, (1977; 120). Fred Payne, 16 Hermitage Way, Sleights, Whitby, N Yorks, YO22 5HG. 01947 810022.

YORK, (1973; 600). Chris Lloyd, 7 School Lane, Upper Poppleton, York, YO26 6JS. 01904 794865; e-mail: chris.a.lloyd@care4free.net www.yorkrspb.org.uk.

Wildlife Hospital
ANIMAL HOUSE WILDLIFE WELFARE, Mrs C Buckroyd, 14 Victoria Street, Scarborough, YO12 7SS. 01723 371256; shop 01723 375162. All species of wild birds. Oiled birds given treatment before forwarding to cleaning stations. Incubators, hospital cages, heat pads, release sites. Birds ringed before release. Prior telephone

call requested. Collection if required. Veterinary support. Charity shop at 127 Victoria Road.

Wildlife Trusts
TEES VALLEY WILDLIFE TRUST, (1979; 4000). Bellamy Pavilion, Kirkleatham Old Hall, Kirkleatham, Redcar, Cleveland, TS10 5NW. 01642 759900; (fax)01642 480401; e-mail: teesvalleywt@cix.co.uk www.wildlifetrust.org.uk/teesvalley

SHEFFIELD WILDLIFE TRUST, (1985; 250). Victoria Hall, 37 Stafford Road, Sheffield S2 2SS. 0114 263 4335; (fax)0114 263 4345; e-mail: sheffieldwt@cix.co.uk www.wildlifetrust.org.uk/sheffield

YORKSHIRE WILDLIFE TRUST, (1946; 8000). 10 Toft Green, York, YO1 6JT. 01904 659570; (fax)01904 613467; e-mail: yorkshirewt@cix.co.uk www.yorkshire-wildlife-trust.org.uk

SCOTLAND

For this section we are following the arrangement of the Scottish recording areas as set out by the Scottish Ornithologists' Club.

WHOLE OF SCOTLAND

Bird Report
See Scottish Ornithologists' Club in National Directory.

Club
See Scottish Ornithologists' Club in National Directory.

SCOTTISH WILDLIFE TRUST (1964; 16,500). Cramond House, Off Cramond Glebe Road, Edinburgh, EH4 6NS, 0131 312 7765; (Fax)0131 312 8705; e-mail: enquiries@swt.org.uk www.swt.org.uk

ANGUS & DUNDEE

Bird Recorder
ANGUS & DUNDEE, Dan A Carmichael, 2a Reres Road, Broughty Ferry, Dundee, DD5 2QA. 01382 779981; e-mail: dan@carmichael2a.fsworld.co.uk

Bird Report
ANGUS & DUNDEE BIRD REPORT (1974-), from Secretary, SOC Tayside Branch.

BTO Regional Representatives & Regional Development Officer
ANGUS RR & RDO, Ken Slater, Braedownie

Farmhouse, Glen Clova, Kirriemuir, Angus, DD8 4RD. 01575 550233

Clubs
ANGUS & DUNDEE BIRD CLUB, (1997; 141). Bob McCurley, 22 Kinnordy Terrace, Dundee, DD4 7NW. 01382 462944; e-mail: bob.mccurley@amserve.net

SOC TAYSIDE BRANCH, (145). James Whitelaw, 36 Burn Street, Dundee, DD3 0LB. 01382 819391.

Ringing Group
TAY RG, Ms S Millar, Edenvale Cottage, 1 Lydox Cottages, Dairsie, Fife, KY15 4RN.

RSPB Local Groups
DUNDEE, (1972;110). Ron Downing, 3 Lynnewood Place, Dundee,DD4 7HB. 01382 451987.

ARGYLL

Bird Recorder
ARGYLL, Paul Daw, Tigh-na-Tulloch, Tullochgorm, Minard, Argyll, PA32 8YQ. e-mail: monedula@globalnet.co.uk

Bird Reports
ARGYLL BIRD REPORT (1984-), From Bill Staley,

16 Glengilp, Ardrishaid, Lochgilphead, Argyll, PA30 8HT. e-mail: pabstaley@freeuk.com

MACHRIHANISH SEABIRD OBSERVATORY REPORT (1992-), from Observatory, see Reserves & Observatories.

BTO Regional Representatives
ARGYLL (MULL, COLL, TIREE AND MORVERN), Richard Evans, C/O RSPB, 25 Ravelston Terrace, Edinburgh, EH4 3TP.
e-mail: rjevans6@freeuk.com

ARGYLL MAINLAND, BUTE AND GIGHA, David Wood, Drover's House, Bellanoch, Lochgilphead, Argyll, PA31 8SN.
e-mail: puffinus@stormie.idps.co.uk

ISLAY, JURA, COLONSAY RR, Dr Malcolm Ogilvie, Glencairn, Bruichladdich, Isle of Islay, PA49 7UN. e-mail: maogilvie@indaal.demon.co.uk

Clubs
ARGYLL BIRD CLUB, (1983;152). Bill Staley, 16 Glengilp, Ardrishaig, Argyll, PA30 8HT.
e-mail: pabstaley@freeuk.com

ISLE OF MULL BIRD CLUB (2001; 105). Len White, Ard Dochas, Lochdon, Isle of Mull, Argyll, Scotland, PA64 6AP. 01680 812335. www. mullbirds.com e-mail: arddochas@aol.com

Ringing Group
TRESHNISH AUK RG, S W Walker, Snipe Cottage, Hamsterley, Bishop Auckland, Co Durham, DL13 3NX. e-mail: snipe@snipe.screaming.net

AYRSHIRE

Bird Recorder
AYRSHIRE, Angus Hogg, 11 Kirkmichael Road, Crosshill, Maybole, Ayrshire, KA19 7RJ.
e-mail: dcgos@globalnet.co.uk

Bird Reports
AYRSHIRE BIRD REPORT (1976-), from Ayrshire Recorder.

BTO Regional Representatives
AYRSHIRE RR, Paul Darnbrough, 65 Loreny Drive, Kilmarnock, Ayrshire, KA1 4RH.
e-mail: pauldarnbrough@hotmail.com

Club
SOC AYRSHIRE BRANCH, (1962; 100). Henry Martin, 9 Shawfield Avenue, Ayr, KA7 4RE. 01292 442086; www.ayrshire-birding.org.uk

RSPB Local Groups
CENTRAL AYRSHIRE, (1978; 70). James Thomson, Sundrum Smithy, Ayr, KA6 6LR. 01292 570351.

NORTH AYRSHIRE, (1976; 180). Duncan Watt, 28 Greenbank, Dalry, Ayrshire, KA24 5AY.

Wildlife Hospital
HESSILHEAD WILDLIFE RESCUE CENTRE, Gay & Andy Christie, Gateside, Beith, Ayrshire, KA15 1HT. 01505 502415
All species. Releasing aviaries. Veterinary support.

BORDERS

Bird Atlas/Avifauna
The Breeding Birds of South-east Scotland, a tetrad atlas 1988-1994 by R D Murray et al. (Scottish Ornithologists' Club, 1998).

Bird Recorder
Ray Murray, 4 Bellfield Crescent, Eddleston, Peebles, EH45 8RQ. 01721 730677;
e-mail: ray.d.murray@ukgateway.net

Bird Report
BORDERS BIRD REPORT (1979-), From Malcolm Ross, The Tubs, Dingleton Road, Melrose, Borders.

BTO Regional Representative & Regional Development Officer
RR, Alex Copland, Keeraun Hill, Banagher, Co Offaly, Ireland;
e-mail: crex@eircom.net

Club
SOC BORDERS BRANCH, (90). Vicky McLellan, 18 Glen Crescent, Peebles, EH45 9BS. 01721 724580.

Ringing Group
BORDERS RG, (1991; 10). Dr T W Dougall, 38 Leamington Terrace, Edinburgh, EH10 4JL. (Fax)0131 469 5599.

RSPB Local Group
BORDERS, (1995; 94). Nancy Marshall, The Birches, Leydon Grove, Clovenfords, Galashiels, TD1 3NF. 01896 850564.

CAITHNESS

Bird Recorders
CAITHNESS, Peter Miler, 10 Harrold Cottages, Reiss, Wick, Caithness, KW1 4RU. 01955 603655.

SCOTLAND

Bird Reports
CAITHNESS BIRD REPORT (1983-), From Julian Smith, St John's, Brough, Dunnet, Caithness; e-mail: designsmith@madasafish.com

BTO Regional Representatives & Regional Development Officers
CAITHNESS, Hugh Clark, Bellfield, 3 Lindsay Place, Wick, Caithness, KW1 4PF. 01955 605372; e-mail: hugh@lindsayplace.fsnet.co.uk

Clubs
SOC CAITHNESS BRANCH, (51). Stan Laybourne, Old Schoolhouse, Harpsdale, Halkirk, Caithness, KW12 6UN. 01847 841244.

CLYDE

Bird Atlas/Avifauna
A Guide to Birdwatching in the Clyde Area (2001) by Cliff Baister and Marin Osler (Scottish Ornithologists' Club, Clyde branch).

Clyde Breeding Bird Atlas (working title). In preparation.

Bird Recorders
CLYDE ISLANDS, Bernard Zonfrillo, 28 Brodie Road, Glasgow,G21 3SB. 0141 557 0791.

CLYDE, Iain P Gibson, 8 Kenmure View, Howwood, Johnstone, Renfrewshire, PA9 1DR. 01505 705874.

Bird Reports
CLYDE BIRDS (1973-), From Jim & Valerie Wilson, 76 Laigh Road, Newton Mearns, Glasgow, G77 5EQ. e-mail: jim.val@btinternet.com

BTO Regional Representatives
ARRAN, BUTE, CUMBRAES, Position vacant.

LANARK, RENFREW, DUMBARTON, Position vacant.

Club
SOC CLYDE BRANCH, (300). Alison Robertson, Flat 2/3, 3 Priorwood Court, Glasgow, G13 1GE. 0141 9581747; e-mail: alison@bogcotton.freeserve.co.uk

Ringing Group
CLYDE RG, (1979; 18). I Livingstone, 57 Strathview Road, Bellshill, Lanarkshire, ML4 2UY. 01698 749844.

RSPB Local Groups
GLASGOW, (1972;153). Jim Coyle, 6 Westerlands, Anniesland, Glasgow, G12 0FB. 0141 579 7565.

HAMILTON, (1976;90). Mrs Isabel Crinean, 15A Central Avenue, Cambuslang, Glasgow, G72 8AY. 0141 641 1292; www.baronshaugh.co.uk

HELENSBURGH, (1975; 62). Alistair McIntyre, Craggan, Rosneath Road, Helensburgh, Dunbartonshire, G84 0EJ. e-mail: almc@jameswatt.co.uk

RENFREWSHIRE, (1986; 200). Ms Alison Purssell, 2 Glencairn Place, High Street, Kilmacolm, PA13 4BT. 01505 872576.

DUMFRIES & GALLOWAY

Bird Recorders
NITHSDALE, ANNANDALE & ESKDALE, 1, Steve Cooper, WWT Caerlaverock, Eastpark Farm, Caerlaverock, Dumfries, DG1 4RS. e-mail: steve.cooper@wwt.org.uk www.wwtck.free-online.co.uk

2, Paul N Collin, Gairland, Old Edinburgh Road, Minnigaff, Newton Stewart, Wigtownshire, DG8 6PL. 01671 402861; e-mail: paul.collin@rspb.org.uk

Bird Report
BIRDS IN DUMFRIES AND GALLOWAY 15 (1985-), From Peter Norman, Low Boreland, Tongland Road, Kirkcudbright, DG6 4UU.

BTO Regional Representatives & Regional Development Officer
DUMFRIES RR, Duncan Irving, 12 Great Eastern Drive, Glancaple, Dumfries. 01387 770265.

DUMFRIES RDO, Ken Bruce, Mallaig, Wellington Street, Glencaple, Dumfries, DG1 4RA. 01387 770336.

KIRKCUDBRIGHT RR, Andrew Bielinski, 41 Main Street, St Johns Town of Dalry, Castle Douglas, Kirkcudbright, DG7 3UP. 01644 430418(eve); 01387 247010(day); e-mail: andrewb@bielinski.fsnet.co.uk

WIGTOWN RR, Geoff Sheppard, The Roddens, Leswalt, Stranraer, Wigtownshire, DG9 0QR. e-mail: geoff_sheppard@lineone.net

Clubs
SOC DUMFRIES BRANCH, (1961; 105). Brian Smith, Rockiemount, Colvend, Dalbeattie, Dumfries, DG5 4QW. 01556 620617.

SOC STEWARTRY BRANCH, (1976; 75). Miss Joan Howie, 60 Main Street, St Johns Town of Dalry, Castle Douglas, Kirkcudbrightshire, DG7 3UW. 01644 430226.

SOC WEST GALLOWAY BRANCH, (1975; 50). Geoff Sheppard, The Roddens, Leswalt, Stranraer, Wigtownshire, DG9 0QR.
e-mail: geoff_sheppard@lineone.net

Ringing Group
NORTH SOLWAY RG, Geoff Sheppard, The Roddens, Leswalt, Stranraer, Wigtownshire, DG9 0QR. e-mail: geoff_sheppard@lineone.net

RSPB Local Group
GALLOWAY, (1985;176). Robert M Greenshields, Nether Linkins, Gelston, Castle Douglas, DG7 1SU. 01556 680217;
e-mail: greenshields@netherlinkins.fsnet.co.uk

FIFE

Bird Recorders
FIFE REGION INC OFFSHORE ISLANDS (NORTH FORTH), Douglas Dickson, 2 Burrelton Court, Bankhead, Glenrothes, Fife, KY7 4UN.
e-mail: douglasdickson@excite.co.uk

ISLE OF MAY BIRD OBSERVATORY, Iain English, 19 Nethan Gate, Hamilton, Lanarkshire, ML3 8NH.
e-mail: i.english@talk21.com

Bird Reports
FIFE BIRD REPORT (1988-) (FIFE & KINROSS BR 1980-87), from Willie McBay, 41 Shamrock Street, Dunfermline, Fife, KY12 0JQ. 01383 723464;
e-mail: wmcbay@aol.com

ISLE OF MAY BIRD OBSERVATORY REPORT (1985-), From David Thorne, Craigurd House, Blyth Bridge, West Linton, Peeblesshire, EH46 7AH.

BTO Regional Representative
FIFE & KINROSS RR, Norman Elkins, 18 Scotstarvit View, Cupar, Fife, KY15 5DX. 01334 654348;
e-mail: jandnelkins@rapidial.co.uk

Clubs
FIFE BIRD CLUB, (1985; 300). Willie McBay, 41 Shamrock Street, Dunfermline, Fife, KY12 0JQ. 01383 723464.

LOTHIANS AND FIFE MUTE SWAN STUDY GROUP, Allan & Lyndesay Brown, 61 Watts Gardens, Cupar, Fife, KY15 4UG.
e-mail: swans@allanwbrown.co.uk

SOC FIFE BRANCH, (1956;180). Fiona Butler, 7 Marionfield Place, Cupar, Fife, KY15 5JN. 01334 654895.

Ringing Groups
ISLE OF MAY BIRD OBSERVATORY, D Robertson, Woodlands, Bandrum, Nr Carnock, Dunfermline, KY12 9HR.
e-mail: derek@woodlandstudios.fsnet.co.uk

TAY RG, Ms S Millar, Edenvale Cottage, 1 Lydox Cottages, Dairsie, Fife, KY15 4RN.

Wildlife Hospital
SCOTTISH SPCA WILD LIFE REHABILITATION CENTRE, Middlebank Farm, Masterton Road, Dunfermline, Fife, KY11 8QN. 01383 412520. All species. Open to visitors, groups and school parties. Illustrated talk on oiled bird cleaning and other aspects of wildlife rehabilitation available. Veterinary support.

FORTH

Bird Recorder
FORTH AREA, Dr C J Henty, Edgehill East, 7b Coneyhill Road, Bridge of Allan, Stirling, FK9 4EL. 01786 832166.

Bird Report
CENTRAL REGION BIRD REPORT (1976-), From Lindsay Corbett, 30 Dunmar Drive, Alloa, Clacks.

BTO Regional Representative
Neil Bielby, 56 Ochiltree, Dunblane, Perthshire, FK15 0DF. e-mail: neil.bielby@ntlworld.com

Club
SOC STIRLING BRANCH, (1968; 90). Ian Wilson, 100 Causewayhead Road, Stirling FK9 5HJ. 01786 473877.

RSPB Local Group
FORTH VALLEY, (1996; 150). Alex Downie, 2 St Lawrence Avenue, Dunblane, Perthshire, FK15 9DE. 01786 825228.

HIGHLAND

Bird Atlas/Avifauna
The Birds of Sutherland by Alan Vittery (Colin Baxter Photography Ltd, 1997).

Birds of Skye by Andrew Currie. In preparation.

Bird Recorders
ROSS-SHIRE, INVERNESS-SHIRE, SUTHERLAND, Colin Crooke, RSPB, Etive House, Beechwood Park, Inverness, IV2 3BW. 01463 715000.

Bird Reports
HIGHLAND BIRD REPORT (1991-), from Recorder.

SUTHERLAND BIRD REVIEW (2002-), from Alan Vittery, C/O 164 West Clyne, Brora, Sutherland, KW9 6NH. 01408 621827.

BTO Regional Representatives & Regional Development Officers
INVERNESS & SPEYSIDE RR & RDO, Hugh Insley, 1 Drummond Place, Inverness,IV2 4JT. e-mail: hugh.insley@tinyworld.co.uk

RUM, EIGG, CANNA & MUCK RR & RDO, Bob Swann, 14 St Vincent Road, Tain, Ross-shire, IV19 1JR. e-mail: bob.swann@freeuk.com

ROSS-SHIRE RR, David Butterfield, 1 Calrichie Cottages, Kindeace, Invergordon, Ross-shire, IV18 0LN. 01349 854434 evgs; e-mail: dave.birder@freeuk.com

SUTHERLAND, Position vacant.

SKYE RR & RDO, Position vacant.

Clubs
EAST SUTHERLAND BIRD GROUP, (1976; 80). Alan Vittery, 164 West Clyne, Brora, Sutherland, KW9 6NH. 01408 621827.

SOC HIGHLAND BRANCH, (1955; 171). Janet Crummy, Coalhaugh, Tomatin, Inverness, IV13 7YS. 01808 511261.

Ringing Groups
EAST ROSS RG, Ivan Brockway, Courthill, Tain, Ross-shire, IV19 1NE. 01349 852521.

HIGHLAND RG, Bob Swann, 14 St Vincent Road, Tain, Ross-shire, IV19 1JR. e-mail: bob.swann@freeuk.com

RSPB Local Group
HIGHLAND, (1987; 214). Richard Prentice, Lingay, Lewiston, Drumnadrochit, Inverness, IV63 6UW. 01456 450526.

LOTHIAN

Bird Atlas/Avifauna
The Breeding Birds of South-east Scotland, a tetrad atlas 1988-1994 by R D Murray et al. (Scottish Ornithologists' Club, 1998).

Bird Recorder
David J Kelly, 20 Market View, Tranent, East Lothian, EH32 9AX. e-mail: dj_kelly@btinternet.com

Bird Reports
LOTHIAN BIRD REPORT (1979-), from Recorder.

WEST LOTHIAN BIRD CLUB REPORT (1991-), From Secretary, West Lothian Bird Club.

BTO Regional Representative
Alan Heavisides, 9 Addiston Crescent, Balerno, Edinburgh, EH14 7DB. e-mail: a.heavisides@napier.ac.uk

Clubs
EDINBURGH NATURAL HISTORY SOCIETY, (1869; 200). Michael Osborne, 2 Old Woodside, Bush Estate, Penicuik, Midlothian, EH26 0PQ. 0131 445 3824.

FOULSHIELS BIRD GROUP, (1991; 7). Frazer Henderson, 2 Elizabeth Gardens, Stoneyburn, W Lothian, EH47 8BP. 01501 762972.

LOTHIANS AND FIFE MUTE SWAN STUDY GROUP, Allan & Lyndesay Brown, 61 Watts Gardens, Cupar, Fife, KY15 4UG. e-mail: swans@allanwbrown.co.uk

SOC LOTHIAN BRANCH, (1936; 440). Ian Thomson, 4 Craigielaw, Longniddry, E Lothian, EH32 0PY. 01875 870588; mail: imt.aberlady@ic24.net

 WEST LOTHIAN BIRD CLUB, (1990; 20). Alan Paterson, 17 Main Street, Winchburgh, Boxbugh, W Lothian.

Ringing Group
LOTHIAN RG, A F Leitch, 2 Burgess Terrace, Edinburgh, EH9 2BD.

RSPB Local Group
EDINBURGH, (1974;450). Hugh Connor, 22 Tippett Knowes, Winchburgh,West Lothian, EH52 6UW. e-mail: h.m.conner@hw.ac.uk http://www.cee.hw.ac.uk/~hmc/rspb.edin/index.html

MORAY & NAIRN

Bird Atlas/Avifauna
The Birds of Moray and Nairn by Martin Cook (Mercat Press, 1992).

Bird Recorders
NAIRN, Martin J H Cook, Rowanbrae, Clochan, Buckie, Banffshire, AB56 5EQ. 01542 850296; e-mail: martin.cook9@virgin.net

SCOTLAND

MORAY, Martin J H Cook, Rowanbrae, Clochan, Buckie, Banffshire, AB56 5EQ. 01542 850296.

Bird Report
MORAY & NAIRN BIRD REPORT (1985-), from Moray Recorder.

BTO Regional Representatives & Regional Development Officer
MORAY AND NAIRN RR, Bob Proctor, 94 Reid Street, Bishopmill, Elgin, Moray, IV30 4HH. e-mail: bob.proctor@rspb.org.uk

NORTH EAST SCOTLAND

Bird Atlas/Avifauna
The Birds of North East Scotland by S T Buckland, M V Bell & N Picozzi (North East Scotland Bird Club, 1990).

Bird Recorder
NORTH-EAST SCOTLAND, Andrew Thorpe, 30 Monearn Gardens, Milltimber, Aberdeen, AB13 0EA. e-mail: andrewthorpe@tinyworld.co.uk

Bird Reports
NORTH-EAST SCOTLAND BIRD REPORT (1974-), From Dave Gill, Drakemyre Croft, Cairnorrie, Methlick, Aberdeenshire, AB41 0JN. 01651 806252; e-mail: dave@drakemyre.freeserve.co.uk

NORTH SEA BIRD CLUB ANNUAL REPORT (1979-), from NSBC Recorder, see below.

BTO Regional Representatives & Regional Development Officer
ABERDEEN RDO, Kath Hamper, 9 Mid Street, Inverallochy, Fraserburgh, Aberdeenshire, AB43 8YA. 01346 583015.

ABERDEEN NORTH RR, Peter Walker, Westgate House, Udny, Ellon, Aberdeenshire, AB41 6SD. e-mail: pkwalkers@aol.com

KINCARDINE & DEESIDE, Graham Cooper, Westbank, Beltie Road, Torphins, Banchory, Aberdeen, AB31 4JT. 01339 882706.

Clubs
NORTH SEA BIRD CLUB, (1979; 200). Andrew Thorpe, (Recorder), Ocean Laboratory and Centre for Ecology, Aberdeen University, Newburgh, Ellon, Aberdeenshire, AB41 6AA. e-mail: nsbc@abdn.ac.uk

SOC GRAMPIAN BRANCH, (1956; 110). John Wills, Bilbo, Monymusk, Inverurie, Aberdeenshire, AB51 7HA. e-mail: bilbo@monymusk.freeserve.co.uk

Ringing Groups
ABERDEEN UNIVERSITY RG, Andrew Thorpe, Ocean Laboratory and Centre for Ecology, Aberdeen University, Newburgh, Aberdeenshire, AB41 6AA. e-mail: nsbc@abdn.ac.uk

GRAMPIAN RG, R Duncan, 86 Broadfold Drive, Bridge of Don, Aberdeen, AB23 8PP.

RSPB Local Group
ABERDEEN, (1977; 180). Bob Littlejohn, 28 Seafield Drive East, Aberdeen, AB15 7UR. 01224 313576.

Wildlife Hospital
GRAMPIAN WILDLIFE REHABILITATION TRUST, 40 High Street, New Deer, Turriff, Aberdeenshire, AB53 6SX. 01771 644489.
Veterinary surgeon. Access to full practice facilities. Will care for all species of birds.

ORKNEY

Bird Atlas/Avifauna
The Birds of Orkney by CJ Booth et al (The Orkney Press, 1984).

Bird Recorder
Jim Williams, Frurholm, Finstown, Orkney, KW17 2EQ. 01856 761317;
e-mail: jim@geniefea.freeserve.co.uk

Bird Report
ORKNEY BIRD REPORT (inc North Ronaldsay Bird Report) (1974-), from EJ Williams, Fairholm, Finstown, Orkney, KW17 2EQ.
e-mail: jim@geniefea.freeserve.co.uk

BTO Regional Representative & Regional Development Officer
Colin Corse, Garrisdale, Lynn Park, Kirkwall, Orkney, KW15 1SL. e-mail: ccorse@aol.com

Club
SOC ORKNEY BRANCH, (1993; 15). Stuart Williams, Crafty, Firth, Orkney, KW17 2ES. e-mail: stuart@gavia.freeserve.co.uk

Ringing Groups
NORTH RONALDSAY BIRD OBSERVATORY, Ms A E Duncan, Twingness, North Ronaldsay, Orkney, KW17 2BE. e-mail: alison@nrbo.prestel.co.uk
www.nrbo.f2s.com

ORKNEY RG, Colin J Corse, Garrisdale, Lynn Park, Kirkwall, Orkney, KW15 1SL. H:01856 874484; W:01856 884156.

SULE SKERRY RG, Dave Budworth, 121 Wood Lane, Newhall, Swadlincote, Derbys, DE11 0LX. 0121 6953384.

RSPB Local Group
ORKNEY, (1985;250). Neil McCance, West End, Burray, Orkney. 01856 731260.

OUTER HEBRIDES

Bird Recorder
OUTER HEBRIDES, Andrew Stevenson, The Old Stores, Bornish, Isle of South Uist HS8 5SA; e-mail: andrewstevenson@snh.gov.uk

WESTERN ISLES, Brian Rabbitts. 01876 580328; e-mail: brian.rabbitts@virgin.net

Bird Report
OUTER HEBRIDES BIRD REPORT (1989-), from Recorder.

BTO Regional Representatives & Regional Development Officer
BENBECULA & THE UISTS RR & RDO, 01876 580328; e-mail: brian.rabbitts@virgin.net

LEWIS & HARRIS RR. 1, Tony Pendle, 3 Linsiadar, Isle of Lewis,HS2 9DR.
e-mail: ellerpendle@madasafish.com

LEWIS & HARRIS RR. 2, Chris Reynolds, 11 Reef, Isle of Lewis, HS2 9HU.
e-mail: juliareynolds@btinternet.com

Ringing Group
SHIANTS AUK RG, David Steventon, Welland House, 207 Hurdsfield Road, Macclesfield, Cheshire, SK10 2PX. 01625 421936.

PERTH & KINROSS

Bird Recorder
PERTH & KINROSS, Ron Youngman, Blairchroisk Cottage, Ballinluig, Pitlochry, Perthshire, PH9 0NE. 01796 482324; e-mail: blairchroisk@aol.com

Bird Report
PERTH & KINROSS BIRD REPORT (1974-), from Recorder.

BTO Regional Representatives & Regional Development Officer
PERTHSHIRE RR, Andrew Wight, 01783 710623; e-mail: perth@interramp.co.uk

Clubs
PERTHSHIRE SOCIETY OF NATURAL SCIENCE (Ornithological Section), (1964; 60). Miss Esther Taylor, 23 Verena Terrace, Perth,PH2 0BZ. 01738 621986.

RSPB Local Groups
TAYSIDE, (1988; 160). Alan Davis, 6 Grey Street, Perth,PH2 0JJ. 01738 622480.

SHETLAND

Bird Recorders
FAIR ISLE, Deryk Shaw, Bird Observatory, Fair Isle, Shetland, ZE2 9JU.
e-mail: fairisle.birdobs@zetnet.co.uk

SHETLAND, Kevin Osborn, 20 Nederdale, Lerwick, Shetland, ZE1 0SA. 01595 695974;
e-mail: k.o@virgin.net

Bird Reports
FAIR ISLE BIRD OBSERVATORY REPORT (1949-), From Scottish Ornithologists' Club, 21 Regent Terrace, Edinburgh, EH7 5BT. 0131 556 6042.

SHETLAND BIRD REPORT (1969-) no pre 1973 available, From Martin Heubeck, East House, Sumburgh Lighthouse, Virkie, Shetland, ZE3 9JN. e-mail: martinheubeck@btinternet.com

BTO Regional Representative
Dave Okill, Heilinabretta, Cauldhame, Trondra, Shetland, ZE1 0XL. H:01595 880450; W:01595 696926.

Club
SHETLAND BIRD CLUB, (1973; 200). Reinoud Norde, Lindale, Ireland, Bigton, Shetland, ZE2 9JA. 01950 422467:
e-mail: reinoud.norde@lineone.net

Ringing Groups
FAIR ISLE BIRD OBSERVATORY, Deryk Shaw, Bird Observatory, Fair Isle, Shetland, ZE2 9JU.
e-mail:
fairisle.birdobs@zetnet.co.uk

SHETLAND RG, Dave Okill, Heilinabretta, Cauldhame, Trondra, Shetland, ZE1 0XL. H:01595 880450; W:01595 696926.

WALES

Bird Report
See Welsh Ornithological Society in National Directory.

Club
See Welsh Ornithological Society in National Directory.

EAST WALES

Bird Atlas/Avifauna
Birds of Radnorshire. In preparation.

The Gwent Atlas of Breeding Birds by Tyler, Lewis, Venables & Walton (Gwent Ornithological Society, 1987).

Bird Recorders
BRECONSHIRE, Martin F Peers, Cyffylog, 2 Aberyscir Road, Cradoc, Brecon, Powys, LD3 9PB. 01874 623774.

MONTGOMERYSHIRE, Brayton Holt, Scops Cottage, Pentrebeirdd, Welshpool, Powys, SY21 9DL. 01938 500266.

RADNORSHIRE, Pete Jennings, Penbont House, Elan Valley, Rhayader, Powys, LD6 5HS. H:01597 811522; W:01597 810880; e-mail: petejelanvalley@hotmail.com

Bird Reports
BRECONSHIRE BIRDS (1962-), from Brecknock Wildlife Trust.

GWENT BIRD REPORT (1964-), from Jerry Lewis, Y Bwthyn Gwyn, Coldbrook, Abergavenny, Monmouthshire, NP7 9TD. (H)01873 855091; (W)01633 644856.

MONTGOMERYSHIRE BIRD REPORT (1981-82-), from Montgomeryshire Wildlife Trust.

RADNOR BIRDS (1987/92-), from Radnorshire Recorder.

BTO Regional Representatives & Regional Development Officer
BRECKNOCK RR, John Lloyd, Cynghordy, Llandovery, Carms, SA20 0LN.
e-mail; thelloyds@dial.pipex.com

MONTGOMERY RR, Brayton Holt (retiring end 2002), Scops Cottage, Pentrebeirdd, Welshpool, Powys, SY21 9DL. 01938 500266.

RADNORSHIRE RR & RDO, Pete Jennings, Penbont House, Elan Valley, Rhayader, Powys, LD6 5HS. H:01597 811522; W:01597 810880; e-mail: petejelanvalley@hotmail.com

Clubs
MONTGOMERYSHIRE FIELD SOCIETY, (1946; 170). Maureen Preen, Ivy House, Deep Cutting, Pool Quay, Welshpool, Powys, SY21 9LJ. Tel: Mary Oliver, 01686 413518.

MONTGOMERYSHIRE WILDLIFE TRUST BIRD GROUP, (1997; 104). A M Puzey, Four Seasons, Arddleen, Llanymynech, Powys, SY22 6RU. 01938 590578.

RADNOR BIRD GROUP, (1986). Pete Jennings, Penbont House, Elan Valley, Rhayader, Powys, LD6 5HS. H:01597 811522; W:01597 810880; e-mail: petejelanvalley@hotmail.com

Ringing Groups
GOLDCLIFF RG, Vaughan Thomas, Gilgal Cottage, Gilfach, Llanvaches, S Wales, NP26 3AZ. 01633 817161.

LLANGORSE RG, Jerry Lewis, Y Bwthyn Gwyn, Coldbrook, Abergavenny, Monmouthshire, NP7 9TD. H:01873 855091; W:01633 644856

Wildlife Trusts
BRECKNOCK WILDLIFE TRUST, (1963; 900). Lion House, Bethel Square, Brecon, Powys, LD3 7AY. 01874 625708; (fax)01874 610552. e-mail: brecknockwt@cix.co.uk www.waleswildlife.co.uk

MONTGOMERYSHIRE WILDLIFE TRUST, (1982; 1,000). Collot House, 20 Severn Street, Welshpool, Powys, SY21 7AD. 01938 555654; (fax)01938 556161. e-mail: montwt@cix.co.uk www.wildlifetrust.org.uk/montgomeryshire

RADNORSHIRE WILDLIFE TRUST, (1987; 789). Warwick House, High Street, Llandrindod Wells, Powys, LD1 6AG. 01597 823298; (fax)01597 823274. e-mail: radnorshirewt@cix.co.uk www.waleswildlife.co.uk

WALES

NORTH WALES

Bird Atlas/Avifauna
The Birds of Caernarfonshire by John Barnes
(1998, from Lionel Pilling, 51 Brighton Close, Rhyl
LL18 3HL).

Bird Recorders
ANGLESEY, Stephen Culley, Millhouse, Penmynydd
Road, Menai Bridge, Anglesey, LL59 5RT. 01248
713091. e-mail: SteCul10@aol.com

CAERNARFON, John Barnes, Fach Goch, Waunfawr,
Caernarfon, LL55 4YS. 01286 650362.

DENBIGHSHIRE & FLINTSHIRE, Norman Hallas, 63
Park Avenue, Wrexham, LL12 7AW. 01978 290522.

MEIRIONNYDD, D L Smith, 3 Smithfield Lane,
Dolgellau, Gwynedd, LL40 1BU. 01341 421064.

Bird Reports
BARDSEY BIRD OBSERVATORY ANNUAL REPORT,
from Warden, see Reserves.

*CAMBRIAN BIRD REPORT (sometime Gwynedd
Bird Report) (1953-)*, from Rhion Pritchard, Pant
Afonig, Hafod Lane, Bangor, Gwynedd, LL57 4BU.
e-mail: rhion@pritchardr.freeserve.co.uk

CLWYD BIRD REPORT, from Dr Anne Brenchley,
Tyr Fannog, 43 Black Brook, Sychdyn, Mold, Flints,
CH7 6LT. 01352 750118.

*MEIRIONNYDD BIRD REPORT Published in
Cambrian Bird Report (above).*

*WREXHAM BIRDWATCHERS' SOCIETY ANNUAL
REPORT (1982-)*, from Secretary, Wrexham
Birdwatchers' Society.

**BTO Regional Representatives & Regional
Development Officer**
ANGLESEY RR, Position vacant.

CAERNARFON RR, John Barnes, Fach Goch,
Waunfawr, Caernarfon, LL55 4YS. 01286 650362.

CLWYD EAST RR, Anne Brenchley, Ty'r Fawnog, 43
Black Brook, Sychdyn, Mold, CH7 6LT.
e-mail: ian.anne@imsab.idps.co.uk

CLWYD WEST RR, Mel ab Owain, 31 Coed Bedw,
Abergele, Conwy, LL22 7EH. 01745 826528;
e-mail: malabowain@cix.co.uk

MEIRIONNYDD RR, Peter Haveland, Ty
Manceinion, Penmachno, Betws-y-Coed, Gwynedd,
LL24 0UD. e-mail: peter.haveland@tesco.net

Clubs
BANGOR BIRD GROUP, (1947; 100). Secretary,

Bangor Bird Group, Treborth Botanic Gardens,
University of Wales, Bangor, LL57 2RQ.
e-mail: n.brown@bangor.ac.uk

CAMBRIAN ORNITHOLOGICAL SOCIETY, (1952;
162). Rhion Pritchard, Pant Afonig, Hafod Lane,
Bangor, Gwynedd, LL57 4BU. 01248 671301;
http://cos.users3.50megs.com/

CLWYD ORNITHOLOGICAL SOCIETY, (1956; 45).
Miss Lynn Davies, Preswylfa, Berthen Rd, Lixwm,
Holywell, Flints, CH8 8LT. 01852 781106.

DEE ESTUARY CONSERVATION GROUP, (1973; 22
grps). N J Friswell, 8 Oaklands Crescent,
Tattenhall, Chester, CH3 9QT. 01829 770463.

DEESIDE NATURALISTS' SOCIETY, (1973; 500).
Roy Hamer, 13 Parc Gorsedd, Gorsedd, Holywell,
Flints, CH8 8RP. 01352 716273.

WREXHAM BIRDWATCHERS' SOCIETY, (1974; 90).
Miss Marian Williams, 10 Lake View, Gresford,
Wrexham, Clwyd, LL12 8PU. 01978 854633.

Ringing Groups
BARDSEY BIRD OBSERVATORY, Steven Stansfield,
Bardsey Island, off Aberdaron, Pwllheli, Gwynedd,
LL53 8DE. 07855 204151;
e-mail: steve@bbfo.freeserve.co.uk

MERSEYSIDE RG, P Slater, 45 Greenway Road,
Speke, Liverpool, L24 7RY.

SCAN RG, D J Stanyard, Court Farm, Groeslon,
Caernarfon, Gwynedd, LL54 7UE.01286 881 669.

RSPB Local Group
NORTH WALES, (1986; 130). Paul Braid, 01492
516260; e-mail: p.braid@virgin.net

Wildlife Trust
NORTH WALES WILDLIFE TRUST, (1963; 2,700).
376 High Street, Bangor, Gwynedd, LL57 1YE.
01248 351541; (fax)01248 353192.
e-mail: nwwt@cix.co.uk
www.wildlifetrust/northwales

SOUTH WALES

Bird Atlas/Avifauna
An Atlas of Breeding Birds in West Glamorgan by
David M Hanford et al (Gower Ornithological
Society, 1992).

Birds of Glamorgan by Clive Hurford and Peter
Lansdown (Published by the authors, c/o National
Museum of Wales, Cardiff, 1995).

Bird Recorders
GLAMORGAN (EAST), Steve Moon, 36 Rest Bay

WALES

Close, Porthcawl, Bridgend, CF36 3UN.
e-mail: moonsj@bridgend.gov.uk

GOWER (WEST GLAMORGAN), Robert Taylor, 285 Llangyfelach Road, Brynhyfryd, Swansea, SA5 9LB. 01792 464780; mobile 07970 567007.

GWENT, Chris Jones, 22 Walnut Drive, Caerleon, Newport, Gwent, NP6 1SB. 01633 423439.

Bird Reports
EAST GLAMORGAN BIRD REPORT (title varies 1963-95) 1996-2001, from Richard G Smith, 35 Manor Chase, Gwaun Miskin, Pontypridd, Rhondda Cynon Taff, S Wales.CF38 2JD.
e-mail: rgsmith@birdpix.freeserve.co.uk

GOWER BIRDS (1965-), from Audrey Jones, 24 Hazel Road, Uplands, Swansea, SA2 0LX. 01792 298859.

BTO Regional Representatives & Regional Development Officer
EAST GLAMORGAN (former Mid & South Glam) RR, Rob Nottage, 32 Village Farm, Bonvilston, Cardiff, CF5 6TY. e-mail: rob@nottages.freeserve.co.uk

WEST RR, Bob Howells, Ynys Enlli, 14 Dolgoy Close, West Cross, Swansea, SA3 5LT.
e-mail: bobhowells31@hotmail.com

GWENT RR, Jerry Lewis, Y Bwthyn Gwyn, Coldbrook, Abergavenny, Monmouthshire, NP7 9TD. H:01873 855091; W:01633 644856

Clubs
CARDIFF NATURALISTS' SOCIETY, (1867; 225). Stephen R Howe, Department of Geology, National Museum of Wales, Cardiff, CF10 3NP.
e-mail: steve.howe@nmgw.ac.uk

GLAMORGAN BIRD CLUB, (1990; 170). Steve Moon, Kenfig National Nature Reserve, Ton Kenfig, Pyle, Bridgend, CF33 4PT.
e-mail: moonsj@bridgend.gov.uk

GOWER ORNITHOLOGICAL SOCIETY, (1956; 120). Audrey Jones, 24 Hazel Road, Uplands, Swansea, SA2 0LX. 01792 298859.

GWENT ORNITHOLOGICAL SOCIETY, (1964; 350). T J Russell, The Pines, Highfield Road, Monmouth, Gwent, NP25 3HR. 01600 716266.

Ringing Groups
FLAT HOLM RG, Brian Bailey, Tamarisk House, Wards Court, Frampton-on-Severn, Glos, GL2 7DY.
e-mail: brianhbailey98@freeserve.co.uk

KENFIG RG, Mr D.G. Carrington, 25 Bryneglwys Gardens, Porthcawl, Bridgend, Mid Glamorgan, CF36 5PR.

RSPB Local Groups
CARDIFF & DISTRICT, (1973; 4,500). Mrs Margaret Read, 121 Lavernock Road, Penarth, South Wales, CF64 3QG. 02920 709537;
e-mail: mereadcmt@aol.com

WEST GLAMORGAN, (1985; 421). Maggie Cornelius, 01792 229244.

Wildlife Hospitals
GOWER BIRD HOSPITAL, Karen Kingsnorth and Simon Allen, Valetta, Sandy Lane, Pennard, Swansea, SA3 2EW. 01792 371630. All species of wild birds, also hedgehogs and small mammals. Prior phone call essential. Gower Bird Hospital cares for sick, injured and orphaned wild birds and animals with the sole intention of returning them to the wild. Post release radio tracking projects, gull ringing scheme. Contact us for more information. e-mail: gbh@valetta.u-net.com

LLEWELLYN, Paul, 104 Manselfield Road, Murton, Swansea, SA3 3AG.
e-mail: p.j.llewellyn@swansea.ac.uk
All species of birds but specialist knowledge of raptors. Veterinary support.

Wildlife Trust
GWENT WILDLIFE TRUST, (1963;4500). 16 White Swan Court, Church Street, Monmouth, Gwent, NP25 3NY. 01600 715501; (fax)01600 715832.
e-mail: gwentwildlife@cix.co.uk
www.wildlifetrust.org.uk/gwent

SOUTH AND WEST WALES, (1961; 1300). Nature Centre, Fountain Road, Tondu, Bridgend, CF32 0EH. e-mail: glamorganwt@cix.co.uk
www.wildlifetrust.org.uk/glamorgan

WEST WALES

Bird Atlas/Avifauna
Birds of Pembrokeshire by Jack Donovan and Graham Rees (Dyfed Wildlife Trust, 1994).

Bird Recorders
CARMARTHENSHIRE, Tony Forster, Ffosddu, Salem, Llandeilo, Carmarthenshire, SA19 7NS. 01558 824237; e-mail: tony-forster@supanet.com.

CEREDIGION, Hywel Roderick, 32 Prospect Street, Aberystwyth, Ceredigion, SY23 1JJ.
e-mail: hywel@adar.freeserve.co.uk

PEMBROKESHIRE. 1, Jack Donovan MBE, The Burren, 5 Dingle Lane, Crundale, Haverfordwest, Pembrokeshire, SA62 4DJ. 01437 762673.

PEMBROKESHIRE.2, Graham Rees, 22 Priory Avenue, Haverfordwest, Pembrokeshire, SA61 1SQ. 01437 762877.

Bird Reports

CARMARTHENSHIRE BIRDS (1982-), from Carmarthenshire Recorder.

CEREDIGION BIRD REPORT (biennial 1982-87; annual 1988-), from Wildlife Trust West Wales.

PEMBROKESHIRE BIRD REPORT (1981-), from TJ Price, 2 Wordsworth Ave, Haverfordwest, Pembrokeshire, SA61 1SN.

THE ISLAND NATURALIST, from the secretary, Friends of Skokholm and Skomer (one issue contains bird report for islands).

BTO Regional Representatives & Regional Development Officer

CARDIGAN RR, Moira Convery, 41 Danycoed, Aberystwyth,SY23 2HD. e-mail: moira@mconvery.freeserve.co.uk

CARMARTHEN RR, David Poulter, Ty Isaf, Pentrepoeth, Idole, Carmarthen, SA32 8DH. e-mail: d.poulter@tiscali.co.uk

PEMBROKE RR, Roderick Hadfield, 104 Nun Street, St David's, Haverfordwest, SA62 6NX. 01437 720572.

Clubs

FRIENDS OF SKOKHOLM & SKOMER (1981; 310). The Secretary, Wildlife Trust of South & West Wales, Fountain Road, Tondu, Bridgend, CF32 0EH. 01656 726985.

LLANELLI NATURALISTS, (1971; 100). Richard Pryce, Trevethin, School Road, Pwll, Llanelli, Carmarthenshire, SA15 4AL. e-mail: pryceeco@aol.com

PEMBROKESHIRE BIRD GROUP, (1993; 60). T J Price, 2 Wordsworth Ave, Haverfordwest, Pembs, SA61 1SN. 01437 779667.

Ringing Group

PEMBROKESHIRE RG, J Hayes, 3 Wades Close, Holyland Road, Pembroke, SA71 4BN. 01646 687036.

Wildlife Hospitals

NEW QUAY BIRD HOSPITAL, Jean Bryant, Penfoel, Cross Inn, Llandysul, Ceredigion, SA44 6NR. 01545 560462. All species of birds. Fully equipped for cleansing oiled seabirds. Veterinary support.

WEST WILLIAMSTON OILED BIRD CENTRE, Mrs J Hains, Lower House Farm, West Williamston, Kilgetty, Pembs, SA68 0TL. 01646 651236. Facilities for holding up to 200 Guillemots, etc. for short periods. Initial treatment is given prior to despatch to other washing centres during very large oil spills; otherwise birds are washed at the Centre with intensive care and rehabilitation facilities. Also other species. Veterinary support.

Wildlife Trust
(see also South Wales)

WILDLIFE TRUSTOF SOUTH & WEST WALES, (1938). Welsh Wildlife Centre, Cilgerran, Cardigan, Ceredigion SA43 2TB. 01239 621212; (fax) 001239 613211. e-mail: wildlife@wtww.co.uk www.wildlife-wales.org.uk

NORTHERN IRELAND

Bird Recorder
George Gordon, 2 Brooklyn Avenue, Bangor, Co Down, BT20 5RB. 028 9145 5763; e-mail: gordon@ballyholme2.freeserve.co.uk

Bird Reports
NORTHERN IRELAND BIRD REPORT, from Secretary. Northern Ireland, Birdwatchers' Association (see, National Directory).

IRISH BIRD REPORT, Included in *Irish Birds*, BirdWatch Ireland in National, Directory.

COPELAND BIRD OBSERVATORY REPORT, from see Reserves.

BTO Regional Representatives
BTO IRELAND OFFICER, Ken Perry, 43 Portstewart Road, Coleraine, Co Londonderry, BT52 1RW. 028 7034 2985; fax: 028 7032 8053; e-mail: kennethwilliamperry@hotmail.com

ANTRIM & BELFAST, Position vacant,

ARMAGH, David W A Knight, 20 Mandeville Drive, Tandragee, Craigavon, Co Armagh, BT62 2DQ. 028 38 840658

DOWN, Position vacant,

LONDONDERRY, Charles Stewart, Bravallen, 18 Duncrun Road, Bellarena, Limavady, Co Londonderry, BT49 0JD.028 77 750468

TYRONE SOUTH & FERMANAGH, Philip S Grosse, 30 Tullybroom Road, Clogher, Co Tyrone, BT76 0UW. 028 8554 8606; e-mail: phigro@aol.com

TYRONE NORTH, Mary Mooney, 20 Leckpatrick Road, Ballymagorry, Strabane, Co Tyrone, BT82 0AL. 028 7188 2442; e-mail: memooney@foxlodge.healthnet.co.uk

Clubs
NORTHERN IRELAND BIRDWATCHERS' ASSOCIATION, see National Directory.

NORTHERN IRELAND ORNITHOLOGISTS' CLUB, see National Directory.

CASTLE ESPIE BIRDWATCHING CLUB, (1995; 60). Mrs Dot Blakely, 31 Clandeboye Way, Bangor, Co Down, BT19 1AD. 028 9145 0784.

Ringing Groups
ANTRIM & ARDS RG, M McNeely, 35 Balleyvalley Heights, Banbridge, Co Down, BT32 4AQ.028 406 29823.

COPELAND BIRD OBSERVATORY, C W Acheson, 28 Church Avenue, Dunmurry, Belfast, BT17 9RS.

NORTH DOWN RG, Hugh Thurgate, 24 Church Court, Clough, Downpatrick, Co Down, BT30 8QX.

RSPB Local Groups
ANTRIM, (1977; 23). Agnes Byron, 59 Tirgracey Road, Mucamore, Co Antrim, BT41 4PS. 028 9446 2207.

BANGOR, (1973; 45). Michael Richardson, 10 Belgravia Road, Bangor, Co Down, BT19 6XJ. 028 9146 2705.

BELFAST, (1970; 130). Ron Houston, 7 Kingsdale Park, Belfast,BT5 7BY. 028 9079 6188.

COLERAINE, (1978; 45). John Clarke, 48 Shelbridge Park, Coleraine, Co Londonderry, BT52 2HP. 028 7032 1239.

FERMANAGH, (1977; 28). Doreen Morrison, 91 Derrin Road, Cornagrade, Enniskillen, Co Fermanagh, BT74 6BA. 028 6632 6654.

LARNE, (1974; 55). Jimmy Christie, 314 Coast Road, Ballygally, Co Antrim, BT40 2QZ028 2858 3223.

LISBURN, (1978; 28). David McCreedy, 10 Downside Avenue, Banbridge, Co Down, BT32 4BP. 028 4062 6125.

Wildlife Hospital
TACT WILDLIFE CENTRE, Mrs Patricia Nevines, 2 Crumlin Road, Crumlin, Co Antrim, BT29 4AD. Tel/ fax 028 944 22900; e-mail: t.a.c.t@care4free.net All categories of birds treated and rehabilitated; released where practicable, otherwise given a home. Visitors (inc. groups) welcome by prior arrangement. Veterinary support.

Wildlife Trust
ULSTER WILDLIFE TRUST, (1978; 2,100). 3 New Line, Crossgar, Co Down, BT30 9EP. 028 4483 0282; fax 028 4483 0888; e-mail: info@ulsterwildlifetrust.org.uk www.ulsterwildlife.org.uk

REPUBLIC OF IRELAND

Bird Recorders
1, Oran O'Sullivan, BirdWatch Ireland, Ruttledge House, 8 Longford Place, Monkstown, Co Dublin; +353 (0)1 2804322; (fax)+353 (0)1 2844407; e-mail: bird@indigo.ie

2. Rarities, Paul Milne, 100 Dublin Road, Sutton, Dublin 13, +353 (0)1 8325653; e-mail: paul.milne@oceanfree.net

Bird Reports
Contact Birdwatch Ireland for the following:
IRISH BIRD REPORT.

CAPE CLEAR BIRD OBSERVATORY ANNUAL REPORT.

CORK BIRD REPORT (1963-71; 1976-).

EAST COAST BIRD REPORT (1980-).

BTO Regional Representative
BTO IRELAND OFFICER, Ken Perry, 43 Portstewart

Road, Coleraine, Co Londonderry, BT52 1RW. From Eire: (048) 7034 2985; fax(048) 7032 8053; From UK: (028) 7034 2985; fax (028) 7032 8053; e-mail: kennethwilliamperry@hotmail.com

BirdWatch Ireland Branches
Branches may be contacted in writing via BirdWatch Ireland HQ.

Ringing Groups
CAPE CLEAR BIRD OBSERVATORY, S Wing, 30 Irsher Street, Appledore, Devon, EX39 1RZ.

GREAT SALTEE RS, O J Merne, 20 Cuala Road, Bray, Co Wicklow,

MUNSTER RG, K P Collins, Ballygambon, Lisronagh, Clonmel, Co Tipperary; e-mail: kevcoll@indigo.ie

SHANNON WADER RG, P A Brennan, The Crag, Stonehall, Newmarket-on-Fergus, Co Clare.

CHANNEL ISLANDS

BTO Regional Representative
Jamie Hooper, 1 Trinity Cottages, Torteval,
Guernsey, GY8 0QD. Tel/fax 01481 266924.

Ringing Group
The Channel Islands ringing scheme is run by the
Société Jersiaise.

ALDERNEY

Bird Recorder
Mark Atkinson, 4 Ferndale Estate, Newtown,
Alderney GY9 3BH. 01481 823286.
http://jillwatson.members.beeb.net

Bird Report
*ALDERNEY SOCIETY ORNITHOLOGY REPORT
(1992-)*, from Recorder.

GUERNSEY

Bird Atlas/Avifauna
Birds of the Bailiwick of Guernsey (working title).
In preparation.

Bird Recorder
Mark Lawlor, Pentland, 15 Clos des Pecqueries, La
Passee, St Sampson's, Guernsey, GY2 4TU. 01481
258168. e-mail: mplawlor@gtonline.net

Bird Report
*REPORT & TRANSACTIONS OF LA SOCIÉTÉ
GUERNESIAISE (1882-)*, from Recorder.

Clubs
LA SOCIÉTÉ GUERNESIAISE (Ornithological
Section), (1882; 30). Vic Froome, La Cloture,
Coutil de Bas Lane, St Sampsons, Guernsey, GY2
4XJ. 01481 254841. www.societe.org.gg

RSPB Local Group
GUERNSEY, (1975; 1,200+). Michael Bairds, Le
Quatre Vents, La Passee, St Sampsons, Guernsey,
GY2 4TS. 01481 255524; www.rspbguernsey.co.uk
e-mail: mikebairds@gtonline.net

Wildlife Hospital
GUERNSEY. GSPCA ANIMAL SHELTER, Mrs Jayne
Le Cras, Rue des Truchots, Les Fiers Moutons, St
Andrews, Guernsey, Channel Islands, GY6 8UD.
01481 57261. All species. Modern cleansing unit
for oiled seabirds. 24-hour emergency service.
Veterinary support.

JERSEY

Bird Recorder
Tony Paintin, 16 Quennevais Gardens, St Brelade,
Jersey, Channel Islands, JE3 8FQ. 01534 741928;
e-mail: cavokjersey@hotmail.com

Bird Report
JERSEY BIRD REPORT, from Secretary
(Publications), Société Jersiaise.

Club
SOCIÉTÉ JERSIAISE (Ornithological Section),
(1948; 40). Roger Noel, 7 Pier Road, St Helier,
Jersey, JE2 4XW. 01534 758314.

RSPB Local Group
JERSEY, Robert Burrow, 1 Southlands, Green Road,
St Clements, Jersey, JE2 6QA. 01534 32167.

Wildlife Hospital
JERSEY. JSPCA ANIMALS' SHELTER, Pru Bannier,
89 St Saviour's Road, St Helier, Jersey, JE2 4GJ.
01534 724331; fax 01534 871797. All species.
Expert outside support for owls and raptors. Oiled
seabird unit. Veterinary surgeon on site.
Educational Centre. e-mail: jspca@super.net

ISLE OF MAN

Bird Report
Manx Bird Atlas. 2002 is fifth year of five year
research programme. Contact: Chris Sharpe (see
below, BTO).

Bird Recorder
Dr Pat Cullen, Troutbeck, Cronkbourne, Braddan,
Isle of Man, IM4 4QA. Home: 01624 623308;
Work 01624 676774; e-mail: bridgeen@mcb.net

Bird Reports
MANX BIRD REPORT (1947-), published in
Peregrine. From G D Craine, 8 Kissack Road,
Castletown, Isle of Man, IM9 1NP.
e-mail: g.craine@advsys.co.uk

*CALF OF MAN BIRD OBSERVATORY ANNUAL
REPORT*, from Secretary. Manx National Heritage,
Manx Museum, Douglas, Isle of Man, IM1 3LY.

BTO Regional Representative & Regional Development Officer
RR, Dr Pat Cullen, as above, 01624 623308.

RDO, Chris Sharpe, 33 Mines Road, Laxey, Isle of Man, IM4 7NH. 01624 861130;
e-mail: chris@manxbirdatlas.org

Club
MANX ORNITHOLOGICAL SOCIETY, (1967; 150).
Mrs A C Kaye, Cronk Ny Ollee, Glen Chass, Port St Mary, Isle of Man, IM9 5PL. 01624 834015.

Ringing Group
CALF OF MAN BIRD OBSERVATORY, Tim Bagworth, Calf of Man, c/o Kionsleau, Plantation Road, Port St Mary, Isle of Man, IM9 5AY. Mobile 07624 462858.

Wildlife Trust
MANX WILDLIFE TRUST, (1973; 900).
Conservation Centre, Tynwald Mills, St Johns, Isle of Man, IM4 3AE. 01624 801985; fax 01624 801022; e-mail: manxwt@cix.co.uk
www.wildlifetrust.org.uk/manxwt

ARTICLES IN BIRD REPORTS

Avon Bird Report 2001
Seabirds, A Review of their Status in the Upper Severn Estuary by B Lancastle
Avon Breeding Survery 2000 by J.Tully
Avon Ringing Report 2000 by LF Roberts
House Sparrow Nesting Survey, Southmead 2000 by J.Tully
Species New to Avon, Cory's Shearwater and Lesser Scaup, by B Lancastle and NR Milbourne
The Avon List, 200 by HE Rose

Ayrshire Bird Report 2001
The Birds of Turnberry by A Hogg
The Kestrel in Ayrshire by G Riddle

Birds of Moray and Nairn 2001
The Canada Goose near Lossiemouth on 16th April 1988 by Bob Proctor
NE Scotland Breeding Bird Atlas
Recent Trends in numbers of some common Farmland Finches by Ian Francis and Martin Coook

Borders Bird Report 2000
Ringing in the Scottish Borders by TW Dougal
Gola Water Waterways Bird Census by Mr Holling

Breconshire Birds 2001
The Willlow Tit in Breconshire by Martin Peers

Brian Unwin 2000
An Exceptional Day (Barnacle Geese passage) by Brian Unwin
Memories of a Phenomenal Wetland by Brian Unwin

Cambridgeshire Bird Report 2000
Isabelline Shrike at Nene Washes - New to Cambridgeshire by JP Taylor
A Survey of the Hobby and Kestrel in

the old County of Cambridgeshire by GMS Easy
Recovery of Magpie at two Sites in the Huntingdon Area by AS Cooke
The Identification of a 'Red-tailed' Shrike at Marsh Lane GP by JS Clark

Cleveland Bird Report 2001
Red-Flanked Bluetail - New to Cleveland by DA Money
Great North Park, Norton by I Lawson

Clwyd Bird Report 2000
What is the future for NE Wales Farmland Birds? By Nick Thomas
Hard to Swallow by Ron Plummer
Sea-watching at the POA by Gareth Stamp

Isles of Scilly Bird and Natural History Review 2001
Thrushes on Scilly by Ren Hathway and Peter Clement
Bats on Scilly by Dave Mawer
Butterflies on Scilly by Mike Hicks
Cetaceans in Scillonian Waters by Amanda Martin
Dragonflies on Scilly by Keith Pellow
Moths on Scilly by Mike Hicks
Plants on Scilly by Rosemary Parslow

Derbyshire Bird Report 2000
Wetland Bird Surveys, Winter 2000-2001 by Chris Burnett
A Partially Albinistic Water Pipit *Anthus spinoletta*, at Willington GP by Rodney Key
Computerisation of Records by Dave Richardson
Honey Buzzards *Pernis Apivorus* in Derbyshire during Sept 2000 by Rodney Key
Ortolan Bunting *Emberiza hortulana* at Aston-on-Trent GP: a new species for Derbyshire by Rodney Key

Devon Bird Report 2001
First's for Devon:

Black-faced Bunting by Richard Patient and Steve Cooper
'Siberian' Stonechat by Mike Langman and Bill MacDonald
Looking Back by Leonard Hurrell
Redpoll Species - Topsham by Mattthew Knott
Visible Migration at Staddon Point, Plymouth Sound by Simon Geary

Dorset Bird Report 2000
Rare and Scarce Birds in Dorset in 2000 by Shaun Robson
Cliff Swallow at The Verne, Portland by Jon Stirling and Dave Chown
Dorset Farmland Project - Lapwing 2000 by Dante Munns and John Selby
Marsh Sandpiper at Stanpit by Ian Prophet
Report on Bird Ringing in Dorset in 2000 by Roger Peart
RSPB Arne-based Reserves by Neil Gartshore
The Syke's Warbler at Portland by Martin Cade

Fife Bird Report 2000
Status of Lesser and Mealy Redpolls in Fife by DS Fotheringham
Hume's Warbler - First for Fife by Rab Shand
Recent Committee Decisions by DE Dickson
Ringing Report by BH Little
The 1994 Shag Wreck and its Consequences by Sarah Wanless and Mike Harris
White-tailed Eagle - First Record for 134 Years by Allister Todd
Yellow Legged Gull - First for Fife by KD Shaw and AW Cauder

Guernsey Bird Report 2000
Rarity Reports:
Black-headed Bunting and Griffon Vulture by W Turner
Fan-tailed Warblers and Little Swift by M Lawlor

ARTICLES IN BIRD REPORTS

Hampshire Bird Report 2000
Species New to Hampshire by JM Clark
Hampshire Song Thrush Breeding Survey by NE Wald and N Pratt
October 1st 2000 - One of Those Days by D Powell
Record Numbers of Manx Shearwaters off the Hampshire Coast by M Moody

The Calf of Man Bird Observatory Annual Report 2001
Systematic List, Ringing Report, Butterfly Report, Moth Report, Cetacean and Shark report by Tim Bagworth

Kent Bird Report 2000
Nightingale Survey by Andrew Henderson
Birds of Palmarsh Gravel Pit in the Last 50 Years by Roger Norman
Raptor Survey - a summary of their breeding status by Rob Clements

Lancashire Bird Report 2001
Bearded Tits at Leighton Moss by J Wilson

Lancashire Bird Report 2000
Common Scoters in Liverpool Bay by SJ White
Mammals of Lancashire by S Cross

Leicester & Rutland Bird Report 2001
Review of the year by Rob Fray
Anglian Water Opsprey Project Update by Helen Dixon
Colour-ringed Cormorants at Rutland Water in 2001 by Steve Lister
Eye Brook Reservoir Ringing Report by Dean Rolzer
North-West Leicestershire Ringing Group Report by Andy Smith
Priory Water Ringing Report by Dave Gamble (data by John Martin)
Shore Lark - New to the County List by Mick Ketley

London Bird Report 1999
Ringing Report by R Taylor
A Raptor Study Group for London? by MR Paice
The Breeding Bird Survey in London, 1999 by DA Coleman

NE Scotland Bird Report 2000
Grampian RG 2000 Ringing Summary by R Duncan
Eastern Race Olivaceous Warbler, Collieston Aberdeenshire 13-21 Sept 2000.
Recent Trends in Numbers of some Bird Species in NE Scotland by Dr I Francis

Swinhoe's Storm Petrel - A New Bird for Scotland by PAA Baxter
Tawny Owls in NE Scotland 2000 by J Massie

Norfolk Bird Report 2000
Ringing Report
Breydon Water and its Birdlife
Eleonora's Falcon at Hickling Broad, July 1987 - first record for Norfolk
Isabelline Wheatear at Blakeney Point - the second record for Norfolk
Norfolk Birdwatchng in 1950 Remembered
Seventy-five years ago - anecdotes from Norfolk birdwatchers in 1925
Slender-billed Gulls at Cley - the second record for Norfolk
The Burgh Castle Bee-eaters - a long-awaited opportunity for Norfolk Birdwatchers
The House Sparrow in Norwich during Autumn/Winter 2000 - a population study
Twenty-five years ago - Memories of 1975

Northamptonshire Bird Report 2001
Review of the Year 2001
Barn Owl Survery in the Oundle Area
Conservation Landscaping at Ditchford/Stanwich CP
Nene Valley Wetlands Conservation Project (provisional)
Overview of Daventry CP
Ringing Report

Birds in Northumbria 2001
Post-Breeding Ringed Plovers in Northumberland by Steve Holliday and Les Robson
Additions to the County List:
Birding Sites IX - Seaton Sluice by Maurice Hepple
Birding Sites X - South Tyne Valley by Graeme Bowman
Decline of Coots at Bigwater by Graeme Bowman
Little Auks - 2001 in perspective by Ian Fisher
Pallid Swift by Mike Catt
Red Squirrel, Large Pine Weevil and Natterer's Bat in Long-Eared Owl Diets by Steve Holliday and Martin Davison
Slender-billed Curlew by Terry Cleeves
Spotted Sandpiper by Terry Mitcham
The County Records Committee 2001 by Ian Fisher
The Tyne Estuary: Changes in Wintering Birds 1995-2002 by Daniel M Turner

Wetland Bird Survey by Roger Norman and Steve Holliday

Orkney Bird Report 2000
Breeding Skuas, Terns and Gulls in Orkney 2000 by Jim Williams
Two Hundred into Two Thousand Does Go by Ian Dillon

Shropshire Bird Report 2000
Long Mynd Breeding Bird Project, Ring Ouzel Update by Leo Smith
Blackbird Feeding a Brood of Robins by John Hawkins
Common Crane at Higginswood by Tony Butter
Dartford Warbler on the Stiperstones by Graham Walker
Ellesmere Wildfowl Counts by Allan Dawes
Venus Pool 2000 by Geof Holmes

Surrey Bird Report 1999
Nightingales Breeding in Surrey in 1999 by Hugh Evans
Nightingales in Scrub at Bookham Common: their habitat and conservation by Alan Prouse

The Sussex Bird Report 2002
The Sussex Ringing Report for 2000 by Sarah Dawkins
A County Review of the Hen Harrier *circus cyaneus* with Special Reference to Roost Sites found on River Valleys and Downland by Martin Kalaher
Little Egret roost at Thorney Deeps by Barry Collins and Tony Cocks
The 1999-2000 Sussex Breeding Swift Survey, Comparison with the 1968-70 Survey and Conservation Issues by Graham Roberts
The Distribution and Status of the Hobby *Falco subbuteo* in Sussex in 2000 by Martin Kalaher
The influx of Honey Buzzards and other Raptors in Sussex during Autumn 2000 by John Cooper

West Midland Bird Report 2000
Changes Affecting Staffordshire's Breeding Birds from 1800 to 2000 by Frank C Gribble MBE
Caspian Gull *larus (a.) cachinnans* at Batley and Frankley Reservoirs by Alan R Dean
Melodious Warbler at Brandon Marsh by Andy Hales, Fred Stokes and Dave Stone
Nightjars on Cannock Chase - year 2000 by Bevan Craddock and Peter K Dedicoat
The Honey Buzzard Invasion: A Once in a Lifetime Event by Steven Nuttall

NATIONAL
DIRECTORY

A pair of Stonechats was selected by Richard Johnson as part of his entry for the BB prize.

ARMY ORNITHOLOGICAL SOCIETY
(1960; 250).
Open to MOD employees and civilians who have an interest in their local MOD estate. Activities include field meetings, expeditions, the preparation of checklists of birds on Ministry of Defence property, conservation advice and an annual bird count. Annual journal *The Osprey*, published with the RNBWS and RAFOS from easter 2001. Bulletins/newsletters twice a year.
Contact: Hon Secretary, Lt Col P S Bennett, SO1 DEF LOG(OPS/EX), HQ DLO, Room 409/11, MOD Metropole Building, Northumberland Avenue, London, W2CN 5EP, 020 7218 6750.

ASSOCIATION FOR THE PROTECTION OF RURAL SCOTLAND (1926).
Works to protect Scotland's countryside from unnecessary or inappropriate development, recognising the needs of those who live and work there and the necessity of reconciling these with the sometimes competing requirements of recreational use.
Contact: Director, Mrs Joan Geddes, Gladstone's Land, 3rd Floor, 483 Lawnmarket, Edinburgh, EH1 2NT, 0131 225 7012; (Fax)0131 225 6592; e-mail: aprs@aprs.org.uk

ASSOCIATION OF COUNTY RECORDERS AND EDITORS (1993; 120).
The basic aim of ACRE is to promote best practice in the business of producing county bird reports, in the work of Recorders and in problems arising in managing record systems and archives. Organises periodic conferences and publishes *newsACRE*.
Contact: Secretary, M J Rogers, 2 Churchtown Cottages, Towednack, St Ives, Cornwall, TR26 3AZ, 01736 796223; e-mail: judith@gmbirds.freeserve.co.uk

BARN OWL TRUST
Registered charity. Aims to conserve the Barn Owl and its environment through conservation, education, research and information. Free leaflets on all aspects of Barn Owl conservation. Educational material inc. video and resource pack. Book '*Barn Owls on Site*', a guide for planners and developers (priced). Works with and advises landowners, farmers, planners, countryside bodies and others to promote a brighter future for Britain's Barn Owls. Currently pursuing proactive conservation schemes in SW England to secure breeding sites and form a stable basis for population expansion. Open to phone calls Mon-Fri (9.30-5.30). Send SAE for information.
Contact: Secretary, Barn Owl Trust, Waterleat, Ashburton, Devon, TQ13 7HU, 01364 653026; e-mail: info@barnowltrust.org.uk
www.barnowltrust.org.uk

BIRD OBSERVATORIES COUNCIL (1970).
Objectives are to provide a forum for establishing closer links and co-operation between individual autonomous observatories and to help co-ordinate the work carried out by them. All accredited bird observatories affiliated to the Council undertake a ringing programme and provide ringing experience to those interested, most also provide accommodation for visiting birdwatchers.
Contact: Secretary, Peter Howlett, c/o Dept of Biodiversity, National Museums & Galleries, Cardiff, CF10 3NP, 0292 057 3233; (Fax)0292 023 9009; e-mail: peter.howlett@nmgw.ac.uk

BIRD STAMP SOCIETY (1986; 250).

Quarterly journal *Flight* contains philatelic and ornithological articles. Lists all new issues and identifies species. Runs a quarterly Postal Auction; number of lots range from 400 to 800 per auction.
Contact: Secretary, Graham Horsman, 9 Cowley Drive, Worthy Down, Winchester, Hants, SO21 2QW, 01962 889381; (Fax)01962 887423.

BIRDWATCH IRELAND (1968; 5,000).
The trading name of the Irish Wildbird Conservancy, a voluntary body founded in 1968 by the amalgamation of the Irish Society for the Protection of Birds, the Irish Wildfowl Conservancy and the Irish Ornithologists' Club. Now the BirdLife International partner in Ireland with 21 voluntary branches. Conservation policy is based on formal research and surveys of birds and their habitats. Owns or manages an increasing number of reserves to protect threatened species and habitats. Publishes *Wings* quarterly and *Irish Birds* annually, in addition to annual project reports and survey results.
Contact: Oran O'Sullivan, Ruttledge House, 8 Longford Place, Monkstown, Co Dublin, Ireland, +353 (0)1 2804322; (Fax)+353 (0)1 2844407; e-mail: bird@indigo.ie
www.birdwatchireland.ie

BRITISH BIRDS RARITIES COMMITTEE (1959).
The Committee adjudicates records of species of rare occurrence in Britain (marked 'R' in the Log Charts). Its annual report is published in *British Birds*. The BBRC also assesses records from the Channel Islands. In the case of rarities trapped for ringing, records should be sent to the Ringing Office of the British Trust for Ornithology, who will

Figures appearing in brackets following the names of organisations indicate the date of formation and, if relevant, the current membership.

in turn forward them to the BBRC.
Contact: Hon Secretary, M J Rogers, 2 Churchtown Cottages, Towednack, St Ives, Cornwall, TR26 3AZ, 01736 796223.
www.bbrc.org.uk

BRITISH FALCONERS' CLUB (1927; 1,200).
Largest falconry club in Europe, with regional branches. Its aim is to encourage responsible falconers and conserve birds of prey by breeding, holding educational meetings and providing facilities, guidance and advice to those wishing to take up the sport. Publishes *The Falconer* annually and newsletter twice yearly.
Contact: Director, Ian A Timmins, Home Farm, Hints, Tamworth, Staffs, B78 2DW, Tel/(Fax)01543 481737; e-mail: falconers@zetnet.co.uk
www.users.zetnet.co.uk/bfc

BRITISH MUSEUM (NAT HIST) see Walter Rothschild Zoological Museum

BRITISH ORNITHOLOGISTS' CLUB
(1892; 600).
Membership open only to members of the British Ornithologists' Union. A registered charity, the Club's objects are 'the promotion of scientific discussion between members of the BOU, and others interested in ornithology, and to facilitate the publication of scientific information in connection with ornithology'. The Club maintains a special interest in avian systematics, taxonomy and distribution. About eight dinner meetings are held each year. Publishes the *Bulletin of the British Ornithologists' Club* quarterly, also (since 1992) a continuing series of occasional publications.
Contact: Hon Secretary, Cdr M B Casement OBE RN, Dene Cottage, West Harting, Petersfield, Hants, GU31 5PA, 01730 825280; e-mail: mbcasement@aol.com.uk

BRITISH ORNITHOLOGISTS' UNION
(1858; 2,000).
Founded by Professor Alfred Newton FRS and one of the world's oldest and most respected ornithological societies. It aims to promote ornithology within the scientific and birdwatching communities, both in Britain and around the world. This is largely achieved by the publication of its quarterly international journal, *Ibis* (1859-), featuring work at the

cutting edge of our understanding of the world's birdlife. An active programme of meetings, seminars and conferences inform birdwatchers and ornithologists about the work being undertaken around the world. This often includes research projects that have received financial assistance from the BOU's ongoing programme of Ornithological Research Grants, which includes student sponsorship. The BOU also runs the Bird Action Grant scheme to assist projects aimed at conserving or researching species on the UK's Biodiversity Action Plan (BAP) list.
Contact: Administrator, Steve Dudley, c/o Natural History Museum, Akeman Street, Tring, Herts, HP23 6AP, 01442 890080; (Fax)0207 942 6150; e-mail: bou@bou.org.uk
www.bou.org.uk www.ibis.ac.uk

BRITISH ORNITHOLOGISTS' UNION RECORDS COMMITTEE
The BOURC is a standing committee of the British Ornithologists' Union. Its function is to maintain the British List, the official list of birds recorded in Great Britain. Up-to-date versions are published annually as *The British List*. Where vagrants are involved it is concerned only with those which relate to potential additions to the British List (ie first records). In this it differs from the British Birds Rarities Committee (qv). In maintaining the British List, it also differs from the BBRC in that it examines, where necessary, important pre-1950 records, monitors introduced species for possible admission to or deletion from the List, and reviews taxonomy and nomenclature generally. BOURC reports are published in *Ibis*. Decisions contained in these reports which affect the List are also announced via the popular birdwatching press and incorporated in *The British List*.
Contact: Secretary, Dr Tim Melling, c/o The Natural History Museum, Akeman Street, Tring, Herts, HP23 6AP, 01442 890080; (Fax)0207 942 6150; e-mail: bourc.sec@bou.org.uk

BRITISH TRUST FOR ORNITHOLOGY
(1933; 12,500).
A registered charity governed by an elected Council, it has a rapidly growing membership and enjoys the support of a large number of county and local birdwatching clubs and societies through the BTO/Bird Clubs Partnership. Its aims are: 'To promote and encourage the wider understanding, appreciation and conservation of birds through scientific studies using the combined skills and enthusiasm of its members, other birdwatchers and staff.' Through the fieldwork of its members and other birdwatchers, the BTO is responsible for the majority of the monitoring of British birds, British bird population and their habitats. BTO

surveys include the National Ringing Scheme, the Nest Record Scheme, the Breeding Bird Survey (in collaboration with JNCC and RSPB), and the Waterways Breeding Bird Survey - all contributing to an integrated programme of population monitoring. The BTO also runs projects on the birds of farmland and woodland, also (in collaboration with WWT, RSPB and JNCC) the Wetland Bird Survey, in particular Low Tide Counts. Garden BirdWatch, which started in 1995, now has more than 14,000 participants. The Trust has 140 voluntary regional representatives (see County Directory) who organise fieldworkers for the BTO's programme of national surveys in which members participate. The results of these co-operative efforts are communicated to government departments, local authorities, industry and conservation bodies for effective action. For details of current activities see National Projects. Members receive *BTO News* six times a year and have the option of subscribing to the thrice-yearly journal, *Bird Study* and twice yearly *Ringing & Migration*. Local meetings are held in conjunction with bird clubs and societies; there are regional and national birdwatchers' conferences, and specialist courses in bird identification and modern censusing techniques. Grants are made for research, and members have the use of a lending and reference library at Thetford and the Alexander Library at the Edward Grey Institute of Field Ornithology (qv).
Contact: Director,Dr Jeremy J D Greenwood, British Trust for Ornithology, The Nunnery, Thetford, Norfolk, IP24 2PU, 01842 750050; (fax)01842 750030; www.bto.org e-mail: btostaff@bto.org

BRITISH WATERFOWL ASSOCIATION

The BWA is an association of enthusiasts interested in keeping, breeding and conserving all types of waterfowl, including wildfowl and domestic ducks and geese. It is a registered charity, without trade affiliations, dedicated to educating the public about waterfowl and the need for conservation as well as to raising the standards of keeping and breeding ducks, geese and swans in captivity.
Contact: Mrs Rachel Boer, Oaklands, Blind Lane, Tamworth in Arden, Solihull, B94 5HS, Tel/ (Fax)01564 741821. www.waterfowl.org.uk

BRITISH WILDLIFE REHABILITATION COUNCIL (1987).

Its aim is to promote the care and rehabilitation of wildlife casualties through the exchange of information between people such as rehabilitators, zoologists and veterinary surgeons who are active in this field. Organises an annual symposium or

workshop. Publishes a regular newsletter. Supported by many national bodies including the Zoological Society of London, the British Veterinary Zoological Society, the RSPCA, the SSPCA, and the Vincent Wildlife Trust.
Contact: Secretary, Tim Thomas, Wildlife Department, RSPCA, Causeway, Horsham, W Sussex, RH12 1HG, 0870 010 1181. www.nimini.demon.co.uk/bwrc

BTCV (formerly British Trust for Conservation Volunteers) (1959).

Involves people of all ages in practical conservation work, much of which directly affects bird habitats. There are more than 2,500 local conservation groups affiliated to BTCV, which also provides a service to many other bodies including the JNCC, RSPB, WWT and county wildlife trusts, national parks, water authorities, local authorities and private landowners. More than 750 training courses are run annually on the theory of management and practical techniques, for example woodland and wetland management, hedging, etc. Runs working holidays in UK and overseas. Publishes a quarterly newsletter, *The Conserver*, a series of practical handbooks and a wide range of other publications. Further information and a list of local offices is available from the above address.
Contact: Chief Executive, Tom Flood, 80 York Way, London, N1 9NG, 020 7713 5327; (Fax)020 7278 8967; e-mail: tflood@btcv.org.uk www.btcv.org.uk

BTCV SCOTLAND

Runs 7-14 day 'Action Breaks' in Scotland during which participants undertake conservation projects; weekend training courses in environmental skills; midweek projects in Edinburgh, Glasgow, Aberdeen, Stirling and Inverness.
Contact: Balallan House, 24 Allan Park, Stirling, FK8 2QG, 01786 479697; (Fax)01786 465359; e-mail: stirling@btcv.org.uk www.btcv.org.uk

CAMPAIGN FOR THE PROTECTION OF RURAL WALES

Its aims are to help the conservation and enhancement of the landscape, environment and amenities of the countryside, towns and villages of rural Wales and to form and educate opinion to ensure the promotion of its objectives. It recognises the importance of the indigenous cultures of rural Wales and gives advice and information upon matters affecting protection, conservation and improvement of the visual environment.

Contact: Director, Merfyn Williams, Ty Gwyn, 31 High Street, Welshpool, Powys, SY21 7YD, 01938 552525/556212; (Fax)552741; www.cprw.org.uk e-mail: info@cprw.org.uk

CANADA GOOSE STUDY GROUP

No longer active in ringing, the Group still functions to monitor records.

Contact: Dr C B Thomas, Dept of Chemistry, University of York, Heslington, York, YO10 5DD, 01904 432532; (Fax)01904 432516; e-mail: cbt1@york.ac.uk

CENTRE FOR ECOLOGY & HYDROLOGY (CEH)

The work of the CEH, a component body of the Natural Environment Research Council, includes a range of ornithological research, covering population studies, habitat management and work on the effects of pollution. The CEH has a long-term programme to monitor pesticide and pollutant residues in the corpses of predatory birds sent in by birdwatchers, and carries out detailed studies on affected species. The Biological Records Centre (BRC), which is part of the CEH, is responsible for the national biological data bank on plant and animal distributions (except birds).

Contact: Director, Prof Pat Nuttall, Monks Wood, Abbots Ripton, Huntingdon, PE28 2LS, 01487 772400. www.ceh.ac.uk

COUNTRY LANDOWNERS' ASSOCIATION

(50,000).

The CLA is at the heart of rural life and is the voice of the countryside for England and Wales, campaigning on issues which directly affect those who live and work in rural communities. Its members together manage 60% of the countryside. CLA members range from some of the largest landowners, with interests in forest, moorland, water and agriculture, to some of the smallest with little more than a paddock or garden.

Contact: Secretary, 16 Belgrave Square, London, SW1X 8PQ, 020 7235 0511.

COUNTRYSIDE AGENCY

Advises the Government on countryside issues and is the leading organisation concerned with landscape conservation and public access to the countryside, as well as promoting social equity and economic opportunity for the people who live there. The Agency works by leading with research and advice, influencing others, especially central and local government and demonstrating ways forward through practical projects. Its responsibilities include designating national parks, areas of outstanding natural beauty and national trails.

Contact: Chief Executive, Richard Wakeford, John Dower House, Crescent Place, Cheltenham, Glos, GL50 3RA, 01242 521381; (Fax)01242 584270.

Offices:

North East Region. Cross House, Westgate Road, Newcastle upon Tyne NE1 4XX, 0191 269 1600; (Fax)0191 269 1601.

North West Region. 7th Floor, Bridgewater House, Whitworth Street, Manchester M1 6LT. 0161 237 1061; (Fax)0161 237 1062.

South West Region. Bridge House, Sion Place, Clifton Down, Bristol BS8 4AS. 0117 973 9966; (Fax)0117 923 8086.

Yorkshire & The Humber Region. 4th Floor Victoria Wharf, No 4 The Embankment, Sovereign Street, Leeds LS1 4BA. 0113 246 9222; (Fax)0113 246 0353.

East Midlands Region. Regional Office 18, Market Place, Bingham, Nottingham NG13 9AP. 01949 876200; (Fax)01949 876222.

West Midlands Region. 1st Floor, Vincent House, Tindal Bridge, 92-93 Edward Street, Birmingham B1 2RA. 0121 233 9399: (Fax)0121 233 9286

Eastern Region. Ortona House, 110 Hills Road, Cambridge CB2 1LQ. 01223 354462, (Fax)01223 313850.

South East Region. Dacre House, Dacre Street, London SW1H 0DH, 020 7340 2900; (Fax)020 7340 2911.

COUNTRYSIDE COUNCIL FOR WALES

The Government's statutory adviser on wildlife, countryside and maritime conservation matters in Wales. It is the executive authority for the conservation of habitats and wildlife. Through partners, CCW promotes protection of landscape, opportunities for enjoyment, and support of those who live, work in, and manage the countryside. It enables these partners, including local authorities, voluntary organisations and interested individuals, to pursue countryside management projects through grant aid. CCW is accountable to the National Assembly for Wales which appoints its Council members and provides its annual grant-in-aid.

Contact: Maes-y-Ffynnon, Penrhosgarnedd, Bangor, Gwynedd, 01248 385500; (Fax)01248 355782; (Enquiry unit)0845 1306229. www.ccw.gov.uk

Area Offices:

West Area. Plas Gogerddan, Aberystwyth, Ceredigian, SY23 3EE. 01970 821100.

North West Area. Llys y bont, Ffordd y Parc, Parc Menai, Bangor, Gwynedd, LL57 4BH. 01248 672500.

South Area. Unit 4, Castleton Court, Fortran Road, St Mellons, Cardiff CF3 0LT. 02920 772400
East Area. Eden House, Ithon Road, Llandrindod, Powys, LD1 6AS, 01597 827400
North East Area. Victoria House, Grosvenor Street, Mold CH7 1EJ. 01352 706600

THE COUNTRYSIDE RESTORATION TRUST
(5,000+).
A charity dedicated to the protection and restoration of a countryside where quality food is produced using farming methods that encourage wildlife and enable more people to earn their living from the land. It protects traditional farms and acquires, for restoration, farmland that has been managed over-intensively.
Contact: The Secretary, Barton, Cambridge, CB3 7AG, Tel/Fax: 01223 870932;
e-mail: info@crtbarton.org.uk
www.crtbarton.org.uk

CPRE (formerly Council for the Protection of Rural England) (1926; 45,000).
Patron HM The Queen. CPRE now has 43 county branches and 200 local groups. It seeks to provide well researched and practical solutions to problems affecting the English countryside. Membership open to all.
Contact: Director, Ms K Parminter, Warwick House, 25 Buckingham Palace Road, London, SW1W 0PP, 020 7976 6433; (Fax)020 7976 6373;
e-mail: info@cpre.org.uk
www.cpre.org.uk

DEPARTMENT OF THE ENVIRONMENT FOR NORTHERN IRELAND
Responsible for the declaration and management of National Nature Reserves, the declaration of Areas of Special Scientific Interest, the administration of Wildlife Refuges, the classification of Special Protection Areas under the EC Birds Directive, the designation of Special Areas of Conservation under the EC Habitats Directive and the designation of ramsar sites under the Ramsar Convention. It administers the Nature Conservation and Amenity Lands (Northern Ireland) Order 1985, the Wildlife (Northern Ireland) Order 1985, the Game Acts and the Conservation (Natural Habitats, etc) Regulations (NI) 1995.
Contact: Bob Bleakley, Environment and Heritage Service, Commonwealth House, 35 Castle Street, Belfast, BT1 1GU, 028 9054 6521;
e-mail: bob.bleakley@doeni.gov.uk

DISABLED BIRDER'S ASSOCIATION
The DBA is a registered charity and international movement, which aims to promote access to reserves and other birding places and to a range of services, so that people with different needs can follow the birding obsession as freely as able-bodied people. Membership is currently free and open to all, either disabled or able-bodied. We are keen for new members to help give a strong voice to get our message across to those who own and manage nature reserves to ensure that they think access when they are planning and improving their facilities. We are also seeking to influence those who provide birdwatching services and equipment.
Contact: DBA, 18 St Mildreds Road, Cliftonville, Margate, Kent, CT9 2LT;
e-mail: bo@fatbirder.com
www.disabledbirdersassociation.org.uk

EDWARD GREY INSTITUTE OF FIELD ORNITHOLOGY (1938).
The EGI takes its name from Edward Grey, first Viscount Grey of Fallodon, a life-long lover of birds and former Chancellor of the University of Oxford, who gave his support to an appeal for its foundation capital. The Institute now has a permanent research staff; it usually houses some 12-15 research students, two or three senior visitors and post-doctoral research workers. The EGI also houses Prof Sir John Krebs's Ecology & Behaviour Group, which study the ecology, demography and conservation of declining farmland birds. Field research is carried out mainly in Wytham Woods near Oxford and on the island of Skomer in West Wales. In addition there are laboratory facilities and aviary space for experimental work and members of the Institute have access to departmental and university computers. The Institute houses the Alexander Library, one of the largest collections of 20th century material on birds in the world. The library is supported by the British Ornithologists Union which provides much of the material.
Contact: Director, Dr BC Sheldon, Department of Zoology, South Parks Road, Oxford, OX1 3PS, 01865 271274, Alexander Library 01865 271143.
web-sites:
(EGI): http://egiwcruzool.zoo.ox.ac.uk/EGI/egihome.htm
(library) http://users.ox.ac.uk/~zoolib/

ENGLISH NATURE (1991)
Advises Government on nature conservation in England. It promotes, directly and through others, the conservation of England's wildlife and geology within the wider setting of the UK and its international responsibilities. It selects, establishes and manages National Nature Reserves (many of which are described in Reserves and Observatories), and identifies and notifies Sites of Special Scientific Interest. It provides advice and

ENGLISH NATURE

information about nature conservation and supports and conducts research relevant to these functions. Through the Joint Nature Conservation Committee (qv), English Nature works with sister organisations in Scotland and Wales on UK and international nature conservation issues.

Contact: Northminster House, Peterborough, PE1 1UA, 01733 455100; (Fax)01733 455103; e-mail: enquiries@english-nature.org.uk www.english-nature.org.uk

Local Teams

Bedfordshire and Cambridgeshire. Ham Lane House, Ham Lane, Nene Park, Orton Waterville, Peterborough PE2 5UR, 01733 405850; (Fax)01733 394093; e-mail: beds.cambs.nhants@english-nature.org.uk

Cheshire and Lancashire. Pier House, 1st Floor, Wallgate, Wigan WN3 4AL. 01942 820342; (Fax)01942 820364; e-mail: northwest@english-nature.org.uk

Cornwall & Isles of Scilly. Trevint House, Strangways Villas, Truro TR1 2PA. 01872 265710; (Fax)01872 262551; e-mail: cornwall@english-nature.org.uk

Cumbria. Juniper House, Murley Moss, Oxenholme Road, Kendal LA9 7RL. 01539 792800; (Fax)01539 792830; e-mail; cumbria@english-nature.org.uk

Devon. Level 2, Rensdale House, Bonhay Rd, Exeter, EX4 3AW, 01392 889770; (Fax)01392 437999; e-mail: devon@english-nature.org.uk

Dorset. Slepe Farm, Arne, Wareham, Dorset BH20 5BN. 01929 557450; (Fax)01929 554752; e-mail: dorset@english-nature.org.uk

Eastern Area. The Maltings, Wharf Road, Grantham, Lincs NG31 6BH. 01476 584800; (Fax)01476 570927; e-mail: eastmidlands@english-nature.org.uk

Essex, London and Hertfordshire. Harbour House, Hythe Quay, Colchester CO2 8JF. 01206 796666; (Fax)01206 794466; e-mail; essex.herts@english-nature.org.uk

Hampshire and Isle of Wight. 1 Southampton Road, Lyndhurst, Hants SO43 7BU. 02380 283944; (Fax)02380 283834; e-mail: hants.iwight@english-nature.org.uk

Hereford and Worcester. Bronsil House, Eastnor, Nr Ledbury HR8 1EP. 01531 638500; (Fax)01531 638501; e-mail: HerefordandWorcester@ english-nature.org.uk

Humber to Pennines. Bull Ring House, Northgate, Wakefield, W Yorks WF1 1HD. 01924 334500; (Fax)01924 201507; e-mail; humber.pennines@english-nature.org.uk

Kent. The Countryside Management Centre, Coldharbour Farm, Wye, Ashford, Kent TN25 5DB. 01233 812525; (Fax)01233 812520; e-mail: kent@english-nature.org.uk

Norfolk. 60 Bracondale, Norwich NR1 2BE. 01603 598400; (Fax)01603 762552; e-mail: norfolk@english-nature.org.uk

North and East Yorkshire. Genesis 1, University Road, Heslington, York YO10 5ZQ. 01904 435500; (Fax)01904 435520; e-mail: york@english-nature.org.uk

North Mercia (Shrops, Staffs, Warks, W Mid). Attingham Park, Shrewsbury SY4 4TW. 01743 709611; (Fax)01743 709303; e-mail: North Mercia @english-nature.org.uk

Northumbria. Stocksfield Hall, Stocksfield, Northumberland NE4 7TN. 01661 845500; (Fax)01661 845501; e-mail: northumbria@english-nature.org.uk

Peak District and Derbyshire. Manor Barn, Over Haddon, Bakewell, Derbyshire DE45 1JE. 01629 816640; (Fax)01629 815091; e-mail: peak.derbys@english-nature.org.uk.

Somerset and Gloucester. Roughmoor, Bishop's Hull, Taunton, Somerset TA1 5AA. 01823 283211; (Fax)01823 272978; e-mail: somerset@english-nature.org.uk

Suffolk. Regent House, 110 Northgate Street, Bury St Edmunds, Suffolk IP33 1HP. 01284 762218; (Fax)01284 764318; e-mail: suffolk@english-nature.org.uk

Sussex and Surrey. Phoenix House, 32-33 North Street, Lewes, E Sussex BN7 2PH. 01273 476595; (Fax)01273 483063; e-mail: sussex.surrey@english-nature.org.uk

Thames and Chilterns. Foxhold House, Thornford Road, Crookham Common, Thatcham, Berks RG19 8EL. 01635 268881; (Fax)01635 268940; e-mail: thames.chilterns@english-nature.org.uk

Wiltshire. Prince Maurice Court, Hambleton Avenue, Devizes, Wilts SN10 2RT. 01380 726344; (Fax)01380 721411; e-mail: wiltshire@english-nature.org.uk

ENVIRONMENT AGENCY (THE) (1996)
A non-departmental body that aims to protect and improve the environment and to contribute towards the delivery of sustainable development through the integrated management of air, land and water. Functions include pollution prevention and control, waste minimisation, management of water resources, flood defence, improvement of salmon and freshwater fisheries, conservation of aquatic species, navigation and use of inland and coastal waters for recreation. Sponsored by the Department of the Environment, Transport and the

NATIONAL DIRECTORY

Regions, MAFF and the Welsh Office.
Contact: Rio House, Waterside Drive, Aztec West, Almondsbury, Bristol, BS32 4UD, 01454 624400; (Fax)01454 624409;
www.environment-agency.gov.uk
Regional Offices:
Anglian. Kingfisher House, Goldhay Way, Orton Goldhay, Peterborough PE2 5ZR. 01733 371811; (Fax)01733 231840.
North East. Rivers House, 21 Park Square South, Leeds LS1 2QG. 0113 244 0191; (Fax)0113 246 1889.
North West. Richard Fairclough House, Knutsford Road, Warrington WA4 1HG. 01925 653999; (Fax)01925 415961.
Midlands. Sapphire East, 550 Streetsbrook Road, Solihull B91 1QT. 0121 711 2324; (Fax)0121 711 5824.
Southern. Guildbourne House, Chatsworth Road, Worthing, W Sussex BN11 1LD. 01903 832000; (Fax)01903 821832.
South West. Manley House, Kestrel Way, Exeter EX2 7LQ. 01392 444000; (Fax)01392 444238.
Thames. Kings Meadow House, Kings Meadow Road, Reading RG1 8DQ. 0118 953 5000; (Fax)0118 950 0388.
Wales. Rivers House, St Mellons Business Park, St Mellons, Cardiff CF3 0EY. 029 2077 0088; (Fax)029 2079 8555.

FARMING AND WILDLIFE ADVISORY GROUP (FWAG) (1969).
An independent UK registered charity led by farmers and supported by government and leading countryside organisations. Its aim is to unite farming and forestry with wildlife and landscape conservation. Active in most UK counties. There are 85 Farm Conservation Advisers who give practical advice to farmers and landowners to help them integrate environmental objectives with commercial farming practices. Technical Director, Richard Knight.
Contact: Chief Executive, Robert Bettley-Smith, National Agricultural Centre, Stoneleigh, Kenilworth, Warwickshire, CV8 2RX, 024 7669 6699; (Fax)024 7669 6760;
e-mail: info@fwag.org.uk
www.fwag.org.uk

FIELD STUDIES COUNCIL (1943).
Manages centres where students from schools, universities and colleges of education, as well as individuals of all ages, could stay and study various aspects of the environment under expert guidance. The courses include many for birdwatchers, providing opportunities to study birdlife on coasts, estuaries, mountains and islands. There are some courses demonstrating bird ringing and others for

members of the Wildlife Explorers. The length of the courses varies: from a weekend up to seven days' duration. Research workers and naturalists wishing to use the records and resources are welcome. FSC Overseas includes birdwatching options in its programme of overseas courses.
Contact: Cathy Preston, Preston Montford, Montford Bridge, Shrewsbury, SY4 1HW, 01743 852100; (Fax)01743 852101;
e-mail: fsc.headoffice@field-studies-council.org
www.field-studies-council.org
Centres:
Blencathra Field Centre, Threlkeld, Keswick, Cumbria CA12 4SG, 017687 79601;
e-mail:fsc.blencathra@ukonline.co.uk
Castle Head Field Centre, Grange-over-Sands, Cumbria LA11 6QT, 015395 34300,
e-mail:fsc,castlehead@ukonline.co.uk
Dale Fort Field Centre, Haverfordwest, Pembs SA62 3RD, 01646 636205,
e-mail: fsc.dalefort@ukonline.co.uk
Epping Forest Field Centre, High Beach, Loughton, Essex, IG10 4AF, 020 8508 7714,
e-mail:fsc.epping@ukonline,co.uk
Flatford Mill Field Centre, East Bergholt, Suffolk, CO7 6UL, 01206 298283,
e-mail:fsc.flatford@ukonline.co.uk
FSC Derrygonnelly, Tir Navar, Creamery St, Derrygonnelly, Co Fermanagh, BT93 6HN
Juniper Hall Field Centre, Dorking, Surrey, RH5 6DA, 0845 458 3507,
e-mail:fsc.juniper@ukonline.co.uk
Malham Tarn Field Centre, Settle, N Yorks, BD24 9PU, 01729 830331,
e-mail:fsc.malham@ukonline.co.uk
Nettlecombe Court, The Leonard Wills Field Centre, Williton, Taunton, Somerset, TA4 4HT, 01984 640320,
e-mail:fsc.nettlecombe@ukonline.co.uk
Orielton Field Centre, Pembroke, Pembs,SA71 5EZ, 01646 661225,
e-mail:fsc.orielton@ukonline.co.uk
Preston Montford Field Centre, Montford Bridge, Shrewsbury, SY4 1DX, 01743 850380,
e-mail:fsc.montford@ukonline.co.uk
Rhyd-y-creuau, the Drapers' Field Centre Betws-y-coed, Conwy, LL24 0HB, 01690 710494,
e-mail:fsc.ryc@ukonline.co.uk
Slapton Ley Field Centre, Slapton, Kingsbridge, Devon, TQ7 2QP, 01548 580466,
e-mail:fsc.slapton@ukonline.co.

NATIONAL ORGANISATIONS

FLIGHTLINE
Northern Ireland's daily bird news service. Run under the auspices of the Northern Ireland Birdwatchers' Association (qv).
Contact: George Gordon, 2 Brooklyn Avenue, Bangor, Co Down, BT20 5RB, 028 9146 7408.

FORESTRY COMMISSION
The Forestry Commission of Great Britain is the government department responsible for the protection and expansion of Britain's forests and woodlands. It has two executive agencies, Forest Enterprise (launched on the 1 April 1996) and Forest Research (launched on the 1 April 1997), which work to targets set by Commissioners and Ministers. Forest Enterprise has four territorial offices and 32 district offices. Its objectives are to protect Britain's forests and woodlands, expand Britain's forest area, enhance the economic value of forest resources, conserve and improve the biodiversity, landscape and cultural heritage of forests and woodlands, develop opportunities for woodland recreation and increase public under-standing and community participation in forestry.
Contact: Forestry Commission Headquarters, 231 Corstorphine Road, Edinburgh, EH12 7AT, 0845 3673787; (Fax) 0131 334 3047; Media enquiries: 0131 314 6550;
e-mail: enquiries@forestry.gsi.gov.uk
www.forestry.gov.uk
Forestry Commission National Offices:
England: Great Eastern House, Tenison Road, Cambridge CB1 2DU. 01223 314546; (Fax)01223 460699, e-mail: fc.nat.off.eng@forestry.gsi.gov.uk
Scotland: Address as HQ above, 0131 334 0303, (Fax)0131 314 615,
e-mail: as.nat.office@forestry.gsi.gov.uk
Wales: Victoria Terrace, Aberystwyth, Ceredigion SY23 2DQ. 01970 625866; (Fax)01970 626177.
Forest Enterprise Territorial Offices
England: 340 Bristol Business Park, Coldharbour Lane, Bristol BS16 1AJ. 0117 906 6000; (Fax)0117 931 2859
Scotland: North.1 Highlander Way, Inverness Retail and Business Park, Inverness, IV2 7GB, 01463 232811; (Fax)01463 243846.
South: 55/57 Moffat Road, Dumfries DG1 1NP. 01387 272440; (Fax)01387 251491
Wales: As above.

FRIENDS OF THE EARTH (1971; 150,000).
The largest international network of environmental groups in the world, represented in 68 countries. It is one of the leading environmental pressure groups in the UK. It has a unique network of campaigning local groups, working in 250 communities in England, Wales and Northern Ireland. It is largely funded by supporters with more than 90% of income coming from individual donations, the rest from special fundraising events, grants and trading.
Contact: 26/28 Underwood Street, London, N1 7JQ, 020 7490 1555; (Fax)020 7490 0881;
e-mail: info@foe.co.uk
www.foe.co.uk

GAME CONSERVANCY TRUST (1933; 27,000).
A registered charity which researches the conservation of game and other wildlife in the British countryside. More than 60 scientists are engaged in detailed work on insects, pesticides, birds (30 species inc. raptors) mammals (inc. foxes), and habitats. The results are used to advise government, landowners, farmers and conservationists on practical management techniques which will benefit game species, their habitats, and wildlife. Each June an *Annual Review* of 100 pages lists about 60 papers published in the peer-reviewed scientific press.
Contact: Director General, Dr G R Potts, Fordingbridge, Hampshire, SP6 1EF, 01425 652381; (Fax)01425 651026; www.gct.org.uk
e-mail: info@gct.org.uk

GAY BIRDERS CLUB (300-400).
A voluntary society for lesbian, gay and bisexual birdwatchers, their friends and supporters, over the age of consent, in the UK and worldwide. The club has 3-400 members and a network of regional contacts. It organises day trips, weekends and longer events at notable birding locations in the UK and abroad; about 200+ events in a year. Members receive a quarterly newsletter with details of all events. There is a Grand Get Together every 18 months. Membership £12 waged and £5 unwaged.
Contact: GeeBeeCee, BCM-Mono, London, WC1N 3XX; e-mail: enquiries@gbc-online.org.uk
www.gbc-online.org.uk

GOLDEN ORIOLE GROUP (1987).
Organises censuses of breeding Golden Orioles in parts of Cambridgeshire, Norfolk and Suffolk. Maintains contact with a network of individuals in other parts of the country where Orioles may or do breed. Studies breeding biology, habitat and food requirements of the species.
Contact: Jake Allsop, 5 Bury Lane, Haddenham, Ely, Cambs, CB6 3PR, 01353 740540;
e-mail: jakeallsop@aol.com

313

HAWK AND OWL TRUST (1969).
Registered charity dedicated to the conservation and appreciation of all birds of prey, including owls. Publishes a *Peregrine* newsletter and educational materials for all ages. The Trust achieves its major aim of creating and enhancing wild habitats for birds of prey through projects which involve practical research, creative conservation and education. Projects are often conducted in close partnership with landowners, farmers and others. Members are invited to take part in population studies, field surveys, etc. Studies of Barn and Little Owls, Hen Harrier, and Goshawk are in progress. The Trust's National Conservation and Education Centre at Newland Park, Gorelands Lane, Chalfont St Giles, Bucks, is now open to the public and offers schools and other groups cross-curricular environmental activities.
Contact: Director, Colin Shawyer, c/o Zoological Society of London, Regents Park, London, NW1 4RY, (Tel/Fax)01582 832182;
Membership administration: 11 St Mary's Close, Abbotskerswell, Newton Abbot, Devon, TQ12 5QF;
e-mail: hawkandowltrust@aol.com
www.hawkandowl.org

IRISH RARE BIRDS COMMITTEE (1985).
Assesses records of species of rare occurrence in the Republic of Ireland. Details of records accepted and rejected are incorporated in the Irish Bird Report, published annually in *Irish Birds*. In the case of rarities trapped for ringing, ringers in the Republic of Ireland are required to send their schedules initially to the National Parks and Wildlife Service, 51 St Stephen's Green, Dublin 2. A copy is taken before the schedules are sent to the British Trust for Ornithology.
Contact: Hon Secretary, Paul Milne, 100 Dublin Road, Sutton, Dublin 13, +353 (0)1 8325653;
e-mail: pjmilne@hotmail.com

JOINT NATURE CONSERVATION COMMITTEE (1990).
A committee of the three country agencies (English Nature, Scottish Natural Heritage, and the Countryside Council for Wales), together with independent members and representatives from Northern Ireland and the Countryside Agency. It is supported by specialist staff. Its statutory responsibilities include the establishment of common standards for monitoring, the analysis of information and research; advising Ministers on the development and implementation of policies for or affecting nature conservation; the provision of advice and the dissemination of knowledge to any persons about nature conservation; and the undertaking and commissioning of research relevant to these functions. JNCC additionally has the UK responsibility for relevant European and wider international matters. The Species Team, located at the HQ address below, is responsible for terrestrial bird conservation.
Contact: Monkstone House, City Road, Peterborough, PE1 1JY, 01733 562626; (Fax)01733 555948;
e-mail: feedback@jncc.gov.uk
www.jncc.gov.uk

LINNEAN SOCIETY OF LONDON (1788).
Named after Carl Linnaeus, the 18th century Swedish biologist, who created the modern system of scientific biological nomenclature, the Society promotes all aspects of pure and applied biology. It houses Linnaeus's collection of plants, insects and fishes, library and correspondence. The Society has a major reference library of some 100,000 volumes. Publishes the *Biological, Botanical and Zoological Journals*, and the *Synopses of the British Fauna*.
Contact: Executive Secretary, Dr J C Marsden, Burlington House, Piccadilly, London, W1J 0BF, 020 7434 4479; (Fax)020 7287 9364;
e-mail: john@linnean.org
www.linnean.org

LITTLE OWL STUDY GROUP (2002; 37).
Formed to promote the study and conservation of Little Owls (*Athene noctua*) in Britain and to develop a population monitoring network for Little Owls. The LOSG is part of the International Little Owl Working Group, a Europe wide organisation networking Little Owl Research and Conservation. The Little Owl is declining at an alarming rate across Europe and is endangered in at least three Western European countries. To combat this, a European Species Action Plan is being developed, to put in place the necessary monitors, conservation, and education measures for its long term survival. Project *Athene* is the British leg of this SAP. (See National Projects).
Contact: Roy Leigh, c/o Biota, Ascot Court, 71-73 Middlewich Road, Northwich, Cheshire, CW9 7BP, 01606 333296; (Fax)01606 333297;
e-mail: RSL@biota.co.uk

THE MAMMAL SOCIETY
The voice for British mammals and the only organisation solely dedicated to the study and conservation of all British mammals. They seek to raise awareness of mammals, their ecology and their conservation

needs, to survey British mammals and their habitats to identify the threats they face, to promote mammal studies in the UK and overseas, to advocate conservation plans based on sound science, to provide current information on mammals through its publications, to involve people of all ages in their efforts to protect mammals, to educate people about British mammals and to monitor mammal population changes.
Contact: The Secretary, 15 Cloisters House, 8 Battersea Park Road, London, SW8 4BG, 020 7498 4358; (Fax)020 7622 8722; www.mammal.org.uk e-mail: enquiries@mammal.org.uk

MANX ORNITHOLOGICAL SOCIETY see County Directory

MANX WILDLIFE TRUST see County Directory

NATIONAL BIRDS OF PREY CENTRE (1967). Concerned with the conservation and captive breeding of all raptors. Approx 85 species on site. Birds flown daily. Open Feb-Nov.
Contact: Mrs J Parry-Jones MBE, Newent, Glos, GL18 1JJ, 0870 9901992;
e-mail: jpj@nbpc.demon.co.uk
www.nbpc.co.uk

NATIONAL SOUND ARCHIVE WILDLIFE SECTION (1969).
(Formerly BLOWS - British Library of Wildlife Sounds). The most comprehensive collection of bird sound recordings in existence: over 130,000 recordings of more than 8,000 species of birds worldwide, available for free listening. Copies or sonograms of most recordings can be supplied for private study or research and, subject to copyright clearance, for commercial uses. Contribution of new material and enquiries on all aspects of wildlife sounds and recording techniques are welcome. Publishes *Bioacoustics* journal, CD and cassette guides to bird songs. Comprehensive catalogue available on-line at http:\\cadensa.bl.uk
Contact: Curator, Richard Ranft, British Library, National Sound Archive, 96 Euston Road, London, NW1 2DB, 020 7412 7402/3;
e-mail: nsa-wildsound@bl.uk
www.bl.uk/nsa

NATIONAL TRUST (1931; 2.6 mill.).
Charity depending on voluntary support of its members and the public. Largest private landowner with over 603,862 acres of land and nearly 600 miles of coast. Works for the preservation of places of historic interest or natural beauty, in England, Wales and N Ireland. The Trust's coast and countryside properties are open to the public at all times, subject only to the needs of farming, forestry and the protection of wildlife. Over a quarter of the Trust's land holding is designated SSSI or ASSI (N Ireland) and about 10% of SSSIs in England and Wales are wholly or partially owned by the Trust, as are 31 NNRs (eg Blakeney Point, Farne Islands, Wicken Fen and large parts of Strangford Lough, N Ireland). Fifteen per cent of Ramsar sites include Trust land, as do 27% of SPAs. 71 of the 117 bird species listed in the UK Red Data Book are found on Trust land.
Contact: Emily Brooks, Communications, 36 Queen Anne's Gate, London, SW1H 9AS, 020 7222 9251. www.nationaltrust.org.uk
Head of Nature Conservation:, Dr H J Harvey, Estates Dept, 33 Sheep Street, Cirencester, Glos GL7 1RQ. 01285 651818.
Northern Ireland Office: Rowallane House, Saintfield, Ballynahinch, Co. Down BT24 7LH. 028 975 10721.
Welsh Office: Trinity Square, Llandudno, LL30 2DE, 01492 860123; (Fax)01492 860233.

NATIONAL TRUST FOR SCOTLAND (1931; 230,000).
An independent charity, its 90 properties open to the public are described in its annual guide.
Contact: Head of Public Affairs, Ian Gardner, Wemyss House, 28 Charlotte Square, Edinburgh, EH2 4ET, 0131 243 9300. www.nts.org.uk

NATURE PHOTOGRAPHERS' PORTFOLIO (1944).
A society for photographers of wildlife, especially birds. Circulates postal portfolios of prints and transparencies.
Contact: Hon Secretary, A Winspear-Cundall, 8 Gig Bridge Lane, Pershore, Worcs, WR10 1NH, 01386 552103.

NORTHERN IRELAND BIRDWATCHERS' ASSOCIATION (1991; 90).
The NIBA Records Committee, established in 1997, has full responsibility for the assessment of records in N Ireland. NIBA also publishes the *Northern Ireland Bird Report*.
Contact: Hon Secretary, William McDowell, 4 Gairloch Park, Holywood, Co Down, BT18 0LZ, 028 9059 4390;
e-mail: williamm.mcdowell@ntlworld.com

NORTHERN IRELAND ORNITHOLOGISTS' CLUB (1965; 150).
Operates two small reserves in Co Down. Operates a Barn Owl nestbox scheme and a winter feeding programme for Yellowhammers. Has a regular programme of lectures and field trips for members. Publishes *The Harrier* quarterly.
Contact: Gary Wilkinson, The Roost, 139 Windmill Road, Hillsborough, Co Down, BT26 6NP, 028 9263 9254. www.nioc.fsnet.co.uk

PEOPLE'S DISPENSARY FOR SICK ANIMALS (1917).
Registered charity. Provides free veterinary treatment for sick and injured animals whose owners qualify for this charitable service.
Contact: Director General, Mrs Marilyn Rydstrom, Whitechapel Way, Priorslee, Telford, Shrops, TF2 9PQ, 01952 290999; e-mail: pr@pdsa.org.uk www.pdsa.org.uk

RARE BREEDING BIRDS PANEL (1973).
An independent body funded by the JNCC and RSPB. Both bodies are represented on the panel, as are BTO and ACRE. It collects all information on rare breeding birds in the United Kingdom, so that changes in status can be monitored as an aid to present-day conservation and stored for posterity. Special forms are used (obtainable free from the secretary) and records should if possible be submitted via the county and regional recorders. Since 1996 the Panel also monitors breeding by scarcer non-native species and seeks records of these in the same way. Annual report published in *British Birds*. For details of species covered by the Panel see Log Charts.
Contact: Secretary, Dr Malcolm Ogilvie, Glencairn, Bruichladdich, Isle of Islay, PA49 7UN, 01496 850218;
e-mail: rbbp@indaal.demon.co.uk

ROYAL AIR FORCE ORNITHOLOGICAL SOCIETY (1965: 291).
RAFOS organises regular field meetings for members, carries out ornithological census work on MOD properties and mounts major expeditions annually to various UK and overseas locations. It publishes a newsletter twice a year, and in conjuction with the the the Army Ornithological Society, publishes *The Osprey* journal annually; in addition, it publishes reports on its expeditions and surveys.
Contact: Squadron Leader Nick Smith, RAFOS General Secretary, Room 24, D Block, Copenacre, JSU Corsham, Chippenham, Wilts, SN13 9NR. 01225 813636 (Fax)01225 813172.
www.rafos.org.uk
e-mail: spchibt-km2@a.dii.mod.uk

ROYAL NAVAL BIRDWATCHING SOCIETY (1946; 167 full and 93 associate members and library).
Cover all main ocean routes, the Society has developed a system for reporting the positions and identity of seabirds and landbirds at sea by means of standard sea report forms, much of the system being computerised. Members are encouraged to photograph birds while at sea and a library of photographs and slides is maintained. Publishes a Bulletin and an annual report entitled *The Sea Swallow*.
Contact: Hon Secretary, FS Ward Esq. 16 Cutlers Lane, Stubbington, Fareham, Hants, PO14 2JW.

ROYAL PIGEON RACING ASSOCIATION (46,000).
Exists to promote the sport of pigeon racing and controls pigeon racing within the Association. Organises liberation sites, issues rings, calculates distances between liberation sites and home lofts, and assists in the return of strays. May be able to assist in identifying owners of ringed birds caught or found.
Contact: General Manager, RPRA, The Reddings, Cheltenham, GL51 6RN, 01452 713529;
e-mail: gm@rpra.org or strays@rpra.org
www.rpra.org

ROYAL SOCIETY FOR THE PREVENTION OF CRUELTY TO ANIMALS (1824).
In addition to its animal homes, the Society also runs a woodland study centre and nature reserve at Mallydams Wood in East Sussex and specialist wildlife rehabilitation centres at West Hatch, Taunton, Somerset TA3 5RT (01823 480156), at Station Road, East Winch, King's Lynn, Norfolk PE32 1NR (01553 842336), and London Road, Stapeley, Nantwich, Cheshire CW5 7JW (0870 4427102). Inspectors are contacted through their Regional Communications Centres, which can be reached via the Society's 24-hour national cruelty and advice line: 08705 555 999.
Contact: RSPCA Headquarters, Willberforce Way, Horsham, West Sussex, RH13 9RS, 0870 0101181; (Fax)0870 7530048. www.rspca.org.uk

ROYAL SOCIETY FOR THE PROTECTION OF BIRDS (1889; 1,022,090).
UK partner of BirdLife International, is Europe's largest voluntary wildlife conservation body. The RSPB, a registered charity, is governed by

an elected body (see also RSPB Phoenix and RSPB Wildlife Explorers). Its work in the conservation of wild birds and habitats covers the acquisition and management of nature reserves; research and surveys; monitoring and responding to development proposals, land use practices and pollution which threaten wild birds and biodiversity; and the provision of an advisory service on wildlife law enforcement.

Work in the education and information field includes formal education in schools and colleges, and informal activities for children through Wildlife Explorers; publications (including *Birds*, a quarterly magazine for members, *Bird Life*, a bi-monthly magazine for RSPB Wildlife Explorers, *Wild Times* for under-8s); displays and exhibitions; the distribution of moving images about birds; and the development of membership activities through Members' Groups.

The RSPB currently manages 176 nature reserves in the UK, covering more than 299,000 acres; 53% of this area is owned. Sites are carefully selected, mostly as being of national or international importance to wildlife conservation. The aim is to conserve a countrywide network of reserves with all examples of the main bird communities and with due regard to the conservation of plants and other animals. Visitors are generally welcome to most reserves, subject to any restrictions necessary to protect the wildlife or habitats. Current national projects include extensive work on agriculture, and conservation and campaigning for the conservation of the marine environment and to halt the illegal persecution of birds of prey. Increasingly, there is involvement with broader environmental concerns such as climate change and transport.

The RSPB's International Dept works closely with Birdlife International and its partners in other countries and is involved with numerous projects overseas, especially in Europe and Asia.

Contact: Chief Executive, Graham Wynne, The Lodge, Sandy, Beds, SG19 2DL, 01767 680551; (Fax)01767 692365; e-mail: (firstname.name)@rspb.org.uk www.rspb.org.uk

Regional Offices:
RSPB North England, 4 Benton Terrace, Sandyford Road, Newcastle upon Tyne NE2 1QU. 0191 281 3366.
RSPB North West, Westleigh Mews, Wakefield Road, Denby Dale, Huddersfield HD8 8QD. 01484 861148.
RSPB Central England, 46 The Green, South Bar, Banbury, Oxon OX16 9AB. 01295 253330.
RSPB East Anglia, Stalham House, 65 Thorpe Road, Norwich NR1 1UD. 01603 661662.
RSPB South East, 2nd Floor, Frederick House, 42 Frederick Place, Brighton BN1 4EA. 01273 775333.
RSPB South West, Keble House, Southernhay Gardens, Exeter EX1 1NT. 01392 432691.
RSPB Scotland HQ, Dunedin House, 25 Ravelston Terrace, Edinburgh EH4 3TP. 0131 311 6500.
RSPB North Scotland, Etive House, Beechwood Park, Inverness IV2 3BW. 01463 715000.
RSPB East Scotland, 10 Albyn Terrace, Aberdeen AB1 1YP. 01224 624824.
RSPB South & West Scotland, Unit 3.1, West of Scotland Science Park, Kelvin Campus, Glasgow G20 0SP. 0141 576 4100.
RSPB North Wales, Maes y Ffynnon, Penrhosgarnedd, Bangor, Gwynedd LL57 2DW. 01248 363800.
RSPB South Wales, Sutherland House, Castlebridge, Cowbridge Road East, Cardiff CF11 9AB. 029 2035 3000.
RSPB Northern Ireland, Belvoir Park Forest, Belfast BT8 7QT. 028 9049 1547.

RSPB WILDLIFE EXPLORERS and RSPB PHOENIX (formerly YOC) (1965; 140,000). Junior section of the RSPB. There are more than 300 groups run by almost 1,200 volunteers. Activities include projects, holidays, roadshows, competitions, and local events for children, families and teenagers. Publishes two bi-monthly magazines, *Bird Life* (aimed at 8-12-year-olds) and *Wild Times* (aimed at under 8s) and a` quarterly magazine *Wingbeat* (aimed at teenagers).
Contact: Principal Youth Officer, David Chandler, RSPB Youth Unit, The Lodge, Sandy, Beds, SG19 2DL, 01767 680551; e-mail: explorers@rspb.org.uk and phoenix@rspb.org.uk www.rspb.org.uk/youth

SCOTTISH BIRDS RECORDS COMMITTEE (1984).
Set up by the Scottish Ornithologists' Club to ensure that records of species not deemed rare enough to be considered by the British Birds Rarities Committee, but which are rare in Scotland, are fully assessed; also maintains the official list of Scottish birds.
Contact: Secretary, R W Forrester, The Gables, Eastlands Road, Rothesay, Isle of Bute, PA20 9JZ. www.the-soc.org.uk

SCOTTISH FIELD STUDIES ASSOCIATION (1950).
Offers residential courses on a variety of environmental subjects, including birdwatching in spring, summer and autumn; weekend and week-long courses.
Contact: Director, SFSA, Kindrogan Field Centre, Enochdhu, Blairgowrie, Perthshire, PH10 7PG, 01250 881286; (Fax)01250 881433;

e-mail: kindrogan@btinternet.com
www.kindrogan.com

SCOTTISH NATURAL HERITAGE (1991).
Statutory body established by the Natural Heritage (Scotland) Act 1991 and responsible to Scottish Ministers. Its aim is to promote Scotland's natural heritage, its care and improvement, its responsible enjoyment, its greater understanding and appreciation and its sustainable use.
Contact: Chief Executive, SNH, Ian Jardine, 12 Hope Terrace, Edinburgh, EH9 2AS, 0131 447 4784; www.snh.org.uk

SCOTTISH ORNITHOLOGISTS' CLUB (1936; 2250).
The Club has 14 branches (see County Directory), each with a programme of winter meetings and field trips throughout the year. The SOC organises an annual weekend conference in the autumn and a joint SOC/BTO one-day birdwatchers' conference in spring. Publishes quarterly newsletter *Scottish Bird News*, the bi-annual *Scottish Birds*, the annual *Scottish Bird Report* and the *Raptor Round Up*. The SOC is developing a new resource centre in Scotland, details of which can be found on the website.
Contact: Development Manager, Bill Gardner MBE, Harbout Point, Newhailes Road, Musselburgh, EH21 6SJ, 0131 653 0653; (Fax)0131 6530654; www.the-soc.org.uk
e-mail: mail@the-soc.org.uk

SCOTTISH SOCIETY FOR THE PREVENTION OF CRUELTY TO ANIMALS (1839).
Represents animal welfare interests to government, local authorities and others. Educates young people to realise their responsibilities. Maintains an inspectorate to patrol and investigate and to advise owners about the welfare of animals and birds in their care. Maintains 13 welfare centres, two of which include oiled bird cleaning centres. Bird species, including birds of prey, are rehabilitated and where possible released back into the wild.
Contact: Chief Executive, Ian Gardiner, Braehead Mains, 603 Queensferry Road, Edinburgh, EH4 6EA, 0131 339 0222; (Fax)0131 339 4777; e-mail: enquiries@scottishspca.org
www.scottishspca.org

SCOTTISH WILDLIFE TRUST (1964; 16,500).
Has members' groups throughout Scotland. Aims to conserve all forms of wildlife and has over 123 reserves, many of great birdwatching interest, covering some 55,555 acres. Member of The Wildlife Trusts partnership and organises Scottish Wildlife Watch. Publishes *Scottish Wildlife* three times a year.
Contact: Chief Executive, Steve Sankey, Cramond House, Off Cramond Glebe Road, Edinburgh, EH4 6NS, 0131 312 7765; (Fax)0131 312 8705; e-mail: enquiries@swt.org.uk www.swt.org.uk

SEABIRD GROUP (1966; 350).
Concerned with conservation issues affecting seabirds. Co-ordinates census and monitoring work on breeding seabirds; has established and maintains the Seabird Colony Register in collaboration with the JNCC; organises triennial conferences on seabird biology and conservation topics. Small grants available to assist with research and survey work on seabirds. Publishes the *Seabird Group Newsletter* every four months and the journal, *Atlantic Seabirds*, quarterly in association with the Dutch Seabird Group.
Contact: Bob Swann, 14 St Vincent Road, Tain, Ross-shire, IV19 1JR, 01862 894329; e-mail: bob.swann@freeuk.com

SOCIETY OF WILDLIFE ARTISTS (1964).
Registered charity. Annual exhibitions held in Sept/ Oct at the Mall Galleries, London.
Contact: President, Bruce Pearson, Federation of British Artists, 17 Carlton House Terrace, London, SW1Y 5BD, 020 7930 6844. www.swla.co.uk

SWAN SANCTUARY (THE)
Founded by Dorothy Beeson BEM. A registered charity which operates nationally, with six rescue centres in the UK and one in Ireland. Has a fully equipped swan hospital with an operating theatre, two treatment rooms, x-ray facilities and a veterinary   surgeon. Present site has three lakes and 10 rehabilitation ponds where some 3,000 swans a year are treated. 24-hour service operated, with volunteer rescuers on hand to recover victims of oil spills, vandalism etc. A planned new site will allow visitors. Provides education and training.
Contact: Secretary, Field View, Pooley Green, Egham, Surrey, TW20 8AT, 01784 431667; (Fax)01784 430122; www.swanuk.org.uk
e-mail: swans@swanuk.org.ukt

SWAN STUDY GROUP (80).
An association of both amateur and professionals, from around the UK. Most are concerned with Mute Swans, but Bewick's and Whooper Swan

biologists are also active members. The aim of the Group is to provide a forum for communication and discussion, and to help co-ordinate co-operative studies. Annual meetings are held at various locations in the UK at which speakers give presentations on their own fieldwork.
Contact: Helen Chisholm, 14 Buckstone Howe, Edinburgh, EH10 6XF, 0131 445 2351.

This study of a Fulmar was one of Alessandro Troisi's entries into the BB competition.

A.T.

UK400 CLUB (1981).
Serves to monitor the nation's leading twitchers and their life lists, and to keep under review contentious species occurrences. Publishes a bi-monthly magazine *Rare Birds*. Membership open to all.
Contact: L G R Evans, 8 Sandycroft Road, Little Chalfont, Amersham, Bucks, HP6 6QL, 01494 763010; e-mail: lgre@uk400clubonline.co.uk
www.uk400clubonline.co.uk

ULSTER WILDLIFE TRUST see County Directory

WADER STUDY GROUP (1970; 600).
An association of wader enthusiasts, both amateur and professional, from all parts of the world. The Group aims to maintain contact between them, to help in the organisation of co-operative studies, and to provide a vehicle for the exchange of information. Publishes the Wader Study Group Bulletin three times a year and holds annual meetings throughout Europe.
Contact: Membership Secretary, Wader Study Group, Rod West, c/o BTO, The Nunnery, Thetford,

Norfolk, IP24 2PU;
e-mail: rodwest@ndirect.co.uk

WALTER ROTHSCHILD ZOOLOGICAL MUSEUM
Founded by Lionel Walter (later Lord) Rothschild, the Museum displays British and exotic birds (1,500 species) including many rarities and extinct species. Galleries open all year except 24-26 Dec. Adjacent to the Bird Group of the Natural History Museum - with over a million specimens and an extensive ornithological library, an internationally important centre for bird research.
Contact: Akeman Street, Tring, Herts, HP23 6AP, 020 7942 6171.
www.nhm.nc.uk/museum/tring

WELSH KITE TRUST (1996).
A registered charity that undertakes the conservation and annual monitoring of Red Kites in Wales. It attempts to locate all the breeding birds, to compile data on population growth, productivity, range expansion etc. The Trust liaises with landowners, acts as consultant on planning issues and with regard to filming and photography, and represents Welsh interests on the UK Kite Steering Group. Provides a limited rescue service for injured kites and eggs or chicks at risk of desertion or starvation. Publishes a newsletter *Boda Wennol* twice a year, sent free to members of Friends of the Welsh Kite and to all landowners with nesting Kites.
Contact: Tony Cross, Samaria, Nantmel, Llandrindod Wells, Powys, LD1 6EN, 01597 860524; e-mail: tony.cross@welshkitetrust.org
www.welshkitetrust.org

WELSH ORNITHOLOGICAL SOCIETY (1988; 250).
Promotes the study, conservation and enjoyment of birds throughout Wales. Runs the Welsh Records Panel which adjudicates records of scarce species in Wales. Publishes the journal *Welsh Birds* twice a year, along with newsletters, and organises an annual conference.
Contact: Paul Kenyon, 196 Chester Road, Hartford, Northwich, CW8 1LG, 01606 77960; e-mail: pkenyon196@aol.com
www.members.aol.com/welshos/cac

WETLAND TRUST
Set up to encourage conservation of wetlands and develop study of migratory birds, and to foster international relations in these fields. Destinations for recent expeditions inc. Senegal, The Gambia, Guinea-Bissau, Nigeria, Kuwait, Thailand, Greece and Jordan. Large numbers of birds are ringed each year in Sussex and applications are invited

from individuals to train in bird ringing or extend their experience.
Contact: AJ Martin, Elms Farm, Pett Lane, Icklesham, Winchelsea, E Sussex, TN36 4AH, 01797 226374; e-mail: alan@wetlandtrust.org

WILDFOWL & WETLANDS TRUST (THE)
(1946; 100,000 members and 4,500 bird adopters). Registered charity founded by the late Sir Peter Scott. It has nine centres with reserves (see Arundel, Caerlaverock, Castle Espie, Llanelli, Martin Mere, Slimbridge, Washington, Welney, and The London Wetland Centre in Reserves and Observatories section). The centres are nationally or internationally important for wintering wildfowl; they also aim to raise awareness of and appreciation for wetland species, the problems they face and the conservation action needed to help them. Programmes of walks and talks are available for visitors with varied interests - resources and programmes are provided for school groups. Centres, except Caerlaverock and Welney, have wildfowl from around the world, inc. endangered species. Research Department works on population dynamics, species management plans and wetland ecology. The Wetland Advisory Service (WAS) undertakes contracts, and Wetland Link International promotes the role of wetland centres for education and public awareness.
Contact: Managing Director, Tony Richardson, Slimbridge, Glos, GL2 7BT, 01453 890333; (Fax)01453 890827; e-mail: enquiries@wwt.org.uk www.wwt.org.uk

WILDLIFE SOUND RECORDING SOCIETY
(1968; 327).
Works closely with the Wildlife Section of the National Sound Archive. Members carry out recording work for scientific purposes as well as for pleasure. A field weekend is held each spring, and members organise meetings locally. Four CD sound magazines of members' recordings are produced for members each year, and a journal, *Wildlife Sound*, is published twice a year.
Contact: Hon Membership Secretary, WSRS, Mike Iannantuoni, 36 Wenton Close, Cottesmore, Oakham, Rutland, LE15 7DR, 01572 812447.

WILDLIFE TRUSTS (THE)
A nationwide network of 46 local Wildlife Trusts and 100 urban Wildlife Groups which work to protect wildlife in town and country. The Wildlife Trusts manage more than 2,300 nature reserves, undertake a wide range of other conservation and education activities, and are dedicated to the achievement of a UK richer in wildlife. Publ *Natural World*. See also Wildlife Watch.
Contact: Director-General, Dr Simon Lyster, The Kiln, Waterside, Mather Road, Newark, NG24 1WT, 01636 677711; (Fax)01636 670001; e-mail: info@wildlife-trusts.cix.co.uk www.wildlifetrusts.org

WILDLIFE WATCH (1971; 24,000+).
The junior branch of The Wildlife Trusts (see previous entry). It supports 1,500 registered volunteer leaders running Watch groups across the UK. Publishes *Watchword* and *Wildlife Extra*.
Contact: Development Officer, Avril Rawson, The Wildlife Trusts, The Kiln, Waterside, Mather Road, Newark, NG24 1WT, 0870 0367711; (Fax)00870 0360101; e-mail: watch@wildlife-trusts.cix.co.uk www.wildlifewatch.org/watch

WWF-UK (1961).
WWF is the world's largest independent conservation organisation, comprising 27 national organisations. It works to conserve endangered species, protect endangered spaces, and address global threats to nature by seeking long-term solutions with people in government and industry, education and civil society. Publishes *WWF News* (quarterly magazine).
Contact: Chief Executive, Robert Napier, Panda House, Weyside Park, Catteshall Lane, Godalming, Surrey, GU7 1XR, 01483 426444; (Fax)01483 426409; www.wwf-uk.org

ZOOLOGICAL PHOTOGRAPHIC CLUB (1899).
Circulates black and white and colour prints of zoological interest via a series of postal portfolios.
Contact: Hon Secretary, Martin B Withers, 93 Cross Lane, Mountsorrel, Loughborough, Leics, LE12 7BX, 0116 229 6080.

ZOOLOGICAL SOCIETY OF LONDON (1826).
Carries out research, organises symposia and holds scientific meetings. Manages the Zoological Gardens in Regent's Park (first opened in 1828) and Whipsnade Wild Animal Park near Dunstable, Beds, each with extensive collections of birds. The Society's library has a large collection of ornithological books and journals. Publications include the *Journal of Zoology, Animal Conservation, The Symposia* and *The International Zoo Yearbook*.
Contact: Director General, Dr Michael Dixon, Regent's Park, London, NW1 4RY, 020 7722 3333. www.zsl.org

NATIONAL PROJECTS

NOTICE TO BIRDWATCHERS

National ornithological projects depend for their success on the active participation of amateur birdwatchers. In return they provide birdwatchers with an excellent opportunity to contribute in a positive and worthwhile way to the scientific study of birds and their habitats, which is the vital basis of all conservation programmes. The following entries provide a description of each particular project and a note of whom to contact for further information (full address details are in the previous section).

BEWICK'S SWAN RESEARCH
A WWT project

Recognition of individual Bewick's Swans by their black and yellow bill markings has been used for an extensive study of the flock wintering at Slimbridge, Gloucestershire since 1964. The swans show a high level of both site and mate fidelity; 10 to 50% of the birds identified each season have been recorded at Slimbridge in previous years. Factors affecting the life cycle of individual birds can therefore be analysed in detail.

A regular ringing programme was introduced in 1967 to identify staging sites used during migration to and from the Russian breeding grounds, and to continue monitoring individuals that transferred to other wintering sites. Bewick's Swans have also been caught and ringed at Caerlaverock (Dumfries & Galloway) and Welney (Norfolk) since 1979, and at Martin Mere (Lancashire) since 1990.

Since 1991 staff have made one or two expeditions to the Russian arctic each summer, to study the swans' breeding biology in collaboration with scientists from Russia, the Netherlands and Denmark. Sightings of marked birds are invaluable for maintaining the life-history records of individual swans.

Contact: Eileen Rees, WWT.

BREEDING BIRD SURVEY
Supported by the BTO, JNCC and the RSPB.

Begun in 1994, the BBS is designed to keep track of the changes in populations of our common breeding birds. It is dependent on volunteer birdwatchers throughout the country who can spare about five hours a year to cover a 1x1km survey square. There are just two morning visits to survey the breeding birds each year.

Survey squares are picked at random by computer to ensure that all habitats and regions are covered. Since its inception it has been a tremendous success, with more than 2,200 squares covered and more than 200 species recorded each year. Contact: Mike Raven, BTO, or your local BTO Regional Representative (see County Directory).

BTO/JNCC WINTER FARMLAND BIRDS SURVEYS
A BTO project funded by a partnership of the BTO and the JNCC.

Three winters of full surveys 1999/2000, 2000/01,

2001/02. They concentrate on a suite of species found on farmland in winter, including Tree Sparrow, Linnet, Bullfinch, Yellowhammer, Redwing and Fieldfare, Lapwing and Golden Plover. The surveys involve several components, including coverage of random squares, counts along standard routes and casual records. The final winter of the random square survey postponed due to Foot & Mouth outbreak. Now going ahead in 2002/03. Contact: Simon Gillings, e-mail: wfbs@bto.org.

CORE MONITORING CENSUS
A BTO project. This BTO project has developed from the Common Birds Census, which ran from 1962 to 2000 and was supported by JNCC. A small group of core plots have been selected and they will continue to be surveyed using the CBC's mapping method. Volunteer fieldworkers make ten breeding-season visits each year to a plot of farmland or woodland. Maps are prepared showing the locations of birds' territories on each plot. These are of value both locally and nationally. The BTO uses the data to study the relationships of breeding birds with their habitats. No new participants are needed at present. Contact: Richard Thewlis, BTO.

CONCERN FOR SWIFTS
A Concern for Swifts Group project.

Endorsed by the BTO and the RSPB, the Group monitors Swift breeding colonies, especially where building restoration and maintenance are likely to cause disturbance. Practical information can be provided to owners, architects, builders and others, as well as advice on nest boxes and the use of specially adapted roof tiles. The help of interested birdwatchers is always welcome. Contact: Jake Allsop, 01353 740540; fax 01353 741585.

CONSTANT EFFORT SITES SCHEME
A BTO project for bird ringers, funded by a partnership of the BTO, the JNCC, Duchas the Heritage Service - National Parks & Wildlife Service (Ireland) and the ringers themselves.

Participants in the Scheme monitor common songbird populations by mist-netting throughout the summer at more than 130 sites across Britain and Ireland. Changes in numbers of adults captured provide an index of population changes

between years, while the ratio of juveniles to adults gives a measure of productivity. Between-year recaptures of birds are used to study variations in adult survival rates. Information from CES complements that from other long-term BTO surveys.
Contact: Dawn Balmer, BTO.

CORMORANT ROOST SITE INVENTORY AND BREEDING COLONY REGISTER
R. Sellers and WWT.
Daytime counts carried out under the Wetland Bird Survey provide an index of the number of Cormorants wintering in Great Britain, but many birds are known to go uncounted on riverine and coastal habitats.
Dr Robin Sellers, in association with WWT, therefore established the Christmas Week Cormorant Survey which, through a network of volunteer counters, sought to monitor the numbers of Cormorants at about 70 of the most important night roosts in GB. In 1997, this project was extended to produce a comprehensive Cormorant Roost Site Inventory for Great Britain. Over 100 county bird recorders and local bird experts helped compile the inventory, which currently lists 291 night roosts, mostly in England.
In 1990, Robin Sellers also established the Cormorant Breeding Colony Survey to monitor numbers and breeding success of Cormorants in the UK at both coastal and inland colonies. Some 1,500 pairs of Cormorants, representing perhaps 15% of the local UK population, now breed inland. New colonies are forming every year as the population inland increases annually by 19%.
The first European-wide Cormorant survey will be undertaken in January 2003, organised in the UK by WWT. Anyone wishng to take part in either roost or breeding surveys should contact Colette Hall at WWT.

GARDEN BIRD FEEDING SURVEY
A BTO project.
The 2001/02 season completed 32 years of the GBFS. Each year 250 observers record the numbers and variety of garden birds fed by man in the 26 weeks between October and March. It is the longest running survey of its type in the world. Gardens are selected by region and type, from city flats, suburban semis and rural houses to outlying farms.
Contact: David Glue, BTO.

GARDEN BIRDWATCH
A BTO project, supported by C J WildBird Foods.
Started in January 1995, this project is a year-round survey that monitors the use that birds make of gardens. Approximately 14,000 participants from all over the UK and Ireland keep a weekly log of species using their gardens. The data collected are used to monitor regional, seasonal and year-to-year changes in the garden populations of our commoner birds. To cover costs there is an annual registration fee of £12. There is a quarterly volunteers magazine and all new joiners receive a full-colour, 80 page garden bird handbook.
Contact: Jacky Prior/Carol Povey, BTO.

GOLDEN ORIOLE CENSUS
A Golden Oriole Group project.
With support from the RSPB, the Golden Oriole Group has undertaken a systematic annual census of breeding Golden Orioles in the Fenland Basin since 1987. In recent years national censuses have been made, funded by English Nature and the RSPB, in which some 60 volunteer recorders have participated. The Group is always interested to hear of sightings of Orioles and to receive offers of help with its census work. Studies of breeding biology, habitat and food requirements are also carried out. Contact: Jake Allsop, Golden Oriole Group.

GOOSE CENSUSES
A WWT project.
Britain and Ireland support internationally important goose populations. During the day, many of these feed away from wetlands and are therefore not adequately censused by the Wetland Bird Survey. Additional surveys are therefore undertaken to provide estimates of population size. These primarily involve roost counts, supplemented by further counts of feeding birds.
Most populations are censused up to three times a year, typically during the autumn, midwinter, and spring. In addition, counts of the proportion of juveniles in goose flocks are undertaken to provide estimates of annual productivity. Further volunteers are always needed. In particular, counters in Scotland, Lancashire and Norfolk are sought. For more information contact: Richard Hearn, WWT, e-mail richard.hearn@wwt.org.uk.

HERONRIES CENSUS
A BTO project.
This survey started in 1928 and has been carried out under the auspices of the BTO since 1934. It represents the longest continuous series of population data for any European breeding bird.
  Counts are made at a sample of heronries each year, chiefly in England and Wales, to provide an index of the current population level; data from Scotland and Northern Ireland are scant and more contributions from these countries would be especially welcomed. Herons may be hit hard during periods of severe weather but benefit by increased survival over mild winters. Their position at the top of a food chain makes them particularly vulnerable to pesticides and pollution. Additional fieldwork is being planned for 2003 to mark the scheme's 75th anniversary.
Contact: John Marchant, BTO.

HERON SURVEY, 75TH ANNIVERSARY
The 75th Anniversary Heron Survey is planned for spring 2003, aiming to obtain better coverage of heronries in England, Wales, Scotland and N Ireland. The survey will be run from Thetford mainly through the regional volunteer network, as well as data received via the web.
Contact: John Marchant, BTO.

HOUSE SPARROW SURVEYS

An eighteen month survey, commencing in March 2003, will investigate how House Sparrows use our gardens. Volunteers will also look in detail at the species' distributions within towns and villages in different areas of the country. House Sparrow counters should contact the Garden BirdWatch Team, BTO, The Nunnery, Thetford, Norfolk, IP24 2PU.

IRISH WETLAND BIRD SURVEY (I-WeBS)

A joint project of BirdWatch Ireland, the National Parks & Wildlife Service of the Dept of Arts, Culture & the Gaeltacht, and WWT, and supported by the Heritage Council and WWF-UK.

Established in 1994, I-WeBS aims to monitor the numbers and distribution of waterfowl populations wintering in Ireland in the long term, enabling the population size and spatial and temporal trends in numbers to be identified and described for each species.

Methods are compatible with existing schemes in the UK and Europe, and I-WeBS collaborates closely with the Wetland Bird Survey (WeBS) in the UK. Synchronised monthly counts are undertaken at wetland sites of all habitats during the winter. Counts are straightforward and counters receive a newsletter and full report annually. Additional help is always welcome, especially during these initial years as the scheme continues to grow. Contact: Kendrew Colhoun, BirdWatch Ireland.

LITTLE OWLS - PROJECT *ATHENE*

Little Owl Study Group

The Little Owl is declining at an alarming rate across Europe and is endangered in at least three Western European countries. To combat this, a European Species Action Plan is being developed, to put in place the necessary monitors, conservation, and education measures for its long term survival. Project *Athene* is the British leg of this plan.

It is a two-tier monitoring programme that anybody can become involved with. To monitor numbers of Little Owls a playback method is employed using standardised protocol. Nest site recording provides a more in-depth information on the population dynamics of the owls. You can join the LOSG and dependant on your time and expertise, carry out Little Owl surveys in your own patch. Contact Roy Leigh: Little Owl Study Group, C/O Biota, 71-73 Ascot Court, Middlewich Road, Northwich, Cheshire CW9 7BP. 01606 333296; e-mail: RSL@biota.co.uk for further information

LOW TIDE COUNTS SCHEME

see Wetland Bird Survey

MANX CHOUGH PROJECT

A Manx registered charitable trust.

Established in 1990 to help the conservation of the Chough in the Isle of Man, leading to its protection and population increase. The main considerations are the maintenance of present nest sites, provision of

suitable conditions for the reoccupation of abandoned sites and the expansion of the range of the species into new areas of the Island. Surveys and censuses are carried out. Raising public awareness of and interest in the Chough are further objects. Contact: Allen S Moore, Lyndale, Derby Road, Peel, Isle of Man IM5 1HH. 01624 843798.

MIGRATION WATCH

A BTO/BirdWatch Ireland project for all birdwatchers, sponsored by Northumbrian Water Ltd and in association with Bird Watching magazine.

Migration Watch, a three-year project that started in 2002, uses the latest Internet technology to record the timing and pattern of arrival for a wide range of spring migrants. The website is launched on 1st March each year and all birdwatchers are welcome to take part. Once online, you can record all the migrant birds you see (and those that you don't see!) at your birdwatching sites such as your garden, the local park or a nature reserve. The results are displayed on the website (www.bto.org/migwatch) in a variety of ways including animated maps, tables and graphs and are provided at a national level. Contact: Dawn Balmer, BTO (E-mail: migwatch.organiser@bto.org)

MUTE SWAN CENSUS 2001

A WWT/JNCC project, in collaboration with BTO, Swan Study Group, SOC and others.

This national census of Mute Swans is scheduled to take place in spring 2001, repeating the previous one conducted in 1990. Mute Swans are widespread during the breeding season on all manner of wetlands, including small lakes and particularly on rivers, habitats little visited by waterbird surveys. Complete coverage will be attempted for the most densely populated regions, with options to assist organisers and counters elsewhere. The census will require large numbers of observers. Contact: Peter Cranswick at WWT.

NEST RECORD SCHEME

A BTO project, funded by a partnership of the BTO, the JNCC.

All birdwatchers can contribute to this scheme by completing easy-to-use Nest Record Cards for any nesting attempt they find. The aim is to provide a picture of how Britain's birds are faring in town and countryside, in a way that no single observer could ever do. Even one card is a useful addition. Prospective new participants can obtain a free introductory pack.

Contact: Andy Simpkin, BTO.

PREDATORY BIRDS MONITORING SCHEME

A Centre for Ecology and Hydrology project

Scientists at the CEH, Monks Wood have been monitoring the levels of various pollutants, including pesticides, in predatory birds for over 35 years. This work relies largely on members of the public sending in any predatory bird carcases they find. Species required include: Sparrowhawk, Kestrel, Barn Owl, Heron, Kingfisher, Great-crested Grebe, Merlin,

Peregrine, Buzzard and other large birds of prey. They are interested in receiving all carcases of these birds, even if the cause of death is known, such as window collisions and roadkills.

Whole specimens found dead should be packed in a sealed plastic bag, placed inside a padded envelope or small box, (mark the outside of the package 'PERISHABLE GOODS') and sent by FIRST CLASS post to; Heath Malcolm, CEH, Monks Wood, Abbots Ripton, Huntingdon, Cambs, PE28 2LS. Personal postage costs will be refunded in stamps. Please enclose the following information: Name and address of finder, date bird was found, location and circumstances in which the bird was found. A report of the cause of death and analytical results will be sent to the finder once examinations are complete. If you require additional information, please do not hesitate to get in touch, either by telephone, 01487 772498 or e-mail: hmm@ceh.ac.uk

The success of the Centre's work depends on the contribution of volunteers.

RAPTOR AND OWL RESEARCH REGISTER

A BTO project

The Register has helped considerably over the past 26 years in encouraging and guiding research, and in the co-ordination of projects. There are currently almost 500 projects in the card index file through which the Register operates.

The owl species currently receiving most attention are Barn and Tawny. As to raptors, the most popular subjects are Kestrel, Buzzard, Sparrowhawk, Hobby and Peregrine, with researchers showing increasing interest in Red Kite, and fewer large in-depth studies of Goshawk, Osprey and harriers. Contributing is a simple process and involves all raptor enthusiasts, whether it is to describe an amateur activity or professional study. The nature of research on record varies widely – from local pellet analyses to captive

Short-eared Owl sightings always excite. This drawing is from Graham Brittain.

breeding and rehabilitation programmes to national surveys of Peregrine, Buzzard and Golden Eagle. Birdwatchers in both Britain and abroad are encouraged to write for photocopies of cards relevant to the species or nature of their work. The effectiveness of the Register depends upon those running projects (however big or small) ensuring that their work is included. Contact: David Glue, BTO.

RED KITE RE-INTRODUCTION PROJECT

An English Nature/SNH/RSPB project supported by Forest Enterprise, Yorkshire Water and authorities in Germany and Spain

The project involves the translocation of birds from Spain, Germany and the expanding Chilterns population for release at sites in England and Scotland. Records of any wing-tagged Red Kites in England should be reported to Ian Carter at English Nature, Northminster House, Peterborough, PEI IUA (tel 01733 455281). Scottish records should be sent to Brian Etheridge at RSPB's North Scotland Regional Office, Etive House, Beechwood Park, Inverness, IV2 3BW (tel 01463 715000).

Sightings are of particular value if the letter/number code (or colour) of wing tags can be seen or if the bird is seen flying low over (or into) woodland. Records should include an exact location, preferably with a six figure grid reference.

RETRAPPING ADULTS FOR SURVIVAL PROJECT

A BTO project for bird ringers, funded by a partnership of the BTO, the JNCC, Duchas the Heritage Service - National Parks & Wildlife Service (Ireland) and the ringers themselves.

This project started in 1998 and is an initiative of the BTO Ringing Scheme. It aims to gather re-trap information for a wide range of species, especially those of conservation concern, in a variety of breeding habitats, allowing the monitoring of survival rates.

Detailed information about survival rates from the RAS Project will help in the understanding of changing population trends. Ringers choose a target species, decide on a study area and develop suitable catching techniques. The aim then is to catch all the breeding adults of the chosen species within the study area. This is repeated each breeding season for a minimum of five years. The results will be relayed to conservation organisations who can use the information to design effective conservation action plans. Contact: Dawn Balmer, BTO.

RINGING SCHEME

A BTO project for bird ringers, funded by a partnership of the BTO, the JNCC, Duchas the Heritage Service - National Parks & Wildlife Service (Ireland) and the ringers themselves.

The purpose of the Ringing Scheme is to study mortality, survival and migration by marking birds with individually numbered metal rings which carry a return address. About 2,000 trained and licensed ringers operate in Britain and Ireland, and together they mark around 750,000 birds each year.

All birdwatchers can contribute to the scheme by reporting any ringed birds they find. On finding a ringed bird the information to note is the ring number, species (if known), when and where the bird was found, and what happened to it. If the bird is dead the ring should be removed, flattened and attached to the letter. Finders who send their name and address will be given details of where and when the bird was ringed. About 12,000 ringed birds are reported each year and an annual report is published.
Contact: Jacquie Clark, BTO.

SIGHTINGS OF COLOUR-MARKED BIRDS
Various bodies.
Studies of movements of colour-marked birds depend heavily on the help of birdwatchers. On sighting a colour-marked bird full details should be recorded and sent to the appropriate contact below. The information will be passed on to the person who marked the bird, who will send details of marking to the observer. Unfortunately some birds cannot be traced, for example, if rings have been lost or are not all seen.
Waders: Wader Study Group, c/o Rob Robinson, BTO.
Wildfowl: Richard Hearn, WWT, Slimbridge, Gloucester GL2 7BT.
Cormorant: Stuart Newson, BTO
Chough: Eric Bignal, Kindrochaid, Bruichladdich, Islay PA44 7PP.
Large gulls: Peter Rock, 59 Concorde Drive, Westbury-on-Trym, Bristol BS10 6PX.
Small gulls: K T Pedersen, Daglykkevej 7, DK-2650 Hridovre, Denmark.
All other species: Linda Milne, Ringing Unit, BTO.

SWIFTS see Concern for Swifts

2003 UK PEREGRINE SURVEY
A joint BTO/Raptor Study Groups project, supported by JNCC/EHS/EN/CCW/SNH/SOC/RSPB.
This is the fifth in a series of ten-yearly surveys of the breeding Peregrine population in the UK. The survey in 1961/62 highlighted the plight of Peregrines, badly affected by organochlorine pesticides such as DDT. Subsequent surveys have shown how the population has recovered as the pesticides were withdrawn from use. In 1991 Peregrines were at least beginning to recolonise the southeast coast of England, but there were worrying declines in the north and west of Scotland.
The survey in 2003 aims to provide solid data about the numbers of Peregrines breeding throughout the UK information that is especially important in the light of perceived conflicts between raptors and game rearing and pigeon racing interests.
The Peregrine is listed on Schedule 1 of the Wildlife and Countryside Act 1981 and a licence is required to disturb a bird at its nest. The survey is being organised on the ground through the network of Raptor Study Groups, where they exist, or through designated regional organisers. Volunteer birdwatchers, with experience of raptor survey, who wish to take part and others, who can provide information on the location of

territorial Peregrines, particularly those birds located in cities, should contact the national organiser, who will put them in touch with their local raptor study group organiser. National Organiser: Humphrey Crick, BTO Scotland.

WATERWAYS BIRD SURVEY
A BTO project
From March to July each year participants survey linear waterways (rivers and canals) to map the position and activity of riparian birds. Results show both numbers and distribution of breeding territories for each waterside species at each site. An annual report on population change is published in *BTO News*. Since 1998, WBS has run parallel with the Waterways Breeding Bird Survey, which uses a transect method. WBS maps show the habitat requirements of the birds and can be used to assess the effects of waterway management. Coverage of new plots is always required, especially in poorly covered areas such as Ireland, Scotland, Wales, SW England and the North East. Contact: John Marchant, BTO.

WATERWAYS BREEDING BIRD SURVEY
A BTO project, supported by the Environment Agency
WBBS uses transect methods like those of the Breeding Bird Survey to record bird populations along randomly chosen stretches of river and canal throughout the UK. Just two survey visits are needed during April-June. WBBS began in 1998 and is currently in a development phase, in which its performance is being assessed against the long established Waterways Bird Survey. Coverage of random sites requires a special boost in 2003-04. Contact BTO Regional Representative (see County Directory) to enquire if any local stretches require coverage, otherwise John Marchant at BTO HQ.

WeBS PILOT DISPERSED WATERBIRDS SURVEY
A WeBS project funded by the BTO, WWT, RSPB and JNCC
Little is known about the numbers of dabbling ducks, Moorhen, Coot, Little Grebe, Heron etc that winter on small water bodies, streams, flooded fields, ditches and dykes, away from Wetland Bird Survey (WeBS) sites. Furthermore, there are no reliable population estimates of wintering Ruff or either species of Snipe. This survey aims to improve the population estimates of these waterbird species on all areas within lowland Britain not counted by other WeBS surveys.
Volunteers are being asked to intensively survey one-kilometre OS grid squares, which have been randomly selected from all lowland one-kilometre squares in Great Britain. Numbers of waterbirds and gulls will be recorded in different broad-scale habitats (*e.g.* river, dry woodland, arable etc). The selection has been stratified according to the proportion of urban and wet areas in the square. WeBS Local Organisers are coordinating counters in their local region, and we are hoping to cover 1,500 squares. Contacts: Michael Armitage, Steve Holloway, BTO; Mark Pollitt, WWT.

WeBS RIVERINE SURVEY

A Wetland Bird Survey project (qv)

Whilst the Wetland Bird Survey (WeBS) achieves excellent coverage of estuaries and inland still waters, rivers are poorly monitored by comparison. Consequently, WeBS undoubtedly misses a significant proportion of the UK populations of several species which use rivers, eg. Little Grebe, Mallard, Tufted Duck, Goldeneye and Goosander. The WeBS Riverine Survey in 2001/02 will be the first national survey of waterbirds on rivers during winter. It aims to estimate total numbers of birds on rivers throughout the UK and to identify particularly important river stretches for birds. Exact methods are being finalised following a pilot last winter, but in essence will involve simply counting the numbers of waterbirds (esp. ducks) on particular stretches of river and canal (sections for counts will probably be 2.5 km long). Many counters in addition to those involved in the pilot will be required. Contact: James Robinson at WWT.

WETLAND BIRD SURVEY

A joint scheme of BTO, WWT, RSPB & JNCC

The Wetland Bird Survey (WeBS) is the monitoring scheme for non-breeding waterbirds in the UK. The principal aims are:
1. to determine the population sizes of waterbirds:
2. to determine trends in numbers and distribution:
3. to identify important sites for waterbirds:
4. to conduct research which underpins waterbird conservation.

WeBS data are used to designate important waterbird sites and protect them against adverse development, for research into the causes of declines, for establishing conservation priorities and strategies and to formulate management plans for wetland sites and waterbirds.

Once monthly, synchronised Core Counts are made at as many wetland sites as possible. Low Tide Counts are made on about 20 estuaries each winter to identify important feeding areas. Counts take just a few hours and are relatively straightforward. The 3,000 participants receive regular newsletters and a comprehensive annual report. New counters are always welcome. Contacts: WeBS Secretariat, WWT (for Core Counts and general enquiries) and Andy Musgrove, BTO (Low Tide Counts).

WHOOPER SWAN RESEARCH

A WWT/Icelandic Museum of Nature History project

WNW's long-term study of Whooper Swans commenced in 1979 with the completion of swan pipes at Caerlaverock (Dumfries & Galloway) and Welney (Norfolk) and the subsequent development of a ringing programme for this species. Whooper Swans have been ringed at Martin Mere (Lancashire) from 1990 onwards. Since 1988, staff have made regular expeditions to Iceland where they collaborate with Icelandic ornithologists in monitoring clutch and brood sizes, and in catching the families and non-breeding flocks. The study aims to determine factors affecting the reproductive success of the Icelandic-breeding Whooper Swan population which winters mainly in Britain and Ireland. Relocating the families in winter is important for assessing the number of cygnets that survive autumn migration. Efforts made by birdwatchers to read Whooper Swan rings and to report the number of juveniles associated with ringed birds, are therefore particularly useful. The first and last dates on which ringed birds are seen at a site are also valuable for monitoring the movements of the swans in winter. Contact: Eileen Rees, WWT.

WILDFOWL COLOUR RINGING

A WWT project

The Wildfowl & Wetlands Trust co-ordinates all colour ringing of swans, geese and ducks on behalf of the BTO. The use of unique coloured leg-rings enables the movements and behaviour of known individuals to be observed without recapture. The rings are usually in bright colours with engraved letters and/or digits showing as black or white, and can be read with a telescope at up to 200m. Colour-marked neck collars, and plumage dyes, have also been used on geese and swans. Any records of observations should include species, location, date, ring colour and mark, and which leg the ring was on (most rings read from the foot upwards). The main study species are Mute Swan, Bewick's Swan, Whooper Swan, Pink-footed Goose, Greylag Goose, Greenland and European White-fronted Geese, Barnacle Goose, Brent Goose, Shelduck and Wigeon. Records will be forwarded to the relevant study, and when birds are traced ringing details will be sent back to the observer. All sightings should be sent to: Research Dept (Colour-ringed Wildfowl), WWT.

WINTER FARMLAND BIRDS SURVEYS see BTO/
JNCC Winter Farmland Bird Surveys.

WOODCOCK SURVEY

Following on from the 2002 pilot survey, there will be a full survey in 2003. The survey will monitor random plots of suitable woodland. Contact: Deborah Lang, BTO, The Nunnery, Thetford, Norfolk, IP24 2PU.

WOODLAND RE-SURVEY PROJECT

A Woodland Bird Group project undertaken by the BTO and RSPB, funded by DEFRA, Forestry Commission, English Nature, RSPB, BTO and Woodland Trust.

Woodland plots originally surveyed either in the 1970's and 80's for the BTO's Common Bird Census or by the RSPB with point counts in the 1980s will be re-surveyed in 2003 and 2004. The aims are to accurately assess the changes in bird populations of a large sample of woods and to attempt to identify regional variations and specific factors (such as habitat change and fragmentation, deer and squirrel impacts) which may be responsible. Survey work will be undertaken by contract fieldworkers and volunteers. Contact: Chris Hewson, BTO.
(email: chris.hewson@bto.org).

INTERNATIONAL
DIRECTORY

A visit to Northern or Southern Europe is always likely to provide sightings of elegant Purple Herons. Illustration by David Thelwell.

The BirdLife Partnership

BirdLife is a Partnership of non-governmental organisations (NGOs) with a special focus on conservation and birds. Each NGO Partner represents a unique geographic territory/country.

The BirdLife Network explained

Partners: Membership-based NGOs who represent BirdLife in their own territory. Vote holders and key implementing bodies for BirdLife's Strategy and Regional Programmes in their own territories.

Partners Designate: Membership-based NGOs who represent BirdLife in their own territory, in a transition stage to becoming full Partners. Non-vote holders.

Affiliates: Usually NGOs, but also individuals, foundations or governmental institutions when appropriate. Act as a BirdLife contact with the aim of developing into, or recruiting, a BirdLife Partner in their territory.

Secretariat: The co-ordinating and servicing body of BirdLife International.

Secretariat Addresses

BirdLife Cambridge Office
BirdLife International
Wellbrook Court
Girton Road
Cambridge CB3 0NA
United Kingdom
Tel. +44 1 223 277 318
Fax +44 1 223 277200
Email birdlife@birdlife.org.uk
http://www.birdlife.net

**BirdLife Americas
Regional Office**
Birdlife International
Vicente Cárdenas 120 y
Japon,
3rd Floor
Quito
Ecuador
Postal address
BirdLife International
Casilla 17-17-717
Quito
Ecuador
Tel. +593 2 453 645

Fax +593 2 459 627
Email birdlife@birdlife.org.ec
http://www.geocities.com/
RainForest/Wetlands/6203

BirdLife Asia Regional Office
Jl. Jend. Ahmad Yani No. 11
Bogor 16161
Indonesia
Postal address
PO Box 310/Boo
Bogor 16003
Indonesia
Tel. +62 251 333 234/+62 251
371 394
Fax +62 251 357 961
Email birdlife@indo.net.id
http://www.kt.rim.or.jp/
~birdinfo/indonesia

**BirdLife European Regional
Office**
Droevendaalsesteeg 3a PO Box
127, NL- 6700 AC, Wageningen
The Netherlands

Tel. +31 317 478831
Fax +31 317 478844
Email birdlife@birdlife.agro.nl

**European Community Office
(ECO)**
BirdLife International
22 rue de Toulouse
B-1040 Brussels
Belgium
Tel. +32 2280 08 30
Fax +32 2230 38 02
Email bleco@ibm.net

**BirdLife Middle East
Regional Office**
BirdLife International
c/o Royal Society for the
Conservation of Nature (RSCN)
PO Box 6354
Amman 11183
Jordan
Tel: +962 6 535-5446
Fax: +962 6 534-7411
Email birdlife@nol.com.jo

FOREIGN NATIONAL ORGANISATIONS

AFRICA

PARTNERS

Burkina Faso
Fondation des Amis de la Nature
(NATURAMA), 01 B.P. 6133,
Ouagadougou 01.
e-mail: naturama@fasonet.bf

Ethiopia
Ethiopian Wildlife and Natural
History Society, PO Box 13303,
Addis Ababa, Pub: *Agazen;
Ethiopian Wildl. and Nat. Hist.
Newsl. (& Annual Report);
Ethiopian Wildl. and Nat. Hist. Soc.
Quarterly News (WATCH); Walia
(WATCH) (Ethiopia).*
e-mail: ewnhs@telecom.net.et
http://ewnhs@telecom.net.et

Ghana
Ghana Wildlife Society, PO Box
13252, Accra, Pub: *Bongo News;
NKO (The Parrots).*
e-mail: wildsoc@ighmail.com

Kenya
Nature Kenya, PO Box 44486,
00100 GPO. Nairobi. Pub: *Bulletin
of the EANHS; Journal of East
African Natural; Kenya Birds.*
e-mail: eanhs@africaonline.co.ke
www.naturekenya.org

Nigeria
Nigerian Conservation Foundation,
PO Box 74638, Victoria Island,
Lagos. Pub: *NCF Matters/News/
Newsletter; Nigerian Conservation
Foundation Annual Report.*
e-mail: ncf@hyperia.com
http://ncf@hyperia.com

Seychelles
Nature Seychelles, BirdLife
Seychelles, P O Box 1310, Suite
202, Aarti Chambers, Mont Fleuri,
Mahe. Pub: *Zwazo - a BirdLife
Seychelles Newsletter.*
e-mail: birdlife@seychelles.net

Sierra Leone
Conservation Society of Sierra
Leone, PO BOX 1292, Freetown.
Pub: *Rockfowl Link, The.*
e-mail: cssl@sierratel.sl

South Africa
BirdLife South Africa, PO Box 515,
Randburg 2125, Pub: *Newsletter
of BirdLife South Africa; Ostrich.*
e-mail: info@birdlife.org.za
www.birdlife.org.za

Tanzania
Wildlife Conservation Society of
Tanzania, PO Box 70919, Dar es
Salaam, Pub: *Miombo.*
e-mail: wcst@africaonline.co.tz

Uganda
Nature Uganda, PO Box 27034,
Kampala. Pub: *Naturalist - A
Newsletter of the East Africa Nat.
His. Soc.*
e-mail: eanhs@infocom.co.ug

PARTNERS DESIGNATE

Tunisia
Association "Les Amis des
Oiseaux", Avenue 18 Janvier 1952,
Ariana Centre, App. C209, 2080
Ariana, Tunis. Pub: *Feuille de
Liaison de l'AAO; Houbara, l'.*
e-mail: aao.bird@planet.tn
http://aao.bird@planet.tn

Zimbabwe
BirdLife Zimbabwe, PO Box CY
161, Causeway, Harare. Pub:
*Babbler (WATCH) (Zimbabwe);
Honeyguide.*
e-mail: birds@zol.co.zw

AFFILIATES

Botswana
Botswana Bird Club, IUCN Private
Bag 00300, Gaborone, Pub:
Babbler (WATCH) (Botswana).

Burundi
Association Burundaise pour la
Protection des Oiseaux, P O Box
7069, Bujumbura
e-mail: aboburundi@yahoo.fr

Cameroon
Cameroon Ornithological Club,
PO Box 3055, Messa, Yaoundé.
e-mail: coc@iccnet.cm

Egypt
Sherif Baha El Din, 3 Abdala El
Katib St, Dokki, Cairo.
e-mail: baha@internetegypt.com

Rwanda
Association pour la Conservation
de la Nature au Rwanda, P O Box
4290, Kigali,
e-mail: acnr_@hotmail.com

Zambia
Zambian Ornithological Society,
Box 33944, Lusaka 10101, Pub:
*Zambian Ornithological Society
Newsletter.*
e-mail: zos@zamnet.zm
www.fisheagle.org

AMERICAS

PARTNERS

Argentina
Aves Argentina / AOP, 25 de Mayo
749, 2 piso, oficina 6, 1002 Buenos
Aires. Pub: *Hornero; Naturaleza &
Conservacion; Nuestras Aves;
Vuelo de Pajaro.*
e-mail: info@avesargentinas.org.ar
http://members.tripod.com/
~HARPIA/aop.html

Belize
The Belize Audubon Society, 12
Fort Street, PO Box 1001, Belize
City. Pub: *Belize Audubon Society
Newsletter.*
e-mail: base@btl.net
www.belizeaudubon.org

Bolivia
Asociacion Armonia, Calle Mexico
110, esquina Ecuador, Casilla 3081,
Santa Cruz de la Sierra. Pub: *Aves
en Bolivia.*
e-mail: armonia@scbbs-bo.com
http://armonia@scbbs-bo.com

Canada
Bird Studies Canada, PO Box/160,
Port Rowan, Ontario N0E 1M0.
Pub: *Bird Studies Canada - Annual
Report; Birdwatch Canada.*
e-mail: mbradstreet@bsc-eoc.org
www.bsc-eoc.org

Canada
Canadian Nature Federation (CNF),
1 Nicholas Street, Suite 606,
Ottawa, Ontario, K1N 7B7. Pub:
*Grass 'n Roots; IBA News Canada;
Nature Canada; Nature Matters;
Nature Watch News (CNF).*
e-mail: cnf@cnf.ca www.cnf.ca

Ecuador
Fundación Ornithológica del
Ecuador, La Tierra 203 y Av. de los
Shyris, Casilla 17-17-906, Quito.
e-mail: cecia@uio.satnet.net
www.geocities.com/RainForest/
Jungle/7633/ingles.html

Jamaica
BirdLife Jamaica, 2 Starlight
Avenue, Kingston 6, Pub:
Broadsheet: BirdLife Jamaica;
Important Bird Areas Programme
Newsletter.
e-mail: birdlifeja@yahoo.com
www.birdelifejamaica.com

Panama
Panama Audubon Society,
Apartado 2026, Ancón, Balboa.
Pub: *Toucan.*
e-mail: audupan@psi.net.pa
www.pananet.com/audubon

Venezuela
Sociedad Conservacionista
Audubon de, Apartado 80.450,
Caracas 1080-A, Venezuela. Pub:
Audubon (Venezuela) (formerly
Boletin Audubon).
e-mail: audubondevenezuela
@audubondevenezuela.org

PARTNERS DESIGNATE

Mexico
CIPAMEX, Apartado Postal 22-012,
D.F. 14091, Mexico. Pub: *AICA's;*
Cuauhtli Boletin de Cipa Mex.
e-mail: cipamex@
campus.iztacala.unam.mx
http://coro@servidor.unam.mx

Paraguay
Guyra Paraguay,, Coronel Rafael
Franco 381 c/ Leandro Prieto,
Casilla de Correo 1132, Asunción.
Pub: *Boletin Jara Kuera.*
e-mail: guyra@highway.com.py
www.mbertoni.org.py

United States
National Audubon Society, 700
Broadway, New York, NY, 10003.
Pub: *American Birds; Audubon*
(USA); Audubon Field Notes;
Audubon Bird Conservation
Newsletter.
e-mail: jwells@audobon.org
www.audubon.org

Chile
Union de Ornitologis de Chile
(UNORCH), Casilla 13.183,
Santiago 21. Pub: *Boletin Chileno*
de Ornitologia; Boletin Informativo
(WATCH) (Chile).
e-mail: unorch@entelchile.net
www.geocities.com/RainForest/
4372

AFFILIATES

Bahamas
Bahamas National Trust, PO Box
N-4105, Nassau. Pub: *Bahamas*
Naturalist; Currents; Grand
Bahama Update.
e-mail: bnt@bahamas.net.bs
http://bnt@bahamas.net.bs
www.bahamas.net.bs/environment

Cuba
Dr Martín Acosta, Museo Historia
Natural, Facultad de Biologia, U.H.,
25 e/J e I Vedado, La Habana
e-mail: poey@comuh.uh.cu

El Salvador
SalvaNATURA, 33 Avenida Sur
#640, Colonia Flor Blanca, San
Salvador.
e-mail: salvanatura@saltel.net

Falkland Islands
Falklands Conservation, PO Box
26, Stanley,. or Falklands
Conservation, 1 Princes Avenue,
Finchley, London N3 2DA, UK.
Pub: *Falklands Conservation.*
e-mail: conservation@
horizon.co.fk
www.
falklands-nature.demon.co.uk

Honduras
Sherry Thorne, c/o Cooperación
Técnica, Apdo 30289 Toncontín,
Tegucigalpa.
e-mail: pilar_birds@yahoo.com

Suriname
Foundation for Nature Preservation
in Suriname, Cornelis
Jongbawstraat 14, PO BOX 12252,
Paramaribo
e-mail: stinasu@sr.net

Uruguay
GUPECA, Casilla de Correo 6955,
Correo Central, Montevideo. Pub:
Achara. e-mail: gupeca@
adinet.com.uy
www.
uruguayos.nu/gupeca/achara.htm

ASIA

PARTNERS

Japan
Wild Bird Society of Japan (WBSJ),

International Centre-WING, 2-35-2
Minamidaira, Hino City, Tokyo,
191-0041, Japan. Pub: *Strix; Wild*
Birds; Wing.
e-mail: int.center@
wing-wbsj.or.jp

Malaysia
Malaysian Nature Society, PO Box
10750, 50724 Kuala Lumpur. Pub:
Enggang; Suara Enggang; Malayan
Nature Journal; Malaysian
Naturalist.
e-mail: natsoc@po.jaring.my
www.mns.org.my

Philippines
Haribon Foundation, Suites 401-
404 Fil-Garcia Bldg, 140 Kalayaan
Avenue cor. Mayaman St, Diliman,
Quezon CIty 1101. Pub: *Haribon*
Foundation Annual Report; Haring
Ibon; Philippine Biodiversity.
e-mail: birdlife@haribon.org.ph
www.haribon.org.ph

Singapore
Nature Society (Singapore), The
Sunflower, 510 Geylang Road, 02-
05, The Sunflower, 398466. Pub:
Nature News; Nature Watch
(Singapore).
e-mail: natsoc@singnet.com.sg
www.post1.com/home/
naturesingapore

Taiwan
Wild Bird Society of Taiwan, 1F,
No. 3, Lane 36 Chinglung St., 116
Taipei, Taiwan. Pub: *Yuhina Post.*
e-mail: wbst@ms12.hinet.net
http://wildbird.hinet.net/taipei

Thailand
Bird Conservation Society of
Thailand, 69/12 Soi Ramindra, 24
Jarakheebua Lardprao, Bangkok,
10230. Pub: *Bird Conservation*
Society of Thailand.
e-mail: bcst@box1.a-net.net.th

PARTNER DESIGNATE

India
Bombay Natural History Society,
Hornbill House, Shaheed Bhagat
Singh Road, Mumbai-400 023.
Pub: *Buceros; Hornbill; Journal of*
the Bombay Natural History
Society.
e-mail: bnhs@bom4.vsnl.net.in
www.museums.or.ke/eanhs/
eanhs.html

AFFILIATES

Hong Kong
The Hong Kong Birdwatching
Society, GPO BOX 12460. Pub:
Hong Kong Bird Report.
e-mail: hkbws@hkbws.org.uk
http://hkbws@hkbws.org.uk
www.hkbws.org.hk

Nepal
Bird Conservation Nepal, GPO
12465, Kathmandu. Pub: *Bird
Conservation Nepal (Danphe);
Ibisbill.*
e-mail: birdlife@mos.com.np
http://birdlife@mos.com.np

Pakistan
Ornithological Society of Pakistan,
PO Box 73, 109D Dera Ghazi Khan,
32200. Pub: *Pakistan Journal of
Ornithology.*
e-mail: osp@mul.paknet.com.pk

Sri Lanka
Field Ornithology Group of Sri
Lanka, Dept of Zoology, University
of Colombo, Colombo 03. Pub:
*Malkoha - Newsletter of the Field
Ornithology Group of Sri Lanka.*
e-mail: fogsl@slt.lk
http://fogsl@slt.lk

EUROPE

PARTNERS

Austria
BirdLife Austria, Museumplatz 1/
10/8, AT-1070 Wien. Pub: *Egretta;
Vogelschutz in Osterreich.*
e-mail: birdlife@blackbox.at

Belgium
BirdLife Belgium (BNVR-RNOB-
BNVS), Kardinaal, Mercierplein 1,
2800 Mechelen, Belgium.
e-mail: wim.vandenbossche@
natuurpunt.be
www.natuurreservaten.be

Bulgaria
Eesti Ornitiliigiaühing (EOÜ), PO
Box 50, BG-1111, Sofia. Pub:
Neophron (& UK).
e-mail: bspb_hq@bspb.org

Czech Republic
Czech Society for Ornithology
(CSO), Hornomecholupska 34, CZ-

102 00 Praha 10. Pub: *Ptaci Svet;
Sylvia; Zpravy Ceske Spolecnosti
Ornitologicke.*
e-mail: cso@birdlife.cz

Denmark
Dansk Ornitologisk Forening
(DOF), Vesterbrogade 138-140,
1620 Kobenhavn V. Pub: *DAFIF -
Dafifs Nyhedsbrev; Dansk
Ornitologisk Forenings Tidsskrift;
Fugle og Natur.* e-mail: dof@dof.dk
www.dof.dk

Estonia
Estonian Ornithological Society
(EOU), PO Box 227, Vesti Str. 4,
EE-50002 Tartu, Estonia. Pub:
Hirundo Eesti Ornitoogiauhing.
e-mail: jaanus.elts@eoy.ee
www.loodus.ee/hirundo

Finland
BirdLife SUOMI Finland, Annankatu
29 A, PO Box 1285, FI 00101,
Helsinki. Pub: *Linnuston-Suojelu;
Linnut; Tiira.*
e-mail: office@birdlife.fi
www.birdlife.fi

France
Ligue pour la Protection des
Oiseaux (LPO), La Corderie Royale,
BP 263, FR-17305, Rochefort
Cedex. Pub: *Lettre Internationale;
Ligue Francaise Pour La Protection
des Oiseaux; Oiseau, L' (LPO);
Outarde infos.*
e-mail: lpo@lpo-birdlife.asso.fr
http://lpo@lpo-birdlife.a

Germany
Naturschutzbund Deutschland,
Herbert-Rabius-Str. 26, D-53225
Bonn, Germany. Pub: *Naturschutz
Heute (NABU) Naturschutzbund
Deutschland.* e-mail:
Naturschutz.heute@NABU.de
NABU@NABU.de

Gibraltar
Gibraltar Ornithological and Nat.
History Society, Jew's Gate, Upper
Rock Nature Reserve, PO Box 843,
GI. Pub: *Alectoris; Gibraltar Nature
News.* e-mail: gohns@gibnet.gi
www.gibraltar.gi/gonhs

Greece
Hellenic Ornithological Society
(HOS), Vas. Irakleiou 24, GR-
10682 Athens, Greece, GR-10681,

Athens. Pub: *HOS Newsletter.*
e-mail: birdlife-gr@
ath.forthnet.gr
www.ornithologiki.gr

Hungary
Hungarian Orn. and Nature Cons.
Society (MME), Kolto u. 21, Pf.
391, HU-1536, Budapest. Pub:
*Madartani Tajekoztato;
Madartavlat; Ornis Hungarica;
Tuzok.* e-mail: mme@mme.hu
www.mme.hu

Iceland
Icelandic Society for the Protection
of Birds, Fuglaverndarfélag
Islands, PO Box 5069, IS-125
Reykjavik, Iceland.
e-mail: fuglavernd@fuglavernd.is

Ireland
BirdWatch Ireland, Ruttledge
House, 8 Longford Place,
Monkstown, Co. Dublin. Pub: *Irish
Birds; Wings (IWC Birdwatch
Ireland).*
e-mail: bird@indigo.ie
www.birdwatchireland.ie

Israel
Society for the Protection of
Nature in Israel, Hashsela 4,
Tel-Aviv 66183. Pub: *SPNI News.*
e-mail: ioc@netvision.net.il
http://ioc@netvision.net.il

Italy
Lega Italiana Protezione Uccelli
(LIPU), Via Trento 49, IT-43100,
Parma. Pub: *Ali Giovani; Ali
Notizie.*
e-mail: lipusede@box1.tin.it
www.lipu.it

Latvia
Latvijas Ornitologijas Biedriba
(LOB), Ak 1010 Riga-50, LV 1050.
Pub: *Putni Daba.*
e-mail: putni@parks.lv

Luxembourg
Letzebuerger Natur-a
Vulleschutzliga (LNVL), Kraizhaff,
route de Luxembourg.L-1899
Kockelscheuer. Pub: *Regulus
(WATCH); Regulus Info (& Annual
Report) (WATCH); Regulus
Wissenschaftliche Berichte
(WATCH).*
e-mail: secretary@luxnatur.lu
www.luxnatur.lu

FOREIGN NATIONAL ORGANISATIONS

Malta
BirdLife Malta, 57 Marina Court, Flat 28, Triq Abate Rigord, MT-Ta' Xbiex, MSD 12, MALTA. Pub: *Bird Talk (WATCH) (Malta); Bird's Eye View (WATCH) (Malta); Il-Merill.*
e-mail: info@birdlifemalta.org
www.birdlifemalta.org

Netherlands
Vogelbescherming Nederland, PO Box 925, NL-3700 AX Zeist. Pub: *Vogelniews; Vogels.*
e-mail: birdlife@vogelbescherming.nl

Norway
Norsk Ornitologisk Forening, Sandgata 30 B, N 7012 Trondheim, Norway. Pub: *Fuglearet; Fuglefauna; Var; Ringmerkaren.*
e-mail: nof@birdlife.no
www.birdlife.no

Poland
Polish Society for the Protection of Birds (OTOP), PO Box 335, PL-80-958, Gdansk 50. Pub: *Ptaki; Ptasie Ostoje.*
e-mail: office@otop.most.org.pl

Portugal
Sociedade Portuguesa para o Estuda das, Aves (SPEA), Rua da Vitoria, 53-2 Dto, 1100-618, Lisboa. Pub: *Pardela.*
e-mail: spea@ip.pt
www.spea.pt

Romania
Romanian Ornithological Society (SOR), Str. Gheorghe Dima RO-3400 Cluj. Pub: *Alcedo; Buletin AIA; Buletin de Informare Societatea Ornitologica Romana; Milvus (Romania).*
e-mail: sorcj@codec.ro
http://sorcj@codec.ro

Slovakia
Soc. for the Prot. of Birds in Slovakia (SOVS), PO Box 71, 093 01 Vranov nad Topl'ou. Pub: *Spravodaj SOVS; Vtacie Spravy.*
e-mail: sovs@changenet.sk
www.sovs.miesto.sk

Slovenia
BirdLife Slovenia (DOPPS), Drustvo Za Opazovanje in Proucevanje Ptic Slovenije. Pub: *Acrocephalus; Svet Ptic.*
e-mail: dopps@dopps-drustvo.si

Spain
Sociedad Espanola de Ornitologia (SEO), C/Melquiades Biencinto 34, E-28053, Madrid. Pub: *Ardeola; Areas Importantes para las Aves.*
e-mail: seo@seo.org
www.seo.org

Sweden
Sveriges Ornitologiska Forening (SOF), Ekhagsvagen 3, SE 104-05, Stockholm. Pub: *Fagelvarld; var; Ornis Svecica.*
e-mail: birdlife@sofnet.org
www.sofnet.org

Switzerland
Schweizer Vogelschutz (SVS), BirdLife Schweiz, Postfach, 8036 Zurich. Pub: *Oiwvos Ornis; Ornis Junior; Ornithologische Beobachter; Der Ornithos; Steinadler.*
e-mail: svs@birdlife.ch
www.birdlife.ch

Turkey
Dogal Hayati Koruna Dernegi (DHKD), Buyuk Postane Caddesi No.: 43-45, Kat: 5-6 Bahcekapi 34420, Istanbul. Pub: *Kelaynak; Kuscu Bulteni.*
e-mail: kelaynak@dhkd.org
www.dhkd.org

United Kingdom
Royal Society for the Protection of Birds, The Lodge, Sandy, Bedfordshire, SG19 2DL.
e-mail: info@RSPB.org.UK

PARTNERS DESIGNATE

Albania
Albanian Society for the Protection of Birds, Museum of Natural Science, Rr. E. Kavajes 132, Tirana
e-mail: mns@albmail.com

Belarus
Bird Conservation Belarus (APB), PO Box 306, BY 220050. Pub: *Subbuteo - The Belarusian Ornithological Bulletin.*
e-mail: APB-Minsk@mail.ru

Storms at sea often blow Little Auks onto inland waters. Illustration by George Brown

FOREIGN NATIONAL ORGANISATIONS

Iceland
Icelandic Institute of Natural History, PO Box 5320, IS-125 Reykjavik. Pub: *Bliki*.
e-mail: bliki@ni.is
http://ni.is/bliki.htm

Lithuania
Lietuvos Ornitologu Draugija (LOD), Naugarduko St. 47-3, LT-2006, Vilnius, Lithuania. Pub: *Baltasis Gandras*.
e-mail: lod@birdlife.lt
www.birdlife.lt

Russian Federation
Russian Bird Conservation Union (RBCU), Building 1, Shosse Entuziastov 60, 111123, RU-Moscow. Pub: *Newsletter of the Russian Bird Conservation Union*.
e-mail: rbcu@online.ru
http://rbcu@online.ru

Ukraine
Ukrainian Union for Bird Conservation (UTOP), PO Box 33, Kiev, 1103, UA. Pub: *Life of Birds*.
e-mail: utop@iptelecom.net.ua
http://utop@iptelecom.net.ua

AFFILIATES

Liechtenstein
Botanish-Zoologische Gesellschaft, Im Bretscha 22, FL-9494 Schaan, Liechtenstein.
e-mail: broggi@pingnet.li or renat@pingnet.li

Andorra
Associacio per a la Defensa de la Natura, Apartado de Correus Espanyols No 96, Andora La Vella, Principat d'Andorra. Pub: *Aiguerola*.
e-mail: and@andorra.ad

Croatia
Croatian Society for Bird and Nature Protection, Iiirski Trg 9, HR-10000 Zagreb, Croatia. Pub: *Troglodytes*.
e-mail: jasmina@mahazu.hazu.hr
http://jasmina@mahazu.hazu.

Cyprus
Cyprus Ornithological Society, PO Box 28076, CY-Nicosia 2090, Cyprus.
e-mail: melis@cytanet.com.cy

Georgia
Georgian Centre for the Conservation of Wildlife, 1 Mosashvili Str, 99 Tbilisi GE-380073, Georgia.
e-mail: Ramaz_Gokhelashvili@dai.com

Switzerland
UNEP/Global Resource Information Database, International Environment House (IEH), 11 Chemin des Anemones, 1219 Chatelaine, Geneva. Pub: *GRID - Geneva Quarterly Bulletin*.
e-mail: info@grid.unep.ch
www.grid.unep.ch/

MIDDLE EAST

PARTNERS

Jordan
Royal Society of the Conservation of Nature, PO Box 6354, Jubeiha-Abu-Nusseir Circle, Amman 11183. Pub: *Al Reem*.
e-mail: adminrscn@rscn.org.jo
www.rscn.org.jo

Lebanon
Society for the Protection of Nature and Natural Resources in Lebanon, PO Box 11-8281, Beirut, Lebanon.
e-mail: r-jaradi@cyberia.net.lb

PARTNER DESIGNATE

Palestine
Wildlife Palestine Association, PO BOX 89, Beit Sahour. Pub: *Palestine Wildlife Society - Annual Report*. www.wildlife-pal.org
e-mail: wildlife@palnet.com

AFFILIATES

Bahrain
Dr Saeed A. Mohamed, PO Box 40266, Bahrain.
e-mail: sam53@batelco.com.bh

Iran, Islamic Republic of
Dr Jamshid Mansoori, Head, Ornithology Unit, Department of the Environment, PO Box: 5181, Tehran 15875, Iran.
e-mail: birdlifeiran@hotmail.com

Saudi Arabia
National Commission for Wildlife Cons & Dev, NCWDC, PO Box 61681, Riyadh 11575. Pub: *Phoenix; The*.
e-mail: ncwcd@zajil.net

PACIFIC

PARTNER

Australia
Birds Australia, 415 Riversdale Road, Hawthorn East, VIC 3123, Australia. Pub: *Australia Garcilla; Birds Australia Annual Report; Eclectus; Emu; Wingspan (WATCH) (Australia); from wingspan@birdsaustralia.com.au*.
e-mail: mail@birdsaustralia.com.au
www.birdsaustralia.com.au

AFFILIATES

Fiji
Dr Dick Watling, c/o Environment Consultants Fiji, P O Box 2041, Government Buildings, Suva, Fiji.
e-mail: watling@is.com.fj

French Polynesia
Société d'Ornithologie de Polynésie "Manu", B.P. 21 098, Papeete, Tahiti.
e-mail: sop.manu@mail.pf

Palau
Palau Conservation Society, PO BOX 1811, Koror, PW96940. Pub: *Ngerel a Biib*.
e-mail: pcs@palaunet.com

Samoa
O le Si'osi'omaga Society Incorporated, O le Si'osi'omaga Society Inc., P O Box 2282, Apia, Western Samoa. e-mail: ngo_siosiomaga@samoa.ws

New Zealand
Royal Forest & Bird Protection Society of, PO Box 631, Wellington. Pub: *Forest & Bird; Forest & Bird Annual Report; Forest & Bird Conservation News*.
e-mail: l.bates@wn.forest-bird.org.nz
www.forest-bird.org.nz

INTERNATIONAL ORGANISATIONS

AFRICAN BIRD CLUB.
c/o Birdlife International as below.
e-mail (general): keithbetton@hotmail.com
(membership and sales):
Moira.Y.Hargreaves@btinternet.com
www.africanbirdclub.org
Pub: *Bulletin of the African Bird Club.*

BIRDLIFE INTERNATIONAL.
Wellbrook Court, Girton Road, Cambridge, CB3
ONA, +44 (0)1223 277318; fax +44 (0)1223
277200,
Pub: *World Birdwatch.* www.birdlife.net

EAST AFRICA NATURAL HISTORY SOCIETY
see Kenya in preceding list.

EURING (European Union for Bird Ringing).
Euring Data Bank, NIOO Centre for Terrestrial
Ecology, PO Box 40, NL-6666 ZG Heteren,
Netherlands.
www.nioo.knaw.nl/euring.htm.

**EUROPEAN WILDLIFE REHABILITATION
ASSOCIATION (EWRA).**
Les Stocker MBE, c/o Wildlife Hospital Trust, Aston
Road, Haddenham, Aylesbury, Bucks, HP17 8AF,
+44 (0)1844 292292; fax +44 (0)1844 292640,
www.sttiggywinkles.org.uk

FAUNA AND FLORA INTERNATIONAL.
Great Eastern House, Tenison Road, Cambridge,
CB1 2TT, +44 (0)1223 571000; fax +44 (0)1223
461481,
Pub: *Fauna & Flora News; Oryx.* www.ffi.org.uk

**LIPU-UK
(the Italian League for the Protection of
Birds).**

David Lingard, Fernwood,
Doddington Road, Whisby,
Lincs, LN6 9BX, +44
(0)1522 689030,
e-mail:
david@lipu-uk.org
www.lipu-uk.org
Pub: *The Hoopoe,*
annually, *Ali
Notizie,* quarterley.

NEOTROPICAL BIRD CLUB.
As OSME below. Pub: *Cotinga.*
www.neotropicalbirdclub.org

ORIENTAL BIRD CLUB.
As OSME below. Pub: *The Forktail; Bull OBC.*
www.orientalbirdclub.org

**ORNITHOLOGICAL SOCIETY OF THE MIDDLE
EAST (OSME).**
c/o The Lodge, Sandy, Beds, SG19 2DL.
Pub: *Sandgrouse.*
www.osme.org

**TRAFFIC International (formerly Wildlife
Trade Monitoring Unit).**
219 Huntingdon Road, Cambridge, CB3 ODL, +44
(0)1223 277427; fax +44 (0)1223 277237.
Pub: *TRAFFIC Bulletin.*
e-mail: traffic@trafficint.org

**WEST AFRICAN ORNITHOLOGICAL
SOCIETY.**
R E Sharland, 1 Fisher's Heron, East Mills, Hants,
SP6 2JR. Pub: *Malimbus.*

WETLANDS INTERNATIONAL.
PO Box 471, 6700 AL Wageningen, Netherlands,
+31 317 478854; fax +31 317 478850,
Pub: *Wetlands.*
www.wetlands.org

WORLD OWL TRUST.
The World Owl Centre, Muncaster Castle,
Ravenglass, Cumbria, CA18 1RQ, +44 (0)1229
717393; fax +44 (0)1229 717107,
www.owls.org

WORLD PHEASANT ASSOCIATION.
PO Box 5, Lower Basildon, Reading, RG8 9PF, +44
(0)118 984 5140; fax +44 (0)118 984 3369,
Pub: *WPA News.* www.pheasant.org.uk

WORLD WIDE FUND FOR NATURE.
Avenue du Mont Blanc, CH-1196 Gland,
Switzerland, +41 22 364 9111; fax +41 22 364
5358,
www.panda.org

QUICK REFERENCE SECTION

Plan your Dawn Chorus visits by checking sunrise times on page 342.
This singing Sedge Warbler was drawn by David Thelwell

TIDE TABLES: USEFUL INFORMATION

BRITISH SUMMER TIME

In 2003 BST applies from 0100 on 30 March to 0100 on 26 October.

Note that all the times in the following tables are GMT. **During British Summer Time one hour should be added.**

Predictions are given for the times of high water at Dover throughout the year.

The times of tides at the locations shown here may be obtained by adding or subtracting their 'tidal difference' as shown opposite (subtractions are indicated by a minus sign).

Tidal predictions for Dover have been computed by the Proudman Oceanographic Laboratory. Copyright reserved.

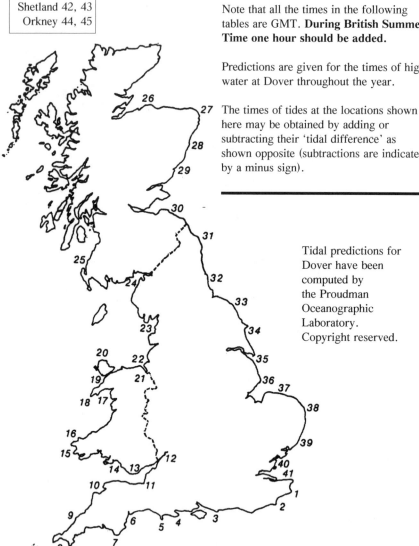

Shetland 42, 43
Orkney 44, 45

Map showing locations for which tidal differences are given on facing page.

TIDE TABLES 2003

Example 1

To calculate the time of first high water at Girvan on February 16
1. Look up the time at Dover (10 35)* = 10.35 am
2. Add the tidal difference for Girvan = 0.54
3. Therefore the time of high water at Girvan = 11.29 am

Example 2

To calculate the time of second high water at Blakeney on June 7
1. Look up the time at Dover (16 08) = 4.08 pm
2. Add 1 hour for British Summer Time (17 08) = 5.08 pm
3. Subtract the tidal difference for Blakeney = - 4.07
4. Therefore the time of high water at Blakeney = 1.01 pm

*All Dover times are shown on the 24-hour clock.
Thus, 08 14 = 08.14 am; 14 58 = 2.58
Following the time of each high water the height of the tide is given, in metres.

(Tables for 2004 are not available at the time of going to press.)

TIDAL DIFFERENCES

1	Dover	See pp 338-340	
2	Dungeness		-0 12
3	Selsey Bill		0 09
4	Swanage (lst H.W.Springs)		-2 36
5	Portland		-4 23
6	Exmouth (Approaches)		-4 48
7	Salcombe		-5 23
8	Newlyn (Penzance)		5 59
9	Padstow		-5 47
10	Bideford		-5 17
11	Bridgwater		-4 23
12	Sharpness Dock		-3 19
13	Cardiff (Penarth)		-4 16
14	Swansea		-4 52
15	Skomer Island		-5 00
16	Fishguard		-3 48
17	Barmouth		-2 45
18	Bardsey Island		-3 07
19	Caernarvon		-1 07
20	Amlwch		-0 22
21	Connahs Quay		0 20
22	Hilbre Island (Hoylake/West Kirby)		-0 05
23	Morecambe		0 20
24	Silloth		0 51
25	Girvan		0 54
26	Lossiemouth		0 48
27	Fraserburgh		1 20
28	Aberdeen		2 30
29	Montrose		3 30
30	Dunbar		3 42
31	Holy Island		3 58
32	Sunderland		4 38
33	Whitby		5 12
34	Bridlington		5 53
35	Grimsby		-5 20
36	Skegness		-5 00
37	Blakeney		-4 07
38	Gorleston		-2 08
39	Aldeburgh		-0 13
40	Bradwell Waterside		1 11
41	Herne Bay		1 28
42	Sullom Voe		-1 34
43	Lerwick		0 01
44	Kirkwall		-0 26
45	Widewall Bay		-1 30

NB. Care should be taken when making calculations at the beginning and end of British Summer Time. See worked examples above.

Time Zone GMT

TIDE TABLES 2003

Tidal Predictions : HIGH WATERS 2003   Units METRES

Datum of Predictions = Chart Datum : 3.67 metres below Ordnance Datum (Newlyn)

British Summer Time : 30th March to 26th October

DOVER — January

Day	Morning hr min	m	Afternoon hr min	m
1 W	09 26	6.4	22 00	6.3
2 Th	10 19	6.5	22 49	6.5
3 F	11 09	6.6	23 35	6.6
4 Sa	11 55	6.5	** **	**
5 Su	00 18	6.6	12 39	6.4
6 M	00 57	6.5	13 19	6.3
7 Tu	01 36	6.4	13 59	6.1
8 W	02 16	6.3	14 41	5.8
9 Th	02 58	6.1	15 27	5.6
10 F	03 44	5.8	16 21	5.4
11 Sa	04 38	5.6	17 23	5.2
12 Su	05 42	5.4	18 33	5.1
13 M	06 51	5.3	19 42	5.2
14 Tu	07 56	5.4	20 38	5.4
15 W	08 49	5.6	21 26	5.7
16 Th	09 34	5.8	22 06	6.0
17 F	10 14	6.0	22 43	6.2
18 Sa	10 52	6.2	23 21	6.4
19 Su	11 33	6.4	** **	**
20 M	00 02	6.6	12 15	6.5
21 Tu	00 44	6.7	13 00	6.5
22 W	01 28	6.7	13 45	6.5
23 Th	02 11	6.6	14 31	6.3
24 F	02 56	6.5	15 20	6.1
25 Sa	03 46	6.3	16 15	5.9
26 Su	04 42	6.1	17 17	5.7
27 M	05 48	5.9	18 29	5.6
28 Tu	07 01	5.8	19 48	5.6
29 W	08 17	5.8	20 59	5.8
30 Th	09 23	6.0	21 56	6.1
31 F	10 18	6.2	22 42	6.3

DOVER — February

Day	Morning hr min	m	Afternoon hr min	m
1 Sa	11 04	6.3	23 24	6.5
2 Su	11 45	6.4	** **	**
3 M	00 02	6.6	12 23	6.4
4 Tu	00 39	6.6	13 00	6.3
5 W	01 14	6.5	13 34	6.2
6 Th	01 48	6.3	14 07	6.1
7 F	02 21	6.1	14 42	5.8
8 Sa	02 56	6.0	15 19	5.6
9 Su	03 34	5.7	16 04	5.3
10 M	04 25	5.4	17 06	5.0
11 Tu	05 34	5.1	18 29	4.9
12 W	06 58	5.1	19 55	5.1
13 Th	08 11	5.3	20 24	5.4
14 F	09 11	5.6	21 43	5.8
15 Sa	09 54	6.0	22 24	6.2
16 Su	10 35	6.3	23 03	6.5
17 M	11 16	6.5	23 44	6.7
18 Tu	11 58	6.7	** **	**
19 W	00 25	6.9	12 41	6.8
20 Th	01 09	6.9	13 25	6.7
21 F	01 49	6.7	14 09	6.5
22 Sa	02 31	6.5	14 54	6.3
23 Su	03 18	6.4	15 44	6.0
24 M	04 12	6.1	16 46	5.7
25 Tu	05 20	5.7	18 04	5.4
26 W	06 46	5.5	19 38	5.3
27 Th	08 17	5.5	20 54	5.6
28 F	09 25	5.8	21 49	5.9

DOVER — March

Day	Morning hr min	m	Afternoon hr min	m
1 Sa	10 15	6.0	22 29	6.2
2 Su	10 55	6.2	23 07	6.4
3 M	11 30	6.3	23 41	6.6
4 Tu	** **	**	12 04	6.4
5 W	00 16	6.6	12 34	6.4
6 Th	00 49	6.5	13 05	6.3
7 F	01 18	6.3	13 34	6.2
8 Sa	01 45	6.1	13 59	6.0
9 Su	02 10	6.1	14 27	5.8
10 M	02 41	5.9	15 04	5.5
11 Tu	03 22	5.5	15 57	5.1
12 W	04 28	5.1	17 23	4.9
13 Th	06 06	4.9	19 08	5.0
14 F	07 41	5.1	20 24	5.4
15 Sa	08 44	5.6	21 16	5.8
16 Su	09 32	6.0	21 58	6.3
17 M	10 12	6.4	22 39	6.6
18 Tu	10 53	6.7	23 19	6.9
19 W	11 35	6.8	** **	**
20 Th	00 01	7.1	12 19	6.9
21 F	00 43	7.1	13 01	6.8
22 Sa	01 24	7.0	13 45	6.6
23 Su	02 06	6.8	14 30	6.4
24 M	02 54	6.4	15 20	6.0
25 Tu	03 50	6.0	16 24	5.6
26 W	05 03	5.6	17 45	5.3
27 Th	06 41	5.4	19 26	5.3
28 F	08 16	5.4	20 40	5.6
29 Sa	09 18	5.7	21 30	5.9
30 Su	10 03	6.0	22 10	6.2
31 M	10 36	6.2	22 43	6.4

DOVER — April

Day	Morning hr min	m	Afternoon hr min	m
1 Tu	11 07	6.3	23 17	6.5
2 W	11 38	6.4	23 49	6.6
3 Th	** **	**	12 08	6.4
4 F	00 20	6.6	12 36	6.3
5 Sa	00 46	6.5	13 00	6.2
6 Su	01 08	6.3	13 24	6.1
7 M	01 32	6.1	13 50	5.9
8 Tu	02 02	5.9	14 27	5.7
9 W	02 44	5.6	15 18	5.4
10 Th	03 49	5.2	16 43	5.1
11 F	05 33	5.0	18 27	5.1
12 Sa	07 08	5.2	19 48	5.4
13 Su	08 14	5.7	20 42	5.9
14 M	09 04	6.1	21 29	6.3
15 Tu	09 46	6.5	22 10	6.7
16 W	10 28	6.7	22 50	7.0
17 Th	11 10	6.9	23 33	7.1
18 F	11 54	6.9	** **	**
19 Sa	00 16	7.1	12 39	6.8
20 Su	01 00	6.9	13 24	6.6
21 M	01 46	6.6	14 11	6.4
22 Tu	02 37	6.3	15 04	6.0
23 W	03 37	5.8	16 05	5.6
24 Th	04 52	5.4	17 24	5.3
25 F	06 32	5.4	19 00	5.3
26 Sa	07 53	5.4	20 09	5.6
27 Su	08 51	5.7	20 59	5.9
28 M	09 33	5.9	21 39	6.1
29 Tu	10 07	6.1	22 14	6.3
30 W	10 38	6.2	22 49	6.4

TIDE TABLES 2003

Time Zone GMT   Units METRES

Tidal Predictions : HIGH WATERS 2003

Datum of Predictions = Chart Datum : 3.67 metres below Ordnance Datum (Newlyn)

British Summer Time : 30th March to 26th October

DOVER — May

Date	Day	Morning hr min	m	Afternoon hr min	m
1	Th ●	11 10	6.3	23 21	6.4
2	F	11 41	6.3	23 51	6.4
3	Sa	** **		12 09	6.3
4	Su	00 16	6.3	12 34	6.2
5	M	00 41	6.2	13 01	6.1
6	Tu	01 08	6.1	13 32	6.0
7	W	01 42	5.9	14 11	5.8
8	Th ⌒	02 28	5.6	15 06	5.5
9	F	03 37	5.4	15 52	5.4
10	Sa	05 10	5.2	17 07	5.3
11	Su	06 33	5.4	18 30	5.6
12	M	07 38	5.8	20 08	6.0
13	Tu	08 30	6.1	20 54	6.4
14	W	09 16	6.4	21 39	6.7
15	Th	10 01	6.6	22 24	6.9
16	F ○	10 48	6.8	23 09	7.0
17	Sa	11 34	6.8	23 56	6.9
18	Su	** **		12 23	6.7
19	M	00 44	6.7	13 11	6.6
20	Tu	01 35	6.5	13 59	6.3
21	W	02 27	6.1	14 49	6.0
22	Th	03 23	5.8	15 46	5.7
23	F	04 32	5.4	16 53	5.5
24	Sa ⌣	05 54	5.3	18 12	5.4
25	Su	07 10	5.4	19 22	5.6
26	M	08 06	5.5	20 17	5.8
27	Tu	08 52	5.9	20 55	5.9
28	W	09 32	6.0	21 41	6.1
29	Th	10 08	6.0	22 19	6.2
30	F	10 43	6.1	22 53	6.2
31	Sa ●	11 16	6.2	23 26	6.2

DOVER — June

Date	Day	Morning hr min	m	Afternoon hr min	m
1	Su ●	11 48	6.2	23 55	6.2
2	M	** **		12 20	6.2
3	Tu	00 26	6.1	12 54	6.1
4	W	01 01	5.9	13 31	6.0
5	Th	01 41	5.8	14 14	5.8
6	F	02 31	5.6	15 06	5.7
7	Sa ⌒	03 33	5.6	16 08	5.7
8	Su	04 45	5.6	17 17	5.7
9	M	05 55	5.6	18 23	5.8
10	Tu	06 58	5.8	19 25	6.1
11	W	07 56	6.0	20 20	6.3
12	Th	08 49	6.3	21 12	6.5
13	F	09 41	6.4	22 03	6.7
14	Sa	10 32	6.6	22 53	6.7
15	Su ○	11 24	6.6	23 45	6.7
16	M	** **		12 13	6.6
17	Tu	00 36	6.5	13 01	6.5
18	W	01 25	6.3	13 45	6.4
19	Th	02 13	6.1	14 30	6.2
20	F	03 02	5.8	15 19	6.0
21	Sa	03 58	5.6	16 12	5.8
22	Su ⌣	05 00	5.4	17 16	5.6
23	M	06 09	5.3	18 23	5.5
24	Tu	07 12	5.4	19 26	5.7
25	W	08 09	5.5	20 21	5.8
26	Th	08 58	5.6	21 09	5.9
27	F	09 40	5.8	21 51	6.0
28	Sa	10 19	6.0	22 29	6.0
29	Su ●	10 56	6.1	23 04	6.1
30	M	11 31	6.2	23 40	6.2

DOVER — July

Date	Day	Morning hr min	m	Afternoon hr min	m
1	Tu	** **		12 08	6.3
2	W	00 18	6.2	12 46	6.3
3	Th	00 57	6.1	13 26	6.3
4	F	01 41	6.1	14 09	6.2
5	Sa	02 27	5.9	14 55	6.1
6	Su	03 18	5.9	15 44	6.1
7	M ⌒	04 14	5.8	16 41	6.0
8	Tu	05 16	5.8	17 42	6.0
9	W	06 19	5.8	18 47	6.0
10	Th	07 25	5.8	19 52	6.1
11	F	08 31	6.0	20 55	6.3
12	Sa	09 32	6.2	21 54	6.4
13	Su	10 28	6.4	22 49	6.5
14	M ○	11 17	6.5	23 40	6.5
15	Tu	** **		12 02	6.6
16	W	00 27	6.4	12 46	6.5
17	Th	01 10	6.3	13 25	6.4
18	F	01 52	6.2	14 04	6.2
19	Sa	02 33	6.0	14 45	6.2
20	Su	03 16	5.8	15 30	6.0
21	M	04 05	5.5	16 21	5.7
22	Tu ⌣	05 02	5.3	17 20	5.5
23	W	06 09	5.2	18 29	5.3
24	Th	07 21	5.2	19 39	5.5
25	F	08 29	5.4	20 40	5.5
26	Sa	09 15	5.6	21 27	5.7
27	Su	09 58	5.9	22 08	5.9
28	M ●	10 35	6.1	22 45	6.1
29	Tu	11 11	6.3	23 21	6.3
30	W	11 48	6.5	** **	
31	Th	00 01	6.4	12 27	6.6

DOVER — August

Date	Day	Morning hr min	m	Afternoon hr min	m
1	F	00 41	6.5	13 08	6.6
2	Sa	01 24	6.4	13 50	6.6
3	Su	02 07	6.3	14 31	6.5
4	M	02 52	6.2	15 15	6.4
5	Tu	03 41	6.0	16 07	6.2
6	W ⌒	04 39	5.8	17 09	6.0
7	Th	05 47	5.6	18 20	5.8
8	F	07 05	5.7	19 41	5.9
9	Sa	08 28	5.7	20 56	5.9
10	Su	09 33	6.0	21 57	6.2
11	M ○	10 24	6.3	22 48	6.3
12	Tu	11 11	6.5	23 31	6.4
13	W	11 47	6.6	** **	
14	Th	00 07	6.4	12 23	6.7
15	F	00 47	6.3	13 00	6.6
16	Sa	01 22	6.1	13 35	6.5
17	Su	01 56	6.1	14 09	6.4
18	M ⌣	02 31	6.0	14 44	6.2
19	Tu	03 08	5.7	15 22	5.5
20	W	03 51	5.4	16 19	5.5
21	Th	04 52	5.1	17 19	5.1
22	F	06 19	5.0	18 51	5.0
23	Sa	07 48	5.1	20 10	5.2
24	Su	08 48	5.4	21 05	5.6
25	M ●	09 33	5.8	21 47	5.9
26	Tu	10 11	6.1	22 24	6.2
27	W	10 48	6.5	22 59	6.5
28	Th	11 24	6.7	23 38	6.6
29	F	** **		12 04	6.9
30	Sa	00 18	6.7	12 43	6.9
31	Su	00 58	6.7	13 22	6.9

TIDE TABLES 2003

Units **METRES**

Tidal Predictions : **HIGH WATERS 2003**

Datum of Predictions = **Chart Datum : 3.67 metres below Ordnance Datum (Newlyn)**

British Summer Time : **30th March to 26th October**

DOVER — September

Day		Morning hr:min	m	Afternoon hr:min	m
1	M	01 41	6.6	14 02	6.7
2	Tu	02 23	6.4	14 45	6.5
3	W ◐	03 12	6.1	15 37	6.2
4	Th	04 11	5.8	16 43	5.8
5	F	05 24	5.5	18 08	5.5
6	Sa	07 03	5.4	19 49	5.5
7	Su	08 30	5.6	21 05	5.8
8	M	09 29	6.0	21 58	6.1
9	Tu	10 12	6.3	22 39	6.3
10	W ○	10 49	6.5	23 14	6.4
11	Th	11 24	6.6	23 47	6.5
12	F	11 58	6.7	** **	6.7
13	Sa	00 19	6.5	12 32	6.6
14	Su	00 50	6.6	13 01	6.6
15	M	01 19	6.3	13 29	6.4
16	Tu	01 46	6.1	13 56	6.2
17	W	02 14	5.9	14 26	5.9
18	Th ◑	02 49	5.6	15 04	5.5
19	F	03 39	5.2	16 07	4.9
20	Sa	05 09	4.9	17 58	5.1
21	Su	07 00	5.0	19 36	5.4
22	M	08 14	5.4	20 37	5.5
23	Tu	09 04	5.8	21 19	6.0
24	W	09 43	6.3	21 57	6.4
25	Th	10 19	6.6	22 32	6.6
26	F ●	10 56	6.9	23 10	6.8
27	Sa	11 34	7.1	23 51	6.9
28	Su	** **	**	12 13	7.1
29	M	00 32	6.9	12 53	7.0
30	Tu	01 14	6.7	13 34	6.8

DOVER — October

Day		Morning hr:min	m	Afternoon hr:min	m
1	W	01 57	6.5	14 20	6.5
2	Th ◐	02 48	6.1	15 16	6.1
3	F	03 50	5.7	16 27	5.6
4	Sa	05 10	5.4	18 11	5.3
5	Su	06 58	5.3	19 55	5.5
6	M	08 19	5.7	20 59	5.8
7	Tu	09 12	6.1	21 46	6.1
8	W	09 51	6.3	22 21	6.3
9	Th ○	10 25	6.5	22 50	6.5
10	F	10 57	6.7	23 28	6.5
11	Sa	11 30	6.7	23 49	6.7
12	Su	** **	**	12 01	6.7
13	M	00 19	6.5	12 29	6.6
14	Tu	00 46	6.4	12 54	6.4
15	W	01 11	6.2	13 18	6.2
16	Th ◑	01 38	6.0	13 46	5.9
17	F	02 10	5.8	14 23	5.6
18	Sa	02 56	5.4	15 22	5.2
19	Su	04 19	5.1	17 11	4.9
20	M	06 06	5.1	18 51	5.1
21	Tu	07 28	5.4	19 57	5.6
22	W	08 24	5.9	20 45	6.0
23	Th	09 08	6.3	21 25	6.4
24	F	09 46	6.7	22 03	6.7
25	Sa ●	10 24	7.0	22 43	6.9
26	Su	11 04	7.1	23 24	7.0
27	M	11 45	7.2	** **	**
28	Tu	00 08	6.9	12 29	7.0
29	W	00 53	6.8	13 14	6.8
30	Th	01 42	6.5	13 54	6.4
31	F	02 34	6.2	15 06	5.9

DOVER — November

Day		Morning hr:min	m	Afternoon hr:min	m
1	Sa ◐	03 36	5.8	16 21	5.5
2	Su	04 52	5.5	18 04	5.3
3	M	06 30	5.4	19 34	5.5
4	Tu	07 48	5.7	20 33	5.8
5	W	08 40	6.0	21 04	6.0
6	Th	09 20	6.2	21 51	6.2
7	F	09 56	6.4	22 21	6.4
8	Sa	10 29	6.5	22 53	6.5
9	Su	11 03	6.6	23 24	6.4
10	M	11 34	6.5	23 55	6.3
11	Tu	** **	**	12 04	6.1
12	W	00 50	6.4	12 29	5.9
13	Th	01 19	6.2	12 54	5.7
14	F	01 55	6.1	13 26	5.4
15	Sa	02 44	5.6	14 07	5.2
16	Su	03 53	5.4	15 06	5.3
17	M ◑	05 16	5.3	16 34	5.2
18	Tu	06 33	5.5	18 01	5.3
19	W	07 36	5.9	19 10	5.6
20	Th	08 26	6.2	20 03	6.0
21	F	09 11	6.4	20 49	6.3
22	Sa	09 54	6.6	21 34	6.6
23	Su ●	10 39	6.9	22 19	6.8
24	M	11 26	7.0	23 06	6.9
25	Tu	** **	**	12 15	6.8
26	W	00 43	6.7	13 05	6.9
27	Th	01 32	6.5	13 59	6.6
28	F	02 23	6.2	14 56	6.3
29	Sa	03 18	6.0	16 01	5.9
30	Su	04 19	5.8	17 12	5.6

DOVER — December

Day		Morning hr:min	m	Afternoon hr:min	m
1	M	04 21	5.7	17 21	5.4
2	Tu	05 37	5.6	18 43	5.4
3	W	06 53	5.6	19 45	5.6
4	Th	07 53	5.8	20 34	5.7
5	F	08 42	6.0	21 16	5.9
6	Sa	09 25	6.1	21 54	6.1
7	Su	10 04	6.2	22 29	6.2
8	M ○	10 41	6.3	23 04	6.3
9	Tu	11 14	6.3	23 38	6.3
10	W	11 45	6.3	** **	**
11	Th	00 09	6.3	12 16	6.2
12	F	00 41	6.2	12 47	6.1
13	Sa	01 15	6.2	13 24	6.0
14	Su	01 53	6.1	14 04	5.8
15	M	02 37	5.9	14 55	5.7
16	Tu ◑	03 29	5.8	15 58	5.5
17	W	04 32	5.7	17 09	5.5
18	Th	05 40	5.8	18 18	5.6
19	F	06 44	5.9	19 18	5.8
20	Sa	07 43	6.1	20 16	6.1
21	Su	08 40	6.4	21 11	6.3
22	M	09 33	6.6	22 04	6.5
23	Tu ●	10 25	6.7	22 57	6.7
24	W	11 17	6.8	23 48	6.7
25	Th	** **	**	12 11	6.7
26	F	00 36	6.7	13 00	6.5
27	Sa	01 22	6.6	13 49	6.3
28	Su	02 07	6.4	14 37	6.1
29	M	02 54	6.2	15 29	5.8
30	Tu ◐	03 44	6.0	16 26	5.5
31	W	04 42	5.7	17 31	5.4

SEA AREAS

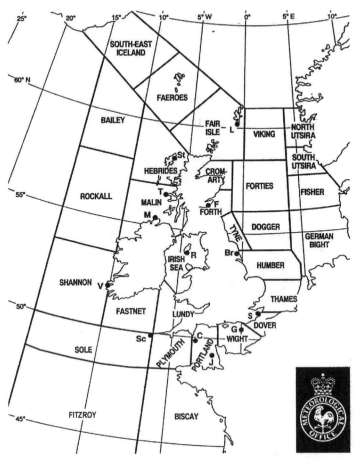

STATIONS WHOSE LATEST REPORTS ARE BROADCAST IN THE 5-MINUTE FORECASTS

Br Bridlington; C Channel Light-Vessel Automatic; F Fife Ness; G Greenwich Light-Vessel Automatic; J Jersey; L Lerwick; M Malin Head; R Ronaldsway; S Sandettie Light-Vessel Automatic; Sc Scilly Automatic; St Stornoway; T Tiree; V Valentia

From information kindly supplied by the Meteoroligical Office

REVISION OF SEA AREAS

On 4 February 2002, the southern boundary of areas Plymouth and Sole, and the northern boundary of areas Biscay and Finisterre were realigned along the Metarea I/II boundary at 48°27' North. At the same time, sea area Finisterre was renamed FitzRoy.

Did you know that the new FitzRoy shipping area is named after the founder of the Met Office?

341

SUNRISE AND SUNSET TIMES

Predictions are given for the times of sunrise and sunset on every Sunday throughout the year. For places on the same latitude as the following, add 4 minutes for each degree of longitude west (subtract if east).

These times are in GMT, except between 01 00 on Mar 30 and 01 00 on Oct 26, when the times are in BST (1 hour in advance of GMT).

		London Rise	London Set	Manchester Rise	Manchester Set	Edinburgh Rise	Edinburgh Set
Jan	5	08 06	16 06	08 24	16 05	08 42	15 54
	12	08 02	16 16	08 20	16 15	08 37	16 05
	19	07 56	16 27	08 13	16 26	08 29	16 18
	26	07 48	16 39	08 04	16 39	08 19	16 32
Feb	2	07 38	16 51	07 53	16 53	08 06	16 47
	9	07 26	17 04	07 41	17 07	07 52	17 03
	16	07 14	17 17	07 27	17 21	07 37	17 18
	23	07 00	17 29	07 11	17 34	07 20	17 33
Mar	2	06 45	17 42	06 56	17 48	07 03	17 48
	9	06 29	17 54	06 39	18 01	06 45	18 03
	16	06 14	18 06	06 22	18 14	06 27	18 17
	23	05 58	18 18	06 05	18 27	06 08	18 32
	30	06 42	19 30	06 48	19 40	06 50	19 46
Apr	6	06 26	19 42	06 32	19 53	06 32	20 00
	13	06 10	19 53	06 15	20 05	06 14	20 15
	20	05 55	20 05	05 59	20 18	05 56	20 29
	27	05 41	20 17	05 44	20 31	05 39	20 43
May	4	05 28	20 28	05 29	20 43	05 24	21 57
	11	05 16	20 39	05 16	20 56	05 09	21 11
	18	05 05	20 50	05 05	21 07	04 56	21 24
	25	04 56	20 59	04 55	21 18	04 45	21 36

Reproduced, with permission, from data supplied by HM Nautical Almanac Office, Copyright Council for the Central Laboratory for the Research Councils.

SUNRISE AND SUNSET TIMES

		London Rise	Set	Manchester Rise	Set	Edinburgh Rise	Set
Jun	1	04 50	21 08	04 47	21 27	04 36	21 46
	8	04 45	21 15	04 42	21 34	04 30	21 55
	15	04 43	21 19	04 39	21 40	04 26	22 00
	22	04 43	21 22	04 40	21 42	04 26	22 03
	29	04 46	21 22	04 43	21 42	04 30	22 02
Jul	6	04 51	21 19	04 48	21 39	04 36	21 59
	13	04 58	21 14	04 56	21 33	04 44	21 52
	20	05 07	21 06	05 05	21 25	04 55	21 42
	27	05 16	20 57	05 16	21 14	05 07	21 31
Aug	3	05 27	20 46	05 27	21 02	05 20	21 17
	10	05 37	20 34	05 39	20 49	05 33	20 02
	17	05 48	20 20	05 51	20 34	05 47	20 46
	24	06 00	20 06	06 03	20 18	06 01	20 29
	31	06 11	19 50	06 15	20 02	06 14	20 11
Sep	7	06 22	19 35	06 28	19 45	06 28	19 53
	14	06 33	19 19	06 40	19 28	06 41	19 34
	21	06 44	19 02	06 52	19 11	06 55	19 16
	28	06 56	18 46	07 04	18 54	07 09	18 57
Oct	5	07 07	18 30	07 17	18 37	07 23	18 39
	12	07 19	18 15	07 30	18 21	07 37	18 21
	19	07 31	18 00	07 42	18 05	07 51	18 04
	26	06 43	16 46	06 56	16 49	07 06	16 47
Nov	2	06 55	16 33	07 09	16 35	07 21	16 31
	9	07 07	16 21	07 22	16 22	07 36	16 17
	16	07 20	16 11	07 36	16 11	07 50	16 04
	23	07 31	16 02	07 48	16 02	08 04	15 54
	30	07 42	15 56	08 00	15 55	08 17	15 45
Dec	7	07 51	15 52	08 10	15 51	08 28	15 40
	14	07 59	15 52	08 18	15 49	08 36	15 38
	21	08 04	15 53	08 23	15 51	08 42	15 40
	28	08 06	15 58	08 25	15 56	08 44	15 44

GRID REFERENCES

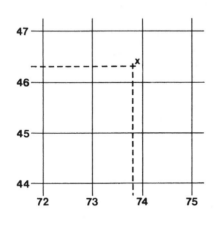

A grid reference is made up of letters and numbers. Two-letter codes are used for 100km squares on the National Grid (opposite) and single-letter codes on the Irish Grid (below).

The squares may be further subdivided into squares of 10km, 1km or 100m, allowing for increasingly specific references. On a given map the lines forming the squares are numbered in the margins, those along the top and bottom being known as 'eastings' and those along the sides as 'northings'. A reference number is made up of the relevant letter code plus two sets of figures, those representing the easting followed by the northing. According to the scale of the map they can either be read off directly or calculated by visually dividing the intervals into tenths. For most purposes three-figure eastings plus three-figure northings are adequate.

The example above, from an Ordnance Survey 'Landranger' map, illustrates how to specify a location on a map divided into 1km squares: the reference for point X is 738463. If that location lies in square SP (see map opposite), the full reference is SP738463.

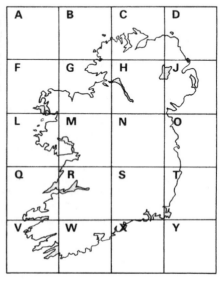

**LETTER CODES FOR
IRISH GRID 10km
SQUARES**

**LETTER CODES FOR
NATIONAL GRID
100km SQUARES**

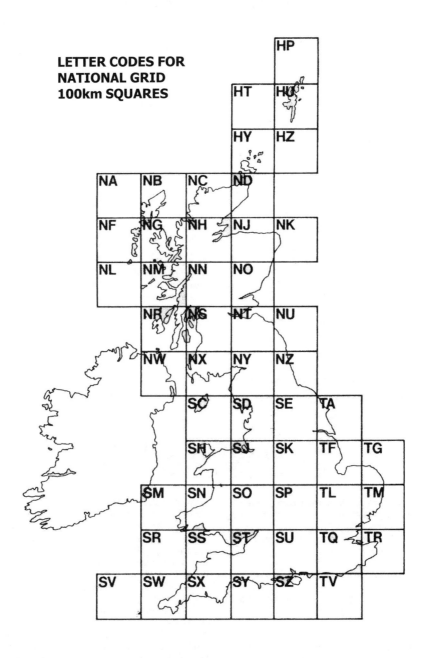

SCHEDULE 1 SPECIES

Under the provisions of the Wildlife and Countryside Act 1981 the following bird species (listed in Schedule 1 - Part I of the Act) are protected by special penalties at all times.

Avocet,
Bee-eater
Bittern
Bittern, Little
Bluethroat
Brambling
Bunting, Cirl
Bunting, Lapland
Bunting, Snow
Buzzard, Honey
Chough
Corncrake
Crake, Spotted
Crossbills (all species)
Curlew, Stone
Divers (all species)
Dotterel
Duck, Long-tailed
Eagle, Golden
Eagle, White-tailed

Falcon, Gyr
Fieldfare
Firecrest
Garganey
Godwit, Black-tailed
Goshawk
Grebe, Black-necked
Grebe, Slavonian
Greenshank
Gull, Little
Gull, Mediterranean
Harriers (all species)
Heron, Purple
Hobby
Hoopoe
Kingfisher
Kite, Red
Merlin
Oriole, Golden
Osprey

Owl, Barn
Owl, Snowy
Peregrine
Petrel, Leach's
Phalarope, Red-necked
Plover, Kentish
Plover, Little Ringed
Quail, Common
Redstart, Black
Redwing
Rosefinch, Scarlet
Ruff
Sandpiper, Green
Sandpiper, Purple
Sandpiper, Wood
Scaup
Scoter, Common
Scoter, Velvet
Serin
Shorelark

Shrike, Red-backed
Spoonbill
Stilt, Black-winged
Stint, Temminck's
Swan, Bewick's
Stone-curlew
Swan, Whooper
Tern, Black
Tern, Little
Tern, Roseate
Tit, Bearded
Tit, Crested
Treecreeper, Short-toed
Warbler, Cetti's
Warbler, Dartford
Warbler, Marsh
Warbler, Savi's
Whimbrel
Woodlark
Wryneck

The following birds and their eggs (listed in Schedule 1 - Part II of the Act) are protected by special penalties during the close season, which is Feb 1 to Aug 31 (Feb 21 to Aug 31 below high water mark), but may be killed outside this period.

Goldeneye, Greylag Goose (in Outer Hebrides, Caithness, Sutherland, and Wester Ross only), Pintail.

THE BIRDWATCHER'S CODE OF CONDUCT

1. Welfare of birds must come first
Whether your particular interest is photography, ringing, sound recording, scientific study or just birdwatching, remember that the welfare of birds must always come first.

2. Habitat protection
A birds's habitat is vital to its survival and therefore we must ensure that our activities do not cause damage.

3. Keep disturbance to a minimum
Birds' tolerance of disturbance varies between species and seasons. Therefore, it is safer to keep all disturbance to a minimum. No birds should be disturbed from the nest in case the opportunities for predators to take eggs or young are increased. In very cold weather, disturbance to birds may cause them to use vital energy at a time when food is difficult to find. Wildfowlers impose bans during cold weather: birdwatchers should exercise similar discretion.

4. Rare breeding birds
If you discover a rare breeding bird and feel that protection is necessary, inform the appropriate RSPB Regional Officer, or the Species Protection Department at the RSPB, The Lodge, Sandy, Beds

SG19 2DL. Otherwise, it is best in almost all circumstances to keep the record strictly secret to avoid disturbance by other birdwatchers and attacks by egg-collectors. Never visit known sites of rare breeding birds unless they are adequately protected. Even your presence may give away the site to others and cause so many other visitors that the birds may fail to breed successfully. Disturbance at or near the nest of species listed on the First Schedule of the Wildlife and Countryside Act 1981 is a criminal offence.

5.   Rare migrants
Rare migrants or vagrants must not be harassed. If you discover one, consider the circumstances carefully before telling anyone. Will an influx of birdwatchers disturb the bird or others in the area? Will the habitat be damaged? Will problems be caused with the landowner?

6.   The law
The bird protection laws, as now embodied in the Wildlife and Countryside Act 1981, are the result of hard campaigning by previous generations of birdwatchers. As birdwatchers, we must abide by them at all times and not allow them to fall into disrepute.

7.   Respect the rights of landowners
The wishes of landowners and occupiers of land must be respected. Do not enter land without permission. Comply with permit schemes. If you are leading a group, do give advance notice of the visit, even if a formal permit scheme is not in operation. Always obey the Country Code.

8.   Keeping records
Much of today's knowledge about birds is the result of meticulous record keeping by our predecessors. Make sure you help to add to tomorrow's knowledge by sending records to your county bird recorder.

9.   Birdwatchng abroad
Behave abroad as you would at home. This code should be firmly adhered to when abroad (whatever the local laws). Well behaved birdwatchers can be important ambassadors for bird protection.

(Reprinted with permisson from the RSPB)

NATIONAL AND REGIONAL BIRDLINES

Birdline name	To obtain information	To report sightings (hotlines)
National		
Bird Information Service	09068 700222	01263 741140
www.birdingworld.co.uk		
Flightline (Northern Ireland)	028 9146 7408	
Regional		
Northern Ireland	028 9146 7408	
Scotland*	09068 700 234	01292 611 994
Wales *	09068 700 248	01492 544 588
East Anglia	09068 700 245	01603 763 388
www.birdnews.co.uk		or 08000 830 803
Midlands *	09068 700 247	01905 754 154
North East*	09068 700 246	01426 983 963
North West *	09068 700 249	0151 336 6188
South East	09068 700 240	07626 933 933
www.southeastbirdnews.co.uk		or 08000 377 240
South West	09068 700 241	01426 923 923

* www.uk-birding.co.uk
Charges
At the time of compilation, calls to 09068 numbers cost 60p per minute.

COUNTY BIRDWATCH TALLIES

The County Birdrace has become an institution in British birdwatching – providing both a personal challenge to those seeking to break records for species seen in one day, but also raising money via sponsorship for local and national conservation projects. For information on how to participate in 2003, contact *Birdwatch* magazine, Solo Publishing, 3D/F Leroy House, 436 Essex Road, Islington, London N1 3QP.

Rules

1. Teams shall comprise four members, all resident in the geographical area of the birdwatch, one of whom may be a driver and/or record-keeper.
2. Geographical areas shall generally be those used by the network of Bird Recorders.
3. A tally must be achieved on one calendar day.
4. No species shall be included in the tally unless seen or heard by at least three members of the team.
5. Team members and birds must be within the defined area at the time of recording.
6. Admitted species shall be those on the relevant official country list (eg. the British List for England, Scotland and Wales), plus Feral Pigeon; rarities must be accepted by the appropriate (county or national) Rarities Committee. Schedule D species shall be excluded.
7. Escapes, sick, injured or oiled birds shall not be admitted.
8. Attracting birds with a tape recording shall not be allowed.
9. The Birdwatchers' Code of Conduct shall be strictly observed.

Tallies opposite are accepted and published in good faith. A listing does not imply that the above rules have been adhered to, nor that any authentication or adjudication has been made. A county or region's best record is used in determining its position in the table. If the same total has been reached in more than one year, only the first is given.

( ) Numbers within curved brackets indicate the latest known total number of species on the county or region's list. In order to ensure consistency as to which species should be included on the list, Rule 6 should be applied.

If the same total has been reached by more than one county or region the names are listed alphabetically and a joint position indicated by an 'equals' sign (=).

Sightings of common wildfowl species or migrants such as Black Tern are equally valuable in bird races. Illustration by Simon Patient

348

COUNTY BIRDWATCH TALLIES

	County	Race total	County total	Year		County	Race total	County total	Year
1	Norfolk	162	(412)	2000	39 =	Carmarthen	122	(293)	1991
2	Dorset	158	(403)	1989	39 =	Gloucs	122	(307)	1998
3	Yorkshire	155	(428)	1998	41 =	Berkshire	121	(309)	1990
4	Kent	153	(402)	1999	41 =	Caithness	121	(292)	1994
5	Grampian	152	(352)	1999	41 =	Moray &			
6	Hampshire	151	(357)	1994		Nairn	121	(291)	1993
7	Cheshire	149	(338)	1993	44 =	Eire	119	(425)	1996
8	Suffolk	148	(371)	1992	44 =	Wexford	119	(?)	1992
9	Highland	146	(246)	1988	46 =	Manchester	118	(300)	1992
10 =	Cleveland	142	(354)	1994	46 =	Wiltshire	118	(308)	1989
10 =	Durham	142	(354)	1999	48	Merioneth	117	(263)	1989
10 =	Northumb	142	(392)	2000	49 =	Dumfries &			
13	Lancs & N					Galloway	115	(279)	1986
	Merseyside	141	(345)	1996	49 =	Glams (Old)	115	(300)	1986
14 =	Cumbria	140	(344)	1996	49 =	Pembroke	115	(355)	1995
14 =	Devon	140	(412)	2001	49 =	Surrey	115	(325)	1995
16 =	Highland,				53 =	Northants	114	(314)	1998
	NE Scotland	136	(?)	1993	53 =	Oxon	114	(297)	2000
16 =	Sussex	136	(380)	1996	53 =	Shetland	114	(419)	1992
16 =	Anglesey	136	(307)	1987	53 =	Worcs	114	(287)	1995
19	Gwynedd				57 =	Bucks	113	(276)	1990
20	(old county)	135	(349)	1989	57 =	Isle of Wight	113	(321)	1989
20 =	Tayside, Angus/				57 =	London	113	(352)	1994
	Dundee	134	(304)	1994	60 =	Montgomery	112	(227)	1991
20 =	Highland,				60 =	Rutland	112	(277)	1994
	N Scotland	134	(?)	1988	62 =	Bedfordshire	111	(287)	1996
22	N Ireland	133	(309)	1993	62 =	Glams,East	111	(298)	1993
23 =	Fife (excl				62 =	Gwent	111	(290)	1991
	Isle of May)	130	(305)	1996	62 =	Warwicks	111	(295)	1993
23 =	Cambs	130	(330)	2000	66	Glams,West	110	(288)	1991
23 =	Cambs/Hunts/				67	Leics	109	(293)	1998
	P'boro	130	(330)	2000	68 =	Central	108	(248)	1996
26	Derbyshire	129	(308)	1998	68 =	Herts	108	(299)	1989
27 =	Cornwall	128	(451)	1992	70	Ceredigion	107	(290)	1986
27 =	Lincolnshire	128	(369)	1988	71 =	Merseyside	105	(?)	1993
27 =	Lothian	128	(343)	1994	71 =	Western Isles	105	(341)	1985
30	Ayrshire	127	(288)	1991	73	Avon	104	(320)	1993
31 =	Caernarf.	126	(351)	1993	74	Shropshire	103	(263)	1989
31 =	Notts	126	(308)	1991	75	Cornwall,			
33 =	Clwyd	125	(296)	1995		Scilly	102	(407)	2000
33 =	Staffordshire	125	(293)	1993	76	Radnorshire	97	(235)	1988
35 =	Borders	124	(294)	2000	77	Guernsey	96	(306)	1992
35 =	Somerset	124	(336)	2000	78	Breconshire	95	(251)	1991
35 =	Yorkshire,E	124	(353)	1993	79	West Mid	92	(265)	1995
38	Essex	123	(365)	1996	80	Hereford	90	(253)	1994

The following do not have a one-day tally but are listed for their County total.
Alderney(267), Argyll (316), Clyde (287), Fife, Isle of May (273), Highland, Sutherland (268), Isle of Man (287), Jersey (303), Orkney (364), Shetland, Fair Isle (354).

INDEX TO BIRD RESERVES AND OBSERVATORIES

INDEX TO RESERVES

INDEX TO RESERVES